Professional
SQL Server™ 2005 XML

Scott Klein

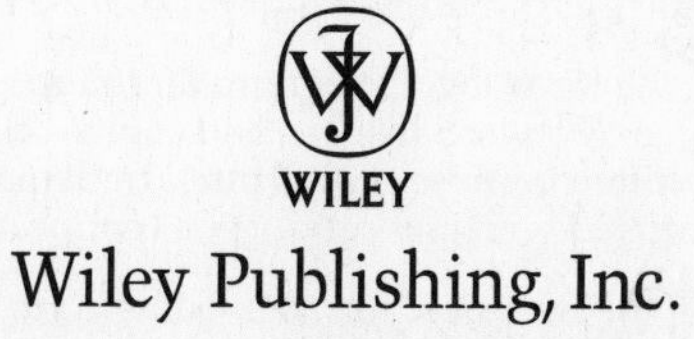

Wiley Publishing, Inc.

Professional SQL Server™ 2005 XML

Published by
Wiley Publishing, Inc.
10475 Crosspoint Boulevard
Indianapolis, IN 46256
www.wiley.com

Copyright © 2006 by Wiley Publishing, Inc., Indianapolis, Indiana

Published simultaneously in Canada

ISBN-13: 978-0-7645-9792-3
ISBN-10: 0-7645-9792-2

Manufactured in the United States of America

10 9 8 7 6 5 4 3 2 1

1MA/SR/RS/QV/IN

Library of Congress Cataloging-in-Publication Data:
Klein, Scott, 1966-
Professional SQL Server 2005 XML / Scott Klein.
p. cm.
Includes index.
ISBN-13: 978-0-7645-9792-3 (paper/website)
ISBN-10: 0-7645-9792-2 (paper/website)
1. SQL server. 2. Client/server computing. 3. XML (Document markup language) I. Title.
QA76.9.C55K545 2005
005.2'768--dc22
2005029721

No part of this publication may be reproduced, stored in a retrieval system or transmitted in any form or by any means, electronic, mechanical, photocopying, recording, scanning or otherwise, except as permitted under Sections 107 or 108 of the 1976 United States Copyright Act, without either the prior written permission of the Publisher, or authorization through payment of the appropriate per-copy fee to the Copyright Clearance Center, 222 Rosewood Drive, Danvers, MA 01923, (978) 750-8400, fax (978) 646-8600. Requests to the Publisher for permission should be addressed to the Legal Department, Wiley Publishing, Inc., 10475 Crosspoint Blvd., Indianapolis, IN 46256, (317) 572-3447, fax (317) 572-4355, or online at http://www.wiley.com/go/permissions.

LIMIT OF LIABILITY/DISCLAIMER OF WARRANTY: THE PUBLISHER AND THE AUTHOR MAKE NO REPRESENTATIONS OR WARRANTIES WITH RESPECT TO THE ACCURACY OR COMPLETENESS OF THE CONTENTS OF THIS WORK AND SPECIFICALLY DISCLAIM ALL WARRANTIES, INCLUDING WITHOUT LIMITATION WARRANTIES OF FITNESS FOR A PARTICULAR PURPOSE. NO WARRANTY MAY BE CREATED OR EXTENDED BY SALES OR PROMOTIONAL MATERIALS. THE ADVICE AND STRATEGIES CONTAINED HEREIN MAY NOT BE SUITABLE FOR EVERY SITUATION. THIS WORK IS SOLD WITH THE UNDERSTANDING THAT THE PUBLISHER IS NOT ENGAGED IN RENDERING LEGAL, ACCOUNTING, OR OTHER PROFESSIONAL SERVICES. IF PROFESSIONAL ASSISTANCE IS REQUIRED, THE SERVICES OF A COMPETENT PROFESSIONAL PERSON SHOULD BE SOUGHT. NEITHER THE PUBLISHER NOR THE AUTHOR SHALL BE LIABLE FOR DAMAGES ARISING HEREFROM. THE FACT THAT AN ORGANIZATION OR WEBSITE IS REFERRED TO IN THIS WORK AS A CITATION AND/OR A POTENTIAL SOURCE OF FURTHER INFORMATION DOES NOT MEAN THAT THE AUTHOR OR THE PUBLISHER ENDORSES THE INFORMATION THE ORGANIZATION OR WEBSITE MAY PROVIDE OR RECOMMENDATIONS IT MAY MAKE. FURTHER, READERS SHOULD BE AWARE THAT INTERNET WEBSITES LISTED IN THIS WORK MAY HAVE CHANGED OR DISAPPEARED BETWEEN WHEN THIS WORK WAS WRITTEN AND WHEN IT IS READ.

For general information on our other products and services please contact our Customer Care Department within the United States at (800) 762-2974, outside the United States at (317) 572-3993 or fax (317) 572-4002.

Trademarks: Wiley, the Wiley logo, Wrox, the Wrox logo, Programmer to Programmer, and related trade dress are trademarks or registered trademarks of John Wiley & Sons, Inc. and/or its affiliates, in the United States and other countries, and may not be used without written permission. All other trademarks are the property of their respective owners. Wiley Publishing, Inc., is not associated with any product or vendor mentioned in this book.

Wiley also publishes its books in a variety of electronic formats. Some content that appears in print may not be available in electronic books.

About the Author

Scott Klein is a software developer and architect, and his passion for SQL Server, .NET, and all things XML led him to Greenville, South Carolina, where he currently works as a SQL/.NET developer for CSI, a software solutions company. He has written several articles for TopXML (`www.TopXLM.com`) and is a frequent speaker at SQL Server and .NET user groups around Greenville and the surrounding areas. When he is not sitting in front of a computer or spending time with his family, he can usually be found aboard his Yamaha at the local motocross track.

Acknowledgments

Writing a book is a daunting task. Writing your first book is just downright intimidating. The better the support people you have assisting and guiding you, the easier the task becomes. Therefore, it is only appropriate to thank those individuals who made this project much easier than it could have been.

First and foremost, Clay Andres for sticking with the book idea when it seemed like the idea wasn't going anywhere.

A huge thanks to the folks at Wiley for making this book happen. Brian Herrmann, my awesome development editor, was truly that. With my being a first time book author, Brian was a tremendous help and a sheer delight to work with. Thanks, Brian.

Thanks also to Jim Minatel, for accepting the book idea and letting me write it, and to Derek Comingore, for technically reviewing this book and providing priceless feedback and help. Thank you, Derek.

I would be remiss if I didn't mention the following individuals for their assistance in providing information. Primarily, I must thank Irwin Dolobowsky, my main contact at Microsoft. Irwin was my go-to guy, a life saver on many occasions. If he didn't know the answer, he knew who did or would find out who did. Also included in the list of Microsoft people to thank are Michael Rys, Arpan Desai, Srik Raghavan, Mark Fussell, Vineet Rao, and Beysim Sezgin. Thank you, to all of you.

Enough cannot be said about the love and support of my family. For my wife, Lynelle, who held the house together for the 8+ months I spent upstairs. And to my children, who were patient with their father knowing that they soon would get their dad back. I love you all.

I can only hope the next book is less daunting.

Credits

Senior Acquisitions Editor
Jim Minatel

Development Editor
Brian Herrmann

Technical Editor
Derek Comingore

Production Editors
Jonathan Coppola
Tim Tate

Copy Editor
Kathryn Duggan

Editorial Manager
Mary Beth Wakefield

Production Manager
Tim Tate

Vice President and Executive Group Publisher
Richard Swadley

Vice President and Executive Publisher
Joseph B. Wikert

Project Coordinator
Kristie Rees

Graphics and Production Specialists
Carrie A. Foster
Lauren Goddard
Denny Hager
Joyce Haughey
Jennifer Heleine
Alicia B. South

Quality Control Technicians
Laura Albert
John Greenough

Proofreading and Indexing
TECHBOOKS Production Services

Contents

Introduction

I have a new favorite word, courtesy of a 1961 Robert Heinlein novel titled *Stranger in a Strange Land*, and emphasized by Rod Paddock in the March/April 2005 *CoDe Magazine* article titled "Grokking .NET." The word is *Grok*, and not only is the meaning profound, the word is just fun to say.

In the novel, the word *Grok* is Martian and means to "understand so thoroughly that the observer becomes a part of the observed," but it applies to this book as well because this book is intended to help you *Grok* the new XML technologies in SQL Server 2005.

Microsoft is serious about XML and it could not be more evident than with the release of SQL Server 2005, supporting a full-blown new `xml` data type. This new data type can be used as a column or in variables and stored procedures. It also supports technologies such as XQuery and XML Data Manipulation Language, which provides full query and data modification capabilities on the `xml` data type.

The same focus has been taken to support the new `xml` data type on the client, and significant changes and enhancements have been made in version 2.0 of the .NET Framework as well as Visual Studio 2005. Why put all the work into the backend when you can't utilize it from the client? For this reason, this the focus of the book's energy is on those changes and improvements.

Microsoft also made some significant improvements to SQLXML, and SQL Server 2005 comes with SQLXML 4.0. The majority of these changes were made to support the new `xml` data type, but some improvements were also made in the security and performance areas to give you a better experience when dealing with XML.

Whom This Book Is For

This book is for developers with a desire to learn about this new and exciting technology and how it can be a benefit in their environment. While a previous knowledge of SQL Server 2000, T-SQL, and previous versions of SQLXML will come in handy, it is certainly not a perquisite to reading this book.

A decent understanding about XML and related technologies (such as XQuery) will also be useful when reading this book, but it isn't necessary.

What This Book Covers

This focus of this book is in three primary areas. First and foremost is the new `xml` data type and server-side XML processing with associated topics such as indexing and querying of the `xml` data type. The book then turns its focus on the client-side processing of the `xml` data type with an emphasis on the new and enhanced technologies found in SQLXML 4.0. Lastly, the book takes a look at the new enhancements and changes to the .NET Framework and ADO.NET for the support of the new `xml` data type and CLR integration in SQL Server 2005.

How This Book Is Structured

The book is organized into a number of parts and sections to help you better grasp the new technology coming in SQL Server. The first couple of parts, focusing on SQL Server 2005, lay the foundation for the rest of the book, which builds on that foundation by discussing how the new version of the .NET Framework, Visual Studio 2005, and the integration of the CLR can add tremendous benefit to your environment.

This book is structured as follows.

Part I—Introduction to SQL Server 2005 XML

- Chapter 1, "What's New in Version 2.0 of the .NET Framework for XML," takes a look at a few of the new features included in the new version of the .NET Framework as it pertains to XML.
- Chapter 2, "What's New in SQL Server 2005 XML," provides an overview of the changes and enhancements between SQL Server 2000 and SQL Server 2005.
- Chapter 3, "Installing SQL Server 2005," provides a quick walkthrough and explanation to installing SQL Server 2005.

Part II—Server-Side XML Processing in SQL Server 2005

- Chapter 4, "xml data type," introduces the `xml` data type.
- Chapter 5, "Querying and Modifying XML Data in SQL Server 2005," discusses how to query and modify the `xml` data type.
- Chapter 6, "Indexing XML Data in SQL Server 2005," discusses indexing on the `xml` data type.
- Chapter 7, "XML Schemas in SQL Server 2005," discusses XML schemas and XML schema collections.
- Chapter 8, "Transact-SQL Enhancements to FOR XML and OPENXML," talks about the T-SQL changes and enhancements in SQL Server 2005.
- Chapter 9, "CLR Support in SQL Server 2005," provides an overview of the CLR integration in SQL Server 2005.

Part III—Client-Side XML Processing in SQL Server 2005

- Chapter 10, "Client-Side Support for the xml data type," discusses the support of the `xml` data type from the client with topics such as SQLXML classes.
- Chapter 11, "Client-Side XML Processing with SQLXML 4.0," talks about the changes and enhancements to SQLXML 4.0 with a focus on the new SQL Native Client.

- Chapter 12, "Creating and Querying XML Views," talks about XML views and XSD schemas.
- Chapter 13, "Updating the XML View Using Updategrams," digs into the changes and improvements to updategrams.
- Chapter 14, "Bulk Loading XML Data Through the XML View," talks about the XML Bulk Load utility and discusses changes provided by SQLXML 4.0.
- Chapter 15, "SQLXML Data Access Methods," discusses more about the SQL Native Client and other data access methods such as ADO, OLE DB, and ODBC.
- Chapter 16, "Using XSLT in SQL Server 2005," provides an overview and introduction of XSLT.

Part IV—SQL Server 2005, SqlXml, and SOAP

- Chapter 17, "Web Service (SOAP) Support in SQL Server 2005," introduces and discusses SQL Server 2005 endpoints (Web Services).
- Chapter 18, "SOAP at the Client," builds on Chapter 18, discussing how to consume and use a SQL Server 2005 endpoint.
- Chapter 19, "Web Service Description Language (WSDL)," introduces and discusses WSDL files, using the built-in files and what to consider when you want to create your own WSDL file.

Part V—SQL Server 2005 and Visual Studio 2005

- Chapter 20, "SQL Server 2005 SQLXML Managed Classes," introduces SQLXML managed classes and how to use them from the client with Visual Studio 2005.
- Chapter 21, "Working with Assemblies," introduces assemblies and discusses how to create and use them in SQL Server 2005 and Visual Studio 2005.
- Chapter 22, "Creating .NET Routines," introduces .NET routines and discusses how to create and use them in SQL Server 2005 and Visual Studio 2005.
- Chapter 23, "ADO.NET," discusses some of the changes and enhancements to ADO.NET 2.0, such as asynchronous command operations, query notifications, and support of the `xml` data type.
- Chapter 24, "ADO.NET 2.0 Guidelines and Best Practices," provides some guidelines and best practices for ADO.NET 2.0.
- Chapter 25, "Case Study — Putting It All Together," provides a case in which most of the technologies discussed in this book are used.
- Appendix A, "XQuery in SQL Server 2005," provides a brief introduction to the support, syntax, and usage of XQuery in SQL Server 2005.

What You Need to Use This Book

All of the examples in this book require the following:

- ❑ SQL Server 2005
- ❑ Visual Studio 2005

While it is possible to run the products on separate computers, the examples in this book were done with both products running on the same computer.

Book Conventions

To help you get the most from the text and keep track of what's happening, we've used a number of conventions throughout the book.

> **Boxes like this one hold important, not-to-be forgotten information that is directly relevant to the surrounding text.**

Tips, hints, tricks, and asides to the current discussion are offset and placed in italics like this.

As for styles in the text:

- ❑ We *italicize* new terms and important words when we introduce them.
- ❑ We show keyboard strokes like this: Ctrl+A.
- ❑ We show file names, URLs, and code within the text like so: `persistence.properties`.
- ❑ We present code in two different ways:

```
In code examples we highlight new and important code with a gray
background.
```

```
The gray highlighting is not used for code that's less important in the present
context, or has been shown before.
```

Source Code

As you work through the examples in this book, you may choose either to type in all the code manually or to use the source code files that accompany the book. All of the source code used in this book is available for download at `http://www.wrox.com`. Once at the site, simply locate the book's title (either by using the Search box or by using one of the title lists) and click the Download Code link on the book's detail page to obtain all the source code for the book.

Because many books have similar titles, you may find it easiest to search by ISBN; for this book, the ISBN is 0-7645-9792-2.

Once you download the code, just decompress it with your favorite compression tool. Alternately, you can go to the main Wrox code download page at `http://www.wrox.com/dynamic/books/download.aspx` to see the code available for this book and all other Wrox books.

Errata

We make every effort to ensure that there are no errors in the text or in the code. However, no one is perfect, and mistakes do occur. If you find an error in one of our books, like a spelling mistake or faulty piece of code, we would be very grateful for your feedback. By sending in errata you may save another reader hours of frustration and at the same time you will be helping us provide even higher quality information.

To find the errata page for this book, go to `http://www.wrox.com` and locate the title using the Search box or one of the title lists. Then, on the book details page, click the Book Errata link. On this page, you can view all errata that has been submitted for this book and posted by Wrox editors. A complete book list including links to each book's errata is also available at `www.wrox.com/misc-pages/booklist.shtml`.

If you don't spot "your" error on the Book Errata page, go to `www.wrox.com/contact/techsupport.shtml` and complete the form there to send us the error you have found. We'll check the information and, if appropriate, post a message to the book's errata page and fix the problem in subsequent editions of the book.

p2p.wrox.com

For author and peer discussion, join the P2P forums at `p2p.wrox.com`. The forums are a Web-based system for you to post messages relating to Wrox books and related technologies and interact with other readers and technology users. The forums offer a subscription feature to e-mail you topics of interest of your choosing when new posts are made to the forums. Wrox authors, editors, other industry experts, and your fellow readers are present on these forums.

At `http://p2p.wrox.com` you will find a number of different forums that will help you not only as you read this book, but also as you develop your own applications. To join the forums, just follow these steps:

1. Go to `p2p.wrox.com` and click the Register link.
2. Read the terms of use and click Agree.
3. Complete the required information to join as well as any optional information you wish to provide and click Submit.
4. You will receive an e-mail with information describing how to verify your account and complete the joining process.

You can read messages in the forums without joining P2P, but in order to post your own messages, you must join.

Once you join, you can post new messages and respond to messages other users post. You can read messages at any time on the Web. If you would like to have new messages from a particular forum e-mailed to you, click the Subscribe to this Forum icon by the forum name in the forum listing.

For more information about how to use the Wrox P2P, be sure to read the P2P FAQs for answers to questions about how the forum software works as well as many common questions specific to P2P and Wrox books. To read the FAQs, click the FAQ link on any P2P page.

Part I: Introduction to SQL Server 2005 XML

1

What's New in Version 2.0 of the .NET Framework for XML

You are probably saying to yourself, "Whoa, wait a minute, I thought this book was about XML technology in SQL Server 2005." Yes, that is true. So why start the book off with a chapter about the XML technology found in version 2.0 of the .NET Framework?

Since the inception of the .NET Framework, Microsoft has taken a serious approach to supporting XML, a fact proven by looking at the amount of functionality provided in the System.Xml namespace, a group of classes specifically designed for the reading, writing, and updating of XML. Even in the first version of the .NET Framework, the support for XML was tremendous. The list of supported XML functionality included, but was not limited to, the following:

- Integration with ADO.NET
- Compliance with W3C standards
- Data source querying (XQuery)
- XML Schema support
- Ease of use

Microsoft set out to create a technology that dealt with data access using XML. Users of System.Xml in version 1.x of the .NET Framework agree that, on the whole, the technology contained a great number of useful classes that made dealing with XML and its related technologies a delight.

Even with all of the great advantages with version 1.1, it was not without its shortcomings. First and foremost, performance was an issue. Because of the way XML is processed, any obstacle or holdup in processing had a performance effect on the rest of the application. Security was another issue. For example, in the XML 1.0 specification, no precaution was taken to secure XML, which led to Denial of Service attacks via DTDs. Not good. The `XmlTextReader` had its own problems in that it could be subclassed and run in semitrusted code.

The inclusion of the CLR (Common Language Runtime) in SQL Server 2005 further strengthens the importance of understanding the XML technology from both sides, server and client. While the primary focus of this book is the support of XML in SQL Server 2005, a small handful of chapters focus on uncovering and understanding XML support in version 2.0 of the .NET Framework, and more important, how to utilize this technology in conjunction with SQL Server 2005 XML to get the most power and efficiency out of your application.

The entire goal of XML in version 2.0 of the .NET Framework boils down to a handful of priorities, with performance and W3C compliance at the top of the list. These are immediately followed by topics such as ease of use, or *pluggable,* meaning that the components are based on classes in the .NET Framework that can be easily substituted. Also included in the list is tighter integration with ADO.NET, which allows for datasets to read and write XML using the `XmlReader` and `XmlWriter` classes.

This chapter outlines some of the major feature enhancements made to the System.xml namespace in version 2.0 of the .NET Framework. If you look at all the changes made to the System.xml namespace, that list could possibly take up a very large portion of a book. The goal of this chapter, however, is to highlight the handful of significant changes that you will most likely use on a day-to-day basis to help improve your XML experience.

System.xml Version 2.0 Enhancements and New Features

The following list contains the System.xml enhancements that are covered in this chapter:

- Performance
- Type support
- XPathDocument
- XPathEditableNavigator
- XML query architecture
- `XmlReader`, `XmlWriter`, and `XmlReaderSettings`

Ideally, this list would include XQuery support. Unfortunately, in a January 2005 MSDN article, Microsoft announced that it would be pulling client-side XQuery support in version 2.0 of the .NET Framework. While the pains of realization set in, their reasons are justifiable. The main reason for pulling XQuery support was for the simple reason of timing. XQuery has yet to become a W3C recommendation and since it has not yet, this opens XQuery up for some changes. This put Microsoft in the peculiar situation of trying to meet the requests of its customers while trying to keep with future compatibility. Microsoft did not want to support a technology that could possibly change. That is not to say, however, that you won't ever see support for client-side XQuery. Microsoft's goal is to add it back in once XQuery has reached recommendation — which I hope will happen quickly.

Time to dig right in. The following section deals with arguably the most important enhancement to version 2.0 of the .NET Framework: performance.

Performance

You have to admit that developers like it when things go fast, and the faster the better. Developers absolutely hate waiting. XML performance is no different. This section, then, discusses the places where Microsoft focused the majority of the performance improvements. There isn't any code in this section to try out, but feel free to run some performance tests using some of the concepts discussed in this section.

XMLTextWriter and XMLTextReader

To begin with, the `XMLTextWriter` and `XMLTextReader` have been significantly re-written to cut these two call times nearly in half. Both of these classes have been completely rewritten to use a common code path.

XMLReader and XMLWriter

The `XmlReader` and `XMLWriter` classes can now be created via the `Create` method. In fact, they outperform the `XmlTextReader` and `XmlTextWriter` and as is discussed a little bit later, the `Create` method is now the preferred method of reading and writing XML documents.

XSLT Processing

XSLT processing performance has dramatically increased in version 2.0 of the .NET Framework. To understand why, you need to understand the `XslTransform` class. The `XslTransform` class, found in the System.Xml.Xsl namespace, is the brains behind XSLT. Its job is to transform the contents of one XML document into another XML document that is different in structure. The `XslTransform` class *is* the XSLT processor.

In version 1.1 of the .NET Framework, the `XslTransform` class was based on version 3.0 of the MSXML XSLT processor. Since then, version 4.0 of the MSXML XSLT processor came out and included enhancements that vastly improved the performance of the XSLT processor. So what's up with version 2.0 of the .NET Framework?

The idea with version 2.0 of the .NET Framework was to improve better yet the XSLT processing beyond that of the MSXML 4.0 XSLT processor. In order to do this, Microsoft completely rebuilt the XSLT processor from the ground up. The new processor is now called the `XslCompileTransform` class and lives in the System.Xml.Xsl namespace.

This new class has the same query runtime architecture as does the CLR, which means that it is compiled down to intermediate format at compile time. There is an upside and downside to this. The downside is that it will take longer to compile your XSLT style sheet. The upside is that the runtime execution is much faster.

Because there is no XQuery support at this time, performance improvements in the `XslCompileTransform` class are critical since XML filter and transformation still need to use XSLT and XPath. To help with this, Microsoft added XSLT debugger support in Visual Studio 2005 to debug style sheets. This comes in handy.

XML Schema Validation

There is one major reason why XML Schema validation performance has improved, and that is type support. Type support will be defined in more detail in the next section; however, for XML Schema validation, type support comes into play in a huge way when you try to load or transform an XML document.

When an XML document is loaded into a reader and a schema applied to it, CLR types are used to store the XML. This is useful because xs:long is now stored as a CLR long. First, the XML stores better this way. Second, there's no more of this useless untyped string stuff.

Type support also applies when creating an `XPathDocument` by applying XSLT to an original `XPathDocument`. In this scenario, the types are passed from one document to another without having to copy to an untyped string and then reparse them back the original type. This in itself is a tremendous performance boost, especially when linking multiple XML components.

Conversion between schema types and CLR types was possible in version 1.1 using the `XmlConverter` helper class, but conversion support is now extended to any `XmlReader`, `XmlWrite`, and `XPathNavigator` class, discussed in the next section.

Type Support

While XQuery support has been removed from version 2.0 of the .NET Framework, type support for many of the XML classes now offers type conversions. Classes such as the `XmlReader`, `XmlWrite`, and `XPathNavigator` are all now type-aware, and support conversion between CLR types and XML schema types.

In version 1.0 of the .NET Framework, type conversion was done by using the `xmlConvert` method, which enabled the conversion of a schema data type to a CLR (or .NET Framework) data type.

For example, the following code demonstrates how to convert an `xml` string value to a CLR Double data type using the `XmlConvert` in version 1.0 of the .NET Framework:

```
Imports System.Xml

 'declare local variables
Dim xtr As XmlTextReader = New XmlTextReader("c:\testxml.xml")
Dim SupplierID As Integer

'loop through the xml file
Do While xtr.Read()
    If xtr.NodeType = XmlNodeType.Element Then
        Select Case xtr.Name
            Case "SupplierID"
                SupplierID = XmlConvert.ToInt32(xtr.ReadInnerXml())
        End Select
    End If
Loop
```

While converting an untyped value of an XML node to a .NET Framework data type is still supported in version 2.0 of the .NET Framework, you can accomplish this same thing via a single method call new to version 2.0 of the .NET Framework. Using the `ReadValueAs` method call provides improved performance (because of the single method call) and is easier to use.

For example, you could rewrite the previous code as follows:

```
Imports System.Xml

  'declare local variables
Dim xtr As XmlTextReader = New XmlTextReader("c:\testxml.xml")

Dim SupplierID As Integer

 'loop through the file
 Do While xtr.Read()
     If xtr.NodeType = XmlNodeType.Element Then
         Select Case xtr.Name
             Case "SupplierID"
                 SupplierID = xtr.ReadElementContentAsInt()
         End Select
     End If
 Loop
```

The same principle can be applied to attributes and collections as well. For example, element values (as long as they are separated by spaces) can be read into an array of values such as the following:

```
Dim I as integer
Dim elementvalues() as integer = xtr.ReadValueAs(TypeOf(elementvalues())
For each I in elementvalues()
 Console.WriteLine(i)
Next I
```

So far the discussion has revolved around untyped values, meaning that all the values have been read from the XML document and stored as a Unicode string value that are then converted into a .NET Framework data type.

An XML document associated with an XML schema through a namespace is said to be *typed*. Type conversion applies to typed XML as well because the types can be stored in the native .NET Framework data type. For example, xs:double types are stored as .NET Double types. No conversion is necessary; again, improving performance.

All the examples thus far have used the `XmlReader`, and as much fairness should be given to the `XmlWriter` for Type conversion, which it has. The new `WriteValue` method on the `XmlWriter` class accomplishes the same as the `ReadValueAs` does for the `XmlReader` class.

In the following example, the `WriteValue` method is used to write CLR values to an XML document:

```
Imports System.Xml

Dim BikeSize As Integer = 250
Dim Manufacturer As String = "Yamaha"
```

```
Dim xws As XmlWriterSettings = New XmlWriterSettings
xws.Indent = True
Dim xw As XmlWriter = XmlWriter.Create("c:\motocross.xml", xws)
xw.WriteStartDocument()
xw.WriteStartElement("Motocross")
xw.WriteStartElement("Team")
xw.WriteStartAttribute("Manufacturer")
xw.WriteValue(Manufacturer)
xw.WriteEndAttribute()
xw.WriteStartElement("Rider")
xw.WriteStartAttribute("Size")
xw.WriteValue(BikeSize)
xw.WriteEndAttribute()
xw.WriteElementString("RiderName", "Tim Ferry")
xw.WriteEndElement()
xw.WriteEndElement()
xw.WriteEndDocument()
xw.Close()
```

Running this code produces the following results in the `c:\testmotocross.xml` file:

```
<?xml version"1.0" encoding="utf-8" ?>
<Motocross>
 <Team Manufacturer="Yamaha">
        <Rider Size="250">
               <RiderName>Tim Ferry</RiderName>
        <Rider>
 </Team>
</Motocross>
```

Now that a lot of the XML classes are type-aware, they are able to raise the schema types with additional conversion support between the schema types and their CLR type counterparts.

XPathDocument

The `XPathDocument` was included in version 1 of the .Net Framework as an alternative to the DOM for XML Document storage. Built on the XPath data model, the primary goal of `XPathDocument` was to provide efficient XSLT queries.

If the purpose of the `XPathDocument` is for XML Document storage, then what happened to the DOM? The DOM is still around and probably won't be going away any time soon. However, there are reasons why an alternative was necessary. First, the acceptance of XML is moving at an extremely fast rate, much faster than the W3C can keep up with the DOM recommendations. Second, the DOM was never really intended for use with XML as a data storage facility, specifically when trying to query the data. The DOM was created at the time when XML was just being adopted and obtaining a foothold in the development communities. Since then, XML acceptance has accelerated greatly and the DOM has not made the adjustments necessary to keep up in improvements. For example, XML documents are reaching high levels of capacity and the DOM API is having a hard time adapting to these types of enterprise applications.

Basically, the DOM has three shortcomings. First, the DOM API is losing its hold on the XML neighborhood with the introduction of `XmlReader` and `XmlWriter` as ways to read and write XML documents. Most developers are ready to admit that the DOM is not the friendliest technology to grasp. The `System.Xml` class provided an easy way to read and write XML documents. Second, the DOM data model is based on XML syntax and query language syntax is not. This makes for inefficient XML document querying. Lastly, application modifications are a must when trying to find better ways to store XML in the application. This is primarily due to the fact that there is no way to store XML documents. Version 2.0 of the .NET Framework has greatly improved the `XPathDocument` by building on better query support and `XPathNavigator` API found in version 1.

The goal of the `XPathDocument` in version 2.0 was to build a much better XML store. To do that, a number of improvements were made, including the following:

- `XmlWriter` to write XML content
- Capability to load and save XML documents
- Capability to accept or reject XML document changes
- XML store type support

What you will find is that the `XPathDocument` has all of the capabilities of the `XmlDocument` class with the added features of great querying functionality. On top of that, you can work in a disconnected state and track the changes made to the XML document.

The next section includes a number of examples to demonstrate loading, editing, and saving XML documents.

XPathNavigator

The `XPathNavigator` class provides a mechanism for the navigation and editing of XML content and providing methods for the editing of nodes in the XML tree.

In version 1.1 of the .NET Framework, the `XPathNavigator` *class was based purely on version 1.0 of the XPath data model. In version 2.0 of the .NET Framework, the* `XPathNavigator` *class is based on the XQuery 1.0 and XPath 2.0 data models.*

As part of the `System.Xml.XPath` namespace, the XPathNavigator class allows for very easy XML document navigation and editing. Using the XML document example created previously, the following code loads that XML document and appends a new `Rider` element using the `XmlWriter` and `XPathNavigator` classes:

```
Dim xpd as XPathDocument = New XPathDocument("c:\motocross.xml")
Dim xpn as XPathDocument = xpd.CreateNavigator

Xpen.MoveToFirstChild()
Xpen.MoveToNext()

Using xw As XmlWriter = xpn.AppendChild
 xw.WriteStartElement("Bike")
```

```
    xw.WriteAttributeString("Size", "250")
    xw.WriteElementString("RiderName", "Chad Reed")
    xw.WriteEndElement()
    xpd.Save("c:\motocross.xml")
End Using
```

The move from version 1.0 of XPath to version 2.0 is important for several reasons. First, there are better querying capabilities. For example, version 1.0 of XPath supported only four types, whereas version 2.0 supports 19 types. The second reason is better performance. XQuery 1.0 and XPath 2.0 nearly share the same foundation; XPath 2.0 is a very explicit subset of the XQuery 1.0 language. Because of this close relationship between the two, once you have learned one, you nearly understand the other.

XML Query Architecture

The XML query architecture provides the capability to query XML documents using different methods such as XPath and XSLT (with XQuery to be provided later). The classes that provide this functionality can be found in the `System.Xml.Xsl` namespace. Part of this functionality is the capability to transform XML data using an XSLT style sheet.

In version 2.0 of the .NET Framework, transforming XML data is accomplished by calling the `XslCompileTransform` class, which is the new XSLT processor. The `XslCompileTransform` class was mentioned previously during the discussion of performance. That section covered the topic of how the `XslCompileTransform` was created to improve XSLT performance. In this section, however, the focus of discussion will be on using the new XSLT processor and its associated methods.

The `XslCompileTransform` class replaces the `XslTransform` class in version 1.0 of the .NET Framework. Therefore, it is needless to say that the `Load` and `Transform` methods of the `XslTransform` class are also obsolete. What replaces them? The `XslCompileTransform` is very similar in architecture to the `XslTransform` class in that it also has two methods: the `Compile` method and the `Execute` method.

The `Transform` method of the `XslCompileTransform` class does exactly what the `Compile` method of the `XsltCommand` class did: it compiles the XSLT style sheet specified by the overload parameter. For example, the following code compiles the style sheet specified by the `XmlReader`:

```
Dim ss as String = "c:\motocross.xsl")
Dim xr as XmlReader = XmlReader.Create(ss)
Xr.ReadToDescendant("xsl:stylesheet")
Dim xct as XslCompiledTransform = new  XslCompiledTransform
 xct.Transform(xw)
```

In this example, you create the `XmlReader`, and then use its `ReadToDescendant` property to advance the `XmlReader` to the next descendant element using the qualified name. The `XslCompileTransform` is then created and the `Transform` method is called with the Reader.

The next step is to call the `Execute` method to execute the transform using the compiled style sheet. Using the previous example, add the following code:

```
Dim ss as String = "c:\motocross.xsl")
Dim xr as XmlReader = XmlReader.Create(ss)
Xr.ReadToDescendant("xsl:stylesheet")
Dim xct as XslCompileTransform = new  XslCompileTransform
 xct.Transform(xw)
Dim xpd as XPathDocument = New XPathDocument("c:\motocross2.xml")
Dim xw as XmlWriter = XmlWriter.Create(Console.Out)
Xs.Execute(New XPathDocument("c:\motocross2.xml"), xw)
Xw.close
```

The `Execute` method takes two input types for the source document: the `IXPathNavigatable` interface or a string URI.

The `IXPathNavigatable` interface is implemented in the `XmlNode` or `XPathDocument` classes and represents an in-memory cache of the XML data. Both classes provide editing capabilities.

The other option is to use the source document URI as the XSLT input. If this is the case, you will need to use an `XmlResolver` to resolve the URI (which is also passed to the `Execute` method).

Transformations can be applied to an entire document or a node fragment. However you're transforming a node fragment, you need to create an object containing the node fragment and pass that object to the `Execute` *method.*

XmlReader, XmlReaderSettings, XmlWriter, and XmlWriterSettings

Throughout this chapter you have seen a number of examples of how to use the `XmlReader` and `XmlWriter` classes. This section highlights a number of new methods that complement the existing methods of both of these classes.

The static `Create` method on both the `XmlReader` and `XmlWriter` classes is now the recommended way to create `XmlReader` and `XmlWriter` objects. The `Create` method provides a mechanism in which features can be specified that you want both of these classes to support.

As seen previously, when combined with the `XmlReaderSettings` class, you can enable and disable features by using the properties of the `XmlReaderSettings`, which are then passed to the `XmlReader` and `XmlWriter` classes.

By using the `Create` method together with the `XmlReaderSettings` class, you get the following benefits:

- You can specify the features you want the `XmlReader` and `XmlWriter` objects to support.
- You can add features to existing `XmlReader` and `XmlWriter` objects. For example, you can use the `Create` method to accept another `XmlReader` or `XmlWriter` object and you don't have to create the original object via the `Create` method.
- You can create multiple `XmlReaders` and `XmlWriters` using the same settings with the same functionality. The reverse of that is also true. You can also modify the `XmlReaderSettings` and create new `XmlReader` and `XmlWriter` objects with completely different feature sets.

- You can take advantage of certain features only available on `XmlReader` and `XmlWriter` objects when created by the `Create` method, such as better XML 1.0 recommendation compliance.
- The `ConformanceLevel` property of the `XmlWriterSettings` class configures the `XmlWriter` to check and guarantee that the XML document being written complies with XML rules. Certain rules can be set so that, depending on the level set, you can check the XML document to make sure it is a well-formed XML document. There are three levels:
  - **Auto:** This level should be used only when you are absolutely sure that the data you are processing will always be well-formed.
  - **Document:** This level ensures that the data stream being read or written meets XML 1.0 recommendation and can be consumed by any XML processor; otherwise an exception will be thrown.
  - **Fragment:** This level ensures that the XML data meets the rules for a well-formed XML fragment (basically, a well-formed XML document that does not have a root element). It also ensures that the XML document can be consumed by any XML processor.

Reading this list, you would think that it couldn't get any better. To tell you the truth, there are additional benefits with some of the items. For example, in some cases when you use the `ConformanceLevel` property, it automatically tries to fix an error instead of throwing an exception. If it finds a mismatched open tag, it will close the tag.

It is time to finish this chapter off with an example that utilizes a lot of what you learned:

```
Dim BikeSize As Integer = 250
Dim Manufacturer As String = "Yamaha"
Dim xws As XmlWriterSettings = New XmlWriterSettings
xws.Indent = True
xws.ConformanceLevel = ConformanceLevel.Document
Dim xw As XmlWriter = XmlWriter.Create("c:\motocross.xml", xws)
xw.WriteStartDocument()
xw.WriteStartElement("Motocross")
xw.WriteStartElement("Team")
xw.WriteStartAttribute("Manufacturer")
xw.WriteValue(Manufacturer)
xw.WriteEndAttribute()
'First Rider
xw.WriteStartElement("Rider")
xw.WriteStartAttribute("Size")
xw.WriteValue(BikeSize)
xw.WriteEndAttribute()
xw.WriteElementString("RiderName", "Tim Ferry")
xw.WriteEndElement()
'Second Rider
xw.WriteStartElement("Rider")
xw.WriteStartAttribute("Size")
xw.WriteValue(BikeSize)
xw.WriteEndAttribute()
xw.WriteElementString("RiderName", "Chad Reed")
xw.WriteEndElement()
xw.WriteEndDocument()
xw.Close()
```

The preceding example creates an XML document and writes it to a file. That file is then reloaded, and using the `XPathEditableNavigator` and `XPathNavigator`, a new node is placed in the XML document and resaved.

Summary

Now that you have an idea of the new XML features that appear in version 2.0 of the .NET Framework, you should also understand why this chapter was included in the book. Microsoft is taking a serious stance on XML technology and it is really starting to show with a lot of the features covered in this chapter.

Performance in XML is imperative to overall application performance, so this was a great place to start. As discussed, many improvements were made in this area so that XML performance was not the bottleneck in application performance. You also spent a little bit of time looking at where those performance improvements were made, such as modifications to certain classes sharing the same code path and complete class re-writes.

You read about the new type support added to the `XmlReader`, `XmlWriter`, and `XmlNavigator` classes, which contributes to the overall performance of XML, but more important, makes it much easier to read and write XML without the headaches of data type conversions.

You will probably agree that the `XPathDocument` and `XPathEditableNavigation` were fun to read and put to test. This is some absolutely cool technology that will make working with XML much easier and a lot more fun than in the past as compared to the DOM. The DOM isn't going away, but these technologies are far better suited for XML storage.

The enhancements to the `XmlWriter`, `XmlReader`, `XmlReaderSettings`, and `XmlWriterSettings` are a welcomed improvement, as you learned how easy it is to read, write, and modify XML documents.

Last, the topic of XML query architecture was discussed, along with the new `XslCompiledTransform` class, which replaces the `XslTransform` class, as well as how to use the new methods on that class.

In the next chapter you discover what's new in SQL Server 2005 XML (which is why you bought the book, right?) and all the new XML support it provides.

2

What's New in SQL Server 2005 XML

SQL Server 2000 made great strides in supporting XML and related technologies. When it first came out, it supported the following:

- Exposing relational data as XML
- Shredding XML documents into row sets
- Using XDR schemas to map XML schemas to database schemas
- Using XPath to query XML
- Using HTTP to query SQL Server data

Subsequent SQLXML web releases were blessed with additional features such as the following:

- updategrams
- Client-side FOR XML
- SQLXML managed classes
- Support for Web Services
- Support for XSD schemas

With the most recent release, SQLXML Service Pack 3, there were many additions such as building a web service with SQL Server 2000, querying relational data with XPath, and the inclusion of .NET managed classes, to name a few. This release was a welcome event to developers who were looking to extend this functionality and take it to higher grounds.

While each service pack provided better XML support, some very nice and needed enhancements and additions were made to SQL Server 2005 that let developers know that Microsoft is serious in supporting XML and XML technologies.

This chapter examines the new XML features in SQL Server 2005 and some of the enhancements made to SQL Server 2005 that existed in SQL Server 2000. All of these items are discussed in detail in later chapters, but the focus of this chapter is to highlight the new and improved XML features of this release of SQL Server.

With SQL Server 2005 there are six major improvements for XML support:

- New `xml` data type
- Indexes on `xml` type columns
- XQuery support
- XML DML (XML Data Modification Language)
- Transact-SQL enhancements (FOR XML and OPENXML)
- HTTP SOAP Access

Each topic is discussed in greater detail later in the book, so the goal of this chapter is to familiarize you with these six topics. The first point of discussion is the new `xml` data type.

xml data type

One of the most important new features of SQL Server 2005 is the addition of an `xml` data type. This new data type supports the storing of XML documents and XML fragments (discussed in Chapter 4) in a SQL Server database, as well as storing XML in Transact-SQL variables.

Overall, there are four major uses for the `xml` data type:

- Column type
- Variable type
- Parameter type
- Function return type

Realistically, there is a fifth use — using the `xml` data type in a `CAST` or `CONVERT` function used to convert an expression from one data type to another — which is covered in detail in Chapter 4.

The `xml` data type supports both typed and untyped XML. Simply put, when a collection of XML schemas is associated with the `xml` data type column, parameter, or variable, it is said to be typed. Otherwise is said to be untyped.

Nothing can really happen without the `xml` data type, so the following section introduces the `xml` data type column.

xml data type Column

Selecting the `xml` data type is just like selecting the `int` or `varchar` data type when you add a column to a table. It is a built-in data type just like all the other types. Simply select the `xml` data type from the drop down list as shown in Figure 2-1.

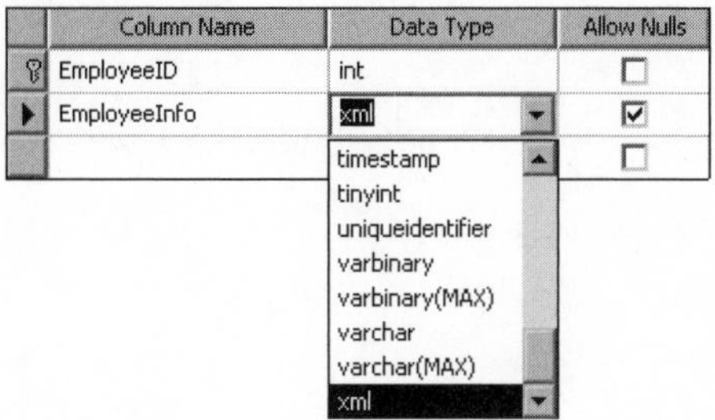

Figure 2-1

If you are not a visual person and like to sling code, you can also add it by using the following code:

```
CREATE TABLE Employees (EmployeeID int, EmployeeInfo xml)
```

Alternatively, if the table is already created and you want to add an `xml` data type column, you can use this code:

```
ALTER TABLE Employees ADD EmployeeInfo xml
```

You don't have to do anything special when setting the properties of the `xml` data type. However, you should be aware of one property: the XML schema `namespace` property. This property is a built-in function that accepts the namespace of a target XML schema, an XML schema collection, or the name of a relational schema. If this value is left empty, an XML instance is automatically mapped that has the necessary XML schemas. It does not return the predefined XML schemas.

xml Variable

Use of the `xml` data type goes far beyond simply creating a table. You can also use it as a variable.

The following syntax demonstrates how to use it as a variable:

```
DECLARE @xmlVar xml
```

The declaration of an `xml` variable is easy, nothing really complex. The `xml` data type has numerous uses as a variable. For example, Figure 2-2 shows how you can create a stored procedure that uses the `xml` data type as a variable in that stored procedure:

```
CREATE PROCEDURE GetEmployeeInfo
  @EmployeeID [int]
WITH EXECUTE AS CALLER
AS

  DECLARE @EmployeeInfo xml
```

Looking briefly at this stored procedure, an xml type variable is declared, which is used to store an XML document or fragment.

In addition to using the xml data type as a variable, you can also use it as a parameter, which is the subject of the next section.

XML Parameter

Using the same stored procedure as an example, modify it as follows:

```
CREATE PROCEDURE GetEmployeeInfo
  @EmployeeID [int],
  @EmployeeInfo [xml] OUTPUT
WITH EXECUTE AS CALLER
AS
```

This example uses the xml data type as an output parameter. The calling application, whether it is SQL Server itself or a .NET application, calls this stored procedure and passes XML to it.

Function Return

Similar to the variable, the xml data type can also be used as a return value. The following example uses the xml data type to return the results of a SELECT statement in this function. The return value is set as the xml data type, which is then returned via the RETURN statement:

```
CREATE FUNCTION dbo.ReturnXML()
RETURNS xml
WITH EXECUTE AS CALLER
AS
BEGIN
  DECLARE @EmployeeInfo xml
  SET @EmployeeInfo = '
   <Employee>
    <FirstName>Scott</FirstName>
    <LastName>Klein</LastName>
   </Employee>'
  RETURN(@EmployeeInfo)
END
GO
```

With the function created, it can now be executed as follows:

```
SELECT dbo.ReturnXML()
```

The results returned look like the following:

```
<Employee><FirstName>Scott</FirstName><LastName>Klein</LastName></Employee>
```

In this example, the return value was hard coded into the stored procedure, but the purpose was to illustrate the functionality of the `xml` data type. In Chapter 4, you learn how to query the `xml` data type, which you can also build into a function such as the example here.

These examples have been quite easy, but in the real world the amount of data being queried is not so little. That is why it is also possible to index the `xml` data type.

Indexes on the xml data type

The importance of indexes on the `xml` data type is crucial because `xml` data type columns are stored as binary large objects, or BLOB's. When you query `xml` data type columns, these BLOB's are shredded at runtime to evaluate the query if there are no indexes on the column. If there is a lot of data, this can be extremely costly in terms of performance and processing.

For this reason, SQL Server 2005 has introduced indexes on the `xml` data type columns.

Primary Index

There are two types of indexes: primary XML and secondary XML indexes. Creating these indexes is not rocket science as shown here:

```
CREATE PRIMARY XML INDEX PriI_Employee_EmployeeInfo
ON Employees(EmployeeInfo)
```

This example created a primary index on the Employee table on the EmployeeInfo column. A primary XML index is a shredded version of what is in the `xml` column. When this index is created, it writes several rows of data for each XML BLOB in the column.

A clustered index must already exist on the primary key of the table on which the XML index is being created. This is explained in more detail in Chapter 6.

Typically, when a table is dropped from a database, all the columns associated with that table are dropped as well. Not so with an `xml` column. An `xml` column with an associated index cannot be deleted or dropped from a table. The index must be removed first before the table can be deleted.

Secondary Index

You can further improve performance by creating a secondary XML index on the same column. It is not required, but could really improve performance on large amounts of data.

A primary index must exist before a secondary index can be created for a specific column.

This chapter shows only syntax, as Chapter 6 is dedicated to XML indexes and contains plenty of hands-on examples.

There are three types of secondary XML indexes: PATH, VALUE, and PROPERTY.

PATH

Use this index when you want to index the paths and node values as the key fields. This can significantly increase query performance. You create a PATH index using the following syntax:

```
CREATE XML INDEX SecI_Employee_EmployeeInfo_PATH
ON Employees (EmployeeInfo)
USING XML INDEX PriI_Employee_EmployeeInfo
FOR PATH
```

In a PATH secondary index, the `path` and `node` values are key columns that provide a more efficient search for searching paths.

VALUE

There are two reasons why you would want to use the VALUE index. First, if your queries are based on values, and second, if the path includes a wild card character or isn't fully specified. As with the PATH index, using the VALUE index in these situations increases query performance. The key columns for the VALUE index are the `node` and `path` values of the primary XML index.

Creating a VALUE index is not that much different from creating a PATH index. You need to make some simple changes to the previous code:

```
CREATE XML INDEX SecI_Employee_EmployeeInfo_VALUE
ON Employees (EmployeeInfo)USING XML INDEX PriI_Employee_EmployeeInfo
FOR VALUE
```

If your query is retrieving values from an XML document and you don't know the element or attribute names that contain the values, the VALUE index can come in very useful.

You'll notice that in each of these syntax examples, the secondary index was created using the primary index as the "primary" index. This means that these indexes are not individually acting indexes but that they work in tandem to improve query performance.

PROPERTY

The PROPERTY index is built on the key columns of the primary XML index such as Primary Key, path, or node values. The syntax is as follows:

```
CREATE XML INDEX SecI_Employee_EmployeeInfo_PROPERTY
ON Employees (EmployeeInfo)
USING XML INDEX PriI_Employee_EmployeeInfo
FOR PROPERTY
```

The PROPERTY index is beneficial when your query returns one or multiple values from a single XML instance, such as when you use the `value()` method of the `xml` data type.

XQuery

For SQL Server 2005, Microsoft has added server-side support for XQuery. Based on the existing XPath query language, XQuery is a language that can query structured, and even semi-structured, XML data. Coupled with the `xml` data type, this allows for quick and efficient storage and retrieval of XML data.

> **As of this writing, SQL Server 2005 Beta 2 comes with the XQuery language based on the November 2003 Last Call working draft. What does that mean? Primarily, it means that the XQuery found in SQL Server 2005 may be a bit different from the specifications of the final recommendation from the W3C. Not to worry though; the differences are covered later on in the book, as well as what you might find in the final release of SQL Server 2005.**
>
> **Also as of this writing, Microsoft has decided not to ship a client-side XQuery support in the .NET Framework 2.0. Again, what does this mean? It means you get to continue to use all that XSLT and XPath knowledge and experience, at least for the short term. And you thought it wouldn't pay off.**

Server-side support for XQuery means that you get all the added benefits of the XPath language plus additional support for things like better iteration, sorting of results, and the ability to shape the results of your queried XML (typically called *construction*). The XQuery data model is what drives the XQuery language, which means, just like the `xml` data type, you can have typed or untyped results as well as XML fragments.

XQuery Structure

In its simplistic form, an XQuery expression contains a query prolog (your namespace declaration) and the actual query expression. What follows is a simple example of an XQuery expression:

```
SELECT Instructions.query('declare namespace MSAW="http://schemas.microsoft.com/
Sqlserver/2004/07/adventure-works/ProductModelManuInstructions";
/MSAW:root/MSAW:Location[LocationID=50]')
AS Result
FROM Production.ProductModel
WHERE ProductModelID = 10
```

The first two lines are actually one line of code and should be entered as such. A hard return was used here to separate them for line continuation and readability only. If you type this syntax in exactly as shown (as two lines), you will receive an error.

Before getting deeper into the discussion of XQuery's structure, run the following SQL statement against the AdventureWorks database:

```
SELECT Instructions FROM Production.ProductModel WHERE ProductModelID = 10
```

Take the results of the above SQL query statement and save them to your hard drive as Production.xml for future reference.

There are basically two parts to this query. The first part contains the namespace declaration (`declare namespace ...`) and the actual query (`/MSAW:root/MSAW:Location[LocationID=50]`).

The results of this query are shown in Figure 2-2.

```
- <MSAW:Location
    xmlns:MSAW="http://schemas.microsoft.com/sqlserver/2004/07/adventure-
    works/ProductModelManuInstructions" LaborHours="3" LotSize="1"
    SetupHours="0.25" LocationID="50">
    Work Center 50 - SubAssembly The following instructions pertain to Work
    Center 50. (Setup hours = .25, Labor Hours = 3, Machine Hours = 0, Lot
    Sizing = 1)
  - <MSAW:step>
      Add
      <MSAW:material>Seat Assembly</MSAW:material>
      .
    </MSAW:step>
  - <MSAW:step>
      Add
      <MSAW:material>Brake assembly</MSAW:material>
      .
    </MSAW:step>
  - <MSAW:step>
      Add
      <MSAW:material>Wheel Assembly</MSAW:material>
      .
    </MSAW:step>
    <MSAW:step>Inspect Front Derailleur.</MSAW:step>
    <MSAW:step>Inspect Rear Derailleur.</MSAW:step>
  </MSAW:Location>
```

Figure 2-2

What you see is a section (or fragment) of the XML stored in the Instruction column. By specifying the query piece you were able to return just the section of the XML you were looking for. The namespace—a group or collection of elements and attributes with a unique name—is equally important. Namespaces provide the mechanism for mapping elements and attributes within an XML document to an associated schema. Running this query without the namespace would result in an error, such as the following:

```
There is no element named '{http://}'
```

Additional Concepts

There are a few concepts that you need to understand in order to fully grasp how XQuery works. An introduction to XQuery can be found in Chapter 5. Those concepts are the following:

- Sequence
- Atomization
- Quantification
- Type promotion

The first of these concepts, sequence, is discussed in the next section.

Sequence

A sequence is simply the result of an XQuery expression that contains a list of XML nodes and fragments as well as XSD types. An *item* is an individual entry in the sequence and can be a node of one of the following types:

- Element
- Attribute
- Text
- Comment
- Document
- Processing instruction

The following example demonstrates how to construct a query that will return a single element sequence:

```
SELECT Instructions.query('
<Test>This is a test </Test>')
AS Result
FROM Production.ProductModel
WHERE ProductModelID = 10
```

The result of this query returns the following:

```
<Test>This is a test</Test>
```

Not very impressive, but it does demonstrate that you have the ability to retrieve specific information from within your XML document. For example, the following query returns the first step (previously shown in Figure 2-2) from your original query:

```
SELECT Instructions.query('declare namespace MSAW="http://schemas.microsoft.com/_
Sqlserver/2004/07/adventure-works/ProductModelManuInstructions";
FOR $Inst in /MSAW:root
Return
 (
 <step1> {string(($Inst/MSAW:Location[LocationID=50]/MSAW:step[1][1]} </step1>
 )
') AS Result
FROM Production.ProductModel
WHERE ProductModelID = 10
```

You should see the following results:

```
<step1>Insert aluminum sheet MS-6061 into tool T-99 framing tool</step1>
```

This query is almost identical to your original query, but what you told it to do was retrieve a more specific value (or sequence) from the XML document.

Atomization

Atomization is the process of retrieving the typed value of an item, and many times it is implied. In certain scenarios, atomization allows you to return the value of an item without having to query for it again. The following example queries the `MachineHours` attribute from the previous example and returns multiple values. The first value is the original queried value. The second value uses the `data()` function to extract the same value and increments it by 1 (adds 1 to it). The third value matches the second value, but is returned automatically using atomization instead of using the `data()` function again.

```
SELECT Instructions.query ('declare namespace MSAW="http://schemas.microsoft.com/_
Sqlserver/2004/07/adventure-works/ProductModelManuInstructions";
FOR $AW in / MSAW:root/ MSAW:Location[2]
Return
 <AW OriginalMachineHours = "{$AW/@MachineHours}"
 NewMachineHours = "{data{$AW/@MachineHours} +1}"
 NewMachineHours1 = "{$AW/@MachineHours +1}></AW>"
')
FROM Production.ProductModel
WHERE ProductModelID = 10
```

This says, "Take a look at the second Location node and return the MachineHours attribute. Now add 1 to it and return that value." Your results should look similar to the following:

```
<AW OriginalMachineHours="1.75" NewMachineHours="2.75" NewMachineHours1="2.75/>
```

Quantification

There are two types of quantification, Existential and Universal, which specify semantics for Boolean operators when applied to two sequences.

A quantified expression in XQuery uses the following syntax:

```
{ some | every } <variable> in <Expression> satisfies <Expression>
```

Existential

The Existential quantifier says that for any two sequences, if an item in the first sequence has a match in the second sequence based on the comparison operator used, then the return value is true. In other words, if a value in the first sequence matches a value in the second sequence based on a specific comparison operator, then the return value is true.

Look at the following example:

```
SELECT Instructions.query ('declare namespace MSAW="http://schemas.microsoft.com/_
sqlserver/2004/07/adventure-works/ProductModelManuInstructions";
 if (every $AW in // MSAW:Location
        Satisfies $AW/@MachineHours)
 then
        <return>All Locations have Machine Hours</return>
 else
        <return>Not all Locations have Machine Hours</return>
')
FROM Production.ProductModel
WHERE ProductModelID = 10
```

When you run this, you get the following in return:

```
<return>Not all locations have Machine Hours</return>
```

If you still have your Production.xml file open, take a look at each `<Location>` element and notice that not every `<Location>` element has a `MachineHours` attribute, so your results are correct.

Now make the following changes to the `then` and `else` clauses and run the query again:

```
SELECT Instructions.query ('declare namespace MSAW="http://schemas.microsoft.com/_
sqlserver/2004/07/adventure-works/ProductModelManuInstructions";
 if (every $AW in // MSAW:Location
        satisfies $AW/@LocationID)
 then
        <return>All Locations have a LocationID</return>
 else
        <return>Not all Locations have a LocationID</return>
')
FROM Production.ProductModel
WHERE ProductModelID = 10
```

What results did you get? What you should get back is a little bit different message than the first example, stating that all locations have a LocationID, as follows:

```
<return>All Locations have a LocationID</return>
```

The reason for this is because in this last example the existential quantifier returned a value of true, meaning that for each location, a LocationID was found. That was not the case in the first example.

Universal

The Universal quantifier says that for any two sequences, if all items in the first sequence have a match in the second sequence, then the return value is true.

The following example looks to see if any of the pictures in the Product table has an angle of front:

```
SELECT CatalogDescription.value ('declare namespace
MSAW="http://schemas.microsoft.com/_
sqlserver/2004/07/adventure-works/ProductModelManuInstructions";
 if (some $AW in //MSAW: ProductDescription/MSAW:Picture
        satisfies $AW/@MSAW:Angle="front"
 then
        "True"
 else
        "False"
', 'varchar(5)') as PictureAngleFront
FROM Production.ProductModel
WHERE ProductModelID = 35
```

Your results should look like the following:

```
PictureAngleFront
TRUE
```

There are two changes in this code you need to be aware of. First is the schema declaration. Second, you are looking to see if any of pictures have an `Angle` of `front`, so your XQuery statement uses `some` instead of `every`. If you had used `every` and not all of the Picture elements had an `Angle` of `front` then your return value would be `False`.

Type Promotion

Type promotion allows for type casting for numeric expressions if one of the values is untyped or for numeric types.

For example, you may want to compare numerical values and determine which value is higher or lower. In these cases, you can implicitly cast the two numbers similar to the following:

```
Max(xs:long("1.0"), xs:integer("2.0"))
```

In the preceding example, both values were typed, but what if you needed to type cast an untyped value with a typed value? The following example shows how to cast a typed value with an untyped value:

```
Max(xtd:untypedatomic(35), xs:integer("2.0"))
```

This section barely touched these topics, but for good reason: Chapter 5 and Appendix A are dedicated to XPath, XQuery, and the querying of the `xml` data type and how they are used in SQL Server 2005. This chapter is just intended to whet your appetite.

XML Data Modification Language

XQuery is a very powerful language intended to allow for querying XML data, and while it is very useful and powerful, it does have its limitations. The biggest limitation is the inability to modify XML documents. To compensate for the shortcomings of XQuery, Microsoft has added on to the XQuery implementation in SQL Server 2005 by giving developers the ability to insert, update, and delete XML documents and fragments.

Microsoft did this by creating the XML Data Modification Language (or XML DML). The XML DML is built on and around the XQuery language as defined by the W3C, but it enhances XQuery by allowing full-on insert, update, and delete access anywhere the xml data type is used.

Using XML DML is as simple as adding one of the three following words to your XQuery statement:

- Insert
- Delete
- Update

The following sections show you some easy examples.

Insert

The basic syntax for inserting a node or nodes into an XML document looks like this:

```
INSERT
 Expression1 (
        {as first | as last } into | after | before
Expression2
         )
```

Now take a look at an example that inserts an element into an XML document. Suppose you had the following XML document:

```
<Root>
 <Employee EmployeeID="1">
        <EmployeeInformation>
        </EmployeeInformation>
 </Employee>
</Root>
```

You want to insert some employee information into the XML document. The following example inserts a `firstname` element into the XML document underneath the `EmployeeInformation` element:

```
INSERT <FirstName>Evel</FirstName>
Into (/ROOT/ProductDescription/EmployeeInformation)[1]
```

Your XML document now looks like the following:

```
<Root>
 <Employee EmployeeID="1">
        <EmployeeInformation>
                <FirstName>Evel</FirstName>
        </EmployeeInformation>
 </Employee>
</Root>
```

To try this example, type the following code into Query Builder and execute it:

```
DECLARE @xmldoc xml
SET @xmldoc =
'<Root>
 <Employee EmployeeID="1">
        <EmployeeInformation>
        </EmployeeInformation>
 </Employee>
</Root>'
SET @xmldoc.modify('
insert <FirstName>Evel</FirstName>
into (/ROOT/Employee/EmployeeInformation)[1]')
GO
```

You didn't need to specify first or last because it was the first child added. The `as first` and `as last` keywords are saved for Chapter 5 when this is discussed in depth. In that chapter, added attributes are discussed as well.

Delete

The syntax for deleting a node or nodes is really simple:

```
DELETE expression
```

Use the previous example and delete the element you just added. Here is the original code with the `delete` code added (shown with a gray screen background):

```
DECLARE @xmldoc xml
SET @xmldoc =
'<Root>
 <Employee EmployeeID="1">
        <EmployeeInformation>
        </EmployeeInformation>
 </Employee>
</Root>'
SELECT @xmldoc
SET @xmldoc.modify('
insert <FirstName>Evel</FirstName>
into (/ROOT/Employee/EmployeeInformation)[1]')
SELECT @xmldoc
SET @xmldoc.modify('
delete /Root/Employee/EmployeeInformation/FirstName')
SELECT @xmldoc
GO
```

Execute this in Query Builder. Each `SELECT @xmldoc` returns a row that you can click and see the results of the query. When you click on the first result you see the original query. Click the second result and you see the same information but with the `<FirstName>` element added. Click the third result and you see the `<FirstName>` element has been removed.

As with the `Insert`, you can delete attributes and much more.

Update

You can update the contents of an XML document with the `modify` method. The syntax looks like this:

```
Replace value of Expression1 with Expression2
```

`Expression1` is the node whose value you want to update. `Expression2` is the new value of the node.

It doesn't make sense to update a node or element. Typically you just delete the offending node. The `replace value of` syntax is used to update the *value* of a node.

Use your previous XML document to illustrate updating the value of a node in an XML document. Make the appropriate changes to the XML as follows:

```
DECLARE @xmldoc xml
SET @xmldoc =
'<Root>
<Employee EmployeeID="1">
        <EmployeeInformation>
                <FirstName>Scott</FirstName>
        </EmployeeInformation>
 </Employee>
</Root>'
SELECT @xmldoc
SET @xmldoc.modify('
replace value of (/Root/Employee/EmployeeInformation/FirstName/text())[1]
with "Calvin"
')
SELECT @xmldoc
GO
```

Execute this in Query Builder. When you click the first result, you see the original query with the value of `<FirstName>` element of `Scott`. Click the second result and you see the same information but with the value of the `<FirstName>` element updated to `Calvin`.

While you have barely scratched the surface of the XML DML topic, you should start to see the flexibility and power it adds to XQuery. You'll learn more about this in Chapter 5.

Transact-SQL Enhancements

For those of you who have used `FOR XML` and `OPENXML` before, you'll whole-heartedly welcome the Transact-SQL changes to both of these. SQL Server 2000 introduced `FOR XML` and `OPENXML` as a clause to the `SELECT` statement. The `FOR XML` clause supported three modes — `RAW`, `AUTO`, and `EXPLICIT`. The `RAW` mode created a single element per row returned. It did not allow nesting. The `AUTO` mode generated nesting based on the `SELECT` statement. The `EXPLICIT` mode gave you greater control over the shape of your XML.

The downside to using pre-SQL Server 2005 `FOR XML` clauses was that `FOR XML` could be used only on the client side. And it wasn't the easiest thing to figure out, especially if you were trying to generate somewhat complex `EXPLICIT` structures.

Fortunately, there is SQL Server 2005. This section covers the changes and enhancements to `FOR XML` and `OPENXML` in the new version of SQL Server.

FOR XML

In SQL Server 2005 many improvements and new features were added to make `FOR XML` more useful, including the following:

- Integrating FOR XML with the xml data type
- Nesting FOR XML expressions
- The new PATH mode
- Assigning FOR XML results

This section covers these enhancements in the order in which they appear in the list, beginning with integration of FOR XML with the xml data type.

xml data type Integration

The addition of the xml data type in SQL Server provides the capability to directly generate XML. You can request that the query results of a FOR XML query be returned as an xml data type by specifying the new TYPE directive. For example:

```
SELECT EmployeeID, FirstName, LastName
FROM Employees
Order By EmployeeID
FOR XML AUTO, TYPE
```

Your results look like this:

```
<Employees EmployeeID="1" FirstName="Sarah" LastName="Adams" />
<Employees EmployeeID="2" FirstName="Joe" LastName="Arnet" />
<Employees EmployeeID="3" FirstName="Dale" LastName="Arbuckle" />
```

Nesting FOR XML Expressions

SQL Server 2000 supported the capability to specify the FOR XML clause at the top level of the SELECT statement only. This meant that any results returned to you were in need of further manipulation. SQL Server 2005 now provides the capability to generate FOR XML queries that return results in the xml data type for server side processing. This means that you can write nested queries where the inner query returns the results to the outer query as an xml data type.

For this example, drop and create the following two tables and associated data:

```
DROP TABLE Employees
GO

CREATE TABLE [dbo].[Employees](
 [EmployeeID] [int] NOT NULL,
 [FirstName] [varchar](25) NULL,
 [LastName] [varchar](25) NULL
) ON [PRIMARY]

GO

CREATE TABLE [dbo].[EmployeePhone](
 [EmployeePhoneID] [int] NOT NULL,
 [EmployeeID] [int] NOT NULL
```

```
  [CellPhoneNumber] [varchar](15) NULL,
  [HomePhoneNumber] [varchar](15) NULL
) ON [PRIMARY]

GO

INSERT INTO Employees (EmployeeID, FirstName, LastName)
 VALUES (1, 'Fred', 'Flintstone')
GO

INSERT INTO Employees (EmployeeID, FirstName, LastName)
 VALUES (2, 'Barney', 'Rubble')
GO

INSERT INTO EmployeePhone (EmployeePhoneID, EmployeeID, CellPhoneNumber,
HomePhoneNumber)
 VALUES (1, 1, '555-BED-ROCK', '555-555-5555')
GO
```

The following example illustrates a nested query using `FOR XML`:

```
SELECT EmployeeID, FirstName, LastName
 (SELECT CellPhoneNumber, HomePhoneNumber
 FROM EmployeePhone ep
 WHERE ep.EmployeeID = e.EmployeeID
 FOR XML AUTO, TYPE)
FROM Employees
WHERE EMPLOYEEID = 23
FOR XML AUTO, TYPE
```

In the preceding example, the inner `SELECT` statement queries the employee phone number and returns it in XML format to the outer query by supplying the `FOR XML` expression. It is guaranteed to be well-formed because the `TYPE` directive was supplied. The outer query then runs its query, combining its results with those of the inner results to provide a well-formed XML document.

PATH Mode

The `PATH` mode is a new addition to `FOR XML` in SQL Server 2005. Do you remember how difficult it was to find your way around the `EXPICIT` mode? Wouldn't it be nice to provide the same flexibility and functionality without the complications of the `EXPLICIT` mode? Fortunately, that is what the `PATH` mode does. It provides the flexibility of the `EXPLICIT` mode in a much easier fashion.

The PATH mode treats column names and column aliases as XPath expressions, indicating how the values are mapped to XML. The following example, while quite simple, illustrates the syntax of the PATH mode.

```
SELECT ContactID, FirstName, LastName
FROM Person.Contact
WHERE ContactID = 218
FOR XML PATH
```

The PATH mode generates element-centric results by default, so the results from this query look like the following:

```
<row>
  <ContactID>218</ContactID>
  <FirstName>Scott</FirstName>
  <LastName>Colvin</LastName>
</row>
```

Namespaces are not supported when generating XML using the PATH mode.

The PATH mode and the rest of the `FOR XML` enhancements are discussed in much more detail in Chapter 8.

Assigning FOR XML Results

`FOR XML` queries can now return assigned values that allow you to assign the results of a `FOR XML` query to a variable, as well as insert them into an `xml` data type column.

For example, you could assign the following `FOR XML` query result to a variable as follows:

```
CREATE TABLE [dbo].[Vendor](
 [VendorID] [int] NOT NULL,
 [VendorName] [varchar](25) NULL,
 [VendorAddress] [varchar](25) NULL,
 [VendorContact] [varchar](25) NULL
) ON [PRIMARY]

GO

DECLARE @xmlvar xml
SET @xmlvar = SELECT VendorID, VendorName, VendorAddress, VendorContact FROM Vendor
FOR XML AUTO, TYPE
```

Just as easily, you can insert the results of a `FOR XML` query directly into a table as follows:

```
CREATE TABLE [dbo].[VendorInfo](
 [VendorInfoID] [int] IDENTITY(1, 1) NOT NULL,
 [VendorInfo] xml NULL,
) ON [PRIMARY]

GO

INSERT INTO Products (VendorInfo) (SELECT VendorName, VendorAddress, VendorContact
FROM Vendors FOR XML AUTO, TYPE)
GO
```

In the preceding example, the VendorInfo column is an `xml` data type column.

In addition to these enhancements, additional enhancements have been made to the `RAW` and `EXPLICIT` modes. These `FOR XML` enhancements allow you to do the following:

- Specify a row element name
- Retrieve element-centric XML
- Specify the root element

The `OPENXML` enhancements include the following:

- CDATA directive with an element name
- `elementxsinil` column mode

All of these enhancements are discussed in detail in Chapter 8, so stay tuned.

HTTP SOAP Access

SQL Server 2005 provides the capability to send HTTP `SOAP` requests directly to SQL Server without going through an IIS server. This includes the capability to execute Transact-SQL statements and stored procedures (including extended stored procedures) as well as user-defined functions.

This functionality works only if SQL Server 2005 is running on Windows Server 2003.

Just as important, SQL Server has the capability to function as its own Web Service, which provides the capability to allow any Web Service application to access SQL Server, reduce the need for a firewall with its built-in security, and utilize the Web Service infrastructure by applying predefined schemas to query results in native XML format.

No examples are given in this chapter, but Chapters 17 and 18 are dedicated specifically to HTTP `SOAP` access.

Summary

The main purpose of this chapter was to give you brief look into the new features and enhancements in SQL Server 2005. A large portion of the chapter examined the new `xml` data type as it applies to columns, variables, and parameters, and the impact it has on the rest of the XML topics.

You spent some time looking at how you can index the `xml` data type to gain performance using primary and secondary indexes. You also learned how SQL Server 2005 stores `xml` instances and what that means when querying these columns, especially when dealing with large amounts of data.

Additionally, this chapter included enough coverage of XQuery to give you a basic understanding of its functionality. However, because XQuery is such an integral part of SQL Server 2005 that you'll spend a good portion of Chapter 5 on it.

XQuery can't be introduced without also introducing the XML Data Modification Language. As you discovered in this chapter, XML DML makes up for some of the things lacking in XQuery and how you can put the functionality of the data modification language to good use. Like XQuery, though, a couple of pages do not do XML DML justice, so it is also covered in more depth in Chapter 5.

After discussing the `xml` data type, XQuery, and XML DML, you learned about the Transact-SQL enhancements to `FOR XML`. As you have probably figured out by now, these improvements could not have come at a better time. `FOR XML`'s integration with the `xml` data type was a great blessing, and together with the `PATH` directive and other enhancements, your `FOR XML` life just got a lot easier. This chapter barely scratched the surface, though, and FOR XML is covered in detail in Chapter 8.

Last, you learned a little bit about the HTTP `SOAP` capabilities in SQL Server 2005. Chapters 17 and 18 are dedicated to this topic, so this chapter simply introduced you to some of the highlights and features that SQL Server 2005 supports in this area.

In the next chapter, you'll learn how to install and configure SQL Server 2005.

3

Installing SQL Server 2005

The first two chapters of the book highlighted some of the features that are new to SQL Server 2005 and XML, as well as what you can look forward to in the .NET Framework 2.0. Both of those topics will come in very handy later on in the book, so keep all of that newfound information in the back of your mind when reading later chapters.

This chapter walks you through the installation of SQL Server 2005 step by step so that you can put it to good use throughout the rest of the book. Fortunately, you will find that the installation is not significantly different from previous versions of SQL Server. If you have already installed it or don't want to try it out on your own, you can skip to Chapter 4. However, there are a few major differences pertaining to the installation of SQL Server 2005, so you might want to read this chapter to become familiar with those differences.

The version used throughout this book is SQL Server 2005 Developers Edition Beta 2, build 3790. Installation requirements aren't covered in this book, but you can find information regarding hardware and software requirements on Microsoft's website at `www.microsoft.com/sql/` *or on the SQL Server installation CD.*

Where to Get SQL Server 2005 Beta 2 Express Edition

Unless you have an MSDN subscription (Universal, Enterprise, or Professional) the only thing to work with is the SQL Server 2005 Beta 2 Express Edition, available at `www.microsoft.com/downloads/details.aspx?FamilyID=62B348BB-0458-4203-BB03-8BE49E16E6CD&displaylang=en`.

The SQL Server Express Edition is the next version of MSDE. The Beta 2 version is an evaluation version and is good up to 18 months from the date of installation. After the evaluation period is over, no SQL Server services will start.

Like its bigger brothers (SQL Server 2005 Enterprise Edition and SQL Server 2005 Developer Edition), the Express Edition also needs the .NET Framework 2.0. But unlike its bigger brothers, the Express Edition does not install it. You have to do that yourself—at least in Beta 2.

You can get the .NET Framework 2.0 from `www.microsoft.com/downloads/details.aspx?familyid=B7ADC595-717C-4EF7-817B-BDEFD6947019&displaylang=en`.

Installing SQL Server 2005

Begin the installation by running the `Setup.exe` in the root of the CD/DVD or if Autorun does not automatically begin the installation.

The first screen to appear is the Welcome/Start screen. Here you have several options. This is a good place to review the requirements for running SQL Server 2005 by selecting the Review hardware and software requirements link.

To begin the actual installation, click the Run the SQL Server Installation Wizard link shown in Figure 3-1.

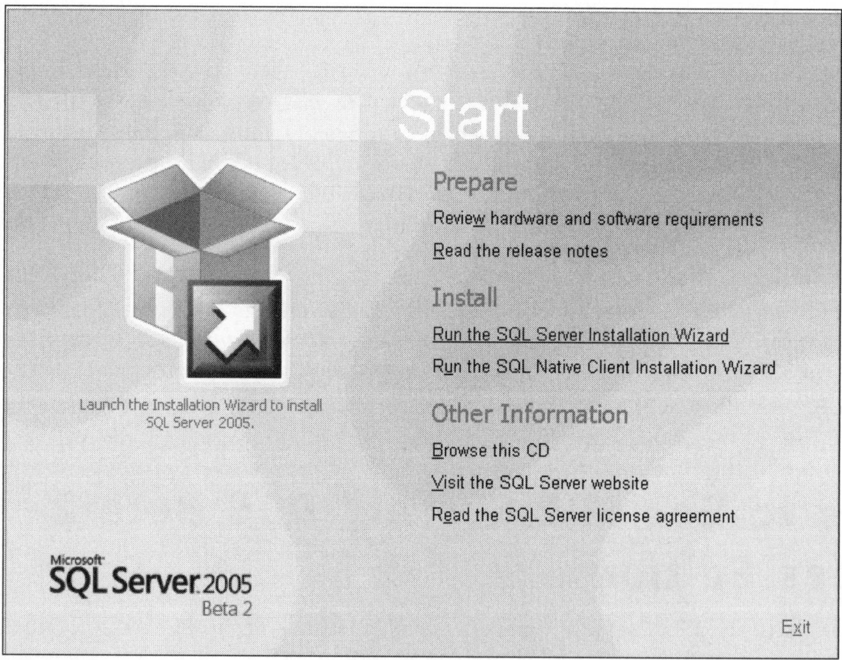

Figure 3-1

The first part of the installation installs software that is necessary prior to installing SQL Server 2005. Three components are required before the installation of SQL Server 2005 can begin: the .NET Framework 2.0, Microsoft SQL Native Client, and Microsoft SQL Server 2005 Beta 2 Setup Support Files, as shown in Figure 3-2.

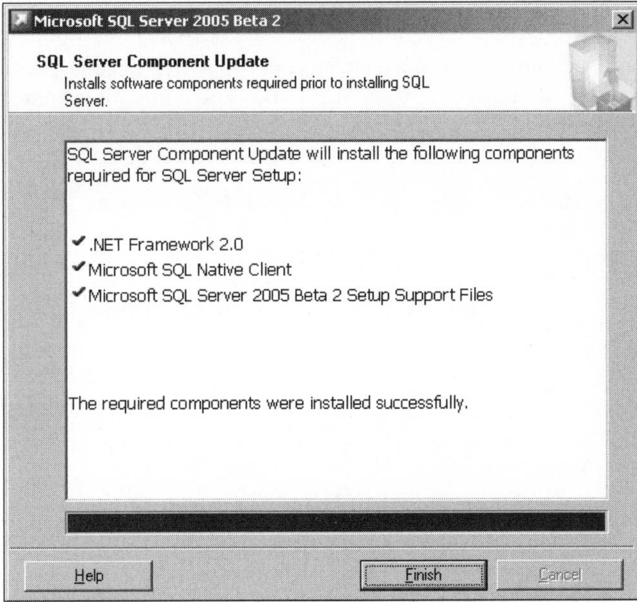

Figure 3-2

The first prerequisite component is the .NET Framework 2.0. As discussed in Chapter 1, SQL Server 2005 uses version 2.0 of the .NET Framework. Luckily, SQL Server 2005 installs version 2.0 for you.

Once all the perquisite components have been installed, click Finish. At this point the SQL Server installation begins, as shown in Figure 3-3.

Figure 3-3

Click Next to begin the installation of SQL Server 2005.

Figure 3-4 shows an important step in the installation process: the System Configuration Check, or SCC. It verifies a total of twelve items of your system to make sure that your system on which to install SQL Server is configured correctly.

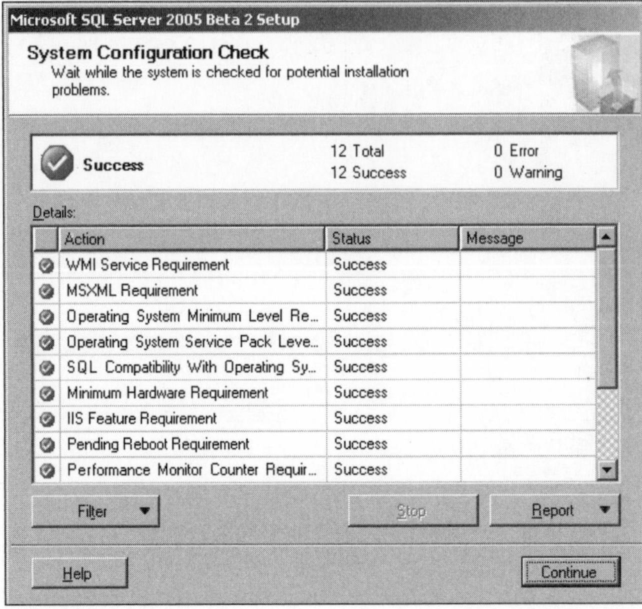

Figure 3-4

We're lucky this process does not take long and it actually makes multiple checks at one time. The SCC is quite thorough and does not allow the installation to continue if certain requirements are not met. For example, it generates a warning if the computer that SQL Server 2005 is being installed on is less than 600 MHz, but it will not stop the installation.

As another example, if the system on which SQL Server 2005 is being installed on has less than 128MB of RAM, it does not allow the installation to continue. It also generates a warning if the amount of memory is between 128MB and 256MB of RAM.

For a complete list of SCC checks, see the online help under the topic *system configuration checker*.

The Continue button is available only if all check results are successful, or if failed checks are non-fatal. For any failed check items, resolution to blocking issues is included with results in the report.

If everything passes and you are given the green light, click Continue.

The next screen, shown in Figure 3-5, allows you to choose which components you want to install. Obviously you want to choose the first option, SQL Server, as that is the minimum required component to run SQL Server 2005. You may also want to select the Workstation components, Books Online and development tools option, which installs some of the components and tools with which to administer SQL Server 2005. Selecting one of these components selects the minimum features necessary to run SQL Server 2005. It is similar to selecting a Typical installation.

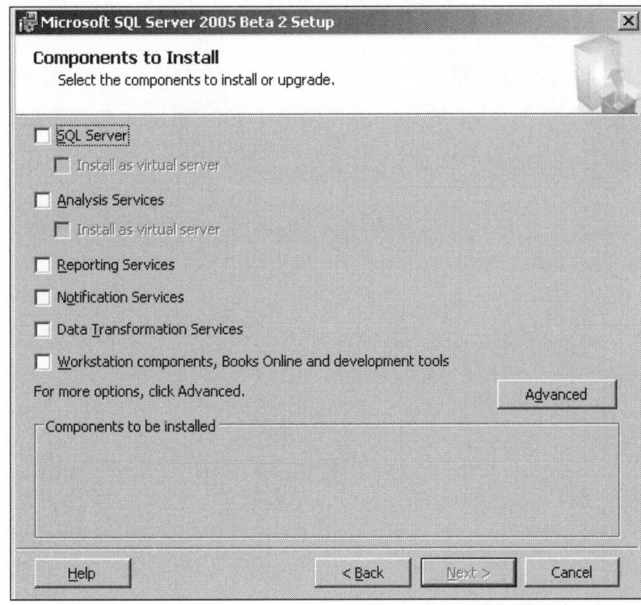

Figure 3-5

One of the new features in the installation is the capability to install SQL Server 2005 as a virtual server. Virtual server enables you to run multiple instances of an OS on a single computer. Think of it as running multiple computers on a single computer. You can select the Install as virtual server option if you want SQL Server to support it.

Also included in the installation is Reporting Services, which was a separate installation for SQL Server 2000.

For a more detailed installation, click the Advanced button, which displays a detailed list of items, shown in Figure 3-6. This option allows you to select which features you want based on the components you selected in the previous step, as well as allowing you to select more detailed features as opposed to a generic component on the previous screen. For example, selecting the SQL Server component on the previous screen basically tells the installer that you want to install SQL Server 2005. This screen lets you select detailed installation options for the SQL Server component such as Replication and Full-Text Search.

If you overlooked a component you wanted to install on the previous installation step, you can either select it here or click the Back button to select the desired component. Selecting the components on the Feature Selection screen is preferable over going back because you can select the features for that component and not have to go back.

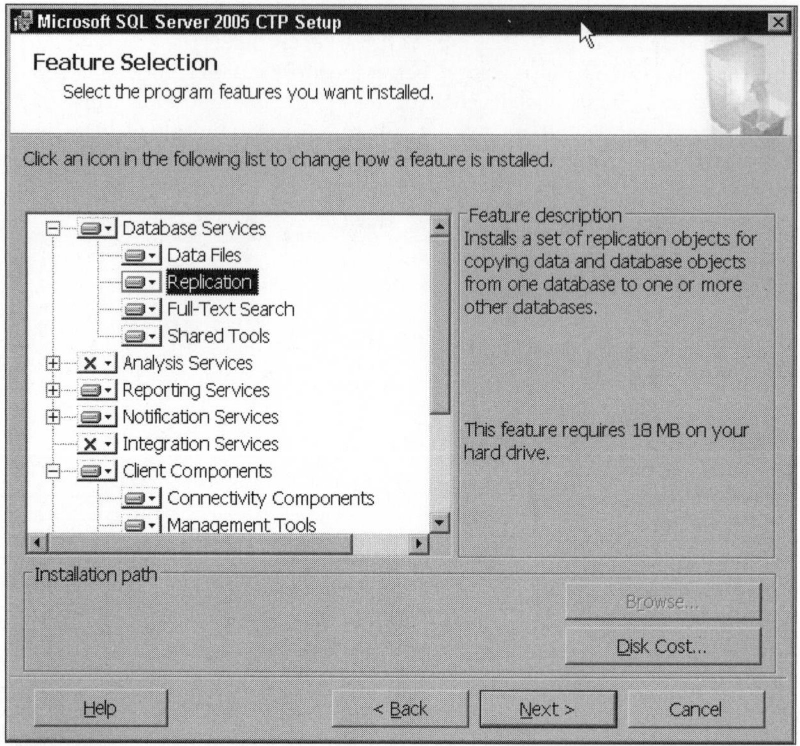

Figure 3-6

Any feature preceded by a red X means that component will not be installed. Any feature preceded by a white box means that feature will be installed. Any feature preceded by a gray box typically means that you can expand that node and select subfeatures. Most likely, some of those subfeatures have not been selected for installation. You should expand that tree node and preview those subfeatures, as there might be some that you want to install.

> **Be sure that you install the sample databases, primarily the AdventureWorks database, because you will be working with them throughout the book. They can be installed by expanding the Documentation and Samples node and selecting the Databases node.**

If you have already installed SQL Server 2005 and are running the installation again, this screen is used to add and remove features.

Click the Next button once you are satisfied with your feature selection.

The next screen in the installation process, shown in Figure 3-7, allows you to select the instance in which you would like to install SQL Server 2005. Just like SQL Server 2000, you can run multiple instances of SQL Server 2005 on a computer.

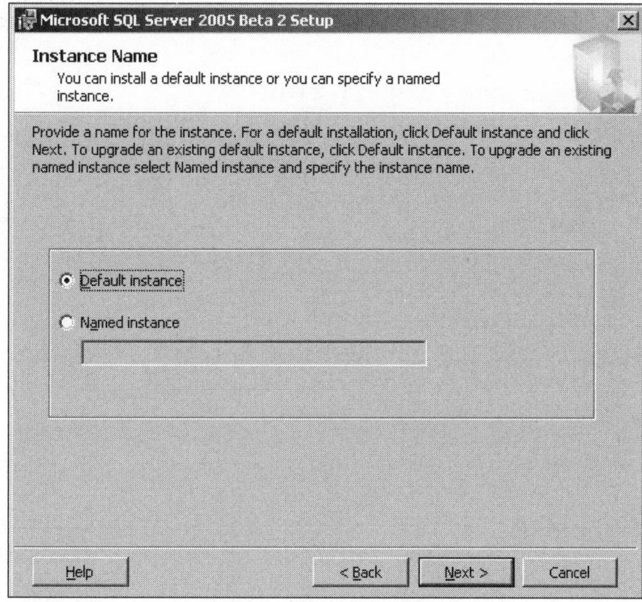

Figure 3-7

The Default instance is the default selection. If you install SQL Server 2005 a second time and select the Default instance, the installation will ask you if you want to upgrade your existing Default instance. The same goes for a Named instance. If you type in a Named instance that already exists, the installer will ask you if you would like to upgrade that instance.

Each instance of SQL Server runs in its own specific space. In other words, it has its own set of services with its own settings, such as collation and other options.

Except for the first installation, you should select a Named instance for each subsequent installation and give that installation a unique instance name, unless you plan on upgrading the desired instance to add or remove features.

Once you have selected the instance in which to install SQL Server, click Next.

The next step in the installation process is the Service Account setup. This screen (see Figure 3-8) lets you define which services run under which account. You can customize each service to start under a specific account or you can use the built-in System account. This screen also lets you determine which services are automatically started when the SQL Server 2005 computer is started.

Once you have configured the services, click Next.

The next step in the installation process is the selection of the Authentication Mode, as shown in Figure 3-9. This step defines the credentials with which you will be connecting (authenticating) to SQL Server 2005.

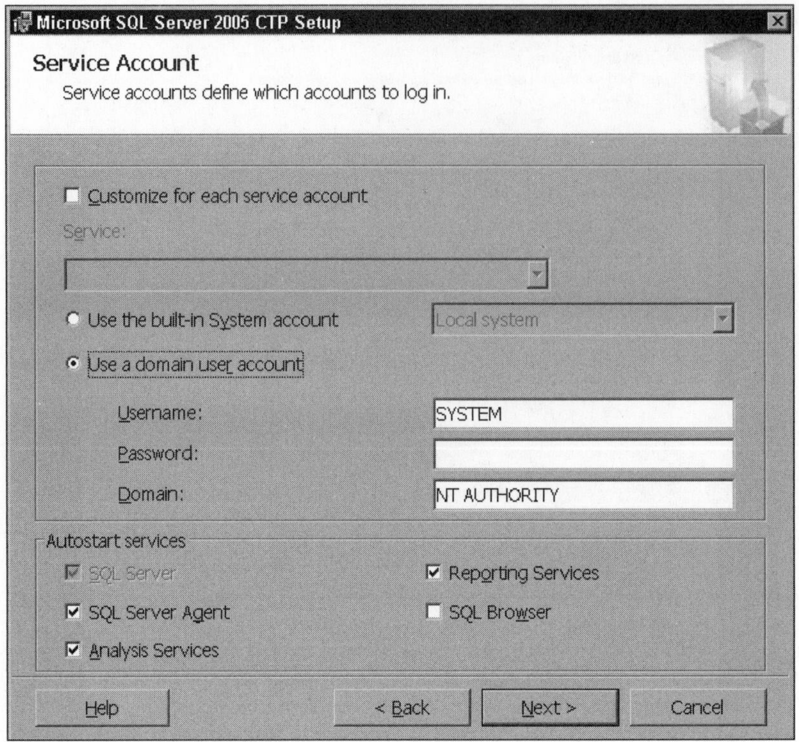

Figure 3-8

Microsoft SQL Server 2005 Beta 2 Setup

Authentication Mode

The authentication mode specifies the security used when connecting to SQL Server.

Select the authentication mode to use for this installation.

Windows Authentication Mode

Mixed Mode (Windows Authentication and SQL Server Authentication)

You must always assign a password for the sa login regardless of which mode you choose. Specify the sa login password below:

Enter password:

****

Confirm password:

****

Help | < Back | Next > | Cancel

Figure 3-9

Just as in the previous version of SQL Server, SQL Server 2005 gives you two options for authentication: Windows Authentication Mode or Mixed Mode authentication.

Windows Authentication connects the user to SQL Server through a Windows user account. SQL Server validates the account credentials (user name and password) via the Windows operating system.

Mixed Mode authentication allows the user to connect either via Windows authentication or SQL Server authentication.

If you select Mixed Mode authentication, be aware that there are some changes in SQL Server 2005. New for this release is Strong Password enforcement. No longer will SQL Server allow you to get away with blank passwords or using "password" as the password.

For example, if you type in "password" for the sa password, you receive the message shown in Figure 3-10.

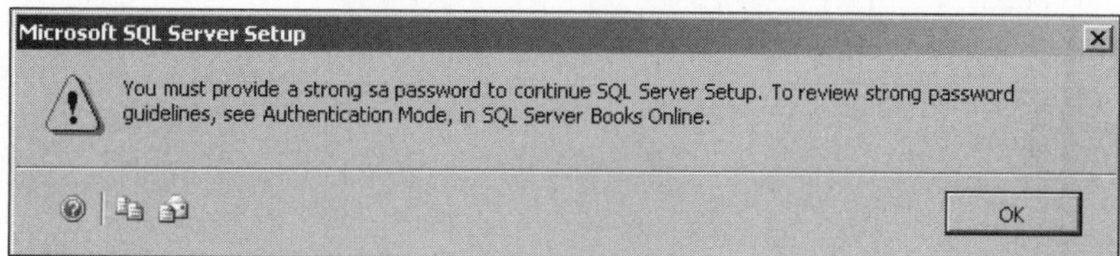

Figure 3-10

In fact, SQL Server 2005 does not allow the following as passwords for the sa account:

- Blank passwords
- The word "Password" or "password"
- The word "Admin" or "admin"
- The word "Administrator" or "administrator"
- The word "sysadmin" or "Sysadmin"
- The acronym "sa"

All passwords used must meet a certain set of requirements before SQL Server lets you use them. Any password must meet three of the following four requirements:

- Must contain uppercase letters
- Must contain lowercase letters
- Must contain numbers
- Must contain non-alphanumeric characters, such as #, $, &, or @

As the error message suggests, see Authentication Mode in the Books Online for more information on strong passwords. The read is well worth your time.

Once you have set your authentication mode, click Next.

The final step in the installation process is setting the collation. Figure 3-11 shows the options available for setting collation and sort order for SQL Server 2005. Collation specifies the SQL Server sorting behavior, meaning how character strings are sorted and compared.

If you don't have any specific sorting or case-sensitivity needs, the default sort order works for most installations.

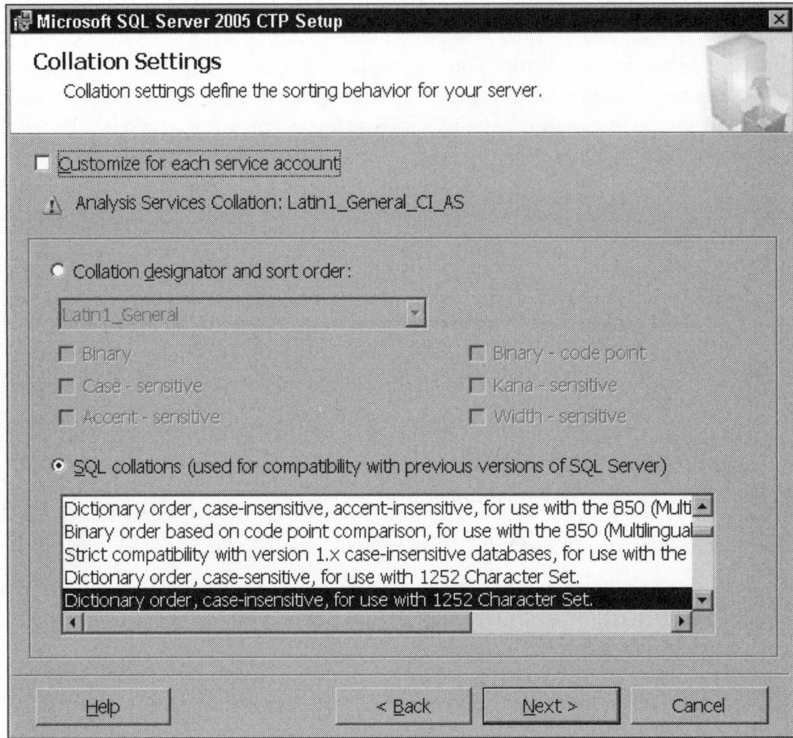

Figure 3-11

Use the top part of this screen when the installation of SQL Server must match the collation settings of another instance of SQL Server or if it must match the Windows local settings of another computer running SQL Server.

Use the SQL collation section for backward compatibility with earlier versions of SQL Server. You should select this option if you want to match compatible settings with SQL Server 8.0 (SQL Server 2000), 7.0, or earlier.

SQL collation cannot be used with Analysis Services. If you select to install SQL Server Analysis Services, SQL Server tries to match the best Windows collation for Analysis Services, based on the SQL collation you select. If the SQL Server collation and Analysis Services collation do not match, your results may not be consistent. Your best bet is to use Windows collation for both.

To select separate collation settings for SQL Server and Analysis Services, select the Customize for each service account check box. This enables the drop-down list of services from which to select the desired service. Select the service, and then select your collation and sort order.

After you select the appropriate sort order, click Next.

The next screen in the installation is the Report Server setup. If you did not select to install the Reporting Services on the Feature Selection screen, you will not see the screen. If you did select Reporting Services, this step allows you specify how a Report Service instance is installed.

You can install the default configuration, which installs and configures Report Server for you, or you can install the Report Server, and after the installation is complete you can configure Reporting Services via the Reporting Services Configuration Tool.

If you select the option to install the default configuration, clicking the Details button displays a screen with information for the default configuration (see Figure 3-12).

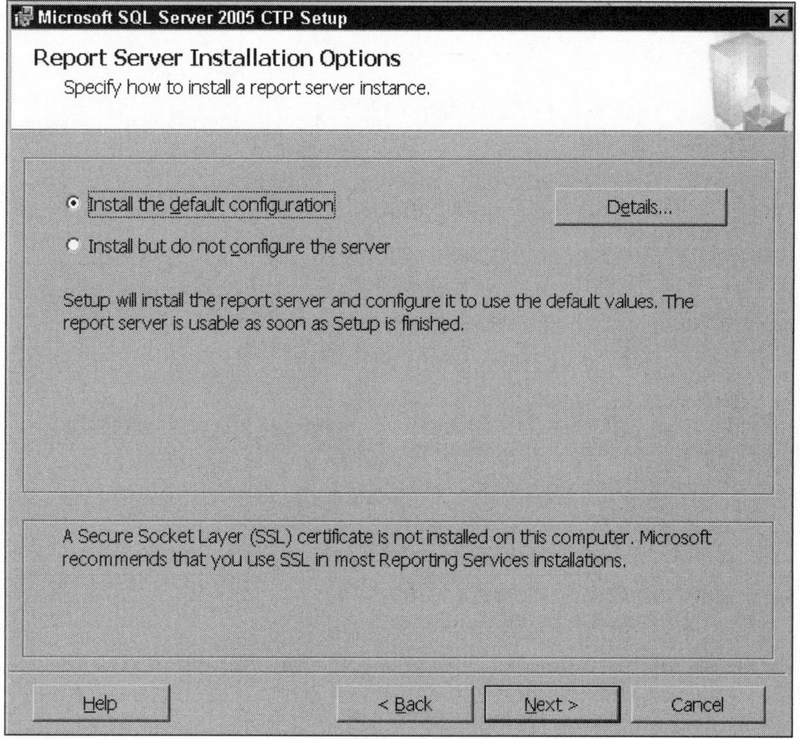

Figure 3-12

After you configure this screen, click Next.

The next screen in the wizard is the Error and Usage Report Settings (see Figure 3-13), which allows you to automatically send feedback to Microsoft for any errors generated or features used.

Microsoft uses these error reports to improve SQL Server functionality. All information is treated as confidential.

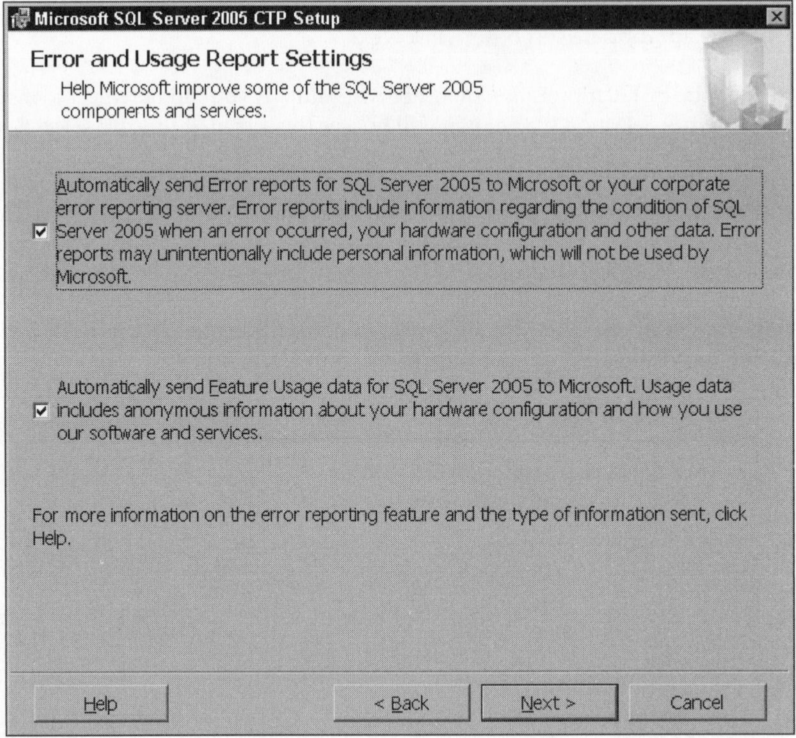

Figure 3-13

If you select to send Feature Usage data (the second checkbox in Figure 3-13), SQL Server is configured to occasionally send a report to Microsoft containing information about how you are using SQL Server 2005. This information is also treaded confidentially.

After you make your selections on this screen, click Next.

The next screen in the setup wizard is the overview of the options you selected during the configuration of the setup (see Figure 3-14). You can look over the items you selected, and by clicking the Back button you can change any items.

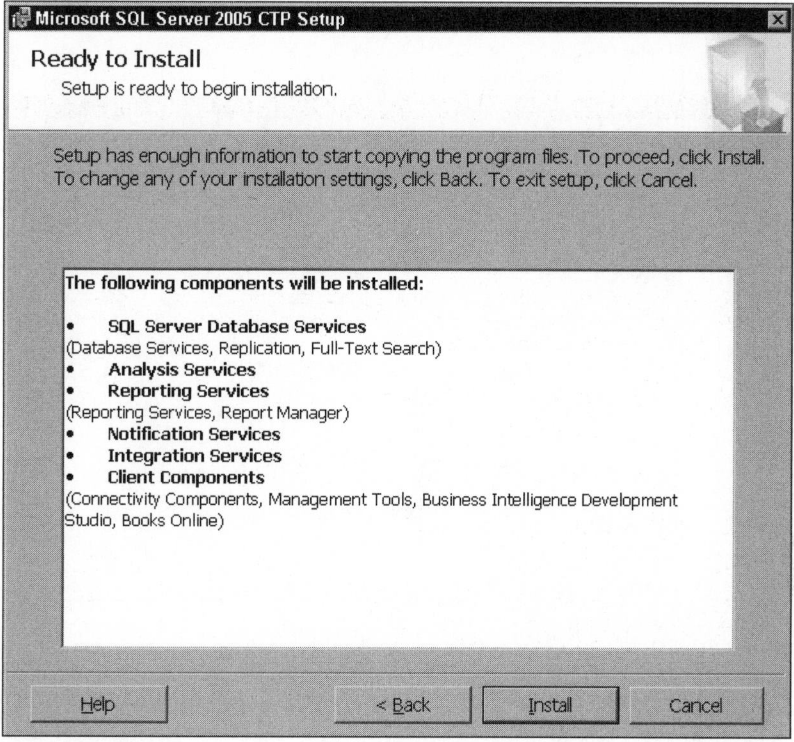

Figure 3-14

If you are satisfied with the selections you made, click Install. At this point the installation begins and you should see a screen that displays the installation progress, similar to Figure 3-15.

At the end of the installation, you may be required to reboot. At this point, SQL Server 2005 is installed and you are almost ready to go. Why almost? You need to set a couple of configuration items before you use some of the examples in this book. As well, if you are using SQL Server 2005 and Visual Studio on separate machines, you need to tell SQL Server about it.

By default, SQL Server 2005 does not accept remote connections. So if you plan to run SQL Server 2005 and Visual Studio 2005 on separate computers, you need to tell SQL Server that connections will be coming in from a remote computer.

You can find this configuration, along with most other SQL Server 2005 configuration items, by opening the Surface Area Configuration form, shown in Figure 3-16.

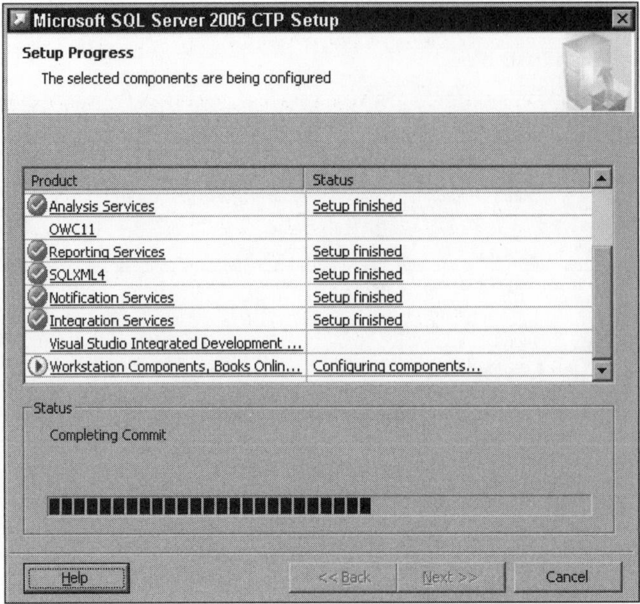

Figure 3-15

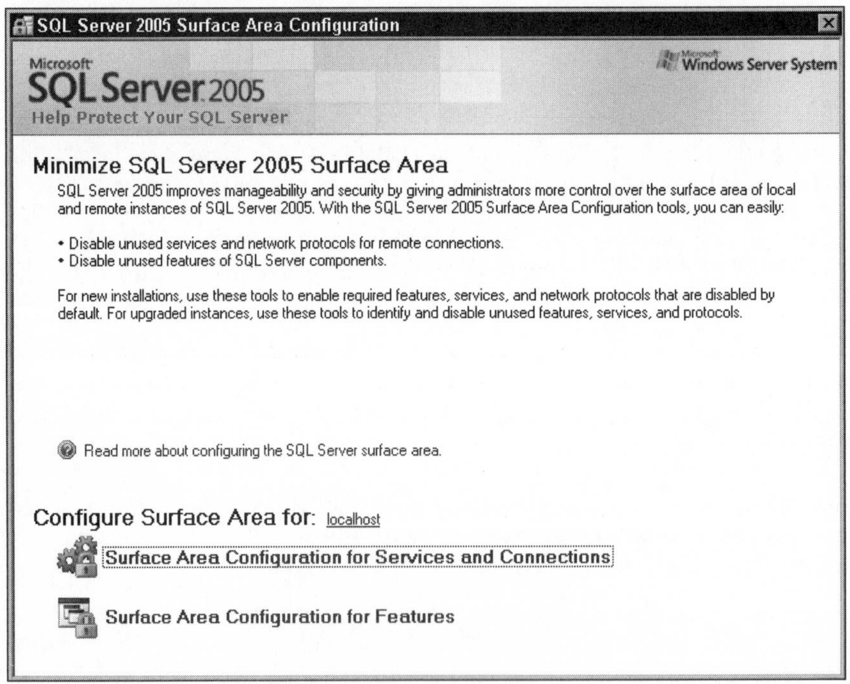

Figure 3-16

First, to tell SQL Server to accept remote connections, select the top option, Surface Area Configuration for Services and Connections. This opens the corresponding form, shown in Figure 3-17.

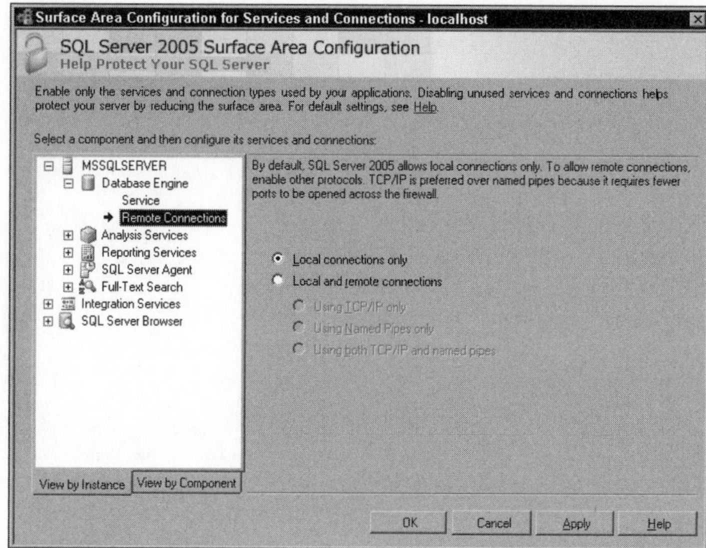

Figure 3-17

To enable remote connections, select the Remote Connections option on the left side of the form. You will notice that by default, SQL Server accepts only local connections. To enable remote connections, click the Local and Remote Connections radio button. This will allow you to select three connection options. Typically, using TCP/IP only will suffice, but if your environment requires a different selection, make the selection and click OK.

The next step is to enable the CLR, which is turned off by default. Back on the main screen (shown previously in Figure 3-16), select the bottom option, Surface Area Configuration for Features to open the form displayed in Figure 3-18.

To enable the CLR, select the CLR Integration option on the left and then click the Enable CLR Integration check box on the right. Click OK to save the changes.

Now you are ready to go!

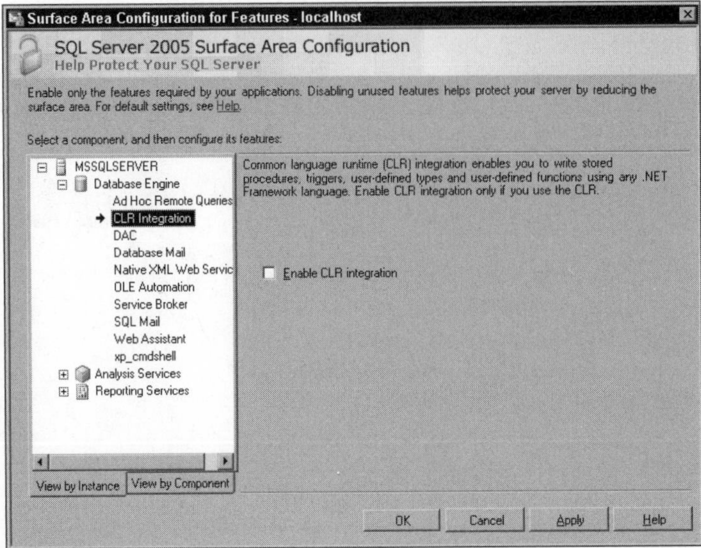

Figure 3-18

Summary

This chapter walked you through basic steps of installing SQL Server 2005 and highlighted some areas of detail, as well as pointed out some differences between SQL Server 2005 and previous versions of SQL Server. With SQL Server installed, you can now easily work with the examples throughout the book.

By now you should have good grasp of what's new in SQL Server 2005 and an idea of what's coming up in later chapters. The next few chapters deal with topics that, while not directly specific to SQL Server, will be of great benefit to you in the last half of this book. In particular, the next chapter covers the new `xml` data type.

Part II: Server-Side XML Processing in SQL Server 2005

xml data type

In Chapter 2, you learned about the `xml` data type and some of the functionality that it exposed, such as some of the `xml` data type methods and untyped versus typed XML. This chapter, however, discusses aspects of the `xml` data type not covered in Chapter 2, as well as elaborates on most of the topics introduced in that chapter.

The addition of the `xml` data type provides tremendous support for XML data processing including native support for XML. This means that XML documents, fragments, and values can be stored natively in SQL Server using the `xml` data type. The `xml` data type also simplifies modifying XML Data.

The goals of this chapter are to examine the `xml` data type in depth and to expose much more of the functionality that it provides. This chapter covers the following topics:

- Typed versus untyped XML
- Altering the `xml` data type column
- `xml` data type methods
- Defaults, constraints, and computed columns on `xml` data type columns
- Creating views
- XML settings options
- Best practices

A lot of the examples throughout this book use the AdventureWorks database that comes with SQL Server 2005. However, some of the examples require the creation of new tables and other objects and refer to a database called Wrox. If you prefer not to use the AdventureWorks database for these examples, feel free to create a new database called Wrox.

untyped versus typed XML

XML comes in two flavors, untyped and typed, and the `xml` data type in SQL Server 2005 supports them both. This section highlights the differences between untyped and typed XML, as well as some scenarios when you would want to use one over the other.

untyped XML

In simple terms, untyped XML means that no schema is associated with an XML document. In reality though, you may have a schema that is perfectly valid for an XML document but have chosen for one reason or another not to associate the schema with the XML document. There are number of reasons you would not want to associate a schema with an XML document, and in a lot of cases it makes sense not to make the association. For example:

- Client-side XML validation
- Unsupported server schema components
- Not well-formed or invalid XML

It is also perfectly suitable to use untyped XML when there is no schema present at all. In any of these cases, the XML document is checked to see if it is well-formed prior to mapping to the `xml` data type.

> *Be aware that there will be performance issues when using untyped XML because of the node conversions at runtime. Node values are stored as strings internally and a conversion needs to be made before it is added to the* `xml` *data type.*

In Chapter 2, you saw some examples that showed you how to create untyped XML such as columns, variables, and parameters. The `xml` data type column that was created in the Employee table had no schema or schema collection associated with it, so it is an untyped XML data type column.

As explained previously, creating an `xml` column in a table is fairly straightforward, as shown here:

```
CREATE TABLE Employee (
    [EmployeeID] [int] NOT NULL,
    [EmployeeInfo] [xml] NOT NULL
) ON [PRIMARY]
GO
```

Inserting into an untyped XML data type column is not rocket science either, as shown in the following example:

```
DECLARE @xmlvar varchar(200)
SET @xmlvar =
'<Employee><FirstName>Horatio</FirstName><LastName>Hornblower</LastName><HireDate>0
5/01/1850</HireDate></Employee>'

INSERT INTO Employee (EmployeeID, EmployeeInfo)
VALUES (1, @xmlvar)
GO
```

If you were to then query the new Employee table, the results shown in Figure 4-1 would be returned.

	EmployeeID	EmployeeInfo
1	1	<Employee><FirstName>Horatio</FirstName><LastName>Hornblower</LastName><HireDate>03/01...

Figure 4-1

Chapter 2 also discussed using the `xml` data type as variables and parameters, and Figure 4-1 demonstrates how to use the `xml` data type in a variable, as well as inserting the untyped XML into an `xml` data type column.

Also in Chapter 2, you saw a portion of a stored procedure that accepts an `xml` data type parameter. Using that code, combined with the preceding code example, the following example demonstrates using the `xml` data type as a parameter.

Using the following code, create a stored procedure called AddEmployee:

```
CREATE PROCEDURE AddEmployee
    @xmlvar [xml]
    WITH EXECUTE AS OWNER
AS

INSERT INTO Employee (EmployeeID, EmployeeInfo)
VALUES (2, @xmlvar)
```

Then in a query window execute the following code:

```
DECLARE @xmlvar varchar(200)
SET @xmlvar =
'<Employee><FirstName>Hortense</FirstName><LastName>Powdermaker</LastName><HireDate
>03/01/1932</HireDate></Employee>'

EXEC AddEmployee @xmlvar
GO
```

Again, if you were to query the Employee table you would see the results shown in Figure 4-2.

	EmployeeID	EmployeeInfo
1	1	<Employee><FirstName>Horatio</FirstName><LastName>Hornblower</LastName><HireDate>05/01/18...
2	2	<Employee><FirstName>Hortense</FirstName><LastName>Powdermaker</LastName><HireDate>03/0...

Figure 4-2

While untyped XML may have its place, there are a number of good reasons why you should consider typed XML storage.

typed XML

When a schema collection that describes XML data is associated with an XML document, the XML document is said to be *typed*. In reality, this is the best scenario because it allows for the association of a collection of XML schemas with an XML column, which automatically validates the XML.

There are several advantages to using an XML schema. First, XML validation is automatic. Regardless if you are assigning XML to a variable or inserting XML into an XML column, SQL Server automatically applies the schema to the XML for validation. The result of this is better performance because node values are not converted at runtime.

Second, XML storage is minimized because the information about the types of elements and attributes is provided in the schema itself, thus providing better conversion interpretation about the values stored.

Using typed XML is not all that different from using an untyped `xml` data type other than the fact that a schema collection is required to have a typed `xml` data type. This applies to the XML column, parameter, and variable.

The untyped examples used previously can be modified to be typed very easily. For example, given the following XML document and schema, creating a table that has a schema collection associated to the `xml` data type column is quite easy.

Suppose you wanted to store the following XML in the `xml` data type column in your Employee table:

```
<Employee EmployeeID = "1">
  <FirstName></FirstName>
  <LastName></LastName>
  <Address></Address>
  <City></City>
  <State></State>
  <Zip></Zip>
</Employee>
```

The first step is to create the necessary schema used to create an XML schema collection. The schema collection you create is then used when you create the table. Based on the above XML document, create the following schema:

```
<xs:schema xmlns="" xmlns:xs="http://www.w3.org/2001/XMLSchema"
xmlns:msdata="urn:schemas-microsoft-com:xml-msdata" id="NewDataSet">
 <xs:element name="Employee">
  <xs:complexType>
   <xs:sequence>
   <xs:element name="FirstName" type="xs:string" minOccurs="0" msdata:Ordinal="0"/>
    <xs:element name="LastName" type="xs:string" minOccurs="0" msdata:Ordinal="1"/>
    <xs:element name="Address" type="xs:string" minOccurs="0" msdata:Ordinal="2"/>
    <xs:element name="City" type="xs:string" minOccurs="0" msdata:Ordinal="3"/>
    <xs:element name="State" type="xs:string" minOccurs="0" msdata:Ordinal="4"/>
    <xs:element name="Zip" type="xs:string" minOccurs="0" msdata:Ordinal="5"/>
   </xs:sequence>
   <xs:attribute name="EmployeeID" type="xs:string"/>
  </xs:complexType>
 </xs:element>
```

```
  <xs:element name="NewDataSet" msdata:IsDataSet="true"
msdata:UseCurrentLocale="true">
    <xs:complexType>
      <xs:choice minOccurs="0" maxOccurs="unbounded">
        <xs:element ref="Employee"/>
      </xs:choice>
    </xs:complexType>
  </xs:element>
</xs:schema>
```

You then use the `CREATE XML SCHEMA COLLECTION` statement to create the schema collection, named `EmployeeSchemaCollection`. The XML schema must exist prior to associating it with an `xml` data type column, parameter, or variable. XML schema collections are discussed in detail in Chapter 7.

After you've created the XML schema collection, you can then use it in the creation of your new table, as illustrated in the following code. The process of associating the schema collection to the `xml` data type column now makes the column a typed column:

```
CREATE TABLE Employee (
[EmployeeID] [int] NOT NULL,
[EmployeeInfo] [xml] (EmployeeSchemaCollection) NOT NULL
) ON [PRIMARY]
GO
```

The other method of associating a schema or schema collection to an `xml` data type column is via the SQL Server Management Studio when creating the table or adding a column, as shown in Figure 4-3.

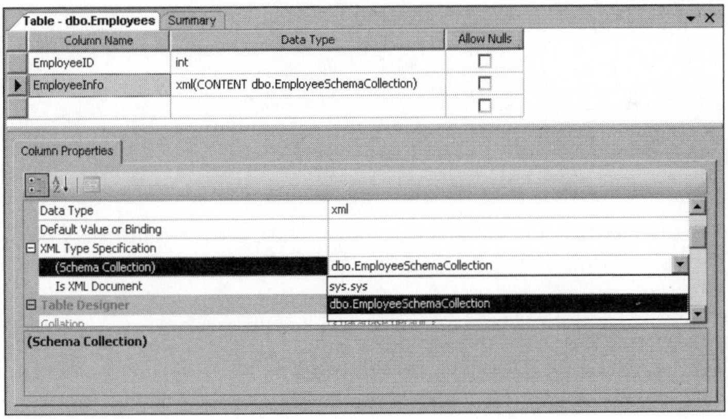

Figure 4-3

The default selection is to have no schema collection, which makes the column untyped. This is perfectly acceptable and the pros and cons of doing so were explained earlier in the chapter. The preferred option is to select a schema collection to associate to the column.

Any schema collections created prior to creating the table (or adding the column to the table) appear in the drop-down list available for selection.

The sys.sys schema collection is the default schema collection if one is not specified and helps determine how well-formed an XML instance is.

Schema collections are discussed in Chapter 7. In this chapter, it is only necessary to discuss associating a schema collection to an xml data type.

Making Changes to the xml data type Column

Altering the xml data type column is completely allowable, with support provided by the ALTER TABLE statement. An xml data type column can be changed from untyped to typed and vice versa, as well as changed from a character string type column to an xml data type column (typed or untyped).

The following example illustrates how to alter a column from a string type to an xml type:

```
/* create the original table */
CREATE TABLE Customer (
    [CustomerID] [int] PRIMARY KEY,
    [CustomerName] [varchar] (100)
    )
GO

/* Insert data into the table */
INSERT INTO Customer (CustomerID, CustomerName)
VALUES (1, '<Data><Team Manufacturer="KTM"></Team></Data>')
GO

/* Change the CustomerName column type to XML type */
ALTER TABLE Customer
ALTER COLUMN CustomerName xml
GO
```

This change is allowed because the value inserted into the CustomerName column prior to changing the data type is well-formed XML and is accepted by the xml data type. The following is also allowed:

```
/* create the original table */
CREATE TABLE Customer (
    [CustomerID] [int] PRIMARY KEY,
    [CustomerName] [varchar] (100)
    )
GO

/* Insert data into the table */
INSERT INTO Customer (CustomerID, CustomerName)
VALUES (2, 'Fast Freddys Five Finger Discount')
GO

/* Change the CustomerName column type to XML type */
ALTER TABLE Customer
ALTER COLUMN CustomerName xml
GO
```

Querying the Customer table returns results similar to Figure 4-4.

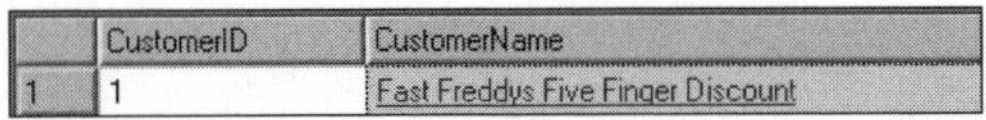

Figure 4-4

The statements executed without error, but why did they work? The reason this example works is because no schema was specified when the column was altered to an xml data type column, thus making it untyped.

Converting from untyped to typed

An xml data type column can be changed from one type to another (untyped to typed and vice versa). The following example illustrates changing an xml data type column from untyped to typed:

```
'First, create the table untyped (no XML schema associated with the xml column)
CREATE TABLE Employee (
[EmployeeID] [int] NOT NULL,
[EmployeeInfo] [xml] NOT NULL
) ON [PRIMARY]
GO

'Now, make it a typed column - THE SCHEMA COLLECTION MUST EXIST FIRST!
ALTER TABLE Employee
ALTER COLUMN EmployeeInfo xml ( EmployeeSchemaCollection)
GO
```

As the comments in the code state and as explained in the previous section, the XML schema collection must exist prior to associating it with an xml data type column, parameter, or variable.

When this statement is executed, all XML data in the CustomerName column is validated against the schemas in the specified schema collection. There are two things to keep in mind when converting to a typed XML column. First, if any invalid XML documents are found during the validation, the conversion from untyped to typed halts and the conversion does not take place. Second, when altering an xml column from a string or untyped type, the conversion could take awhile on tables with large amounts of data.

It should be obvious that the preferred choice is to create the column as typed to begin with, but it is perfectly acceptable to create untyped columns as needs dictate.

xml data type Methods

The xml data type comes with five methods that support the querying and modification of XML instances. These xml data type methods are extremely useful when they are used together. Very rarely will you use these methods by themselves, and as the examples demonstrate, the real power and flexibility behind the xml data type is when these methods are used together.

This section examines these five methods:

- ❑ `query()`
- ❑ `value()`
- ❑ `exist()`
- ❑ `nodes()`
- ❑ `modify()`

The following section discusses each of these methods in detail, beginning with the `query()` method.

query()

If your goal is to return parts or sections of an XML instance, then the `query()` method is the method of choice. The `query()` method executes a query by evaluating an XQuery expression against the elements and attributes in an XML instance. Results are returned as untyped XML.

The syntax for the `query()` method is as follows:

```
query('XQueryExpression')
```

The `query()` method can be run against any XML instance, such as an `xml` data type variable or column. For example, the following example uses the `query()` method to return a portion of an XML instance from a `xml` data type variable:

```
DECLARE @xmlvar xml
SET @xmlvar =
'<Motocross>
    <Team Manufacturer="Yamaha">
        <Rider Size="250">
            <RiderName>Tim Ferry</RiderName>
        </Rider>
        <Rider Size="250">
            <RiderName>Chad Reed</RiderName>
        </Rider>
    </Team>
</Motocross>'

SELECT @xmlvar.query('/Motocross/Team/Rider')
```

In the preceding example, an `xml` data type variable is declared and an XML instance is assigned to that variable. The last line of code uses the `query()` method to specify an XQuery expression against the `xml` data type variable and select a portion of the XML instance.

The XQuery expression in the example is asking for everything under the Team node; thus the query returns all of the Rider information. The results are shown in Figure 4-5.

	(No column name)
1	<Rider Size="250"><RiderName>Tim Ferry</RiderName></Rider><Rider Size="250"><RiderName>Chad Reed</RiderName></Rider>

Figure 4-5

The `query()` method can also be used when querying an `xml` data type column. The following example uses the `query()` method to return a section of an XML instance from an `xml` data type column:

```
SELECT Instructions.query('declare namespace
MSAW="http://schemas.microsoft.com/sqlserver/2004/07/adventure-
works/ProductModelManuInstructions";
<Location>{ /MSAW:root/MSAW:Location[1] }</Location>
') as Result
FROM Production.ProductModel
WHERE ProductModelID=7
```

A portion of the results looks like the following:

```
<Location>
  <MSAW:Location
xmlns:MSAW="http://schemas.microsoft.com/sqlserver/2004/07/adventure-
works/ProductModelManuInstructions" LaborHours="2.5" LotSize="100" MachineHours="3"
SetupHours="0.5" LocationID="10">Work Center - 10 Frame FormingThe following
instructions pertain to Work Center 10.
...
</Location>
```

Like the other `query()` method examples, this example uses an XPath expression to query the first (as denoted by the `[1]` predicate) location node from the Instructions column in the Production.ProductModel table.

A predicate is somewhat similar to a `WHERE` clause. It provides further filtering on a node-set. In the previous example, the predicate said, "where the location is the first Location."

The `query()` method is very valuable and flexible when querying the `xml` data type and the goal is to return a portion of an XML document.

value()

The `value()` method is useful when you want to extract node values from an XML instance, particularly an `xml` data type column, variable, or parameter. It returns the value that the XQuery expression evaluates to. The syntax for this method is as follows:

```
value(XQueryExpression, SQLType)
```

The first parameter is the XQuery expression that looks for the node value within the XML instance. The second parameter is the string literal value converted to the SQL type specified by this parameter.

The following example uses the `value()` method to extract an attribute from an XML instance:

```
DECLARE @xmlvar xml
DECLARE @Team varchar(50)
SET @xmlvar =
'<Motocross>
    <Team Manufacturer="Yamaha">
        <Rider Size="250">
            <RiderName>Tim Ferry</RiderName>
```

```
        </Rider>
        <Rider Size="250">
            <RiderName>Chad Reed</RiderName>
        </Rider>
    </Team>
</Motocross>'

SET @Team = @xmlvar.value('(/Motocross/Team/@Manufacturer)[1]', 'varchar(50)')
SELECT @Team
```

The result returned from this is the word `Yamaha`. The XQuery expression in this example specifies the first attribute in the /Motocross/Team path and returns the attribute for that node.

The next example uses the `value()` method to return a node value from the XML instance:

```
DECLARE @xmlvar xml
DECLARE @Team varchar(50)
SET @xmlvar =
'<Motocross>
    <Team Manufacturer="Yamaha">
        <Rider Size="250">
            <RiderName>Tim Ferry</RiderName>
        </Rider>
        <Rider Size="250">
            <RiderName>Chad Reed</RiderName>
        </Rider>
    </Team>
</Motocross>'

SET @Team = @xmlvar.value('(/Motocross/Team/Rider/RiderName)[1]', 'varchar(50)')
SELECT @Team
```

The result returned from this statement is the name of the first rider, `Tim Ferry`. Just like the previous example, the XQuery expression in the `value()` method specifies the first `RiderName` node, signified by the `[1]` predicate, from which to obtain the results.

In the `SET @Team` statement, change the code to look like the following:

```
SET @Team = @xmlvar.value('(/Motocross/Team/Rider/RiderName)[2]', 'varchar(50)')
```

Now rerun the entire code. The results should now be the second rider, Chad Reed. This is called *static typing,* which determines an expression's return type, and is covered in Chapter 5.

Both of the preceding examples used the `value()` method to query an `xml` data type variable. More common scenarios require the querying of data in an `xml` data type column. So, the following example uses the `value()` method to query an `xml` data type column:

```
SELECT Instructions.value('declare namespace msaw
="http://schemas.microsoft.com/sqlserver/2004/07/adventure-
works/ProductModelManuInstructions";
       (//msaw:Location/@LocationID)[1]', 'int') as Result
FROM Production.ProductModel
WHERE Instructions IS NOT NULL
```

The results from this query list all `LocationIDs` from the Instruction column.

Type Conversion

The `value()` method uses, when necessary, the `CONVERT` function of T-SQL to implicitly convert XQuery expression results from the XSD type to its corresponding SQL type.

In the following table, the XSD data type to SQL Server 2005 data type mappings are shown to help make the necessary conversion in your program.

XSD	SQL Server
boolean	bit
decimal	numeric
double	float
float	real
string	nvarchar(4000), nvarchar(max)
NOTATION	nvarchar
Qname	nvarchar
Duration	varbinary
Datetime	Varbinary
Time	Varbinary
Date	Varbinary
gYearMonth	Varbinary
gYear	Varbinary
gMonthDay	Varbinary
gDay	Varbinary
gMonth	Varbinary
hexBinary	Varbinary
Base64Binary	Varbinary
anyURI	Varbinary

The `value()` method is a very versatile component of the `xml` data type and when combined with other `xml` data type methods, it proves to be even more valuable.

exist()

The `exist()` method allows you to check for the existence of a specific XML fragment in an XML instance. The return result is 1 if it exists, and 0 if it does not.

The syntax for the `exist()` method is as follows:

```
exist('XQeuryExpression')
```

Consider the following example:

```
DECLARE @xmlvar xml
DECLARE @bitvar bit
SET @xmlvar = '
<Motocross>
    <Team Manufacturer="Yamaha">
        <Rider Size="250">
            <RiderName>Tim Ferry</RiderName>
        </Rider>
        <Rider Size="250">
            <RiderName>Chad Reed</RiderName>
        </Rider>
    </Team>
</Motocross>'
SET @bitvar = @xmlvar.exist('/Motocross/Team[@Manufacturer eq
xs:string("Yamaha")]')
SELECT @bitvar
```

In the execution of this code, the `exist()` method returns a 1 because it finds the value of `Yamaha` in the XML instance. Change the manufacturer to `Suzuki` and run the code again. The `exist()` method returns a 0 because it does not find a value of `Suzuki` in the XML instance.

Using that same example, the `exist()` method can look for node values as well, as illustrated by the following code:

```
DECLARE @xmlvar xml
DECLARE @bitvar bit
SET @xmlvar = '
<Motocross>
    <Team Manufacturer="Honda">
        <Rider Size="250">
            <RiderName>Kevin Windham</RiderName>
        </Rider>
        <Rider Size="250">
            <RiderName>Mike LaRocco</RiderName>
        </Rider>
        <Rider Size="250">
            <RiderName>Jeremy McGrath</RiderName>
        </Rider>
    </Team>
</Motocross>'
SET @bitvar = @xmlvar.exist('/Motocross/Team/Rider/RiderName[text()[1] eq
xs:string("Kevin Windham")]')
SELECT @bitvar
```

As with the first example, the `exist()` method in this example returns a 1 because it finds `Kevin Windham` in the XML instance.

The following two examples use the `exist()` method with a typed XML instance (the previous examples used untyped XML instances). The first uses the `exist()` method against an XML variable:

```
DECLARE @intvar int
DECLARE @xmlvar xml (Production.ManuInstructionsSchemaCollection)

SELECT @xmlvar = Instructions
FROM Production.ProductModel
WHERE ProductModelID = 7

SET @intvar = @xmlvar.exist(' declare namespace
MSAW="http://schemas.microsoft.com/sqlserver/2004/07/adventure-
works/ProductModelManuInstructions";
    /MSAW:root/MSAW:Location[@LocationID=30]
')

SELECT @intvar
```

As with the previous examples, the `exist()` method returns a 1. By changing the `@LocationID` variable to a value, such as `80`, then rerunning the code, the `exist()` method returns a 0 because it cannot find a `Location` node with an attribute of `LocationID` with a value of `80`, but it did find one with a value of `30`.

The second example modifies the previous example, still using the `exist()` method, but against an `xml` data type column:

```
SELECT Instructions.exist(' declare namespace
MSAW="http://schemas.microsoft.com/sqlserver/2004/07/adventure-
works/ProductModelManuInstructions";
  /MSAW:root/MSAW:Location[@LocationID=50]
')
FROM Production.ProductModel
WHERE ProductModelID = 10
```

The results of this query also return a value of 1 because the XPath expression inside the `exist()` method finds a `LocationID` with a value of 50.

The `exist()` method can also be used in the `WHERE` clause, as follows:

```
SELECT ProductModelID, Name
FROM Production.ProductModel
WHERE Instructions.exist(' declare namespace
MSAW="http://schemas.microsoft.com/sqlserver/2004/07/adventure-
works/ProductModelManuInstructions";
    /MSAW:root/MSAW:Location[@LocationID=60]
') = 1
```

In this example the SELECT statement selects non-XML columns with the WHERE clause supplying the XQuery expression in the exist() method. The query says to return the ProductModelID and Name columns where a LocationID value of 60 exists within the XML in the Instructions column.

The results return two rows:

```
ProductModelID      Name
7                   HL Touring Frame
10                  LL Touring Frame
```

The exist() method is preferred over the value() method when comparing *predicates*, expressions that evaluate to TRUE or FALSE. UNKOWN is even considered to be a predicate, and in these cases where the expression is returning one of these three, it is good practice to use the exist() method rather than the value() method.

For example, if you know for certain that the query expression is returning a value (non-TRUE/FALSE) then the value() method is the way to go. On the other hand, if you are checking to see if a certain node, attribute, or value exists, use the exist() method.

The xml data type methods so far have dealt with specific values within an XML instance, but what about the times you need to return the results as relational data? This is where the nodes() method comes in.

nodes()

The term *shredding* in XML terms means converting an xml data type instance into relational data. The nodes() method puts this term to very good use. The purpose of the nodes() method is to specify which nodes are mapped to a new dataset row.

The general syntax of the nodes() method looks like the following:

```
Nodes (XQuery) as Table(Column)
```

The XQuery parameter specifies the XQuery expression. If the expression returns nodes, then the nodes are included in the result set. Likewise, if the result of the expression is empty, then the result set is also empty. The Table(column) parameter is the name and column of the final result set.

This first example uses an xml data type variable:

```
DECLARE @xmlvar xml
SET @xmlvar='
<Motocross>
    <Team Manufacturer="Yamaha">
        <Rider>Tim Ferry</Rider>
        <Rider>Chad Reed</Rider>
        <Rider>David Vuillemin</Rider>
    </Team>
    <Team Manufacturer="Honda">
        <Rider>Kevin Windham</Rider>
        <Rider>Mike LaRacco</Rider>
```

```
        <Rider>Jeremy McGrath</Rider>
    </Team>
    <Team Manufacturer="Suzuki">
        <Rider>Ricky Carmichael</Rider>
        <Rider>Broc Hepler</Rider>
    </Team>
    <Team Manufacturer="Kawasaki">
        <Rider>James Stewart</Rider>
        <Rider>Michael Byrne</Rider>
    </Team>
</Motocross>'
SELECT Motocross.Team.query('.')
AS RESULT
FROM @xmlvar.nodes('/Motocross/Team') Motocross(Team)
```

The results are returned as a single result set with four rows, as shown in Figure 4-6.

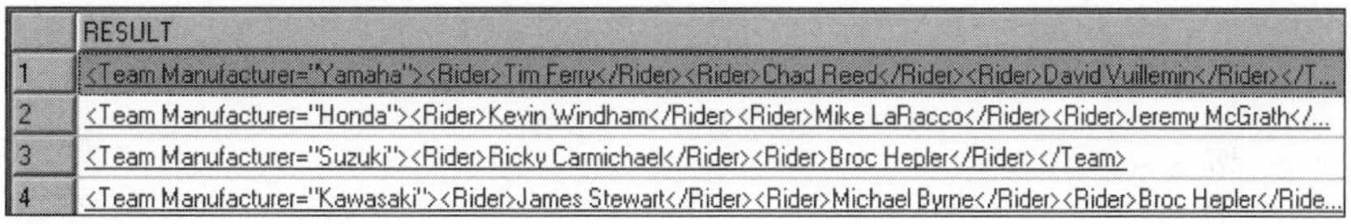

	RESULT
1	<Team Manufacturer="Yamaha"><Rider>Tim Ferry</Rider><Rider>Chad Reed</Rider><Rider>David Vuillemin</Rider></T...
2	<Team Manufacturer="Honda"><Rider>Kevin Windham</Rider><Rider>Mike LaRacco</Rider><Rider>Jeremy McGrath</...
3	<Team Manufacturer="Suzuki"><Rider>Ricky Carmichael</Rider><Rider>Broc Hepler</Rider></Team>
4	<Team Manufacturer="Kawasaki"><Rider>James Stewart</Rider><Rider>Michael Byrne</Rider><Rider>Broc Hepler</Ride...

Figure 4-6

In this example, the `nodes()` method identifies the nodes in the results of the XQuery expression, returning them as a rowset, with each team being a row. The `nodes()` method basically said, "Break out each Team into a row," thus making a result set. Each row in the rowset is a logical copy of the original XML instance. The node in each row, in this case the Team node, matches one of the nodes specified in the XQuery expression.

The `query()` method in this example is used together with the `nodes()` method to return the appropriate results. The `query()` method is the method used to query the XML document, and the `nodes()` method defines how the results are sent back.

The `query()` method can also take an absolute path expression, which means that the query starts on the root node. In the following example, an absolute path expression is used:

```
DECLARE @xmlvar xml
SET @xmlvar='
<Motocross>
    <Team Manufacturer="Yamaha">
        <Rider>Tim Ferry</Rider>
        <Rider>Chad Reed</Rider>
        <Rider>David Vuillemin</Rider>
    </Team>
    <Team Manufacturer="Honda">
        <Rider>Kevin Windham</Rider>
        <Rider>Mike LaRacco</Rider>
        <Rider>Jeremy McGrath</Rider>
    </Team>
    <Team Manufacturer="Suzuki">
        <Rider>Ricky Carmichael</Rider>
```

```
        <Rider>Broc Hepler</Rider>
    </Team>
    <Team Manufacturer="Kawasaki">
        <Rider>James Stewart</Rider>
        <Rider>Michael Byrne</Rider>
    </Team>
</Motocross>'
SELECT Motocross.Team.query('/Motocross/Team')
AS RESULT
FROM @xmlvar.nodes('/Motocross/Team') Motocross(Team)
```

The results are quite a bit different now. The result set from the first query had each Team in its own row. The results from the absolute path query return four rows with all four Teams in each row (basically four rows for every context node, as shown in Figure 4-7).

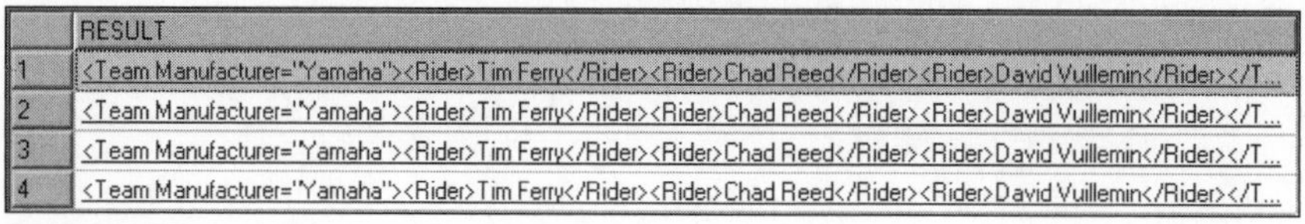

	RESULT
1	<Team Manufacturer="Yamaha"><Rider>Tim Ferry</Rider><Rider>Chad Reed</Rider><Rider>David Vuillemin</Rider></T...
2	<Team Manufacturer="Yamaha"><Rider>Tim Ferry</Rider><Rider>Chad Reed</Rider><Rider>David Vuillemin</Rider></T...
3	<Team Manufacturer="Yamaha"><Rider>Tim Ferry</Rider><Rider>Chad Reed</Rider><Rider>David Vuillemin</Rider></T...
4	<Team Manufacturer="Yamaha"><Rider>Tim Ferry</Rider><Rider>Chad Reed</Rider><Rider>David Vuillemin</Rider></T...

Figure 4-7

You should be starting to see the real power behind these methods. When they are used individually they are extremely powerful. When used together, the functionality they provide is nearly endless.

modify

All the other methods focus on getting data *out* of an XML instance. The `modify()` method's function in life, on the other hand, is to modify `xml` type variables or columns. This method takes a XML Data Modification Language statement as a parameter to perform the necessary operation (insert, update, or delete). XML DML was introduced in Chapter 2 and is covered in greater detail in Chapter 5.

The syntax of the `modify()` method looks like this:

```
Modify(XML DML)
```

The `modify()` method of the `xml` data type allows you to insert, update (replace value of), and delete content within an XML instance. The `modify()` method uses the XML DML to provide those actions on the XML instance.

The following example shows you how to use the `modify()` method:

```
DECLARE @xmldoc xml
SET @xmldoc =
'<Root>
    <Employee EmployeeID="1">
        <EmployeeInformation>
        </EmployeeInformation>
    </Employee>
```

```
</Root>'
SET @xmldoc.modify('
insert <LastName>Knievel</LastName>
into (/Root/Employee/EmployeeInformation)[1]')
SELECT @xmldoc
GO
```

In this example, an `xml` data type variable is defined and an XML document is assigned to that variable. The `modify()` method is then executed against that xml data type variable to insert a new node and value. The results of the `modify()` method on the XML document are as follows:

```
<Root>
    <Employee EmployeeID="1">
        <EmployeeInformation>
            <LastName>Knievel</LastName>
        </EmployeeInformation>
    <Employee>
</Root>
```

If you recall from Chapter 2, a number of examples used the `modify()` method with XML DMLModification to modify the XML content, so this should not be new. While the previous example is fairly simple, don't worry, because an entire section is dedicated to this method and XML DML in Chapter 5. Now that you're somewhat familiar with all the `xml` data type methods, the next section shows you how to combine some of the methods within a single statement.

Combining Methods

The following example combines the `value()`, `query()`, and `nodes()` methods in a single statement against an xml data type variable. The `value()` method gets the `Manufacturer`, the `query()` method gets the riders for the specific `Team`, and the `nodes()` method tells the query to return the results as a rowset:

```
DECLARE @xmlvar xml
SET @xmlvar='
<Motocross>
    <Team Manufacturer="Yamaha">
        <Rider>Tim Ferry</Rider>
        <Rider>Chad Reed</Rider>
        <Rider>David Vuillemin</Rider>
    </Team>
    <Team Manufacturer="Honda">
        <Rider>Kevin Windham</Rider>
        <Rider>Mike LaRacco</Rider>
        <Rider>Jeremy McGrath</Rider>
    </Team>
    <Team Manufacturer="Suzuki">
        <Rider>Ricky Carmichael</Rider>
        <Rider>Broc Hepler</Rider>
    </Team>
    <Team Manufacturer="Kawasaki">
        <Rider>James Stewart</Rider>
        <Rider>Michael Byrne</Rider>
    </Team>
```

```
</Motocross>'
--SELECT Motocross.Team.query('.')
SELECT Motocross.Team.value('@Manufacturer', 'varchar (50)') as Manufacturer,
        Motocross.Team.query('Rider') as Team
FROM @xmlvar.nodes('/Motocross/Team') Motocross(Team)
```

The results of the statement are shown in Figure 4-8.

	Manufacturer	Team
1	Yamaha	<Rider>Tim Ferry</Rider><Rider>Chad Reed</Rider><Rider>David Vuillemin</Rider>
2	Honda	<Rider>Kevin Windham</Rider><Rider>Mike LaRacco</Rider><Rider>Jeremy McGrath</Rider>
3	Suzuki	<Rider>Ricky Carmichael</Rider><Rider>Broc Hepler</Rider>
4	Kawasaki	<Rider>James Stewart</Rider><Rider>Michael Byrne</Rider><Rider>Broc Hepler</Rider>

Figure 4-8

In this example, the `query()`, `value()`, and `nodes()` methods were used to return the results shown. The `query()` method is the method used to query the entire XML instance, the `value()` method is used to return the individual Manufacturer values, and the `nodes()` method is used to format the results as rowsets.

Look at one more example using a combination of some of the `xml` data type methods. The following example uses the `exist()` method to check to see if any of the Teams have any riders, and if they do not, they aren't included in the results:

```
DECLARE @xmlvar xml
SET @xmlvar='
<Motocross>
    <Team Manufacturer="Yamaha">
        <Rider>Tim Ferry</Rider>
        <Rider>Chad Reed</Rider>
        <Rider>David Vuillemin</Rider>
    </Team>
    <Team Manufacturer="Honda">
        <Rider>Kevin Windham</Rider>
        <Rider>Mike LaRacco</Rider>
        <Rider>Jeremy McGrath</Rider>
    </Team>
    <Team Manufacturer="Suzuki">
        <Rider>Ricky Carmichael</Rider>
        <Rider>Broc Hepler</Rider>
    </Team>
    <Team Manufacturer="Kawasaki">
    </Team>
</Motocross>'
--SELECT Motocross.Team.query('.')
SELECT Motocross.Team.value('@Manufacturer', 'varchar (50)') as Manufacturer
FROM @xmlvar.nodes('/Motocross/Team') Motocross(Team)
WHERE Motocross.Team.exist('Rider') = 1
```

The results of the statement appear in Figure 4-9.

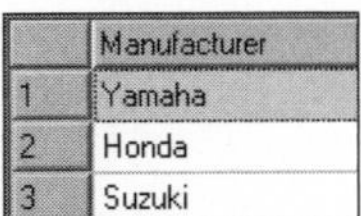

	Manufacturer
1	Yamaha
2	Honda
3	Suzuki

Figure 4-9

In this example, the same query(), value(), and exist() methods are used to determine if any of the manufacturers have riders. The query() method queries the XML instance, the value() method returns the manufacturer value for all manufacturers who have riders, provided by the exist() method. If the result of the exist() method is true for each manufacturer then the value() method returns the name of the manufacturer.

Using Operators with Methods

Operators allow you to use a table-valued function against each row returned by a query expression from an outer table. In simple terms, the APPLY operator creates a second table-column pair with which to compare to the original table-column pair. Each row from each table-column pair is evaluated against each row in the second table-column pair. The final table-column list is the combination of the second table-column pair being added to the original table-column pair.

There are two different APPLY operators: OUTER APPLY and CROSS APPLY.

Considering the previous example, you can obtain the same results by using the APPLY operator. The OUTER APPLY operator applies the nodes() method to each row, but the caveat is that it includes rows that have NULL values. To compensate for this, you need to add an additional clause on the WHERE clause, as follows:

```
DECLARE @xmlvar xml
SET @xmlvar='
<Motocross>
    <Team Manufacturer="Yamaha">
        <Rider>Tim Ferry</Rider>
        <Rider>Chad Reed</Rider>
        <Rider>David Vuillemin</Rider>
    </Team>
    <Team Manufacturer="Honda">
        <Rider>Kevin Windham</Rider>
        <Rider>Mike LaRacco</Rider>
        <Rider>Jeremy McGrath</Rider>
    </Team>
    <Team Manufacturer="Suzuki">
        <Rider>Ricky Carmichael</Rider>
        <Rider>Broc Hepler</Rider>
    </Team>
    <Team Manufacturer="Kawasaki">
    </Team>
</Motocross>'

SELECT DISTINCT Motocross.Team.value('@Manufacturer', 'varchar (50)') as
Manufacturer
FROM @xmlvar.nodes('/Motocross/Team') Motocross(Team)
OUTER APPLY Motocross.Team.nodes('./Rider') AS Motocross2(Team2)
WHERE Motocross2.Team2 IS NOT NULL
```

By adding the OUTER APPLY operator and modifying the WHERE clause, the returned results will look exactly like what was shown in Figure 4-9.

The other APPLY operator, CROSS APPLY, does away with modifying the WHERE clause and applies the nodes() method to each row in the result set, but returns only those rows generated from the nodes() method (much like the exist() method) from the first table-column pair. For example:

```
SELECT Motocross.Team.value('@Manufacturer', 'varchar (50)') as Manufacturer
FROM @xmlvar.nodes('/Motocross/Team') Motocross(Team)
CROSS APPLY Motocross.Team.rows.nodes('./Rider) AS Motocross2(Team2)
```

Any column that the nodes() *method returns cannot be used directly. Meaning, the following is not allowable:*

```
SELECT Motocross.Team
FROM @xmlvar.nodes('/Motocross/Team') Motocross(Team)
```

So far all the examples have dealt with xml data type variables. The following example uses an xml data type column with the nodes() method. In this example, the value() and query() methods are used to return values from the nodes in the result set. For each given location the SELECT clause returns the LocationID and any tools at the given location:

```
SELECT Instruct.value('@LocationID','int') as LocationID,
       Instruct.query('declare namespace
MSAW="http://schemas.microsoft.com/sqlserver/2004/07/adventure-
works/ProductModelManuInstructions";
                 MSAW:step/ MSAW:tool') as Tool
FROM    Production.ProductModel
CROSS APPLY Instructions.nodes('
declare namespace MSAW2 ="http://schemas.microsoft.com/sqlserver/2004/07/adventure-
works/ProductModelManuInstructions";
/MSAW2:root/MSAW2:Location') as PPM(Instruct)
WHERE ProductModelID=53
```

The results are shown in Figure 4-10.

	LocationID	Tool
1	50	<MI:tool xmlns:MI="http://schemas.microsoft.com/sqlserver/2004/07/adventure-works/ProductModel...

Figure 4-10

In this example, the CROSS APPLY is used to return only the rows from the outer table, in this case the Instructions.nodes() query, which produces the result "small wrench." The results are returned through a result set from the table-value function. In this example, the table-value function is the right input and the outer table expression is the left input of the expression.

For every row in the left input, the right input is examined and the resulting rows are joined for the final results.

Time to move on to defaults, constraints, and computed columns as they relate to xml data type columns.

Defaults, Constraints, and Computed Columns

As with any other data type column in a table, an `xml` data type column can have defaults and constraints applied to it, as well as being used as a computed column.

Defaults

There are two ways to apply defaults to an `xml` data type column. The first is to *implicitly* cast the data to an XML type as follows:

```
CREATE TABLE Employee (
    [EmployeeID] [int] NOT NULL,
    [EmployeeInfo] [xml] NOT NULL DEFAULT N'<Employee></Employee>'
) ON [PRIMARY]
GO
```

The second method is to *explicitly* convert the XML using the `CAST` function as follows:

```
CREATE TABLE Employee (
    [EmployeeID] [int] NOT NULL,
   [EmployeeInfo] [xml] NOT NULL DEFAULT CAST(N'< Employee></Employee >' As xml)
) ON [PRIMARY]
GO
```

Seems easy enough, but what purpose would adding a default to an `xml` data type column serve? The answer lies in looking at other data type columns that have defaults, but with much more functionality.

Suppose that in your Employee table you had the columns for the employee first name, last name, hire date, and so on. There really is no downside to this approach, but suppose that instead of all those columns, you had an `xml` data type column called EmployeeInfo and on that column you applied a default that contained a *shell* of an XML instance such as the following:

```
<root><Employee></Employee></root>
```

In this scenario, instead of inserting data into different columns, you could just as easily open the XML instance using XmlReader and insert into the XML document the appropriate nodes, such as the first name and last name nodes using the `update` method of XML DML.

Even better, why not have the entire XML instance stored in the column and use the `update` method of XML DML and just update the appropriate nodes with the data? The XML instance might look like this:

```
<root>
    <employee>
        <FirstName></FirstName>
        <LastName></LastName>
        <Address></Address>
```

```
            <HireDate></HireDate>
            .
            .
            .
        </employee>
    </root>
```

Instead of updating many columns, you are updating only a single column. The result is a performance gain and an easier method of updating an XML document.

Constraints

Constraints allow you to define how you want SQL Server to enforce database integrity. In other words, constraints allow you to specify the type of allowable data to be inserted into the columns in your database.

In SQL Server 2005, you can add constraints to `xml` data type columns, thereby limiting the XML values being added to the column. You can define these constraints by specifying row-level constraints and table-level constraints. These constraints apply to both typed and untyped XML.

Column-Level Constraints

Column-level constraints are applied to the specific column to which you want to limit the data, and can be applied only to a single column. For an `xml` data type column, adding a constraint entails using the `check()` object and specifying the query expression for which to check. For example, the following code demonstrates how to apply a constraint on an `xml` column:

```
CREATE TABLE Employee (
    [EmployeeID] [int] NOT NULL,
    [EmployeeInfo] [xml] check(EmployeeInfo.exist('/Employee/@EmployeeID')=1)
) ON [PRIMARY]
GO
```

This constraint states that any XML instance added to this column must have an `Employee` element with an `EmployeeID` attribute. The XML instance must have both of these in order for the insert to be successful. For example, the following `INSERT` succeeds because of the EmployeeID attribute on the Employee element:

```
INSERT INTO Employee (EmployeeID, EmployeeInfo)
VALUES (1, '<Employee EmployeeID="1"><FirstName>Damon</FirstName></Employee>')
GO
```

The following example, however, does not allow the `INSERT` because the `EmployeeID` attribute is missing:

```
INSERT INTO Employee (EmployeeID, EmployeeInfo)
VALUES (1, '<Employee><FirstName>Damon</FirstName></Employee>')
GO
```

The error message returned from the execution of this statement says that the `INSERT` statement conflicted with the `check()` constraint and therefore the `INSERT` fails because no `EmployeeID` attribute was supplied.

Column-level constraints are also useful when validating node values within the XML document. For example, the following constraint could check to ensure that duplicate values within the given XML document are not found in the `Employee` element:

```
<Employee EmployeeID="1">
    <FirstName>Williams</FirstName>
    <LastName>Williams</LastName>
</Employee>
```

The constraint for this looks like the following:

```
CONSTRAINT NameCheck CHECK (('/Employee[FirstName=LastName]')=0)
```

This constraint says to look at the `FirstName` and `LastName` elements underneath the `Employee` element and make sure their values are not equal.

Table-Level Constraints

A table-level constraint means that more than one column is included in the constraint. These types of constraints are good for further enforcing the integrity of the data in your tables. For example, you could use the `value()` method of the `xml` data type to check the value of an element or attribute of an XML document to see if it contains specific information before inserting or updating a table.

One of the limitations of check constraints, however, is that they do not support any of the `xml` data type methods. As mentioned in Chapter 2, the workaround for this is to create a user-defined function that wraps the `xml` data type method and then use the UDF for the creation of the table.

The following example creates a simple UDF to be used on the Employee table that will be used later:

```
CREATE FUNCTION xmludf(@xmlvar xml)
returns bit
AS
BEGIN
 RETURN @xmlvar.value('EmployeeInfo/@EmployeeID)[1]', 'int') = EmployeeID)
END
GO
```

Once the UDF is created, it can then be applied as a constraint to a table. The following creates an Employee table with a constraint that uses the UDF created earlier:

```
CREATE TABLE Employee (
    [EmployeeID] [int] NOT NULL,
    [EmployeeInfo] [xml]
    CONSTRAINT EmployeeInfoValidate check (dbo.xmludf(EmployeeInfo))
) ON [PRIMARY]
GO
```

The constraint applied to the Employee table specifies that any XML instance stored in the EmployeeInfo column will compare the `EmployeeID` attribute to the corresponding rows value in the EmployeeID column. For example, the following code sample inserts a row into the Employee table with an `EmployeeID` of `1` and an `EmployeeID` attribute of `21`, which will fail:

```
INSERT INTO Employee (EmployeeID, EmployeeInfo)
VALUES (1, '<Employee EmployeeID="21"><FirstName>Damon</FirstName></Employee>')
GO
```

The insert in the previous example fails because the EmployeeID column value does not match the `EmployeeID` attribute of the `Employee` element in the XML document.

However, the following constraint succeeds:

```
INSERT INTO Employee (EmployeeID, EmployeeInfo)
VALUES (1, '<Employee EmployeeID="1"><FirstName>Damon</FirstName></Employee>')
GO
```

This example succeeds because the EmployeeID column value matches the `EmployeeID` attribute of the `Employee` element in the XML document.

Constraints are valuable because they are a great way to enforce the validity of data. Constraints on `xml` data type columns, however, are much more useful because it is possible to enforce XML integrity not only of the existing column, but of your entire table as well.

Computed Columns

Never let it be said that the `xml` data type is not flexible. Not only is it possible to apply defaults and constraints to an `xml` data type column, but the XML contained in the column can be used in creating computed columns as well.

Computed columns are virtual columns, or existing columns, that are computed from an expression or equation using one or more columns in the same table. For example, it is possible to convert the value from a string column to an `xml` column as follows:

```
CREATE TABLE Table1 (
    Column1 varchar(200),
    Column2 as CAST(column1 as xml)
)
GO
```

The preceding example reads the value from `column1` and is used to compute the values for `column2`. The catch in this example is that in order for this to work, the data in `column1` must be well-formed XML.

It is also possible to go the other way as well, meaning you can convert `xml` to a string, as follows:

```
CREATE TABLE Table2 (
    Column1 xml,
    Column2 as CAST(column1 varchar(500))
)
GO
```

The CAST function was used in both of these examples to explicitly convert one data type to another data type.

Although this is nice, the real power comes from the capability to read XML instance node values and use those values to create computed columns.

> xml *data type methods cannot be used to create computed columns directly, so you must utilize other methods in the creation of computed columns, such as using UDFs to wrap the* xml *data type method.*

Since xml data type methods can't be used to create computed columns, the simple solution is to create a user-defined function that queries the value from the XML instance and then uses the function in the CREATE TABLE statement. The first step is to create the user-defined function as follows:

```
CREATE FUNCTION GetNodeValue(@xmlvar xml) RETURNS int
AS BEGIN
RETURN @xmlvar.value('(/Employee/@EmployeeID)[1]', 'int')
END
GO
```

The second step is to create the table:

```
CREATE TABLE Employee (
    EmployeeInfo xml,
    EmployeeID as dbo.GetNodeValue(EmployeeInfo)
)
GO
```

> *You must specify the* dbo *account when specifying the user-defined function during the table creation statement because if it is left off, SQL Server does not recognize it as a built-in function and generates an error.*

The next step is to insert the XML data into the table (the EmployeeInfo column):

```
INSERT INTO Employee (EmployeeInfo)
VALUES ('<Employee EmployeeID="10"><FirstName>Robin</FirstName></Employee>')
GO
```

Now query the Employee table and review the results. The results should look like Figure 4-11.

	EmployeeInfo	EmployeeID
1	<Employee EmployeeID="10"><FirstName>Robin</FirstName></Employee>	10

Figure 4-11

In the previous example, the user-defined function was created and used in the CREATE TABLE statement as the computed column for the second column (EmployeeID). The user-defined function uses the value() method to query the XML instance for a specific value, in this case the EmployeeID attribute of the Employee node. When a record is inserted into the table, the user-defined function pulls the value from the XML instance and is used as the value for the EmployeeID column.

This functionality also makes it possible (and quite simple) to use the `query()` method to query entire XML fragments to be used for computed columns.

Modify the user-defined function as follows:

```
DROP FUNCTION GetElementInfo
GO

CREATE FUNCTION GetElementInfo(@xmlvar xml) RETURNS xml
AS BEGIN
RETURN @xmlvar.query('root/Employee')
END
GO
```

The table also needs to change a bit:

```
DROP TABLE Employee
GO

CREATE TABLE Employee (
    EmployeeInfo xml,
    EmployeeID as dbo.GetElementInfo(EmployeeInfo)
)
GO
```

The last step is to insert a row into the table with a somewhat sizable XML instance:

```
INSERT INTO Employee (EmployeeInfo)
VALUES ('<root><Employee><FirstName>Robin</FirstName></Employee></root>')
GO
```

Query the Employee table again to view the results, as shown in Figure 4-12.

	EmployeeInfo	EmployeeID
1	<root><Employee><FirstName>Robin</FirstName></Employee></root>	<Employee><FirstName>Robin</FirstName></Employee>

Figure 4-12

In this example, the UDF is applied to the EmployeeID column with the data type being set as the user-defined function. The UDF queries and returns the entire XML document, returning the XML document such that when the UDF is applied to the EmployeeID column and data is inserted into the EmployeeInfo table, the UDF executes and sets the value of EmployeeID column equal to what was inserted into the EmployeeInfo column. The Employee column is therefore used as a computed column using the `xml` data type.

By now you should start to have a grasp on computed columns using the `xml` data type column, and you can move on to other matters, such as views, which are covered in the next section.

Creating Views

Views can be created using an `xml` data type column. Since the contents of a view are based on a query, this makes it very enticing to use with the `xml` data type because the view has access to all the `xml` data type functionality, such as the `value()` and `query()` methods.

The following example illustrates building a view that queries an `xml` data type column and uses the `value()` method to return values.

First, a little clean-up:

```
DROP TABLE Motocross
GO

CREATE TABLE Motocross (
 [MotocrossID] [int] NOT NULL,
 [MotocrossInfo] [xml] NOT NULL
) ON [PRIMARY]
GO
```

Now insert some data:

```
INSERT INTO Motocross (MotocrossID, MotocrossInfo)
VALUES (1, '
<Motocross>
    <Team Manufacturer="Yamaha">
        <Rider BikeSize="250">Tim Ferry</Rider>
        <Rider BikeSize="250">Chad Reed</Rider>
        <Rider BikeSize="250">David Vuillemin</Rider>
    </Team>
    <Team Manufacturer="Honda">
        <Rider BikeSize="450">Kevin Windham</Rider>
        <Rider BikeSize="250">Mike LaRacco</Rider>
        <Rider BikeSize="250">Jeremy McGrath</Rider>
    </Team>
    <Team Manufacturer="Suzuki">
        <Rider BikeSize="250">Ricky Carmichael</Rider>
        <Rider BikeSize="125">Broc Hepler</Rider>
    </Team>
    <Team Manufacturer="Kawasaki">
        <Rider BikeSize="250">James Stewart</Rider>
        <Rider BikeSize="125">Michael Byrne</Rider>
    </Team>
</Motocross>
')
GO
```

After inserting the data, the next step is to create the view:

```
CREATE VIEW GetTeamInfo AS
SELECT MotocrossInfo.value('(/Motocross/Team/@Manufacturer)[1]', 'varchar(40)') as
Team,
MotocrossInfo.value('(/Motocross/Team)[1]', 'varchar(40)') as Riders
FROM Motocross
```

Now that the view is created, you can query it:

```
SELECT * FROM GetTeamInfo
```

The results should look like this:

```
Team        Riders
------      -----------------------------------
Yamaha      Tim Ferry Chad Reed David Vuillemin
```

Views are a great way to filter the data coming from the `xml` data type column, and other than not being able to use views in a distributed partitioned view (see the "xml data type Best Practices" and "Limitations" sections), there are no limitations when using the `xml` data type in a view.

A distributed partitioned view is a view that includes a `UNION ALL` *operator, where the tables defined by the* `UNION ALL` *are structured equally. However, the tables are stored as multiple tables within the same instance of SQL Server or a group of independent instances.*

XML Settings Options

Certain settings affect how XML will behave in SQL Server. This behavior applies to `xml` data type variables and columns. The following table lists the settings that must be configured and the appropriate value for each setting. If these settings are not configured as shown in the table, all queries and modifications on `xml` data type will fail.

SET Options	Required Values
NUMERIC_ROUNDABOUT	OFF
ANSI_PADDING	ON
ANSI_WARNING	ON
ANSI_NULLS	ON
ARITHABORT	ON
CONCAT_NULL_YIELDS_NULL	ON
QUOTED_IDENTIFIER	ON

These options can be set by running the appropriate T-SQL. For example:

```
SET ANSI_PADDING ON
GO
```

xml data type Best Practices

As with everything else in technology there are some things to consider when using anything new. XML support in SQL Server 2005 is no different, and while it is a fantastic addition, it is always a good idea to know what some of the best practices and limitations are.

The following sections detail some of things to take into consideration as you plan to move forward with SQL Server 2005.

Why and Where

The intent of this book is not to persuade anyone to use SQL Server 2005 XML technology over relational storage at all. Chances are, however, that if you are reading this you have either started down the path of using XML in your databases or are already doing so.

If you are in the first group, those that are considering using SQL Sever 2005 XML, the purpose of this section is to highlight the reasons and benefits of string XML in SQL Server 2005. Consider using the XML data model if any of the following conditions are met:

- You are "platform independent." XML does not care what platform or operating system you are using.
- There is a lack of consistency in the structure of your data. If your data structure changes frequently, you should strongly consider the XML data model.
- Your data is in hierarchical format, a collection of strictly nested sets or nodes.
- The order of you data is important.

typed versus untyped

This chapter spent quite a bit of time covering the differences between typed and untyped XML, but didn't really discuss which to use in a particular scenario. Thus, the purpose of this section is to give you some guidance as to when you should use one over the other.

Regardless of whether you use typed or untyped, SQL Server is going to check for well-formed XML anyway. At times, however, one method is a better solution over the other.

You should use the untyped XML data type if the following criteria are met:

- There are no schemas associated with the XML data.
- You want data validation to happen on the client rather than on the server.

You should use typed XML under the following conditions:

- You want XML data validation to take place on the server rather than on the client.
- You want to utilize the query optimizations.
- You want to utilize the storage optimizations.
- You want to utilize the compilation of type information.

Constraints

As stated previously, constraints are a great way to limit the type of data that is permitted in an XML instance. For example, consider using a constraint under either of the following conditions:

- Any time business rule logic cannot be included (or is not allowed) in an XML schema. In these circumstances the logic can be moved to a constraint using `xml` data type methods.
- Any time columns other than `xml` data type columns are included in the constraint.

There is a downside to using constraints, and that is that you cannot use any of the `xml` data type methods when you specify a constraint. If you do need to specify a constraint, the solution is to create a UDF around the `xml` data type method. When you create the constraint, you can specify the function in the constraint.

Limitations

As much as XML fans would like to say that the `xml` data type is perfect, there are a few limitations, which are displayed in the following list:

- `xml` data type instance cannot exceed 2GB.
- `xml` data type cannot be used in a distributed partitioned view.
- `xml` data type cannot be used as a `PRIMARY KEY` or `FOREIGN KEY` constraint.
- `xml` data type cannot be used as a `UNIQUE` constraint.
- `xml` data type cannot use the `CAST` or `CONVERT` functions on a `text` or `ntext` data type.
- Since XML has its own encoding, `COLLATE` is not supported.
- `xml` data type cannot be used in a `GROUP BY` statement.
- `xml` data type cannot be part of a clustered or non-clustered index.
- `xml` data type can only cast `string` data type to `xml` data type.
- xml data type does not preserve namespace prefixes.

Summary

This chapter took an in-depth look at the `xml` data type and its implementation in SQL Server 2005, as this is the foundation for the rest of the book.

You delved into typed and untyped XML and learned the importance of determining how XML instances are stored in SQL Server, as well as some of the considerations to keep in mind when making that decision.

Likewise, you learned how to alter the `xml` data type column. This can be very beneficial if you are considering moving toward XML storage or are currently storing XML in your database and would like to migrate to the `xml` data type column.

From there, you focused on the `xml` data type methods and how to use them to query XML instances. Understanding these methods prepares you for the upcoming chapters on querying and modifying XML data using XQuery and XML DML.

Building on the `xml` data type column theme, the chapter's focus shifted to using defaults, constraints, and computed columns to further enhance the `xml` data type column for greater usability, especially when applied to using the `xml` data type methods.

Equally important is understanding the best way to put this new knowledge to use in a given situation, so the last part of the chapter focused on providing some insight on when to use the `xml` data type and outlined some of its limitations.

Building on all of this new knowledge, the next chapter discusses querying and modifying XML data.

5

Querying and Modifying XML Data in SQL Server 2005

A sizable section of Chapter 4 dealt with the `xml` data type methods, which are used to extract data from an XML document. The syntax of those methods, each one of them, except for the `modify()` method, takes an XQuery expression as a parameter. The XQuery expression of those methods is what really determines what data is returned from the XML document.

This chapter focuses on querying the `xml` data type and modifying data in XML instances, both in variables or the `xml` data type column. Both of these topics were introduced briefly in Chapter 2, but it is necessary to spend much more time on each one in order to fully grasp the implementation of XQuery in SQL Server 2005.

The first part of this chapter focuses primarily on the built-in XQuery support in SQL Server 2005, while the second half delves into the modification of XML documents using XML DML.

The intent of this chapter is to give you a good understanding of XQuery implementation in SQL Server 2005. It does not go into every aspect of XQuery, which could fill a book by itself.

XQuery

The XQuery language provides the capability to query well-formed XML documents. Combined with the added benefit of SQL Server 2005 providing native XML storage via the `xml` data type, XML documents can be queried natively in SQL Server. As of SQL Server 2005 Beta 2, the support for XQuery is based on the Last Call working draft of the W3C XQuery Language of November 2003.

Chapter 2 spent a few pages reviewing the structure of an XQuery expression, as well as some of the expressions and terms used in the XQuery language. This section briefly reviews what was introduced in Chapter 2; provides some new information on XQuery Prolog, XQuery Path expressions, and XQuery XML construction; and then introduces topics and examples of other XQuery features, namely the FLOWR statement and XQuery sorting.

XQuery Structure and Concepts Review

The XQuery language is a case-sensitive language defined by the W3C and is built on XPath expressions that allow for the querying of XML documents. This section briefly introduces XQuery and its syntax, and the components that make up an XQuery query.

Here are a few of the syntax rules:

- XQuery is case-sensitive.
- XQuery elements, attributes, and variables must be valid XML names.
- XQuery string values can be within double (" ") or single (' ') quotes.
- XQuery variables are defined by the `$` symbol.

As explained in Chapter 2, there are two main parts to an XQuery query. The first part is the XQuery Prolog (discussed in more detail in the "XQuery Prolog" section), which is simply a namespace declaration, such as the following:

```
declare namespace MSAW="http://schemas.microsoft.com/_
Sqlserver/2004/07/adventure-works/ProductModelManuInstructions");
```

The second part of the XQuery query is the body of the query, the query expression, as follows:

```
/MSAW:root/MSAW:Location[LocationID=50]
```

When put together, the entire XQuery expression looks like the following:

```
SELECT Instructions.Query('declare namespace MSAW="http://schemas.microsoft.com/_
Sqlserver/2004/07/adventure-works/ProductModelManuInstructions";
/MSAW:root/MSAW:Location[@LocationID=50]')
AS Location
FROM Production.ProductModel
WHERE ProductModelID = 47
```

All of these parts are necessary to have a true XQuery expression, including one of the `xml` data type methods, such as the `query()` method shown in the example. The power behind an XQuery expression is its ability to query deep into an XML document and retrieve any piece of information, whether it's from an XML variable or from data stored in an `xml` data type column.

Chapter 2 also touched briefly on some of the concepts and terms of XQuery such as Sequence, Atomization, Quantification, and Type promotion, which are reviewed in subsequent sections.

Sequence

As defined in Chapter 2, a sequence is the result returned from an XQuery expression made up of nodes and fragments called items. For example, consider the following query:

```
SELECT Instructions.query('
declare namespace MSAW="http://schemas.microsoft.com/sqlserver/2004/07/adventure-
works/ProductModelManuInstructions";
 for $Inst in /MSAW:root
 return
     (
     <FirstStep> {string(($Inst/MSAW:Location[@LocationID = 50]/MSAW:step[1])[1]) }
</FirstStep>,
     <SecondStep> {string(($Inst/MSAW:Location[@LocationID = 50]/MSAW:step[2])[1])
} </SecondStep>
     )
') AS Steps
FROM Production.ProductModel
WHERE ProductModelID=47
```

The results are shown in Figure 5-1.

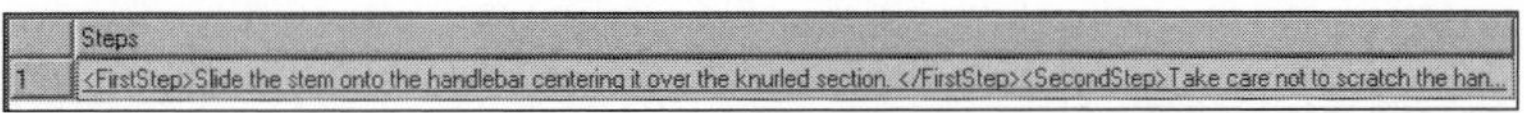

	Steps
1	<FirstStep>Slide the stem onto the handlebar centering it over the knurled section. </FirstStep><SecondStep>Take care not to scratch the han...

Figure 5-1

Taking a look at the XQuery expression, this example is querying the first two `<step>` elements, which are wrapped in parentheses. What would happen if the parentheses are removed? Go ahead and try it. What happened? It returned an error because of the `return` keyword bound to the first element.

The solution to this is to either put the parentheses back, or to remove the second element. The parentheses are important because the parentheses have a higher order of precedence than that of the comma separating the elements.

This is a fairly simple example. However, suppose you were to execute the following query:

```
SELECT Instructions
FROM Production.ProductModel
WHERE ProductModelID = 47
```

A small portion of the results are shown here:

```
<Location LaborHours="3.5" LotSize="1" LocationID="50">Work Center - 50 Frame
FormingThe following instructions pertain to Work Center 10. (Setup hours = .0,
Labor Hours = 3.5, Machine Hours = 0, Lot Sizing = 1)
 <step>Slide the
        <material>stem</material> onto the
        <material>handlebar</material> centering it over the knurled section.
 </step>
 <step>Take care not to scratch the handlebar.</step>
```

Notice that this query returned a lot of information that is difficult to decipher. It's one big XML document from a single column. The preceding results are only a small portion of the entire results returned. Wouldn't it be great if there were a way to query specific data out all of that information?

Well, there is: XQuery. If the schema in the Prolog supported it, the XQuery expression could have queried a level deeper into the XML document and pulled out the material node information.

Atomization

Returning the typed value of an item is called *atomization*. A common scenario of atomization occurs when you use the `data()` function to return a typed value of a specific node.

Going back to the example in Chapter 2, the query expression used atomization to automatically return the value of a node that had already been retrieved via the `data()` function:

```
SELECT Instructions.query ('declare namespace MSAW="http://schemas.microsoft.com/_
Sqlserver/2004/07/adventure-works/ProductModelManuInstructions";
FOR $AW in / MSAW:root/ MSAW:Location[2]
Return
 <AW OriginalMachineHours = "{$AW/@MachineHours}"
 NewMachineHours = "{data{$AW/@MachineHours} +1}"
 NewMachineHours1 = "{$AW/@MachineHours +1}"></AW>
')
FROM Proction.ProductModel
WHERE ProductModelID = 47
```

In this example, the first value is the attribute `MachineHours`. The second value is the same value returned using the `data()` function, and the third value is automatically returned using atomization. Therefore, the `data()` function is not needed.

The use of the `data()` function is completely optional in XQuery, although it does improve the readability of an XQuery expression.

Quantification

Quantification comes in two flavors: Existential and Universal. *Existential* simply means that for any two sequences, a value of `TRUE` will always be returned when any item in the first sequence matches any item in the second sequence. *Universal* means that for any two sequences a return value of `TRUE` will always be returned if every item in the first sequence has a match in the second sequence.

In the following example, a Universal quantified expression uses the `xml` data type `value()` method instead of the `query()` method to compare two sequences, checking to see if every Location (sequence 1) has a `MachineHours` attribute (sequence 2):

```
SELECT Instructions.value ('declare namespace
MSAW="http://schemas.microsoft.com/sqlserver/2004/07/adventure-
works/ProductModelManuInstructions";
( if (every $loc in //MSAW:root/MSAW:Location
   satisfies $loc /@MachineHours)
 then
   "YEP!"
 else
```

```
    "NOPE!"
[1])','varchar(5)') AS ReturnValue
FROM Production.ProductModel
WHERE ProductModelID = 47
```

The results from this query return `NOPE!` because not every `Location` has a `MachineHours` attribute. Change the XQuery quantified expression from `every` to `some` (an Existential quantification) and rerun the query. What are your results?

Type Promotion

Type promotion allows the implicit casting of numeric values, or an untyped value to a typed value. Casting can be Explicit or Implicit; however, there are certain rules that you need to follow when type casting regardless if you are explicitly or implicitly casting values.

Explicit Casting

There are a number of rules you need to follow when explicitly casting. These castings are not supported:

- Casting to or from list types. For example, you cannot cast to or from `xs:ENTITIES`.
- Casting to or from `xs:QNAME` and `xs:NOTATION`.
- Casting to or from duration subtypes `xdt:yearMonthDuration` and `xdt:dayTimeDuration`.

What type of casting is allowed? A built-in type can be cast to another built-in type.

Implicit Casting

The following rules apply when you are implicitly casting values:

- You can cast decimals to a float.
- You can cast a float to a double.
- You can cast numerical types (built-in) to their base type.
- You cannot implicitly cast string types.
- You cannot implicitly cast numeric types to string.

XQuery Prolog

As stated earlier, an XQuery expression contains two parts: the Prolog and the body. The *Prolog* is a combination of namespace and schema declarations that define the query processing *environment*. The *body* of an XQuery expression is what contains the actual expression that specifies which values you want returned from the XML document.

The following example, taken from earlier in this chapter, is used to define the XQuery expression:

```
SELECT Instructions.query('declare namespace MSAW="http://schemas.microsoft.com/
_sqlserver/2004/07/adventure-works/ProductModelManuInstructions";
```

```
/MSAW:root/MSAW:Location/[LocationID=50]')
AS Location
FROM Production.ProductModel
WHERE ProductModelID = 47
```

The first step in setting a Prolog is declaring a namespace prefix. You do this by using the `declare` keyword followed by the name of your namespace prefix. The name is then used in the body of the expression. The following example demonstrates declaring a namespace:

```
declare namespace MSAW
```

The Prolog in the code example is the following:

```
MSAW="http://schemas.microsoft.com/_
sqlserver/2004/07/adventure-works/ProductModelManuInstructions";
```

The Prolog is followed by the body of the expression:

```
/MSAW:root/MSAW:Location/[LocationID=50]
```

The purpose of declaring a namespace is first to define a prefix to use in the body of the query, and second, to associate the prefix with a namespace URI (Uniform Resource Identifier), which in this case points to the corresponding XSD schema. Using the default namespace declaration binds a default namespace for all element names.

In the event that you have been attacked by a severe case of writer's block and for whatever reason you cannot think of a namespace prefix, don't worry; you can always use the `DECLARE DEFAULT ELEMENT namespace`. This is a default namespace that will bind a default namespace for all element names.

The following example illustrates how to use this default namespace:

```
SELECT CatalogDescription.query('
  declare default element namespace
"http://schemas.microsoft.com/sqlserver/2004/07/adventure-
works/ProductModelDescription";
  /ProductDescription/Features
') as Result
FROM  Production.ProductModel
WHERE ProductModelID=28
```

When you run this query, all elements in the results are now prefixed with the default namespace defined in the Prolog. Here's a portion of these results:

```
<Features xmlns="http://schemas.microsoft.com/sqlserver/2004/07/adventure-works/
ProductModelDescription">These are the product highlights.
<p1:Warranty xmlns:p1="http://schemas.microsoft.com/sqlserver/2004/07/
adventure-works/ProductModelWarrAndMain">
<p1:WarrantyPeriod>1 year</p1:WarrantyPeriod><p1:Description>parts and
labor</p1:Description></p1:Warranty>

<p2:Maintenance xmlns:p2="http://schemas.microsoft.com/sqlserver/2004/07/
adventure-works/ProductModelWarrAndMain">
```

```
<p2:NoOfYears>5 years</p2:NoOfYears>
<p2:Description>maintenance contact available through dealer</p2:Description>
</p2:Maintenance>
```

By declaring a default namespace, you can bind each element name to the default namespace without the need to specify a prefix. This lets you write your expression without the need to specify the prefix at every turn, such as the case in the first example in this section where a namespace prefix was declared and used throughout the query.

XQuery Path Expressions

Path expressions in XQuery provide a node location in an XML document. The nodes, regardless of whether they are elements, attributes, and other node types are always returned by the path expression ordered in the same order as in the XML document, without duplicates nodes listed.

When specifying a path expression, the expression can be either relative or absolute. A *relative* path expression contains at least one or more steps separated by slash marks, typically one (/) or two (//). Using the CatalogDescription column in the Production.ProductModel table in the Adventure Works database for this example, a relative expression would look like the following:

```
child::Manufacturer
```

In this example expression, child refers to the current node being searched, which in this example is the `<ProductDescription>` node. It returns the `<Manufacturer>` node of the `<ProductDescription>` node.

Absolute path expressions begin with slashes (one or two) and can be followed by a relative path (the absolute path is optional). For example, using the same table and column, the following is an absolute path expression:

```
/child::ProductDescription/child::Manufacturer
```

Since the expression begins with a slash, which tells the expression to start at the root node, and is then followed by a relative path expression. The expression queries starting at the root node and returns all `<Manufacturer>` nodes of the `<ProductDescription>` nodes of the root node.

Absolute paths that start with a single slash (/) may not necessarily be followed by a relative path expression. For example, if the expression contains a single slash only, the entire XML document is returned.

Path expressions consist of one or more steps. A step is a level in the XML hierarchy. For example, the following expression contains a single step:

```
/MSAW:Location
```

The following expression has two steps:

```
/MSAW:Location/MSAW:Step
```

The first example returns all <Location> nodes underneath the root node element. The second example returns all <Step> child elements for each <Location> element.

Steps in path expressions can of two different types: Axis step or General step. In SQL Server 2005, General steps in path expressions are not supported, so they are not covered in this book.

Axis Step

There are two parts to an Axis step: the axis and the node test. The axis specifies the direction in which to search, and the node test defines the names of the nodes to be selected.

There are six types of axes:

- **Child:** Returns children of the context node.
- **Descendant:** Returns all descendants of the context node.
- **Parent:** Returns the parent of the context node.
- **Attribute:** Returns the attribute of the context node.
- **Self:** Returns its own node.
- **Descendant-or-self:** Returns itself and its children.

The following example illustrates using a child axis to query child nodes of the parent node:

```
SELECT CatalogDescription.query('
declare namespace MSAW="http://schemas.microsoft.com/sqlserver/2004/07/adventure-
works/ProductModelDescription";
  /child::MSAW:ProductDescription/child::MSAW:Manufacturer')
FROM Production.ProductModel
WHERE ProductModelID=35
```

The results are shown in Figure 5-2.

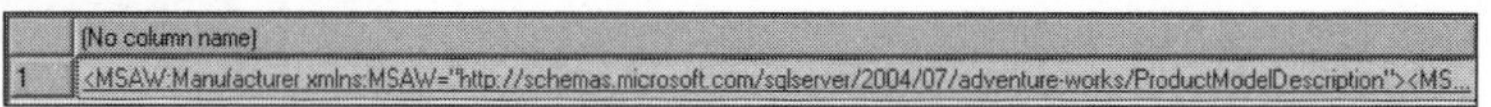

Figure 5-2

In this example, there are two steps in the expression. The first step, <ProductDescription>, is a child of the root node. The second step, <Manufacturer>, is a child of the <ProductDescription> node. The query then returns all children nodes of the <Manufacturer> node.

Node Test

The node test is a test condition in which all the nodes selected in a step must meet the query criteria. For example, the following step example returns only the child elements of the <ProductDescription> node whose element name is Manufacturer:

```
/child::ProductDescription/child::Manufacturer
```

Node test conditions can be specified by either the node name or by node type. For example, the following query expression returns the <name> element by specifying the node name to query:

```
SELECT CatalogDescription.query('
declare namespace PD="http://schemas.microsoft.com/sqlserver/2004/07/adventure-
works/ProductModelDescription";

 /child::PD:ProductDescription/child::PD:Manufacturer/child::PD:Name
')
FROM Production.ProductModel
WHERE ProductModelID=35
```

In this example, the Name node value is returned because the Name element is specified in the path expression. The path expression contains node tests.

The results of this query are as follows:

```
<PD:Name xmlns:PD="http://schemas.microsoft.com/sqlserver/2004/07/adventure-
works/ProductModelDescription">AdventureWorks</PD:Name>
```

A node test can be a node name (illustrated by the example) or a node type. A node test where the condition is of a node type returns only those nodes where the type is specified in the query, such as the following:

```
/child::PD:ProductDescription/child::PD:Manufacturer/child::comment()
```

This query returns all comment types found within the Manufacturer node.

Node tests can be useful when you are not sure exactly what nodes are in your XML document and you want to query and test for specific nodes.

XQuery XML Construction

XQuery construction is permitted using XQuery constructors inside of an XQuery expression. The constructors are accessible to all elements and attributes as well as other components of an XML document. Constructors allow you to build XML-type syntax, defining the construct of your XML.

The concept of dynamically retrieving data from your database is where XML construction comes in handy. For example, the following queries all the manufacturing steps at the second <Location> element and builds or constructs a <Location> element with the returned data:

```
SELECT Instructions.query('
declare namespace MSAW="http://schemas.microsoft.com/sqlserver/2004/07/adventure-
works/ProductModelManuInstructions";
        <Location>
           { / MSAW:root/ MSAW:Location[2]/ MSAW:step }
        </Location>
') as Location
FROM Production.ProductModel
WHERE ProductModelID=47
```

The results are shown in Figure 5-3.

Figure 5-3

Click the link to better view the results (see Figure 5-4). The namespaces have been removed for readability:

```
<Location>
    <MSAW:step xmlns:MSAW="...">Assemble all <MSAW:material>handlebar components</MSAW:material>
    <MSAW:step xmlns:MSAW="...">Weld all components together as shown in illustration <MSAW:diag
    <MSAW:step xmlns:MSAW="...">Inspect all weld joints per Adventure Works Cycles Inspection Sp
</Location>
```

Figure 5-4

The results of the query, which are all of the steps for the second location, were returned inside of the constructed <Location> element.

Constructors also provide the ability to construct attributes. Building on the previous example, modify the expression as follows:

```
SELECT Instructions.query('
declare namespace MSAW="http://schemas.microsoft.com/sqlserver/2004/07/adventure-
works/ProductModelManuInstructions";
    <Location
        LocationID="{ (/MSAW:root/MSAW:Location[2]/@LocationID)[1] }"
        MachineHours = "{ (/MSAW:root/MSAW:Location[2]/@MachineHours)[1] }" >
        { /MSAW:root/MSAW:Location[2]/MSAW:step }
    </Location>
') as Location
FROM Production.ProductModel
WHERE ProductModelID=47
```

The results look the same, except there are two attributes added to the <Location> element, as illustrated in Figure 5-5.

```
<Location LocationID="20" MachineHours="1.75">
    <MSAW:step xmlns:MSAW="...">Assemble all <MSAW:material>handlebar components</MSAW:material>
    <MSAW:step xmlns:MSAW="...">Weld all components together as shown in illustration <MSAW:diag
    <MSAW:step xmlns:MSAW="...">Inspect all weld joints per Adventure Works Cycles Inspection Sp
</Location>
```

Figure 5-5

Make one more modification to get rid of the namespace and return only the string value of the manufacturing step:

```
SELECT Instructions.query('
declare namespace MSAW="http://schemas.microsoft.com/sqlserver/2004/07/adventure-
works/ProductModelManuInstructions";
    <Location
```

```
        LocationID="{ (/MSAW:root/MSAW:Location[2]/@LocationID)[1] }"
        MachineHours = "{ (/MSAW:root/MSAW:Location[2]/@MachineHours)[1] }" >
        {
        for $var in /MSAW:root/MSAW:Location[2]/MSAW:step
        return string($var)
        }
    </Location>
') as Location
FROM Production.ProductModel
WHERE ProductModelID=47
```

The results are shown in Figure 5-6, and have been formatted for better readability.

```
<Location LocationID="20" MachineHours="1.75">
    Assemble all handlebar components following blueprint 1111.
    Weld all components together as shown in illustration 5
    Inspect all weld joints per Adventure Works Cycles Inspection Specification INFS-222.
</Location>
```

Figure 5-6

Computed element and attribute names are not fully supported in this release, but will be supported at product release time. Until then, you can use string literals to define the names.

FLWOR Statement

The FLWOR (pronounced *flower*) statement is the syntax in which you can define XQuery expression iteration within the XML document. FLWOR is an acronym that stands for FOR, LET, WHERE, ORDER BY, and RETURN.

LET *is not supported in the current beta release of SQL Server 2005.*

A FLWOR statement is made up of the following components:

- An input sequence (constructed XML nodes are not accepted as input)
- A FLWOR variable (for example, FOR $var)
- An optional WHERE clause
- An optional ORDER BY clause
- A RETURN expression

Using the code sample from the previous section, the following example queries all the step elements for the second <Location> node:

```
SELECT Instructions.query('
declare namespace MSAW="http://schemas.microsoft.com/sqlserver/2004/07/adventure-
works/ProductModelManuInstructions";
for $var in //MSAW:root/MSAW:Location[2]/MSAW:step
      return
           string($var)
```

```
') as Steps
FROM Production.ProductModel
WHERE ProductModelID=47
```

The results from the query are shown in Figure 5-7.

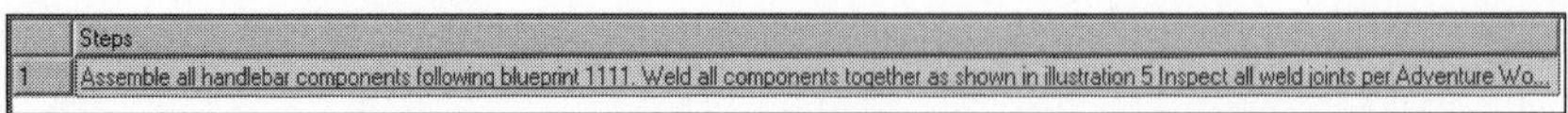

	Steps
1	Assemble all handlebar components following blueprint 1111. Weld all components together as shown in illustration 5 Inspect all weld joints per Adventure Wo...

Figure 5-7

Looking at the query syntax, it follows the FLWOR syntax because it uses a number of the necessary components required for a FLWOR statement. It has the FLWOR statement FOR and the RETURN expression, and it includes the input sequence specified by the XPath expression.

The preceding example uses a single variable bound to a single input sequence. The following example uses the same code sample from earlier, but uses multiple variables, each bound to an input sequence:

```
SELECT Instructions.query('
declare namespace MSAW="http://schemas.microsoft.com/sqlserver/2004/07/adventure-
works/ProductModelManuInstructions";
for $var in //MSAW:root/MSAW:Location[2]/MSAW:step,
  $mat in $var/MSAW:material
      Return
       <Material>
         { $mat }
       </Material>

') as Material
FROM Production.ProductModel
WHERE ProductModelID=47
```

The results are as follows:

```
<Material>
  <MSAW:material
xmlns:MSAW="http://schemas.microsoft.com/sqlserver/2004/07/adventure-
works/ProductModelManuInstructions">handlebar components</MSAW:material>
</Material>
```

The difference between the previous two examples is that the latter defines two variables in the `for` clause. The first expression returns all of the steps for the second location. The second path expression, assigned to the `$mat` variable, returns all results for all the material elements within the `$var` variable. In this example, there is only a single occurrence of the `material` element.

The WHERE clause in the FLWOR statement is not the `where` clause following the FROM clause in the preceding example. The `where` clause is included within the query expression and provides the capability to limit or filter the results returned. For example, the following queries all Locations where the number of step nodes is greater than two:

```
SELECT Instructions.query('
declare namespace MSAW="http://schemas.microsoft.com/sqlserver/2004/07/adventure-
works/ProductModelManuInstructions";
for $var in /MSAW:root/MSAW:Location
where count($var/MSAW:step) > 2
return
    <Location>
        { $var/@LocationID }
    </Location>
') as Location
FROM Production.ProductModel
WHERE ProductModelID=47
```

The results of this query, shown in Figure 5-8, include only those `LocationIDs` where the number of manufacturing steps is greater than 2.

Figure 5-8

This filtering for this query is provided by the `where` clause in the following expression query:

```
where count($var/MSAW:step) > 2
```

XQuery Sorting

Sorting in XQuery is provided by the `GROUP BY` clause of the `FLWOR` statement. In fact, the `GROUP BY` clause can *only* be used in a `FLWOR` statement. If the `GROUP BY` clause is not specified, the results are returned in ascending order by default, but you can specify the optional keywords `ascending` or `descending` as well.

The capability to sort using `GROUP BY` is not limited to sorting by types. For example, a query expression can sort on an element value, attribute value, or element name.

Using the Adventure Works database again, the following example shows how to retrieve all the alternate phone numbers for a specific person and then sort them from the Person.Contact table:

```
SELECT AdditionalContactInfo.query('
declare namespace ct="http://schemas.microsoft.com/sqlserver/2004/07/adventure-
works/ContactTypes";
declare namespace ci="http://schemas.microsoft.com/sqlserver/2004/07/adventure-
works/ContactInfo";
   for $var in /ci:AdditionalContactInfo//ct:telephoneNumber
   order by $var/ct:number[1]
   return $var
') As Result
FROM Person.Contact
WHERE ContactID=1
```

The results are shown in Figure 5-9.

```
<ct:telephoneNumber xmlns:ct="http://schemas.m
   <ct:number>111-111-1111</ct:number>
   <ct:SpecialInstructions>
         Call only after 5PM.
      </ct:SpecialInstructions>
</ct:telephoneNumber>
<ct:telephoneNumber xmlns:ct="http://schemas.m
   <ct:number>112-111-1111</ct:number>
</ct:telephoneNumber>
```

Figure 5-9

In the preceding example, the optional sort (ascending or descending) was left off, which automatically sorted the phone numbers in ascending order.

In the next example, instead of sorting by a node value, the results are sorted by the `MachineHours` attribute:

```
SELECT Instructions.query('
declare namespace MSAW="http://schemas.microsoft.com/sqlserver/2004/07/
adventure-works/ProductModelManuInstructions";
for $MH in /MSAW:root/MSAW:Location
order by $MH/@MachineHours descending
    return
      <Location>
        { $MH/@LocationID }
        { $MH/@MachineHours }
      </Location>
') as Location
FROM Production.ProductModel
WHERE ProductModelID = 47
```

The results (see Figure 5-10) show the `Locations`, the `LocationID` attribute, and the `MachineHours` attribute sorted in descending order by `MachineHours`.

Figure 5-10

This final example shows how to sort by element name. The query expression queries the first manufacturing step of the first location to retrieve all child elements in ascending order:

```
SELECT Instructions.query('
declare namespace
 MSAW="http://schemas.microsoft.com/sqlserver/2004/07/adventure-works/
ProductModelManuInstructions";
    for $var in /MSAW:root/MSAW:Location[1]/MSAW:step[1]/*
    order by local-name($var)
    return $var
') as Result
FROM Production.ProductModel
where ProductModelID=47
```

The results show the element names sorted in ascending order:

```
<MSAW:material>aluminum sheet MS-2259</MSAW:material>
<MSAW:tool>T-50 Tube Forming tool</MSAW:tool>
```

While not nearly a complete discourse on XQuery technology, I hope this section gave you enough information about the XQuery implementation in SQL Server 2005 to be able to readily retrieve data from your XML documents.

XML Data Modification Language

The XML Data Modification Language (XML DML) was introduced in Chapter 2 with some examples to highlight some of its features. The purpose of this section is to discuss the topics that were not covered in Chapter 2, provide more examples, and list any limitations of XML DML.

As listed in Chapter 2, there are three keywords added that need to be added to an XQuery expression to enable XML DML functionality. The keywords are case-sensitive. They are as follows:

- `insert`
- `delete`
- `replace value of`

insert

The `insert` keyword allows for the insertion of one or more nodes into an existing XML document. The placement of the new nodes is determined by the syntax used in the expression. The basic syntax for the `insert` keyword is as follows:

```
INSERT
    Expression1
    (
        (as first | Last) into | after | before
    Expression2
    )
```

`Expression1` is the node or nodes to be inserted into the XML document. This expression can be an XML instance or an XQuery expression. When specifying multiple nodes, you must wrap the nodes in parentheses and separate them by a comma. If `Expression1` contains one or more values, those values are inserted as a single text node.

The `into` keyword signifies that the nodes in `Expression1` are inserted into the identified node in `Expression2` as child nodes. If `Expression2` already has child nodes, then you must include the `as first` or `as last` keyword to specify where in `Expression2` to insert the new nodes. When inserting attributes, the `as first` and `as last` keywords are ignored.

The `before` and `after` keywords determine where in `Expression2` to insert `Expression1`. The `before` keyword inserts the nodes in `Expression1` into `Expression2` before any existing nodes in `Expression2`. The `after` keyword inserts the nodes in `Expression1` into `Expression2` after any existing nodes in `Expression2`.

`Expression2` is the relative node in the XML document into which the nodes in `Expression1` are inserted. As with `Expression1`, `Expression2` can also be an XML instance or an XQuery expression.

In all of the following examples, `Expression1` is the node that is to be inserted. Here's the first example:

```
<FirstName>Evel</FirstName>
```

`Expression2` is the location where the nodes in `Expression1` are added, which is the following:

```
(/Root/Employee/EmployeeInformation)[1]')
```

The XML document used in Chapter 2 to demonstrate the `insert` keyword is used again here:

```
<Root>
 <Employee EmployeeID="1">
        <EmployeeInformation>
        </EmployeeInformation>
 </Employee>
</Root>
```

The first example simply inserts a new node into the listed XML. The following code inserts a new `lastname` node into the XML instance:

```
DECLARE @xmldoc xml
SET @xmldoc =
'<Root>
 <Employee EmployeeID="1">
        <EmployeeInformation>
        </EmployeeInformation>
 </Employee>
</Root>'
SET @xmldoc.modify('
insert <LastName>Knievel</LastName>
into (/Root/Employee/EmployeeInformation)[1]')
SELECT @xmldoc
GO
```

The results of the `SELECT @xmldoc` statement looks like the following:

```
<Root>
    <Employee EmployeeID="1">
        <EmployeeInformation>
            <LastName>Knievel</LastName>
        </EmployeeInformation>
    <Employee>
</Root>
```

Using the `as first` keyword, modify the original code to look like the following:

```
DECLARE @xmldoc xml
SET @xmldoc =
'<Root>
```

```
 <Employee EmployeeID="1">
        <EmployeeInformation>
        </EmployeeInformation>
 </Employee>
</Root>'
--SELECT @xmldoc
SET @xmldoc.modify('
insert <LastName>Knievel</LastName>
into (/Root/Employee/EmployeeInformation)[1]')
SET @xmldoc.modify('
insert <FirstName>Evel</FirstName>
as first
into (/Root/Employee/EmployeeInformation)[1]
')
SELECT @xmldoc
GO
```

Running this query returns the results shown in Figure 5-11.

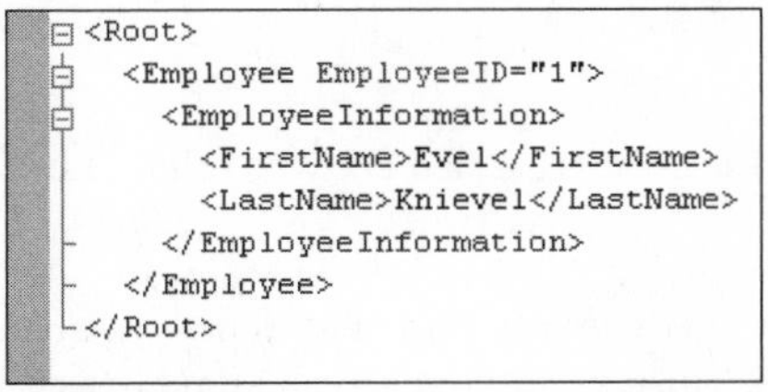

```
<Root>
  <Employee EmployeeID="1">
    <EmployeeInformation>
      <FirstName>Evel</FirstName>
      <LastName>Knievel</LastName>
    </EmployeeInformation>
  </Employee>
</Root>
```

Figure 5-11

The `as first` keyword added the `FirstName` element as the first element in the parent `EmployeeInformation` element.

To finish off this example, make the following changes to the code and rerun the query:

```
DECLARE @xmldoc xml
SET @xmldoc =
'<Root>
 <Employee EmployeeID="1">
        <EmployeeInformation>
        </EmployeeInformation>
 </Employee>
</Root>'
SET @xmldoc.modify('
insert <LastName>Knievel</LastName>
into (/Root/Employee/EmployeeInformation)[1]')
SET @xmldoc.modify('
insert <FirstName>Evel</FirstName>
as first
into (/Root/Employee/EmployeeInformation)[1]
')
```

```
SET @xmldoc.modify('
insert <JobTitle>Daredevil</JobTitle>
as last
into (/Root/Employee/EmployeeInformation)[1]
')
SELECT @xmldoc
GO
```

Figure 5-12 displays the results.

```
<Root>
  <Employee EmployeeID="1">
    <EmployeeInformation>
      <FirstName>Evel</FirstName>
      <LastName>Knievel</LastName>
      <JobTitle>Dare Devil</JobTitle>
    </EmployeeInformation>
  </Employee>
</Root>
```

Figure 5-12

Using the `as last` keyword the `JobTitle` element was inserted into the XML instance as the last element in `Expression2`.

Inserting multiple elements is nearly identical in operation to inserting single elements. The following example takes the original XML instance (`Expression2`) and inserts the `FirstName`, `LastName`, and `JobTitle` elements (`Expresssion1`) into the XML instance:

```
DECLARE @xmldoc xml
SET @xmldoc =
'<Root>
 <Employee EmployeeID="1">
   <EmployeeInformation>
   </EmployeeInformation>
 </Employee>
</Root>'
SET @xmldoc.modify('
insert (
        <FirstName>Evel</FirstName>,
        <LastName>Knievel</LastName>,
        <JobTitle>Daredevil</JobTitle>
       )
into (/Root/Employee/EmployeeInformation)[1]')
SELECT @xmldoc
GO
```

The results of this query are exactly the same as the results shown in Figure 5-12. The difference is that it took only a single `insert` to add the elements into the XML instance.

Adding attributes in not much different from adding elements. The following example inserts an attribute into the XML instance of the previous results:

```
DECLARE @xmldoc xml
SET @xmldoc =
'<Root>
 <Employee EmployeeID="1">
        <EmployeeInformation>
                <FirstName>Evel</FirstName>
                <LastName>Knievel</LastName>
                <JobTitle>Daredevil</JobTitle>
        </EmployeeInformation>
 </Employee>
</Root>'
SET @xmldoc.modify('
insert attribute BusesJumped {"14" }
into (/Root/Employee[@EmployeeID=1])[1] ')
DECLARE @Status varchar(10)
SET @Status ='Success'
SET @xmldoc.modify('
insert attribute JumpStatus {sql:variable("@Status") }
into   (/Root/Employee[@EmployeeID=1])[1] ')
SELECT @xmldoc
GO
```

In this example, two different attributes are added to the XML instance. The first one is added by specifying the literal string value `BusesJumped`. The second attribute is added by assigning the value to a variable and using the `sql:variable` function to pass the variable to the `modify` method.

The attributes are successfully added, as shown in Figure 5-13.

```
<Root>
  <Employee EmployeeID="1" BusesJumped="14" JumpStatus="Success">
    <EmployeeInformation>
      <FirstName>Evel</FirstName>
      <LastName>Knievel</LastName>
      <JobTitle>Daredevil</JobTitle>
    </EmployeeInformation>
  </Employee>
</Root>
```

Figure 5-13

The next example adds a new element into an untyped XML column. The following example uses the Motocross table created earlier to insert an element into the XML instance stored in the `xml` data type column.

The XML instance in the MotocrossInfo column in the Motocross table looks like Figure 5-14 (which shows only the important piece of the XML instance):

```
    <Rider BikeSize="250">Mike LaRacco</Rider>
    <Rider BikeSize="250">Jeremy McGrath</Rider>
  </Team>
  <Team Manufacturer="Suzuki">
    <Rider BikeSize="250">Ricky Carmichael</Rider>
    <Rider BikeSize="125">Broc Hepler</Rider>
  </Team>
  <Team Manufacturer="Kawasaki">
    <Rider BikeSize="250">James Stewart</Rider>
```

Figure 5-14

The following code inserts a new `Rider` element under the `Team Suzuki` node. The new node is the last node using the `as last` keyword, as follows:

```
UPDATE Motocross
SET MotocrossInfo.modify('insert <Rider BikeSize="250">Sebastien Tortelli</Rider>
as last
  into   (/Motocross/Team)[3]
')
GO
```

When you re-query the Motocross table, the results now look like Figure 5-15.

```
    <Rider BikeSize="250">Jeremy McGrath</Rider>
  </Team>
  <Team Manufacturer="Suzuki">
    <Rider BikeSize="250">Ricky Carmichael</Rider>
    <Rider BikeSize="125">Broc Hepler</Rider>
    <Rider BikeSize="250">Sebastien Tortelli</Rider>
  </Team>
  <Team Manufacturer="Kawasaki">
    <Rider BikeSize="250">James Stewart</Rider>
    <Rider BikeSize="125">Michael Byrne</Rider>
```

Figure 5-15

Elements and attributes can also be added using conditional statements, such as the following:

```
SET @xmldoc.modify ('
insert
If (/Root/Employee/[@EmployeeID=1])
Then attribute BusesJumped {"14"}
Else ()
    As first
    into (/Root/Employee[@EmployeeID=1])[1]')
```

This example is very similar to a previous example where you added the `BusesJumped` attribute. The difference here is that in this example, the addition of the attribute was wrapped around a conditional statement. If the `EmployeeID` attribute has a value of `1`, then add the new attribute; otherwise, don't add it.

Deleting elements and attributes is as easy as adding them, as shown in the next section.

delete

You can delete nodes from an XML instance by using the `delete` keyword. As explained in Chapter 2, the syntax is straightforward. Here it is again for your review:

```
Delete Expression
```

The following example deletes a node from an `xml` data type variable:

```
DECLARE @xmldoc xml
SET @xmldoc =
'<Root>
 <Employee EmployeeID="1">
        <EmployeeInformation>
                <FirstName>Evel</FirstName>
                <LastName>Knievel</LastName>
                <JobTitle>Daredevil</JobTitle>
        </EmployeeInformation>
 </Employee>
</Root>'
SET @xmldoc.modify('
  delete /Root/Employee/EmployeeInformation/JobTitle
')
SELECT @xmldoc
```

Running this query removes the `JobTitle` node from the XML instance.

The following example uses the same expression to delete the `EmployeeID` attribute from the XML instance:

```
DECLARE @xmldoc xml
SET @xmldoc =
'<Root>
 <Employee EmployeeID="1">
        <EmployeeInformation>
                <FirstName>Evel</FirstName>
                <LastName>Knievel</LastName>
                <JobTitle>Daredevil</JobTitle>
        </EmployeeInformation>
 </Employee>
</Root>'
SET @xmldoc.modify('
  delete /Root/Employee/EmployeeInformation/JobTitle
')
SET @xmldoc.modify('
  delete /Root/Employee/@EmployeeID
  ')
SELECT @xmldoc
```

Compare the results in Figure 5-16 with those shown previously in Figure 5-13, and you'll notice that both the `EmployeeID` attribute and `JobTitle` node have been removed from the XML instance.

```
<Root>
  <Employee>
    <EmployeeInformation>
      <FirstName>Evel</FirstName>
      <LastName>Knievel</LastName>
    </EmployeeInformation>
  </Employee>
</Root>
```

Figure 5-16

The last example of this section illustrates deleting a node from an `xml` data type column:

```
UPDATE Motocross
SET Motocross.modify(' delete /Root/Team[3]/Rider')
```

When you query the Motocross table, the results show that the `Rider` node with a value of `Sebastien Tortelli` has been deleted.

replace value of

The `update` keyword in conjunction with the `replace value of` keyword allows for the in-place update of a node value in an XML instance. Chapter 2 covered the syntax of the `replace value of` keyword, but it is shown again here for review and additional information:

```
replace value of
  expression1
with
  expression2
```

`Expression1` is the node whose value is being updated. Only a single node can be expressed; if multiple nodes are expressed, an error is generated.

`Expression2` is the new value of the node.

The following example updates a node in an XML instance with a new value. Using the previous Employee example, the `JobTitle` value is updated with a new value as follows:

```
DECLARE @xmldoc xml
SET @xmldoc =
'<Root>
 <Employee EmployeeID="1">
        <EmployeeInformation>
                <FirstName>Evel</FirstName>
                <LastName>Knievel</LastName>
                <JobTitle>Daredevil</JobTitle>
        </EmployeeInformation>
 </Employee>
</Root>'
-- update text in the first manufacturing step
SET @xmldoc.modify('
```

```
  replace value of (/Root/Employee/EmployeeInformation/JobTitle[1]/text())[1]
  with     "Retired"
')
SELECT @xmldoc
```

The results of the SELECT statement (see Figure 5-17) show that the JobTitle value has been changed from Daredevil to Retired:

```
<Root>
  <Employee EmployeeID="1">
    <EmployeeInformation>
      <FirstName>Evel</FirstName>
      <LastName>Knievel</LastName>
      <JobTitle>Retired</JobTitle>
    </EmployeeInformation>
  </Employee>
</Root>
```

Figure 5-17

Attributes can also be updated as shown in the following example (also note the change in information in the XML instance):

```
DECLARE @xmldoc xml
SET @xmldoc =
'<Root>
 <Employee EmployeeID="1">
        <EmployeeInformation>
                <FirstName>Robby</FirstName>
                <LastName>Knievel</LastName>
                <JobTitle>Son</JobTitle>
        </EmployeeInformation>
 </Employee>
</Root>'
-- update text in the first manufacturing step
SET @xmldoc.modify('
  replace value of (/Root/Employee/EmployeeInformation/JobTitle[1]/text())[1]
  with     "Daredevil"
')
SET @xmldoc.modify('
  replace value of (/Root/Employee/@EmployeeID)[1]
  with     "2"
')
SELECT @xmldoc
```

This example updates both the EmployeeID attribute as well as the JobTitle value, as shown in Figure 5-18.

In the previous examples, a [1] is added to the end of the target value being updated. Since only a single node can be updated, the [1] value specifies which node to update. In these examples, the [1] is not really necessary because there is only one <JobTitle> node.

```
<Root>
  <Employee EmployeeID="2">
    <EmployeeInformation>
      <FirstName>Robby</FirstName>
      <LastName>Knievel</LastName>
      <JobTitle>Daredevil</JobTitle>
    </EmployeeInformation>
  </Employee>
</Root>
```

Figure 5-18

However, in the case of multiple nodes with the same name, such as the case with the Motocross examples where there are multiple `<Rider>` nodes, the `[1]` is necessary. A value of `[1]` updates the first `<Rider>` node, while a `[2]` updates the second `<Rider>` node.

For example, the following code updates the second rider `<Rider>` node of the third `Team` node of the Motocross table (the column is untyped):

```
UPDATE Motocross
SET MotocrossInfo.modify ('
  replace value of (/Motocross/Team/Rider/text())[2]
  with "Davi Millsaps" ')
```

This example demonstrates the `replace value of` statement, which updates the name of the second rider for team Suzuki from `Broc Hepler` to `Davi Millsaps`. The modified results are shown here:

```
    <Rider BikeSize="250">Jeremy McGrath</Rider>
  </Team>
  <Team Manufacturer="Suzuki">
    <Rider BikeSize="250">Ricky Carmichael</Rider>
    <Rider BikeSize="125">Davi Millsaps</Rider>
    <Rider BikeSize="250">Sebastien Tortelli</Rider>
  </Team>
  <Team Manufacturer="Kawasaki">
    <Rider BikeSize="250">James Stewart</Rider>
    <Rider BikeSize="125">Michael Byrne</Rider>
```

The first expression identifies the node whose value is to be replaced and must be a single node. An error is generated if multiple nodes are found in the results of the query. Equally, if the results of the first expression are empty, no replacement is made.

The second expression specifies the new value of the node — either a single value or a list of values. In the case where it is a list of values, the old value is replaced with the list.

The last example in this section uses conditional statements to determine the new value. In the following example, the expression queries the number of riders for the first team, and depending on the number of riders found, sets the attribute of the `Team` element to a different value:

```
DECLARE @xmldoc xml
SET @xmldoc = '<Motocross>
  <Team Manufacturer="Yamaha">
```

```
      <Rider BikeSize="250">Tim Ferry</Rider>
      <Rider BikeSize="250">Chad Reed</Rider>
      <Rider BikeSize="250">David Vuillemin</Rider>
    </Team>
    <Team Manufacturer="Honda">
      <Rider BikeSize="450">Kevin Windham</Rider>
      <Rider BikeSize="250">Mike LaRacco</Rider>
      <Rider BikeSize="250">Jeremy McGrath</Rider>
    </Team>
    <Team Manufacturer="Suzuki">
      <Rider BikeSize="250">Ricky Carmichael</Rider>
      <Rider BikeSize="125">Broc Hepler</Rider>
      <Rider>Sebastien Tortelli</Rider>
    </Team>
    <Team Manufacturer="Kawasaki">
      <Rider BikeSize="250">James Stewart</Rider>
      <Rider BikeSize="125">Michael Byrne</Rider>
    </Team>
  </Motocross>'
  SET @xmldoc.modify('
    replace value of (/Motocross/Team[1]/@Manufacturer)[1]
    with (
         if (count(/Motocross/Team[1]/Rider) = 3) then
           "Team Yamaha"
         else
            "Yamaha"
        )
  ')
  SELECT @xmldoc
```

The results shown in Figure 5-19 illustrate that the attribute on the `Team` element for the Yamaha manufacturer has changed for the Yamaha Team.

```
<Motocross>
  <Team Manufacturer="Team Yamaha">
    <Rider BikeSize="250">Tim Ferry</Rider>
    <Rider BikeSize="250">Chad Reed</Rider>
    <Rider BikeSize="250">David Vuillemin</Rider>
  </Team>
  <Team Manufacturer="Honda">
    <Rider BikeSize="450">Kevin Windham</Rider>
    <Rider BikeSize="250">Mike LaRacco</Rider>
    <Rider BikeSize="250">Jeremy McGrath</Rider>
  </Team>
  <Team Manufacturer="Suzuki">
    <Rider BikeSize="250">Ricky Carmichael</Rider>
    <Rider BikeSize="125">Broc Hepler</Rider>
    <Rider>Sebastien Tortelli</Rider>
  </Team>
  <Team Manufacturer="Kawasaki">
    <Rider BikeSize="250">James Stewart</Rider>
    <Rider BikeSize="125">Michael Byrne</Rider>
  </Team>
</Motocross>
```

Figure 5-19

This example used the `count()` function to count the number of child nodes. While this example is fairly simplistic, conditional expressions used in XQuery expressions have to use every XQuery function available at its disposal.

For example, an expression could check the value of a node and the conditional expression could base its decision on the return of that value.

Summary

The entire purpose of this chapter was to build on the related topics that were discussed in Chapter 2. The implementation of XQuery support in SQL Server 2005, with the addition of the XML DML, makes the querying and modification of the `xml` data type quite easy.

The XQuery language is quickly becoming a very popular and common XML querying language, and it would be wise to start learning it. This chapter got you started with that endeavor by explaining the syntax and structure of XQuery and some discussions of the concepts and terms used with XQuery, such as sequences and atomization.

That was followed by an in-depth discussion on the XML DML (Data Modification Language), which is an extension of the XQuery language and used to modify the data within an XML instance. You learned about the three case-sensitive keywords (`insert`, `delete`, and `replace value of`), which allow you to modify XML document content.

From here it is time to learn and understand how to improve performance when querying XML documents by learning about indexing the `xml` data type.

6

Indexing XML Data in SQL Server 2005

Indexing is not new to SQL Server; it has been a feature since the early versions. *Indexing* is the concept of storing a structure associated with a table that allows for quick retrieval of data. This b-tree structure contains keys built from one or multiple columns in a table. With the introduction of the `xml` data type and the associated column in SQL Server 2005, the need to index the `xml` data type column is just as important, if not more important, than an index on any other data type column in a table.

In SQL Server 2005, XML instances are stored as BLOBs (binary large objects) in the `xml` data type column, and the maximum storage size of this column can be up to 2GB. That is *a lot* of XML data. Querying these XML instances can be a serious undertaking, and without an index on the column, the XML instance is converted to relational data when querying. This is called *shredding* and is not the best way to query data from a table.

An XML index does not use a b-tree index. Instead, an XML index is a shredded depiction of the XML instance contained in the `xml` column.

Indexing the `xml` data type was first mentioned in Chapter 2 as an introduction to this topic. This chapter assumes that you have at least a basic understanding of how to create indexes and how they work, so no time is spent covering that, as it is outside the scope of this book. However, this chapter focuses entirely on indexing the `xml` data type in SQL Server 2005 by covering the following:

- ❑ Creating primary and secondary XML indexes
- ❑ Indexing XML content
- ❑ Modifying and deleting XML indexes
- ❑ Option settings for XML indexes
- ❑ Best practices for XML indexes

Primary XML Index

In most of the examples thus far, the queries retrieved data from the Instructions column in the Production.ProductModel table in the AdventureWorks sample database. Looking in SQL Server Management Studio, you can see that there is indeed an index on the Instructions column (see Figure 6-1).

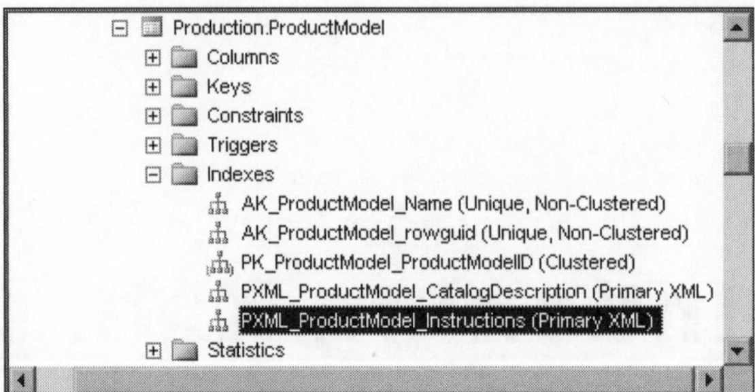

Figure 6-1

Figure 6-2 shows the properties of that index.

Figure 6-2

Looking at Figure 6-2, you can see that it is an index on the Instructions column in the ProductModel table, but the most important piece of information to gather from the figure is that it is a primary XML index. This section discusses creating primary XML indexes.

Take a look at the following query against the Instructions column:

```
SELECT Instructions.query('
declare namespace MSAW="http://schemas.microsoft.com/sqlserver/2004/07/adventure-
works/ProductModelManuInstructions";
  for $var in /MSAW:Location[@LocationID=50]
```

```
  return
      $var
') as Location
FROM Production.ProductModel
WHERE Instructions.exist ('declare namespace
MSAW="http://schemas.microsoft.com/sqlserver/2004/07/adventure-
works/ProductModelManuInstructions";
  //MSAW:Location[@LocationID=50]') = 1
```

Now imagine what would happen if this index did not exist. This example employs the `exist()` method to look at the Instructions column for a LocationID with a value of 50, as expressed in the path expression. Without an index on the Instructions column, the `exist()` method must interrogate every row in the table looking for that value. That is a very time consuming process. Creating indexes on an `xml` data type column greatly improves query performance.

The basic syntax for creating a primary XML index is as follows:

```
CREATE [PRIMARY] XML INDEX Indexname
  ON Tablename (xml_Columnname)
```

`Indexname` is the new name of the primary XML index to be created. `Tablename` is the table on which to create the new primary XML index. Finally, `xml_columnname` is the column on which to create the new primary XML index.

In a query window, run the following SQL, which drops the Employee table if it exists, recreates it, and then adds a primary XML index on the `xml` data type column EmployeeInfo:

```
if  exists (select * from dbo.sysobjects where id = object_id(N'[dbo].[Employee]')
and OBJECTPROPERTY(id, N'IsUserTable') = 1)
DROP TABLE [dbo].[Employee]
GO

CREATE TABLE [dbo].[Employee](
 [EmployeeID] [int] NOT NULL,
 [EmployeeInfo] [xml] NOT NULL,
) ON [PRIMARY]
GO
CREATE PRIMARY XML INDEX PriI_Employee_EmployeeInfo
ON Employee(EmployeeInfo)
GO
```

Didn't work did it? What's missing? Modify the SQL to add the following highlighted section, and then rerun the query:

```
if exists (select * from dbo.sysobjects where id = object_id(N'[dbo].[Employee]')
and OBJECTPROPERTY(id, N'IsUserTable') = 1)
DROP TABLE [dbo].[Employee]
GO

CREATE TABLE [dbo].[Employee](
 [EmployeeID] [int] NOT NULL,
```

```
 [EmployeeInfo] [xml] NOT NULL,
 CONSTRAINT [PK_Employee] PRIMARY KEY CLUSTERED
(
 [EmployeeID] ASC
) ON [PRIMARY]
) ON [PRIMARY]
GO
CREATE PRIMARY XML INDEX PriI_Employee_EmployeeInfo
ON Employee(EmployeeInfo)
GO
```

This time it worked successfully because before a primary XML index can be created, a clustered index must exist on a primary key column (see commandment 4 in the "10 Commandments of XML Index Creation" section later in this chapter). This is for insurance reasons. If the base table is partitioned, the XML index also gets partitioned along with the table.

Figure 6-3 shows the results of the table and index creation.

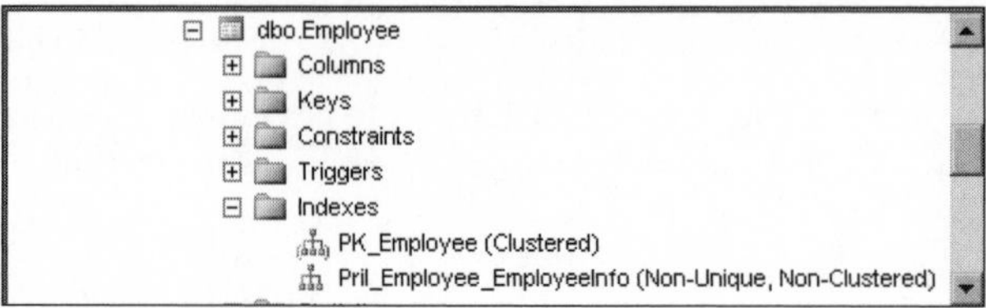

Figure 6-3

As you can see from Figure 6-3, the code created a Non-Clustered index on the EmployeeInfo column. It is not necessary to specify in the `CREATE` statement whether to create a Clustered or Non-Clustered index because by specifying `PRIMARY`, the `CREATE INDEX` statement knew that there was already a Clustered index on the primary key, and to create the `PRIMARY XML` index as Non-Clustered.

Once the index is created you can go into its properties and try to change it to a Clustered index, only to have SQL Server balk at you for trying to drop the existing Clustered index, thus breaking the rule stated previously about needing a clustered primary key to create the index.

Trying to drop the primary index with secondary indexes associated to it also generates an error.

Secondary XML Index

Secondary XML indexes can be added to `xml` data type columns to provide additional query performance. Having a primary index on an `xml` data type column without any secondary XML indexes may not prove to be beneficial, especially for columns with large XML documents. Querying a large XML instance based on path values can be very time consuming, and a single primary index may not provide the best performance. In these cases, adding secondary XML indexes specifically designed for certain query expressions can prove to be very beneficial.

There are three different types of secondary XML indexes depending on what you are querying, but regardless of the secondary XML index type, a primary XML index must exist prior to creating any secondary XML index.

The three types of secondary XML indexes are:

- PATH
- VALUE
- PROPERTY

As shown in Chapter 2, the basic syntax of a secondary XML index looks like the following:

```
CREATE XML INDEX SecondaryXMLIndexName
ON TableName ( xml_ColumName )
USING XML INDEX PrimaryXMLIndexName
FOR [PATH | VALUE | PROPERTY]
```

`SecondaryXMLIndexName` is the new name of the secondary XML index to be created. `TableName` is the table on which to create the new secondary XML index. `ColumnName` is the column on which to create the new secondary XML index. `PrimaryXMLIndexName` is the primary XML index on which to base the secondary XML index.

PATH

You use the `PATH` secondary XML index when using path expressions in your query. You can determine that you need a `PATH` secondary XML index by looking at the `WHERE` clause of your SQL statement. If there is an `exist()` method on the `xml` column, you are using a `PATH` expression and could most likely benefit from this type of index.

For example, the Instructions column in the Production.ProductModel table already has a primary XML index on it, and the following code adds a secondary `PATH` XML index:

```
CREATE XML INDEX SecI_PM_I_PATH ON Production.ProductModel(Instructions)
USING XML INDEX PXML_ProductModel_Instructions
FOR PATH
GO
```

Figure 6-4 shows that the new `PATH` secondary XML index has been created.

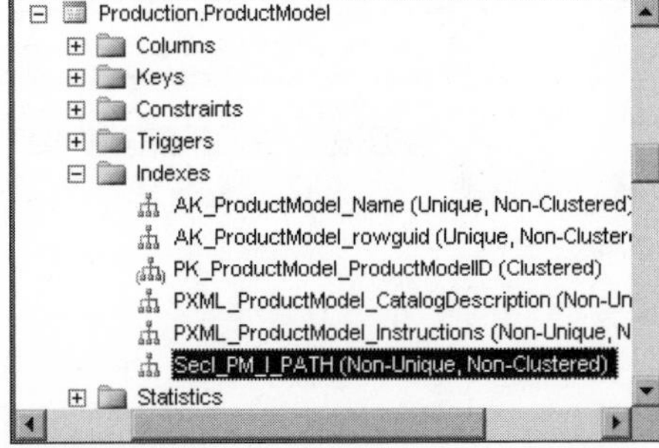

Figure 6-4

The PATH secondary XML index created is based on the primary XML index called PXML_ProductModel_Instructions and improves any path expression queries made on this column. For example, the following query (used previously) uses the exist() method to check for the existence of a location with a LocationID attribute with a value of 50:

```
SELECT Instructions.query('
declare namespace MSAW="http://schemas.microsoft.com/sqlserver/2004/07/adventure-
works/ProductModelManuInstructions";
  for $var in /MSAW:Location[@LocationID="50"]
  return
      $var
') as Location
FROM Production.ProductModel
WHERE Instructions.exist ('declare namespace
MSAW="http://schemas.microsoft.com/sqlserver/2004/07/adventure-works/
ProductModelManuInstructions";
/MSAW:Location[@LocationID="50"]') = 1
```

Since there is now a secondary XML index on the Instructions column, the XML instance does not need to be shredded, making querying the XML instance faster.

VALUE

When querying for specific values in an XML instance, you should use the VALUE index, especially when the name of the node or element isn't exactly known or the path includes a wild card character.

Add a VALUE index onto the Instructions column by running the following SQL statement:

```
CREATE XML INDEX SecI_PM_I_VALUE ON Production.ProductModel(CatalogDescription)
USING XML INDEX PXML_ProductModel_CatalogDescription
FOR VALUE
GO
```

Figure 6-5 shows that the new VALUE secondary XML index was created.

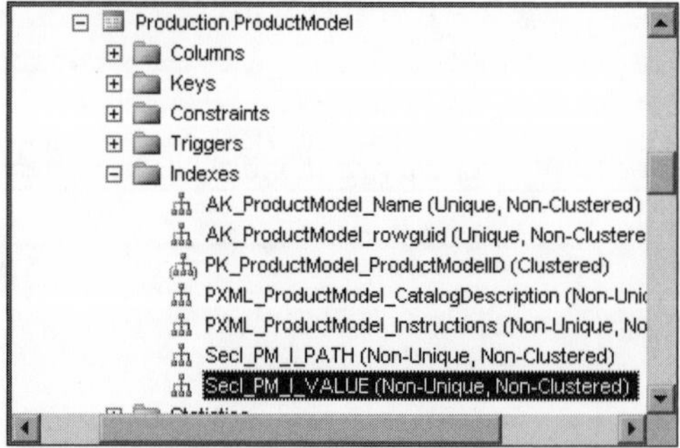

Figure 6-5

Just like the PATH index, the VALUE index was created based on the primary XML index and improves any value expression queries made on this column. For example, the following query executes a value() expression query to return the ProductID and Name columns from the Production.Product table if the picture size "small" is found:

```
WITH XMLNAMESPACES (
  'http://schemas.microsoft.com/sqlserver/2004/07/adventure-
works/ProductModelDescription' AS p1)
SELECT ProductModelID, Name
FROM   Production.ProductModel
WHERE  CatalogDescription.exist('//p1:Picture/Size[.="small"]') = 1
```

In the following partial results, there are a number of ProductID and Name columns containing the value "small":

```
ProductID      Name
19             Mountain-100
23             Mountain-500
25             Road-150
```

There will be times when you are looking for a specific piece of data and want to query off that key piece of information. The VALUE index helps improve query performance when those times arise.

PROPERTY

The intent of the VALUE index is to speed up searches for single values within an XML instance, but if you are searching for multiple values, such as "find all manufacturing steps for a specific Location" or "find the steps and material for a specific Location," the VALUE index for this type of search is not adequate. But the PROPERTY index is made exactly for this type of search.

For this example you need to add a PROPERTY index onto the Instructions column by running the following SQL statement:

```
CREATE XML INDEX SecI_PM_I_PROPERTY ON Production.ProductModel(Instructions)
USING XML INDEX PXML_ProductModel_Instructions
FOR PROPERTY
GO
```

Figure 6-6 shows that the new PROPERTY secondary XML index was created.

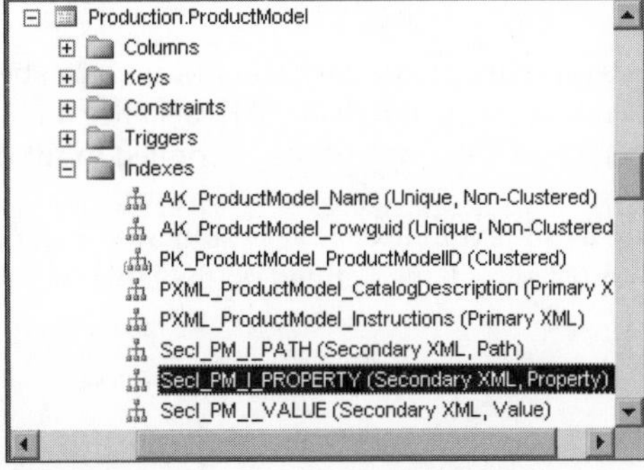

Figure 6-6

Consider the following query:

```
WITH XMLNAMESPACES ('http://schemas.microsoft.com/sqlserver/2004/07/adventure-
works/ProductModelManuInstructions' AS "PD")
SELECT ProductModelID,
 Instructions.value('(/PD:root/PD:Location/@LocationID)[1]', 'int') AS LocationID,
 Instructions.value('(/PD:root/PD:Location/@MachineHours)[1]', 'int') AS MachineHrs
FROM Production.ProductModel
WHERE ProductModelID = 7
```

The results of this query produce three columns, as shown in the following results. The value of the first column is the ProductID, which is returned from the ProductID column in the table. The values of the second and third columns, however, are returned from the XQuery, which retrieved the `LocationID` and `MachineHours` attributes from the first location:

```
ProductID  LocationID  MachineHrs
7          10          3
```

Because multiple values were returned, the `PROPERTY` index was utilized in the query. The `PROPERTY` index kicks into play with the `value()` method of the `xml` data type. It is also beneficial to know the primary key, in this case the ProductID column.

Secondary indexes are a great way to improve query performance, especially when the size of the XML instance is large. Because multiple secondary indexes can be applied to a column, it is a good idea to apply the different types as needed.

The secondary indexes are applied to the `xml` data type to help speed up your queries and return your results to you faster. In addition, indexes can also be applied to content, which is discussed in the next section.

Content Indexing

In addition to creating primary and secondary XML indexes on the `xml` data type column, you can create and use full-text indexes on the column. While the primary and secondary XML indexes index the values and nodes, a full-text index indexes the entire XML instance, ignoring the values, nodes, and other XML syntax.

However, unlike primary and secondary XML indexes, only one full-text index per table is allowed. Not per column, but per table. A full-text index is applied to a column, not a table.

Because both types of indexes (primary/secondary and full-text) can be applied to both a table and a column, they both can be used together to query an XML instance. In the case of a full-text index, the index is applied first, and then an XQuery expression is applied to sift deeper.

The requirements for creating a full-text index are very similar to that of the primary index in that a unique primary key column must already be defined on the table for which the full-text index is created.

The basic syntax for a full-text index is as follows:

```
CREATE FULLTEXT INDEX
ON TableName ( xml_ColumnName )
KEY INDEX IndexName
```

`TableName` refers to the table in which the full-text index is being created. `ColumnName` is the name of the column on which the full-text index will be applied. `IndexName` is the name of the unique primary key index.

Before a full-text index can be created, a full-text catalog must exist in the database, as all full-text indexes are stored in the catalog. A database can contain one or more catalogs.

The following example first creates a full-text catalog in which to store the full-text index, and then creates a full-text index on the Instructions column of the Production.ProductModel table:

```
CREATE FULLTEXT CATALOG FTC AS DEFAULT
GO
CREATE FULLTEXT INDEX
ON Production.ProductModel(Instructions)
KEY INDEX PK_ProductModel_ProductModelID
ON FTC
GO
```

Figure 6-7 displays the results of the `CREATE FULLTEXT CATALOG` statement. The full-text catalog FTC has been created in the AdventureWorks database.

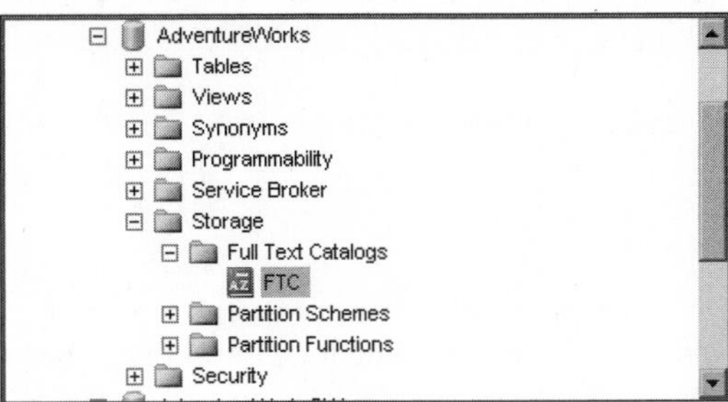

Figure 6-7

Double-click on the FTC full text catalog, or right-click and select Properties to display the FTC Properties page. On the left side of the Properties page, select Tables/Views. This page (see Figure 6-8) shows that a full-text index was created on the Production.ProductModel table using the unique index `PK_ProductModel_ProductModelID` on the Instructions column. Any table that has a full-text index on it is automatically displayed in the list on the right, as it shows only those tables that have a full-text index.

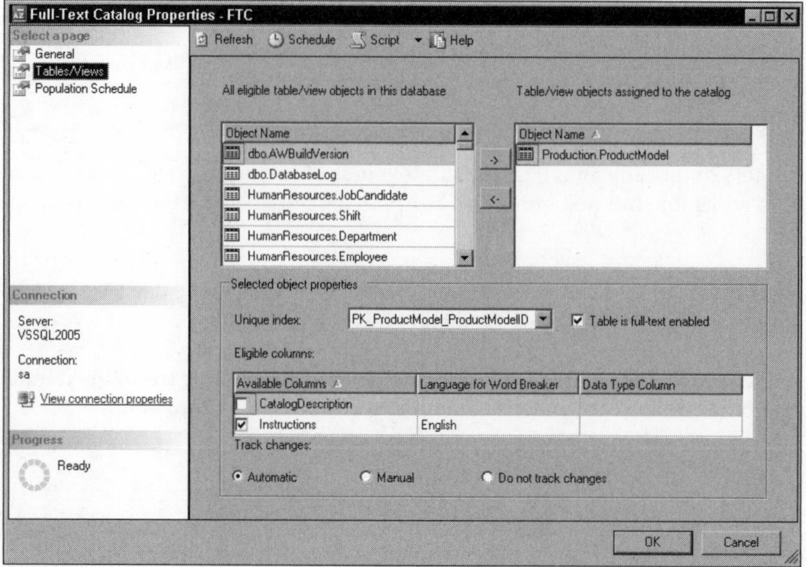

Figure 6-8

To get the best performance out of full-text searches, in certain scenarios it is possible to combine a full-text search with an XML index. The first step is to filter the XML values using the SQL full-text search, and then query the filtered values.

In the following section, you put the full-text index to use.

CONTAINS()

You use the `CONTAINS()` keyword to search character strings looking for word or phrase matches. It also conducts what is called a *proximity* search, looking for a word that is near another word.

For example, the following statement uses the `CONTAINS()` keyword to search the Instructions column of the Production.ProductModel table looking for the phrase "Inspection Specification":

```
SELECT ProductModelID, Instructions
FROM production.productmodel
WHERE CONTAINS(Instructions, '"Inspection Specification"')
```

The results of the query are shown in Figure 6-9.

	ProductModelID	Instructions
1	7	<root xmlns="http://schemas.microsoft.com/sqlserver/2004/07/adventure-works/Pro...
2	10	<root xmlns="http://schemas.microsoft.com/sqlserver/2004/07/adventure-works/Pro...
3	47	<root xmlns="http://schemas.microsoft.com/sqlserver/2004/07/adventure-works/Pro...
4	48	<root xmlns="http://schemas.microsoft.com/sqlserver/2004/07/adventure-works/Pro...

Figure 6-9

In this example, the results returned four rows because the query found four instances of the phrase `"Inspection Specification"` within the Instructions column. The `CONTAINS` predicate in this example searched each row of the Instructions column looking inside each XML document, and returned only those rows that contain the `"Inspection Specification"` phrase.

The results of the query can be defined even further with an additional `AND` clause, such as the following, which would return a single row:

```
SELECT ProductModelID, Instructions
FROM production.productmodel
WHERE CONTAINS(Instructions, '"Inspection Specification"')
AND ProductModelID = 47
```

In the following example, the `CONTAINS` predicate looks for multiple phrases by including an additional `OR` condition:

```
SELECT ProductModelID, Instructions
FROM production.productmodel
WHERE CONTAINS(Instructions, '"Inspection Specification" OR "Securely tighten the
spindle"')
```

The query returns results where the `CONTAINS` predicate finds instructions containing the phrase `"Inspection Specification"` or `"Securely tighten the spindle"`, this time returning the same four rows as previously shown in Figure 6-9 plus an additional row, ProductModelID53.

The next example uses the `NEAR` keyword looking for the word `Inspect` near the word `Specification`. The `NEAR` operator is used to indicate that a word or phrase on the left side of the `NEAR` operator is in close proximity to the word or phrase on the right side of the operator:

```
SELECT ProductModelID, Instructions
FROM production.productmodel
WHERE CONTAINS(Instructions, 'Inspect NEAR Specification')
```

The results from this query return seven rows, as shown in Figure 6-10, indicating that the query found seven instances of the word `Inspect` near the word `Specification`.

	ProductModelID	Instructions
1	7	<root xmlns="http://schemas.microsoft.com/sqlserver/2004/07/adventure-works/ProductModelManuInstructions">...
2	10	<root xmlns="http://schemas.microsoft.com/sqlserver/2004/07/adventure-works/ProductModelManuInstructions">...
3	47	<root xmlns="http://schemas.microsoft.com/sqlserver/2004/07/adventure-works/ProductModelManuInstructions">...
4	48	<root xmlns="http://schemas.microsoft.com/sqlserver/2004/07/adventure-works/ProductModelManuInstructions">...
5	53	<root xmlns="http://schemas.microsoft.com/sqlserver/2004/07/adventure-works/ProductModelManuInstructions">...
6	66	<root xmlns="http://schemas.microsoft.com/sqlserver/2004/07/adventure-works/ProductModelManuInstructions">...
7	67	<root xmlns="http://schemas.microsoft.com/sqlserver/2004/07/adventure-works/ProductModelManuInstructions">...

Figure 6-10

As stated earlier, further filtering can be accomplished by combining the full-text index (using the `CONTAINS()` keyword) with an XQuery expression to filter the results even more. The following example again queries the Instructions column of the Production.ProductModel table to look for a specific value returned from the `CONTAINS()` keyword:

```
SELECT ProductModelID, CatalogDescription.query('
    declare namespace pd="http://schemas.microsoft.com/sqlserver/2004/07/adventure-
works/ProductModelDescription";
      <Prod>
         { /pd:ProductDescription/@ProductModelID }
         { /pd:ProductDescription/pd:Summary }
      </Prod>
 ') as Result
FROM Production.ProductModel
WHERE CatalogDescription.value('declare namespace
pd="http://schemas.microsoft.com/sqlserver/2004/07/adventure-
works/ProductModelDescription";
  contains( (/pd:ProductDescription/pd:Summary//*/text())[1],
            "smooth-shifting")','bit') = 1
```

The results of this query are shown in Figure 6-11.

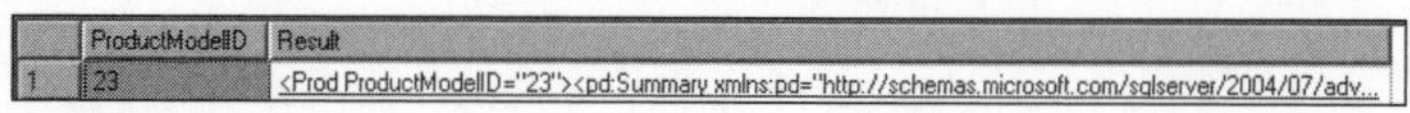

	ProductModelID	Result
1	23	<Prod ProductModelID="23"><pd:Summary xmlns:pd="http://schemas.microsoft.com/sqlserver/2004/07/adv...

Figure 6-11

In this example, a full-text index is combined with an XQuery expression to find and filter the results. The `SELECT` part of the query returns the ProductModelID and the entire `Summary` node based on the results of the `WHERE` clause. The `WHERE` clause is where the filtering takes place using the `CONTAINS` predicate. The `CONTAINS` predicate uses an XQuery to look through the `Summary` node in the CatalogDescription column looking for the text `"smooth-shifting"`. If the query finds what it is looking for, it returns the information requested by the `SELECT` portion of the query.

As you create and use the indexes, you will also find that there will probably be a need to modify those indexes to better fit your application. The topic of modifying indexes is discussed next.

Altering XML Index

Once created, an XML index can be altered. Typically, once an index is in place, it is not necessary to alter it, but if the occasion arises, altering an index is supported with very few exceptions.

The syntax for altering an XML index is as follows:

```
ALTER INDEX IndexName
On TableName
SET ( option )
```

`IndexName` is the name of the index to alter. `TableName` is the table in which the index that is being altered is applied. `Option` is the option that is being altered on the index.

The following is a list of available XML index options:

- PAD_INDEX
- FILLFACTOR
- SORT_IN_TEMPDB
- STATISTICS_NORECOMPUTE
- DROP_EXISTING
- ALLOW_ROW_LOCKS
- ALLOW_PAGE_LOCKS
- MAXDOP
- ONLINE

All but FILLFACTOR and MAXDOP are an ON/OFF value. For example:

```
PAD_INDEX = ON
```

The FILLFACTOR option, an integer value between 0 and 100, defines the percentage that dictates to the SQL Server engine the percentage of free space for each index page when the index is created. For example, the following tells SQL Server to reserve 75 percent of free space:

```
FILLFACTOR = 75
```

The FILLFACTOR option can be used only when the index is first created or rebuilt.

The MAXDOP option, an integer value between 0 and 64, overrides the *max degree of parallelism* option, which limits the number of actual processors used in an execution plan (parallel running). For example, the following sets the MAXDOP option to a value of 1, which executes the plan serially:

```
MAXDOP = 1
```

The following example alters the primary index on the Employee table and sets the SORT_IN_TEMPDB option to ON:

```
ALTER INDEX PriI_Employee_EmployeeInfo
ON Employee
REBUILD WITH ( SORT_IN_TEMPDB = ON )
GO
```

Rebuilding an index drops and recreates the index. This is not a bad thing, as it removes fragmentation and reorders the indexes. If you don't want to completely rebuild the indexes, you can simply use the following syntax:

```
ALTER INDEX PriI_Employee_EmployeeInfo
ON Employee
SET ( SORT_IN_TEMPDB = ON )
GO
```

Several options can be set at one time. For example:

```
ALTER INDEX PriI_Employee_EmployeeInfo
ON Employee
SET ( SORT_IN_TEMPDB = ON, ALLOW_PAGE_LOCKS = ON, IGNORE_DUP_KEY = ON )
GO
```

Each of the options can have an impact on your index and resulting performance, so it would be wise to experiment with some of these options to determine which options will benefit your application and environment best.

Setting Options for XML Indexing

In Chapter 4, you saw a list of settings for the `xml` data type, but they are listed again in the following table because they also apply to indexes on the `xml` data type column.

SET Options	Required Values
NUMERIC_ROUNDABOUT	OFF
ANSI_PADDING	ON
ANSI_WARNING	ON
ANSI_NULLS	ON
ARITHABORT	ON
CONCAT_NULL_YIELDS_NULL	ON
QUOTED_IDENTIFIER	ON

These options must be set as shown when creating an XML index; otherwise, indexes will fail to be created or modified, and no data will be able to be inserted or modified in `xml` data type columns.

Best Practices

There are two main reasons why you would want to index your `xml` data type columns:

- You plan to execute queries against the `xml` data type column.
- The amount of data in the `xml` data type column is large.

Storing XML instances in an `xml` data type column does not automatically necessitate putting an index on that column. If you don't plan to execute queries on that column, then putting an index on the column does not make sense.

However, if the needs of your organization match both of the items listed here, there are a few things to remember when creating an XML index.

Ten Commandments of XML Index Creation

You must adhere to the following when creating an XML index:

- You can only create a primary XML index on one `xml` data type column. For example, column ColA can have its own primary XML index, and column ColB can have its own primary index. However, ColA and ColB cannot share the same primary XML index.
- You cannot modify primary keys of a table if a primary XML index exists on the same table. To modify the primary key, you must drop the XML index prior to modifying the primary key.
- A table cannot have an XML primary index and non-XML index with the same name.
- Any table in which you are creating an XML primary index must already have a Clustered index on the primary key.
- You must drop an XML index prior to changing the `xml` data type column from typed to untyped (or untyped to typed).
- You cannot create XML indexes on `xml` type variables or views with an `xml` type column.
- The same restrictions as the previous bullet apply to XML index names as view names.
- The `ARITHABORT` option cannot have the value of `OFF` when you create an XML index. All queries to an `xml` data type fail if this value equals `OFF`.
- You can only use the `DROP_EXISTING` option to drop and recreate a new primary or secondary index, meaning that you cannot use `DROP_EXISTING` to drop a primary and create a secondary, nor to drop a secondary and create a primary. For example, `DROP_EXISTING` can drop a primary index and create a primary index, or drop a secondary index and create a secondary index.
- You must create an XML index on the same file-group or partition as the table.

Summary

In this chapter, you learned the different types of XML indexes and how they can be applied and used on an `xml` data type column. You also learned in what situations it is beneficial to apply the different types of indexes, as well as how to alter the indexes and the options available when altering an index.

This chapter also talked about the best practices of applying an XML index and the settings options that are needed for creating an XML index. In the next chapter, you learn about XML schema collections.

7

XML Schemas in SQL Server 2005

With the introduction of the `xml` data type in SQL Server 2005, the capability to natively validate XML documents and instances stored internally in SQL Server provides developers with many more XML validation options than they have had in the past. This flexibility helps developers determine how and where XML validation takes place. By having the ability to move XML validation into SQL Server, developers now have more control over how XML is handled, both from the client and the server.

In SQL Server 2005, the concept of XML schema collections is introduced to validate instances of XML in the `xml` data type column or `xml` data type variable. The XML schema collection is just that, a collection of XML schemas that validate XML instances and performs type checking when XML data is stored in the database.

The focus of this chapter is the creation and management of XML schema collections, the XML schema preprocessor tool, and best practices when using XML schema collections. Specifically, this chapter covers the following topics:

- Managing XML schema collections (creating, dropping, and altering)
- Viewing XML schema collections
- Permissions on XML schema collections (grant, deny, and revoke)
- Guidelines and limitations

Managing XML Schema Collections

The management of XML schema collections is provided through enhancements to the DDL (Data Definition Language). Using the DDL, you can create, drop, and alter XML schemas. Likewise, you can manage permissions to the XML schema collections.

The XML schemas are stored internally, associated with `xml` data type columns and variables, and used to validate XML instances, and they ensure that the XML data is typed correctly when stored in the database. When an XML instance is stored in the database, SQL Server uses the schema collection for validation. Depending on the results of the validation, the instance is either accepted and stored, or rejected and not allowed database storage.

Think of an XML schema collection in the same terms as a table or any other object in SQL Server. It can be created and dropped, even altered just like other objects. When creating an XML schema collection, the schemas are automatically imported into the collection. Other schemas can be added to an existing collection; schemas can be removed from a collection as well. All schema collections are stored in SQL Server system tables.

The following section examines the creation, deletion, and modification of XML schema collections.

Creating XML Schema Collections

You create XML schema collections by using the following DDL syntax:

```
CREATE XML SCHMEA COLLECTION RelationalSchema.SqlIdentifier AS Expression
```

In the syntax, `RelationalSchema` is the name of the schema being imported. This is optional, but if a relational schema is not specified, a default is relational schema is supplied. `SqlIdentifier` is the name of the schema collection. `Expression` is the string constant or variable schema syntax of `(n)varchar`, `(n)varbinary`, or `xml` type.

Don't confuse a relational schema with an XML schema. In this case, a relational schema contains database objects such as tables, views, and stored procedures. Relational schemas have database owners, and the owner can be a database user or database role. For example, there is a `dbo` relational schema. The following is an example using a relational schema when creating an XML schema collection:

```
CREATE XML SCHEMA COLLECTION dbo.MotocrossCollectionTest AS...
```

For more information on relational schemas, consult the SQL Server documentation.

Before jumping in to some examples, I should make a few comments regarding the components created when a schema is imported into the database.

When an XML schema collection is created, several components related to the schema are imported into the database. The components are stored in a number of SQL Server system tables and include the following:

- Attributes
- Elements
- Type definitions

What is important to remember is that when a schema is imported into the database, the schema is not stored, but rather the components themselves are stored. Each component falls into one of the following categories:

- ATTRIBUTE
- ELEMENT
- TYPE
- ATTRIBUTE GROUP
- MODELGROUP

These categories define how a schema is stored in the database. When a schema is added or imported in the database, the schema is parsed and each component is stored by its type. The schema itself as a whole is not stored. For example, an `<element>` tag is not stored, but its components—such as values or attributes—are stored by the appropriate type.

The last tidbit of information is that a schema can be imported into the collection with or without a namespace.

For example, the following code creates an XML schema collection and imports a schema that does not contain a namespace:

```
CREATE XML SCHEMA COLLECTION MotocrossCollection AS '
<xs:schema xmlns="" xmlns:xs="http://www.w3.org/2001/XMLSchema"
xmlns:msdata="urn:schemas-microsoft-com:xml-msdata" id="Motocross">
  <xs:element name="Motocross" msdata:IsDataSet="true">
    <xs:complexType>
      <xs:choice minOccurs="0" maxOccurs="unbounded">
        <xs:element name="Team">
          <xs:complexType>
            <xs:sequence>
                    <xs:element name="Rider" minOccurs="0" maxOccurs="unbounded">
                <xs:complexType>
                  <xs:sequence>
                    <xs:element name="Name" type="xs:string" minOccurs="0"msdata:
Ordinal="0"/>
                  </xs:sequence>
                  <xs:attribute name="NationalNumber" type="xs:string"/>
                  <xs:attribute name="Class" type="xs:string"/>
                  <xs:attribute name="Type" type="xs:string"/>
                </xs:complexType>
              </xs:element>
            </xs:sequence>
            <xs:attribute name="Manufacturer" type="xs:string"/>
          </xs:complexType>
        </xs:element>
      </xs:choice>
    </xs:complexType>
  </xs:element>
</xs:schema>'
GO
```

The `CREATE XML SCHEMA COLLECTION` *statement allows you to specify which database to create the schema collection in, so make sure you are in the correct database when creating the schema collection.*

Figure 7-1 shows the newly created schema collection in the appropriate database.

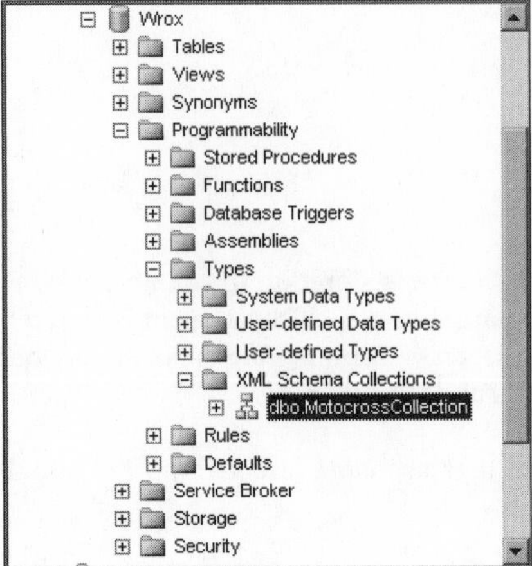

Figure 7-1

In the example, the `Manufacturer`, `NationalNumber`, `Type`, and `Class` attributes belong to the `ATTRIBUTE` category, and the `Team`, `Rider`, and `Name` elements belong to the `ELEMENT` category.

Now that the schema is created, you can use it for XML instance validation. For example, it can be applied to an `xml` data type column, as shown in Figure 7-2.

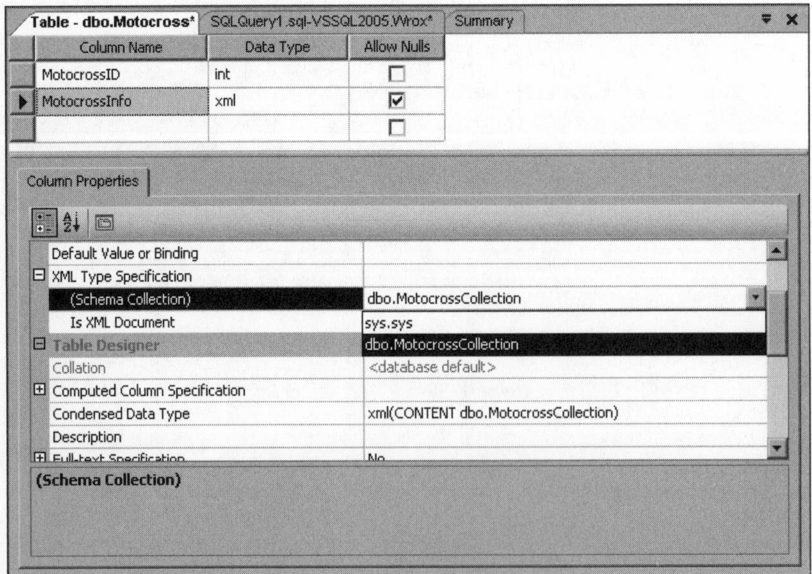

Figure 7-2

Now any time an XML instance is inserted into this column it is validated against the schema collection. If an XML instance passes the validation, it is inserted into the database. For example, the following XML instance passes the validation and is inserted into the table because it contains the appropriate elements and attributes as defined by the XML schema:

```
INSERT INTO Motocross (MotocrossID, MotocrossInfo)
VALUES (1,
'<Motocross>
  <Team Manufacturer="Yamaha">
    <Rider NationalNumber="22" Class="250">
      <Name>Chad Reed</Name>
    </Rider>
    <Rider NationalNumber="12" Class="250">
      <Name>David Vuillemin</Name>
    </Rider>
    <Rider NationalNumber="15" Class="250">
      <Name>Tim Ferry</Name>
    </Rider>
    <Rider NationalNumber="123" Class="125" Type="Support">
      <Name>Kelly Smith</Name>
    </Rider>
    <Rider NationalNumber="18" Class="125" Type="Support">
      <Name>Brock Sellards</Name>
    </Rider>
    <Rider NationalNumber="256" Class="125" Type="Support">
      <Name>Brett Metcalf</Name>
    </Rider>
    <Rider NationalNumber="31" Class="125" Type="Support">
      <Name>Danny Smith</Name>
    </Rider>
  </Team>
  <Team Manufacturer="Kawasaki">
    <Rider NationalNumber="259" Class="250">
      <Name>James Stewart</Name>
    </Rider>
    <Rider NationalNumber="26" Class="250">
      <Name>Michael Byrne</Name>
    </Rider>
  </Team>
  <Team Manufacturer="Suzuki">
    <Rider NationalNumber="4" Class="250">
      <Name>Ricky Carmichael</Name>
    </Rider>
    <Rider NationalNumber="188" Class="125">
      <Name>Davi Millsaps</Name>
    </Rider>
    <Rider NationalNumber="60" Class="125">
      <Name>Broc Hepler</Name>
    </Rider>
    <Rider NationalNumber="103" Class="250">
      <Name>Sebastien Tortelli</Name>
    </Rider>
  </Team>
  <Team Manufacturer="Honda">
    <Rider NationalNumber="2" Class="250">
```

```
      <Name>Jeremy McGrath</Name>
    </Rider>
    <Rider NationalNumber="24" Class="250">
      <Name>Ernesto Fonseca</Name>
    </Rider>
    <Rider NationalNumber="70" Class="250">
      <Name>Travis Preston</Name>
    </Rider>
    <Rider NationalNumber="51" Class="125">
      <Name>Andrew Short</Name>
    </Rider>
    <Rider NationalNumber="5" Class="250" Type="Support">
      <Name>Mike LaRocco</Name>
    </Rider>
    <Rider NationalNumber="14" Class="250" Type="Support">
      <Name>Kevin Windham</Name>
    </Rider>
  </Team>
</Motocross>
')
GO
```

However, the following XML instance does not pass validation, nor is it inserted into the table because each rider has a `BikeSize` attribute, which is not defined by the schema:

```
INSERT INTO Motocross (MotocrossID, MotocrossInfo)
VALUES (2,
'<Motocross>
  <Team Manufacturer="Yamaha">
    <Rider BikeSize="250">Tim Ferry</Rider>
    <Rider BikeSize="250">Chad Reed</Rider>
    <Rider BikeSize="250">David Vuillemin</Rider>
  </Team>
  <Team Manufacturer="Honda">
    <Rider BikeSize="450">Kevin Windham</Rider>
    <Rider BikeSize="250">Mike LaRacco</Rider>
    <Rider BikeSize="250">Jeremy McGrath</Rider>
  </Team>
  <Team Manufacturer="Suzuki">
    <Rider BikeSize="250">Ricky Carmichael</Rider>
    <Rider BikeSize="125">Broc Hepler</Rider>
    <Rider>Sebastien Tortelli</Rider>
  </Team>
  <Team Manufacturer="Kawasaki">
    <Rider BikeSize="250">James Stewart</Rider>
    <Rider BikeSize="125">Michael Byrne</Rider>
  </Team>
</Motocross>
')
GO
```

If you try to insert this XML document, the following error is generated:

```
XML Validation: Undefined or prohibited attribute specified: 'BikeSize'
```

Another way to create the schema collection is to assign the schema to a variable and use that variable in the `CREATE XML SCHEMA` statement. The following example creates an `xml` data type variable, sets the schema syntax to the variable, and then uses the variable in the `CREATE XML SCHEMA` statement (to save space and for better readability, most of the schema syntax has been left out):

```
DECLARE @xmlvar xml
SET @xmlvar = '<xs:schema ...</xs:schema>'
CREATE XML SCHEMA COLLECTION MotocrossCollection AS @xmlvar
```

Before moving on to the next example, look at the results of the `CREATE XML SCHEMA COLLECTION` statement from a system table perspective. Open a query window and run the following query:

```
SELECT sys.xml_schema_collections.name
FROM sys.xml_schema_collections
```

The results return a single column with two rows containing the default `sys` schema collection, and the `MotocrossCollection` schema just added. It should look like the following:

```
Name
----
Sys
MotocrossCollection
```

Now modify the query to look like the following:

```
SELECT sys.xml_schema_collections.name
FROM sys.sys.xml_schema_collections
JOIN sys.xml_schema_namespaces
ON (sys.xml_schema_collections.xml_collection_id =
   sys.xml_schema_namespaces. xml_collection_id)
WHERE sys.xml_schema_collection.name = N''
```

The results of running this query return a single column with a single row, containing the name of the collection you added, as follows:

```
Name
----
MotocrossCollection
```

When the `MotocrossCollection` schema collection was added, no namespace was provided and therefore no system table namespace record exists for the `MotocrossCollection` schema collection.

This next example imports multiple schemas into the collection, both of which contain namespaces:

```
CREATE XML SCHEMA COLLECTION ProductModelSchemaCollection AS
'<xsd:schema
targetNamespace="http://schemas.microsoft.com/sqlserver/2004/07/adventure-works/
ProductModelManuInstructions"
xmlns="http://schemas.microsoft.com/sqlserver/2004/07/adventure-works/
ProductModelManuInstructions"
elementFormDefault="qualified"
attributeFormDefault="unqualified"
xmlns:xsd="http://www.w3.org/2001/XMLSchema">
```

```
<xsd:complexType name="StepType" mixed="true">
  <xsd:choice minOccurs="0" maxOccurs="unbounded">
    <xsd:element name="tool" type="xsd:string" />
    <xsd:element name="material" type="xsd:string" />
    <xsd:element name="blueprint" type="xsd:string" />
    <xsd:element name="specs" type="xsd:string" />
    <xsd:element name="diag" type="xsd:string" />
  </xsd:choice>
</xsd:complexType>
<xsd:element name="root">
<xsd:complexType mixed="true">
<xsd:sequence>
  <xsd:element name="Location" minOccurs="1" maxOccurs="unbounded">
<xsd:complexType mixed="true">
<xsd:sequence>
  <xsd:element name="step" type="StepType" minOccurs="1" maxOccurs="unbounded" />
</xsd:sequence>
    <xsd:attribute name="LocationID" type="xsd:integer" use="required" />
    <xsd:attribute name="SetupHours" type="xsd:decimal" use="optional" />
    <xsd:attribute name="MachineHours" type="xsd:decimal" use="optional" />
    <xsd:attribute name="LaborHours" type="xsd:decimal" use="optional" />
    <xsd:attribute name="LotSize" type="xsd:decimal" use="optional" />
  </xsd:complexType>
      </xsd:element>
    </xsd:sequence>
  </xsd:complexType>
</xsd:element>
</xsd:schema>

<xs:schema
targetNamespace="http://schemas.microsoft.com/sqlserver/2004/07/adventure-works/
ProductModelDescription"
xmlns="http://schemas.microsoft.com/sqlserver/2004/07/adventure-works/
ProductModelDescription"
elementFormDefault="qualified"
xmlns:mstns="http://tempuri.org/XMLSchema.xsd"

xmlns:xs="http://www.w3.org/2001/XMLSchema">
<xs:import namespace="http://schemas.microsoft.com/sqlserver/2004/07/
adventure-works/ProductModelManuInstructions" />
  <xs:element name="ProductDescription" type="ProductDescription" />
    <xs:complexType name="ProductDescription">
      <xs:sequence>
        <xs:element name="Summary" type="Summary" minOccurs="0" />
      </xs:sequence>
      <xs:attribute name="ProductModelID" type="xs:string" />
      <xs:attribute name="ProductModelName" type="xs:string" />
    </xs:complexType>
    <xs:complexType name="Summary" mixed="true" >
      <xs:sequence>
        <xs:any processContents="skip" namespace="http://www.w3.org/1999/xhtml"
minOccurs="0" maxOccurs="unbounded" />
        </xs:sequence>
    </xs:complexType>
  </xs:schema>'
GO
```

The second schema imports the first schema, as illustrated by the following code. This `import` reference is necessary if some of the components you want to add to your collection already exist in the collection. Equally necessary, this `import` statement is required when your components need to reference components in the same target space:

```
<xs:import namespace="http://schemas.microsoft.com/sqlserver/2004/07/adventure-
works/ProductModelManuInstructions" />
```

Now run the following query:

```
SELECT * FROM sys.xml_schema_namespaces
```

The results (see Figure 7-3) show the addition of the namespaces from the two schemas in the system tables.

	xml_collection_id	name	xml_namespace_id
1	1	http://www.w3.org/2001/XMLSchema	1
2	65536		1
3	65539	http://schemas.microsoft.com/sqlserver/2004/07/adventure-works/ProductModelManuInstructions	1
4	65539	http://schemas.microsoft.com/sqlserver/2004/07/adventure-works/ProductModelDescription	2

Figure 7-3

XML schema collections provide instant XML schema validation and data type information. This takes the validation away from the client and in turn provides a performance increase and optimized storage. Are they required? No, not at all, but adding the schema validation wouldn't hurt if the case calls for it.

Dropping XML Schema Collections

Dropping a schema collection is as easy as dropping any other object. The syntax for dropping a schema collection is as follows:

```
DROP XML SCHEMA COLLECTION RelationalSchema.SqlIdentifier
```

`RelationalSchema` is the name of the relational schema. This is optional. `SqlIdentifier` is the name of the schema collection being dropped.

The following example drops the `ProductModelSchemaCollection` that was created in the previous section:

```
DROP XML SCHEMA COLLECTION ProductModelSchemaCollection
```

It doesn't get much easier than that. However, there are a few noteworthy items:

- Any schema collection in use cannot be dropped. For example, if a schema collection is associated to an `xml` data type column, its schema collection cannot be dropped.
- Any schema collection used in a table constraint cannot be dropped. Drop the constraint first, and then drop the schema collection.
- Any schema collection used in a stored procedure or schema bound function cannot be dropped.

Dropping an XML schema collection removes the entire collection, which might not be what you want. A better alternative would be to modify the collection to make specific changes. Modifying XML schema collections is discussed in the next section.

Altering XML Schema Collections

Once XML schema collections are created, you can make modifications to them at many levels. For example, an entire schema can be added to the collection, and individual components can be added to existing schemas in the collection.

This first example creates a schema collection with a single schema entry, and then alters the collection by adding a new complete schema.

The first step in this example is to add back part of the `ProductModelSchemaCollection` schema collection that was dropped in the previous section. Open a query window and run the following `CREATE XML SCHEMA COLLECTION` statement:

```
CREATE XML SCHEMA COLLECTION ProductModelSchemaCollection AS
'<xsd:schema
targetNamespace="http://schemas.microsoft.com/sqlserver/2004/07/adventure-
works/ProductModelManuInstructions"
xmlns="http://schemas.microsoft.com/sqlserver/2004/07/adventure-
works/ProductModelManuInstructions"
elementFormDefault="qualified"
attributeFormDefault="unqualified"
xmlns:xsd="http://www.w3.org/2001/XMLSchema">
  <xsd:complexType name="StepType" mixed="true">
    <xsd:choice minOccurs="0" maxOccurs="unbounded">
      <xsd:element name="tool" type="xsd:string" />
      <xsd:element name="material" type="xsd:string" />
      <xsd:element name="blueprint" type="xsd:string" />
      <xsd:element name="specs" type="xsd:string" />
      <xsd:element name="diag" type="xsd:string" />
    </xsd:choice>
  </xsd:complexType>
  <xsd:element name="root">
  <xsd:complexType mixed="true">
  <xsd:sequence>
    <xsd:element name="Location" minOccurs="1" maxOccurs="unbounded">
  <xsd:complexType mixed="true">
  <xsd:sequence>
    <xsd:element name="step" type="StepType" minOccurs="1" maxOccurs="unbounded" />
  </xsd:sequence>
      <xsd:attribute name="LocationID" type="xsd:integer" use="required" />
      <xsd:attribute name="SetupHours" type="xsd:decimal" use="optional" />
      <xsd:attribute name="MachineHours" type="xsd:decimal" use="optional" />
      <xsd:attribute name="LaborHours" type="xsd:decimal" use="optional" />
      <xsd:attribute name="LotSize" type="xsd:decimal" use="optional" />
    </xsd:complexType>
        </xsd:element>
      </xsd:sequence>
    </xsd:complexType>
```

```
  </xsd:element>
</xsd:schema>
'
```

This statement adds the components from the first schema to the schema collection. The next step is to alter the schema collection. The following example alters the newly created `ProductModelSchemaCollection` schema collection by adding components from another schema.

In the query window, run the following `ALTER` statement:

```
ALTER XML SCHEMA COLLECTION ProductModelSchemaCollection ADD '<xs:schema
targetNamespace="http://schemas.microsoft.com/sqlserver/2004/07/adventure-
works/ProductModelDescription"
xmlns="http://schemas.microsoft.com/sqlserver/2004/07/adventure-
works/ProductModelDescription"
elementFormDefault="qualified"
xmlns:mstns="http://tempuri.org/XMLSchema.xsd"
xmlns:xs="http://www.w3.org/2001/XMLSchema"
xmlns:wm="http://schemas.microsoft.com/sqlserver/2004/07/adventure-
works/ProductModelWarrAndMain" >
<xs:import namespace="http://schemas.microsoft.com/sqlserver/2004/07/adventure-
works/ProductModelWarrAndMain" />
  <xs:element name="ProductDescription" type="ProductDescription" />
    <xs:complexType name="ProductDescription">
      <xs:sequence>
        <xs:element name="Summary" type="Summary" minOccurs="0" />
      </xs:sequence>
      <xs:attribute name="ProductModelID" type="xs:string" />
      <xs:attribute name="ProductModelName" type="xs:string" />
    </xs:complexType>
    <xs:complexType name="Summary" mixed="true" >
      <xs:sequence>
        <xs:any processContents="skip" namespace="http://www.w3.org/1999/xhtml"
minOccurs="0" maxOccurs="unbounded" />
        </xs:sequence>
    </xs:complexType>
  </xs:schema>'
GO
```

This example uses the `ALTER XML SCHEMA COLLECTION` statement to modify the existing XML schema collection, adding a second schema to the collection. This is done by using the `ADD` keyword with the `ALTER` statement and providing the schema to be added.

The final example alters the `ProductModelSchemaCollection` schema collection, adding both an attribute and element to the schema with the target namespace `"http://schemas.microsoft.com/sqlserver/2004/07/adventure-works/ProductModelManuDescription"`:

```
ALTER XML SCHEMA COLLECTION ProductModelSchemaCollection ADD '
<schema xmlns="http://www.w3.org/2001/XMLSchema"
     targetNamespace="http://schemas.microsoft.com/sqlserver/2004/07/
adventure-works/ProductModelManuDescription"
     xmlns:ns="http://schemas.microsoft.com/sqlserver/2004/07/adventure-works/
ProductModelManuDescription">
```

```
    <element name="PartCount" type="string"/>
</schema>'
GO

ALTER XML SCHEMA COLLECTION ProductModelSchemaCollection ADD '
<schema xmlns="http://www.w3.org/2001/XMLSchema"
        targetNamespace="http://schemas.microsoft.com/sqlserver/2004/07/
adventure-works/ProductModelDescription">
<attribute name="EmployeeCount" type="string"/>
</schema>'
GO
```

Had this schema been associated with an XML data type column when the ALTER statement was executed, any existing data in that column would be re-validated against the new schema.

Once the schema collection is associated with an `xml` data type column or variable, all XML must now meet the new requirements, that is, contain a new `"PartCount"` element and `"EmployeeCount"` attribute.

Here are a couple of noteworthy items. First, any existing XML instances in an `xml` data type column are revalidated when a schema collection is altered. Therefore, when altering a schema collection that is associated to an `xml` data type column, if the XML instances within the column do not meet the schema validation process, the schema collection alteration is not applied or saved.

Second, the entire schema in its entirety is not stored in the database, only the components. If you need the schema stored it its entirety for whatever reason, you have two options: store the schema on the local file system or store it in a column in the database.

Viewing XML Schema Collections

In the previous section, you queried the `sys.xml_schema_namespaces` system tables in order to view the schema collection creation results. All it really showed was that, yes, it indeed inserted some data into the system tables. It is informative, but not too useful when you want to view detailed information about the schema collection or to view the schema itself.

The `xml_schema_namespace` function provides a detailed look inside a schema collection. As stated previously, the schema itself is not stored in the collection, but rather it is stored in the schema components. The `xml_schema_namespace` function reconstructs the schema, which returns an `xml` data type instance.

The syntax for the `xml_schema_namespace` function is as follows:

```
Xml_schema_namespace(RelationalSchema, XML_Schema_Collection_Name, [Namespace])
```

The `RelationalSchema` is the relational schema name. The `XML_Schema_Collection_Name` is the name of the XML schema collection to reconstruct. The optional `Namespace` parameter is the namespace URI of the XML schema to be reconstructed.

For example, the following example uses the `xml_schema_namespace` function to reconstruct the `MotocrossCollection` schema collection. Make sure this statement is run against the appropriate database (the first parameter is the name of the `RelationalSchema` when the schema collection was created, if one was supplied; the second parameter is the name of the schema collection):

```
SELECT xml_schema_namespace('', 'MotocrossCollection')
GO
```

Figure 7-4 shows partial results of the call to `xml_schema_namespace`.

```
<xsd:schema xmlns:xsd="http://www.w3.org/2001/XMLSchema">
  <xsd:element name="Motocross">
    <xsd:complexType>
      <xsd:complexContent>
        <xsd:restriction base="xsd:anyType">
          <xsd:choice minOccurs="0" maxOccurs="unbounded">
            <xsd:element name="Team">
              <xsd:complexType>
                <xsd:complexContent>
                  <xsd:restriction base="xsd:anyType">
                    <xsd:sequence>
                      <xsd:element name="Rider" minOccurs="0" maxOccurs="unbou
```

Figure 7-4

In this example, all the schemas in the collection will be reconstructed and returned. Using some of the XQuery information covered in Chapter 5, you can extract information about a specific schema. For example, the following code uses the `query()` method to find a specific schema in the collection:

```
SELECT XML_SCHEMA_NAMESPACE(
'','ProductModelSchemaCollection').query('
/xs:schema[@targetNamespace="http://schemas.microsoft.com/sqlserver/2004/07/adventu
re-works/ProductModelManuInstructions"]
')
GO
```

The other way to do this is to specify the target namespace as the third parameter (it is an optional parameter), as follows:

```
SELECT XML_SCHEMA_NAMESPACE(
'','ProductModelSchemaCollection',
'http://schemas.microsoft.com/sqlserver/2004/07/adventure-
works/ProductModelManuInstructions')

GO
```

Both ways work and return the same results; it is just a matter of personal preference.

Viewing your schemas is an excellent way to view any changes you have made if you have altered them. One thing to remember is that SQL Server does not store the entire document, just the necessary components. Items such as white space and annotations are lost. This means that when the schema is rebuilt for display, it may not look the same.

Now that you know how to create, modify, and view XML schema collections, the next logical step is to apply permissions.

XML Schema Collection Permissions

This section introduces the topic of permissions on XML schema collections. A user must have the necessary rights and privileges to create and load a schema collection as well as alter, execute and use a schema collection. These permissions are applied using the GRANT, DENY, and REVOKE statements.

Just as important, a user must also have the necessary rights and privileges to use a schema collection in a table, variable, or parameter. The following sections cover the aspects of granting, denying, and revoking permissions on an XML schema collection.

Granting Permissions

There are two parts to granting permissions on an XML schema collection. The first part involves granting permission on the XML schema collection itself, and the second part involves granting permission on the XML schema collection object. The first step is to understand the granting of permission on the XML schema collection itself.

Permissions on the XML Schema Collection

The GRANT syntax for granting permissions is as follows:

```
GRANT { XML_schema_collection_permission }
  ON XML SCHEMA COLLECTION::XML_schema_collection_name
  TO DatabasePrinciple
  WITH GRANT OPTION
  AS {Windows Group | Database Role | Application Role }
```

XML_schema_collection_permission is the permission that can be granted on an XML schema, and is one of the following options:

- ALTER: Permission to make changes to the XML schema collection.
- EXECUTE: Permission to query the xml data type column or variables, and validate values inserted or updated against the xml data type.
- TAKE OWNERSHIP: Permission to take ownership, or transfer ownership, of the XML schema collection.
- REFERENCES: Permission to use the XML schema collection.
- VIEW DEFINITION: Permission to view the XML schema collection definitions via XML_SCHEMA_NAMESPACE or via catalog views.
- CONTROL: Principle can perform any operation on the XML schema collection.

XML_schema_collection_name is the name of the XML schema collection in which the permissions are being granted. DatabasePrinciple is the user to which the permission is being granted. A principle can be one or more individuals or a group. A principle can also be a process that can ask for SQL Server resources.

The GRANT OPTION indicates that the principle also has the necessary rights to grant permissions to other principles. The AS clause specifies the Windows group, database role, or application role in which the principle who is executing the DENY statement obtains the rights to grant the permission.

For further clarification, the `REFERENCES` option gives permission to use the XML schema collection, for example, when creating a typed `xml` data type column or using it in an `xml` data type variable.

Creating an XML schema collection requires two permissions. First, at the database level the principle needs `CREATE XML SCHEMA COLLECTION` permission. Second, the principle needs `ALTER` permissions. The second permission is needed because the schema collections are scoped at the relational schema level.

Any of the following permissions satisfy the database level permissions and allow a user to create an XML schema collection:

- `CONTROL` permissions on the server or in the database
- `ALTER` permissions on the database
- `ALTER ANY DATABASE` permission on the server
- `ALTER ANY SCHEMA` and `CREATE XML SCHEMA COLLECTION` permission in the database

Granting Permission on the XML Schema Collection Object

Granting permissions on the XML schema collection object is defined as the permissions necessary to modify the *contents* of an XML schema collection. Here are some guidelines:

- `ALTER` permissions are necessary in order to alter any schema collection.
- To validate values, whether inserted or updated, the `EXECUTE` permissions are necessary.
- `CONTROL` permissions are required when performing any operation on a schema collection, such as granting permission on an XML schema collection.
- To transfer ownership of the schema collection from one principle to another, `TAKE OWNERSHIP` permissions are necessary.
- To view the contents of a schema collection, the `VIEW DEFINITION` permissions are needed.
- To use the schema collection in an `xml` data type column, variable, or constraint, the `REFERENCE` permissions are required.

The following example creates a user called xmluser in the Wrox database, and then assigns that user the necessary permissions to create an XML schema collection. It does this by first granting `ALTER ON SCHEMA` permissions, which grant the user permissions to `ALTER` that particular schema collection, and then grants `CREATE XML SCHEMA COLLECTION` permissions to the xmluser:

```
USE master
GO
CREATE LOGIN xmluser WITH password='xmlrocks'
GO
USE Wrox
go
CREATE USER [xmluser] FOR LOGIN [xmluser]
```

Figure 7-5 shows the new xmluser created in the Wrox database.

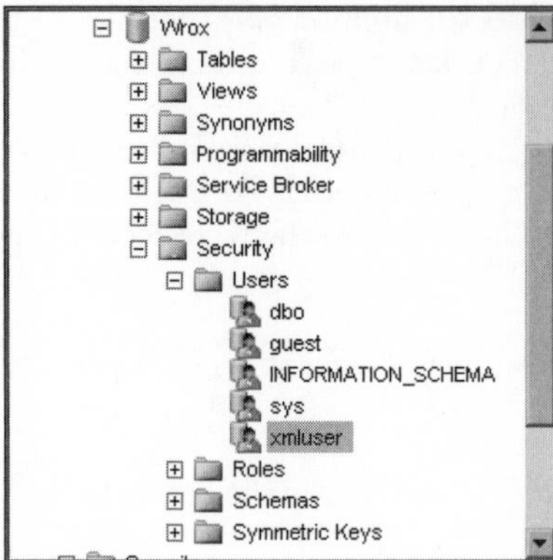

Figure 7-5

Now the user xmluser can successfully create XML schema collections. However, the user does not have permission to use any schema collections, even the collections he or she creates. The following example gives xmluser the necessary permissions to assign a schema collection to a column, insert data, and alter data:

```
GRANT REFERENCES ON XML SCHEMA COLLECTION::MotocrossCollection
TO xmluser
GO
GRANT EXECUTE ON XML SCHEMA COLLECTION::MotocrossCollection
TO xmluser
GO
GRANT INSERT TO xmluser
GO
GRANT SELECT TO xmluser
GO
GRANT ALTER ON XML SCHEMA COLLECTION::MotocrossCollection TO xmluser
GO
```

In this example, the first `GRANT` statement gives xmluser permission to use the schema collection with an `xml` data type column (creating a typed XML column). The second `GRANT` statement gives xlmuser the rights to insert data into an `xml` data type column with an associated schema collection. The third `GRANT` statement gives ownership to xmluser for permissions to insert into the table. The fourth `GRANT` statement gives xmluser the rights to query the `xml` data type column. The final `GRANT` statement gives xmluser the necessary privileges to alter components inside the schema collection.

Denying Permissions

As with granting permissions, denying permissions has two parts: denying permissions on the schema collection and denying permissions on the schema collection objects.

The syntax for denying permission is as follows:

```
DENY { XML_schema_collection_permission }
  ON XML SCHEMA COLLECTION::XML_schema_collection_name
  TO DatabasePrinciple
  CASCADE
  AS {Windows Group | Database Role | Application Role }
```

`XML_schema_collection_permission` is the permission that can be denied on an XML schema, and is one of the following:

- `ALTER`
- `EXECUTE`
- `TAKE OWNERSHIP`
- `REFERENCES`
- `VIEW DEFINITION`
- `CONTROL`

`XML_schema_collection_name` is the name of the XML schema collection in which the permissions are being denied. `DatabasePrinciple` is the user to which the permission is being denied. The `CASCADE` option specifies that all permissions being denied to the principle are also being denied to the other principles which were previously granted to by the principle.

The `AS` clause specifies the Windows group, database role, or application role in which the principle who is executing the `REVOKE` statement obtains the rights to revoke the permission.

To deny permissions on the schema collection, you can deny `ALTER ANY SCHEMA` on the database, deny `ALTER` permissions on the relational schema, and deny `CONTROL` permissions, which denies permissions on all the objects within the relational schema and the schema itself.

Denying permissions to the schema collection objects is the reverse of granting permissions. Instead of granting `ALTER`, `EXECUTE`, `CONTROL`, `OWNERSHIP`, `VIEW OWNERSHIP`, and `REFERENCE` permissions, simply deny the same permissions.

This first example denies the user xmluser the ability to alter or execute the XML schema collection `ProductionModelSchemaCollection`:

```
DENY ALTER ON XML SCHEMA COLLECTION::ProductionModelSchemaCollection
TO xmluser
GO
DENY EXECUTE ON XML SCHEMA COLLECTION::ProductionModelSchemaCollection
TO xmluser
GO
```

However, xmluser still has the ability to insert, reference, and alter existing collections. The following code takes those rights away:

```
DENY REFERENCES ON XML SCHEMA COLLECTION::MotocrossCollection
TO xmluser
GO
DENY EXECUTE ON XML SCHEMA COLLECTION::MotocrossCollection
TO xmluser
GO
DENY INSERT TO xmluser
GO
DENY SELECT TO xmluser
GO
DENY ALTER ON XML SCHEMA COLLECTION::MotocrossCollection
GO
```

Now the xmluser permissions are back where they started.

Revoking Permissions

Revoking permissions takes away rights to permissions previously granted. Like `GRANT` and `DENY`, the underlying principle is the same regarding the parts to revoke permissions.

The syntax for revoking permission is as follows:

```
REVOKE [GRANT OPTION FOR]
  { XML_schema_collection_permission }
  ON XML SCHEMA COLLECTION::XML_schema_collection_name
  { TO | FROM } DatabasePrinciple
  CASCADE
  AS {Windows Group | Database Role | Application Role }
```

`XML_schema_collection_permission` is the permission that can be revoked on an XML schema, and is one of the following options:

- ALTER
- EXECUTE
- TAKE OWNERSHIP
- REFERENCES
- VIEW DEFINITION
- CONTROL

`XML_schema_collection_name` is the name of the XML schema collection in which the permissions are being revoked. `DatabasePrinciple` is the user to which the permission is being revoked. The `CASCADE` option specifies that all permissions being revoked to the principle are also being revoked to the other principles which were previously granted to by the principle.

The `AS` clause specifies the Windows group, database role, or application role in which the principle who is executing the `GRANT` statement obtains the rights to grant the permission.

The following example grants rights to xmluser to create XML schema collections, and then promptly revokes those rights:

```
GRANT ALTER ON SCHEMA::dbo
TO xmluser
GO
GRANT CREATE XML SCHEMA COLLECTION
TO xmluser
GO
REVOKE ALTER ON SCHEMA::dbo FROM xmluser
GO
REVOKE CREATE XML SCHEMA COLLECTION
TO xmluser
GO
```

The final example gives xmluser all the permissions necessary to create, alter, reference, and use XML schema collections and their components, and then, again, promptly revokes them:

```
--GRANT Permissions
GRANT ALTER ON SCHEMA::dbo TO xmluser
GO
GRANT CREATE XML SCHEMA COLLECTION
TO xmluser
GO

GRANT REFERENCES ON XML SCHEMA COLLECTION::MotocrossCollection
TO xmluser
GO
GRANT EXECUTE ON XML SCHEMA COLLECTION::MotocrossCollection
TO xmluser
GO
GRANT INSERT TO xmluser
GO
GRANT SELECT TO xmluser
GO

--Found out permissions were given to the wrong user. Take these away
REVOKE ALTER ON SCHEMA::dbo FROM xmluser
GO
REVOKE CREATE XML SCHEMA COLLECTION
TO xmluser
GO
REVOKE REFERENCES ON XML SCHEMA COLLECTION::MotocrossCollection
TO xmluser
GO
REVOKE EXECUTE ON XML SCHEMA COLLECTION::MotocrossCollection
TO xmluser
GO
REVOKE INSERT TO xmluser
GO
REVOKE SELECT TO xmluser
GO
```

Guidelines and Limitations

The purpose of this section is to highlight some areas of importance when preparing XSD schemas for import into an XML schema collection. They are as follows:

- The `<xsd:include>` element is not supported in the version of SQL Server. Any schema that contains this element will be rejected.
- The `<xsd:key>`, `<xsd:keyref>`, and `<xsd:unique>` constraints are not supported. The `<xsd:unique>` constraint enforces uniqueness; the `<xsd:key>` and `<xsd:keyref>` constraints enforce keys and key references. Any schema imported into SQL Server that contains these constraints receives an error message and the schema is rejected.
- The element `<xsd:redefine>` is not supported. This element provides support for schema component redefinition.
- `NOTATION` Type is not supported. Schemas that contain the `NOTATION` Type are rejected.
- Uniqueness of IDs is enforced in SQL Server on the `<xsd:attribute>` declaration and not on the `<xsd:element>` declaration.
- Empty strings used as a value for a namespace are rejected.
- `"NaN"` values used in `<xsd:simpleType>` declarations are rejected.
- `minOccurs` and `maxOccurs` attribute values must be in 4-byte integers, otherwise they are rejected.
- `date`, `time`, and `datetime` simpleTypes are stored as Greenwich Mean Time (GMT).
- `length`, `minLength`, and `maxLength` values are stored as long types.
- Empty string values used as the enumeration for `xs:string` are rejected by SQL Server.
- Types derived from `xs:QName` are not supported.

Summary

The introduction of XML schema collections in SQL Server 2005 provides the capability to natively validate XML documents. The purpose of this chapter was to provide a thorough and deep introduction to the creation, modification, and deletion of XML schema collections.

Creating and maintaining XML schema collections, as you learned in this chapter, is not a difficult task and provides great usefulness, not only to tables (`xml` data type columns), but to variables and parameters as well.

Likewise, this chapter covered granting, revoking, and denying permissions to XML schema collections. There is great flexibility in applying permissions to schema collections and this will come in handy when planning how and where validation occurs.

The last part of the chapter talked about some of the limitations of the XML schema collections. The list of limitations, while quite long, still does not and should not take away from the power and importance of native schema validation.

8

Transact-SQL Enhancements to FOR XML and OPENXML

When SQL Server 2000 hit the streets, it included some XML functionality that was aimed at helping developers get their hands around easily converting relational data to XML. It was a serious step into continuing the support of XML and is used by a large portion of the developer community.

Subsequent SQLXML service pack releases added some functionality and fixes to further build upon that success. That focus has continued with the release of SQL Server 2005.

This chapter concentrates on the Transact-SQL enhancements and new features added to both the FOR XML and OPENXML statements in SQL Server 2005.

Specifically, this chapter covers the following topics:

- FOR XML
    - The new TYPE directive
    - Enhancements to RAW, AUTO, and EXPLICIT modes
    - PATH mode
    - Nested FOR XML queries
    - XSD schema generation
- OPENXML
    - sp_xml_preparedocument enhancements
    - WITH clause enhancements

FOR XML

The FOR XML statement was added to SQL Server 2000 to provide the capability to turn relational data into usable XML. The FOR XML clause is an add-on to the end of a SELECT statement that returns normal relational data in the form of a rowset.

When FOR XML first hit the big-time, it supported three modes in which a user could specify in what XML format to return the relational data. Those three modes — RAW, AUTO, and EXPLICIT — enabled the user to dictate how the relational data should be transformed into XML. Each mode provides a different result, and the modes range in complexity.

The RAW mode is the easiest to learn, returning results in single <row> elements for each row returned. The AUTO mode allows the user to base the shape of the results of the XML on a query, returning the results as nested elements. The EXPLICIT mode gives the best flexibility in defining how the results are returned, but takes nothing short of a rocket scientist to figure it out.

The purpose of this section is to introduce the new features and enhancements to the FOR XML statement, beginning with the TYPE directive.

The TYPE Directive

With the addition of the xml data type in SQL Server 2005, it only makes sense to make that data type available everywhere XML is concerned. Why should FOR XML be any different? To this end, SQL Server 2005 provides the capability to specify that the results of a FOR XML statement be returned as an xml data type. This is accomplished by adding the TYPE directive to the FOR XML statement at the end of the SELECT statement.

If FOR XML is specified in a SELECT statement without the TYPE directive, the results are returned as an XML instance in a nvarchar(max) data type.

The general syntax of the FOR XML statement using the TYPE directive is as follows:

```
SELECT Columnname(s)
FROM Tablename
FOR XML, TYPE
```

The easiest way to demonstrate this is with examples. The first example selects a couple of columns from the Person.Contact table and returns them as an xml data type using the TYPE directive:

```
SELECT HRE.EmployeeID, PC.FirstName, PC.LastName, HRE.Title
FROM Person.Contact PC, HumanResources.Employee HRE
WHERE PC.ContactID = HRE.ContactID
ORDER BY HRE.EmployeeID
FOR XML RAW, TYPE
```

The results of this query are shown in Figure 8-1.

```
<row EmployeeID="1" FirstName="Guy" LastName="Gilbert" Title="Production Technician - WC60"
<row EmployeeID="2" FirstName="Kevin" LastName="Brown" Title="Marketing Assistant" />
<row EmployeeID="3" FirstName="Roberto" LastName="Tamburello" Title="Engineering Manager" /
<row EmployeeID="4" FirstName="Rob" LastName="Walters" Title="Senior Tool Designer" />      >
<row EmployeeID="5" FirstName="Thierry" LastName="D'Hers" Title="Tool Designer" />
<row EmployeeID="6" FirstName="David" LastName="Bradley" Title="Marketing Manager" />
<row EmployeeID="7" FirstName="JoLynn" LastName="Dobney" Title="Production Supervisor - WC6
<row EmployeeID="8" FirstName="Ruth" LastName="Ellerbrock" Title="Production Technician - W
<row EmployeeID="9" FirstName="Gail" LastName="Erickson" Title="Design Engineer" />
<row EmployeeID="10" FirstName="Barry" LastName="Johnson" Title="Production Technician - WC
```

Figure 8-1

Take off the `TYPE` directive and rerun the query. Notice that the results look exactly the same. The only difference is that by specifying the `TYPE` directive, the results were returned as an `xml` data type whereas by taking off the `TYPE` directive the results were returned as a `nvarchar(max)` data type.

This example used the `RAW` mode, which returned the results as single `<row>` elements.

Applying some of the knowledge learned from previous chapters in the book, this next example uses the `query()` method of the `xml` data type to query the results returned by the `FOR XML` query:

```
SELECT (SELECT FirstName, LastName, EmailAddress, AdditionalContactInfo.query('
declare namespace pc="http://schemas.microsoft.com/sqlserver/2004/07/adventure-
works/ContactTypes";
 //pc:eMail/pc:eMailAddress
') as EmailAddress
FROM Person.Contact
FOR XML AUTO, TYPE).query('/Person.Contact')
```

The results are shown in Figure 8-2.

```
<Person.Contact FirstName="Gustavo" LastName="Achong" EmailAddress="gustavo0@adventure-works.co
  <EmailAddress>
    <pc:eMailAddress xmlns:pc="http://schemas.microsoft.com/...">customer1@xyz.com</pc:eMailAdd
  </EmailAddress>
</Person.Contact>
<Person.Contact FirstName="Catherine" LastName="Abel" EmailAddress="catherine0@adventure-works.
  <EmailAddress>
    <pc:eMailAddress xmlns:pc="http://schemas.microsoft.com/...">Joe@xyz.com</pc:eMailAddress>
  </EmailAddress>
</Person.Contact>
<Person.Contact FirstName="Kim" LastName="Abercrombie" EmailAddress="kim2@adventure-works.com">
  <EmailAddress>
    <pc:eMailAddress xmlns:pc="http://schemas.microsoft.com/...">Customer3@xyz.com</pc:eMailAdd
  </EmailAddress>
</Person.Contact>
<Person.Contact FirstName="Humberto" LastName="Acevedo" EmailAddress="humberto0@adventure-works
  <EmailAddress>
    <pc:eMailAddress xmlns:pc="http://schemas.microsoft.com/...">Customer4@xyz.com</pc:eMailAdd
    <pc:eMailAddress xmlns:pc="http://schemas.microsoft.com/...">Customer4@abc.com</pc:eMailAdd
  </EmailAddress>
```

Figure 8-2

In the results, notice that the `FirstName`, `LastName`, and `EmailAddress` values are returned as attributes. Had the `ELEMENTS` directive been specified on the `FOR XML` clause, these values would have been returned as elements and the results would look quite different.

The `query` method of the `xml` data type is used to return a fourth value, the alternative e-mail address, which as you notice is returned as a separate element because of the `As EmailAddress`. The addition of the `TYPE` directive returns these results as an `xml` data type.

This next example shows the `FOR XML` statement and `TYPE` directive being used with the `xml` data type `query()` method, but all the `xml` data type methods are eligible for use with `FOR XML`.

`FOR XML` can also be applied to variables as shown in the following example. This example queries the Contacts table using `FOR XML`, and the results are placed in an `xml` data type variable:

```
DECLARE @xmlvar xml
SET @xmlvar = (SELECT HRE.ContactID,
    PC.FirstName,
    PC.LastName,
    PC.AdditionalContactInfo.query
('
declare namespace ct="http://schemas.microsoft.com/sqlserver/2004/07/
adventure-works/ContactTypes";
//ct:eMail/ct:eMailAddress
')
as AdditionaleMail
FROM Person.Contact PC, HumanResources.Employee HRE
WHERE PC.ContactID = HRE.ContactID
ORDER BY HRE.ContactID
FOR XML AUTO, TYPE)
SELECT @xmlvar
GO
```

The results are shown in Figure 8-3.

```
<HRE ContactID="1001">
  <PC FirstName="Terri" LastName="Duffy" />
</HRE>
<HRE ContactID="1002">
  <PC FirstName="Roberto" LastName="Tamburello" />
</HRE>
<HRE ContactID="1003">
  <PC FirstName="Michael" LastName="Sullivan" />
</HRE>
<HRE ContactID="1004">
  <PC FirstName="Sharon" LastName="Salavaria" />
</HRE>
```

Figure 8-3

This example is very similar to the previous example. The `FirstName` and `LastName` values are still returned as attributes, as in the previous example. The difference here is that the results are returned as an `xml` data variable.

As a final note on this topic, `FOR XML` can also be combined with `XML DML` statements to provide `UPDATE`, `DELETE`, or `INSERT` functionality. For example, the following code first creates the Employee table with two `xml` data type columns, inserts an XML document into the first `xml` data type column, and then updates the second `xml` data type column using a `FOR XML SELECT` statement and the `query()` method of the `xml` data type:

```
DROP TABLE Employee
GO
CREATE TABLE Employee (EmployeeID int, EmployeeInfo xml, EmployeeInfo2 xml NULL)
GO
INSERT INTO Employee (EmployeeID, EmployeeInfo)
VALUES(1, '<root><EmployeeInfo><Employee
EmployeeID="1"></Employee></EmployeeInfo></root>')
GO
SELECT * FROM Employee
UPDATE Employee SET EmployeeInfo2 = (SELECT EmployeeInfo.query('/root') FROM
Employee row FOR XML AUTO, TYPE)
GO
SELECT * FROM Employee
```

The results from the query are shown in Figure 8-4.

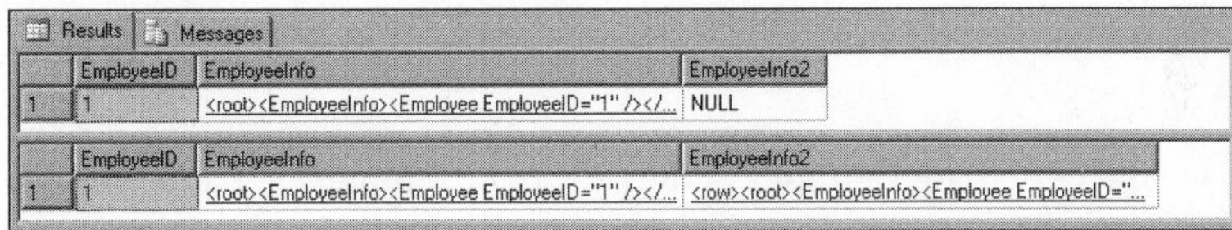

Figure 8-4

In this example, the `query` method of the `xml` data type is used to query all the contents of the `root` node (which in this example is the entire XML document). Those results are then inserted into the EmployeeInfo2 column.

Take a look at the `FROM` clause for a moment, and also look at the EmployeeInfo2 column of the second set of results. Notice that the query specified its own root node called `row`. This means that the `root` node in the EmployeeInfo column is not the `root` node in the EmployeeInto2 column; the `row` node is.

RAW Mode Enhancements

The `RAW` mode is the simplest `FOR XML` mode to use, yet a number of enhancements have been made to make it even more functional. The enhancements made to the `RAW` mode are as follows:

- ❑ Capability to specify the root element in the XML result
- ❑ Capability to specify the `<row>` element name (instead of the default `<row>`)
- ❑ Capability to return element-centric XML

Specifying the <row> Element Name

This first example illustrates renaming the `<row>` element. The code is a modification of the first example in this chapter, as shown in the highlighted line:

```
SELECT Top 10 HRE.EmployeeID, PC.FirstName, PC.LastName, HRE.Title
FROM Person.Contact PC, HumanResources.Employee HRE
WHERE PC.ContactID = HRE.ContactID
ORDER BY HRE.EmployeeID
FOR XML RAW ('Employee'), TYPE, ELEMENTS
```

Figure 8-5 shows the results of the query.

```
<Employee>
   <EmployeeID>1</EmployeeID>
   <FirstName>Guy</FirstName>
   <LastName>Gilbert</LastName>
   <Title>Production Technician - WC60</Title>
</Employee>
<Employee>
   <EmployeeID>2</EmployeeID>
   <FirstName>Kevin</FirstName>
   <LastName>Brown</LastName>
   <Title>Marketing Assistant</Title>
</Employee>
<Employee>
```

Figure 8-5

You should take note of a couple of things in the previous example. First, the `<row>` element has been renamed to `<Employee>`. This was accomplished by specifying the name of the element in the `FOR XML` statement, such as `FOR XML ('Employee')`. The second point is that the results are returned in a nice, neat nested structure. The `ELEMENTS` keyword provided this structure and makes the XML much easier to read. Had the `ELEMENTS` keyword been left off, the results would have looked like the following:

```
<Employee EmployeeID="1" FirstName="Guy" LastName="Gilbert" Title="">
<Employee EmployeeID="2" FirstName="Kevin LastName="Brown" Title="">
<Employee EmployeeID="3" FirstName="Roberto" LastName="Tamburello" Title="">
```

Specifying the Root Element

Using the `ROOT` directive in a `FOR XML` statement allows you to specify a top-level element for the results. When specifying the `ROOT` directive, you must specify an argument containing the name of the top-level element.

Consider the following example query:

```
SELECT top 2 ContactID, FirstName, LastName
FROM Person.Contact
FOR XML RAW, ROOT('Contact'), TYPE, ELEMENTS
GO
```

Figure 8-6 shows the results of this query.

```
<Contact>
  <row>
    <ContactID>1</ContactID>
    <FirstName>Gustavo</FirstName>
    <LastName>Achong</LastName>
  </row>
  <row>
    <ContactID>2</ContactID>
    <FirstName>Catherine</FirstName>
    <LastName>Abel</LastName>
  </row>
</Contact>
```

Figure 8-6

The results in this example contain a top-level root element named `<Contact>`. This example, as with the previous example, specified the `TYPE` directive, which returned the results as an `xml` data type, as well as the `ELEMENTS` directive to format the XML a bit better. Had the `ELEMENTS` directive not been specified, the top-level root element would still be returned, but the nesting would have been lost and each row would be returned in a single `<row>` element.

AUTO Mode Enhancements

The `AUTO` mode provides a bit more flexibility in shaping the results of the XML over the `RAW` mode, but it is still limited as to the control. It uses a query as the basis for how the XML is shaped, determining how elements are nested when returned by comparing the value of the current row against the values of the rows around it.

When multiple tables are specified in the `FROM` clause, each table is specified as an XML element as long as one column from each table is used in the `SELECT` statement. Following this same logic, the order of the tables specified determines the XML hierarchy.

In SQL Server 2000, all but the `image`, `text`, and `ntext` columns were available for value comparison. In SQL Server 2005, this list also includes the `xml` data type, so specifying the `TYPE` directive will have no effect. However, the `varchar(max)`, `nvarchar(max)`, and `varbinary(max)` are compared.

This section shows a few examples of how to use the `AUTO` mode.

The first example uses the `AUTO` mode in a simple query to return four columns, two from the Person.Contact table and two from the HumanResources.Employee table, joined together on the ContactID column:

```
SELECT Top 5 HRE.EmployeeID, PC.FirstName, PC.LastName, HRE.Title
FROM Person.Contact PC, HumanResources.Employee HRE
WHERE PC.ContactID = HRE.ContactID
ORDER BY HRE.EmployeeID
FOR XML AUTO
```

Figure 8-7 shows the results returned. Each column specified in the query is the element name in which each value applied has an attribute.

```
<HRE EmployeeID="1" Title="Production Technician - WC60">
  <PC FirstName="Guy" LastName="Gilbert" />
</HRE>
<HRE EmployeeID="2" Title="Marketing Assistant">
  <PC FirstName="Kevin" LastName="Brown" />
</HRE>
<HRE EmployeeID="3" Title="Engineering Manager">
  <PC FirstName="Roberto" LastName="Tamburello" />
</HRE>
<HRE EmployeeID="4" Title="Senior Tool Designer">
  <PC FirstName="Rob" LastName="Walters" />
</HRE>
<HRE EmployeeID="5" Title="Tool Designer">
  <PC FirstName="Thierry" LastName="D'Hers" />
</HRE>
```

Figure 8-7

While these results are valid, returning the column values as attributes is not the best solution for this query and they could be formatted better for easier reading. Modify the query, as follows, by adding the `ELEMENTS` directive, which will change how the results of the query are formatted:

```
SELECT Top 5 HRE.EmployeeID, PC.FirstName, PC.LastName, HRE.Title
FROM Person.Contact PC, HumanResources.Employee HRE
WHERE PC.ContactID = HRE.ContactID
ORDER BY HRE.EmployeeID
FOR XML AUTO, ELEMENTS
```

This changes the results as shown in Figure 8-8. By adding the `ELEMENTS` directive, the column values are no longer returned as attributes, but rather are returned as elements in the hierarchical format.

```
<HRE>
  <EmployeeID>1</EmployeeID>
  <Title>Production Technician - WC60</Title>
  <PC>
    <FirstName>Guy</FirstName>
    <LastName>Gilbert</LastName>
  </PC>
</HRE>
<HRE>
  <EmployeeID>2</EmployeeID>
  <Title>Marketing Assistant</Title>
  <PC>
    <FirstName>Kevin</FirstName>
    <LastName>Brown</LastName>
  </PC>
</HRE>
```

Figure 8-8

As demonstrated in this section, the XML results returned are based on the query, allowing you to shape the results somewhat. While the shaping is limited, `AUTO` mode does give more flexibility over the `RAW` mode. By adding the `TYPE` directive to the query as follows you can specify to have the results returned as `xml` data type:

```
FOR XML AUTO, TYPE, ELEMENTS
```

EXPLICIT Mode Enhancements

The following two enhancements have been made to the `EXPLICIT` mode:

- `CDATA` directive with an element name.
- `elementxsinil` column mode.

Since an entire chapter, and a large one at that, could be spent on explaining the `EXPLICIT` mode, this section assumes that this mode is not new to you or that you have at least a minimal understanding of the `EXPLICIT` mode. To that end, the examples in this section highlight the enhancements of the `EXPLICIT` mode and try to demonstrate a few more of its features while doing so.

With that, time to jump into some examples.

CDATA

This first example queries the Person.Contact table and builds an XML document with a `CDATA` section wrapped in an `<element>` tag:

```
SELECT
  1 AS Tag,
  0 AS Parent,
  ContactID as [Contact!1!ContactID],
  FirstName as [Contact!1!FirstName],
  LastName  as [Contact!1!LastName],
  '<ContactInformation>Contact information</ContactInformation>'
    as [Contact!1!!cdata]
FROM    Person.Contact
WHERE   ContactID=218
FOR XML EXPLICIT
```

Figure 8-9 shows the results.

```
<Contact ContactID="218" FirstName="Scott" LastName="Colvin">
  <![CDATA[<ContactInformation>Contact information</ContactInformation>]]>
</Contact>
```

Figure 8-9

In this example, ContactID, FirstName, and LastName are added as attributes to the `Contact` element, and the `CDATA` section is within the `<ContactInformation>` element.

Modify the previous example as follows and rerun the query:

```
SELECT
  1 AS Tag,
  0 AS Parent,
  ContactID as [Contact!1!ContactID],
  FirstName as [Contact!1!FirstName!ELEMENT],
  LastName  as [Contact!1!LastName!ELEMENT],
  '<ContactInformation>Contact information</ContactInformation>'
```

```
    as [Contact!1!!cdata]
FROM     Person.Contact
WHERE    ContactID=218
FOR XML EXPLICIT
```

What is the shape of the results now? Adding the `ELEMENTS` directive to the `FOR XML EXPLICIT` statement is not allowed; therefore if you want `FirstName` and `LastName` returned as elements, you need to add the `ELEMENTS` directive to the `SELECT` statement as shown in the example. The results should look like those shown in Figure 8-10.

```
<Contact ContactID="218">
  <FirstName>Scott</FirstName>
  <LastName>Colvin</LastName>
  <![CDATA[<ContactInformation>Contact information</ContactInformation>]]>
</Contact>
```

Figure 8-10

The `CDATA` directive is used to wrap returned data in a `CDATA` section. This directive is useful when you want to include text that typically would not be recognized as markup characters. In the example, the `CDATA` directive was used to add information in its own element.

elementxsinil

The `elementxsinil` directive is used to generate elements for null values, meaning that if the query returns a null value, the `elementxsinil` directive still builds an element for that value with an attribute of `xsi:nil="true"`.

Modify the example from the previous section to include the following:

```
SELECT
  1 AS Tag,
  0 AS Parent,
  ContactID as [Contact!1!ContactID],
  FirstName as [Contact!1!FirstName!ELEMENT],
  MiddleName as [Contact!1!MiddleName!ELEMENTXSINIL],
  LastName  as [Contact!1!LastName!ELEMENT],
  '<ContactInformation>Contact information</ContactInformation>'
    as [Contact!1!!cdata]
FROM     Person.Contact
WHERE    ContactID=483
FOR XML EXPLICIT
```

This example queries the Person.Contact table for a Contact. The MiddleName column uses the `elementxsinil` directive, telling the query that if the `MiddleName` value for the specified ContactID is `NULL`, include an element for it anyway. The results for this query are shown in Figure 8-11.

```
<Contact xmlns:xsi="http://www.w3.org/2001/XMLSchema-instance" ContactID="483">
  <FirstName>Scott</FirstName>
  <MiddleName xsi:nil="true" />
  <LastName>Konersmann</LastName>
  <![CDATA[<ContactInformation>Contact information</ContactInformation>]]>
</Contact>
```

Figure 8-11

Sure enough, the MiddleName for ContactID 483 is NULL, but an element for the MiddleName was included anyway. What happens if the elementxisnil directive is used and a MiddleName is not NULL? Modify the query, changing the WHERE statement to query for ContactID of 218 and rerun the query.

In the case where the elementxisnil directive is specified but the value returned is not NULL, the elementxisnil directive is basically ignored and the value is included in the MiddleName element, as shown in Figure 8-12.

```
<Contact xmlns:xsi="http://www.w3.org/2001/XMLSchema-instance" ContactID="218">
  <FirstName>Scott</FirstName>
  <MiddleName>A.</MiddleName>
  <LastName>Colvin</LastName>
  <![CDATA[<ContactInformation>Contact information</ContactInformation>]]>
</Contact>
```

Figure 8-12

In both examples, using the elementxisnil directive, notice that the root Contact element includes a namespace.

Specifying the TYPE directive is allowed, which lets you return these results as xml data type.

PATH Mode

It is no secret, as you found out in the last section or probably already know: dealing with the EXPLICIT mode is exquisitely painful. The upside to this mode is that it provides the greatest flexibility when shaping XML results. The downside is that the learning curve is *steep*.

The moans and groans from all over the world were heard loud and clear at Microsoft headquarters in Redmond, Washington; thus the PATH mode is introduced in SQL Server 2005 to ease the EXPLICIT mode pains.

The goal of the PATH mode is to provide an easier way to generate XML documents with much easier queries. The PATH mode provides a painless way to mix attributes and elements and can be used to return results as the xml data type using the TYPE directive. And as you will learn about in the next section, it also can be used with nesting FOR XML queries.

The PATH mode takes all columns returned from a SELECT query and maps them to attributes and elements using an XPath-like syntax.

The PATH mode is specified by adding the PATH directive to the FOR XML clause, as follows:

```
FOR XML PATH
```

Jumping right in to examples, the following example queries four columns from the Person.Contact table; the fourth column does not specify a column name, but the PATH mode inserts an XML instance with the returned data in the query:

```
SELECT
  ContactID,
  FirstName,
```

```
   LastName,
   AdditionalContactInfo.query('
   declare namespace PC="http://schemas.microsoft.com/sqlserver/2004/07/adventure-
works/ContactTypes";
   /PC:telephoneNumber/PC:number
   ')
FROM Person.Contact
WHERE ContactID = 10
FOR XML PATH
GO
```

Any column that does not specify a name is included in-line, meaning properly nested within the XML instance, as shown in Figure 8-13.

```
<row>
  <ContactID>10</ContactID>
  <FirstName>Ronald</FirstName>
  <LastName>Adina</LastName>
</row>
```

Figure 8-13

Column names returned in the rowset are mapped case-sensitive to the results in the XML instance. For example, the following code simply queries the Person.Contact table creating an alias column called @PCID:

```
SELECT ContactID as "@PCID",
FirstName,
LastName
FROM Person.Contact
WHERE ContactID = 218
```

The results look like this:

```
@PCID    FirstName    LastName
-----    ---------    --------
218      Scott        Colvin
```

Adding the `FOR XML PATH` statement to the query, as in the following example, the column name from the first query begins with an at symbol (@), and therefore is mapped to an attribute of the `<row>` column with the value associated to it:

```
SELECT ContactID as "@PCID",
FirstName,
LastName
FROM Person.Contact
WHERE ContactID = 218
FOR XML PATH
GO
```

Figure 8-14 shows the resulting XML instance.

```
<row PCID="218">
   <FirstName>Scott</FirstName>
   <LastName>Colvin</LastName>
</row>
```

Figure 8-14

When generating this kind of query, the attribute needs to come before the other columns or else an error is generated. For example, the following will fail:

```
SELECT FirstName,
ContactID as "@PCID"
FROM Person.Contact
WHERE ContactID = 218
FOR XML PATH
GO
```

The basic rule of thumb to remember is that if the column name in the rowset does not begin with @, but begins with a forward slash (/), then XML hierarchy is applied. In the preceding example, the column name began with @; therefore the `PATH` mode mapped it as an attribute.

In the following example, four columns are returned. The first column begins with @, so it is mapped to an attribute. The other three columns contain a /, so the XML hierarchy is applied:

```
SELECT EmployeeID "@EmpID",
       FirstName  "EmpName/First",
       MiddleName "EmpName/Middle",
       LastName   "EmpName/Last"
FROM   HumanResources.Employee E, Person.Contact C
WHERE  E.EmployeeID = C.ContactID
AND    E.EmployeeID=218
FOR XML PATH
```

Figure 8-15 shows the resulting XML instance.

```
<row EmpID="218">
  <EmpName>
    <First>Scott</First>
    <Middle>A.</Middle>
    <Last>Colvin</Last>
  </EmpName>
</row>
```

Figure 8-15

The XML instance can be further shaped by making the following changes to the query:

```
SELECT EmployeeID "@EmpID",
       FirstName  "EmpName/First",
       MiddleName "EmpName/MiddleName/Middle",
       LastName   "EmpName/Last"
FROM   HumanResources.Employee E, Person.Contact C
WHERE  E.EmployeeID = C.ContactID
AND    E.EmployeeID=218
FOR XML PATH
```

The results now look like Figure 8-16.

```
<row EmpID="218">
  <EmpName>
    <First>Scott</First>
    <MiddleName>
      <Middle>A.</Middle>
    </MiddleName>
    <Last>Colvin</Last>
  </EmpName>
</row>
```

Figure 8-16

In this example, the query was modified to have the <Middle> node show up a level deeper, a child of the <MiddleName> node. This was accomplished by telling the results to add another layer for this node.

As you learned earlier, if the query returns a NULL value, the element is not mapped. To generate elements for a NULL value, specify the ELEMENTS XSINIL directive. The ELEMENTS XSINIL directive is very similar to the NULL example given earlier in the chapter except for the placement and slight difference in syntax. The functionality is the same, but in this case the placement of the directive is after the FOR XML clause and it is two words, not one. Note also the change in the ContactID for this example:

```
SELECT EmployeeID "@EmpID",
       FirstName  "EmpName/First",
       MiddleName "EmpName/MiddleName/Middle",
       LastName   "EmpName/Last"
FROM   HumanResources.Employee E, Person.Contact C
WHERE  E.EmployeeID = C.ContactID
AND    E.EmployeeID=236
FOR XML PATH, ELEMENTS XSINIL
```

This next example specifies multiple paths and maps the columns accordingly:

```
SELECT EmployeeID   "@EmpID",
       FirstName    "Contact/First",
       MiddleName   "Contact/Middle",
       LastName     "Contact/Last",
       Birthdate   "Employee/Birthdate",
       HireDate     "Employee/HireDate"
FROM   HumanResources.Employee E, Person.Contact C
WHERE  E.ContactID = C.ContactID
AND    E.EmployeeID=218
FOR XML PATH
```

The results are shown in Figure 8-17.

```
<row EmpID="218">
  <Contact>
    <First>Gary</First>
    <Middle>E.</Middle>
    <Last>Altman</Last>
  </Contact>
  <Employee>
    <Birthdate>1961-03-21T00:00:00</Birthdate>
    <HireDate>2000-01-03T00:00:00</HireDate>
  </Employee>
</row>
```

Figure 8-17

In the previous example the columns were nice and orderly. What happens if that order is tossed around like this:

```
SELECT EmployeeID   "@EmpID",
       FirstName    "Contact/First",
       Birthdate   "Employee/Birthdate",
       MiddleName   "Contact/Middle",
       HireDate     "Employee/HireDate",
       LastName     "Contact/Last"
FROM   HumanResources.Employee E, Person.Contact C
WHERE  E.ContactID = C.ContactID
AND    E.EmployeeID=1
FOR XML PATH
```

The columns are returned as shown in Figure 8-18. The `PATH` directive nests the elements as they appear in the `SELECT` statement, and cannot order them as shown previously in Figure 8-17.

```
<row EmpID="218">
  <Contact>
    <First>Gary</First>
  </Contact>
  <Employee>
    <Birthdate>1961-03-21T00:00:00</Birthdate>
  </Employee>
  <Contact>
    <Middle>E.</Middle>
  </Contact>
  <Employee>
    <HireDate>2000-01-03T00:00:00</HireDate>
  </Employee>
  <Contact>
    <Last>Altman</Last>
  </Contact>
</row>
```

Figure 8-18

The results in Figure 8-18 look different than they do in Figure 8-17 because the `PATH` directive nests the elements as they appear in the SQL statement. In the case of Figure 8-18, because the order was mixed, the query returned the results with each value in its own node instead of grouping them like Figure 8-17.

One more example for this section:

```
SELECT EmployeeID "@EmployeeID",
        'Employee Information'              as "text()",
        'MiddleName is optional'            as "EmpName/text()",
        FirstName                           as "EmpName/First",
        MiddleName                          as "EmpName/Middle",
        LastName                            as "EmpName/Last",
        Birthdate                           as "Employee/Birthdate",
        HireDate                            as "Employee/HireDate"
FROM   HumanResources.Employee E, Person.Contact C
WHERE  E.EmployeeID = C.ContactID
AND    E.EmployeeID=218
FOR XML PATH
```

In this query, an XPath node test of `text()` is used in two places. First, it is used to add a string after the root node `<row>`, and the second use adds a text string after the `<EmpName>` element. The results in Figure 8-19 show the `text()`.

```
<row EmployeeID="218">Employee Information
<EmpName>MiddleName is optional
  <First>Scott</First>
  <Middle>A.</Middle>
  <Last>Colvin</Last>
</EmpName>
<Employee>
  <Birthdate>1961-03-21T00:00:00</Birthdate>
  <HireDate>2000-01-03T00:00:00</HireDate>
  </Employee>
</row>
```

Figure 8-19

The `PATH` mode, as you should be able to tell by now, is a much welcomed addition to SQL Server 2005 and a much simpler method of mixing elements and attributes over the cumbersome `EXPLICIT` mode.

Speaking of new enhancements to SQL Server 2005, it's time to talk about another one.

Nesting FOR XML

The `FOR XML` clause in SQL Server 2000 could only be used on the outer, or top-level, `SELECT` statements, and nesting of `FOR XML` was not supported. The other limitation in SQL Server 2000 was that any further processing of these queries took place on the client, meaning that once the `FOR XML` query was executed, the results were sent to the client for processing.

In SQL Server 2005, however, you have the capability to nest `FOR XML` statements, thus processing the queries internally on the server, returning the results as `xml` data type. The addition of this functionality in SQL Server 2005 provides better shaping of the XML returned by the `FOR XML` queries. Because `FOR XML` queries can be nested, the inner `FOR XML` query can return the results as `xml` data type for further processing by the outer `FOR XML` query, which can then also return the results as an `xml` data type.

In the first example, the inner `SELECT` query, which queries the employee's title and birth date from the Title and Birthdate columns of the HumanResources.Employee table, are returned as `xml` data type as elements as determined by the ELEMENTS directive. Those results are then passed to the outer SELECT query for further processing, which selects the corresponding ContactID, FirstName, and LastName columns from the Person.Contact table as xml data type and combines them:

```
SELECT ContactID, FirstName, LastName,
     (SELECT HumanResources.Employee.Title, HumanResources.Employee.Birthdate
      FROM HumanResources.Employee
      WHERE Employee.ContactID = Contact.ContactID
      FOR XML AUTO, TYPE, ELEMENTS
     )
FROM Person.Contact
WHERE ContactID > 1000
ORDER BY ContactID
FOR XML AUTO, TYPE
```

Figure 8-20 displays the results of the query.

```
<Person.Contact ContactID="1001" FirstName="Terri" LastName="Duffy">
  <HumanResources.Employee>
    <Title>Vice President of Engineering</Title>
    <Birthdate>1961-09-01T00:00:00</Birthdate>
  </HumanResources.Employee>
</Person.Contact>
<Person.Contact ContactID="1002" FirstName="Roberto" LastName="Tamburello">
  <HumanResources.Employee>
    <Title>Engineering Manager</Title>
    <Birthdate>1964-12-13T00:00:00</Birthdate>
  </HumanResources.Employee>
</Person.Contact>
<Person.Contact ContactID="1003" FirstName="Michael" LastName="Sullivan">
  <HumanResources.Employee>
    <Title>Senior Design Engineer</Title>
    <Birthdate>1969-07-17T00:00:00</Birthdate>
  </HumanResources.Employee>
</Person.Contact>
```

Figure 8-20

In this example, the ContactID, FirstName, and LastName values are returned as attributes because the query did not specify to return them as elements. The inner query returned the Title and Birthdate columns as elements because the ELEMENTS directive was specified on the FOR XML clause.

The following example also uses a nested FOR XML statement, but it also uses the XQuery data function to retrieve all the associated SalesOrders for each Contact in the inner SELECT. Those results do not need to be returned as an xml data type, so the TYPE directive is left off. The results are passed to the outer SELECT, which queries the ContactID and FirstName columns of the associated SalesOrders table:

```
SELECT ContactID    as "@ContactID",
       FirstName    as "@ContactName",
       (SELECT SalesOrderID as "data()"
        FROM Sales.SalesOrderHeader
        WHERE SalesOrderHeader.ContactID = Contact.ContactID
        FOR XML PATH ('')) as "@SalesOrderIDs"
FROM Person.Contact
FOR XML PATH('SalesOrders')
```

Partial results from this query are shown in Figure 8-21.

```
<SalesOrders ContactID="1" ContactName="Gustavo" SalesOrderIDs="44132 45579 46389 47454 48395 49495
<SalesOrders ContactID="2" ContactName="Catherine" SalesOrderIDs="53459 58907 65157 71782" />
<SalesOrders ContactID="3" ContactName="Kim" SalesOrderIDs="44110 44772 45550 46358 47409 48349 4946
<SalesOrders ContactID="4" ContactName="Humberto" SalesOrderIDs="44131 44800 45573 46386 47453 48394
<SalesOrders ContactID="5" ContactName="Pilar" SalesOrderIDs="53485 58931 65191 71805" />
<SalesOrders ContactID="6" ContactName="Frances" SalesOrderIDs="43680 44301 45059 45799 46634 47689
<SalesOrders ContactID="7" ContactName="Margaret" SalesOrderIDs="47448 48387 49544" />
<SalesOrders ContactID="8" ContactName="Carla" SalesOrderIDs="43693 44318 45075 45814" />
<SalesOrders ContactID="9" ContactName="Jay" SalesOrderIDs="48382 50734 53561 59058 65311 71884" />
<SalesOrders ContactID="10" ContactName="Ronald" SalesOrderIDs="43887 44532 45312 46070" />
<SalesOrders ContactID="11" ContactName="Samuel" SalesOrderIDs="44084 46328 48303 49453 50709 53543
<SalesOrders ContactID="12" ContactName="James" SalesOrderIDs="51805 63206 69434" />
<SalesOrders ContactID="13" ContactName="Robert" SalesOrderIDs="53533 58979 65168 71787" />
<SalesOrders ContactID="14" ContactName="François" SalesOrderIDs="43683 44308 45064 45804 46647 4769
<SalesOrders ContactID="15" ContactName="Kim" SalesOrderIDs="44123 44789 45567 46376 50732 59056 653
```

Figure 8-21

This query returns everyone from the Person.Contact table, so you can specify an optional `WHERE` clause to further filter the results if necessary.

The final example is a bit more complicated, in that it nests a few `FOR XML` queries within the inner `SELECT` statement:

```
SELECT TOP 5 SalesOrderID, SalesPersonID, CustomerID,
  (SELECT TOP 2 SalesOrderDetail.SalesOrderID, ProductID, OrderQty, UnitPrice
  FROM Sales.SalesOrderDetail, Sales.SalesOrderHeader
  WHERE SalesOrderDetail.SalesOrderID = SalesOrderHeader.SalesOrderID
  FOR XML AUTO, TYPE),
     (SELECT *
     FROM  (SELECT Employee.EmployeeID As SalesPersonID, Contact.FirstName,
Contact.LastName
            FROM Person.Contact, HumanResources.Employee
            WHERE Contact.ContactID = Employee.EmployeeID) As SalesPerson
     WHERE SalesPerson.SalesPersonID = SalesOrderHeader.SalesPersonID
     FOR XML AUTO, TYPE, ELEMENTS)
FROM Sales.SalesOrderHeader
FOR XML AUTO, TYPE
```

A portion of the results are shown in Figure 8-22.

```
<Sales.SalesOrderHeader SalesOrderID="43659" SalesPersonID="279" CustomerID="676">
  <Sales.SalesOrderDetail SalesOrderID="43659" ProductID="776" OrderQty="1" UnitPric
  <Sales.SalesOrderDetail SalesOrderID="43659" ProductID="777" OrderQty="3" UnitPric
  <SalesPerson>
    <SalesPersonID>279</SalesPersonID>
    <FirstName>Carol</FirstName>
    <LastName>Elliott</LastName>
  </SalesPerson>
</Sales.SalesOrderHeader>
<Sales.SalesOrderHeader SalesOrderID="43660" SalesPersonID="279" CustomerID="117">
  <Sales.SalesOrderDetail SalesOrderID="43659" ProductID="776" OrderQty="1" UnitPric
  <Sales.SalesOrderDetail SalesOrderID="43659" ProductID="777" OrderQty="3" UnitPric
  <SalesPerson>
    <SalesPersonID>279</SalesPersonID>
    <FirstName>Carol</FirstName>
    <LastName>Elliott</LastName>
  </SalesPerson>
</Sales.SalesOrderHeader>
```

Figure 8-22

XSD Schema Generation

Just when you think that the new `FOR XML` features can't get any better, the capability to generate an inline schema associated to your `FOR XML` query comes along.

How easy is it, you ask? Simply by adding the `XMLSCHEMA` keyword to the end of the `FOR XML` statement you can quickly and easily generate a nice XSD schema. The syntax looks like this:

```
FOR XML AUTO, XMLSCHEMA
```

However, you need to follow a couple of rules when using the `XMLSCHEMA` keyword:

- You can use the `XMLSCHEMA` keyword only in the `RAW` and `AUTO` modes.
- When nesting `FOR XML` statements, you can use the `XMLSCHEMA` keyword only on the outer, or top-level, query.

When you specify the `XMLSCHEMA` *keyword, both the schema and the XML data results are returned with the schema preceding the XML data.*

The following example returns both an XML instance and the corresponding XSD schema:

```
SELECT ContactID, FirstName, LastName
FROM Person.Contact
WHERE ContactID = 218
FOR XML AUTO, XMLSCHEMA
```

In the following results, the schema precedes the XML data, which is listed at the end of the results:

```
<xsd:schema xmlns:xsd="http://www.w3.org/2001/XMLSchema"
targetNamespace="http://schemas.microsoft.com/sqlserver/2004/sqltypes">
  <xsd:simpleType name="int">
    <xsd:restriction base="xsd:int" />
  </xsd:simpleType>
  <xsd:simpleType name="nvarchar">
    <xsd:restriction base="xsd:string" />
  </xsd:simpleType>
</xsd:schema>
<xsd:schema targetNamespace="urn:schemas-microsoft-com:sql:SqlRowSet1"
xmlns:schema="urn:schemas-microsoft-com:sql:SqlRowSet1"
xmlns:xsd="http://www.w3.org/2001/XMLSchema"
xmlns:sqltypes="http://schemas.microsoft.com/sqlserver/2004/sqltypes"
elementFormDefault="qualified">
  <xsd:import namespace="http://schemas.microsoft.com/sqlserver/2004/sqltypes" />
  <xsd:element name="Person.Contact">
    <xsd:complexType>
      <xsd:attribute name="ContactID" type="sqltypes:int" use="required" />
      <xsd:attribute name="FirstName" use="required">
        <xsd:simpleType sqltypes:sqlTypeAlias="[AdventureWorks].[dbo].[Name]">
          <xsd:restriction base="sqltypes:nvarchar" sqltypes:localeId="1033"
sqltypes:sqlCompareOptions="IgnoreCase IgnoreKanaType IgnoreWidth"
sqltypes:sqlSortId="52">
            <xsd:maxLength value="50" />
          </xsd:restriction>
```

```
        </xsd:simpleType>
      </xsd:attribute>
      <xsd:attribute name="LastName" use="required">
        <xsd:simpleType sqltypes:sqlTypeAlias="[AdventureWorks].[dbo].[Name]">
          <xsd:restriction base="sqltypes:nvarchar" sqltypes:localeId="1033"
sqltypes:sqlCompareOptions="IgnoreCase IgnoreKanaType IgnoreWidth"
sqltypes:sqlSortId="52">
            <xsd:maxLength value="50" />
          </xsd:restriction>
        </xsd:simpleType>
      </xsd:attribute>
    </xsd:complexType>
  </xsd:element>
</xsd:schema>

<Person.Contact xmlns="urn:schemas-microsoft-com:sql:SqlRowSet1" ContactID="218"
FirstName="Scott" LastName="Colvin" />
```

Things to Watch Out For

In dealing with XML, it is possible to have attributes and elements with the same name. For example, the following is perfectly acceptable in XML:

```
<Employee>
  <FirstName>Howard</FirstName>
  <LastName>Hughes</LastName>
    <Supervisor>
      <FirstName>Daffy</FirstName>
      <LastName>Duck</LastName>
    </Supervisor>
</Employee>
```

To test this, run the following query:

```
DECLARE @test xml
SET @test = '<Employee>
 <FirstName>Howard</FirstName>
 <LastName>Hughes</LastName>
  <Supervisor>
   <FirstName>Daffy</FirstName>
   <LastName>Duck</LastName>
  </Supervisor>
</Employee>'
SELECT @test
```

When you run this query, you get the XML shown at the beginning of this section. However, the following query generates an error trying to deal with the same-name columns:

```
SELECT Contact.ContactID,
       SalesOrderHeader.SalesOrderID,
       SalesOrderHeader.ContactID,
       Contact.FirstName
```

```
FROM   Sales.SalesOrderHeader, Person.Contact
WHERE  SalesOrderHeader.ContactID = Contact.ContactID
AND    Contact.ContactID = 218
FOR XML RAW, XMLSCHEMA
```

The solution to this is to simply add the ELEMENTS directive to the FOR XML statement, like so:

```
SELECT Contact.ContactID,
       SalesOrderHeader.SalesOrderID,
       SalesOrderHeader.ContactID,
       Contact.FirstName
FROM   Sales.SalesOrderHeader, Person.Contact
WHERE  SalesOrderHeader.ContactID = Contact.ContactID
AND    Contact.ContactID = 218
FOR XML RAW, XMLSCHEMA, ELEMENTS
```

It is important to remember that using the XSINIL directive is permitted when generating schemas. If a column returns a NULL value it is not included in the schema if the directive is not included. Adding the XSINIL directive ensures that both columns are returned in the results, as well as included in the schema. The following example illustrates this:

```
SELECT Contact.ContactID,
       SalesOrderHeader.SalesOrderID,
       SalesOrderHeader.ContactID,
       Contact.FirstName
       Contact.MiddleName
FROM   Sales.SalesOrderHeader, Person.Contact
WHERE  SalesOrderHeader.ContactID = Contact.ContactID
AND    Contact.ContactID = 226
FOR XML RAW, XMLSCHEMA, ELEMENTS XSINIL
```

The example specifies that if any values returned from the query are found, to still include an element for that value. In this example, the MiddleName column does not have a value, but the column is still included with the following value:

```
<MiddleName xsi:nil="true" />
```

That covers the FOR XML changes. Microsoft made a number of OPENXML changes as well, so on to that.

OPENXML

Two improvements were made to the OPENXML clause in SQL Server 2005. The first is the capability to pass an xml data type to the sp_xml_preparedocument stored procedure. The second enhancement is the capability to use the new data types in the WITH clause.

In the following example, the @xmlvar variable is declared as an xml data type and filled with an XML document, which is then passed to the sp_xml_preparedocument stored procedure. The OPENXML statement is then used to query the XML document to retrieve the Employee attribute of all three employees:

```
DECLARE @xmldocDoc int
DECLARE @xmlvar xml
SET @xmlvar = N'<ROOT>
<Employee EmployeeID="1" ManagerID="2" NationalIDNumber="10708100">
   <Tenor Position="AltoTenor" Solo="Io Conosco un Giardino">
      <FirstName>José</FirstName>
      <LastName>Carreras</LastName>
   </Tenor>
</Employee>
<Employee EmployeeID="2" ManagerID="3" NationalIDNumber="112432117">
   <Tenor Position="BaritoneTenor" Solo="Memories de Danton">
      <FirstName>Plácido</FirstName>
      <LastName>Domingo</LastName>
   </Tenor>
</Employee>
<Employee EmployeeID="3" ManagerID="3" NationalIDNumber="112432117">
   <Tenor Position="Tenor" Solo="Granada">
      <FirstName>Luciano</FirstName>
      <LastName>Pavarotti</LastName>
   </Tenor>
</Employee>
</ROOT>'
-- Create an internal representation of the XML document.
EXEC sp_xml_preparedocument @xmldocDoc OUTPUT, @xmlvar
-- Execute a SELECT statement using OPENXML rowset provider.
SELECT *
FROM OPENXML (@xmldocDoc, '/ROOT/Employee',1)
      WITH (EmployeeID  int,
            ManagerID int,
            NationalIDNumber varchar(15))
EXEC sp_xml_removedocument @xmldocDoc
```

The results of the SELECT statement are shown in Figure 8-23.

	EmployeeID	ManagerID	NationalIDNumber
1	1	2	10708100
2	2	3	112432117
3	3	3	112432117

Figure 8-23

The example demonstrates both enhancements to the OPENXML statement by passing an xml data type variable to the sp_xml_preparedocument stored procedure, and by using the new data types in the WITH clause.

Finally, make the following modifications to the example code:

```
DECLARE @xmldocDoc int
DECLARE @xmlvar xml
SET @xmlvar = N'<ROOT>
<Employee EmployeeID="1" ManagerID="2" NationalIDNumber="10708100">
   <Tenor Position="AltoTenor" Solo="Io Conosco un Giardino">
      <FirstName>José</FirstName>
```

```
      <LastName>Carreras</LastName>
   </Tenor>
</Employee>
<Employee EmployeeID="2" ManagerID="3" NationalIDNumber="112432117">
   <Tenor Position="BaritoneTenor" Solo="Memories de Danton">
      <FirstName>Plácido</FirstName>
      <LastName>Domingo</LastName>
   </Tenor>
</Employee>
<Employee EmployeeID="3" ManagerID="3" NationalIDNumber="112432117">
   <Tenor Position="Tenor" Solo="Granada">
      <FirstName>Luciano</FirstName>
      <LastName>Pavarotti</LastName>
   </Tenor>
</Employee>
</ROOT>'
-- Create an internal representation of the XML document.
EXEC sp_xml_preparedocument @xmldocDoc OUTPUT, @xmlvar
-- Execute a SELECT statement using OPENXML rowset provider.
SELECT *
FROM OPENXML (@xmldocDoc, '/ROOT/Employee/Tenor',1)
      WITH (Position varchar(15),
            Solo varchar(15))
EXEC sp_xml_removedocument @xmldocDoc
```

Now rerun the query. You should see results similar to those shown in Figure 8-24.

	Position	Solo
1	Alto Tenor	lo Conosco un G
2	Baritone Tenor	Memories de Dan
3	Tenor	Granada

Figure 8-24

Using the `OPENXML` clause to go deeper into the XML document, the `Position` and `Solo` attributes were queried and returned, as displayed in the figure.

Summary

In this chapter, you learned about the new improvements to the `FOR XML` and `OPENXML` statements. The `FOR XML` statement comes packed with a lot of new functionality that makes shaping your data and creating XML instances much easier.

The `PATH` mode, as you learned, is much easier to learn than the `EXPLICIT` mode, and the results are just as pleasing with a lot shorter learning curve. The `TYPE` directive is a very nice addition as well, giving you the option of returning the query results as an `xml` data type, with very little restriction. The enhancements to the `RAW` and `AUTO` modes, specifically the capability to specify the root element, return element-centric XML, and specify the row element name come in very useful when you want to determine the shape of your XML results.

Of all the excellent features in this chapter, the two most important are the capability to automatically generate schemas and nesting FOR XML queries. These two alone should make any developer's life infinitely easier, and probably should put the EXPLICIT mode out of business.

Not as many enhancements were made to OPENXML, but the few that were made were very nice, such as the addition of a capability to pass xml data type to the sp_xml_preparedocument stored procedure.

The next chapter discusses CLR enhancements in SQL Server 2005 and how those enhancements benefit you when dealing with XML in SQL Server.

9

CLR Support in SQL Server 2005

If you really look at some of the biggest improvements made to SQL Server 2005, the top two would have to be the addition of native support for the `xml` data type and the integration of the Common Language Runtime (CLR). It's up to you to decide which improvement is most important, but regardless of the order, you have to admit that these are the top two from the developer's perspective.

What is the CLR? Good question. The CLR is the heart and soul of the Microsoft .NET Framework. It provides the environment for the execution of all the .NET Framework code. The CLR is also the foundation for many of the built-in services that are required for your programs to run, such as exception handling, thread and memory management, and JIT (just-in-time compilation — code is compiled when it is needed).

A term that you need to remember is *managed code*. What is managed code? Any code that runs within the CLR is called managed code. When it is compiled, managed code compiles down to native code, which means better performance. Why is this important? By integrating the CLR into SQL Server, developers can now write stored procedures and other objects, compile them into managed code, and use them right from SQL Server.

This does not mean that Microsoft has set out to put every DBA out of job, so before all you DBAs out there panic, continue reading, especially the section "The Great Debate." However, neither this chapter nor this book discusses the CLR in any great detail. There are already books out there that do that.

Up until this chapter, the focus of the book has been on the native `xml` data type support. However, this chapter changes direction and focuses on the integration of the CLR in SQL Server 2005.

When your boss comes to you and says that he or she heard that SQL Server 2005 comes with CLR integration and asks you what you think about using it in some of your application development, how will you answer?

You can't really expect to learn everything there is about the integration of the CLR in a single chapter. That is why this chapter is merely an overview, or introduction, to the integration of the CLR in SQL Server 2005. Integration of the CLR is introduced here as a preface to later chapters in the book, which go into more detail about the topics introduced here, and to simply whet your appetite.

The topics discussed in this chapter are the following:

- Overview of Common Language Runtime integration
- T-SQL language limitations
- Introduction to managed code
- Advantages of CLR integration
- Choosing between T-SQL and managed code
- Security

The Great Debate

The integration of the CLR in SQL Server 2005 has caused a great stir in the development community, both from database administrators and developers as well as the developers writing the front-end application. There have been great debates from those who are for the integration as well as from those who are against the integration, from database administrators and developers alike.

Many rumblings have come from those who say that the integration of the CLR into SQL Server signifies the demise of T-SQL, while the other side of the camp wonders if the integration was even necessary (and possibly dangerous). This book does not jump onto either bandwagon, but rather presents the material in such a way that you will be able to make your own decision, one that is best for your applications.

The purpose of this chapter (and other chapters later in the book) is not to persuade you one way or the other, but rather to give you the information you need to make an intelligent decision of when and how to use the CLR over T-SQL and vice versa. Follow-up chapters later in the book dig into the detail on how to use the CLR in SQL Server 2005.

Nearly every developer, whether they are a SQL or front-end object-oriented developer, agrees that T-SQL is great at data access and the manipulation of that data at the database. SQL Server is awesome — most developers can agree with that. But these same developers should also admit that it is not as complete of a programming language as C# or Visual Basic .NET. The SQL programming language is built around data access and data manipulation at the database level. It does a tremendous job of that, but it has its limitations. This is where an object-oriented programming language can step in and complement T-SQL. Not replace, complement.

Integration Overview

The integration of CLR provides database programmers with the capability to include and use business-oriented languages such as C# and Visual Basic .NET within SQL Server 2005. Using this new integration, database developers can now create database objects such as stored procedures, triggers, and user-defined functions using these common business oriented languages as an alternative to T-SQL.

This integration provides functionality not found before in SQL Server, such as preemptive threading and memory garbage collection (returning unused memory back to the operating system). While SQL Server and the CLR differ in the way they handle issues such as threads and memory, understanding their integration can be an advantage to you as a developer when trying to get the most of your application.

The goals of integrating the CLR in SQL Server 2005 come down to a handful of items. Listed in no particular order, they are as follows:

- Scalability
- Reliability
- Performance
- Security
- Memory management services (such as garbage collection)

Scalability

As mentioned previously, SQL Server and the CLR both have different mechanisms for handling memory and other processes. When running user code inside SQL Server, the last thing you want to do is degrade performance by causing a conflict between two competing processes. For example, SQL Server uses a non-preemptive threading (threads occasionally yield execution) model whereas the CLR uses a preemptive threading model. Another example, the CLR cannot tell the difference between physical and virtual memory, but SQL Server can, because physical memory limits can be set and memory is therefore managed by SQL Server.

Careful thought must be given when writing user code that operates inside SQL Server. Any user code dealing with things like memory and threading will conflict with the same functionality in SQL Server and cause serious scalability issues.

Reliability

Also known as safety, reliability states that any code running in the CLR should not compromise the integrity of the SQL Server database engine in which the process is running. An example of this is a process that changes the structure of a database.

Performance

What good does it do to run .NET code in SQL Server that runs worse than its T-SQL equivalent? Any managed code running in SQL Server must perform as well as, or better than the native T-SQL code.

By taking advantage of the CLR in SQL Server, you can take advantage of the fact that both the data and the code are brought closer together. By doing this, you are taking advantage of the processing power of the server and in many cases you will see an increase in performance.

Security

Any user code running in SQL Server needs a way to access machine resources that are outside of the database engine. One of the main security reasons for utilizing the CLR in SQL Server is that much less data needs to leave the server, lessening the risk of exposing your data.

Managed code running in the database needs to adhere to the same authentication and authorization rules as access database objects such as tables or stored procedures. This ensures that no unwanted processes can gain access to the database engine and database components without going through the correct channels.

Later on in the book, Chapter 21 to be exact, you will learn about Assemblies in SQL Server 2005. As a quick introduction, an assembly is a SQL Server hosted DLL or EXE that when created in SQL Server has one of three levels of security in which context the assembly can run. As you will learn later, each level of security either strengthens or lessens the security context in which the assembly is run. This will have a definite impact on how you utilize the CLR security in your environment, so don't skip that chapter.

Limitations of T-SQL

Most diehard T-SQL developers will tell you that whatever you can do in .NET can be done in T-SQL, and they might go as far as to say that they can do it better. While the validity of that statement will be argued until the end of time, the reality is that other programming languages, such as C# and Visual Basic, are more complete.

That is not to say that T-SQL is inferior by any means. Previously this chapter mentioned what T-SQL did well, and that was data access and set-based operations within a database. In fact, in SQL Server 2005, you have the ability to do *recursive* queries, which is the capability of a common table expression to reference itself. SQL Server 2005 also comes with new analytical functions (such as `RANK` and `ROW_NUMBER`) and relational operators (such as `APPLY`, `PIVOT`, and `UNPIVOT`), which are used to manipulate table-valued expressions into another table.

All of these new features in SQL Server 2005 prove that T-SQL continues to grow and is taken seriously. ANSI SQL is based on open standards that are not owned by a single company, making it easy to be used with any RDBMS that complies with the ANSI standards.

That said, though, SQL Server does have its limitations. For example, the following cannot be done in T-SQL but can easily be done in .NET:

- Arrays
- Collections
- `FOR EACH` loops
- Classes

While this list is by no means complete, it gives you an idea of the major differences between T-SQL and other matured programming languages.

For example, to loop through a list of Product records using T-SQL, a `CURSOR` is required, as shown in the following example:

```
Use AdventureWorks
GO
DECLARE Product_Cursor CURSOR FOR
SELECT ProductID, Name
FROM Production.Product
WHERE Color IS NOT NULL
ORDER BY Name

OPEN Product_Cursor

FETCH NEXT FROM Product_Cursor
WHILE @@FETCH_STATUS = 0
BEGIN
  --DO SOMETHING WITH THE DATA
  FETCH NEXT FROM Product_Cursor
END

CLOSE Product_Cursor
DEALLOCATE Product_Cursor
```

To accomplish this same thing in .NET requires the following:

```
Module Module1
 Sub Main()
  Dim tsql As String = "SELECT ProductID, Name FROM Production.Product WHERE Color
IS NOT NULL ORDER BY Name"

  Dim connstr As String =
"Provider=SQLOLEDB;Server=(local);Database=AdventureWorks;UID=sa;PWD=hackthis"

  Dim conn As New OleDb.OleDbConnection(connstr)
  Dim cmd As New OleDb.OleDbCommand(tsql, conn)

  Try
    conn.Open()

    Dim rdr As OleDb.OleDbDataReader = cmd.ExecuteReader()

    For Each rdr.Item In rdr.c
      rdr.Read()
      Console.WriteLine(rdr.Item(0) + ", " & rdr.Item(1))
    Next

    rdr.Close()
  Catch ex As Exception
    Console.WriteLine(ex.Message.ToString())
  Finally
    conn.Close()
  End Try
 End Sub
End Module
```

The purpose of this section was certainly not to paint the T-SQL language as an inferior language. Actually, it was the opposite: T-SQL is a strong and powerful language for data access and manipulation. The new features in SQL Server 2005 discussed here can attest to that. The integration of the CLR is there as a complement to the already strong SQL language, making it that much stronger. So breathe a sigh of relief DBAs; you're not out of a job.

Introduction to Managed Code

Managed code is simply code that runs within the CLR. Prior to SQL Server 2005, it was not possible to mix database engine processes with the CLR with any amount of success, but SQL Server 2005 has integrated the CLR and provides the capability to run safe user code within the confines of a database engine process.

Every CLR-compliant language compiles its code down to what is called MSIL, or Microsoft Intermediate Language. The CLR can run this compiled source code because implementation differences are gone, regardless of how it is used or presented in the specific language. For example, a `system.string` in one language is a `system.string` in another language when it is compiled.

COM (Component Object Model) was the first great step in not having to write everything from the ground up. COM supplied the foundation for the higher-level software and services. It allowed you to build your application by using components written by others. For example, you could buy a third-party grid or calendar control so you didn't have to create one from scratch. It sped up application development and provided functionality you would have had to otherwise spend the time to develop yourself.

As cool as it is, COM has its limitations. Have you ever tried to pass a string value from a VB application to a C++ application? Typically the work had to be done on the C++ side because VB hates working outside the box.

These limitations don't exist with the CLR and managed code. Even better, running managed code within the CLR has been extended to SQL Server 2005. If you have done any work with the .NET Framework and the CLR, you know how easy it is to work with.

With the CLR integrated into SQL Server 2005, this same flexibility is accessible from right inside the database engine, providing the capability to write stored procedures, triggers, and user-defined functions in managed code. And don't forget user-defined types and aggregates. For example, you can use .NET to create your own type and use it in SQL Server (you'll see an example of this in Chapter 22).

Take the following code, for example:

```
Imports System
Imports System.Data
Imports System.Data.Sql
Imports System.Data.SqlServer
Imports System.Data.SqlTypes

Public Class SampleTestClass
  <SqlProcedure>
```

```
    Public Shared Sub TestMessage()

      Microsoft.SqlServer.Server.SqlContext.Pipe().Send("This Stuff ROCKS!")
    End Sub
  End Class
```

You can compile this simple class into a CLR stored procedure and, using an assembly, execute it via a standard T-SQL stored procedure.

This simple example walks you through how to do just that. Open Visual Studio 2005 and select Create New Project. The New Project screen, depicted in Figure 9-1, is displayed. Under Project Types on the left side of the screen, select Database. Then in the Templates section on the right, select SQL Server Project. Give the project a name (such as TestAssembly), browse to where you want to save the project, and then click OK.

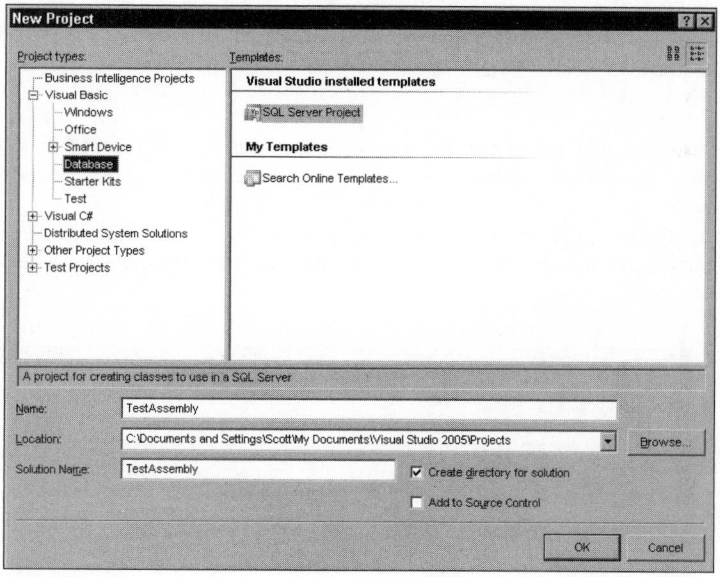

Figure 9-1

After clicking OK, you might get a new dialog window named New Database Reference. This dialog is used to inform your project which SQL Server you want to deploy your project to. The only information required is the server name where SQL Server 2005 is running, the username and password you want to use to connect, and the database in which to deploy your project. After you fill in that information, click OK. The project is then created in Visual Studio.

After the project is created, right-click the solution name in the Solution Explorer window, select Add, and then select New Item from the menu. This opens the Add New Item dialog shown in Figure 9-2.

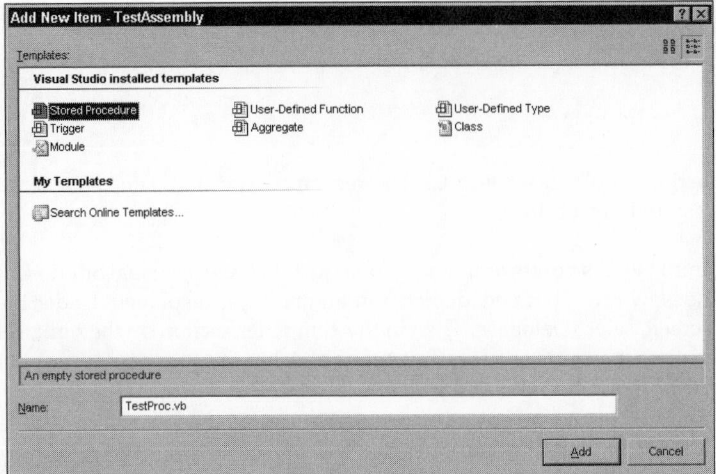

Figure 9-2

In the Add New Item dialog, select Stored Procedure and then give the stored procedure a name. In this example, the stored procedure is called TestProc. After you name the stored procedure, click Add.

When you click Add, Visual Studio automatically opens and displays your stored procedure with a lot of the necessary code already filled in. Figure 9-3 shows what the template looks like when it is first opened and displayed.

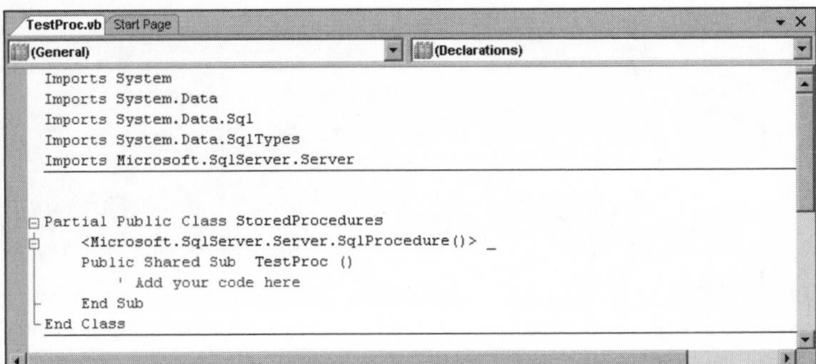

Figure 9-3

The two lines of code to pay attention to in the figure are the following:

```
<Microsoft.SqlServer.Server.SqlProcedure()>
Public Shared Sub TestProc ()
```

The first line tells this assembly that when compiled, it will be compiled into a stored procedure. The second line is the name of the stored procedure when compiled, `TestProc`.

Add the line of code shown in Figure 9-4. Notice that the code in the figure looks similar to the sample code presented at the beginning of this section.

```
TestProc.vb | Start Page
StoredProcedures | TestProc

Imports System
Imports System.Data
Imports System.Data.Sql
Imports System.Data.SqlTypes
Imports Microsoft.SqlServer.Server

Partial Public Class StoredProcedures
    <Microsoft.SqlServer.Server.SqlProcedure()> _
    Public Shared Sub  TestProc ()
        ' Add your code here
        Microsoft.SqlServer.Server.SqlContext.Pipe.Send("This Stuff ROCKS!")
    End Sub
End Class
```

Figure 9-4

The next step is to build the solution, which compiles this code into a DLL (referred to as the *assembly*) behind the scenes. From the Build menu, select Build Solution, as shown in Figure 9-5.

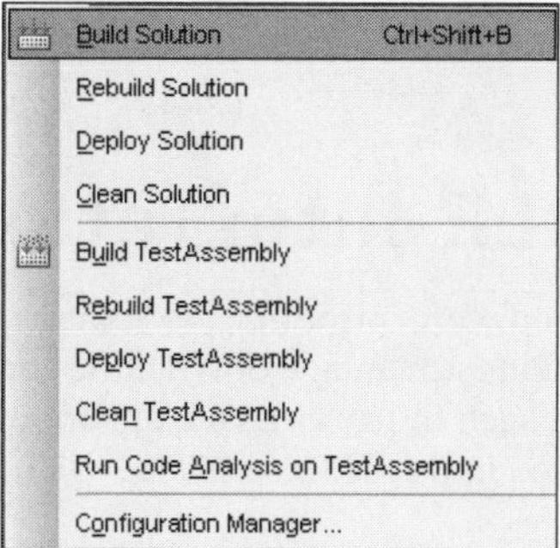

Figure 9-5

The final step in this process is to deploy the assembly. Deploying the assembly automatically creates the assembly reference and the stored procedure in SQL Server 2005. From the Build menu, select Deploy Solution, as shown in Figure 9-6.

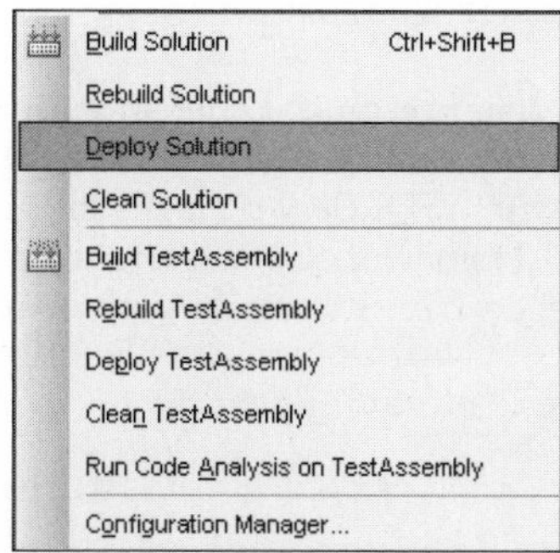

Figure 9-6

Open Microsoft SQL Server Management Studio and open a new query window. Be sure to select the database in which the assembly was deployed. In the query window, execute the following T-SQL statement:

```
EXEC TestProc
```

Figure 9-7 shows the T-SQL statement and the results of the execution of the stored procedure.

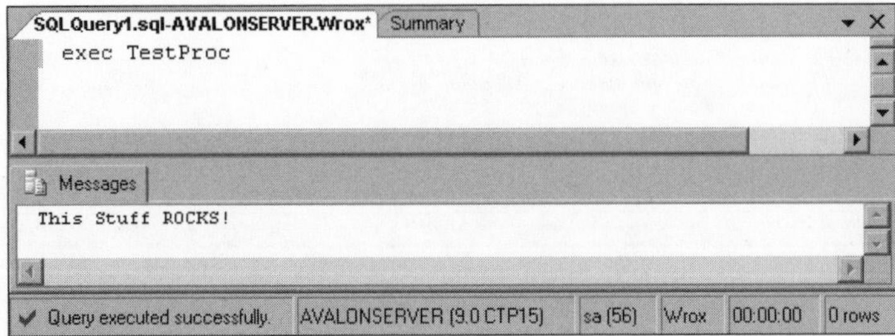

Figure 9-7

While this example was quick and easy, it does a very good job of showing the capabilities of developing SQL Server objects using the .NET Framework.

Advantages of CLR Integration

At the beginning of the chapter, you were introduced to some of the limitations of T-SQL and how those limitations are better served by taking advantage of what the CLR provides. You saw a small list of the shortcomings of T-SQL, including such things as a lack of support for arrays, collections, and other things that are more than supported in the CLR.

This section briefly discusses some of the advantages of using managed code over T-SQL. What you need to understand is that, while there are some definite advantages of using CLR over T-SQL, it is not a "fix all" for every situation or scenario.

T-SQL is specifically designed for quick data access, manipulation, and data management. It is exceptionally good at that. It was not designed, however, to provide support for collections, arrays, or classes, for example. As stated previously, this type of functionality can be imitated using T-SQL, but there are typically performance issues associated with that.

Managed code offers what T-SQL does not: much better support for string manipulation and complex logic, thus bridging the gap between what SQL doesn't do well and what .NET does well, and offering real object-oriented functionality within SQL Server via the integration of the CLR into SQL Server 2005. All of the functionality in the .NET Framework can now be accessed via managed code within SQL Server. Stored procedures and triggers have full access to any class in the .NET Framework, which was not accessible before.

The CLR interrogates all user code before it is executed to verify that it is safe, meaning that it won't break anything when it executes, something that SQL Server does not do. For example, the CLR checks to make sure that any user code being executed does not read into memory that has already been read and written to.

The integration of the CLR also provides some object-oriented capabilities that are not provided in SQL Server 2005. Encapsulation, inheritance, and polymorphism are three object-oriented features that currently do not exist in SQL Server. Each of these is defined in the following list:

- **Encapsulation:** The capability to contain and control a group of related items. For example, a class can contain a number of related methods and properties, controlled by the class. All the methods, properties, and events are treated as a single object.
- **Inheritance:** The capability for one class to *inherit* from another class. In other words, inheritance is the ability to create a new class based on an already existing class. For example, if class B inherits from class A, class B gains access to all the methods and properties of class A, plus any others that it has defined itself.
- **Polymorphism:** The capability to have multiple classes, each with its own methods and properties, which are used in distinct ways even though the names of the methods or properties are the same. A base class may have a method called `GetEmployeeInfo`, for example. Polymorphism lets you create one or more classes from the base class with each new class implementing its own version of the `GetEmployeeInfo` method, with each class being used interchangeably.

Even though these three features do not exist in SQL Server 2005, the CLR extends this function to SQL Server through the CLR integration and provides an extra benefit to the already excellent features of SQL Server.

With all of this information in mind, you must wonder how to choose between T-SQL and the CLR. Well, read on.

Choosing Between T-SQL and Managed Code

With the integration of the CLR in SQL Server 2005, the line that separates what is commonly known as the Business Logic Tier and the Data Tier just got a little fuzzier. That certainly is not meant to be taken negatively; it just means that you will need to do a little more homework when choosing where to do what, and your homework just got a little more complicated.

Choosing where to put middle tier logic and database access logic was fairly easy. It is not so obvious now with the CLR being integrated into SQL Server, but with that comes added functionality and flexibility that can certainly enhance your applications.

Choosing between T-SQL and managed code is not a cut and dried decision. As explained previously, T-SQL does some things phenomenally well, and managed code does other things well. That doesn't mean you should throw all data retrieval functionality into a T-SQL stored procedure.

When doing data retrieval, T-SQL is the way to go. Leave the data manipulation to the managed code side of things — those tasks that SQL doesn't do well — especially if there is complex logic being processed on the returned data. Many developers make decisions like this based on the amount of data being handled. For example, if you know that a certain call to the database always returns a single record, why put that in a stored procedure? Obviously there are other things to consider, such as compiled execution plans that SQL Server provides, but every situation is different and more research is required to find the best-laid plan.

The other thing to take into consideration is where the code is executed. Is the client the best place for certain logic, or does that same logic perform better on the server? With SQL Server 2005, both T-SQL and managed code can be run on the server, bringing the added benefit of server processing power, as well as shortening the gap between data and code. Is your application web-based or Windows-based? This also has an effect on where the logic is placed.

Don't discount the client, as workstation computers are very well powered and can handle a lot of the application processing without bringing the workstation to its knees. This means that a lot of the application processing can be offloaded to the client, freeing up the server for other tasks.

Keep in mind that managed code can run on either the client or the server, but T-SQL can only run on the server.

Security

There are now two security models inside SQL Server 2005. The first is the SQL Server security model, which is built around user-authentication. This is not new — it has been in place since way back. The second security model is the CLR security model, which is a code-access security model. Both of these are combined to support all the features of both SQL Server and the CLR inside SQL Server 2005.

The combination of the two security models secures access between both CLR and non-CLR objects operating in SQL Server. When a call is made between objects running on the server, both models may step in to manage the security of the objects. The calls between these objects are called *links*. There are three types of links:

- Invocation
- Table-access
- Gated

Invocation

Invocation links refer to the invocation of code. This could be from, for example, a CLR stored procedure being executed, or a user calling a T-SQL stored procedure. `EXECUTE` permissions are checked when these types of links are executed.

Table-Access

Table-access links refer to the retrieval or modification of data in a table, view, or value-function. These types of links require `INSERT`, `SELECT`, `DELETE`, or `UPDATE` permissions.

Gated

In gated links, permissions are not checked once relationships have been verified. When a link is made between two objects, permissions on the second object are checked only at the creation of the first object.

In SQL Server 2000, gated links are used for computed columns and fulltext-indexed columns. In SQL Server 2005, gated links are used in the CLR to define a T-SQL entry point into assemblies. This simply means that in order to execute a T-SQL entry point in a CLR-defined assembly, only appropriate permissions are checked on the T-SQL entry point and not the assembly.

CLR Security Integration Goals

Integrating the CLR into SQL Server 2005 was a large process, and the following security goals were at the top of the list:

- Any managed code running in SQL Server should not compromise the integrity and stability of SQL Server.
- Any managed code running in SQL Server should not have unauthorized access to data or other code in the database.
- There should be a method for restricting user code from accessing resources outside of the server.
- Any user code running in SQL Server should not have unauthorized access to system resources simply by running in a SQL Server engine process.

Summary

The same question posed to you at the beginning of the chapter is now asked of you again. If your boss comes to you and says that he heard that SQL Server 2005 comes with CLR integration and asks you what you think about using it in some of your application development, how will you answer now?

Let's hope your answer will be a simple, "It depends," as you then explain to him or her that simply utilizing this technology may not be the best solution for you application and that you need to perform careful research before jumping in.

Using the CLR in SQL Server 2005 can be a great benefit to your application if used wisely and appropriately in certain situations. Finding that "certain situation" takes time, but it can add great benefits when you find it. This chapter marks the end of the section on server-side XML processing.

The next several chapters deal with client-side XML processing. Chapter 10 specifically covers client-side support for the `xml` data type.

Part III: Client-Side XML Processing in SQL Server 2005

10

Client-Side Support for the xml data type

The last nine chapters have focused primarily on the `xml` data type within SQL Server 2005, from the `xml` data type itself to indexing and querying the `xml` data type. By now you should have a good grasp of the `xml` data type from the perspective of SQL Server. It is now time to change focus and look at it from the other side, the client side.

This part of the book deals strictly with XML from the client side, starting with this chapter, which discusses client-side support for the `xml` data type and introduces the `SqlXml` class. The `SqlXml` class is the means by which the client can interface with the `xml` data type.

In this chapter, the following topics will be discussed:

- The `SqlXml` class and the `CreateReader` method
- Updating and inserting data with the `SqlXml` class

SqlXml Class

The `SqlXml` class is a new class in the `System.Data.SqlTypes` namespace. This class represents XML data retrieved from, or stored in, SQL Server.

One of the benefits of the `SqlXml` class is that it contains an instance of the `XmlReader`-derived type, providing fast, forward-only access to XML data. The `SqlXml` class implements the `INullable` interface, allowing `SqlTypes` to contain null values.

The general syntax for using the `SqlXml` class is as follows:

```
Dim xml As SqlXml = SqlDataReader.GetSqlXml([column/index])
```

The `SqlXml` class, a method of the `SqlDataReader` class, returns the value of a specified column as an XML value. It takes a zero-based column ordinal that specifies the column whose data you want to return.

There are various methods available to the `SqlXml` class, but the most important method when dealing with XML is the `CreateReader` method, which is outlined in the following section.

Introducing the CreateReader Method

The `CreateReader` method is a public method on the `SqlXml` class. It is what gets or returns the value of the XML, always in the form of an `XmlReader`. It supports XML documents as well as XML fragments.

The general syntax for using the `CreateReader` method is as follows:

```
Dim sdr As SqlDataReader
Dim xml As SqlXml = sdr.GetSqlXml(0)
Dim xmlrdr As XmlReader = xml.CreateReader
```

The first line creates an instance of the `SqlDataReader`. The second line creates an instance of the `SqlXml` class. The third line uses the `CreateReader` method of the `SqlXml` class to create an `XmlReader`. The `XmlReader` can then be used to read and parse through XML documents and fragments.

Using the SqlXml Class

Before the example begins, the table and data need to be created and populated.

Open a query window in SQL Server Management Studio and execute the following T-SQL statements:

```
DROP TABLE Motocross
GO
CREATE TABLE Motocross (
  [TeamID]  [int] IDENTITY(1,1) NOT NULL,
  [TeamInfo] [xml] NULL,
CONSTRAINT [PK_Motocross] PRIMARY KEY CLUSTERED
(
  [TeamID] ASC
) ON [PRIMARY]
) ON [PRIMARY]
GO

INSERT INTO MOTOCROSS (TeamInfo)
VALUES ('
<Motocross>
  <Team Manufacturer="Yamaha">
    <Rider>
      <Name Class="250">Chad Reed</Name>
      <Number>22</Number>
```

```
    </Rider>
    <Rider>
      <Name Class="250">David Vuillemin</Name>
      <Number>12</Number>
    </Rider>
    <Rider>
      <Name Class="250">Tim Ferry</Name>
      <Number>15</Number>
    </Rider>
    <Rider>
      <Name Class="125">Kelly Smith</Name>
      <Number>123</Number>
    </Rider>
    <Rider>
      <Name Class="125">Brock Sellards</Name>
      <Number>18</Number>
    </Rider>
    <Rider>
      <Name Class="125">Brett Metcalf</Name>
      <Number>256</Number>
    </Rider>
    <Rider>
      <Name Class="125">Danny Smith</Name>
      <Number>31</Number>
    </Rider>
  </Team>
</Motocross> ')
GO

INSERT INTO MOTOCROSS (TeamInfo)
VALUES ('
<Motocross>
  <Team Manufacturer="Kawasaki">
    <Rider>
      <Name Class="250">James Stewart</Name>
      <Number>259</Number>
    </Rider>
    <Rider>
      <Name Class="250">Michael Byrne</Name>
      <Number>26</Number>
    </Rider>
  </Team>
</Motocross> ')
GO

INSERT INTO MOTOCROSS (TeamInfo)
VALUES ('
<Motocross>
  <Team Manufacturer="Suzuki">
    <Rider>
      <Name Class="250">Ricky Carmichael</Name>
      <Number>4</Number>
    </Rider>
    <Rider>
      <Name Class="125">Davi Millsaps</Name>
```

```
        <Number>188</Number>
      </Rider>
      <Rider>
        <Name Class="125">Broc Hepler</Name>
        <Number>60</Number>
      </Rider>
      <Rider>
        <Name Class="250">Sebastien Tortelli</Name>
        <Number>103</Number>
      </Rider>
    </Team>
</Motocross> ')
GO

INSERT INTO MOTOCROSS (TeamInfo)
VALUES ('
<Motocross>
  <Team Manufacturer="Honda">
    <Rider>
      <Name Class="250">Jeremy McGrath</Name>
      <Number>2</Number>
    </Rider>
    <Rider>
      <Name Class="250">Ernesto Fonseca</Name>
      <Number>24</Number>
    </Rider>
    <Rider>
      <Name Class="250">Travis Preston</Name>
      <Number>70</Number>
    </Rider>
    <Rider>
      <Name Class="250">Andrew Short</Name>
      <Number>51</Number>
    </Rider>
  </Team>
</Motocross> ')
GO
```

Now that the data is in place, you are ready to write some code. Open the Visual Studio test application you have been using and open the main form in Design View. Add a new button and text box to the form. Set the following properties for the button:

Property	Value
`Text`	`SqlXml` Class
`Name`	`cmdSqlXml`
`Location`	12, 12

Next, set the properties for the text box as follows:

Property	Value
Name	txtResults
Multiline	True
ScrollBars	Vertical
Location	12, 62
Size	446, 196

With the properties set on the controls, double-click on the button to view the code behind it.

To begin the example, first make sure that the following `Imports` statements are declared in your form in the declaration section:

```
Imports System.Data.SqlClient
Imports System.Data.SqlTypes
Imports System.Xml
```

Next, add the following code in the `click` event of the button:

```
Dim Connection As SqlConnection
Dim Command As SqlCommand

Connection = New SqlConnection
Command = New SqlCommand

Try
  'ENTER YOUR OWN USER NAME AND PASSWORD
  Connection.ConnectionString = "Server=localhost;Database=Wrox;UID=;PWD="

  Connection.Open()

  Command.Connection = Connection
  Command.CommandText = "SELECT TeamInfo FROM Motocross"

  Dim r As SqlDataReader = Command.ExecuteReader
  r.Read()

  Dim xml As SqlXml = r.GetSqlXml(0)
  Dim xmlrdr As XmlReader = xml.CreateReader
  xmlrdr.Read()
  Me.txtResults.Text = xmlrdr.ReadOuterXml()

Catch ex As Exception
  MessageBox.Show(ex.Message)
End Try

Command.Dispose()
Connection.Close()
```

Run the project by pressing F5 or by selecting Start Debugging from the Debug menu. When the form comes up, click the `SqlXml Class` button. Figure 10-1 shows the results of the query.

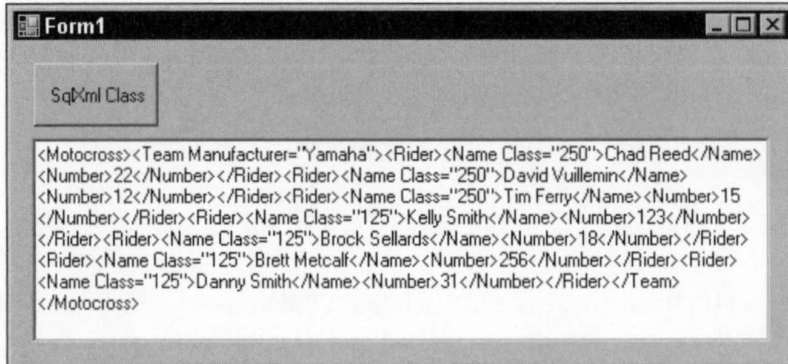

Figure 10-1

In this example, the `SqlDataReader` reads the selected rows from the Motocross table, and then the `GetSqlXml` method is called to retrieve the value from the first column (specified by the value `0`). The `CreateReader` method is then created from the `SqlXml` class to retrieve the XML content of the `SqlXml` as an `XmlReader`, which allows for the reading of the access and reading of the XML document content. The retrieved XML content is then displayed in the text box as shown in the previous figure.

In the example, the results displayed only the first record retrieved from the table, but in actuality all four records were returned by the query. The four records can be displayed by simply looping through the result set and displaying the XML by modifying the code from the example.

The `SqlDataReader`, `XmlReader`, and `SqlXml` class are still necessary to return the data as before, but this time it is necessary loop through the result set.

Modify the `Click` event code for the SqlXml button as follows:

```
Dim Connection As SqlConnection
Dim Command As SqlCommand

Connection = New SqlConnection
Command = New SqlCommand

Try

  'ENTER YOUR OWN USER NAME AND PASSWORD
  Connection.ConnectionString = "Server=vssql2005;Database=Wrox;UID=;PWD="

  Connection.Open()

  Command.Connection = Connection
  Command.CommandText = "SELECT TeamInfo FROM Motocross"

  Dim r As SqlDataReader = Command.ExecuteReader
  Dim xml As SqlXml
  Dim xmlrdr As XmlReader
  Dim StrVal As String = ""
```

```
        Do While r.Read()
          xml = r.GetSqlXml(0)
          xmlrdr = xml.CreateReader
          xmlrdr.Read()
          StrVal += xmlrdr.ReadOuterXml() + Chr(13) + "-----------------------" + Chr(13)
        Loop
        Me.txtResults.Text = StrVal

      Catch ex As Exception
      MessageBox.Show(ex.Message)
      End Try

      Command.Dispose()
      Connection.Close()
```

The changes made to the `Click` event now allow for the display of all the records. A `SqlDataReader` is still created, but the difference in the code is that a `Do-While` loop is used to loop through all the records returned. With each loop of the `Do-While` loop, a `Read()` is executed to read and retrieve the next record from the `SqlDataReader`. Then the same code used in the previous example, the `GetSqlXml` and `CreateReader` methods, are used to read the XML from the first column.

Figure 10-2 shows the results of the TeamInfo column returned from all the rows.

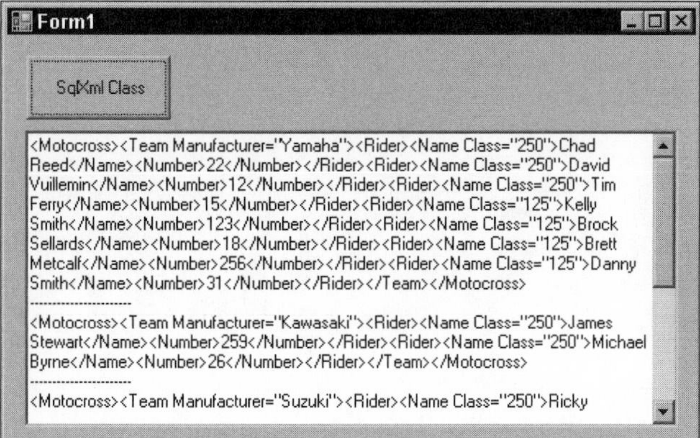

Figure 10-2

Returning the entire XML document of one or all of the records is great functionality if that is the requirement, but what if the requirement is to return a particular value or set of values from the XML document? This can be accomplished just as easily with only a little modification.

In this next example, each rider and their associated bike class is returned for the first row in the table.

Modify the `Click` event code behind the button as follows:

```
Dim Connection As SqlConnection
Dim Command As SqlCommand

Connection = New SqlConnection
```

```
Command = New SqlCommand

Try

  'ENTER YOUR OWN USER NAME AND PASSWORD
  Connection.ConnectionString = "Server=localhost;Database=Wrox;UID=;PWD="

  Connection.Open()

  Command.Connection = Connection
  Command.CommandText = "SELECT TeamInfo FROM Motocross"

  Dim r As SqlDataReader = Command.ExecuteReader
  r.Read()

  Dim xml As SqlXml = r.GetSqlXml(0)
  Dim xmlrdr As XmlReader = xml.CreateReader
  Do While xmlrdr.Read()

     Dim i As Integer
     For i = 0 To xmlrdr.AttributeCount - 1
       xmlrdr.MoveToAttribute(i)

       Me.txtResults.Text += xmlrdr.Name + "=" + xmlrdr.Value + vbCrLf
     Next i
     xmlrdr.MoveToContent()
     If xmlrdr.Name = "Name" Then

       Me.txtResults.Text += xmlrdr.Name + "=" + xmlrdr.ReadElementString + vbCrLf
     End If

     'Move to the next element element.
     xmlrdr.MoveToElement()


  Loop

Catch ex As Exception
  MessageBox.Show(ex.Message)
End Try

Command.Dispose()
Connection.Close()
```

Figure 10-3 shows each rider with his associated bike class. This example uses the same method as the previous examples. A `SqlDataReader` is used to retrieve the data from the `xml` data type column TeamInfo. The `GetSqlXml` method is then used to access the `xml` data field in the rowset of the `SqlDataReader`.

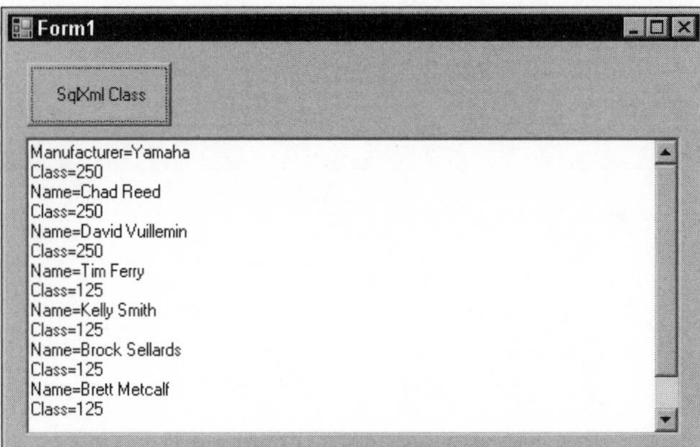

Figure 10-3

The `CreateReader` method is used to retrieve the value of the XML content of the `SqlXml` class as an `XmlReader`, which is then used to read and display the results in the text box as shown in Figure 10-3.

The XML document is read, looping through the document, reading each element and attribute looking for a specific element name. Every time the specified element is found, the value of that element is read, as is the corresponding `Class` attribute, and those values are written to the output window.

Updating and inserting data using the `SqlXml` class is not that much different from the previous examples, and actually is quite easy. The following examples demonstrate updating existing records and inserting new records using the `SqlXml` class.

Updating Data with the SqlXml Class

The first example in this section updates an existing `xml` data type column. First, execute the following SQL statement that inserts a new row into the Motocross table with a `NULL` value for the `xml` data type column. Open a SQL query window in SQL Server Management Studio and execute the following `INSERT` statement:

```
INSERT INTO Motocross SELECT NULL
GO
```

To verify the data in the table, run a query to select all the data from the table. Figure 10-4 shows the table with five rows, including the row with a `NULL` value for the TeamInfo column you just inserted.

	TeamID	TeamInfo
1	1	<Motocross><Team Manufacturer="Yamaha"><Rider><Name Class="250">Chad Reed</Name><Number>22</Number></Rider>...
2	2	<Motocross><Team Manufacturer="Kawasaki"><Rider><Name Class="250">James Stewart</Name><Number>259</Number></...
3	3	<Motocross><Team Manufacturer="Suzuki"><Rider><Name Class="250">Ricky Carmichael</Name><Number>4</Number></Rid...
4	4	<Motocross><Team Manufacturer="Honda"><Rider><Name Class="250">Jeremy McGrath</Name><Number>2</Number></Ride...
5	5	NULL

Figure 10-4

The NULL value in the record just created is updated and replaced with a valid XML document in the following example.

For this next example, add a new button to the form, setting the following properties:

Property	Value
Text	SqlXml Class 2
Name	cmdSqlXml2
Location	118, 12

Double-click the newly added button to view the code behind it, and add the following code:

```
Dim Connection As SqlConnection
Dim Command As SqlCommand

Dim XmlStr As String

Connection = New SqlConnection
Command = New SqlCommand

XmlStr = "<Motocross><Team Manufacturer='Kawasaki' Sponsor='Pro Circuit'>" & _
"<Rider><Name Class='125'>Grant Langston</Name><Number>8</Number>" & _
"</Rider></Team></Motocross>"

Try

  'ENTER YOUR OWN USER NAME AND PASSWORD
  Connection.ConnectionString = "Server=localhost;Database=Wrox;UID=;PWD="

  Connection.Open()

  Command.Connection = Connection
  Command.CommandText = "UPDATE Motocross SET TeamInfo = @xmlvar WHERE TeamID = 5"

  Dim sqlparam As SqlParameter = Command.Parameters.Add("@xmlvar",
Data.SqlDbType.Xml)
  sqlparam.Value = New SqlXml(New XmlTextReader(XmlStr, XmlNodeType.Document,
Nothing))
  Command.ExecuteNonQuery()
Me.txtResults.Text = "SUCCESS!"

Catch ex As Exception
  MessageBox.Show(ex.Message)
End Try

Command.Dispose()
Connection.Close()
```

Save the project and run the program. Click the new button you just added. The word "`SUCCESS!`" will display in the text box to let you know the code has finished running and that the update was successful.

To validate that the insert was successful, open a SQL query window in SQL Server Management Studio and execute a query to return all the rows in the Motocross table. Figure 10-5 shows the results of the update.

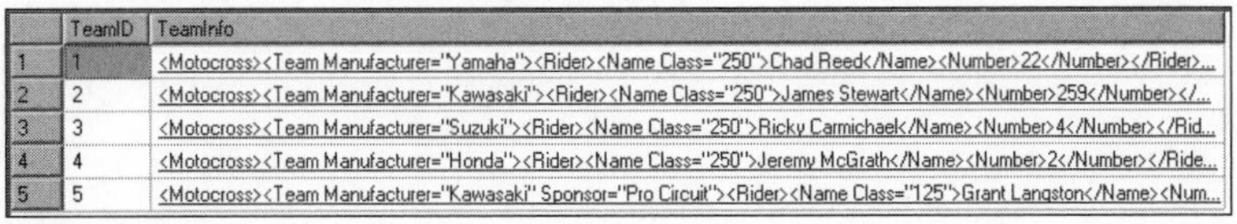

	TeamID	TeamInfo
1	1	<Motocross><Team Manufacturer="Yamaha"><Rider><Name Class="250">Chad Reed</Name><Number>22</Number></Rider>...
2	2	<Motocross><Team Manufacturer="Kawasaki"><Rider><Name Class="250">James Stewart</Name><Number>259</Number></...
3	3	<Motocross><Team Manufacturer="Suzuki"><Rider><Name Class="250">Ricky Carmichael</Name><Number>4</Number></Rid...
4	4	<Motocross><Team Manufacturer="Honda"><Rider><Name Class="250">Jeremy McGrath</Name><Number>2</Number></Ride...
5	5	<Motocross><Team Manufacturer="Kawasaki" Sponsor="Pro Circuit"><Rider><Name Class="125">Grant Langston</Name><Num...

Figure 10-5

In this example, you used the `SqlXml` class together with the `UPDATE` statement to update the `NULL` column for the record recently created. You used the `SqlCommand` class to execute an `UPDATE` statement, which included a variable to hold the place of a `SqlParameter`. You used the `Parameter` property to add a parameter to the `UPDATE` statement, which is set in the `@xmlvar` variable. Notice that you specified the parameter type as an `xml` type by using the `Data.SqlDbType.Xml` property. The update resulted in the replacement of the `NULL` value with the XML document contained in the `XmlStr` variable.

You use the `SqlXml` class to set the parameter value with the `XmlTextReader` class to provide the XML document, held in the `XmlStr` variable, to the `SqlCommand` parameter collection.

When the `UPDATE` statement executes, the `@XmlVar` variable is passed to the `UPDATE` statement to be used, and the value is inserted into the TeamInfo column.

Inserting Data with the SqlXml Class

This next example uses the same technique to insert a new record into the Motocross table. Modify the code behind the `SqlXml Class 2` button used in the previous example as follows:

```
Dim Connection As SqlConnection
Dim Command As SqlCommand

Dim XmlStr As String

Connection = New SqlConnection
Command = New SqlCommand

XmlStr = "<Motocross><Team Manufacturer='Kawasaki' Sponsor='Factory Connection'>"&_
"<Rider><Name Class='250'>Mike LoRocco</Name><Number>5</Number></Rider>" & _
"<Rider><Name Class='250'>Kevin Windham</Name><Number>14</Number></Rider>" & _
"</Team></Motocross>"

Try

  'ENTER YOUR OWN USER NAME AND PASSWORD
```

```
      Connection.ConnectionString = "Server=localhost;Database=Wrox;UID=;PWD="

      Connection.Open()

      Command.Connection = Connection
      Command.CommandText = "INSERT INTO Motocross (TeamInfo) VALUES (@xmlvar)"

      Dim sqlparam As SqlParameter = Command.Parameters.Add("@xmlvar",
    Data.SqlDbType.Xml)
      sqlparam.Value = New SqlXml(New XmlTextReader(XmlStr, XmlNodeType.Document,
    Nothing))
      Command.ExecuteNonQuery()
      Me.txtResults.Text = "SUCCESS!"

    Catch ex As Exception
      MessageBox.Show(ex.Message)
    End Try

    Command.Dispose()
    Connection.Close()
```

Run the program and click the button. As in the previous example, the text box displays "`SUCCESS!`" when the code executes.

In a query window in SQL Server Management Studio, execute a query to select all the rows from the Motocross table. Figure 10-6 shows the newly added record.

	TeamID	TeamInfo
1	1	<Motocross><Team Manufacturer="Yamaha"><Rider><Name Class="250">Chad Reed</Name><Number>22</Number></Rider>...
2	2	<Motocross><Team Manufacturer="Kawasaki"><Rider><Name Class="250">James Stewart</Name><Number>259</Number></...
3	3	<Motocross><Team Manufacturer="Suzuki"><Rider><Name Class="250">Ricky Carmichael</Name><Number>4</Number></Rid...
4	4	<Motocross><Team Manufacturer="Honda"><Rider><Name Class="250">Jeremy McGrath</Name><Number>2</Number></Rider...
5	5	<Motocross><Team Manufacturer="Kawasaki" Sponsor="Pro Circuit"><Rider><Name Class="125">Grant Langston</Name><Num...
6	6	<Motocross><Team Manufacturer="Kawasaki" Sponsor="Factory Connection"><Rider><Name Class="250">Mike LoRocco</Nam...

Figure 10-6

This example was really no different from the previous example. Instead of issuing an `UPDATE` statement, you issued an `INSERT` statement instead. The method of creating and passing the parameters remains the same using the `SqlXml` class and `XmlTextReader`.

Summary

The purpose of this chapter was to introduce you to the `SqlXml` class of the `System.Data.SqlTypes` namespace, and to show you how you can interface with the `xml` data type on the client side. The chapter provided an overview of the `SqlXml` class, introduced the `CreateReader` method, and gave the general syntax, to help provide an idea of how both `SqlXml` and `CreateReader` are used to query and read XML documents on the client. The remainder of the chapter was dedicated to a number of examples using the `SqlXml` class and `CreateReader` method.

In the next chapter, you'll learn about client-side processing with SQLXML 4.0.

11

Client-Side XML Processing with SQLXML 4.0

The previous chapter focused on client-side support for the `xml` data type and briefly introduced the technologies contained in SQLXML. Realistically, the `xml` data type in SQL Server is no good if you can't do anything with it from the client side.

The next few chapters focus on SQLXML and XML processing. When SQLXML 3.0 was released, it provided many welcome capabilities, such as Web Service support, as well as enhancements to existing features like XML bulk load, updategrams, and annotated XSD schemas.

SQLXML 4.0, which comes with SQL Server 2005, adds features such as client-side support for the `xml` data type and the new SQL Native Client provider, and builds on existing features such as client-side formatting with `FOR XML`.

The next five chapters focus entirely on client-side processing with SQLXML 4.0, with the focus of this chapter being the enhancements made to SQLXML and an introduction to the new SQL Native Client. The SQL Native Client is discussed in more detail in Chapter 20 when the topic of SQLXML data access methods is highlighted.

The topics of discussion for this chapter are as follows:

- Introduction to SQL Native Client
- ADO and SQLXML 4.0 classes
- Client-side formatting with `FOR XML`

SQL Native Client

SQL Server 2005 introduces a new technology that combines the earlier data access technologies, such as the ODBC driver and OLE DB provider, and replaces them with the SQL Native Client. This new data access client is an API that combines both the ODBC driver and OLE DB provider into single interface. Besides combining these components, this DLL, called `sqlncli.dll`, also includes additional features such as support for the `xml` data type and UDTs (user-defined types).

In earlier versions of SQLXML, query execution over HTTP was accomplished using SQLXML virtual directories and the SQLXML ISAPI filter. During the installation of previous versions of SQLXML, a utility called the IIS Virtual Directory Management for SQLXML, shown in Figure 11-1, was installed, which gave users the ability to configure IIS virtual directories and run templates via HTTP.

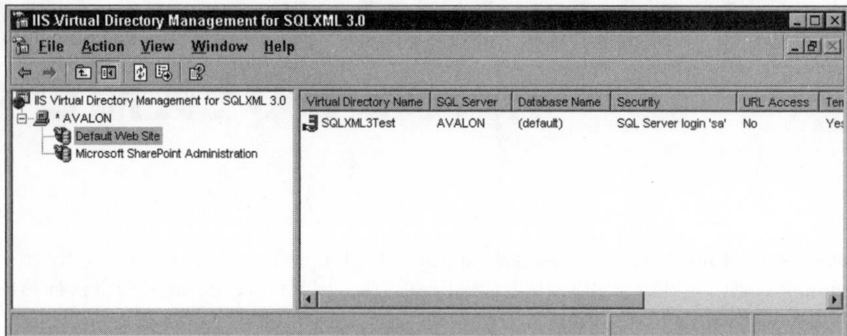

Figure 11-1

Both of these components were removed from SQLXML 4.0 and replaced with two options. The first option is the native SQL Server 2005 Web Service functionality, discussed in detail in Chapter 17. The second option is to utilize the SQL Native Client and the ADO (ActiveX Data Object) extensions built into SQLXML 4.0, which is discussed in this chapter. Both of these technologies accomplish the same task, but give the developer more XML formatting options. Likewise, it does not take a complete application rewrite to accommodate either of these options.

The design goal of the SQL Native Client is to make an easy way to access data from SQL Server, regardless if you are using OLE DB or ODBC. Since the SQL Native Client combines both of those into a single interface, a developer can easily adapt to this new client without completely rewriting the application or changing any of the data access components.

The SQL Native Client uses many of the components of MDAC (Microsoft Data Access Components) and will work with version 2.6 or higher, or any version that is installed with Windows 2000 SP3 or later. As you will see in the next section, the SQL Native Client also works with ADO (ActiveX Data Objects), providing access to all SQL Native Client functionality via ADO.

The following list details the benefits and features of using the SQL Native Client:

- `xml` **data type:** Provides support for the `xml` data type on the client side.
- **User-defined types:** Provides support for UDTs on the client side.
- **Execution of multiple result sets:** Provides the capability to execute and return multiple result sets via a single connection.

- **Asynchronous operation:** Methods are now returned immediately, eliminating calling thread blocking issues.
- **Password expiration:** Users can now change their expired passwords without administrator intervention.

SQL Native Client and MDAC Differences

Both the SQL Native Client and MDAC provide access to SQL Server, but you need to understand the numerous differences between them. The SQL Native Client incorporates many of the MDAC components, but it is specifically designed to work with the new features and enhancements made to SQL Server 2005. For example, MDAC by itself does not support the SQL Server 2005 `xml` data type, but the SQL Native Client does.

Following is a list that highlights some of the areas where the SQL Native Client and MDAC differ:

- SQL Native Client does not support connection pooling, memory management, and other MDAC-accessible features.
- SQL Native Client does not support SQLXML integration.
- SQL Native Client supports only SQL Server version 7.0 and higher.
- SQL Native Client supports only the OLE DB and ODBC interfaces.
- To make distribution easier, all the necessary data access functionality in the SQL Native Client has been included in a single DLL interface.

This list is not exhaustive, as it is intended to highlight the bigger differences between the two technologies. The intent of the SQL Native Client is to simplify data access to SQL Server. The client tools for SQL Server are available for those who need a broader range of data access.

Deployment Considerations

The SQL Native Client is installed by default when you install SQL Server 2005 and you can also install it as a separate component for client installations. The installation file, `SQLNCLI.msi`, is on the SQL Server 2005 installation CD; you use it to install the SQL Native Client on client computers.

By separating this component into its own install component, SQL Native Client can be more easily distributed, and even included in an application's installation routine. For now, the SQL Native Client install runs in silent mode only.

xml Data Type Support

When you query an `xml` data type column using the SQL Native Client, the results are returned either as a text stream or an ISequentialStream.

The ISequentialStream interface is the preferred method for reading and writing BLOBs (Binary Large Objects). If you recall Chapter 4's discussion of the `xml` data type, XML documents and XML instances are stored in the `xml` data type column and BLOBs, and therefore can either be returned on the client side as strings, or by using the ISequentialStream interface.

CreateReader()

The SQLXML class also contains a method called CreateReader(), which returns the results of a query as an XMLReader instance, ready to read the XML. This access is available via ADO.NET 2.0 of the .NET Framework and is discussed in greater detail in Chapter 23.

SQLXML 4.0 Queries with ADO

One of the biggest design goals of SQLXML 4.0 was to make data access easier without having to rewrite an entire application. As stated previously, one of the options for data access is to utilize the ADO extensions built into SQLXML 4.0. These extensions were first introduced in early versions of the Microsoft Data Access Components (MDAC) library, so they are available as long as MDAC 2.6 or later is present.

This section demonstrates a couple of examples using SQLXML with ADO to query data and format the returned information into XML using client-side XML formatting.

Open a query window in SQL Server Management Studio, type in the following T-SQL statement, and execute it against the AdventureWorks database. This code creates a stored procedure called GetProducts, which returns the ProductID and ProductName columns:

```
CREATE PROCEDURE GetProducts
AS
    SELECT   ProductID, Name, ProductNumber
    FROM     Production.Product

GO
```

In Visual Studio 2005, create a new Visual Basic Windows project. Name the project SqlCliTestApp and click OK. The project creates a new form called Form1. Open this form in design view, and from the toolbox on the left side of the designer, drop a text box and button onto the form.

For the text box, set the following properties to the corresponding values:

Property	Value
multiline	True
ScrollBars	Vertical
Width	391
Height	109
Name	txtResults

For the button, set the following properties to the corresponding values:

Property	Value
`Name`	`cmdADOExample`
`Text`	ADO Example

Prior to entering any code, you need to add the appropriate references. From the Project menu, select Add Reference. In the Add Reference dialog, select the COM tab and scroll down and select Microsoft ActiveX Data Objects 2.8 Library (see Figure 11-2). Click OK.

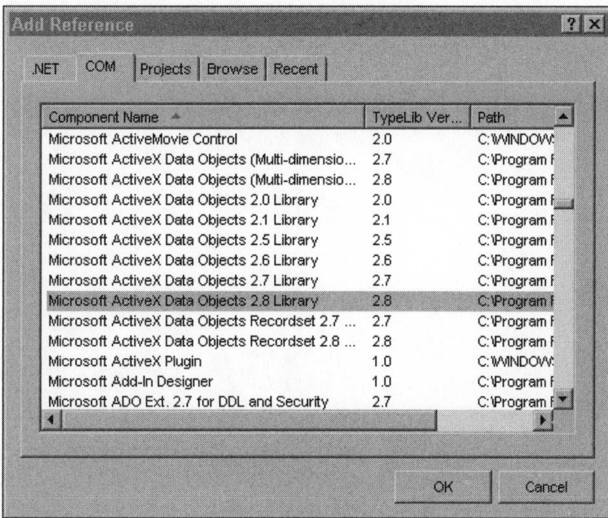

Figure 11-2

Now that you have appropriate references set, double-click the button on Form1 to display the code window. In the `Click` event for the `cmdADOExample` button, enter the following code:

```
Dim InStream As ADODB.Stream
Dim conn As ADODB.Connection
Dim cmd As ADODB.Command
Dim strconn As String
Dim dbGuid As String
Dim Userid As String
Dim Password As String

InStream = New ADODB.Stream
conn = New ADODB.Connection
cmd = New ADODB.Command

dbGuid = "{5d531cb2-e6ed-11d2-b252-00c04f681b71}"

strconn = "Provider=SQLXMLOLEDB;Data Provider=SQLNCLI;Server=localhost;" & _
```

```
        "Database=AdventureWorks"

Userid = "Type your username here"
Password = "Type your password here"

Me.Cursor = Cursors.WaitCursor

Try
  conn.Open(strconn, Userid, Password)
  cmd.ActiveConnection = conn

  cmd.CommandText = "<ROOT xmlns:sql='urn:schemas-microsoft-com:xml-sql'>" & _
  "<sql:query client-side-xml=""1"">EXEC GetProducts FOR XML NESTED" & _
  "</sql:query></ROOT>"

  InStream.Open()

  cmd.Dialect = dbGuid
  cmd.Properties("Output Stream").Value = InStream
  cmd.Execute(, , 1024)

  InStream.Position = 0
  InStream.Charset = "utf-8"

  Me.txtResults.Text = InStream.ReadText()

  conn.Close()

Catch ex As Exception
  MessageBox.Show(ex.Message.ToString)
End Try

Me.Cursor = Cursors.Default
```

To run this example, press F5 or select Start from the Debug menu. When Form1 opens, click the ADO Example button. When you press the button, a connection is made to the specified SQL Server 2005 instance and database. The template query is then passed to the command object and executed.

The first line to notice is the SQLXMLOLEDB provider command object, which can only execute to a Stream; thus the few lines of code set the OutputStream property value to a Stream and execute it to a Stream.

Focus on the template query for a moment. There are two pieces that should stand out. The first is the client-side-xml=1 attribute in the <sql:query> element. This tells the SQL Server that the XML formatting will be done on the client side. When the stored procedure is executed the results are returned to the middle tier for XML formatting.

The second item to take note of is the FOR XML NESTED clause after the stored procedure name. Even though the FOR XML clause is passed to SQL Server, it is ignored because the client-side-xml attribute is set to 1. When the results are retuned from SQL Server, the FOR XML clause is then applied to the results.

The remaining section of code sets the Stream position and Stream Character set, and then displays those results in the text box.

Figure 11-3 shows the results of the query.

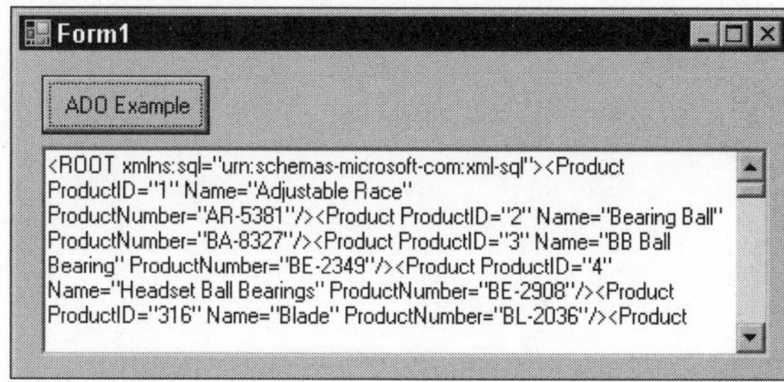

Figure 11-3

The previous example used a SQL Server stored procedure to query and return data from a table, and then passed the results back to the client for formatting. The same can be accomplished by passing in a `T-SQL` statement directly, as shown in the following example:

```
Dim InStream As ADODB.Stream
Dim conn As ADODB.Connection
Dim cmd As ADODB.Command
Dim strconn As String
Dim dbGuid As String
Dim Userid as String
Dim Password as String

InStream = New ADODB.Stream
conn = New ADODB.Connection
cmd = New ADODB.Command

dbGuid = "{5d531cb2-e6ed-11d2-b252-00c04f681b71}"

strconn = "Provider=SQLXMLOLEDB;Data Provider=SQLNCLI;Server=localhost;" & _
"Database=AdventureWorks"

Userid = "Type your SQL Server Login here"
Password = "Type your SQL Server Password HERE"

Me.Cursor = Cursors.WaitCursor

Try
  conn.Open(strconn, Userid, password)
  cmd.ActiveConnection = conn

cmd.CommandText = "<ROOT xmlns:sql='urn:schemas-microsoft-com:xml-sql'>" & _
  "<sql:query client-side-xml=""1"">" & _
  "SELECT ProductID, Name, ProductNumber" & _
  "FROM Production.Product FOR XML NESTED" & _
  "</sql:query></ROOT>"

  InStream.Open()

  cmd.Dialect = dbGuid
  cmd.Properties("Output Stream").Value = InStream
```

```
    cmd.Execute(, , 1024)

    InStream.Position = 0
    InStream.Charset = "utf-8"

    Me.txtResults.Text = InStream.ReadText()

    conn.Close()

  Catch ex As Exception
    MessageBox.Show(ex.Message.ToString)
  End Try

  Me.Cursor = Cursors.Default
```

Run the project by pressing F5. The results are the same; the only difference is that the first executed a stored procedure while the second passed in the T-SQL statement. The main thing to notice between the two is the similarity in the `FOR XML` clause at the end of each. In the first example, the `FOR XML` clause was appended to the end of the stored procedure, telling SQL Server that the XML formatting will be done at the client. The same principle applies to the second example. The `FOR XML` clause was appended to the T-SQL statement, telling SQL Server to return the results to the client and let the client do the XML formatting. In either case, the results of the XML formatting are the same.

This example is really no different from the first example. The entire `T-SQL` statement, including the `FOR XML` clause, is passed to SQL Server for execution, but the `FOR XML` clause is ignored because the `client-side-xml` attribute is set to a value of `1`. Just like the first example, the query is executed on the server and the results are passed back to the middle for formatting, which is then passed to the client. Both of these examples utilize the SQL Native Client as the data provider, which is specified in the connection string.

This section provided a quick introduction to SqlXml 4.0 and ADO and how they can be used to return and format XML on the client. Now that you have the foundation, it is time to dig deeper into client-side formatting with `FOR XML`.

Client-Side Formatting with FOR XML

Formatting XML on the client side is not new. The `FOR XML` clause has been around for quite a while and has provided great benefits when it comes to client-side XML formatting. There are two main reasons why you would want to consider client-side XML formatting.

First, client-side formatting provides a more balanced workload on the server. By letting the client provide the formatting, the server is freed up for other processes.

Second, existing stored procedures do not have to be modified for client-side XML formatting. As long as the stored procedure returns a single result set, client-side XML formatting can be applied to the results returned from the stored procedure. The first example in the previous section used a stored procedure to query data from the Production.Product table using the following syntax:

```
EXEC GetProducts FOR XML NESTED
```

The syntax of the `GetProducts` stored procedure, as seen a few pages ago, contains no XML formatting because the XML formatting happens on the client side. Thus, the `GetProducts` stored procedure did not have to be modified.

This section focuses entirely on the client-side enhancements to `FOR XML` and walks through some examples to help you become familiar with the client-side `FOR XML` clause. The next section begins by discussing the SqlXml architecture and moves on to discussing a deeper discussion of client-side formatting with some examples.

SQLXML Architecture

XML documents can be formatted on either the client side or the server side. In server-side formatting, which was covered in depth in Chapter 8, the command is sent from the client to the server. The server processes the command and formats the results in XML and sends it back to the client.

There are two options when using server-side formatting. The first is to use the `SQLXMLOLEDB` provider, which uses the new `SqlXmo4.dll` that is installed when you install SQLXML 4.0. This new DLL is similar to the previous version of the DLL, sqlxmlx.dll. It provides all the necessary XML formatting capabilities and extensions to format your query results into XML. The second option is to use the `SQLOLEDB` provider, which comes with MDAC (Microsoft Data Access Components) 2.6 or later. The `SQLOLEDB` provider includes the same SQLXML functionality as the previous version of the SqlXml.dll, `Sqlxml.dll` (notice this did not say `Sqlxml4.dll`). In both of these scenarios, SQL Server 2005 is required. If you want to use `SQLOLEDB` and still get the `Sqlxml4` flexibility, the SQLXML version needs to be set in the `SQLOLEDB` connection object. Regardless of what provider you use, the XML is formatted on the server and returned to the client.

For client-side XML formatting, SQLXML 4.0 uses the `SQLXMLOLEDB` provider, which passes the command from the client to the server for execution. The SQL Server 2005 server generates a rowset with the results, and hands it back to the client for formatting, performed against the returned rowset.

Choosing Between Client-Side and Server-Side XML Formatting

There is a handful of formatting differences in SQLXML when deciding between client-side and server-side XML formatting.

First and foremost, the use of queries that generate multiple result sets is not supported. This was true of SQLXML 3.0 and still applies in SQLXML 4.0. For example, the following query generates an error:

```
<Root nsxml:sql="urn:schemas-microsoft-com:xml-sql"
  <sql:query>
    SELECT Name, ProductNumber FROM FROM Production.Product FOR XML NESTED;
    SELECT Description FROM Production.ProductDescription FOR XML NESTED
  </sql:query>
</Root>
```

SQLXML cannot format multiple result sets, so it throws an error. The way to get around this is to execute each query individually.

With variants, variant types are converted to strings (Unicode) when formatting is done on the client side. Because of this, variant subtypes are also not used.

When XML is formatted on the client, the NESTED mode is very similar to the server-side AUTO mode except when you query views. When you query views on the server using the AUTO mode, the view name is returned as the element name when the XML results come back. When you specify client-side using the NESTED mode, the base table names that the view is based on are used as the element name.

FOR XML Modes

The syntax for client-side XML formatting with FOR XML is nearly the same as server-side XML formatting. All the modes are supported, plus an additional mode specific to the client side for XML formatting. This section explains what is new in FOR XML in SQLXML 4.0.

The basic syntax for the FOR XML clause is as follows:

```
FOR XML [mode]
```

The following modes can be used with client-side XML formatting:

- RAW
- EXPLICIT
- NESTED

The RAW and EXPLICIT modes were discussed in detail in Chapter 8, so only the NESTED mode is discussed here. You can also specify AUTO mode; however, the difference with AUTO mode on the client side is that the entire query is sent and executed on the server. This is by design as a convenience.

The NESTED and AUTO modes are very similar, with very few differences between the two.

First, when you use NESTED mode on the client side, the table names are returned as element names in the XML that is returned. More important, when you specify a table alias, the alias name is ignored. For example, the following template query returns the ProductID and Name from the Production.Product table:

```
<ROOT xmlns:sql='urn:schemas-microsoft-com:xml- sql'>
  <sql:query client-side-xml="1">
    SELECT ProductID, Name FROM Production.Product P FOR XML NESTED
  </sql:query>
</ROOT>
```

When you execute this query, the results returned use the table name as element names and the alias is ignored, as follows:

```
<ROOT xmlns:sql="urn:schemas-microsoft-com:xml-sql">
  <Production.Product ProductID="1" Name="Adjustable Race" />
  <Production.Product ProductID="2" Name="Bearing Ball" />
</ROOT>
```

Take the same template query, but change it as follows:

```
<ROOT xmlns:sql='urn:schemas-microsoft-com:xml- sql'>
  <sql:query client-side-xml="0">
    SELECT ProductID, Name FROM Production.Product P FOR XML AUTO
  </sql:query>
</ROOT>
```

When this template query is executed, the table alias name is used as the element name when `FOR XML AUTO` is used and server-side XML formatting is specified:

```
<ROOT xmlns:sql="urn:schemas-microsoft-com:xml-sql">
  <P ProductID="1" Name="Adjustable Race" />
  <P ProductID="2" Name="Bearing Ball" />
</ROOT>
```

Second, querying a view using `AUTO` mode and `NESTED` mode has different results. Open a query window and create a view using the following T-SQL statement:

```
CREATE VIEW vw_ProductInfo AS (
  SELECT ProductID, Name, ProductNumber
  FROM Production.Product)
```

Next, modify the original template query, making the following changes:

```
<ROOT xmlns:sql='urn:schemas-microsoft-com:xml-sql'>
  <sql:query client-side-xml="1">
    SELECT * FROM vw_ProductInfo FOR XML NESTED
  </sql:query>
</ROOT>
```

When you execute this template query, the results will have the table name as the element name, just as in the first example.

```
<ROOT xmlns:sql="urn:schemas-microsoft-com:xml-sql">
  <Production.Product ProductID="1" Name="Adjustable Race" />
  <Production.Product ProductID="2" Name="Bearing Ball" />
</ROOT>
```

Next, modify the template query making the following changes:

```
<ROOT xmlns:sql='urn:schemas-microsoft-com:xml-sql'>
  <sql:query client-side-xml="0">
    SELECT * FROM vw_ProductInfo FOR XML AUTO
  </sql:query>
</ROOT>
```

This time when the query is executed, the view name is used as the element names, as follows:

```
<ROOT xmlns:sql="urn:schemas-microsoft-com:xml-sql">
  <vw_ProductInfo ProductID="1" Name="Adjustable Race" />
  <vw_ProductInfo ProductID="2" Name="Bearing Ball" />
</ROOT>
```

Summary

The intent of this chapter was to introduce you to three important topics that are discussed in more detail later on in the book. The first is the SQL Native Client. This new data access client will surely earn its keep, if only by simplifying data access to SQL Server.

The second topic was using ADO with SQLXML 4.0, and the functionality it replaced over previous versions of SQLXML, plus the new features and enhancements such as the SQL Native Client and support for the `xml` data type. Many of you have experience with the SQLXML IIS configuration tool, which enabled you to configure IIS websites to work with template queries. Again, Microsoft is going after simplicity while reducing the redundancy in the technology. By combining ADO with SQLXML, developers have a single method of data access when they want to use ADO.

There were some changes and improvements made to `FOR XML` on the client side, and the goal for this chapter was simply to point out what is new and help you understand the new architecture and how SQLXML now deals with the new `xml` data type.

In the next chapter, you learn how to create XML views and use them to query relational tables within SQL Server.

12

Creating and Querying XML Views

Some new technology you learned about in the last chapter will be fundamental throughout the next few chapters. The first topic covered in the last chapter dealt with the new SQL Native Client that provides improved data access functionality. The second topic dealt with using ADO to execute SQLXML queries in SQLXML 4.0, which allows for easier query capabilities when you want to format XML results. The information gathered from these two sections will be useful throughout the next few chapters.

This chapter (as well as the next two chapters) focuses on the topic of XML views. This chapter introduces the topic of XML views with the majority focusing on how to create views, how to query views, and how to map views back to the relational data.

Specifically, this chapter covers the following topics:

- Introduction to XML views, annotation, and XSD schemas
- Querying XML views
- Best practices

The first section covers all the information you need to understand and work with XML views, followed by a section full of examples putting all the new knowledge to work learning how to query the views.

XML Views and XSD Schemas

A brief history first. When `FOR XML` was introduced in SQL Server 2000, the only option available for shaping the XML on the client side was the `FOR XML` clause with the `RAW`, `AUTO`, and `EXPLICIT` modes. Each mode provided a different level of shaping and was more complex than the other to work with. As you learned in Chapter 8, using the `EXPLICIT` mode was a major undertaking, but provided the greatest flexibility when shaping XML.

XML views were created with the purpose in mind of giving developers another option to reshape their XML with more complexity, more so than the `RAW` and `AUTO` modes, but on the level of the `EXPLICIT` mode, without having to struggle to understand the `EXPLICIT` mode.

If you are already dealing with XML, then moving to XML views is not overly complicated. In fact, it is quite easy; simply a matter of modifying the schema associated to your XML document, and *voila*, an XML view.

XML views are also known as *annotated schemas* or *mapping schemas* and are created by adding specific annotations to any XSD schema. These annotations provide the *mapping* to the database, specifically the table and columns, on which the schema is based. Or, in other words, the annotations provide a *view* to the relational table.

With these annotations in place, other SQLXML technologies such as XPath can use this XML view to query and update the relational tables on which the XML view is based.

A typical minimal XSD schema looks like this:

```
<xsd:schema xmlns:xsd="http://www.w3.org/2001/XMLSchema"
    Xmlns:sql="urn:schemas-microsoft-com">
    ...
</xsd:schema>
```

When you create a mapping schema, the minimum mapping schema declaration is needed in the XSD schema as follows:

```
<xsd:schema xmlns:xsd="http://www.w3.org/2001/XMLSchema"
    Xmlns:sql="urn:schemas-microsoft-com:mapping-schema">
    ...
</xsd:schema>
```

The only difference is the addition of the `mapping-schema` part of the namespace, which signifies that this schema will map back to the database and table. With the introduction out of the way, the following several sections detail the various annotations available when creating XML views.

sql:field

In its simplest terms, the `sql:field` annotation maps an XML element or attribute to a column in a database table. For example, take the following schema:

```
<xsd:schema xmlns:xsd="http://www.w3.org/2001/XMLSchema">
  <xsd:element name="Product" >
   <xsd:complexType>
     <xsd:sequence>
        <xsd:element name="ProdName"
                     type="xsd:string" />
        <xsd:element name="ProdNum"
                     type="xsd:string" />
     </xsd:sequence>
        <xsd:attribute name="ProdID" type="xsd:integer" />
    </xsd:complexType>
  </xsd:element>
</xsd:schema>
```

Adding annotations to the schema provides mapping back to the table and columns on which the table is based, thus turning this schema into an XML view. The following example modifies the schema above, adding the `sql:field` and `sql:relation` annotations to specify the table and column names that the elements and attributes map to (the `sql:relation` annotation is covered in more detail in the next section):

```
<xsd:schema xmlns:xsd="http://www.w3.org/2001/XMLSchema">
  xmlns:sql="urn:schemas-microsoft-com:mapping-schema">
  <xsd:element name="Product" sql:relation="Production.Product" >
   <xsd:complexType>
     <xsd:sequence>
        <xsd:element name="ProdName"
                     sql:field="Name"
                     type="xsd:string" />
        <xsd:element name="ProdNum"
                     sql:field="ProductNumber"
                     type="xsd:string" />
     </xsd:sequence>
        <xsd:attribute name="ProdID"
                       sql:field="ProductID"
                       type="xsd:integer" />
    </xsd:complexType>
  </xsd:element>
</xsd:schema>
```

Adding annotations in an XSD schema, like the one here, specifies the XML to relational mapping. In the example, the `sql:relation` annotation specifies the table in which this schema retrieves its information. The `sql:field` annotations specify from which columns in the table the schema retrieves its information for the specified elements or attributes.

sql:field cannot specify an empty element.

Now that you've added the annotations, you can query this XML view using XPath returning an XML document. Querying XML views is covered later in this chapter.

sql:relation

You use the `sql:relation` annotation to map a node in the XSD schema to a database table, specifically the table on which the XML document and schema is based. The value of the annotation holds the name of the table.

`sql:relation` annotations, when specified on an element node, apply the annotation to all other elements and attributes within the complex type definition under which the `sql:annotation` is specified.

The syntax for specifying a `sql:relation` annotation is as follows:

```
sql:relation = "tablename"
```

In this example, the `sql:relation` annotation maps the XSD schema to the Production.Product table in the AdventureWorks database by specifying the table name for the value of the annotation as follows:

```
sql:relation="Production.Product"
```

In this example, the `sql:relation` annotation was used to map the Production.Product table to the XML node in the XSD schema:

```
<xsd:schema xmlns:xsd="http://www.w3.org/2001/XMLSchema">
  xmlns:sql="urn:schemas-microsoft-com:mapping-schema">
  <xsd:element name="Product" sql:relation="Production.Product">
   <xsd:complexType>
     ...
    </xsd:complexType>
  </xsd:element>
</xsd:schema>
```

There are times when a table name and column name are valid in SQL Server but not in XML. For example, a valid column name such as Product Name is valid in SQL Server, but invalid in XML. In these cases, the `sql:relation` annotation comes in handy, as the `sql:relation` annotation can be used to specify the mapping to the table:

```
<xsd:element name="Name"
             sql:relation="[Product Name]"
             type="xsd:string" />
```

There is really not much to the `sql:relation` annotation, but you can do a lot more with the XML view. For example, you can relate elements within an XML document to each other with the `sql:relationship` annotation, which is the subject of the next section.

sql:relationship

The `sql:relationship` annotation provides the capability to relate elements within an XML document and nest elements hierarchically. In an XSD schema, this annotation nests the elements by the primary and foreign key relationships of the tables on which the schema is based, or in other words, on which the elements map.

The syntax for using the `sql:relationship` annotation is as follows:

```
<sql:relationship name="relationshipname"
    parent="parenttablename"
    parent-key="parentprimarykey"
    child="childtablename"
    child-key="parentkey"/>
```

When you specify the `sql:relationship` annotation in an XSD schema, the following must be present:

- A parent table and a child table
- A join condition

For example, a product can have multiple product reviews; therefore, a `<product>` element can have `<productreview>` subelements. Continuing the example, the `<product>` element maps to the Production .Product table and the `<productreview>` element maps to the Production.ProductReview table, linked together via the ProductID, thus satisfying the join condition. The relationship between the elements is handled by the `sql:relationship` annotation.

The following list contains the attributes available with the `sql:relationship` annotation, which provide the relationship mapping between the tables. These attributes can be used only with the `sql:relationship` annotation:

- `Name`: The name of the relationship; must be unique.
- `Parent`: The name of the parent table.
- `Child`: The name of the child table.
- `Parent-key`: The parent key (or primary key) of the parent table.
- `Child-key`: The child key (or foreign key) of the child table.

The `Parent` attribute is optional, and when it is not included, the name of the parent table is retrieved from the XML document based on the child hierarchy.

It is possible for the `Parent-key` attribute to contain more than one column, and in these cases the names are included, separated by a space. Position matters here, as the order of the values that are specified correspond, or map, to the corresponding child key.

It is also possible for the `Child-key` attribute to contain more than one column, and just like the `Parent-key` attribute, the names are separated by a space. Again, position matters, as the order of the values map to the corresponding parent key.

The following annotated schema, using a named relationship, illustrates the relationship mapping between the Product and ProductReview tables using the ProductID column as the key linking the two tables, as identified in the `<xsd:appinfo>` element. As stated previously, a product can have multiple product reviews, so in this example the `sql:relationship` annotation is on the `<ProductReview>` subelement:

```
<xsd:schema xmlns:xsd="http://www.w3.org/2001/XMLSchema"
            xmlns:sql="urn:schemas-microsoft-com:mapping-schema">
<xsd:annotation>
  <xsd:appinfo>
    <sql:relationship name="ProdRvw"
          parent="Production.Product"
          parent-key="ProductID"
          child="Production.ProductReview"
          child-key="ProductID" />
  </xsd:appinfo >
</xsd:annotation>

  <xsd:element name="Product" sql:relation="Production.Product" type="ProductLine"
/>
   <xsd:complexType name="ProductLine" >
     <xsd:sequence>
        <xsd:element name="ProductReview"
                     sql:relation="Production.ProductReview"
                    sql:relationship="ProdRvw" >
           <xsd:complexType>
              <xsd:attribute name="ProductReviewID" type="xsd:integer" />
              <xsd:attribute name="ProductID" type="xsd:integer" />
           </xsd:complexType>
```

```
            </xsd:element>
        </xsd:sequence>
            <xsd:attribute name="ProductID" type="xsd:integer" />
      </xsd:complexType>

</xsd:schema>
```

As stated earlier, the example uses a named relationship for the mapping, but the same results could be obtained using an unnamed relationship as follows:

```
<xsd:schema xmlns:xsd="http://www.w3.org/2001/XMLSchema"
            xmlns:sql="urn:schemas-microsoft-com:mapping-schema">

  <xsd:element name="Product" sql:relation="Production.Product" type="ProductType"
/>
    <xsd:complexType name="ProductType" >
      <xsd:sequence>
         <xsd:element name="ProductReview"
                     sql:relation="Production.ProductReview">
            <xsd:annotation>
             <xsd:appinfo>
               <sql:relationship
                 parent="Production.Product"
                 parent-key="ProductID"
                 child="Production.ProductReview"
                 child-key="ProductID" />
             </xsd:appinfo>
            </xsd:annotation>
            <xsd:complexType>
               <xsd:attribute name="ProductReviewID" type="xsd:integer" />
               <xsd:attribute name="ProductID" type="xsd:integer" />
            </xsd:complexType>
         </xsd:element>
      </xsd:sequence>
         <xsd:attribute name="ProductID" type="xsd:integer" />
    </xsd:complexType>

</xsd:schema>
```

In this example, the elements are unnamed, but the results are the same. A portion of the results is shown here:

```
<ROOT xmlns:sql="urn:schemas-microsoft-com:xml-sql">
  <Product ProductID="1"/>
  <Product ProductID="2"/>
  <Product ProductID="3"/>
  <Product ProductID="4"/>
  <Product ProductID="316"/>
  <Product ProductID="317"/>
  <Product ProductID="318"/>
  <Product ProductID="319"/>
  <Product ProductID="320"/>
  ...
</ROOT>
```

In this example, the `sql:relationship` annotation is used to specify the relationship between the Production.Product table and the Production.ProductRreview table. In that annotation, the `parent` and `child` attributes specify the parent and child tables along with the keys on which the two tables are joined.

Don't worry about how to run these examples just yet; they're for explanation purposes and you'll get your hands on some examples shortly.

The next example joins three tables, chaining together the three tables with the `sql:relationship` annotation to create two relationships:

```
<xsd:schema xmlns:xsd="http://www.w3.org/2001/XMLSchema"
            xmlns:sql="urn:schemas-microsoft-com:mapping-schema">
<xsd:annotation>
  <xsd:appinfo>
    <sql:relationship name="ProdCat"
          parent="Production.ProductCategory"
          parent-key="ProductCategoryID"
          child="Production.ProductSubCategory"
          child-key="ProductCategoryID" />

    <sql:relationship name="ProdSubCat"
          parent="Production.ProductSubCategory"
          parent-key="ProductSubCategoryID"
          child="Production.Product"
          child-key="ProductSubCategoryID" />
  </xsd:appinfo>
</xsd:annotation>

  <xsd:element name="ProductCategory" sql:relation="Production.ProductCategory"
sql:key-fields="ProductCategoryID" type="ProductLine" />
   <xsd:complexType name="ProductLine" >
     <xsd:sequence>
        <xsd:element name="Product" sql:relation="Production.Product"
                     sql:key-fields="ProductSubCategoryID"
                     sql:relationship="ProdCat ProdSubCat">
          <xsd:complexType>
             <xsd:attribute name="Name" type="xsd:string" />
          </xsd:complexType>
        </xsd:element>
     </xsd:sequence>
        <xsd:attribute name="ProductCategoryID" type="xsd:integer" />
    </xsd:complexType>
</xsd:schema>
```

In this example, the `sql:key-fields` annotation (more on that in the next section) is used to identify the CategoryID and SubCategoryID columns that uniquely identify each row in the relationship. A portion of the results is shown here:

```
<ROOT xmlns:sql="urn:schemas-microsoft-com:xml-sql">
  <ProductCategory ProductCategoryID="1">
    <Product Name="Mountain-100 Silver, 38"/>
    <Product Name="Mountain-100 Silver, 42"/>
```

```
        <Product Name="Mountain-100 Silver, 48"/>
        ...
      </ProductCategory>
      <ProductCategory ProductCategoryID="2">
        <Product Name="LL Mountain Handlebars"/>
        <Product Name="ML Mountain Handlebars"/>
        <Product Name="HL Mountain Handlebars"/>
        ...
      </ProductCategory>
      <ProductCategory ProductCategoryID="3">
        <Product Name="Men&apos;s Bib-Shorts, S"/>
        <Product Name="Men&apos;s Bib-Shorts, M"/>
        <Product Name="Men&apos;s Bib-Shorts, L"/>
        ...
      </ProductCategory>
      <ProductCategory ProductCategoryID="4">
        <Product Name="Hitch Rack - 4-Bike"/>
        <Product Name="All-Purpose Bike Stand"/>
        <Product Name="Water Bottle - 30 oz."/>
        ...
      </ProductCategory>
    </ROOT>
```

Pay close attention to the `sql:relationship` annotation on the `<product>` element. The annotation specifies two values, which are the name values of the two relationships. As stated previously, the order of these two values is important.

The ProdCat relationship defines the parent-child relationship between the Production.ProductCategory and Production.ProductSubCategory tables. The ProdSubCat relationship defines the parent-child relationship between the Production.ProductSubCategory and Production.Product tables.

You should have a good grasp now of how the `sql:relation` and `sql:relationship` annotations work, so it's time to look at the `sql:key-fields` annotation.

sql:key-fields

There are two reasons why you would use the `sql:key-fields` annotation in a schema. First, it is a great way to ensure that the appropriate nesting hierarchy is created, and in these cases it is best to use the annotation on elements that map to tables.

Second, you use the `sql:key-fields` annotation when an element contains a `sql:relationship` annotation that defines an element and its corresponding child element, but no primary key is specified in the parent element. In these cases the `sql:key-fields` annotation is required to ensure the proper nesting.

The `sql:key-fields` annotation syntax is as follows:

```
sql:key-fields="uniquekeycolumns"
```

The value for this annotation is the column, or columns, that uniquely identify each row in the relationship. If a single column is used it could be the primary key for the primary table. For example, the syntax would look like the following for a single-column value:

```
sql:key-fields="EmployeeID"
```

In a multiple-column value, each key column is separated by a space, as follows:

```
sql:key-fields="EmployeeID FirstName"
```

The following example uses the `sql:key-fields` annotation to produce proper nesting in the results, as there is no hierarchy specified by the `sql:relationship` annotation. The `sql:key-fields` annotation is necessary to identify products in the Production.Product table distinctively:

```
<xsd:schema xmlns:xsd="http://www.w3.org/2001/XMLSchema"
            xmlns:sql="urn:schemas-microsoft-com:mapping-schema">
  <xsd:element name="HumanResources.Employee" sql:key-fields="EmployeeID" >
   <xsd:complexType>
     <xsd:sequence>
        <xsd:element name="Title">
          <xsd:complexType>
            <xsd:simpleContent>
              <xsd:extension base="xsd:string">
                 <xsd:attribute name="EmployeeID" type="xsd:integer" />
              </xsd:extension>
            </xsd:simpleContent>
          </xsd:complexType>
        </xsd:element>
     </xsd:sequence>
   </xsd:complexType>
  </xsd:element>
</xsd:schema>
```

The next example uses the `sql:key-fields` to specify the key fields in both the Production .ProductModel and Production.Product tables to ensure that the two tables have the correct hierarchy and the proper node nesting in the resulting XML:

```
<xsd:schema xmlns:xsd="http://www.w3.org/2001/XMLSchema"
            xmlns:sql="urn:schemas-microsoft-com:mapping-schema">
<xsd:annotation>
  <xsd:appinfo>
    <sql:relationship name="ProdMod"
        parent="Production.ProductModel"
        parent-key="ProductModelID"
        child="Production.Product"
        child-key="ProductModelID" />
  </xsd:appinfo>
</xsd:annotation>
  <xsd:element name="ProductModel" sql:relation="Production.ProductModel"
               sql:key-fields="ProductModelID">
   <xsd:complexType>
     <xsd:sequence>
     <xsd:element name="Product" sql:relation="Production.Product"
                      sql:relationship="ProdMod">
       <xsd:complexType>
         <xsd:attribute name="ProdID" sql:field="ProductID" />
       </xsd:complexType>
```

```
      </xsd:element>
      </xsd:sequence>
      <xsd:attribute name="ProductModelID" type="xsd:integer" />
    </xsd:complexType>
  </xsd:element>
</xsd:schema>
```

In this example, the `sql:key-field` annotation is used to properly establish the hierarchy between the two tables and obtain the appropriate nesting for the results. A portion of the results show the ProductIDs for the corresponding ProductModelIDs:

```
<ROOT xmlns:sql="urn:schemas-microsoft-com:xml-sql">
  <ProductModel ProductModelID="1">
    <Product ProdID="864"/>
    <Product ProdID="865"/>
    <Product ProdID="866"/>
  </ProductModel>
  <ProductModel ProductModelID="2">
    <Product ProdID="712"/>
  </ProductModel>
  <ProductModel ProductModelID="3">
    <Product ProdID="861"/>
    <Product ProdID="862"/>
    <Product ProdID="863"/>
  </ProductModel><ProductModel ProductModelID="4">
    <Product ProdID="858"/>
    <Product ProdID="859"/>
    <Product ProdID="860"/>
  </ProductModel>
  ...
</ROOT>
```

Now that you have a good understanding of how relationships can be used in XML schemas, you're ready to get started with some coding examples.

Querying XML Views

Querying XML views is really no different than the querying you have done in previous chapters. Up until now, you have executed queries primarily using T-SQL statements either via a stored procedure or in-line T-SQL. The queries in the following examples use XML views just like the ones you have learned so far in the chapter.

In a text editor such as Notepad, enter the following and save the file as `SqlField.xml` in the `C:\Wrox\` directory:

```
<xsd:schema xmlns:xsd="http://www.w3.org/2001/XMLSchema">
  xmlns:sql="urn:schemas-microsoft-com:mapping-schema">
  <xsd:element name="Product" sql:relation="Production.Product" >
   <xsd:complexType>
     <xsd:sequence>
        <xsd:element name="ProdName"
```

```
                        sql:field="Name"
                        type="xsd:string" />
            <xsd:element name="ProdNum"
                        sql:field="ProductNumber"
                        type="xsd:string" />
         </xsd:sequence>
            <xsd:attribute name="ProdID"
                          sql:field="ProductID"
                          type="xsd:integer" />
        </xsd:complexType>
     </xsd:element>
   </xsd:schema>
```

In Visual Studio 2005, open the SqlCliTestApp project that you created for the examples in Chapter 11. Open Form1 in Design mode, add a button to the form, and set the caption property to XML View.

Double-click the button you just added to display the code window. In the click event, enter the following code (similar to the code entered in Chapter 11). Make sure the path to the XML document is specified correctly:

```
Dim InStream As ADODB.Stream
Dim conn As ADODB.Connection
Dim cmd As ADODB.Command
Dim strconn As String
Dim dbGuid As String
Dim Userid as String
Dim Password as String


InStream = New ADODB.Stream
conn = New ADODB.Connection
cmd = New ADODB.Command

dbGuid = "{5d531cb2-e6ed-11d2-b252-00c04f681b71}"

strconn = "Provider=SQLXMLOLEDB;Data Provider=SQLNCLI;Server=localhost;" & _
"Database=AdventureWorks"

      Userid = "Type your SQL Server Login HERE"
      Password = "Type your SQL Server Password HERE"

Me.Cursor = Cursors.WaitCursor

Try
  conn.Open(strconn, Userid, password)
  cmd.ActiveConnection = conn

  cmd.CommandText = "<ROOT xmlns:sql='urn:schemas-microsoft-com:xml-sql'>" & _
  "<sql:xpath-query mapping-schema='c:\wrox\sqlfield.xml'>/Product" & _
  "</sql:xpath-query></ROOT>"

  InStream.Open()

  cmd.Dialect = dbGuid
```

```
    cmd.Properties("Output Stream").Value = InStream
    cmd.Execute(, , 1024)

    InStream.Position = 0
    InStream.Charset = "utf-8"

    Me.txtResults.Text = InStream.ReadText()

    conn.Close()

  Catch ex As Exception
    MessageBox.Show(ex.Message)
  End Try

  Me.Cursor = Cursors.Default
```

Figure 12-1 shows the results from the query.

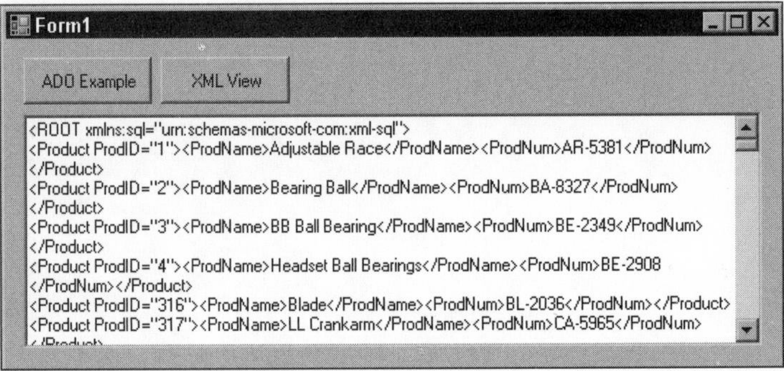

Figure 12-1

As specified in the schema, the `ProductID`, mapped to the ProductID column, is an attribute to the `Product` element. Both the `ProductName` and `ProductNumber` elements are mapped to the Name and ProductNumber columns using the `sql:field` annotation, while the `sql:relation` annotation is used to map the `Product` element to the Production.Product table.

This next example uses the `sql:relationship` annotation to hierarchically nest the schema elements in the result based on the primary and foreign key relationships. Taking from the first `sql:relationship` example preceding, type the following code into your text editor and save it as `sqlrelationship.xml` in the `C:\Wrox` directory:

```
<xsd:schema xmlns:xsd="http://www.w3.org/2001/XMLSchema"
            xmlns:sql="urn:schemas-microsoft-com:mapping-schema">
<xsd:annotation>
  <xsd:appinfo>
    <sql:relationship name="ProdRvw"
          parent="Production.Product"
          parent-key="ProductID"
          child="Production.ProductReview"
          child-key="ProductID" />
  </xsd:appinfo >
```

```
</xsd:annotation>

  <xsd:element name="Product" sql:relation="Production.Product" type="ProductLine"
/>
   <xsd:complexType name="ProductLine" >
     <xsd:sequence>
        <xsd:element name="ProductReview"
                    sql:relation="Production.ProductReview"
                   sql:relationship="ProdRvw" >
           <xsd:complexType>
              <xsd:attribute name="ProductReviewID" type="xsd:integer" />
              <xsd:attribute name="ProductID" type="xsd:integer" />
           </xsd:complexType>
        </xsd:element>
     </xsd:sequence>
        <xsd:attribute name="ProductID" type="xsd:integer" />
    </xsd:complexType>

</xsd:schema>
```

Next, modify the click event code for the XML View button in the SqlCliTestApp project as follows:

```
Dim InStream As ADODB.Stream
Dim conn As ADODB.Connection
Dim cmd As ADODB.Command
Dim strconn As String
Dim dbGuid As String
      Dim Userid as String
      Dim Password as String


InStream = New ADODB.Stream
conn = New ADODB.Connection
cmd = New ADODB.Command

dbGuid = "{5d531cb2-e6ed-11d2-b252-00c04f681b71}"

strconn = "Provider=SQLXMLOLEDB;Data Provider=SQLNCLI;Server=vssql2005;" & _
"Database=AdventureWorks"

      Userid = "Type your SQL Server Login HERE"
      Password = "Type your SQL Server Password HERE"

Me.Cursor = Cursors.WaitCursor

Try
  conn.Open(strconn, Userid, password)
  cmd.ActiveConnection = conn

  cmd.CommandText = "<ROOT xmlns:sql='urn:schemas-microsoft-com:xml-sql'>" & _
  "<sql:xpath-query mapping-schema='c:\wrox\sqlrelationship.xml'>" & _
  "/Product[@ProductID=937]" & _
```

```
    "</sql:xpath-query></ROOT>"

    InStream.Open()

    cmd.Dialect = dbGuid
    cmd.Properties("Output Stream").Value = InStream
    cmd.Execute(, , 1024)

    InStream.Position = 0
    InStream.Charset = "utf-8"

    Me.txtResults.Text = InStream.ReadText()

    conn.Close()

  Catch ex As Exception
    MessageBox.Show(ex.Message)
  End Try

  Me.Cursor = Cursors.Default
```

Clicking the XML View button should display the results shown in Figure 12-2.

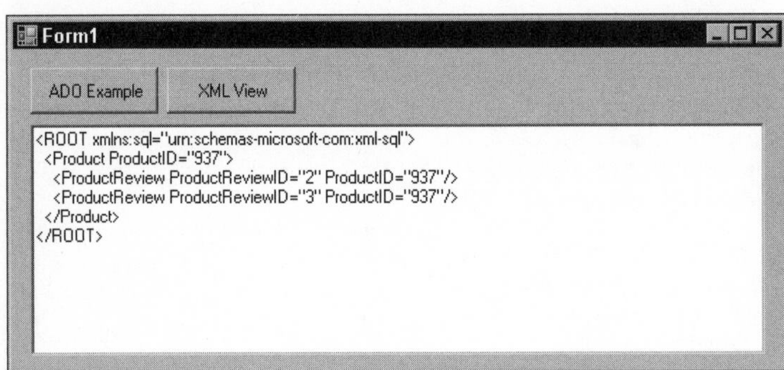

Figure 12-2

The values returned show the relationship between the two tables. The `Product` element comes from the Production.Product table, returning the individual ProductID as an attribute. The `sql:relationship` annotation is used to define the relationship between the Product and ProductReview tables, with the associated ProductReview table and columns being mapped accordingly to the elements and attributes.

This next example builds on the previous example, mapping relationships among three tables, as shown in the second `sql:relationship` annotation example. Open your text editor and type the following schema and save it as `sqlrelationship2.xml`in the `C:\Wrox` directory:

```
<xsd:schema xmlns:xsd="http://www.w3.org/2001/XMLSchema"
            xmlns:sql="urn:schemas-microsoft-com:mapping-schema">
<xsd:annotation>
  <xsd:appinfo>
    <sql:relationship name="ProdCat"
          parent="Production.ProductCategory"
```

```
            parent-key="ProductCategoryID"
            child="Production.ProductSubCategory"
            child-key="ProductCategoryID" />

      <sql:relationship name="ProdSubCat"
            parent="Production.ProductSubCategory"
            parent-key="ProductSubCategoryID"
            child="Production.Product"
            child-key="ProductSubCategoryID" />
    </xsd:appinfo>
  </xsd:annotation>

    <xsd:element name="ProductCategory" sql:relation="Production.ProductCategory"
  sql:key-fields="ProductCategoryID" type="ProductLine" />
     <xsd:complexType name="ProductLine" >
       <xsd:sequence>
          <xsd:element name="Product" sql:relation="Production.Product"
                      sql:key-fields="ProductSubCategoryID"
                      sql:relationship="ProdCat ProdSubCat">
            <xsd:complexType>
               <xsd:attribute name="Name" type="xsd:string" />
            </xsd:complexType>
          </xsd:element>
       </xsd:sequence>
          <xsd:attribute name="ProductCategoryID" type="xsd:integer" />
      </xsd:complexType>
  </xsd:schema>
```

Modify the `click` event code for the XML View button and then run the program:

```
cmd.CommandText = "<ROOT xmlns:sql='urn:schemas-microsoft-com:xml-sql'>" & _
"<sql:xpath-query mapping-schema='c:\wrox\sqlrelationship2.xml'>" & _
"/ProductCategory" & _
"</sql:xpath-query></ROOT>"
```

Clicking the XML View button should display the results shown in Figure 12-3.

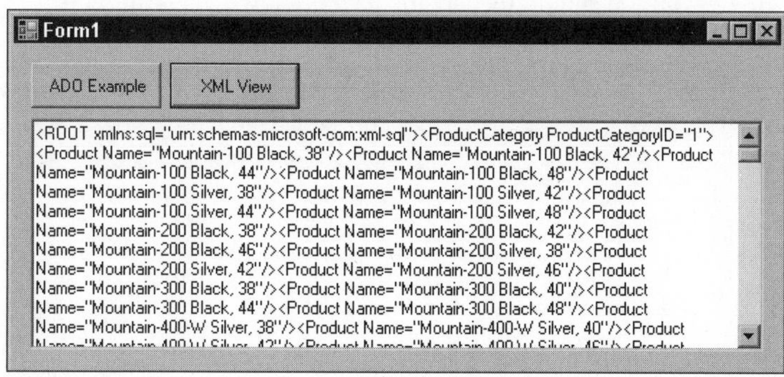

Figure 12-3

In this example, the `sql:relationship` annotation was used to map the relationship among the ProductCategory, ProductSubCategory, and Product tables. For each ProductCategory, the associated product names are returned.

The next two examples use the `sql:key-fields` annotation. The first example uses the annotation to ensure proper nesting. In this example, no `sql:relationship` annotation is specified; thus no hierarchy is defined. To fulfill the requirement of having a distinctly identified key (in this case, the ProductID), it is necessary to specify the `sql:key-fields` annotation. Open your text editor and type the following, saving it as `sqlkeyfield.xml` in the `C:\Wrox` directory:

```
<xsd:schema xmlns:xsd="http://www.w3.org/2001/XMLSchema"
            xmlns:sql="urn:schemas-microsoft-com:mapping-schema">
  <xsd:element name="Production.Product" sql:key-fields="ProductID" >
   <xsd:complexType>
     <xsd:sequence>
        <xsd:element name="Name">
          <xsd:complexType>
            <xsd:simpleContent>
              <xsd:extension base="xsd:string">
                 <xsd:attribute name="ProductID" type="xsd:integer" />
              </xsd:extension>
            </xsd:simpleContent>
          </xsd:complexType>
        </xsd:element>
     </xsd:sequence>
   </xsd:complexType>
  </xsd:element>
</xsd:schema>
```

In the code behind the XML View button, change the following code and then run the program:

```
cmd.CommandText = "<ROOT xmlns:sql='urn:schemas-microsoft-com:xml-sql'>" & _
"<sql:xpath-query mapping-schema='c:\wrox\sqlkeyfield.xml'>" & _
"/Production.Product" & _
"</sql:xpath-query></ROOT>"
```

Clicking the XML View button should display the results shown in Figure 12-4.

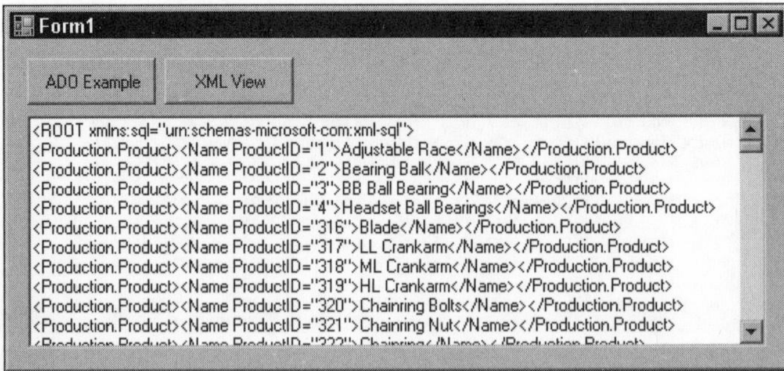

Figure 12-4

In this example, the `sql:key-fields` annotation provides the proper nesting and forming of the results because no `sql:relationship` annotation is specified.

The next example continues with the `sql:key-fields` annotation, but uses it to ensure the proper hierarchy. In this example, you use the `sql:key-fields` annotation to help uniquely identify the proper hierarchy because the `sql:relationship` annotation information does not provide the primary key of the parent table in the parent element.

Open your text editor and type in the following, saving it as sqlkeyfield2.xml in the `C:\Wrox` directory:

```
<xsd:schema xmlns:xsd="http://www.w3.org/2001/XMLSchema"
            xmlns:sql="urn:schemas-microsoft-com:mapping-schema">
<xsd:annotation>
  <xsd:appinfo>
    <sql:relationship name="ProdModel"
        parent="Production.ProductModel"
        parent-key="ProductModelID"
        child="Production.Product"
        child-key="ProductModelID" />
  </xsd:appinfo>
</xsd:annotation>
  <xsd:element name="ProductModel" sql:relation="Production.ProductModel"
               sql:key-fields="ProductModelID">
   <xsd:complexType>
     <xsd:sequence>
     <xsd:element name="Product" sql:relation="Production.Product"
                          sql:relationship="ProdModel">
       <xsd:complexType>
         <xsd:attribute name="ProdID" sql:field="ProductID" />
       </xsd:complexType>
     </xsd:element>
     </xsd:sequence>
     <xsd:attribute name="ProductModelID" type="xsd:integer" />
    </xsd:complexType>
  </xsd:element>
</xsd:schema>
```

Now modify the code behind the XML View button and make the following changes:

```
cmd.CommandText = "<ROOT xmlns:sql='urn:schemas-microsoft-com:xml-sql'>" & _
  "<sql:xpath-query mapping-schema='c:\wrox\sqlkeyfield2.xml'>" & _
  "/ProductModel" & _
  "</sql:xpath-query></ROOT>"
```

Run the SqlCliTestApp program and click the XML View button. The displayed results should look like Figure 12-5.

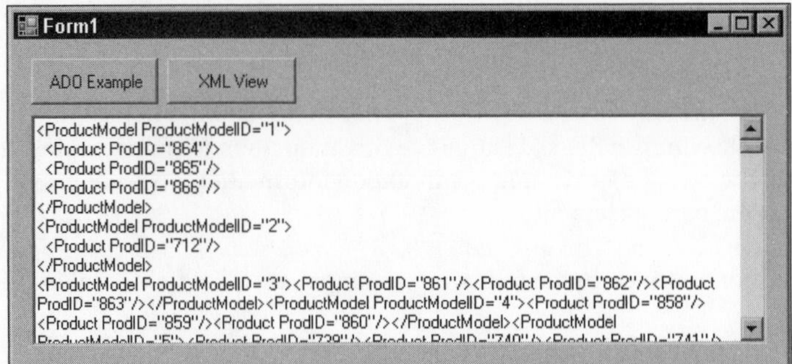

Figure 12-5

The results can be filtered by modifying the XPath statement in a similar way as the following:

```
cmd.CommandText = "<ROOT xmlns:sql='urn:schemas-microsoft-com:xml-sql'>" & _
   "<sql:xpath-query mapping-schema='c:\wrox\sqlkeyfield2.xml'>" & _
   "/ProductCategory[@ProductModelID=20" & _
   "</sql:xpath-query></ROOT>"
```

This example used an XPath query against the XSD schema to return specific information, in this case key information such as the ProductID. Since a `sql:relationship` annotation was also specified, the `sql:key-fields` annotation is used to ensure the correct hierarchy and nesting of the elements.

By now you should have a good grasp on how XML schema views work and how to use the annotations to produce the appropriate relationships and relational mappings. You can now move on to learn how best to use your new knowledge.

Best Practices

Security can be a big factor when using annotated schemas, so there are a few items to consider.

Using default mapping and explicit mapping exposes such database information as the table and column names. Default mapping is an issue because the element and attribute names map to table and column names, respectively, and you must consider the ramifications of making the schemas publicly available if there is such a need.

The alternative is to give non-meaningful names to the elements and attributes in the schema to explicitly map them back to the corresponding tables and attributes.

Summary

The purpose of this chapter was to create the basic foundation and building blocks to understanding XML views and how to query them. You have seen the basic makeup of an XML view, and the requirements necessary to map the elements and attributes back to the corresponding table and columns. You have seen how to define relationships and when two or more tables are included in the schema, and even how to set the appropriate hierarchy when the relationship information is not enough to appropriately define the relationship.

You have also seen how to apply the technology you learned in Chapter 11, using ADO to execute SQLXML queries, query these views, and return the necessary information.

Chapter 13 builds on what you learned in this chapter and discusses using the updategram to update the XML View.

13

Updating the XML View Using Updategrams

This chapter focuses on updating a database directly using updategrams and the XML view. The information in this chapter builds on the previous two chapters in which you learned about using ADO and OLEDB to query a database via the SQL Native Client.

Updategrams, introduced in SQL Server 2000, are another option you can use to update, delete, and insert data into your database. Before updategrams, the first option was to use the OPENXML feature of SQLXML. Both updategrams and OPENXML provide the same results, that is, inserting, deleting, and updating of data. The difference between the two is that updategrams use XML views and the mapping schema, which you learned about in Chapter 12, to provide the functionality. The schema contains the mapping of elements and attributes back to the tables and columns in the database.

In particular, this chapter covers the following topics:

- Overview and structure of updategrams
- Mapping schemas and updategrams
- Using updategrams to modify data
- Passing parameters
- updategram concurrency
- NULL handling
- updategram security
- Guidelines and limitations

Overview and Structure

updategrams offer the capability through XML to modify a database directly without shredding the XML document, as does OPENXML. Although OPENXML is great for dealing with rowset providers by generating operational statements to modify data, updategrams don't do any XML document shredding. updategrams work directly against XML views (which you learned about in Chapter 12) and their associated mapping schemas (which you learned about in Chapter 7). The mapping schemas contain the information that is required to bind, or map, the elements and attributes back to the associated tables and columns for quick and efficient processing.

The structure of an updategram is simply a template with a predefined set of tags that merely give a before and after picture of the data when the updategram is executed.

The basic syntax of an updategram looks like this:

```
<ROOT xmlns:updgrm-"urn:schemas-microsoft-com:xml-updategram">
  <updg:sync [mapping-schema="annotatedschema.xml"]>
    <updg:before>
      ...
    </updg:before>
    <updg:after>
      ...
    </updg:after>
  </updg:sync>
</ROOT>
```

The following list defines each piece of the updategram and explains what the syntax means.

- <sync> **Block:** The <sync> block encompasses the <before> and <after> blocks, and can contain multiple <before> and <after> blocks. If multiple <before> and <after> blocks are within the <sync> block, then each <before> and <after> needs to be designated as a pair.

  An updategram can contain multiple <sync> blocks, each containing a transactional unit. In other words, everything in the <sync> block executes, or nothing executes. The failure of one <sync> block to execute does not affect the execution of other <sync> blocks.

- <before>**:** Defines the state of the data as it currently is, prior to execution. This is commonly known as the *before* state.

- <after>**:** Defines the state of the data after the execution occurs. This is commonly known as the *after* state.

- **Namespace:** The <sync>, <before>, and <after> keywords used in an updategram are provided by the `urn:schemas-microsoft-com:xml-updategram` namespace. The namespace prefix is not predetermined, and can be determined by you. In the previous structure example, the prefix is defined as `updgrm`.

Mapping Schemas and Updategrams

As you learned in Chapter 12, the schema can have either implicit or explicit mapping. *Implicit mapping* simply means that a mapping schema has not been specified, so the updategram takes on implicit mapping. *Explicit mapping* means that the elements and attributes in the updategram have been explicitly mapped to the elements and attributes in the mapping schema.

The default mapping is implicit mapping (covered in the following section), meaning that proper nesting of elements and subelements is essential. Each element in the <before> and <after> blocks maps to a table, and the subelements and attributes map to a column.

Implicit Mapping

The following example illustrates implicit mapping. The <Production.ProductModel> element implicitly maps to the Production.Product table and the Name attribute implicitly maps to the Name column in the Production.Product table:

```
<ROOT xmlns:updgrm="urn:schemas-microsoft-com:xml-updategram">
  <updgrm:sync>
    <updgrm:before>
    </updgrm:before>
    <updgrm:after>
      <Production.ProductModel Name="Widget" />
    </updgrm:after>
  </updgrm:sync>
</ROOT>
```

This next example uses implicit mapping to update the same record:

```
<ROOT xmlns:updgrm="urn:schemas-microsoft-com:xml-updategram">
  <updgrm:sync>
    <updgrm:before>
      <Production.ProductModel ProductModelID="129" />
    </updgrm:before>
    <updgrm:after>
      <Production.ProductModel Name="ExtremeWidget" />
    </updgrm:after>
  </updgrm:sync>
</ROOT>
```

In this example, no mapping schema is associated to the updategram, so it takes on implicit mapping. When you use implicit mapping, the <Production.ProductModel> element maps to the Production .ProductModel table and the Name attribute maps to the corresponding columns in the Production .ProductModel table.

Explicit Mapping

Explicit mapping, as mentioned previously, simply means associating a mapping schema to the updategram. The following example is a mapping schema that is then mapped to an updategram. For the sake of this example, this mapping schema is called exampleupdgrmschema.xml:

```
<xsd:schema xmlns:xsd="http://www.w3.org/2001/XMLSchema"
            xmlns:sql="urn:schemas-microsoft-com:mapping-schema">
  <xsd:element name="Product" sql:relation="Production.Product" >
   <xsd:complexType>
        <xsd:attribute name="ProductID"
                       sql:field="ProductID"
                       type="xsd:string" />
        <xsd:attribute name="ModelID"
                       sql:field="ProductModelID"
                       type="xsd:string" />
        <xsd:attribute name="Name"
                       Sql:field="Name"
                       Type="xsd:string" />
    </xsd:complexType>
  </xsd:element>
</xsd:schema>
```

The next step is to map the schema to an updategram that explicitly maps the elements and attributes to the table and columns. The updategram, referencing the mapping schema in the second line, looks like the following:

```
<ROOT xmlns:updgrm="urn:schemas-microsoft-com:xml-updategram">
  <updgrm:sync mapping-schema="exampleupdgrmschema.xml">
    <updgrm:before>
      <Product ProductID="535" ModelID="" Name="Tension Pulley" />
    </updgrm:before>
    <updgrm:after>
      <Product ProductID="535" ModelID="103" Name="Tension Pulley" />
    </updgrm:after>
  </updgrm:sync>
</ROOT>
```

With the mapping in place, the updategram updates the ModelID column in the Product table with the value specified in the `ModelID` attribute in the `<updgrm:after>` block.

Modifying Data

As with all the examples so far in this book, the examples in this section are executed using the new functionality you learned in Chapter 12, using ADO and SQLXML to execute updategrams.

In order to execute these examples, the SqlCliTestApp application needs to be modified (just so the previous code and examples aren't messed with).

Open the SqlCliTestApp application, and then open the form in design view. Add a button on the form. Set the `Text` property to `"updategram"` and set the `Name` property to `cmdupdategram`.

Double-click the button you just added to display the code window. In the click event for the updategram button, enter the following code:

```
Dim InStream As ADODB.Stream
Dim conn As ADODB.Connection
Dim cmd As ADODB.Command
```

```
Dim strconn As String
Dim dbGuid As String
Dim Userid as String
Dim Password as String
Dim cmdText as String

InStream = New ADODB.Stream
conn = New ADODB.Connection
cmd = New ADODB.Command

dbGuid = "{5d531cb2-e6ed-11d2-b252-00c04f681b71}"

strconn = "Provider=SQLXMLOLEDB;Data Provide=SQLNCLI;Server=localhost; " & _
      "Database=AdventureWorks"

Userid = "Type your SQL Server Login here"
Password = "Type your SQL Server Password HERE"

Me.Cursor = Cursors.WaitCursor

Try
  conn.Open(strconn, Userid, password)
  cmd.ActiveConnection = conn

  cmdText = "" 'This will be filled in later!

  cmd.CommandText = cmdText

  InStream.Open()

  cmd.Dialect = dbGuid
  cmd.Properties("Output Stream").Value = InStream
  cmd.Execute(, , 1024)

  conn.Close()

          MessageBox.Show("Record Inserted")

Catch ex As Exception
  MessageBox.Show(ex.Message)
End Try

Me.Cursor = Cursors.Default
```

Now you are ready for some examples. Most of the examples in this section use implicit mapping, but a few use explicit mapping.

Inserting Data

There are three ways to specify the data you want to insert. They are as follows:

- Attribute-centric
- Element-centric
- Mixed mode

Attribute-Centric

Attribute-centric mapping specifies all the columns in which to insert data as attributes to the table element. For example, the following code uses attribute-centric mapping to add a row to the Production ProductCategory table:

```
<ROOT xmlns:updgrm="urn:schema-microsoft-com:xml-updategram">
  <updgrm:sync>
    <updgrm:before>
    </updgrm:before>
    <updgrm:after>
      <Production.ProductCategory
        Name="Go-Karts" />
    <updgrm:after>
  </updgrm:sync>
</ROOT>
```

In this example, only the Name column needs to be specified because the ProductCategoryID column is an identity column, so the value is automatically generated. The value of the rowguid column is also automatically generated, and the ModifiedDate column in the table has a default set on it so that when a record is inserted into the table, the current date is automatically applied to the column.

A multi-column insert would look like the following:

```
<ROOT xmlns:updgrm="urn:schema-microsoft-com:xml-updategram">
  <updgrm:sync>
    <updgrm:before>
    </updgrm:before>
    <updgrm:after>
      <Sales.SalesPerson
        SalesQuota="10000000.00"
        Bonus="25000.00"
        CommissionPct="10.0"
        SalesYTD="750000.00"
        SalesLastYear="900000.00" />
    <updgrm:after>
  </updgrm:sync>
</ROOT>
```

In both of these examples, the column values are listed as attributes to the table element.

Element-Centric

Element-centric mapping simply means that the column values are listed as subelements of the table element, as follows:

```
<ROOT xmlns:updgrm="urn:schema-microsoft-com:xml-updategram">
  <updgrm:sync>
    <updgrm:before>
    </updgrm:before>
    <updgrm:after>
      <Production.ProductCategory>
        <Name>Go-Karts</Name>
      </Production.ProductCategory>
```

```
    <updgrm:after>
  </updgrm:sync>
</ROOT>
```

Another example of element-centric mapping would appear like the following:

```
<ROOT xmlns:updgrm="urn:schema-microsoft-com:xml-updategram">
  <updgrm:sync>
    <updgrm:before>
    </updgrm:before>
    <updgrm:after>
      <Sales.SalesPerson>
        <SalesQuota>10000000.00</SalesQuota>
        <Bonus>5000.00</Bonus>
        <CommissionPct>10.0</CommissionPct>
        <SalesYTD>750000.00</SalesYTD>
        <SalesLastYear>900000.00</SalesLastYear>
      </Sales.SalesPerson>
    <updgrm:after>
  </updgrm:sync>
</ROOT>
```

Mixed Mode

Mixed mode means that both attribute-centric and element-centric mapping can exist in the same updategram, as shown below:

```
<ROOT xmlns:updgrm="urn:schema-microsoft-com:xml-updategram">
  <updgrm:sync>
    <updgrm:before>
    </updgrm:before>
    <updgrm:after>
      <Sales.SalesPerson
        SalesQuota="10000000.00"
        Bonus="25000.00"
        CommissionPct="10.0"
        <SalesYTD>750000.00</SalesYTD>
        <SalesLastYear>900000.00</SalesLastYear>
      </Sales.SalesPerson>
    <updgrm:after>
  </updgrm:sync>
</ROOT> will
```

Before getting into the examples of mixed mode, you need to insert a record into the Production.Product table. Open a query window in SQL Server Management Studio and run the following query against the AdventureWorks database:

```
INSERT INTO Production.ProductCategory ([NAME]) VALUES ('Burritos')
GO
```

In this case, when you insert data with an updategram, the `<before>` block is left empty, signifying that a new row is being added. The first example inserts a row into the Product.ProductModel table. Modify the code behind the updategram button, changing the `cmd.CommandText` syntax to look like the following:

```
cmdText = "<ROOT xmlns:updgrm='urn:schemas-microsoft-com:xml-updategram'>" & _
"<updgrm:sync>" & _
"<updgrm:before>" & _
"</updgrm:before>" & _
"<updgrm:after>" & _
"<Production.ProductCategory Name='Go-Karts' />" & _
"</updgrm:after>" & _
"</updgrm:sync>" & _
"</ROOT>"
```

Run the application and click the updategram button. When the code is executed and the record is inserted, you get a message box showing the record was created successfully. To verify this, open a query window in SQL Server Management Studio and query the Production.ProductCategory table. You will see that the new record has been added, as shown in Figure 13-1.

	ProductCategoryID	Name	rowguid	ModifiedDate
1	1	Bikes	CFBDA25C-DF71-...	1998-06-01 00:00...
2	2	Components	C657828D-D808-...	1998-06-01 00:00...
3	3	Clothing	10A7C342-CA82-...	1998-06-01 00:00...
4	4	Accessories	2BE3BE36-D9A2-...	1998-06-01 00:00...
5	5	Burritos	20B5686E-7ABB-...	2005-04-05 23:51...
6	7	Go-Karts	D93E74EF-77CD-...	2005-04-05 23:47...

Figure 13-1

updategrams can be used to insert multiple records at a time, and there are multiple ways to do it. This example uses a single <sync> block to insert three records into the Production.ProductCategory table:

```
<ROOT xmlns:updgrm='urn:schemas-microsoft-com:xml-updategram'>
  <updgrm:sync>
    <updgrm:before>
    </updgrm:before>
    <updgrm:after>
      <Production.ProductCategory Name='Hang Gliders' />
    </updgrm:after>
    <updgrm:before>
    </updgrm:before>
    <updgrm:after>
      <Production.ProductCategory Name='Dirt Bikes' />
    </updgrm:after>
    <updgrm:before>
    </updgrm:before>
    <updgrm:after>
      <Production.ProductCategory Name='Guitars' />
    </updgrm:after>
  </updgrm:sync>
</ROOT>
```

A second way to insert multiple records is to wrap each insert in a separate <sync> block, as follows:

```
<ROOT xmlns:updgrm='urn:schemas-microsoft-com:xml-updategram'>
  <updgrm:sync>
    <updgrm:before>
    </updgrm:before>
```

```
    <updgrm:after>
      <Production.ProductCategory Name='Hang Gliders' />
    </updgrm:after>
  </updgrm:sync>
  <updgrm:sync>
    <updgrm:before>
    </updgrm:before>
    <updgrm:after>
      <Production.ProductCategory Name='Dirt Bikes' />
    </updgrm:after>
  <updgrm:sync>
  </updgrm:sync>
    <updgrm:before>
    </updgrm:before>
    <updgrm:after>
      <Production.ProductCategory Name='Guitars' />
    </updgrm:after>
  </updgrm:sync>
</ROOT>
```

As stated earlier in the chapter, one `<sync>` block is not dependent on the other, so if one fails, the others still execute.

ReturnID and at-identity Attributes

When inserting into a table that has an identity column, it is possible to retrieve the newly generated value. The `at-identity` attribute is used to obtain the new value and stores it in a placeholder value. The following example inserts into the Production.ProductCategory table, which has an identity column and returns the newly generated identity value. This example also uses explicit mapping.

First, generate the mapping schema, as follows:

```
<xsd:schema xmlns:xsd="http://www.w3.org/2001/XMLSchema"
            xmlns:sql="urn:schemas-microsoft-com:mapping-schema">
  <xsd:element name="Production.ProductCategory" >
   <xsd:complexType>
        <xsd:attribute name="Name" type="xsd:string" />
    </xsd:complexType>
  </xsd:element>
</xsd:schema>
```

Save this mapping schema as `C:\Wrox\identitymapschema.xml`. Now you're ready to create the updategram. You place the `at-identity` attribute as an attribute on the table element, which retrieves the newly generated identity value and stores it in a placeholder variable of `x`. You place the `ReturnID` attribute on the `<after>` block, which simply returns the new generated identity value (retrieving it from the placeholder variable) when the updategram is executed, and returns it as output.

The updategram for this example looks like the following:

```
<ROOT xmlns:updgrm="urn:schemas-microsoft-com:xml-updategram">
  <updgrm:sync mapping-schema="identitymapschema.xml">
    <updgrm:before>
    </updgrm:before>
    <updgrm:after updgrm:returnid="x">
```

```
        <Production.ProductCategory
             updgrm:at-identity="x" Name="Dirt Bikes" />
      </updgrm:after>
    </updgrm:sync>
</ROOT>
```

In the SqlCliTestApp application, replace the code within the `Try` block of the updategram click event with the following:

```
conn.Open(strconn, Userid, password)
cmd.ActiveConnection = conn

  cmdText = "<ROOT xmlns:updgrm='urn:schemas-microsoft-com:xml-updategram'>" & _
  "<updgrm:sync mapping-schema='c:\Wrox\identitymapschema.xml'>" & _
  "<updgrm:before>" & _
  "</updgrm:before>" & _
  "<updgrm:after updgrm:returnid='x'>" & _
  "<Production.ProductCategory updgrm:at-identity='x' Name='Dirt Bikes' />" & _
  "</updgrm:after>" & _
  "</updgrm:sync>" & _
  "</ROOT>"

cmd.CommandText = cmdText

InStream.Open()

cmd.Dialect = dbGuid
cmd.Properties("Output Stream").Value = InStream
cmd.Execute(, , 1024)

  InStream.Position = 0
  InStream.Charset = "utf-8"

  Me.txtResults.Text = Instream.ReadText()

conn.Close()

MessageBox.Show("Record Inserted")
```

Press F5 to start the program. When the form opens, click the updategram button. Figure 13-2 shows the results that come back from the execution of the updategram. As you can see, the new record was inserted and the identity value of the new row was returned via the `updgrm:returned` attribute.

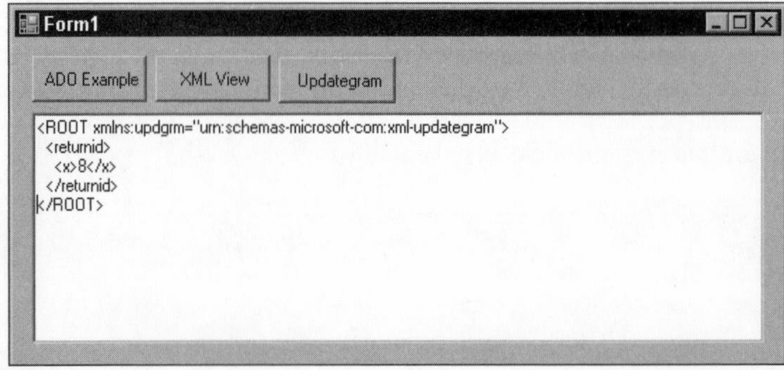

Figure 13-2

To verify the results, open a query window in SQL Server Management Studio and run a query to select all the records from the Production.ProductCategory table, as follows:

```
SELECT * FROM Production.ProductCategory
```

The results look like Figure 13-3.

	ProductCategoryID	Name	rowguid	ModifiedDate
1	1	Bikes	CFBDA25C-DF71-...	1998-06-01 00:00...
2	2	Components	C657828D-D808-...	1998-06-01 00:00...
3	3	Clothing	10A7C342-CA82-...	1998-06-01 00:00...
4	4	Accessories	2BE3BE36-D9A2-...	1998-06-01 00:00...
5	5	Burritos	20B5686E-7ABB-...	2005-04-05 23:51...
6	7	Go-Karts	D93E74EF-77CD-...	2005-04-05 23:47...
7	8	Dirt Bikes	5EEC73B6-13C5-...	2005-04-06 22:38...

Figure 13-3

Last, what's the use of having an `xml` data type column if you can't use an updategram to insert data into it? The final example inserts into an `xml` data type column of the Employee table using implicit mapping.

First, you need to create the employee table:

```
Use AdventureWorks
GO

CREATE TABLE Employee (
  [EmployeeID] [int] IDENTITY(1,1) NOT NULL,
  [EmployeeInfo] [xml] NULL
) ON [PRIMARY]
```

The second step is to create the schema. In your favorite text editor, type the following:

```
<xsd:schema xmlns:xsd="http://www.w3.org/2001/XMLSchema"
  <xsd:element name="Emp"  sql:relation="Employee" >
     <xsd:complexType>
       <xsd:sequence>
          <xsd:element name="Info" sql:field="EmployeeInfo" sql:datatype="xml">
           <xsd:complexType>
            <xsd:sequence>
              <xsd:element name="Employee">
              </xsd:element>
            </xsd:sequence>
           </xsd:complexType>
          </xsd:element>
       </xsd:sequence>
       <xsd:attribute name="EmployeeID" sql:field="EmployeeID"/>
     </xsd:complexType>
  </xsd:element>
</xsd:schema>
```

Save this schema as `C:\Wrox\xmlinsertschema.xml`. Next, replace the `cmdText` assignment statement in the updategram button's click event, as follows:

```
cmdText = "<ROOT xmlns:updg="urn:schemas-microsoft-com:xml-updategram">
 <updg:sync mapping-schema="c:\wrox\xmlinsertschema.xml" >
  <updg:before>
  </updg:before>
  <updg:after>
  </updg:after>
    <Employee @EmployeeID="1">
      <FirstName>Scott</FirstName>
      <MiddleName>L</MiddleName>
      <LastName>Klein</LastName>
      <Email>ScottKlein@TopXML.com</Email>
      <Phone>555-555-5555</Phone>
      <Title>geek</Title>
    </Employee>
  </updg:sync>
</ROOT>"
```

Run the application and click the updategram button. When the execution is finished, open a query window and execute the following query against the AdventureWorks database:

```
SELECT * FROM Employee
```

Figure 13-4 shows the results of the updategram just executed.

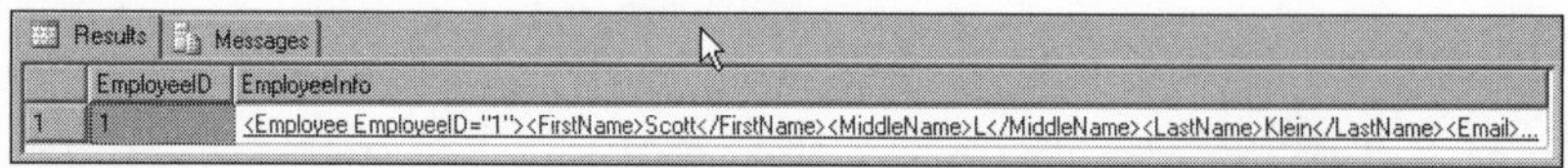

	EmployeeID	EmployeeInfo
1	1	<Employee EmployeeID="1"><FirstName>Scott</FirstName><MiddleName>L</MiddleName><LastName>Klein</LastName><Email>...

Figure 13-4

In this updategram example, no `<before>` value is specified, so the updategram knows that this is an insert operation. When the updategram is executed, the XML document contained in the `<after>` block is inserted into the Employee table. It knows to insert into the EmployeeInfo column of the Employee table by the mapping schema reference in the updategram. The mapping schema contains the mapping information back to the database for the corresponding table and column.

With data now in the tables, it would be nice to be able to delete data also, if the need arises. That's the next topic.

Deleting Data

Deleting data using an updategram is just as easy as inserting, if not easier. In fact, it is nearly the opposite of an insert updategram. In a delete updategram, the `<before>` block contains data, and the `<after>` block is empty.

The same updategram syntax is used when deleting records; the only difference is that the `<before>` block contains the information about the data you want to delete, and the `<after>` block is empty.

For example, the following updategram illustrates using an updategram to delete the row from the Production.ProductCategory table where the value in the Name column is `Burritos`, using implicit mapping:

```
<ROOT xmlns:updgrm="urn:schema-microsoft-com:xml-updategram">
  <updgrm:sync>
    <updgrm:before>
      <Production.ProductCategory Name="Burritos" />
    </updgrm:before>
    <updgrm:after>
    <updgrm:after>
  </updgrm:sync>
</ROOT>
```

To run this example, modify the updategram button’s click event within the `Try` block, as follows:

```
conn.Open(strconn, Userid, password)
cmd.ActiveConnection = conn

cmdText = "<ROOT xmlns:updgrm='urn:schemas-microsoft-com:xml-updategram'>" & _
"<updgrm:sync>" & _
"<updgrm:before>" & _
"<Production.ProductCategory Name='Burritos' />" & _
"</updgrm:before>" & _
"<updgrm:after>" & _
"</updgrm:after>" & _
"</updgrm:sync>" & _
"</ROOT>"

cmd.CommandText = cmdText

InStream.Open()

cmd.Dialect = dbGuid
cmd.Properties("Output Stream").Value = InStream
cmd.Execute(, , 1024)

  InStream.Position = 0
  InStream.Charset = "utf-8"

  Me.txtResults.Text = Instream.ReadText()

conn.Close()

MessageBox.Show("Record Deleted")
```

Clicking the updategram button executes the updategram, deleting the record specified in the updategram from the table. SQL Server determined that because there was information in the `<before>` block and no instructions in the `<after>` block that it needed to delete the row from the table. Figure 13-5 shows the results of the execution on the form.

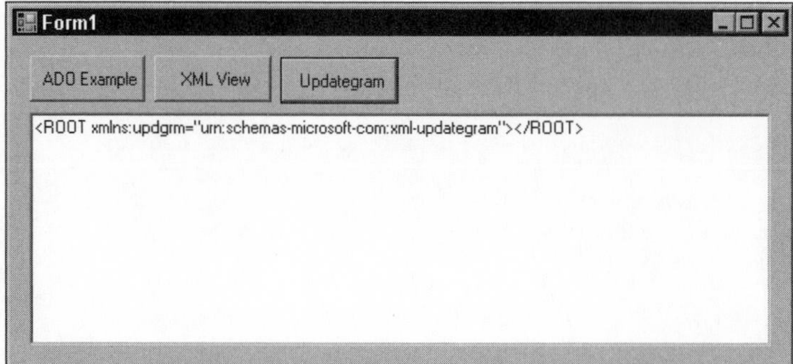

Figure 13-5

Realistically, the code behind the button didn't need to return results, but the code to return results was left in to show what is brought back from the execution of the updategram.

For verification, query the Production.Product table, which displays the results shown in Figure 13-6.

	ProductCategoryID	Name	rowguid	ModifiedDate
1	1	Bikes	CFBDA25C-DF71-...	1998-06-01 00:00...
2	2	Components	C657828D-D808-...	1998-06-01 00:00...
3	3	Clothing	10A7C342-CA82-...	1998-06-01 00:00...
4	4	Accessories	2BE3BE36-D9A2-...	1998-06-01 00:00...
5	7	Go-Karts	D93E74EF-77CD-...	2005-04-05 23:47...
6	8	Dirt Bikes	5EEC73B6-13C5-...	2005-04-06 22:38...

Figure 13-6

Notice that the Burritos record has been deleted.

A mapping schema can also be applied to a delete updategram, as follows:

```
<xsd:schema xmlns:xsd="http://www.w3.org/2001/XMLSchema"
            xmlns:sql="urn:schemas-microsoft-com:mapping-schema">
  <xsd:element name="Product" sql:relation="Production.ProductCategory" >
   <xsd:complexType>
        <xsd:attribute name="ProdCatID"
                       sql:field="ProductCategoryID"
                       type="xsd:integer" />
    </xsd:complexType>
  </xsd:element>
</xsd:schema>
```

Save this schema as `C:\Wrox\sampdelschema.xml`, and then in the `commandtext` assignment statement in the updategram button's click event, reference the schema in the updategram, as follows:

```
<ROOT xmlns:updgrm="urn:schemas-microsoft-com:xml-updategram">
  <updgrm:sync mapping-schema="C:\Wrox\sampdelschema.xml">
    <updgrm:before>
      <Product ProdCatID="9" />
```

```
    </updgrm:before>
    <updgrm:after>
    </updgrm:after>
  </updgrm:sync>
</ROOT>
```

When the updategram is executed, the record in the Production.ProductCategory table with a ProductCategoryID of 9 is deleted.

Updating Data

When you use an updategram to update existing data, both the `<before>` and `<after>` blocks within a `<sync>` block must contain information. The `<before>` block describes the current state of the data and identifies the data that is going to be changed, and the `<after>` block describes the data after the execution of the updategram.

The requirements for update updategrams are identical to insert and delete updategrams, such as attaching mapping schemas. Let's forgo all that and just jump right in to the examples.

The first example combines both an insert and an update transaction in a single updategram. Each `<before>` and `<after>` block pair is wrapped in its own `<sync>` block. The first `<before>` and `<after>` block inserts a record into the Production.ProductCategory table with a category name of `Burritos`. The second `<before>` and `<after>` block pair updates the category name from the newly inserted record from `Burritos` to `Manly Power Tools`.

```
<ROOT xmlns:updgrm='urn:schemas-microsoft-com:xml-updategram'>
  <updgrm:sync>
    <updgrm:before>
    </updgrm:before>
    <updgrm:after>
      <Production.ProductCategory Name='Burritos' />
    </updgrm:after>
  </updgrm:sync>
  <updgrm:sync>
    <updgrm:before>
      <Production.ProductCategory Name='Burritos' />
    </updgrm:before>
    <updgrm:after>
      <Production.ProductCategory Name='Manly Power Tools' />
    </updgrm:after>
  </updgrm:sync>
</ROOT>
```

In the updategram button's click event, modify the code within the Try block, as follows:

```
conn.Open(strconn, Userid, password)
cmd.ActiveConnection = conn
```

```
cmdText = "<ROOT xmlns:updgrm='urn:schemas-microsoft-com:xml-updategram'>" & _
          "<updgrm:sync>" & _
          "<updgrm:before>" & _
          "</updgrm:before>" & _
```

```
            "<updgrm:after>" & _
            "<Production.ProductCategory Name='Burritos' />" & _
            "</updgrm:after>" & _
            "</updgrm:sync>" & _
            "<updgrm:sync>" & _
            "<updgrm:before>" & _
            "<Production.ProductCategory Name='Burritos' />" & _
            "</updgrm:before>" & _
            "<updgrm:after>" & _
            "<Production.ProductCategory Name='Manly Power Tools' />" & _
            "</updgrm:after>" & _
            "</updgrm:sync>" & _
            "</ROOT>"

    cmd.CommandText = cmdText

    InStream.Open()

    cmd.Dialect = dbGuid
    cmd.Properties("Output Stream").Value = InStream
    cmd.Execute(, , 1024)

      InStream.Position = 0
      InStream.Charset = "utf-8"

    Me.txtResults.Text = Instream.ReadText()

    conn.Close()

    MessageBox.Show("Record Updated")
```

Run the program and execute this updategram by clicking the updategram button. If you left the code in that writes to the text box, you receive a message similar to what was previously shown in Figure 13-4. To view the results, query the Production.ProductCategory table, which displays the newly inserted and updated records, as shown in Figure 13-7.

	ProductCategoryID	Name	rowguid	ModifiedDate
1	1	Bikes	CFBDA25C-DF71-...	1998-06-01 00:00...
2	2	Components	C657828D-D808-...	1998-06-01 00:00...
3	3	Clothing	10A7C342-CA82-...	1998-06-01 00:00...
4	4	Accessories	2BE3BE36-D9A2-...	1998-06-01 00:00...
5	7	Go-Karts	D93E74EF-77CD-...	2005-04-05 23:47...
6	8	Dirt Bikes	5EEC73B6-13C5-...	2005-04-06 22:38...
7	10	Manly Power Tools	98098569-530A-4...	2005-04-07 20:03...

Figure 13-7

Although this example used two <sync> blocks, you can obtain the same results by using a single <sync> block.

The next example uses a mapping schema to update a record in the Production.ProductCategory table. Before you begin this example, run the following T-SQL statement against the AdventureWorks database in a query window in SQL Server management studio:

```
SELECT * FROM Production.ProductReview
```

The results from this query should return four records. Take a look at the last record, where the ProductReviewID is 4. This is the record the next example will update, specifically the Rating column. Currently the value for that column is 5. The example will update and change that value.

First, create the following mapping schema in your favorite text editor and save it as `C:\Wrox\updatemapschema.xml`:

```
<xsd:schema xmlns:xsd="http://www.w3.org/2001/XMLSchema"
            xmlns:sql="urn:schemas-microsoft-com:mapping-schema">
<xsd:annotation>
  <xsd:appinfo>
    <sql:relationship name="ProdRvw"
          parent="Production.Product"
          parent-key="ProductID"
          child="Production.ProductReview"
          child-key="ProductID" />
  </xsd:appinfo >
</xsd:annotation>

  <xsd:element name="Product" sql:relation="Production.Product" type="ProductLine"
/>
   <xsd:complexType name="ProductLine" >
     <xsd:sequence>
        <xsd:element name="ProductReview"
                     sql:relation="Production.ProductReview"
                    sql:relationship="ProdRvw" >
           <xsd:complexType>
              <xsd:attribute name="ProductReviewID" type="xsd:integer" />
              <xsd:attribute name="ProductID" type="xsd:integer" />
        <xsd:attribute name="Rating" type="xsd:integer" />
           </xsd:complexType>
        </xsd:element>
     </xsd:sequence>
        <xsd:attribute name="ProductID"   type="xsd:integer" />
    </xsd:complexType>

</xsd:schema>
```

Next, in the updategram button's click event, modify the code in the `Try` block as follows:

```
conn.Open(strconn, Userid, password)
cmd.ActiveConnection = conn
```

```
cmdText = "<ROOT xmlns:updgrm='urn:schemas-microsoft-com:xml-updategram'>" & _
          "<updgrm:sync mapping-schema='c:\Wrox\updatemapschema.xml'>" & _
            "<updgrm:before>" & _
              "<ProductReview ProductID = '798' />" & _
            "</updgrm:before>" & _
            "<updgrm:after>" & _
                "<ProductReview ProductID = '798' Rating ='4'/>" & _
            "</updgrm:after>" & _
```

```
            "</updgrm:sync>" & _
            "</ROOT>"
```

```
    cmd.CommandText = cmdText

    InStream.Open()

    cmd.Dialect = dbGuid
    cmd.Properties("Output Stream").Value = InStream
    cmd.Execute(, , 1024)

    InStream.Position = 0
    InStream.Charset = "utf-8"

    Me.txtResults.Text = Instream.ReadText()

    conn.Close()

    MessageBox.Show("Record Updated")
```

Run the program and click the updategram button to execute the updategram. When the execution is complete, query the Production.ProductReview table to view that indeed the Rating for ProductID 798 has been changed from a value of 5 to a value of 4, as shown in Figure 13-8.

	ProductReviewID	ProductID	ReviewerName	ReviewDate	EmailAddress	Rating
1	1	709	John Smith	2003-10-20 00:00...	john@fourthcoffee.com	5
2	2	937	David	2003-12-15 00:00...	david@graphicdesignin...	4
3	3	937	Jill	2003-12-17 00:00...	jill@margiestravel.com	2
4	4	798	Laura Norman	2003-12-17 00:00...	laura@treyresearch.net	4

Figure 13-8

As you have seen, updating data is quite simple yet very versatile. Before moving on to passing parameters in updategrams, there is one more quick topic to cover.

When using update updategrams, there is an attribute called `updg:id` that links records in the `<before>` and `<after>` blocks. The purpose of this attribute is to help associate a record in the `<before>` block with its `<after>` block partner.

You use the `updg:id` attribute to mark and link rows in the `<before>` and `<after>` blocks. When the updategram is processed, the processor uses this attribute to link a row in the `<before>` block with a row in the `<after>` block.

To use the `updg:id` attribute, simply specify a value for the attribute, as follows:

```
    updg:id="linkvalue"
```

In this syntax, `linkvalue` is the value that links the `<before>` and `<after>` rows.

For example, the following code creates a link between the elements in the `<before>` and `<after>` blocks using the `updg:id` attribute, specified by the value of `a`, and then inserts a new record into the same table:

```
<ROOT xmlns:updg="urn:schemas-microsoft-com:xml-updategram">
  <updg:sync >
    <updg:before>
       <Production.ProductCategory updg:id="a" Name="Manly Power Tools" />
    </updg:before>
    <updg:after>
      <Production.ProductCategory updg:id="a" Name="Very Manly Power Tools" />
      <Production.ProductCategory updg:id="b" Name="Sissy Tools" />
    </updg:after>
  </updg:sync>
</ROOT>
```

The `updg:id` attribute is not necessary if the elements in the mapping schema are defined with the `sql:key-fields` attribute, and if there is a unique value provided to the key fields in the updategram.

You should have a good grasp of updategrams by now, so it is time to complicate things a bit and discuss the topic of passing parameters to updategrams.

Passing Parameters

As you have probably deduced by now, updategrams look exactly like templates because that is what they are. Because they are templates, updategrams inherit the functionalities that are given to templates, especially the capability to pass parameters to them.

This is not new functionality, not even to updategrams. Passing parameters to templates has been around in SQL Server and SQLXML for quite a while. However, in SQLXML 4.0, passing a parameter is a bit different than in previous versions.

The first step to passing parameters is to create the updategram that accepts parameters. You do this by using the `updg:param` element and passing value to the name attribute. The syntax is as follows:

```
<updg:param name="parametername"/>
```

`parametername` is the name of the parameter used in the updategram `<before>` and `<after>` blocks.

The following example takes two parameters with which to update the Production.ProductReview table. The first parameter is the ProductReviewID, used to identify the row to be updated. The second parameter is the value of the Rating to update. Inside the updategram, the values are held in two variables, `ProdCatID` and `ProdName`. Those variables are then used in the `<before>` and `<after>` blocks when the updategram is executed:

```
<ROOT xmlns:updg="urn:schemas-microsoft-com:xml-updategram">
<updg:header>
  <updg:param name="ProdCatID"/>
  <updg:param name="ProdName" />
</updg:header>
  <updg:sync >
    <updg:before>
       <Production.ProductCategory ProductCategoryID="$ProdCatID" />
    </updg:before>
```

```
    <updg:after>
      <Production.ProductCategory Name="$ProdName" />
    </updg:after>
  </updg:sync>
</ROOT>
```

This example is used to set the `Rating` value set a few examples ago back to the original value of 5. If you remember, you used an updategram to change the value of the `Rating` from 5 to a value of 4 for ProductReviewID 4 in the Production.ProductReview table.

In the updategram button's click event, modify the code in the `Try` block as follows:

```
conn.Open(strconn, Userid, password)
cmd.ActiveConnection = conn

cmdText = "<ROOT xmlns:updg="urn:schemas-microsoft-com:xml-updategram">" & _
"<updg:header>" & _
"<updg:param name="ProdRevID"/>" & _
"<updg:param name="Rating" />" & _
"</updg:header>" & _
"<updg:sync >" & _
"<updg:before>" & _
"<Production.ProductReview ProductReviewID="$ProdRevID" />" & _
"</updg:before>" & _
"<updg:after>" & _
"<Production.ProductReview ProductReviewID="$ProdRevID" Rating="$Rating" />" & _
"</updg:after>" & _
"</updg:sync>" & _
"</ROOT>"

cmd.CommandText = cmdText

InStream.Open()

cmd.Dialect = dbGuid
cmd.Properties("Output Stream").Value = InStream
cmd.NamedParameters = True

cmd.Parameters.Append(cmd.CreateParameter("@ProdRevID",_
ADODB.DataTypeEnum.adInteger, ADODB.ParameterDirectionEnum.adParamInput, 4))

cmd.Parameters.Append(cmd.CreateParameter("@Rating", ADODB.DataTypeEnum.adInteger,_
ADODB.ParameterDirectionEnum.adParamInput, 5))

cmd.Execute(, , 1024)

  InStream.Position = 0
  InStream.Charset = "utf-8"

conn.Close()

MessageBox.Show("Record Updated")
```

Run the program and click the updategram button to execute the updategram. When the execution is complete, query the Production.ProductReview table to view that indeed the Rating for ProductID 798 has been changed back to a value of 5 from a value of 4.

To verify the results, run the following T-SQL in a query window:

```
SELECT * FROM Production.ProductReview
```

The `Rating` value for ProductReviewID 4 is back to a value of 5.

Passing parameters is quite simple and provides you with a great amount of flexibility when dealing with updategrams. However, even with all of the flexibility that updategrams provide, there still remains an issue of concurrency, that is, multiple people updating or modifying the same record at the same time, no matter what the technology you use to update data. That topic is discussed next.

Updategram Concurrency

Concurrency is the process of dealing with the issue of multiple people updating the same record in a multi-user environment. This applies to anything in SQL Server that updates data, even updategrams.

SQL Server uses what is called Optimistic Concurrency Control, a method of data integrity that ensures that the data you request has not changed between the time you requested the data and the time you issue the update.

In updategrams, concurrency control is done by including the original values in the `<before>` block. When it comes time to update the database with the value of the `<after>` block, the updategram checks the values of the `<before>` block with the values in the database.

There are three levels of control offered by the Optimistic Concurrency Control, and you can determine which level you use by the type of updategram. The three levels are outlined in the following sections.

Low-Level Concurrency Protection

Low-level concurrency protection is a simple update, commonly called a *blind* update. This type of update does not check the value of the database against the value in the `<before>` block, regardless of any updates made to the data between the time you requested the data and the time you issue the update.

In a low-level update, only primary key columns are specified in the `<before>` block, which simply identifies the record to be updated.

The following example illustrates a low-level updategram:

```
<ROOT xmlns:updgrm="urn:schemas-microsoft-com:xml-updategram">
  <updgrm:sync>
    <updgrm:before>
      <Production.ProductModel ProductModelID="20" />
```

```
      </updgrm:before>
      <updgrm:after>
        <Production.ProductModel ProductModelID="20" Name="ExtremeWidget" />
      </updgrm:after>
    </updgrm:sync>
  </ROOT>
```

This updategram updates the Name column regardless of any updates made to it prior to this update being applied, and regardless of any other updates made to the records specified since the record was first read. Therefore it is low-level concurrency.

Medium-Level Concurrency Protection

Medium-level protection compares the current database column values with the `<before>` block values in the updategram, checking to see if the values in the database have been updated by another process prior to being read by your transaction.

To ensure this level of protection, the `<before>` block needs to specify not only the key column or columns, but the value or values of the columns you are updating as well.

The following illustrates a medium- (or intermediate-) level protection updategram:

```
<ROOT xmlns:updgrm="urn:schemas-microsoft-com:xml-updategram">
  <updgrm:sync>
    <updgrm:before>
      <Production.ProductModel ProductModelID="20" Name="ExtremeWidget"/>
    </updgrm:before>
    <updgrm:after>
      <Production.ProductModel ProductModelID="20" Name="Power Packs" />
    </updgrm:after>
  </updgrm:sync>
</ROOT>
```

In this example, if the value of Name has been changed since the request of your transaction, the update fails. In the `<before>` block, the value of the Name column is specified so that when the updategram is executed, that value is compared against the value in the database to make sure it has not changed. Therefore, it is a medium- or intermediate-level of concurrency.

High-Level Concurrency Protection

The best level of concurrency protection is the highest level of protection, which guarantees that the record has not changed since your transaction has read the record. Realistically, this does not prevent other users from changing the data, as that would spark a mutiny aboard ship from your users. What it does do is stop your update from taking place because your data in the updategram and the data in the database no longer match.

There are two things you can do to obtain this level of protection. The first is to include multiple columns in the `<before>` block. When the updategram is executed, it compares all the values in the `<before>` block with the values in the database. If any of the column values have changed, the update does not occur. It's as simple as that. The more columns you specify in the `<before>` block, the higher the level of protection.

Second, you can compare datetime or timestamp values. This requires that the table you are operating against has a `datetime` or `timestamp` data type column. In this case, you simply include the primary key column and the datetime or timestamp column in the `<before>` block (instead of all the other columns as discussed in the first option). When the updategram is executed, it compares the value in the `<before>` block with the value in the database. If they match, the update takes place. If they differ, the update does not happen.

The following illustrates an updategram using the timestamp option:

```
<ROOT xmlns:updgrm="urn:schemas-microsoft-com:xml-updategram">
  <updgrm:sync>
    <updgrm:before>
      <Production.ProductModel ProductModelID="34" ModifiedDate="2002-11-20
09:56:38.273"/>
    </updgrm:before>
    <updgrm:after>
      <Production.ProductModel Name="Power Packs" />
    </updgrm:after>
  </updgrm:sync>
</ROOT>
```

In this example, the updategram compares the ModifiedDate value in the `<update>` block against the value in the ModifiedDate column in the database for ProductModelID 34. If they match, the update occurs. If they do not match, the record has been modified, and the update does not take place.

NULL Handling

SQLXML allows you specify `NULL` for an element or attribute in an updategram. This is accomplished by using the `updg:nullvalue` attribute.

Specifying a `NULL` value for an attribute or element is done via the `updg:nullvalue` attribute. The syntax for this attribute is as follows:

```
Updg:nullvalue="nullvalue"
```

`nullvalue` specifies the `NULL` value for an element or attribute.

The following example uses the `updg:nullvalue` attribute to set the value of Name column in the Production.ProductModel table to `NULL` where the value of ProductModelID is `34`:

```
<ROOT xmlns:updgrm="urn:schemas-microsoft-com:xml-updategram">
  <updgrm:sync updg:nullvalue="ISNULL">
    <updgrm:before>
      <Production.ProductReview ProductReviewID="4" Rating="4"/>
    </updgrm:before>
    <updgrm:after>
      <Production.ProductReview Rating="ISNULL" />
    </updgrm:after>
  </updgrm:sync>
</ROOT>
```

To test NULL values, replace the cmdText assignment statement in the updategram button's click event in the Try block with the following code:

```
cmdText = "<ROOT xmlns:updgrm='urn:schemas-microsoft-com:xml-updategram'>" & _
"<updgrm:sync updg:nullvalue='ISNULL'>" & _
"<updgrm:before>" & _
"<Production.ProductReview ProductReviewID='4' Rating='4'/>" & _
"</updgrm:before>" & _
"<updgrm:after>" & _
"<Production.ProductReview Rating='ISNULL' />" & _
"</updgrm:after>" & _
"</updgrm:sync>" & _
"</ROOT>"

cmd.CommandText = cmdText
```

When you run the application and click the updategram button, you receive an error stating that the column does not allow NULLs. You receive this error on any column you are trying to update that does not allow NULLs. To remedy this situation, run the following T-SQL statement in a query window:

```
ALTER TABLE Production.ProductReview
  ALTER COLUMN Rating int NULL
GO
```

This time when you run the application and click the updategram button, you get a message box stating that the update succeeded. To verify the results, query the Production.ProductReview table as follows:

```
SELECT * FROM Production.ProductReview WHERE ProductReviewID = 4
```

Take a look at the Rating column for ProductReviewID 4. There should be no value in that column for ProductReviewID 4, so the update succeeded.

The updg:nullvalue attribute works both ways. In the previous example, it sets a column to NULL, but it can also be used to set a column to a value where the original value is NULL.

```
<ROOT xmlns:updgrm="urn:schemas-microsoft-com:xml-updategram">
  <updgrm:sync updg:nullvalue="ISNULL">
    <updgrm:before>
      <Production.ProductReview ProductReviewID="4" Rating="ISNULL"/>
    </updgrm:before>
    <updgrm:after>
      <Production.ProductModel Rating="4" />
    </updgrm:after>
  </updgrm:sync>
</ROOT>
```

This updategram looks for a NULL value in the Rating column for ProductReviewID 4 and updates it back to its original value.

As a last comment, NULL can also be passed as a parameter by using this same attribute, updg:nullvalue, in the <updg:header> element block.

Updategram Security

You should keep two issues of security in mind when using updategrams.

First, avoid using default mapping if at all possible. As explained at the beginning of this chapter, default mapping means an element name maps to a database table name, and attributes map to columns. This poses a potential security risk. Using explicit mapping solves this issue, as the mapping schemas are normally stored out of harm's way, and you can use arbitrary table and column names in the updategram.

Second, store the updategrams as templates on the server rather than creating them dynamically. This makes it unnecessary for users to have to create and execute their own updategrams, which could potentially expose the database.

Guidelines and Limitations

As with other functionalities in SQL Server 2005, the use of updategrams comes with its own guidelines and limitations, outlined in the following list:

- Unlike earlier versions of SQLXML, SQLXML 4.0 requires that updategrams have all the column values mapped explicitly in the referenced schema, generating the XML view for the updategram child elements.
- Any values that contain spaces and other special characters being used with the `sql:relation` and `sql:field` annotations must be enclosed in brackets. For example, "Sales Person" should be written as `"[Sales Person]"`.
- Passing `image` data types as parameters is not permitted during update operations.
- You can exclude the `<before>` block in an updategram for insert transactions if you specify a single `<after>` block. If you use multiple `<before>` and `<after>` blocks, all blocks must be included. Similarly, you can omit the `<after>` block when using a single `<before>` delete updategram transaction.
- Relationship chaining is not supported in updategrams. Commonly referred to as a cross-reference table, if table X is related to table Z via table Y in an updategram, the updategram fails.
- When modifying a binary column, you must use a mapping schema that includes the server data type (`text`, `ntext`, and `image`) and `xml` data type (`dt:type="binhex"` or you must specify `dt:type="binbase(64))`. Similarly, the data for the column must be included in the updategram.

Summary

The purpose of this chapter was three-fold. First, the chapter gave an introduction to updategrams to those who are new to the technology. An updategram is another option of updating SQL Server data.

Second, as mentioned at the start of the chapter, updategrams have been around a while, so this chapter also intended to explain the new features of updategrams in SQLXML 4.0. updategrams have been updated to handle the introduction of the `xml` data type in SQL Server 2005. The other features and enhancements to updategrams in SQLXML 4.0 include XSD schema mapping behavior when dealing with child elements and relationships.

Third, this chapter showed you how to use the new SQL Native Client to execute updategrams to insert, update, and delete data. Executing these types of operational statements prior to the SQL Native Client meant dealing with IIS and configuring the SQLXML Virtual Directory Manager. What this means now, however, is that you no longer need IIS and can do updategrams via SQLXML and .NET.

Overall, updategrams provide a very efficient way of modifying data without the learning curve and performance hits (shredding can potentially be costly when dealing with large XML documents) of OPENXML.

In the next chapter, you learn about bulk loading XML data through the XML view.

14

Bulk Loading XML Data Through the XML View

There are many ways to get data into a database, from the simple `INSERT` statement that inserts a single record, the `BULK INSERT` statement that inserts multiple records, or the BCP utility that has been around almost since the dawn of time and is used by DBAs to load large amounts of data. All of these tools accomplish the same task, but each has its idiosyncrasies.

XML has quickly become accepted as standard data storage and transfer mechanism, and the need to move large amounts of XML-formatted data in and out of a database becomes greater with each passing year. SQLXML provides the functionality of loading XML-formatted data into SQL Server 2005 through the SQLXML Bulk Load utility.

This chapter will cover SQLXML Bulk Load using XML views to load data into SQL Server 2005. The topics covered in this chapter are as follows:

- Bulk Load overview
- Bulk Load object model
- Using Bulk Load in a .NET environment
- Security issues
- Guidelines and limitations

Bulk Load Overview

The SQLXML Bulk Load is a separate utility that enables the import of well-formed XML-formatted documents or XML instances into Microsoft SQL Server. The SQLXML Bulk Load uses an annotated XSD schema, which maps the XML elements and attributes to the database tables and columns to manage the importing of the data and ensure the integrity of data load.

Prior to the bulk load operation, the Bulk Load utility checks to see if the XML document is well-formed. If it is not well-formed, the bulk load operation is cancelled and errors are generated. XML fragments do not fit within this criterion as long as the `XMLFragment` property is set to `TRUE` (the `XMLFragment` property is covered in greater detail later in the chapter).

The SQLXML Bulk Load utility has the added benefit of being able to load into more than one table at a time, unlike the limitation of the BCP utility or the `BULK INSERT` statement. The often-used `INSERT` statement, in conjunction with the `OPENXML` function, provides the same functionality as the SQLXML Bulk Load utility, but the SQLXML Bulk Load utility provides better performance when importing large amounts of data.

The SQLXML Bulk Load utility is provided by the SQLXML BulkLoad 4.0 Type Library, a COM object contained in the `xblkld4.dll` file.

This chapter first discusses some basics of the SQLXML Bulk Load utility, and then toward the end of the chapter is a complete section with examples covering all the topics previously discussed.

XML Data Streaming

The SQLXML Bulk Load utility works by streaming the data from the XML document instead of reading the entire document at once. As the XML document is streamed, the Bulk Load utility reads and interprets the document, determining which tables it needs to deal with, and then generates the records for insertion.

Streaming works well in all bulk load situations, especially when dealing with large XML documents. Imagine trying to load a very large XML document into memory and then trying to process it. This is why the Bulk Load utility streams the XML documents — they are more efficient and better performing.

The downside to streaming is the potential that the XML document does not need to be well-formed. For example, the Bulk Load utility will load an XML document missing a root node.

Bulk Load Operation Modes

The SQLXML Bulk Load utility can be executed in two separate modes: Transacted and Non-transacted. These modes define at a transactional level how the records are imported into SQL Server.

Transacted

The *Transacted mode* basically states that the entire bulk load process is a single transaction. The bulk load will either succeed or fail. If the transaction succeeds, the bulk load import is committed and saved. If any part of the data import fails, the transactions are rolled back.

As the Bulk Load utility reads the XML document for the tables it needs to handle, the Transacted mode tells the Bulk Load utility to create a temporary file for each of the tables it finds. The Bulk Load utility then stores the data in the temporary file for each corresponding table then initiates a `BULK INSERT` statement for each temporary file. You specify the location for these temporary files by using the `TempFilePath` property.

The Transacted mode reads the data twice: once to read and write the data to the temporary files and a second time reading from the temporary files to insert into the database. From a performance perspective, this is not the most efficient method. However, if your goal is simply to get the data in and you're not worried about partially loaded data, this is your best option.

To use Transacted mode, you must set the `Transaction` property of the SQLXML Bulk Load object to `TRUE`.

Non-Transacted

The Non-transacted mode is the default mode, and the most performance is gained with this mode. The Non-transacted mode does not create temporary files, as the data is imported directly into the tables from the XML documents.

The SQL Native Client in the OLEDB provider implements the `IRowsetFastLoad` interface. This interface carries support for bulk load operations, which provides faster importing of data into a SQL Server table.

Since this mode does not operate with transactions, a rollback of the data is not guaranteed if an error in the import occurs. In this mode, the Bulk Load utility uses a default internal transaction that is committed upon completion of the data insertion. If the `Transaction` property is set to `TRUE`, this default internal transaction is not used.

Unless your target tables are empty when beginning the bulk load operation, this mode is not recommended since it cannot guarantee the integrity of the data when the operation is complete.

Bulk Load Object Model

The SQLXML Bulk Load functionality comes from the `SQLXMLBulkLoad` object. This object contains a number of methods and properties supporting the bulk loading of XML-formatted data into an SQL Server table. The following sections detail the methods and properties contained in the SQLXML Bulk Load object.

Execute Method

The `Execute` method loads the schema file and associated data file, which are passed as parameters. The syntax for using the `Execute` method is as follows:

```
Dim objBulkLoad As SQLXMLBULKLOADLib.SQLXMLBulkLoad4Class = New_
SQLXMLBULKLOADLib.SQLXMLBulkLoad4Class

objBulkLoad.Execute("C:\Wrox\MotocrossBulkLoadSchema.xml",
"C:\Wrox\MotocrossBulkLoad.xml")
```

The first parameter is the XML schema file (XML view) that contains the mapping schema. The Bulk Load utility examines the schema with its annotations, and maps the elements and attributes to the appropriate tables and columns in the database.

The second parameter is the XML document or fragment. This can be either a file name or an input stream.

BulkLoad Property

The Boolean `BulkLoad` property tells the Bulk Load utility whether or not to import the data. If this property is set to `FALSE`, the associated database schemas (tables and columns) are created (if they do not exist), but the Bulk Load operation is not executed (the data is not imported). If it the property is set to `TRUE`, the Bulk Load operation executes.

The syntax for the `BulkLoad` property is as follows:

```
Dim objBulkLoad As SqlXmlBulkLoad.SQLXMLBulkLoad4Class = New _
SqlXmlBulkLoad.SQLXMLBulkLoad4Class

objBulkLoad.BulkLoad = True
```

The default value for the `BulkLoad` property is `TRUE`.

CheckConstraint Property

The Boolean `CheckConstraint` property specifies whether the Bulk Load utility should recognize or ignore column constraints in the database. If this property is set to `FALSE`, all constraints are ignored during an insert. If you set this property to `TRUE`, each column constraint is checked for each value inserted. When you set this property to `TRUE` and a value is inserted into a column that violates a constraint, an error is generated. Depending on the transaction mode (transacted or non-transacted) the bulk load either rolls back or continues (resulting in invalid data).

The syntax for the `CheckConstraint` property is as follows:

```
Dim objBulkLoad As SqlXmlBulkLoad.SQLXMLBulkLoad4Class = New _
SqlXmlBulkLoad.SQLXMLBulkLoad4Class

objBulkLoad.CheckConstraints = False
```

The default value for this property is `FALSE`.

ConnectionCommand Property

The `ConnectionCommand` property identifies the connection that the Bulk Load utility should use for its load operations. You can specify this property or the `ConnectionString` property (covered in the next section). It is not necessary to specify both. If both are specified, the Bulk Load utility uses the last property specified.

The syntax for the `ConnectionCommand` property is as follows:

```
Dim objBulkLoad As SqlXmlBulkLoad.SQLXMLBulkLoad4Class = New _
SqlXmlBulkLoad.SQLXMLBulkLoad4Class

Dim cmd as New ADODB.Command

objBulkLoad.ConnectionCommand = cmd
```

When you use the ConnectionCommand property, you must set the Transaction property to TRUE.

The default value for the ConnectionCommand property is NULL.

ConnectionString Property

As an alternative to the ConnectionCommand property, the ConnectionString property defines the OLE DB connection information required to make a connection to SQL Server. As with the ConnectionCommand property, if both are specified, the Bulk Load utility uses the last property specified.

The syntax for the ConnectionString property is as follows:

```
Dim objBulkLoad As SqlXmlBulkLoad.SQLXMLBulkLoad4Class = New _
SqlXmlBulkLoad.SQLXMLBulkLoad4Class

objBulkLoad.ConnectionString = "Provider=SQLOLE DB;data
source=localhost;database=wrox"
```

The default value for this property is NULL.

ErrorLogFile Property

The ErrorLogFile property specifies the path and file name to which all bulk load errors and messages are written. If no value is specified, no logging is performed.

The syntax for the ErrorLogFile property is as follows:

```
Dim objBulkLoad As SqlXmlBulkLoad.SQLXMLBulkLoad4Class = New _
SqlXmlBulkLoad.SQLXMLBulkLoad4Class

objBulkLoad.ErrorLogFile = "C:\Wrox\ErrorLog.txt"
```

ForceTableLock Property

This Boolean property specifies whether the Bulk Load utility locks the table into which it is currently importing data. If you set the ForceTableLock property to TRUE, the Bulk Load utility locks the table from the time it starts the import until the time it finishes, or commits, the import. If you set this value to FALSE, the table is locked per record insert.

The syntax for the ForceTableLock property is as follows:

```
Dim objBulkLoad As SqlXmlBulkLoad.SQLXMLBulkLoad4Class = New _
SqlXmlBulkLoad.SQLXMLBulkLoad4Class

objBulkLoad.ForceTableLock = True
```

The default value for the ForceTableLock property is FALSE.

IgnoreDuplicateKeys Property

The Boolean IgnoreDuplicateKeys property tells the Bulk Load utility what to do when a duplicate key value is inserted into a key column. When you set this property to FALSE, the bulk load fails if attempting to insert a duplicate key. If you set it to TRUE, only the record being inserted fails but the bulk load continues with the next record.

The syntax for the IgnoreDuplicateKeys property is as follows:

```
Dim objBulkLoad As SqlXmlBulkLoad.SQLXMLBulkLoad4Class = New _
SqlXmlBulkLoad.SQLXMLBulkLoad4Class

objBulkLoad.IgnoreDuplicateKeys = True
```

This property has performance ramifications if set to TRUE. For each insert an internal COMMIT is performed, drastically reducing performance. You can set the IgnoreDuplicateKeys property to TRUE only when the Transaction property is set to FALSE. Otherwise, a transaction conflict would occur.

The default value for the IgnoreDuplicateKeys property is FALSE.

KeepIdentity Property

The KeepIdentity property dictates how the Bulk Load utility handles key, or identity, columns. A Boolean property, when you set it to FALSE, ignores identity column values specified in the XML document, allowing SQL Server to generate the value. If you set the Bulk Load Utility to TRUE, it uses the values in the XML document for the identity column.

The syntax for the KeepIdentity property is as follows:

```
Dim objBulkLoad As SqlXmlBulkLoad.SQLXMLBulkLoad4Class = New _
SqlXmlBulkLoad.SQLXMLBulkLoad4Class

objBulkLoad.KeepIdentity = True
```

The default for the KeepIdentity property is TRUE.

SchemaGen Property

The SchemaGen property dictates whether the target tables are created prior to performing the bulk load operation. When you set this property to TRUE, the Bulk Load utility retrieves the list of tables and column names from the mapping schema and creates them prior to the bulk load operation.

The syntax for the SchemaGen property is as follows:

```
Dim objBulkLoad As SqlXmlBulkLoad.SQLXMLBulkLoad4Class = New _
SqlXmlBulkLoad.SQLXMLBulkLoad4Class

objBulkLoad.SchemaGen = True
```

This property does not create the PRIMARY KEY constraints when the tables are created, but it does create the FOREIGN KEY constraints for any sql:relationship and sql:field matches it finds in the mapping schema.

The default value for the SchemaGen property is FALSE.

SGDropTables Property

The SGDropTables property is used together with the SchemaGen property and dictates whether the target tables should be dropped prior to the bulk load operation. When you set this property to FALSE, the target tables are not dropped. If you set it to TRUE, the target tables are dropped and recreated.

The syntax for the SGDropTables property is as follows:

```
Dim objBulkLoad As SqlXmlBulkLoad.SQLXMLBulkLoad4Class = New _
SqlXmlBulkLoad.SQLXMLBulkLoad4Class

objBulkLoad.SGDropTables = True
```

The default value for this property is FALSE.

SGUseID Property

When you set the SGUseID property to TRUE, it investigates the mapping schema to establish the fields that make up the primary key fields of the target table being created, thus, the SchemaGen property must also be set to TRUE. Any attributes in the mapping schema with a dt:type="id" type are used by the SchemaGen property to add the PRIMARY KEY.

The syntax for the SGUseID property is as follows:

```
Dim objBulkLoad As SqlXmlBulkLoad.SQLXMLBulkLoad4Class = New _
SqlXmlBulkLoad.SQLXMLBulkLoad4Class

objBulkLoad.SGUseID = True
```

The default value for this property is FALSE.

TempFilePath Property

The TempFilePath property identifies the path where the temporary files are created during a Transacted Bulk Load operation. If you set the Transaction property to TRUE and do not specify a TempFilePath property value, the TEMP environment value is used.

The syntax for the TempFilePath property is as follows:

```
Dim objBulkLoad As SqlXmlBulkLoad.SQLXMLBulkLoad4Class = New _
SqlXmlBulkLoad.SQLXMLBulkLoad4Class

objBulkLoad.TempFilePath = "C:\Wrox\"
```

If you do not specify a path in this property, the XML Bulk Load utility stores files in the location specified in the TEMP environment variable. If the path specified for this property is not on the local server, the path must be a valid UNC path. For example:

```
objBulkLoad.TempFilePath = "\\MyServer\MyPath"
```

Transaction Property

The Transaction property indicates the Bulk Load operation mode. A value of TRUE indicates that the Bulk Load operation will be transactional, whereas a value of FALSE will not. The default is FALSE.

The syntax for the Transaction property is as follows:

```
Dim objBulkLoad As SqlXmlBulkLoad.SQLXMLBulkLoad4Class = New _
SqlXmlBulkLoad.SQLXMLBulkLoad4Class

objBulkLoad.Transaction = True
```

If you set this property to TRUE and the ConnectionString property sets or defines the connection string, XML Bulk Load manages the transaction operations such as starting and committing the transaction, or rolling back the transaction if needed.

If you set this property to FALSE, the XML Bulk Load utility uses the OLE DB interface IRowsetFastLoad to load the data.

The SQL Native Client OLE DB provider provides the IRowSetInterface. The IRowSetInterface supports the memory-based bulk copying and provides the COMMIT method (discussed previously in the "IgnoreDuplicateKeys Property" section).

If you set this property to FALSE, you cannot use the ConnectionObject. The default value for the Transaction property is FALSE.

XMLFragment Property

The Boolean value XMLFragment property, when set to FALSE, basically tells the Bulk Load utility that the incoming XML document is well-formed.

The syntax for the XMLFragment property is as follows:

```
Dim objBulkLoad As SqlXmlBulkLoad.SQLXMLBulkLoad4Class = New _
SqlXmlBulkLoad.SQLXMLBulkLoad4Class

objBulkLoad.XMLFragment = True
```

The default value for this property is FALSE.

Bulk Load in a .NET Environment

This section shows you how to use SQLXML Bulk Load in the .NET Framework. As explained earlier, the SQLXML Bulk Load utility is a separate component of SqlXml 4.0.

The first step is to reference the SQLXML Bulk Load `COM` object. Open the SqlCliTestApp application and from the Project menu, select Add Reference. On the Add Reference dialog, select the COM tab. Scroll down the list of components, looking for SqlXmlBulkLoad. Click the component to highlight it and then click OK, as shown in Figure 14-1.

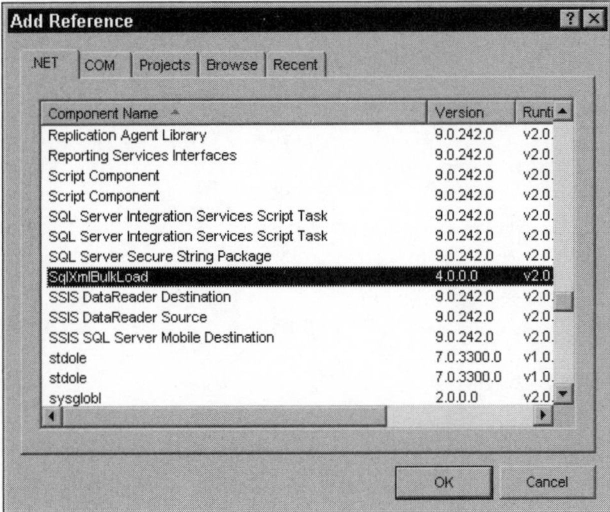

Figure 14-1

Figure 14-2 shows the added reference in Visual Studio 2005.

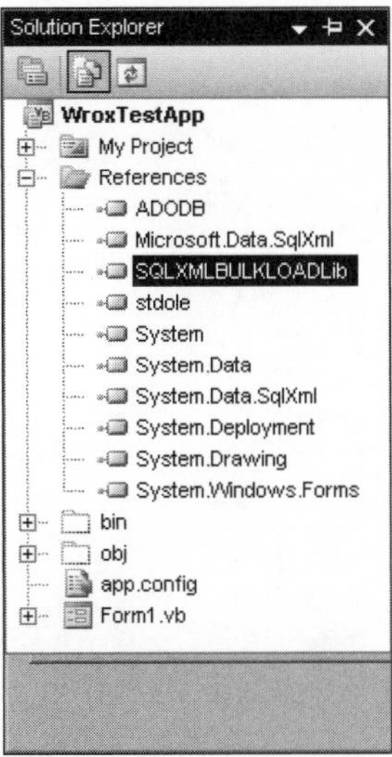

Figure 14-2

Next, you need to create the target database tables. In SQL Server Management Studio, open a query window and execute the following T-SQL:

```
USE [Wrox]
GO

CREATE TABLE [dbo].[Team](
 [TeamID] [int] IDENTITY(1,1) NOT NULL,
 [TeamName] [varchar](15) ,
PRIMARY KEY CLUSTERED
(
 [TeamID] ASC
) ON [PRIMARY]
) ON [PRIMARY]

GO

CREATE TABLE [dbo].[Rider](
 [RiderID] [int] NOT NULL,
 [TeamID] [int] NOT NULL,
 [RiderName] [varchar](25) ,
  [Class] [varchar] (3) NOT NULL,
 [NationalNumber] [int] NULL,
 CONSTRAINT [PK_Rider] PRIMARY KEY CLUSTERED
(
 [RiderID] ASC
) ON [PRIMARY]
) ON [PRIMARY]

GO
```

Next, open your favorite text editor and create the following XML document, saving it as `C:\Wrox\MotocrossBulkLoad.xml`:

```
<ROOT>
  <Team TeamID="1" TeamName="Yamaha">
    <Rider RiderID="1" RiderName="Chad Reed" Class="250" NationalNumber="22" />
    <Rider RiderID="2" RiderName="David Vuillemin" Class="250" NationalNumber="12"
/>
    <Rider RiderID="3" RiderName="Tim Ferry" Class="250" NationalNumber="15" />
  </Team>
  <Team TeamID="2" TeamName="Kawasaki">
    <Rider RiderID="4" RiderName="James Stewart" Class="250" NationalNumber="259"
/>
    <Rider RiderID="5" RiderName="Michael Byrne" Class="250" NationalNumber="26" />
  </Team>
  <Team TeamID="3" TeamName="Suzuki">
    <Rider RiderID="6" RiderName="Ricky Carmichael" Class="250" NationalNumber="4"
/>
    <Rider RiderID="7" RiderName="Davi Millsaps" Class="125" NationalNumber="188"
/>
    <Rider RiderID="8" RiderName="Broc Hepler" Class="125" NationalNumber="60" />
    <Rider RiderID="9" RiderName="Sebastien Tortelli" Class="250"
NationalNumber="103" />
  </Team>
```

```
    <Team TeamID="4" TeamName="Suzuki">
      <Rider RiderID="10" RiderName="Jeremy McGrath" Class="250" NationalNumber="2"
  />
      <Rider RiderID="11" RiderName="Ernesto Fonseca" Class="125" NationalNumber="24"
  />
      <Rider RiderID="12" RiderName="Travis Preston" Class="125" NationalNumber="70"
  />
      <Rider RiderID="13" RiderName="Andrew Short" Class="250" NationalNumber="51" />
      <Rider RiderID="14" RiderName="Mike LaRocco" Class="125" NationalNumber="5" />
      <Rider RiderID="15" RiderName="Kevin Windham" Class="250" NationalNumber="14"
  />
    </Team>
  </ROOT>
```

Now you need to create the mapping schema. In your text editor, create the following schema, saving it as `C:\Wrox\MotocrossBulkLoadSchema.xml`:

```
<xsd:schema xmlns:xsd="http://www.w3.org/2001/XMLSchema"
            xmlns:sql="urn:schemas-microsoft-com:mapping-schema">
<xsd:annotation>
  <xsd:appinfo>
    <sql:relationship name="TeamInfo"
          parent="Team"
          parent-key="TeamID"
          child="Rider"
          child-key="TeamID" />
  </xsd:appinfo>
</xsd:annotation>

  <xsd:element name="Team" sql:relation="Team"
                           sql:key-fields="TeamID" >
   <xsd:complexType>
     <xsd:sequence>
        <xsd:element name="Rider" sql:relation="Rider"
                     sql:key-fields="RiderID"
                     sql:relationship="TeamInfo">
          <xsd:complexType>
             <xsd:attribute name="RiderID" type="xsd:int" />
             <xsd:attribute name="RiderName" type="xsd:string" />
      <xsd:attribute name="Class" type="xsd:string" />
      <xsd:attribute name="NationalNumber" type="xsd:int" />
          </xsd:complexType>
        </xsd:element>
     </xsd:sequence>
        <xsd:attribute name="TeamID"   type="xsd:integer" />
        <xsd:attribute name="TeamName"   type="xsd:string" />
    </xsd:complexType>
  </xsd:element>
</xsd:schema>
```

Next, modify the Visual Studio test application. Add a new button on the form with the following properties:

Property	Value
Text	"Bulk Load"
Name	cmdBulkLoad

Last, double-click the Bulk Load button and add the following code in the `click` event (be sure to put the correct username and password in the connection string):

```
Try
  Dim objBulkLoad As SQLXMLBULKLOAD.SQLXMLBulkLoad4Class = New_
SQLXMLBULKLOAD.SQLXMLBulkLoad4Class
  objBulkLoad.ConnectionString = "Provider=SQLOLE DB;Data Provider=SQLNCLI;
Server=localhost;Database=Wrox;UID=sa;PWD=putpasswordhere"
  objBulkLoad.ErrorLogFile = "C:\Wrox\ImportError.xml"
  objBulkLoad.KeepIdentity = True
  objBulkLoad.Execute("C:\Wrox\MotocrossBulkLoadSchema.xml",
"C:\Wrox\MotocrossBulkLoad.xml")

  SET objBulkLoad = Nothing

  Me.txtResults.Text = "ImportSuccessful! "

Catch ex As Exception
  MessageBox.Show(ex.Message.ToString)
End Try
```

Run the program and click the Bulk Load button. The Bulk Load runs, and if it is successful an "Import Successful!" message is displayed in the output window, as shown in Figure 14-3.

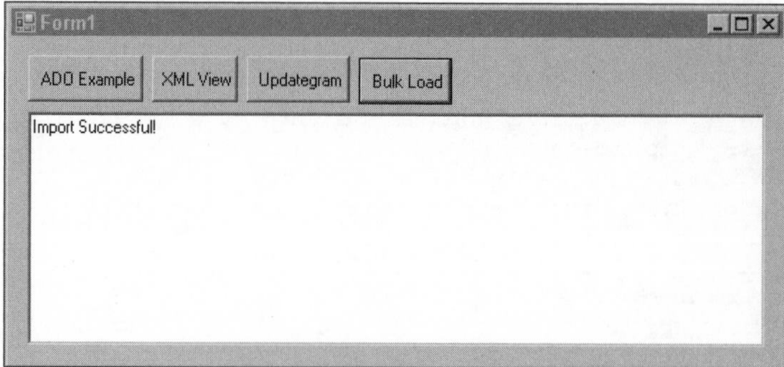

Figure 14-3

To verify the results, open a query window in SQL Server Management Studio and run the following query:

```
SELECT * FROM Team
GO
SELECT * FROM Rider
GO
```

Figure 14-4 shows the results of the Bulk Load import. The mapping schema provided the mapping between the tables and columns in the XSD annotated schema to the elements and attributes in the XML data document. When the bulk load operation began it determined which tables it needed to deal with by examining the mapping schema. Once the Bulk Load utility determined that it knew which tables and columns it needed, it brought in the data.

	TeamID	TeamName
1	1	Yamaha
2	2	Kawasaki
3	3	Suzuki
4	4	Suzuki

	RiderID	TeamID	Class	RiderName	NationalNumber
1	1	1	250	Chad Reed	22
2	2	1	250	David Vuillemin	12
3	3	1	250	Tim Ferry	15
4	4	2	250	James Stewart	259
5	5	2	250	Michael Byrne	26
6	6	3	250	Ricky Carmichael	4
7	7	3	125	Davi Millsaps	188
8	8	3	125	Broc Hepler	60
9	9	3	250	Sebastien Tortelli	103
10	10	4	250	Jeremy McGrath	2
11	11	4	125	Ernesto Fonseca	24
12	12	4	125	Travis Preston	70
13	13	4	250	Andrew Short	51
14	14	4	125	Mike LaRocco	5
15	15	4	250	Kevin Windham	14

Figure 14-4

In this example, the database schema already existed and all the Bulk Load utility had to do was import the data.

Go into SQL Server Management Studio and delete the Team and Rider tables using the following T-SQL:

```
DROP TABLE Team
GO

DROP TABLE Rider
GO
```

Next, modify the click event code behind the Bulk Load button as follows:

```
objBulkLoad.ErrorLogFile = "C:\Wrox\ImportError.xml"
objBulkLoad.KeepIdentity = True
objBulkLoad.SchemaGen = True
```

Rerun the application and click the Bulk Load button. When the application finishes execution, go back to your query window in SQL Server Management Studio and execute the following code:

```
SELECT * FROM Team
GO

SELECT * FROM Rider
GO
```

Because the SchemaGen property is now set to `True`, you can see that the tables were implicitly created.

The next topic discusses security as it pertains to the Bulk Load utility and some ideas that you should consider when using the Bulk Load utility.

Security Issues

The following is a list of security issues related to the Bulk Load utility:

- The error log file is overwritten each time the Bulk Load utility is run. Any data from a previous bulk load process is deleted and replaced.
- The Bulk Load utility can and may create temporary tables in the database as needed. Any temporary tables created are created with the same permissions that are being used to connect to the database.
- Bulk Load, when used in Transacted mode, may create and delete temporary files. The permissions used for the creation and deletion are the same permissions that the bulk load process is operating in.
- There is no preset time limit or setting to designate the amount of time for the Bulk Load utility to complete the import process. It runs until the process is complete and a `COMMIT` is issued or until an error occurs.
- The Bulk Load utility does not care about the amount of data being inserted.
- Data may be left in an incomplete state if the Bulk Load utility is run in Non-transacted mode.
- No permission settings are set within the Bulk Load utility itself. Permissions are passed to Bulk Load, which are then used for database access.
- Bulk load errors returned to the user may contain database information such as table and column names. It is good practice to catch these errors and return messages without database information.

Guidelines and Limitations

The following list contains some guidelines and limitations related to the Bulk Load utility:

- When setting the `Transaction` property to `TRUE` and specifying a path using the `TempFilePath` property, make sure the SQL Server account used to do the bulk load has access to the path specified in the `TempFilePath` property.
- For best performance when you are bulk loading into a table, disable all indexes on the target table.

- In the mapping schema, primary key tables must be defined before the tables that contain the corresponding foreign key. If they aren't, the Bulk Load utility will fail.
- Do not use SQL Server reserved words for element and attribute names in the mapping schema. If you set the `SchemaGen` property to `TRUE`, the Bulk Load utility uses these values to create the corresponding table and column names.
- Inline schemas, such as `xmlns="x:schema"`, are ignored by the XML Bulk Load utility.
- XML documents are not validated against any DTD or schema specified in the XML file.
- If you do not specify a `sql:overflow-field` annotation in the schema, any data in the XML document not specified in the schema is ignored.
- All information before and after the `<ROOT>` and `</ROOT>` elements is ignored.
- Any default attribute values specified in the mapping schema are used if the XML source does not provide a value for the corresponding attribute.
- `sql:url-encode` annotations are not supported.
- The `SchemaGen` property provides basic schema generation (tables and columns) when you use annotated XSD schemas.
- If multiple relationships exist between two tables, `SchemaGen` attempts to generate a single relationship using the keys from the multiple relationships. This could lead to T-SQL generated errors.

Summary

The purpose of this chapter was to provide information on how to use the SQXML Bulk Load utility in SQLXML 4.0. Understanding the SQLXML Bulk Load object model and its different methods and properties is essential to get the best performance and usage out of this utility.

Likewise, a good portion of this chapter was dedicated to showing you how to use the SQLXML Bulk Load utility in a .NET environment. With the improvements in the SQL Native Client, the Bulk Load utility is very fast and efficient and much easier to use.

Last, you learned about some security issues that will come in very useful when implementing the Bulk Load utility, as well as some guidelines and limitations of the Bulk Load utility.

The next chapter deals with the data access methods that you can use when executing SQLXML.

15

SQLXML Data Access Methods

When SQL Server 2000 first came on the scene, it was limited as to the amount of XML support it provided, especially from the client side. Since then there have a number of updates to SQLXML that provide additional functionality. The most prominent release was SQLXML 3.0, the Web release that provided more client-side functionality, as well as XSD schemas, the XML Bulk Load, updategrams, and Web Service (SOAP) support.

SQLXML 4.0, introduced in SQL Server 2005, provides even more of that same rich functionality, the most important being the support of the native `xml` data type and the capability to execute SQLXML queries via ADO.NET.

Also introduced with SQL Server 2005 is the SQL Native Client, a data access technology that combines both the SQL OLE DB provider and the SQL ODBC driver into a single API. This new client provides a new set of functionality that is completely separate from the already existing Microsoft Data Access Components (MDAC). The SQL Native Client is what allows applications to take advantage of the new SQL Server 2005 features, such as the `xml` data type, UDTs (user-defined types), and MARS (Multiple Active Result Sets).

This chapter focuses distinctly on data access methods using SQLXML 4.0 technology. You may already be familiar with some of this technology, such as SQLXML Managed Classes and Web Services, since they are not new to SQL Server 2005. What is discussed here are the new features added to these technologies in SQLXML 4.0.

The main topics discussed in this chapter are as follows:

- SQL Native Client
- SQLXML Managed Classes
- Web Services

SQL Native Client

Back in Chapter 11, you learned a little bit about the SQL Native Client and some of its capabilities. This section reviews the information in Chapter 11, but builds on it and delves deeper into the SQL Native Client.

SQL Server 2005 introduces a new technology that combines the earlier data access technologies, such as the ODBC driver and OLE DB provider, and replaces them with the SQL Native Client. This new data access client is an API that combines both the ODBC driver and OLE DB provider into a single interface. Besides combining these components, this DLL, called *sqlncli.dll*, also adds features such as support for the `xml` data type, UDTs (user defined types), and MARS (Multiple Active Result Sets).

SQL Native Client versus MDAC

Both the SQL Native Client and MDAC provide access to SQL Server, but there are a number of differences between them that you need to understand. The SQL Native Client incorporates many of the MDAC components, but it is specifically designed to work with the new features and enhancements made to SQL Server 2005.

For example, MDAC by itself does not support the SQL Server 2005 `xml` data type, but the SQL Native Client does.

The following is a list that highlights some of the areas where the SQL Native Client and MDAC differ:

- SQL Native Client does not support features such as connection pooling, memory management, and other MDAC-accessible features.
- SQL Native Client does not support SQLXML integration.
- SQL Native Client supports only SQL Server version 7.0 and higher.
- SQL Native Client supports only the OLEDB and ODBC interfaces.
- To make distribution easier, all the necessary data-access functionality in the SQL Native Client is included in a single DLL interface.

This is not quite a complete list—it merely highlights the bigger differences between the two technologies. The intent of the SQL Native Client is to simplify data access to SQL Server. The client tools for SQL Server are available for those who need a broader range of data access.

SQL Native Client Benefits

The design goal of the SQL Native Client is to make an easy way to access data from SQL Server, regardless of whether you are using OLEDB or ODBC. Because it combines both of these into a single interface, a developer can easily adapt to this new client without completely rewriting the application or changing any of the data access components.

The SQL Native Client uses many of the components of MDAC and works with version 2.6 or higher, or any version that is installed with Windows 2000 SP3 or later. The SQL Native Client also works with ADO (ActiveX Data Objects), providing access to all SQL Native Client functionality via ADO.

The following list explains the benefits and features of using the SQL Native Client:

- `xml` **data type:** Provides support for the `xml` data type on the client side.
- **User-Defined Types:** Provides support for UDTs on the client side.
- **Execution of multiple result sets:** Provides the capability to execute and return multiple result sets via a single connection.
- **Asynchronous operation:** Methods are now returned immediately, eliminating calling thread blocking issues.
- **Password expiration:** Users can now change their expired passwords without administrator intervention.

Deployment Considerations

The SQL Native Client is installed by default when you install SQL Server 2005 and can also be installed as a separate component for client installations. The installation file, SQLNCLI.msi, is found on the SQL Server 2005 installation CD and is used to install the SQL Native Client on client computers.

Separating this component into its own install component means it can be more easily distributed and even included in an application's installation routine. For now, the SQL Native Client install runs only in silent mode.

xml Data Type Support

When you query an `xml` data type column using the SQL Native Client, the results are returned either as a text stream or an ISequentialStream.

The ISequentialStream interface is the preferred method for reading and writing BLOBs (Binary Large Objects). As mentioned in the discussion of the `xml` data type in Chapter 4, XML documents and XML instances are stored in the `xml` data type column as BLOBs, and therefore can either be returned on the client side as strings or by using the ISequentialStream interface.

SQLXMLOLEDB Provider

The SQL Native Client cannot be used by itself when the goal is to work with XML from the client side. The purpose of the SQL Native Client is to provide access to SQL Server, not to provide SQLXML functionality. The `SQLXMLOLEDB` provider is an OLEDB provider that exposes the SQLXML functionality via ActiveX Data objects (ADO).

In addition, the provider is not a rowset provider; therefore, it can only execute commands via the Output Stream mode.

In Chapter 11, you saw an example that executed the `GetProducts` stored procedure. Here it is again:

```
dbGuid = "{5d531cb2-e6ed-11d2-b252-00c04f681b71}"

strconn = "Provider=SQLXMLOLEDB.4.0;Data Provider=SQLNCLI;Server=localhost;" & _
"Database=AdventureWorks"

Userid = "Type your SQL Server Login here"
```

```
Password = "Type your SQL Server Password HERE"

Me.Cursor = Cursors.WaitCursor

Try
  conn.Open(strconn, Userid, password)
  cmd.ActiveConnection = conn

  cmd.CommandText = "<ROOT xmlns:sql='urn:schemas-microsoft-com:xml- sql'>" & _
  "<sql:query client-side-xml=""1"">EXEC GetProducts FOR XML NESTED" & _
  "</sql:query></ROOT>"

  InStream.Open()

  cmd.Dialect = dbGuid
  cmd.Properties("Output Stream").Value = InStream
  cmd.Execute(, , 1024)

  InStream.Position = 0
  InStream.Charset = "utf-8"

  Me.txtResults.Text = InStream.ReadText()

  conn.Close()

Catch ex As Exception
  MessageBox.Show(ex.Message)
End Try
```

In this example, the `Provider` specified is the `SQLXMLOLEDB` provider with the SQL Native Client being used as the Data Provider. In Chapter 11, you learned that when this example is run, the ProductID, Name, and ProductNumber are returned and formatted properly by the `FOR XML` clause.

However, what happens when you modify the connection string and remove the `SQLXMLOLEDB` provider and execute the code? Modify the connection string as follows:

```
strconn = "Provider=SQLNCLI;Server=localhost;Database=AdventureWorks"
```

When you run the program and click the button, a message box similar to the one shown in Figure 15-1 is displayed.

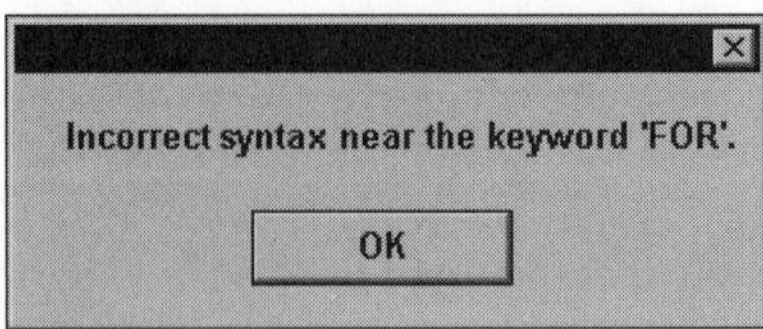

Figure 15-1

If you step through the code, you will notice a connection is indeed made to the database, but the error is generated when you attempt to execute the query. What you have essentially done is remove the part that provides the SQLXML functionality.

There are two parts to the connection string: `Provider` and `Data Provider`.

The correct connection string from the original example contains both a `Provider` and `Data Provider`, as follows:

```
Dim strconn As String

strconn = "Provider=SQLXMLOLEDB;Data Provider=SQLNCLI;Server=localhost;" & _
"Database=AdventureWorks"
```

The `Provider` is what provides the SQLXML functionality and exposes the provider-specific connection property. Without this provider, any SqlXml statements are rejected when executed.

The `Data Provider`, the SQL Native Client, is what executes the command. It provides the ProgID of the Provider that is contained within the SQL Native Client.

In the example, the `SQLXMLOLEDB` provider is what provides the SQLXML functionality. Removing this provider is what caused the error in Figure 15-1 to be generated because the SQL Native Client is for SQL Server access. It does not understand SQLXML commands, which are provided by the `SQLXMLOLEDB` provider.

Requirements

The requirements for using the `SQLXMLOLEDB` provider are straightforward. They are the following:

- Microsoft ActiveX Data Objects 2.6 and higher library
- SQLXML 4.0 SQL Native Client

SQLXMLOLEDB Provider Properties

There are eight properties exposed by the `SQLXMLOLEDB` provider, one of which you have already seen in Chapter 11 and again earlier in this chapter: the `ClientSideXML` property.

For example, the following code sets the `ClientSideXML` property to `True`, telling the provider that the formatting of XML will take place on the client:

```
Dim conn As New ADODB.Connection
Dim cmd As New ADODB.Command

Conn.Open("Provider=SQLXMLOLEDB;Data
Provider=SQLNCLI;Server=localhost;Database=AdventureWorksUID=Wrox;PWD=Wrox")

cmd.ActiveConnection = conn
cmd.Properties("ClientSideXML").Value = True
```

In the example, an ADO command object is created, and then the `ClientSideXML` property is set on the command object.

The following section explains each property of the SQLXMLOLEDB provider and provides examples for each property. While these properties are properties of the provider, they are exposed via the provider as provider-specific command properties.

Base Path

The Base Path property specifies the location of the XSLT style sheet or mapping schema files. The syntax for setting this property is as follows:

```
cmd.Properties("Base Path").Value = "C:\Wrox\Chapter15\"
```

In this example, the "Base Path" property is used to set the root, or base, location of any mapping schemas or XSL style sheets.

ClientSideXML

You have seen the ClientSideXML property in previous examples. It specifies whether you want the data from a result set converted at the client instead of the server. The syntax for setting this property is as follows:

```
cmd.Properties("ClientSideXML").Value = False
```

The default for this property is False.

Mapping Schema

The Mapping Schema property specifies the name and location of the mapping schema when executing an XPath query. The syntax for setting this property is as follows:

```
cmd.Properties("Mapping Schema").Value = "C:\Wrox\Chapter15\Motocross.xml"
```

Both relative and absolute paths are allowed. If no path is specified, the relative path is that of the current directory. URLs are also allowed, but WinHTTP must be configured to access HTTP and HTTPS through a proxy server.

The default for this property is NULL.

namespaces

The namespaces property provides the capability to execute XPath queries that use namespaces. The syntax for setting this property is as follows:

```
cmd.Properties("namespaces").Value = "xmlns:sql='urn:schema:products'"
```

When schema elements are qualified with a namespace, the XPath queries that are executed against the schema must specify that namespace. This becomes a problem when specifying a wildcard character (signified by an asterisk [*]), because SQLXML 4.0 does not support wildcard characters. The solution for this is to use the namespaces property to specify the namespace and appropriate binding.

xml root

The xml root property defines a root tag for the resulting XML document. The syntax for setting this property is as follows:

```
cmd.Properties("xml root").Value = "rootvalue"
```

rootvalue defines the root tag for the resulting XML. This property can be used to add a root tag when your resulting XML document does not contain a single root element.

xsl

You use the `xsl` property to specify the file name of the XSLT style sheet when executing a transformation on an XML document. The syntax for setting this property is as follows:

```
cmd.Properties("xsl").Value = "C:\Wrox\Chapter15\Intro.xsl"
```

Both relative and absolute paths are allowed. If you do not specify a path, the relative path is that of the current directory.

Executing SQL Queries

Executing queries using the `SQLXMLOLEDB` provider also requires the use of the SQL Native Client. The following example queries the Production.Product table for the ProductID, Name, and ProductNumber columns from the AdventureWorks database.

Open the Visual Studio project and form you have been using and add a button to the form. Set the `Text` property of the button to `"SQLXMLOLEDB"`. In the code behind the button, enter the following code:

```
Dim InStream As ADODB.Stream
Dim conn As ADODB.Connection
Dim cmd As ADODB.Command
Dim strconn As String

InStream = New ADODB.Stream
conn = New ADODB.Connection
cmd = New ADODB.Command

strconn = "Provider=SQLXMLOLEDB.4.0;Data Provider=SQLNCLI;Server=localhost;" & _
"Database=AdventureWorks"

Me.Cursor = Cursors.WaitCursor

Try
  'Be sure to enter your login name and password
  Dim LoginName As String = ""
  Dim Password As String = ""

  conn.Open(strconn, LoginName, Password)
  cmd.ActiveConnection = conn

  cmd.Properties("ClientSideXML").Value = True
  cmd.CommandText = "SELECT ProductID, Name, ProductNumber FROM Production.Product
FOR XML AUTO"

  InStream.Open()

  cmd.Properties("Output Stream").Value = InStream
```

```
        cmd.Properties("xml root").Value = "Root"
        cmd.Execute(, , 1024)

        InStream.Position = 0
        InStream.Charset = "utf-8"

        Me.txtResults.Text = InStream.ReadText()

        conn.Close()

    Catch ex As Exception
        MessageBox.Show(ex.Message)
    End Try

    Me.Cursor = Cursors.Default
```

In the example, notice the use of the `ClientSideXML` property. Even though the SQL statement contains the `FOR XML` clause, the `ClientSideXML` property tells SQL Server that the formatting of XML will happen on the client and not the server.

Run the program and click the button you just added. In Figure 15-2, you can see the root node `"Root"` in the results returned from the query. Supplying a value to the `"xml root"` property provides the root node, as shown in the previous example.

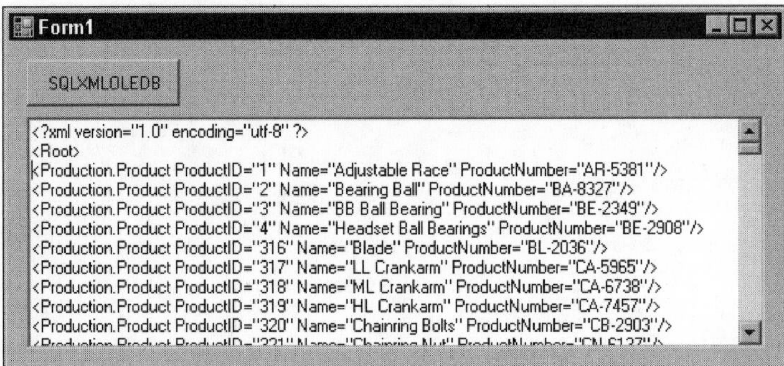

Figure 15-2

The `SQLXMLOLEDB` provider returns results via output streams; results are not returned as rowsets.

XPath Queries

You can also use the `SQLXMLOLEDB` provider to execute XPath queries against XSD schemas. In the following example, you use the `"Base Path"` and `"Mapping Schema"` properties to specify the location and name of the mapping schema.

First, open your favorite text editor and enter the following code, saving it as `C:\Wrox\Chapter15\Products.xml`:

```
<xsd:schema xmlns:xsd='http://www.w3.org/2001/XMLSchema'
   xmlns:sql='urn:schemas-microsoft-com:mapping-schema'>
 <xsd:element name= 'Root' sql:is-constant='1'>
```

```
      <xsd:complexType>
         <xsd:sequence>
           <xsd:element ref = 'Products'/>
         </xsd:sequence>
      </xsd:complexType>
   </xsd:element>
   <xsd:element name='Products' sql:relation='Production.Product'>
       <xsd:complexType>
            <xsd:attribute name='ProductID' type='xsd:integer' />
            <xsd:attribute name='Name' type='xsd:string'/>
            <xsd:attribute name='ProductNumber' type='xsd:string' />
    <xsd:attribute name='Color' type='xsd:string' />
      </xsd:complexType>
    </xsd:element>
</xsd:schema>
```

Next, modify the click event code behind the SQLXMLOLEDB button as follows:

```
Dim InStream As ADODB.Stream
Dim conn As ADODB.Connection
Dim cmd As ADODB.Command
Dim strconn As String

InStream = New ADODB.Stream
conn = New ADODB.Connection
cmd = New ADODB.Command

strconn = "Provider=SQLXMLOLEDB.4.0;Data Provider=SQLNCLI;Server=localhost;" & _
"Database=AdventureWorks"

Me.Cursor = Cursors.WaitCursor

Try
  'Be sure to enter your login name and password
  Dim LoginName As String = ""
  Dim Password As String = ""

  conn.Open(strconn, LoginName, Password)
  cmd.ActiveConnection = conn

  cmd.Properties("ClientSideXML").Value = True

  cmd.CommandText = "Root"

  InStream.Open()

  cmd.Dialect = "{ec2a4293-e898-11d2-b1b7-00c04f680c56}"
  cmd.Properties("Output Stream").Value = InStream
  cmd.Properties("Base Path").Value = "c:\Wrox\Chapter15\"
  cmd.Properties("Mapping Schema").Value = "Products.xml"
  cmd.Properties("Output Encoding").Value = "utf-8"
  cmd.Execute(, , 1024)

  InStream.Position = 0
```

```
        InStream.Charset = "utf-8"

        Me.txtResults.Text = InStream.ReadText()

        conn.Close()

    Catch ex As Exception
        MessageBox.Show(ex.Message)
    End Try

    Me.Cursor = Cursors.Default
```

In the code, notice the reference to the XPath dialect. Since an XPath query is being specified directly, the specific XPath dialect is required. As before, you specify the `ClientSideXML` property to let SQL Server know that any XML formatting will take place on the client.

Figure 15-3 shows the results of the query.

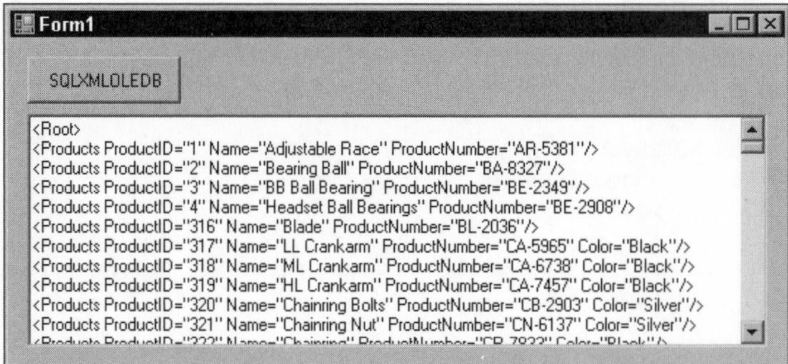

Figure 15-3

In this example, a number of the SQLXMLOLEDB provider properties were used. First, the `ClientSideXML` property was used to tell the provider that any necessary XML formatting would happen on the client. Second, the `Base Path` property was used to specify location of the Products.xml schema. Last, the `mapping schema` property was used to specify the name of the mapping schema against which the XQuery was executed.

Because the query was an XPath query, the dialect property is accordingly for XPath.

XSL Transform Using the SQLXMLOLEDB Provider

In the following example, the data is returned from SQL Server and formatted to XML using the `ClientSideXML` property. The `"xsl"` property is specified in the following example, which specifies the name of the XSLT style sheet to be applied to the resulting XML formatting. The same `"Base Path"` property is used to set the location of the style sheet. When you execute the query, the transformation takes place using the value specified in the `"xsl"` property.

In your text editor, type the following code and save this as `C:\Wrox\Products.xsl`:

```
<?xml version='1.0' encoding='UTF-8'?>
 <xsl:stylesheet xmlns:xsl="http://www.w3.org/1999/XSL/Transform" version="1.0">
```

```
    <xsl:template match = 'Production.Product'>
      <TR>
        <TD><xsl:value-of select = '@ProductID' /></TD>
        <TD><xsl:value-of select = '@Name' /></TD>
        <TD><B><xsl:value-of select = '@ProductNumber' /></B></TD>
      </TR>
    </xsl:template>
    <xsl:template match = '/'>
    <HTML>
      <HEAD>
        <STYLE>th { background-color: #0066ff }</STYLE>
      </HEAD>
      <BODY>
        <TABLE border='0' style='width:300;'>
          <TR><TH colspan='3'>Products</TH></TR>
          <TR><TH >Product ID</TH>
            <TH >Product Name</TH>
            <TH>Product Number</TH>
          </TR>
          <xsl:apply-templates select = 'ROOT' />
        </TABLE>
      </BODY>
    </HTML>
   </xsl:template>
  </xsl:stylesheet>
```

Modify the code behind the button again, this time making the following changes:

```
Dim InStream As ADODB.Stream
Dim conn As ADODB.Connection
Dim cmd As ADODB.Command
Dim strconn As String

InStream = New ADODB.Stream
conn = New ADODB.Connection
cmd = New ADODB.Command

strconn = "Provider=SQLXMLOLEDB.4.0;Data Provider=SQLNCLI;Server=localhost;" & _
"Database=AdventureWorks"

Me.Cursor = Cursors.WaitCursor

Try
  'Be sure to enter your login name and password
  Dim LoginName As String = ""
  Dim Password As String = ""

  conn.Open(strconn, LoginName, Password)
  cmd.ActiveConnection = conn

  cmd.Properties("ClientSideXML").Value = True
```

```
  cmd.CommandText = "<ROOT xmlns:sql='urn:schemas-microsoft-com:xml-sql' >" & _
  "<sql:query> " & _
  "SELECT ProductID, Name, ProductNumber FROM Production.Product FOR XML AUTO " & _
```

```
      "</sql:query> " & _
      " </ROOT> "

      InStream.Open()

      cmd.Dialect = "{5d531cb2-e6ed-11d2-b252-00c04f681b71}"
      cmd.Properties("Output Stream").Value = InStream
      cmd.Properties("Base Path").Value = "c:\Wrox\Chapter15\"
      cmd.Properties("xsl").Value = "Products.xsl"
      cmd.Execute(, , 1024)

      InStream.Position = 0
      InStream.Charset = "utf-8"

      Me.txtResults.Text = InStream.ReadText()

      conn.Close()

    Catch ex As Exception
      MessageBox.Show(ex.Message)
    End Try

    Me.Cursor = Cursors.Default
```

Notice the change in the command dialect. This change is required because the SQL query is specified in a template; therefore, a different command dialect is required notifying SQL Server that a template query is being executed.

Figure 15-4 shows the results of the query.

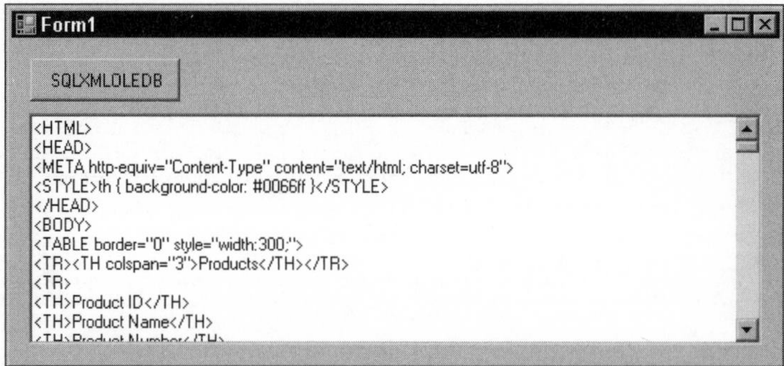

Figure 15-4

Select all the results in the text box and copy them to the clipboard. In Windows Explorer, create a new text file named Products.html and edit the file. Paste the contents of the clipboard into the file and save the file. Double-click the file to open it up in your default browser. Figure 15-5 shows what the results of the transformation look like in Windows Internet Explorer.

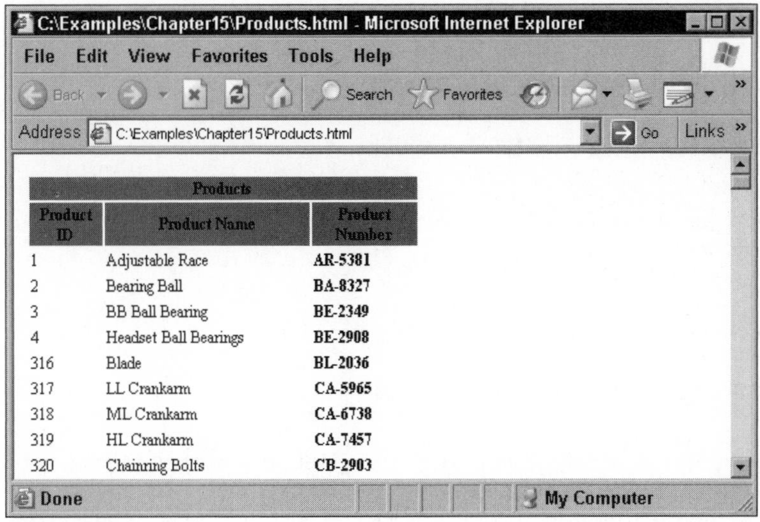

Products		
Product ID	Product Name	Product Number
1	Adjustable Race	**AR-5381**
2	Bearing Ball	**BA-8327**
3	BB Ball Bearing	**BE-2349**
4	Headset Ball Bearings	**BE-2908**
316	Blade	**BL-2036**
317	LL Crankarm	**CA-5965**
318	ML Crankarm	**CA-6738**
319	HL Crankarm	**CA-7457**
320	Chainring Bolts	**CB-2903**

Figure 15-5

Different browsers may display the results differently. The results in Figure 15-5 are displayed using Microsoft Internet Explorer 6.0.

This example uses the `xsl` property to apply an XSL style sheet to the results. The template query was specified directly in the `commandtext` property, and the `base path` and `xsl` attributes values specified the location and name of the style sheet.

The next section goes into further detail about executing template queries.

Executing Template Queries

`SQLXMLOLEDB` supports the capability to execute a template query, which is an XML template that contains a SQL query executed on the server. Template queries were discussed in Chapter 11, but the difference here is that the results are returned in a Stream and the XML formatting is applied on the client.

This first example contains an XML template with a standard SQL statement inside it. Even though the `FOR XML` clause is specified in the query, the XML formatting is applied at the client because the `ClientSideXML` property is set to `True`. Modify the code behind the button again, with the following changes:

```
Dim InStream As ADODB.Stream
Dim conn As ADODB.Connection
Dim cmd As ADODB.Command
Dim strconn As String

InStream = New ADODB.Stream
conn = New ADODB.Connection
```

```
cmd = New ADODB.Command

strconn = "Provider=SQLXMLOLEDB.4.0;Data Provider=SQLNCLI;Server=localhost;" & _
"Database=AdventureWorks"

Me.Cursor = Cursors.WaitCursor

Try
  'Be sure to enter your login name and password
  Dim LoginName As String = ""
  Dim Password As String = ""

  conn.Open(strconn, LoginName, Password)
  cmd.ActiveConnection = conn

  cmd.Properties("ClientSideXML").Value = True

  cmd.CommandText = "<ROOT xmlns:sql='urn:schemas-microsoft-com:xml-sql' >" & _
  "<sql:query> " & _
  "SELECT ProductID, Name, ProductNumber FROM Production.Product FOR XML AUTO " & _
  "</sql:query> " & _
  " </ROOT> "

  InStream.Open()

  cmd.Dialect = "{5d531cb2-e6ed-11d2-b252-00c04f681b71}"
  cmd.Properties("Output Stream").Value = InStream
  cmd.Execute(, , 1024)

  InStream.Position = 0
  InStream.Charset = "utf-8"

  Me.txtResults.Text = InStream.ReadText()

  conn.Close()

Catch ex As Exception
  MessageBox.Show(ex.Message)
End Try

Me.Cursor = Cursors.Default
```

As with the previous example, the command dialect did not change because this example also uses a template query. The results of the query are shown in Figure 15-6.

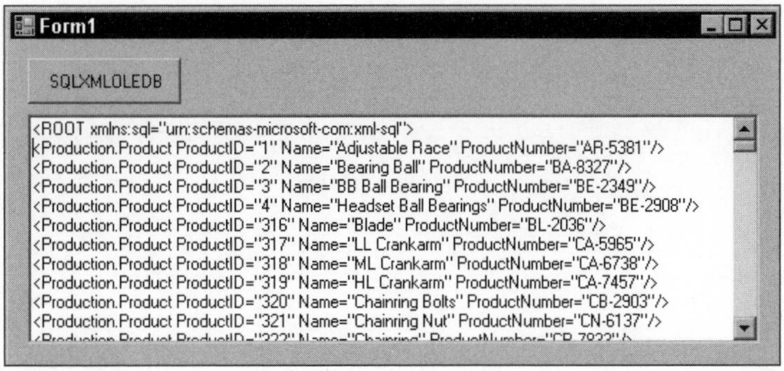

Figure 15-6

Taking a couple of pieces from each of the previous examples to demonstrate template queries and returning results, this example includes the `ClientSideXML` property, which despite the `FOR XML` clause being included in the `SELECT` statement, is sent to the server. The server, however, executes the query and returns the results back to the client where the client then applies the `FOR XML` formatting to the result set.

The `SELECT` statement is wrapped in a template query specifying a root element. Since a root element is already specified, the `xml root` property is not needed.

The next example also uses a template query, but it differs in that the template query contains an XPath query that points to an XSD mapping schema. The mapping schema provides the mapping to the table and columns in the database in which the query is executed. The schema is the same as the one that was used a few examples earlier.

The `"Base Path"` and `"Mapping Schema"` properties supply the location and file name of the mapping schema. Again, modify the code behind the button with the following changes:

```
Dim InStream As ADODB.Stream
Dim conn As ADODB.Connection
Dim cmd As ADODB.Command
Dim strconn As String

InStream = New ADODB.Stream
conn = New ADODB.Connection
cmd = New ADODB.Command

strconn = "Provider=SQLXMLOLEDB.4.0;Data Provider=SQLNCLI;Server=localhost;" & _
"Database=AdventureWorks"

Me.Cursor = Cursors.WaitCursor

Try
  'Be sure to enter your login name and password
  Dim LoginName As String = ""
  Dim Password As String = ""

  conn.Open(strconn, LoginName, Password)
```

```
        cmd.ActiveConnection = conn

        cmd.Properties("ClientSideXML").Value = True

        "<sql:xpath-query mapping-schema='c:\Wrox\Chapter15\Products.xml' > " & _
        " Root " & _
        "    </sql:xpath-query> " & _
        " </ROOT> "

        InStream.Open()

        cmd.Dialect = "{5d531cb2-e6ed-11d2-b252-00c04f681b71}"
        cmd.Properties("Output Stream").Value = InStream
        cmd.Properties("Base Path").Value = "c:\Wrox\Chapter15\"
        cmd.Properties("Mapping Schema").Value = "c:\wrox\chapter15\Products.xsl"
        cmd.Properties("Output Encoding").Value = "utf-8"
        cmd.Execute(, , 1024)

        InStream.Position = 0
        InStream.Charset = "utf-8"

        Me.txtResults.Text = InStream.ReadText()

        conn.Close()

      Catch ex As Exception
        MessageBox.Show(ex.Message)
      End Try

      Me.Cursor = Cursors.Default
```

The XPath query specified in the template simply contains an XPath query `"Root"`, which as you can see in Figure 15-7, becomes the root node.

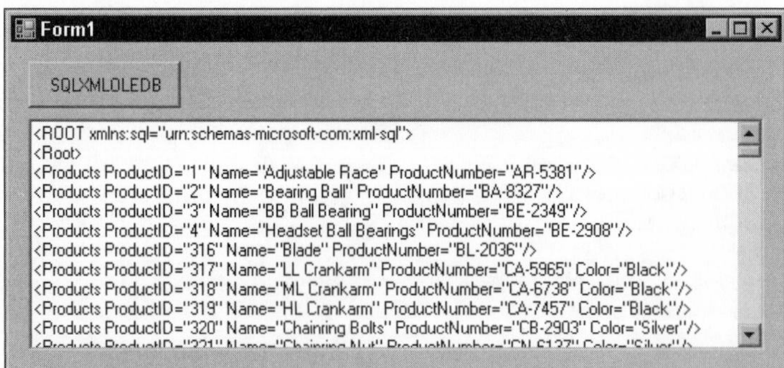

Figure 15-7

As you can see, the `SQLXMLOLEDB` provider is extremely robust and the performance is exceptional. The examples in this section did not filter any records, as they returned all the rows from the Production.Product table.

SQLXML Managed Classes

If you've been using SQLXML 3.0 at all, you are familiar with the SQLXML Managed Classes. They are not new to SQLXML 4.0, but they are enhanced to work with SQL Server 2005 and the .NET Framework version 2.0. This section provides a few examples to help demonstrate SQLXML connectivity using Managed Classes. SQL Managed Classes are discussed in depth in Chapter 20.

SQLXML Managed Classes expose the functionality of SQLXML 4.0 inside the .NET Framework. With this exposed functionality, the ability to access XML data from within SQL Server and bring it into the .NET Framework is completely possible. Once the data is passed from SQL Server to the .NET Framework, it can be updated or changed and sent back to SQL Server.

This first example creates a SQLXML Managed Class, passing a simple SQL statement to SQL Server, and returns the data to the client. The XML formatting takes place on the server in this example.

Open your text editor, enter the following code, and save it as `C:\Wrox\Chapter15\Products.vb`

```
Imports System
Imports System.IO
Imports Microsoft.Data.SqlXml

Public Class Products

  Public Shared Function Main() As Integer

    Dim InStream As Stream

    'Be sure to use the correct username and password
    Dim cmd As SqlXmlCommand = New
SqlXmlCommand("Provider=SQLOLEDB;Server=localhost;Database=AdventureWorks;UID=Wrox;
PWD=Wrox")

cmd.CommandText = "SELECT ProductID, Name, ProductNumber FROM" & _
"Production.Product FOR XML AUTO"

    Try
      InStream = cmd.ExecuteStream
      InStream.Position = 0
      Dim sr As StreamReader = New StreamReader(InStream)
      Console.WriteLine(sr.ReadToend)

    Catch ex As SqlXmlException
      Dim Results As String
      ex.ErrorStream.Position = 0
      Results = New StreamReader(ex.ErrorStream).ReadToEnd
      System.Console.WriteLine(Results)
    End Try

  End Function

End Class
```

Next, open a command prompt and browse to the .NET Framework 2.0 directory. At the time of this writing, the latest release is 2.0.50215. The .NET Framework directory is located in the `C:\WINDOWS\Microsoft.NET\Framework` directory.

After you navigate to the correct directory, execute the `vbc` command. This command creates an executable using the `vb` class you will pass it. The syntax is as follows:

```
Vbc /reference:Microsoft.Data.SqlXml.dll PathToProducts.vb
```

For example, Figure 15-8 illustrates how to use the `vbc` command to create an executable passing it the path of the location of the Products.vb file created previously. The syntax is as follows:

```
Vbc /reference:Microsoft.Data.SqlXml.dll c:\Wrox\chapter15\products.vb
```

Figure 15-8 also shows the results when the execution is finished. In this example, a file called Products.exe is created in the `c:\Wrox\chapter15` directory.

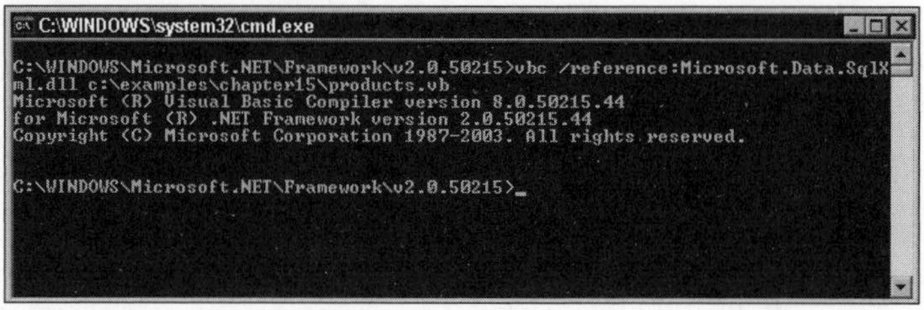

```
C:\WINDOWS\system32\cmd.exe

C:\WINDOWS\Microsoft.NET\Framework\v2.0.50215>vbc /reference:Microsoft.Data.SqlX
ml.dll c:\examples\chapter15\products.vb
Microsoft (R) Visual Basic Compiler version 8.0.50215.44
for Microsoft (R) .NET Framework version 2.0.50215.44
Copyright (C) Microsoft Corporation 1987-2003. All rights reserved.

C:\WINDOWS\Microsoft.NET\Framework\v2.0.50215>_
```

Figure 15-8

After you create the executable, navigate to the `c:\Wrox\chapter15` directory in the `command` prompt. Once there, execute the executable by typing the following command at the command prompt:

```
Products
```

Figure 15-9 shows the results of executing the Managed Class.

```
Visual Studio 2005 Command Prompt
ID="980" Name="Mountain-400-W Silver, 38" ProductNumber="BK-M38S-38"/><Productio
n.Product ProductID="981" Name="Mountain-400-W Silver, 40" ProductNumber="BK-M38
S-40"/><Production.Product ProductID="982" Name="Mountain-400-W Silver, 42" Prod
uctNumber="BK-M38S-42"/><Production.Product ProductID="983" Name="Mountain-400-W
 Silver, 46" ProductNumber="BK-M38S-46"/><Production.Product ProductID="984" Nam
e="Mountain-500 Silver, 40" ProductNumber="BK-M18S-40"/><Production.Product Prod
uctID="985" Name="Mountain-500 Silver, 42" ProductNumber="BK-M18S-42"/><Producti
on.Product ProductID="986" Name="Mountain-500 Silver, 44" ProductNumber="BK-M18S
-44"/><Production.Product ProductID="987" Name="Mountain-500 Silver, 48" Product
Number="BK-M18S-48"/><Production.Product ProductID="988" Name="Mountain-500 Silv
er, 52" ProductNumber="BK-M18S-52"/><Production.Product ProductID="989" Name="Mo
untain-500 Black, 40" ProductNumber="BK-M18B-40"/><Production.Product ProductID=
"990" Name="Mountain-500 Black, 42" ProductNumber="BK-M18B-42"/><Production.Prod
uct ProductID="991" Name="Mountain-500 Black, 44" ProductNumber="BK-M18B-44"/><P
roduction.Product ProductID="992" Name="Mountain-500 Black, 48" ProductNumber="B
K-M18B-48"/><Production.Product ProductID="993" Name="Mountain-500 Black, 52" Pr
oductNumber="BK-M18B-52"/><Production.Product ProductID="994" Name="LL Bottom Br
acket" ProductNumber="BB-7421"/><Production.Product ProductID="995" Name="ML Bot
tom Bracket" ProductNumber="BB-8107"/><Production.Product ProductID="996" Name="
HL Bottom Bracket" ProductNumber="BB-9108"/><Production.Product ProductID="997"
Name="Road-750 Black, 44" ProductNumber="BK-R19B-44"/><Production.Product Produc
tID="998" Name="Road-750 Black, 48" ProductNumber="BK-R19B-48"/><Production.Prod
uct ProductID="999" Name="Road-750 Black, 52" ProductNumber="BK-R19B-52"/>

C:\Examples\Chapter15>
```

Figure 15-9

The SQL statement executed, the data was formatted into XML at the server and sent back to the .NET Framework environment, and the results were output to the console window.

This next example provides the same functionality but accomplishes the task with two differences. First, instead of sending a SQL statement to SQL Server, the code executes a stored procedure. Second, the `ClientSideXML` property is set so that the results are returned to the client for XML formatting.

The `GetProducts` stored procedure that was created in Chapter 11 should still exist in the AdventureWorks database. If it does not, open a query window in SQL Server Management Studio and execute the following SQL query:

```
CREATE PROCEDURE GetProducts
AS
    SELECT   ProductID, Name, ProductNumber
    FROM     Production.Product

GO
```

Next, open the Products.vb file and modify it as follows, saving the changes as Products2.vb:

```
Imports System
Imports System.IO
Imports Microsoft.Data.SqlXml

Public Class Products1

    PUblic Shared Function Main() As Integer

        Dim InStream As Stream

        Dim cmd As SqlXmlCommand = New
SqlXmlCommand("Provider=SQLOLEDB;Server=localhost;Database=AdventureWorks;UID=sa;PW
D=hackthis")
 cmd.ClientSideXML = True

        cmd.CommandText = "EXEC GetProducts FOR XML NESTED"

        Try
            InStream = cmd.ExecuteStream
     InStream.Position = 0
            Dim sr As Streamreader = New StreamReader(InStream)
            Console.WriteLine(sr.ReadToend)

        Catch ex As SqlXmlException
            Dim Results As String
            ex.ErrorStream.Position = 0
            Results = New StreamReader(ex.ErrorStream).ReadToEnd
            System.Console.WriteLine(Results)
        End Try

    End Function

End Class
```

Just like the previous example, open a command prompt and compile Products2.vb into an executable using the syntax shown earlier.

After you create the executable, navigate to the directory where it was created and run the executable. Figure 15-10 shows the results of running the executable.

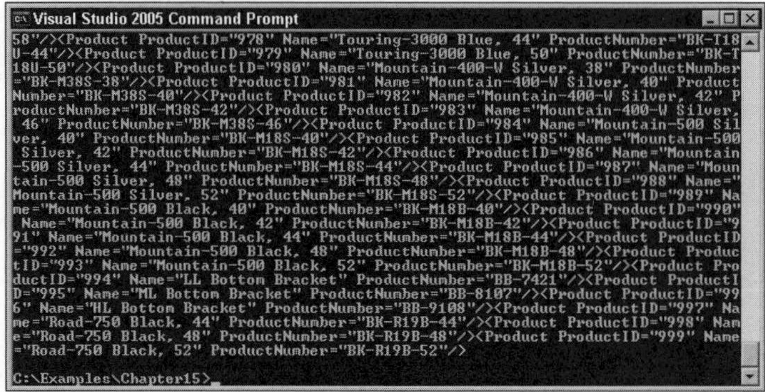

Figure 15-10

In this example, the Managed Class executed the `GetProducts` stored procedure and returned the data to the client for XML formatting. The results were then displayed to the console window.

While these examples are fairly simple, they should give you an introductory idea of how Managed Classes work. The purpose with these examples was to show you how Managed Classes can be used on the client side to access SQL Server.

Web Services

This section briefly introduces Web Services in SQL Server 2005, and Chapter 17 is dedicated to this topic. Through its database engine, SQL Server 2005 provides native XML Web Services with support for the open standard protocols. Those protocols are as follows:

- HTTP
- SOAP
- WSDL

With the introduction of native Web Service support in SQL Server 2005, a number of benefits come into play that improve functionality and performance. The primary benefit is that now any application utilizing Web Services can access SQL server. Any application that supports XML and HTTP can access SQL Server.

A second benefit is improved security. The built-in support for HTTP and SOAP offers a new level of Web access. Anonymous user access is prohibited, and administrative privileges are now needed to create endpoints.

Third, the inclusion of Web Services results in much better support for wireless clients. This follows what has been called "Anytime, Anywhere" access, being able to connect and process requests at any given time.

Additional benefits are discussed in Chapter 17, but you should start to see some of the great benefits of SQL Server 2005's support of Web Services.

Summary

With the release of SQL Server 2005, more options became available for accessing data using SQLXML. With the introduction of the SQL Native Client, you can take advantage of the new native `xml` data type, which MDAC and other access technologies cannot. SQLXML provides a very robust access technology that includes support for the SQL Native Client, and support for the `xml` data type and other data types new to SQL Server 2005.

This chapter outlined several differences between MDAC and the SQL Native Client, and from those differences, you should be able to determine the course of action to take when deciding which technology to use. Of course, MDAC does not support the `xml` data type and related functionality, so if you want to take advantage of those features, you need to go with the SQL Native Client.

The `SQLXMLOLEDB` provider is a new addition to SQLXML 4.0, whose sole purpose is to provide SQLXML functionality via ADO. When combined with the SQL Native Client, it is the perfect match for building high-performing applications that need SQLXML functionality.

From there, you learned about SQLXML Managed Classes, which provide a whole new level of data access for SQLXML, exposing the functionality of SQLXML 4.0 inside of the .NET Framework. While this chapter did not go into a whole lot of detail about SQL Managed Classes, I hope provided a good foundation so you are better prepared for Chapter 20.

Last, you were introduced to native Web Service support in SQL Server 2005 and the many benefits it provides. Just like Managed Classes, an entire chapter is dedicated to this topic later on, but it was included here to provide an insight as to the many benefits Web Services provide for client access.

16

Using XSLT in SQL Server 2005

This part of the book on client-side XML processing would not be complete without including a chapter on the changes and new features that support XSLT in version 2.0 of the .NET Framework. Until now, the focus of each chapter in this part was querying and retrieving XML from the client. Now that the client has the data in XML format, it would be really nice to be able to format it so that it can be nicely displayed instead of showing the raw XML. What user wants to see that, let alone would be able to read it and understand it?

This chapter briefly introduces XSLT style sheets, but spends the majority of the time discussing the changes made to the `System.Xml.Xsl` class. There have been some significant changes and enhancements to this class, some of which require you to migrate some of your existing code if you are using existing XSLT client-side processing code in current versions of the .NET Framework.

This chapter provides a brief overview of XSLT, and then moves on to discuss what is new for XSLT in version 2.0 of the .NET Framework.

Specifically, this chapter discusses the following topics:

- Overview of XSLT
- Changes and enhancements to XSLT
- Moving to version 2.0 of System.Xml.Xsl
- Guidelines

XSLT Overview

Before digging in, a quick example is in order. Open up your favorite text editor and type the following:

```
<?xml version="1.0"?>
<?xml-stylesheet type="text/xsl" href="C:\Wrox\Intro.xsl"?>
<xsltsample>
  <scroll>Is XSLT cool, or what?</scroll>
  <message>Welcome to XSLT</message>
  <message2>4 out of 5 dentists recommend XSLT over CSS</message2>
</xsltsample>
```

Save this as `C:\Wrox\Intro.xml`. Next, you need to create the style sheet. Open a new document and type the following:

```
<?xml version="1.0"?>
<xsl:stylesheet
    xmlns:xsl="http://www.w3.org/1999/XSL/Transform"
    version="1.0">
  <xsl:template match="/xsltsample">
    <HTML>
      <HEAD>
        <TITLE>An XSLT Example</TITLE>
      </HEAD>
      <BODY>
        <H1><Center><xsl:value-of select="message"/></Center></H1>
        <xsl:apply-templates select="scroll"/>
        <xsl:apply-templates select="message2"/>
      </BODY>
    </HTML>
  </xsl:template>
  <xsl:template match="scroll">
      <Marquee><I><xsl:value-of select="."/></I></Marquee>
  </xsl:template>
  <xsl:template match="message2">
      <H3><I><xsl:value-of select="."/></I></H3>
  </xsl:template>
</xsl:stylesheet>
```

Save this as `C:\Wrox\Intro.xsl`. In Windows Explorer, navigate to the `C:\Wrox` directory and double-click the `Intro.xml` file. Your results should look like Figure 16-1.

Figure 16-1

In this simple example, the XML document Intro.xml holds the instructions that link it to the XSLT style sheet, Intro.xsl. It is the XSLT file that contains the information on how to transform the XML document into an HTML document.

When the Intro.xml file is opened, the browser processes the XML and finds a reference to the Intro.Xsl file. The style sheet is then applied to the XML and the results rendered in the Web browser. The rendering is applied because of the instructions in the XSL style sheet. For example, the style sheet contains a node called `<xsl:template>` with an attribute called `match`. The value of the name attribute, `"scroll"`, points to an element name in the XML file of the same value. This is called a Match Template and is explained in more detail later in the chapter. When the match between the style sheet and XML document is made, the browser reads the XML file and processes the instructions of the XML, which say to scroll the value of the `<scroll>` element. The same process happens with the `<xsl:template>` nodes in the XSL document.

This section briefly discusses the components that make up an XSLT style sheet and how to create XSLT style sheets. It does not go into any deep discussions on XSLT, as that is outside the scope of this book. There are complete books dedicated to this topic, and some really good ones are *Beginning XSLT* and *XSLT 2.0 Programmer's Reference, 3rd Edition*, both from Wrox.

XSLT is a language that enables the manipulation and display of an XML document. It provides the capability to create a new document based on the original document without changing or modifying the original document.

For example, the Intro.xml file contains the information that provides the location of the XSLT transformation, which is in the following line:

```
<?xml-stylesheet type="text/xsl" href="Intro.xsl"?>
```

If this line were removed from the XML document, the results would look like Figure 16-2 when displayed in your browser.

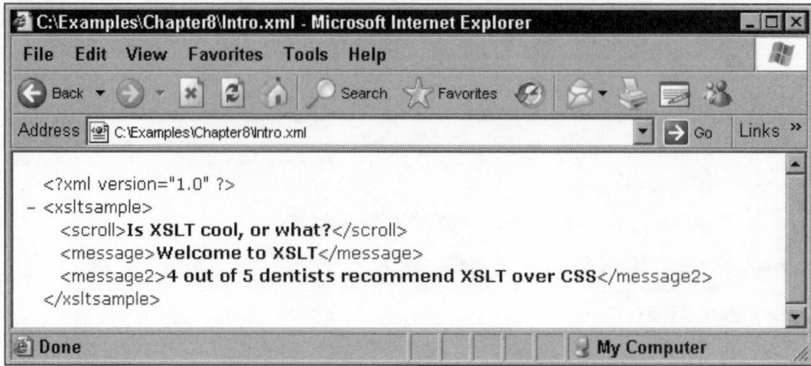

Figure 16-2

In its simplest terms, an XSLT document, or *transform*, is an XML document that contains instructions how to display the XML document. This transform is made up of a set of templates that hold the display instructions. When the document is opened, the parser attempts to map a given template pattern to the top node of the XML document. XPath expressions are then used to select sub-items in the XSLT document, which are then mapped to the corresponding parts of the XML document. This is not a one-time process; it occurs until no matches can be found within the document.

An XSLT document is made up of several required components. The first is the document declaration, which informs the processor that it is an XML file:

```
<?xml version="1.0"?>
```

The second requirement is the root element. In its simplest form, it looks like this:

```
<xsl:stylesheet>
```

In the example earlier in this section, the root element has a number of attributes:

```
<xsl:stylesheet
    xmlns:xsl="http://www.w3.org/1999/XSL/Transform"
    version="1.0">
```

The `version` attribute defines the version of the XSLT specification, and the `xmlns:xsl` attribute defines the namespace used throughout the XSLT document.

The final requirement is the `template` element and template rules declared within the `template` element:

```
<xsl:template match="/xsltsample">
  <HTML>
    <HEAD>
      <TITLE>An XSLT Example</TITLE>
    </HEAD>
```

```
      <BODY>
        <H1><Center><xsl:value-of select="message"/></Center></H1>
        <xsl:apply-templates select="scroll"/>
        <xsl:apply-templates select="message2"/>
      </BODY>
    </HTML>
  </xsl:template>
  <xsl:template match="scroll">
      <Marquee><I><xsl:value-of select="."/></I></Marquee>
  </xsl:template>
  <xsl:template match="message2">
      <H3><I><xsl:value-of select="."/></I></H3>
  </xsl:template>
</xsl:stylesheet>
```

Templates are described in detail shortly, but first an understanding of nodes is in order.

Nodes

A *node* in basic terms is a single element item within an XML document tree that contains data. For example, in the following XML document, the element `<Name>` contains the value `"Chad Reed"`. Moving up the document tree, the `<Rider>` node contains attributes and sub-elements:

```
<?xml version="1.0" encoding="UTF-8"?>
<Motocross >
  <Team Manufacturer="Yamaha">
    <Rider NationalNumber="22" Class="250">
      <Name>Chad Reed</Name>
    </Rider>
    ...
```

Current Node

The *current* node is the node that is currently being processed as you navigate through the document tree. For example, if you are processing the information and data of the `<Rider>` node, the `<Rider>` node is the current node.

This terminology also applies when you are matching templates and XML documents. When a node in an XML document matches an XSLT template, that node becomes the current node. This is to help keep track of the processing of nodes.

Context Node

A *context* node is a node that is part of an expression, in which that expression is operating on a specific node.

In the following example, the context node is the `<Name>` node when the path expression is requesting the rider's name:

```
<xsl:value-of select="Team/Rider/Name">
```

Templates

In an XSLT style sheet, templates hold the formatting instructions that will be executed when the template is called, or when it is matched to a node in the XML document. If templates didn't exist, you would have to write a lot of code to accomplish what templates do. Imagine the amount of code you would have to write to do what the XSLT processor accomplishes, such as node matching. The benefit of using templates eliminates the need for you to write all of this yourself, and makes it very easy to reuse templates, as well as matching complex node expressions. The basic format of a template is as follows:

```
<xsl:stylesheet
 xmlns:xsl="http://www.w3.org/1999/XSL/Transform"
 version="1.0">
  <xsl:template match="">
  <xsl:value-of select=".">
  </xsl:template>
</xsl:stylesheet>
```

The `xsl:stylesheet` element is the root node or element of a style sheet. The `xsl:template` element defines a unit of processing that produces an output template. The output template can be called either by name or by matching pattern. This element is a top-level element and can only be used as a child as the `xsl:stylesheet` element. The `xsl:value-of` element inserts a value of an expression into the output. It can appear anywhere in the body of the template.

You can call templates in either of two ways. As mentioned earlier, you can call them when the template finds a matching node in the XML document. This type of template is called a *Match Template*. You perform the match by specifying an XPath expression in the `match` attribute, as follows (taken from the chapter's first example):

```
<xsl:template match="scroll">
```

A more elaborate expression can be used to return a rider's name from the Motocross.xml file. For example, the following `match` attribute value returns the rider's name:

```
<xsl:template match="Team/Rider/Name">
```

When a template executes, the elements inside the template are executed in the order in which they appear in the template.

You can also execute a template explicitly. Called *Named Templates*, you can call these types from another template instead of matching them to a node. In order to call this type of template, you must name it uniquely within the style sheet. To accomplish this, you add a `name` attribute to the Named Template and call it by adding `xsl:call-template` element.

In the following example, the top template contains the `xsl:call-template` element, referencing the second template that contains the `name` attribute, distinguishing it as the Named Template. The value of the `xsl:call-template` element must match the value of the `name` attribute in the Named Template:

```
<xsl:template match="Team">
  <xsl:call-template name="Rider">
</xsl:template>
```

```
<xsl:template name="Rider">
  <xsl:value-of select="Team/Rider/Name">
</xsl:template>
```

When you call a Named Template from a Match Template, the context node does not change. This is not the case when you navigate through an XML document and apply templates using `xsl:apply-template`. The context node changes the very instant an `xsl:apply-template` is issued.

XSLT Changes

Okay, enough of the background, it's time to move into what's new. Version 2.0 of the .NET Framework provides a number of changes to the `System.Xml.Xsl` namespace. These changes focus on performance and usability, and include new classes (`XslCompiledTransform` and `XsltSettings`) and enhancements to existing classes.

XslCompiledTransform

The `XslCompiledTransform` class is a new class that offers performance gains over its predecessor, the `XslTransform` class. This new XSLT processor supports the XSLT 1.0 syntax, and even the structure of the `XslCompiledTransform` class is very similar to the now obsolete `XslTransform` class.

The performance gains are achieved by compiling the XSLT style sheet down to a common interface format, allowing it to be cached and reused. This process is similar to what the CLR (Common Language Runtime) does for other programming languages.

Out of the box, support for the `document()` method is disabled by default, but you can enable it by creating an `XslSettings` object and passing it the `Load` method. XSLT scripting is also disabled for security reasons. For more information, see the "Guidelines" section later in this chapter.

Just like its predecessor, the `Load` method takes an XSLT style sheet and compiles it. The `Transform` method then executes the transform, taking an XML document as input resulting in an HTML document.

The following example takes the same files used in the first example in this chapter. The `Load` method loads and compiles the Intro.xsl style sheet. The `Transform` method then executes the transform on the Intro.xml document resulting in a new file, Intro.html.

Open up the Visual Studio test application you've been using and add a new button to the form, setting the text property of the button to `"Xslt"`.

In the Solution Explorer of your Visual Studio 2005 application, expand the References node and make sure you have a reference to the `System.Xml` namespace, as shown in Figure 16-3.

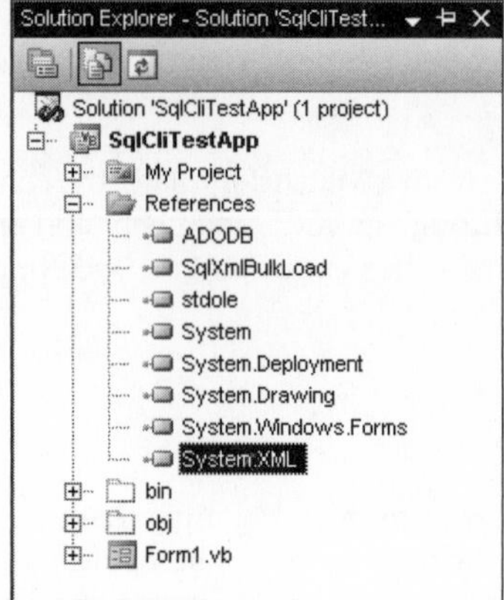

Figure 16-3

If you do not have the `System.Xml` reference, right-click the references node and select Add Reference. The Add Reference dialog box is displayed. Make sure the .NET tab is selected and scroll down until you see `System.Xml`, as shown in Figure 16-4.

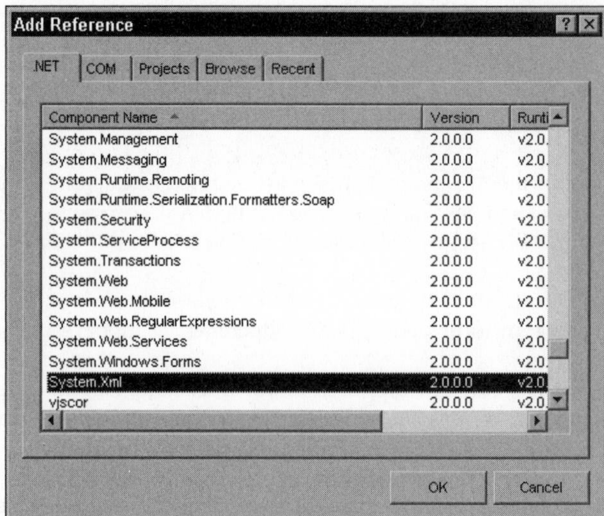

Figure 16-4

Select the `System.Xml` namespace and click OK to add a reference to this namespace.

Next, double-click the Xslt button you just added to the form, and in the click event of that button, add the following code:

```
Dim xslt As New XslCompiledTransform()

Try

  xslt.Load("c:\Wrox\Intro.xsl")

xslt.Transform("c:\Wrox\Intro.xml", "c:\Wrox\Intro.html")

  Me.txtResults.Text = "SUCCESS!"

Catch ex As Exception
  MessageBox.Show(ex.Message)
End Try
```

Last, scroll up to the declaration section of the form and add the following lines to the declaration section:

```
Imports System.Xml.Xsl
Imports System.Xml
Imports System.Xml.XPath
Imports System.IO
```

Run the project and click the button you just added. When the code has run successfully, the text box on the form displays the `Success!` message.

In Windows Explorer, you should see the new Intro.html file (see Figure 16-5) created as the result of the transform.

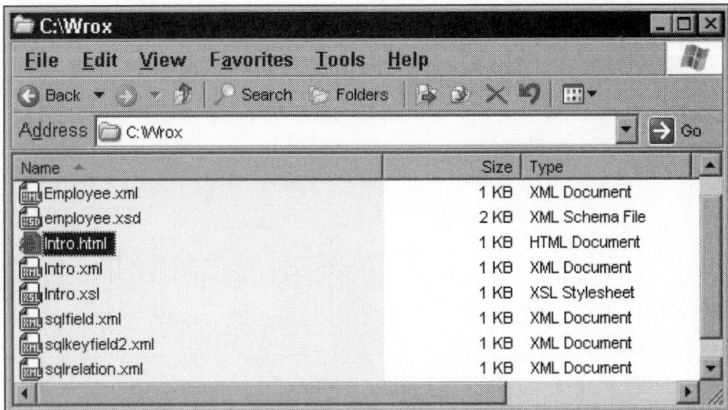

Figure 16-5

Right-click Intro.html and select Edit. Figure 16-6 shows the code for the Intro.html document generated by the `Transform` method.

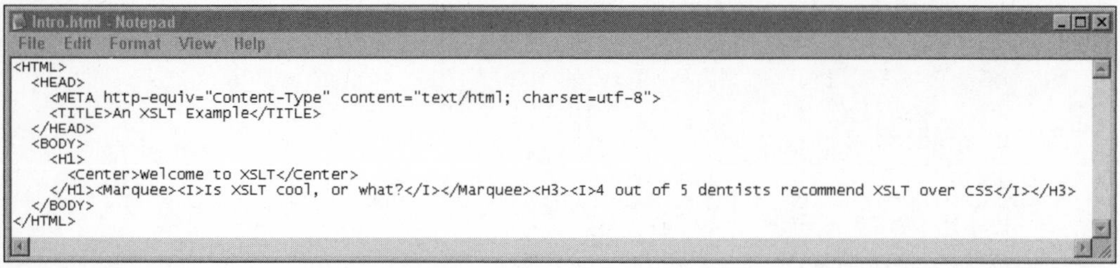

Intro.html - Notepad

File Edit Format View Help

```
<HTML>
  <HEAD>
    <META http-equiv="Content-Type" content="text/html; charset=utf-8">
    <TITLE>An XSLT Example</TITLE>
  </HEAD>
  <BODY>
    <H1>
      <Center>Welcome to XSLT</Center>
    </H1><Marquee><I>Is XSLT cool, or what?</I></Marquee><H3><I>4 out of 5 dentists recommend XSLT over CSS</I></H3>
  </BODY>
</HTML>
```

Figure 16-6

Double-clicking the Intro.html file opens it in your default browser, displaying the same results as you saw in Figure 16-1.

Transform Method Input

The `Transform` method can take three input types as the source for the source document. The first is an object that supports the IXPathNavigatable interface. In version 1.1 of the .NET Framework, the `XPathNavigator` class was based on the XPath 1.0 data model, while version 2.0 of the .NET Framework `XPathNavigator` class is based on the XQuery 1.0 and XPath 2.0 data model.

The `XPathDocument` class is an in-memory cache representation of the XML data. It is read-only and is the recommended method for XSLT processing, as it provides the fastest performance over the `XmlNode` class, which is not read-only, allowing editing of the data.

This example loads a style sheet that is held in an `XPathDocument` object, and then uses the `XmlWriter` object to write the output to the console:

```
Dim xct As New XslCompiledTransform()
Try
  xct.Load("c:\Wrox\Intro.xsl")

  Dim xmldoc As New XPathDocument("C:\Wrox\Intro.xml")

  Dim xw As XmlWriter = XmlWriter.Create("C:\Wrox\Console.Out")

  xct.Transform(xmldoc, xw)
  xw.close
```

The second input parameter on the `Transform` method is of type `XmlWriter`, which allows for the results of the transform to be written to the specified file.

When you pass in an `XmlReader` object, the position of the `XmlReader` is on the next node after the end of the context document once the `Transform` method has completed execution, as follows:

```
Dim xr As XmlReader = XmlReader.Create("Intro.xsl")
Xr.ReadToDescendant("xsl:stylesheet")

Dim xct As New XslCompiledTransform()
xct.Load(xr)
```

The third input type is a string URI. This type of input takes an `XmlUrlResolver` to resolve the URI, which can then be passed to the `Transform` method. The `XmlUrlResolver` class in this example uses the `Credentials` property to authenticate Web requests. The credentials it uses comes from the `CredentialCache` class, which is used to store users' credentials. This class comes from the `System.Net` namespace, as follows:

```
Dim Transform as XslCompiledTransform = New XslCompiledTransform ()
Dim Resolver as XmlUrlResolver = New XmlUrlResolver()
Resolver.Credentials = System.Net.CredentialCache.DefaultCredentials
Transform.Load("Intro.xsl", XsltSettings.Default, Resolver)
```

All of these input methods accomplish the same task depending on your requirements and the source of your XML document.

Transform Method Output

The `Transform` method can output four available types. The first type is an `XmlWriter`:

```
Dim xct As New XslCompiledTransform()
xct.Load("c:\Wrox\Intro.xsl")

Dim xw As XmlWriter = XmlWriter.Create("C:\Wrox\Results.xml", xct.OutputSettings)

xct.Transform("c:\Wrox\Intro.xml", xw)
xw.close
```

In this example, an instance of the `XmlWriter` class is created, passing it the name of the file to be created when the transform is executed. The results of the transform are sent to the `XmlWriter`, which writes the results of the transform to the Results.xml file.

The second output type is a string that contains the URI of the output file. In the example used earlier in this section, the `Transform` method passed a string URI as the output of the transform, as follows:

```
xslt.Transform("c:\Wrox\Intro.xml", "cWrox\Intro.html")
```

The third type is a `Stream` type. The following example outputs the results of the XSLT transformation to a FileStream:

```
Dim xct As New XslCompiledTransform()
Xct.Load("c:\Wrox\Intro.xsl")
Dim FileStrm As New FileStream("c:\Wrox\NewFile.xml", FileMode.Create)
Xct.Transform(New XPathDocument("c:\Wrox\.xml"), Nothing, FileStrm)
```

The fourth type is a `TextWriter` type. The following example sends the XSLT transformation output to a string:

```
Dim xct As New XslCompiledTransform()
Xct.Load("c:\Wrox\Intro.xsl")
Dim StrOutput as String
Dim StrWrtr As New StringWriter()
Xct.Transform("c:\examplesWrox\Intro.xml", Nothing, StrWrtr)
StrOutput = StrWrtr.ToString()
```

You can execute all of these examples in your test application. You can send the `Stream` and `TextWriter` outputs to the text box by sending the results to the txtResult text box. For example, the following code displays the results of `StrOutput` to the text box on the form:

```
Dim xct As New XslCompiledTransform()
Xct.Load("c:\Wrox\Intro.xsl")
Dim StrOutput as String
Dim StrWrtr As New StringWriter()
Xct.Transform("c:\Wrox\Intro.xml", Nothing, StrWrtr)
StrOutput = StrWrtr.ToString()
Me.txtResult.Text = StrOutput
```

Figure 16-7 shows the results of `StrOutput`.

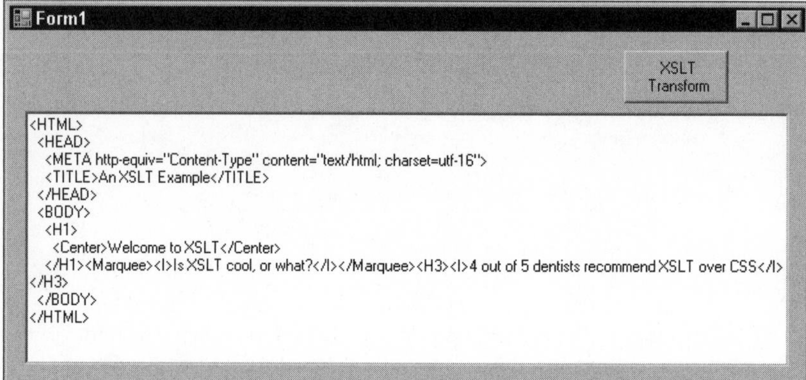

Figure 16-7

In this example, you use the `StringWriter` class to capture the results of the transform. The style sheet is loaded, an instance of the `StringWriter` is created, and then the transform is executed, sending the results of the transform to the `StringWriter`. The contents of the `StringWriter` are then written to the text box.

XsltSettings

Also new in version 2.0 of the .NET Framework is the `XsltSettings` class. When you compile and execute an XSLT style sheet, the responsibility of the `XsltSettings` class is to specify which features are supported for that execution.

By default, embedded script blocks and the XSLT `document()` function are disabled and the `XsltSettings` class is used to enable or disable these features. At execution time, the `XsltSettings` object is then passed to the `Load` method of the `XslCompiledTransform` class.

The `XsltSettings` class takes two parameters, both Boolean. The first parameter specifies whether or not the XSLT `document()` function is enabled, and the second parameter specifies whether script blocks are enabled. For example, the following disables both the XSLT document function and embedded script blocks:

```
Dim xslSettings As New XsltSettings(False, False)
```

You then pass the XsltSettings object to the Load method as follows:

```
Dim xslSettings As New XsltSettings(False, False)
Dim Resolver As XmlUrlResolver = New XmlResolver()
Resolver.Credentials = System.Net.CredentialCache.DefaultCredentials
Dim xct As New XslCompiledTransform()
Xct.Load("Intro.xsl", xslSettings,Resolver)
```

There have been a number of new additions and enhancements to the System.Xml.Xsl namespace, which the following section discusses.

Moving to the New

As discussed previously, the new XslCompiledTransform class is very similar to the XslTransform class. The changes made were to improve performance and security. This section outlines the differences between the two classes and the necessary changes you need to make to migrate your existing code from the XslTransform class to the XslCompiledTransform class.

You use the Transform method of the XslTransform class as follows:

```
Dim Transform as XslTransform = New XslTransform
Transform.Load("c:\Wrox\Intro.xsl")
Transform.Transform("c:\Wrox\Intro.xml", "Intro.html")
```

The new XslCompiledTransform class looks like this:

```
Dim xct As New XslCompiledTransform()
xct.Load("c:\Wrox\Intro.xsl")
xct.Transform("c:\Wrox\Intro.xml", "c:\Wrox\Intro.html")
```

As you can see, it is not a whole lot different. In version 2.0 of the .NET Framework, the new XslCompiledTransform class replaces the now obsolete XslTransform class. However, the functionality is the same, so there's nothing new to learn. Instead of using the XslTransform class to transform the XML data, you now use the XslCompiledTransform class to accomplish the same thing. They both contain the Load method, which compiles the style sheet, and they both contain a Transform method, which executes the transform. The difference is that the XslCompiledTransform class has been completely rewritten to include performance gains over the old XslTransform class. As noted previously, XSLT scripting is disabled by default.

In this next example, both the XslTransform class and the new XslCompiledTransform class are used to enable scripting.

This example illustrates how scripting was accomplished using the XslTransform class:

```
Dim Transform as XslTransform = New XslTransform
Transform.Load("c:\Wrox\Intro.xsl")
Transform.Transform("c:\Wrox\Intro.xml", "Intro.html")
```

Using the XslCompiledTransform class, XSLT, you enable scripting as follows:

```
Dim Settings As XsltSetting = New XsltSettings(False, True)
Dim xct As XslCompiledTransform = New XslCompiledTransform
xct.Load("c:\Wrox\Intro.xsl", Settings, New XmlUrlResolver)
xct.Transform("c:\Wrox\Intro.xml", "c:\Wrox\Intro.html")
```

Guidelines

The following lists a few guidelines to consider when deploying XSLT:

- Scripting comes disabled by default. Enable scripting only when you know that the style sheet comes from a source you trust. If the source cannot be trusted, use a value of `NULL` for XSLT settings arguments.
- The `document()` function is disabled by default. Enable this function only when the style sheet comes from a trusted source.
- Specify a value of `NULL` for the `XmlResolver` argument to ensure that no external resources are accessed.
- You can customize the `XmlResolver` class to implement your own behavior for accessing resources.

Summary

The purpose of this chapter was to give a brief overview of XSLT and the components that make up an XSLT style sheet. Granted, there is so much more that could have been covered, but the purpose of this chapter was to give a basic foundation to style sheets so that you have a clear understanding of how they are compiled and mapped.

Two new classes were introduced in version 2.0 of the .NET Framework, and you learned how to use these new classes as well as how to migrate your existing code to be able utilize the new functionality provided in these new classes. The first class, `XslCompiledTransform`, is the replacement for the `XslTransform` class. The `XslCompiledTransform` class offers better security and, more important, a big performance improvement. The second class, `XsltSettings`, lets you specify which features are supported for a given transformation: specifically, the enabling and disabling of the embedded script blocks and the XSLT `document()` function.

A few guidelines were mentioned that should provide you with some insight as to the security issues when using the `XslCompiledTransform` class.

The part of this book on client-side XML processing ends with this chapter. In the next part, you'll learn about SQLXML and SOAP support in SQL Server 2005 and the new technologies in that area. In particular, the next chapter deals with Web Service (SOAP) support in SQL Server 2005.

Part IV: SQL Server 2005, SqlXml, and SOAP

17

Web Service (SOAP) Support in SQL Server 2005

When SQLXML Web release 3.0 for SQL Server 2000 was released in 2001, it came with a number of great new client-side features such as updategrams, XML Bulk Load, and XSD schemas. Not to be left out is one of the most important additions to SQLXML 3.0: support for Web Services and SOAP.

Subsequent service packs have been released since then, the latest being Service Pack 3 released in October 2004. This service pack included additional Web Service SOAP functionality with the ability to build Web Services with SQL Server 2000.

SQL Server 2005 introduces the native XML Web Service that supports many new features and enhancements, including support of the `xml` data type and related functionality. This chapter covers Web Service (SOAP) support in SQL Server 2005.

The topics discussed in this chapter are as follows:

- An overview of SOAP
- Configuring SOAP
- Best practices

SOAP Overview

According to the SOAP specification at `www.w3c.com`, the purpose of SOAP is to exchange information in a distributed environment using XML technologies. It is designed as a lightweight protocol that defines an extensible messaging framework that allows different programs, written in different languages, and running on different platforms, to talk to one another regardless of the protocol.

At times, understanding SOAP can be overwhelming and intimidating. In simple terms, SOAP is the specification that defines the format of XML messages that are exchanged between different environments. A SOAP message is simply a well-formed XML document wrapped in a few SOAP elements. Granted, there is much more needed for applications to be able to communicate with each other, but the underlying premise is that if your application talks XML, you have won half the battle.

There are two primary goals of SOAP. The first is to make it simple to use (thus, the first letter in the acronym). To accomplish this, a lot of duplicate functionality has been removed that was also found in the distributed systems, such as security, reliability, and routing. In addition, SOAP defines a framework that specifies how to move XML messages from one location to another.

The second goal is to make it extensible. The capability to use SOAP over any transport protocol is key to providing pure extensibility, and the SOAP specification lays out the requirements for a framework for such a task.

At its incarnation, SOAP stood for Simple Object Access Protocol. The goal of SOAP was to quickly and easily access objects on distributed systems and environments. However, since then the purpose of SOAP has grown to support much more than that; its acronym just doesn't do it justice anymore. Rather than confusing people, the acronym stays for now, but no more spelling it out.

SOAP in SQL Server 2005

New to SQL Server 2005 is the support for native XML Web Services provided by the SQL database engine. With this new support comes a support for a variety of standard protocols, which allows a wide array of clients to communicate with SQL Server.

SOAP is one of these standards that define the use of XML and HTTP when you access data and objects within SQL Server. Through the use of native XML, you can send SOAP requests to SQL Server over HTTP to execute stored procedures, user-defined functions, and T-SQL batch statements.

Native support for the HTTP listener is provided only on Windows Server 2003 and Windows XP with Service Pack 2.

How Native XML Works

Native XML mode in SQL Server 2005 allows HTTP-based clients to query the server through a *gateway* created on the server. This gateway is an HTTP endpoint on the server that allows stored procedures and user-defined functions to be accessed, as well as allowing other stored procedures and user-defined functions to be created.

Web Methods are the enabling of these stored procedures and functions. The process of enabling makes them available for clients. A group of Web Methods designed to be used together is called a Web Service.

When a client accesses a Web Service, SQL Server generates and returns information about the Web Service in the form of a WSDL file. These WSDL files can be automatically generated by SQL Server or custom-generated to fit your specific client requirements. You can also configure the endpoint to not answer any WSDL requests.

WSDL

WSDL (Web Service Definition Language) files are dynamically generated XML documents that define the Web interface for any functions defined on the HTTP endpoint. If any SQL batch functionality exists for that endpoint, the WSDL file describes those as well.

The WSDL file is requested by the client, which in turn generates requests from the server using the created and configured gateways, or endpoints. When the initial connection is made via the HTTP endpoint, the WSDL file is returned to the server by the client that made the connection request.

WSDL files come in two flavors: default and customized. The default WSDL file supports two WSDL file types, the first being the extended format, the second being the simplified format. The extended WSDL format adds features such as an XSD schema, which provides a better description of the information exposed by the endpoint. The simplified format uses a very scaled-down XSD schema and has support for older clients.

If neither of these types of files (extended or simplified format) meets your requirements, SQL Server provides the capability to create a customized version of a WSDL file with which you can update the server. Both default and customized WSDL files are supported by SQL Server 2005.

At the point and time the endpoint is created and defined, the WSDL argument is used to specify whether a WSDL file is generated on the server. It also defines if the file is returned so that the endpoint can inform the client of its interface. The basic WSDL argument syntax is as follows:

```
WSDL = {NONE | DEFAULT | 'sp_name'}
```

A WSDL file is not generated or returned if you specify a value of `NONE` for this argument. If you specify `DEFAULT`, a default WSDL file is generated and returned to the client that submitted the query to the endpoint. Optionally, if you are creating a custom WSDL file, you can supply a name of a stored procedure that can generate the custom WSDL. As mentioned previously, if you specify `DEFAULT`, you specify one of two types to determine the format of the WSDL file returned.

Default

The default WSDL is the full extended version of the WSDL file and is returned to the client when you specify the following URL: `http://server/endpointpath?wsdl`.

The full version of the WSDL file contains XSD-derived types to provide proper mapping to the SQL Server types.

Simple

The simple WSDL file is a scaled-down version of the default WSDL file, mapping all native XSD types to SQL Server types. It is returned to the client when you specify the following URL: `http://server/endpointpath?wsdlsimple`.

You can also specify custom WSDL files when neither the default nor simple WSDL files fulfill the client requirements.

Native XML Access Versus SQLXML

Prior to the introduction of SOAP, if clients wanted to connect to SQL Server, they needed to install MDAC. SQLXML 3.0 eased that a little bit by providing a middle-tier layer that gave the clients a Web-based method of accessing SQL Server. The downside to that was the need to deploy IIS. For clients running Microsoft Windows, they required a proprietary protocol called TDS (Tabular Data Stream) as well as MDAC. TDS is an application-level protocol specific to SQL Server and is built by the Microsoft OLE DB Provider.

Through SQL Server 2005 and native XML access, users can access SQL Server through an HTTP/SOAP combination. This method gives a much wider range of clients wanting to access SQL Server a better alternative. In addition, it requires nothing to be installed on the client such as MDAC or SQLXML.

Native XML Access Benefits

Chapter 15 listed a few benefits of native XML access. This section revisits those and lists a few more. Running XML Web Services natively in SQL Server has several benefits, including:

- **Any application utilizing Web Services can access SQL Server:** Of all the benefits of using native XML access, this is one of the biggest. Now any device that can submit HTTP requests, receive HTTP responses, and parse XML has capability to access SQL Server. This is especially useful in diverse environments.
- **Better support for mobile clients:** Now mobile clients can access SQL Server from anywhere, making mobile application development easier. Clients are also capable of connecting any time, enabling connection-monitoring once a connection has been established.
- **Built-in level of security:** HTTP endpoints prohibit anonymous user access, which is provided by a level of security built in to SQL Server. To accomplish this, administrative privileges are required to create endpoints and then only those methods you make available publicly are exposed by the endpoint.
- **Better Microsoft and third-party web development toolset integration:** With query results being returned in XML format from SQL Server 2005 Native XML Web Services, third-party developers make the most of the built-in schemas and the Native XML Web Services by using development environments such as Visual Studio 2005 to build applications that don't depend on a specific language or environment.

Native XML Support Requirements

In order for the native XML to be supported, the HTTP listener must be installed in your environment. This listener comes in the form of a file called Http.sys and only gets installed with Windows 2003 and Windows XP Service Pack 2. Http.sys provides the HTTP support needed by the Native XML Web Services.

SOAP, discussed in the next section, defines how XML and HTTP work together to access the information and services you need, no matter what the environment is.

SOAP Configuration

Configuring SOAP in SQL Server 2005 requires the creation of endpoints that can listen and receive requests from clients, allowing clients to send requests directly to SQL Server.

When SQL Server receives a SOAP request, it is received by the endpoint, which then looks at the URL to determine the registered endpoint and forwards the request to the SQL Server. IIS is never in the picture, thus eliminating the extra step and improving performance.

The following section details the configuration and creation of native XML Web Services in SQL Server 2005.

Web Methods

Web Methods are existing stored procedures or user-defined functions (UDFs) that can be selected to be exposed to the endpoint. Alluded to in this section's introduction, they are exposed using the `CREATE ENDPONT` statement specifying the name of the stored procedure or user-defined function as the method.

In this section, you create a couple of stored procedures and user-defined functions for use later in the chapter when you create the endpoint.

Stored Procedures

You will be using the AdventureWorks database for the examples in this section. In SQL Server Management Studio, expand the databases node in the Object Explorer window. Select the AdventureWorks database, expand that node by clicking on the plus (+) next to the database name, and then expand the Programmability node. Expand the Stored Procedures node as well, as shown in Figure 17-1. If a stored procedure does not exist with the name GetProducts, you need to create one for the examples in this chapter.

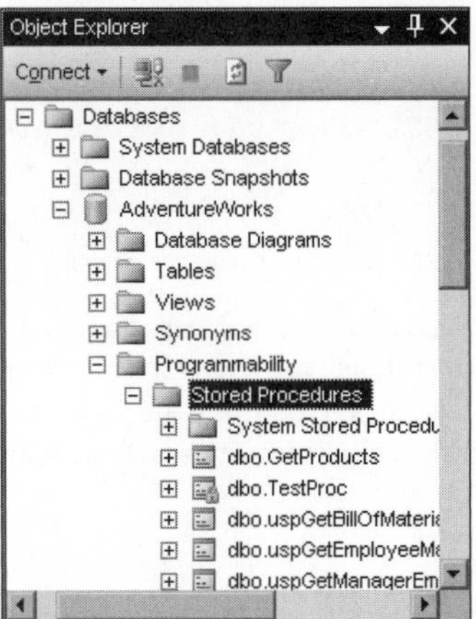

Figure 17-1

Open a query window and enter the following T-SQL code:

```
DROP PROCEDURE GetProducts
GO
CREATE Procedure GetProducts
AS
  SELECT ProductID, Name, ProductNumber
  FROM Production.Product
  ORDER BY Name
```

You use the name of the stored procedure when creating the endpoint as the `WEBMETHOD` argument. You learn how this is used later in this chapter.

Next, create a second stored procedure called `GetProductsByID`. In the query window, enter the following T-SQL statement:

```
CREATE Procedure GetProductByID
@ProductID int
AS
  SELECT Name, ProductNumber
  FROM Production.Product
  WHERE ProductID = @ProductID
```

This stored procedure will be used when the endpoint is altered to add a Web Method.

User Defined Functions

You can also utilize user-defined functions when creating endpoints:

```
CREATE FUNCTION GetProductCount (@ProductModelID int)
RETURNS int
AS
BEGIN
 DECLARE @RowCount int
 SET @RowCount = (SELECT COUNT(*) FROM Production.Product WHERE ProductModelID =
@ProductModelID);
    RETURN @RowCount;
END;
```

User-defined functions are routines written in any Microsoft.NET programming language. The routines can take a parameter and return a result, as well as perform any action available to the .NET programming language. As you will read about in Chapter 22, there are two flavors of .NET routines: scalar routines, which return a single value, and table-valued routines, which return one or multiple rows.

Endpoints

In order for SQL Server to be able to listen for SOAP requests, you must set up SQL Server as a Web Service, which means creating and defining HTTP endpoints and their related properties and methods that the endpoint exposes.

DDL Revisited

You use T-SQL DDL (Data Definition Language) statements to create and manage endpoints. There are three T-SQL DDL statements used for creating and managing endpoints: `CREATE ENDPOINT`, `ALTER ENDPOINT`, and `DROP ENDPOINT`. Each of these statements is discussed in subsequent sections.

Creating Endpoints

You create endpoints via the `CREATE ENDPOINT` statement. This statement creates and defines the endpoint and all the methods that the endpoint exposes, which the client can send SOAP requests to. It also defines the authentication for the endpoint.

The general syntax for creating an endpoint is as follows:

```
CREATE ENDPOINT endpointname [AUTHORIZATION login]
STATE = {STARTED | STOPPED | DISABLED }
AS {TCP | HTTP}
(
  <protocol specific items>
)
FOR {SOAP | TSQL | SERVICE_BROKER | DATABASE_MIRRORING}
(
  <language specific items>
)
```

The `endpointname` argument is the name of the endpoint to be created.

The `AUTHORIZATION` argument determines the owner of the endpoint that is being created. If you do not supply this argument, by default the owner of the endpoint is the login in which the endpoint is created. To change ownership of the endpoint, use the `ALTER ENDPOINT` statement discussed a bit later.

The `STATE` argument determines the state of the endpoint when it is created. A value of `STARTED` means that the endpoint is started and listening for connections. A value of `DISABLED` means that the server is not listening to the endpoint port and will not respond to any requests received by the endpoint. A value of `STOPPED` means that the server will listen to requests but will respond with an error back to the client. The value of `STOPPED` is the default value supplied if you do not specify one during the creation of the endpoint. To change the `STATE` value, use the `ALTER ENDPOINT` statement discussed a few sections hence.

The easiest way to understand endpoints is to break the syntax into two separate parts: the `AS` part and the `FOR` part.

AS

The `AS` part of the `CREATE ENDPOINT` syntax defines transport protocol-specific information using either TCP or HTTP and the port on which the endpoint listens. In this part, the authentication for the endpoint is also defined, and a list of restricted IP addresses can be listed here as well.

HTTP protocol-specific items include the following:

- AUTHENTICATION: The authentication type used when authenticating users logging into SQL Server. The available values are BASIC, DIGEST, and INTEGRATED:
  - You should use the BASIC authentication only as a last resort because content can be easily decoded. It contains a BASE64-encoded username and password, which are separated by a colon.
  - DIGEST authentication contains a one-way hashed username and password, which is then sent to the server. In this scenario, the server can either read the raw password or compare the hashed password sent by the client to the stored MD5 hash value created when the password was created.
  - Endpoints created using the INTEGRATED authentication support both NTLM and Kerberos authentication types. The server attempts to authenticate the client using whichever type the client has requested. This is the preferred method of authentication, as the Kerberos method is the Internet standard of authentication, and NTLM is supported by Windows 9x, Windows NT, and Windows 2000 or later.
- PATH: This is the URL path that specifies the endpoint location on the host computer. If you specify a SITE argument value (discussed later in this chapter), the host computer is specified as the PATH.
- PORTS: The port or ports listening on the endpoint. Ports can be clear ports, SSL ports, or a mix of both. Since there can be a mix, the incoming requests must match the type of ports specified. For example, clear ports listen for incoming requests using HTTP, while SSL ports listen to requests from HTTPS.
- AUTH_REALM (optional): If you specify the value of DIGEST as the authentication type, this is the hint returned to the client that sent the request. The default value is NONE.
- CLEAR_PORT (optional): The clear port number. Port 80 is the default port if you do not specify a port number.
- COMPRESSION (optional): If you set the value of this argument to ENABLED, SQL Server accepts the gzip encoding and returns compressed responses to the client. The default value is DISABLED.
- DEFAULT_LOGON_DOMAIN (optional): If you specify the value of BASIC as the authentication type, this is the default login domain. The default value is NONE.
- SITE (optional): There are three available values for this argument. The first value is the actual name of the HOST computer. The second value is the plus sign (+), which means that a listening operation applies to all possible host names for the computer in which the XML Web Service is running. An asterisk (*) signifies that the HTTP endpoint is listening on all host names, including those not explicitly reserved, for the computer in which the XML Web Service is running. The asterisk value is the default if you do not specify a value for the SITE argument.
- SSL_PORT (optional): The SSL port number. Port 443 is the default port if you do not specify a port number.

TCP-specific items include the following:

- LISTENER_PORT: This is the port number that the TCP/IP protocol that Service Broker listens to for connections. If you do not specify a value, the default is 4022.
- LISTENER_IP: This is the IP address on which the endpoint listens. This parameter has a default value of ALL, meaning that all IP addresses are valid and can submit requests.

The following items apply to both TCP and HTTP protocol:

- RESTRICT_IP (optional): Specifies which IP addresses are allowed to send SOAP requests to the endpoint. Either of the following values is permitted: NONE followed by a list of IP addresses that are not allowed to the endpoint (except for those specified in the EXCEPT_IP parameter), or ALL followed by a list of IP addresses that can submit SOAP requests to the endpoint.
- EXCEPT_IP (optional): Specifies the list of IP addresses that can or cannot send SOAP requests to the endpoint as specified in the RESTRICT_IP parameter.

FOR

The FOR part of the CREATE ENDPOINT syntax specifies the type of content that is supported by the endpoint. The available content type values are SOAP, T-SQL, Service Broker, and Database Mirroring. This part also specifies information specific to the language used in the endpoint, such as SOAP—which, as you'll find out shortly, allows you to specify a stored procedure to expose on your endpoint—or TSQL, which allows you to specify T-SQL statements on your endpoint.

The following sections outline the available arguments for the specific FOR values.

SOAP

The SOAP value takes the following arguments:

- WEBMETHOD (optional): The name in which the client sends HTTP SOAP requests to the endpoint for the corresponding method. For multiple Web Methods being exposed, you can supply multiple WEBMETHOD arguments. The reason this argument is optional is because you can create an endpoint with no methods, but add methods at a later point using the ALTER ENDPOINT statement.
- NAME: The name of the stored procedure or user-defined function that corresponds to the value indicated in the WEBMETHOD argument. The format of the value of this argument must follow the three-part name format, database.owner.name.
- SCHEMA (optional): For the corresponding WebMethod clause, this specifies whether an XSD schema is returned to the client for the called Web Method in the SOAP response. The values for this argument are DEFAULT, NONE, and STANDARD.
- FORMAT (optional): This argument specifies the additional information returned along with the result set. The values for this argument are as follows:
    - NONE: Returns no SOAP-specific markup from the server.
    - ALL_RESULTS: Returns row count, error messages, and warnings along with the result set in the SOAP message. This is the default value if you do not specify a value.
    - ROWSETS_ONLY: Returns only the result set.
- LOGIN_TYPE: Specifies the authentication mode for SQL Server on the endpoint. Available values are as follows:
    - WINDOWS: Uses only Windows authentication to authenticate to the endpoint.
    - MIXED: Uses either Windows or SQL authentication to authenticate to the endpoint. If you specify this value but SQL is installed using Windows mode, an error is generated.

- BATCHES: Specifies whether ad-hoc queries are supported by the endpoint. The values for this argument are ENABLED and DISABLED.
- WSDL: Specifies whether WSDL document-generation is supported by the endpoint.
- SESSIONS (optional): Specifies whether multiple SOAP requests can be sent in as a single session. The values for this argument are ENABLED and DISABLED.
- SESSION_TIMEOUT (optional): The amount of time in seconds before a SOAP session expires. The timer begins once the server has completed sending the response to the client. If no more requests are received before the timer expires, the session is terminated.
- DATABASE (optional): The name of the database against which the SOAP request is executed. If omitted, the default database associated to the login is used.
- NAMESPACE (optional): The endpoint namespace. If a namespace is not supplied, the value of http://tempura.org is used.
- SCHEMA (optional): For the endpoint, this specifies the XSD schema returned by the endpoint with the SOAP results. The values for this argument are STANDARD and NONE.
- CHARACTER_SET (optional): Specifies the behavior when results are returned with invalid XML characters. The values for this argument are SQL and XML. Specifying XML returns an error if characters in the result are not valid XML characters. Specifying SQL encodes the offending characters and returns them in the results.

Service Broker

There are a number of arguments that the SERVICE_BROKER and DATABASE_MIRRORING options share. Those arguments are listed under "Shared Arguments." The following arguments pertain solely to the SERVICE_BROKER option:

- MESSAGE_FORWARDING: For any messages received by the endpoint, this argument specifies that the endpoint forwards messages that are meant for services located elsewhere. This argument has two options:
  - ENABLED: Messages received by this endpoint are forwarded.
  - DISABLED: Messages received by this endpoint are not forwarded.
- MESSAGE_FORWARD_SIZE: This option specifies the maximum storage size, in MB (megabytes), allotted for storing messages that are to be forwarded.

Database Mirroring

The single argument that pertains solely to the DATABASE_MIRRORING option is ROLE. It identifies and sets the role used by the endpoint when participating in a mirrored SQL Server database. (For more information regarding the different types of roles, see the SQL Server Books Online help file.) The available values are as follows:

- WITNESS: This value specifies that the endpoint acts in the role of witness when database-mirroring.
- PARTNER: This value specifies that the endpoint acts in the role of partner when database-mirroring.
- ALL: This value specifies that the endpoint acts in both roles, as witness and partner when database-mirroring.

Shared Arguments

The following arguments are shared by both the SERVICE_BROKER and DATABASE_MIRRORING options, and they share the same general syntax.

The SERVICE_BROKER arguments are as follows (those arguments already discussed are highlighted):

```
FOR SERVICE_BROKER (
  [ AUTHENTICATION = {
    WINDOWS [ { NTLM | KERBEROS | NEGOTIATE } ]
    | CERTIFICATE certificate_name
    | WINDOWS [ { NTLM | KERBEROS | NEGOTIATE } ] CERTIFICATE certificate_name
    | CERTIFICATE certificate_name WINDOWS [ { NTLM | KERBEROS | NEGOTIATE } ]
  } ]
   [ , ENCRYPTION = { DISABLED | SUPPORTED | REQUIRED }
   [ ALGORITHM { RC4 | AES | AES RC4 | RC4 AES } ]
  ]
  [ , MESSAGE_FORWARDING = { ENABLED | DISABLED* } ]
  [ , MESSAGE_FORWARD_SIZE = forward_size ]
)
```

The DATABASE_MIRRORING syntax is as follows (those arguments already discussed are highlighted):

```
FOR DATABASE_MIRRORING (
  [ AUTHENTICATION = {
    WINDOWS [ { NTLM | KERBEROS | NEGOTIATE } ]
    | CERTIFICATE certificate_name
  } ]
  [ [ , ] ENCRYPTION = { DISABLED |SUPPORTED | REQUIRED }
  [ ALGORITHM { RC4 | AES | AES RC4 | RC4 AES } ]
 ]
 [,] ROLE = { WITNESS | PARTNER | ALL }
)
```

This section discusses the arguments shared by the options. They are as follows:

- AUTHENTICATION: This argument specifies the authentication requirements when authenticating to an endpoint. The default value for this argument is WINDOWS, which tells the endpoint that connections made to it will be using Windows authentication to authenticate. There are also three authorization methods that can be specified for this argument: NTLM, KERBEROS, and NEGOTIATE. NEGOTIATE is the default value if an authorization method is not specified. The following example illustrates the syntax for specifying an authentication method for the SERVICE_BROKER argument:

```
FOR SERVICE_BROKER (
  AUTHENTICATION = WINDOWS KERBEROS)
```

- CERTIFICATE: When connections are made to an endpoint, this argument specifies the name of the certificate, in the certificate_name value, which the endpoint uses to authenticate the connection.

- ENCRYPTION: Specifies the type of encryption used. There are three options:
    - DISABLED: Any data sent over the connection is not encrypted.
    - SUPPORTED: Data encryption is supported. If you are using database mirroring, the opposite endpoint has encryption set to use either REQUIRED or SUPPORTED.
    - REQUIRED: Any data sent over the connection is required to be encrypted. This is the default value if one is not specified.
- ALGORITHM: This argument is used to optionally manage the use of algorithms by each endpoint. The available values are as follows:
    - RC4: The endpoint must use the RC4 algorithm. If you do not specify a no value for the ALGORITHM argument, this value is defaulted.
    - AES: The endpoint must use the AES algorithm.
    - AES RC4: When you specify this option, the two endpoints negotiate for an encryption algorithm. The endpoint in which this value is being set uses the AES algorithm preference.
    - RC4 AES: When you specify this option, the two endpoints negotiate for an encryption algorithm. The endpoint in which this value is being set uses the RC4 algorithm preference.

With all of this newfound knowledge under your belt, it is time to create an endpoint. Open a query window in SQL Server Management Studio and enter the following DDL statement:

```
CREATE ENDPOINT wrox_endpoint
STATE = STARTED
AS HTTP(
   PATH = '/wrox',
   AUTHENTICATION = (DIGEST),
   PORTS = ( CLEAR ),
   SITE = 'vssql2005'
   )
FOR SOAP (
   WEBMETHOD 'GetProducts'
            (name='AdventureWorks.dbo.GetProducts',
             SCHEMA=STANDARD ),
   WSDL = DEFAULT,
   SCHEMA = STANDARD,
   DATABASE = 'AdventureWorks'
   )
GO
```

If you are running this on Windows XP, you might receive the following error:

```
An error occurred while attempting to register the endpoint 'wrox_endpoint'. One
or more of the ports specified in the CREATE ENDPOINT statement may be bound to
another process. Attempt the statement again with a different port of use netstat
to find the application currently using the port and resolve the conflict.
```

If you receive this message, it is because both IIS and SQL Server are fighting over port 80. For more information and a workaround, see the "Guidelines and Limitations" section at the end of this chapter.

If you didn't receive the error, you see the following message:

```
Command(s) completed successfully.
```

This next example creates an endpoint with multiple Web Methods, one being a stored procedure and the other a function:

```
CREATE ENDPOINT wrox_endpoint
STATE = STARTED
AS HTTP(
   PATH = '/wrox',
   AUTHENTICATION = (DIGEST),
   PORTS = ( CLEAR ),
   SITE = 'vssql2005'
   )
FOR SOAP (
   WEBMETHOD 'GetProducts'
            (name='AdventureWorks.dbo.GetProducts',
             SCHEMA=STANDARD ),
   WEBMETHOD 'GetProductCount'
            (name='AdventureWorks.dbo.GetProductCount'),
   WSDL = DEFAULT,
   SCHEMA = STANDARD,
   DATABASE = 'AdventureWorks'
   )
GO
```

One more endpoint needs to be created for purposes of this chapter. This endpoint is nearly an exact duplicate of the previous one, but some examples later in the chapter use this endpoint. Run the following `CREATE ENDPOINT` statement to create the `wrox_endpoint2` endpoint.

```
CREATE ENDPOINT wrox_endpoint2
STATE = STARTED
AS HTTP(
   PATH = '/wrox2',
   AUTHENTICATION = (DIGEST),
   PORTS = ( CLEAR ),
   CLEAR_PORT = 81,
   SITE = 'vssql2005'
   )
FOR SOAP (
   WEBMETHOD 'GetProducts'
            (name='AdventureWorks.dbo.GetProducts',
             SCHEMA=STANDARD ),
   WEBMETHOD 'GetProductCount'
            (name='AdventureWorks.dbo.GetProductCount'),
   WSDL = DEFAULT,
   SCHEMA = STANDARD,
   DATABASE = 'AdventureWorks'
   )
GO
```

The next section discusses altering endpoints to add Web Methods and other arguments to the endpoint.

There are a number of system tables that can be queried, which provide some excellent information about created endpoints. For example:

- The `sys.endpoints` system table contains detailed information about HTTP endpoints such as the `SITE` and `URL` information.
- The `sys.soap.endpoint` system table contains SOAP-specific information about endpoints.
- The `sys.endpoint_webmethod` system table contains information regarding the SOAP methods defined on the endpoint.

The following T-SQL shows the syntax for querying the `sys.endpoints` system table:

```
SELECT *
FROM   sys.endpoints
```

Figure 17-2 shows the results of querying the `sys.endpoints` table once the `CREATE ENDPOINT` statements are executed.

	name	endpoint_id	principal_id	protocol	protocol_desc	type	type_desc	state	state_desc
1	Dedicated Admin Connection	1	1	2	TCP	2	TSQL	0	STARTED
2	TSQL Local Machine	2	1	4	SHARED_MEMORY	2	TSQL	0	STARTED
3	TSQL Named Pipes	3	1	3	NAMED_PIPES	2	TSQL	0	STARTED
4	TSQL Default TCP	4	1	2	TCP	2	TSQL	0	STARTED
5	TSQL Default VIA	5	1	5	VIA	2	TSQL	0	STARTED
6	Wrox_EndPoint	65536	1	1	HTTP	1	SOAP	0	STARTED

Results | Messages

Figure 17-2

Altering Endpoints

Altering endpoints allows you to change permission information, add new methods to an existing endpoint, modify or delete an existing method from an endpoint, and change properties of an existing endpoint.

The syntax for altering endpoints is very similar to that of creating endpoints, so a thorough examination of the arguments is not required here.

The general syntax for altering an endpoint is as follows:

```
ALTER ENDPOINT endpointname
[AFFINITY = {NONE | ADMIN | <64bit_integer>} ]
STATE = {STARTED | STOPPED | DISABLED }
AS {TCP | HTTP}
(
  <protocol specific items>
)
FOR {SOAP | TSQL | SERVICE_BROKER | DATABASE_MIRRORING}
(
  <language specific items>
)
```

The following arguments are available when altering an endpoint:

- ADD EXCEPT_IP: Contains a list of IP addresses that can or cannot send SOAP requests to the endpoint, depending on the values specified in the RESTRICT_IP list, that are added to the endpoint.
- DROP EXCEPT_IP: Contains a list of IP addresses that can or cannot send SOAP requests to the endpoint, depending on the values specified in the RESTRICT_IP list, that are removed from the endpoint.
- ADD WEBMETHOD: Adds a new method endpoint.
- ALTER WEBMETHOD: Changes the definition of an existing method endpoint.
- DROP WEBMETHOD: Removes an existing method endpoint.

Altering endpoints does not change current values that were previously set unless specified in the ALTER ENDPOINT statement.

The following example adds a method to the endpoint created earlier in this section. It specifies a Web Method name and the name of the actual stored procedure or user-defined function:

```
ALTER ENDPOINT wrox_endpoint
FOR SOAP
(
  ADD WEBMETHOD 'GetProductsByID' (name='AdventureWorks.dbo.GetProductByID',
FORMAT=NONE)
)
```

This next example removes a Web Method from an endpoint:

```
ALTER ENDPOINT wrox_endpoint
FOR SOAP
(
  DROP WEBMETHOD 'GetProductCount')
)
```

Deleting Endpoints

Deleting endpoints is pretty simple. The thing to remember is that proper permissions are necessary to remove endpoints.

The syntax for removing endpoints is as follows:

```
DROP ENDPOINT EndPointName
```

For example, the following code deletes the second endpoint created in this section's first example:

```
DROP ENDPOINT Wrox_EndPoint2
```

As previously stated, the correct permissions are required in order to remove an endpoint. The owner of the endpoint may delete the endpoint, as well as members of the Sysadmin role and any users who have been given CONTROL permissions on the endpoint.

Endpoint Permissions

Endpoint permissions are set by using DDL statements, which allow for the creation, altering, connecting, and transfer of ownership of endpoints. You must execute any of these permission statements against the master database.

In SQL Server Management Studio, expand the Security node in the Object Explorer window. Right-click Logins and select New Login from the context menu, shown in Figure 17-3.

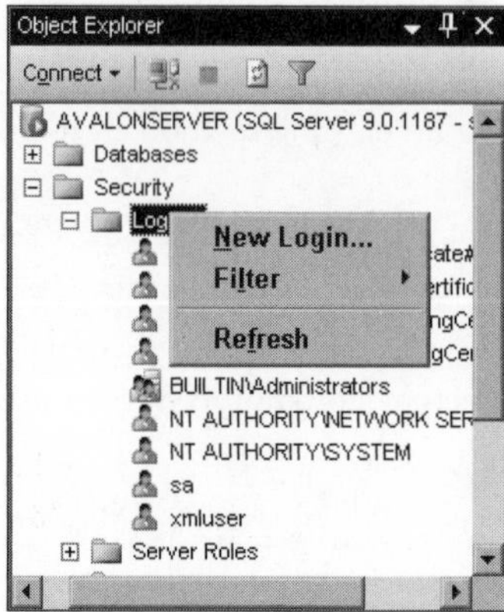

Figure 17-3

This brings up the Login - New dialog, shown in Figure 17-4. Select the SQL Server authentication option, and for the login name enter **WroxSQLLogin**. Enter **PassWord1** for the password.

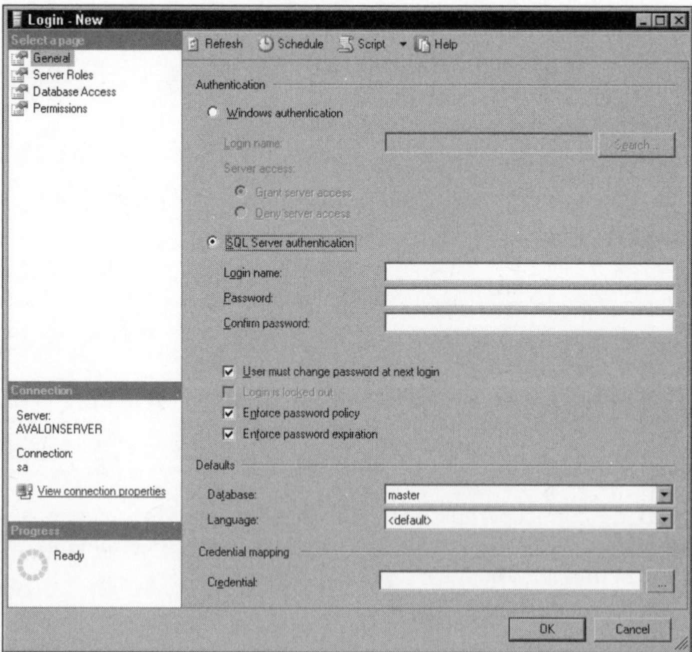

Figure 17-4

Repeat the process to create a user called TempSQLLogin. Both of these logins will be used to discuss endpoint permissions throughout the rest of this chapter.

CREATE

`CREATE` permissions can be given or taken away using `CREATE ENDPOINT TO` statement. The general syntax is as follows:

```
{ GRANT | DENY | REVOKE } CREATE ENDPOINT TO login
```

The following example grants `CREATE ENDPOINT` permissions to the WroxSQLLogin that you created. Open a query window and enter the following statement:

```
GRANT CREATE ENDPOINT TO WroxSQLLogin
```

Once `CREATE` permissions have been given, they can be taken away using `REVOKE`. The following example takes away the `CREATE` permissions just given to the WroxSQLLogin user:

```
REVOKE CREATE ENDPOINT TO WroxSQLLogin
```

`CREATE` permissions can be denied for a specific user. The following example denies `CREATE` permissions for the WroxSQLLogin user:

```
DENY CREATE ENDPOINT TO WroxSQLLogin
```

Endpoints are securable at a server level, so denying permission to an endpoint removes all implied endpoint and server permission on a specific endpoint.

ALTER

Giving `ALTER` permissions to a user allows that user to alter an endpoint. You can give `ALTER` permissions without giving `CREATE` permissions. This section outlines the different `ALTER` permissions that can be given.

`ALTER ANY ENDPOINT` gives the user the ability to modify any endpoint on the selected server. The general `ALTER ANY ENDPOINT` syntax is as follows:

```
{ GRANT | DENY | REVOKE } ALTER ANY ENDPOINT TO login
```

The following example gives the WroxSQLLogin users the ability to alter any endpoint on the local server:

```
GRANT ALTER ANY ENDPOINT TO WroxSQLLogin
```

You can revoke or deny the permissions to alter any endpoint by using the following statements:

```
REVOKE ALTER ANY ENDPOINT TO WroxSQLLogin

DENY ALTER ANY ENDPOINT TO WroxSQLLogin
```

ALTER ON ENDPOINT gives the user the ability to modify a specific endpoint on the local server. The general syntax for ALTER ON ENDPOINT is as follows:

```
{ GRANT | DENY | REVOKE } ALTER ON ENDPOINT::endpointname TO login
```

For example, the following statement grants the WroxSQLLogin user the ability to alter the Wrox_EndPoint:

```
GRANT ALTER ON ENDPOINT::Wrox_EndPoint TO WroxSQLLogin
```

Likewise, the following statement revokes and denies the user WroxSQLLogin the ability to alter the Wrox_EndPoint.

```
REVOKE ALTER ON ENDPOINT::Wrox_EndPoint TO WroxSQLLogin

DENY ALTER ON ENDPOINT::Wrox_EndPoint TO WroxSQLLogin
```

CONTROL ON ENDPOINT controls whether a user can alter or delete an endpoint, as well as transfer ownership of the endpoint. The general syntax for CONTROL ON ENDPOINT is as follows:

```
{ GRANT | DENY | REVOKE } CONTROL ON ENDPOINT::endpointname TO login
```

The following example grants CONTROL permission of the Wrox_EndPoint to the WroxSQLLogin user:

```
GRANT CONTROL ON ENDPOINT::Wrox_EndPoint TO WroxSQLLogin
```

As with the other ALTER statements, you can revoke or deny the CONTROL permission, as follows:

```
REVOKE CONTROL ON ENDPOINT::Wrox_EndPoint TO WroxSQLLogin

DENY CONTROL ON ENDPOINT::Wrox_EndPoint TO WroxSQLLogin
```

CONNECT

The CONNECT argument specifies whether a login can or cannot execute requests against a specific endpoint. The syntax for the CONNECT argument is as follows:

```
{ GRANT | DENY | REVOKE } CONNECT ON ENDPOINT::endpointname TO login
```

The following example grants CONNECT permissions on the Wrox_EndPoint to the user WroxSQLLogin:

```
GRANT CONNECT ON ENDPOINT:: Wrox_EndPoint TO WroxSQLLogin
```

TAKE OWNERSHIP

The TAKE OWNERSHIP argument gives permissions to a user who then takes over ownership of the specified endpoint. This works in conjunction with the AUTHORIZATION clause. When ownership is transferred between users, the user to which the permissions are being transferred must accept ownership by executing ALTER ENDPOINT and specifying the AUTHORIZATION statement. Meaning, the TAKE OWNERSHIP argument determines if a login can be specified in the AUTHORIZATION clause of the endpoint.

The general syntax is as follows:

```
{ GRANT | DENY | REVOKE } TAKE OWNERSHIP ON ENDPOINT::endpointname TO login
```

The following example script transfers ownership of the endpoint from the WroxSQLLogin user to the TempSQLLogin user. This script assumes that the correct `ALTER` permissions have been given to the TempSQLLogin user:

```
SETUSER
GO

SETUSER 'WroxSQLLogin'
GO

GRANT TAKE OWNERSHIP ON ENDPOINT::Wrox_EndPoint TO TempSQLLogin
GO

SETUSER
GO

SETUSER 'TempSQLLogin'
GO

ALTER AUTHORIZATION ON ENDPOINT::Wrox_EndPoint TO TempSQLLogin
GO
```

In this example, the owner of the `Wrox_EndPoint`, WroxSQLLogin, grants ownership of the endpoint to the TempSQLLogin user by issuing the `GRANT TAKE OWNERSHIP` permission. The TempSQLLogin then changes the ownership of the endpoint to himself using the `ALTER AUTHORIZATION` statement. The TempSQLLogin user now has ownership of the `Wrox_Endpoint` endpoint and can manage the endpoint accordingly.

Guidelines and Limitations

The following lists several guidelines and limitations that apply to native XML Web Services and HTTP SOAP requests:

- When attempting to create an endpoint on Windows XP running SQL Server 2005, you might receive the following error:

```
An error occurred while attempting to register the endpoint 'wrox_endpoint'. One or
more of the ports specified in the CREATE ENDPOINT statement may be bound to
another process. Attempt the statement again with a different port of use netstat
to find the application currently using the port and resolve the conflict.
```

  This is due to a conflict between SQL Server and IIS because IIS listens on port 80. As a workaround to this problem, try executing the `CREATE ENDPOINT` statement again, this time specifying a specific port number as illustrated by this `CREATE ENDPOINT` statement fragment:

```
          AS HTTP (
           CLEAR_PORT = 81
           )
```

- Native XML Web Services only function on SQL Server 2005 that is running on versions of Windows that support the HTTP API, which are currently Windows 2003 and Windows XP with Service Pack 2. This API is in the Http.sys file. Any attempts to create native XML Web Services on operating systems that do not support this API result in failed DDL statement execution. Http.sys is in the C:\Windows\System32\Drivers directory.
- Table valued user-defined functions are not supported. This is a function that returns a table rather than a scalar value (such as an integer).
- You can configure endpoints can be configured to use multiple ports, but you cannot configure endpoints to use two ports of the same type. For example, one clear port and one SSL port is acceptable. Two clear ports or two SSL ports are not.
- When you specify a namespace during the creation of an endpoint, make sure it does not match any namespaces used in endpoint `xml` data type schemas. This allows for better interoperability with Visual Studio 2005.
- There is a difference between the SOAP specification and SQL Server in the way that XML processing is handled. The SOAP specification allows for the handling of XML processing instructions found in a request or response. This is not enforced by SQL Server and if found in SOAP request, any processing instructions are ignored by the server, due in part to the fact that some client applications may not be able to understand the `xml` data type.

Best Practices

This section outlines some best practices when considering native XML Web Services in SQL Server 2005.

Performance

From a performance perspective, there are a number of things to keep in mind:

- Not every scenario requires a native XML Web Service. If you already have Web Services deployed via IIS, native XML Web Services are not meant to be an end-all replacement solution. Consider native XML Web Services if:
    - Your application currently reads and writes XML.
    - You are looking for better performance and are currently using SQLXML as a mid-tier solution.
    - Your current application uses stored procedures.
    - You have SOAP in mind. In this scenario, a combination of your current Web Services solutions and SQL Server Web Services provides optimal performance and connection alternatives, especially in a heterogeneous environment.
- SOAP uses additional server resources and thus has more overhead than the normal TDS protocol. Therefore, you should consider additional server hardware resources.
- Consider the correct WSDL option for your organization prior to deploying native XML Web Services. The Simple WSDL file is recommended in environments where there are non-Windows clients, whereas the Default WSDL file is recommended for environments where strictly Windows clients are found. However, do not rule out Customized WSDL if the requirements call for it.

Performance Counters

SQL Server 2005 adds several performance counters that can be monitored to help determine the current state and performance of your SQL Server 2005 environment.

To add the performance counters, open the Performance Monitor application, shown in Figure 17-5, by selecting the Performance program from the Administrative Tools menu; or by selecting Start ➪ Run, typing **Perfmon** in the dialog box, and then clicking OK.

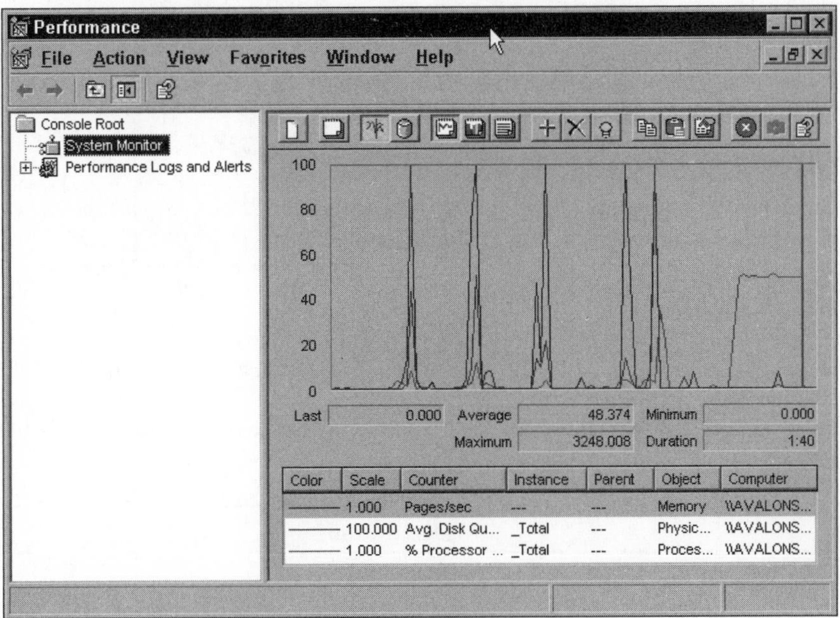

Figure 17-5

Add the counters by right-clicking in the monitor pane and selecting Add Counters, or by clicking the Add button (the plus sign), as shown in Figure 17-6.

Figure 17-6

This opens up the Add Counters dialog. To add the SOAP counters, select SQLServer:General Statistics from the Performance Object drop-down menu, as shown in Figure 17-7.

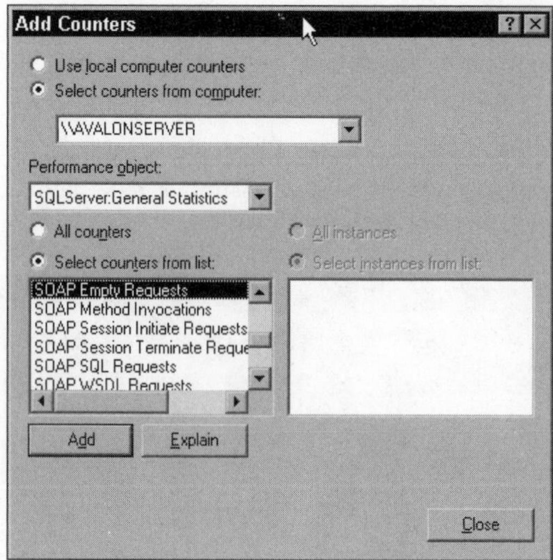

Figure 17-7

To add the individual counters, select the desired counter and click the Add button.

The following table details the SQL Server SOAP counters available for monitoring. Each of these counters resets every second.

Name	Description
HTTP Authenticated Request	Number of authenticated HTTP requests per second using Integrated, Digest, or Basic. Requests received during a challenge are not counted.
SOAP Batch SQL Requests	Number of ad hoc SOAP batch requests per second. Requests received during a challenge are not counted.
SOAP Method Invocations	Number of individual SOAP method calls started per second. Requests received during a challenge are not counted.
SOAP WSDL Requests	Number of SOAP WSDL requests per second. Requests received during a challenge are not counted.
SOAP Requests Executing	Number of SOAP requests being processed by the server per second. When a request begins, the number is incremented. When a process finishes, the number is decremented.
SOAP Requests Failed	Number of failed SOAP request (SOAP faults) per second.
SOAP Requests Succeeded	Number of successfully executed SOAP requests per second.

Security

From a security point of view, consider the following.

Use a Firewall

Native XML Web Services should *only*, and *always*, be used behind a firewall. Any port specified in the endpoint setup should also be protected by the firewall.

SSL

The purpose of SSL is to provide the encryption and decryption of data between the client and server. You must secure any data via the SSL protocol. To enable SSL and encryption, you need to configure a certificate first. Once the certificate is configured, you can configure the endpoint to provide SSL encryption.

Keep in mind that any certificate you use for SSL might also be used for other applications. This means that there is the possibility that the same certificate could be securing traffic on your IIS server over the same port, which could lead to some security implications.

Disable the Windows Guest Account

As a matter of habit, always make sure that the Windows Guest account is disabled on the server on which SQL Server is installed and running. On Windows NT and Windows 2000, this account is enabled by default. On Windows 2003, it is disabled by default.

Kerberos Authentication

Previously, this chapter detailed the different authentication types to be used when creating an endpoint. When you create an endpoint, the recommended authentication method is either `KERBEROS` or `INTEGRATED` as follows:

```
AUTHENTICATION = KERBEROS
AUTHENTICATION = INTEGRATED
```

`KERBEROS` authentication supports only Kerberos as the mode of authentication, meaning that SQL Server must associate a Server Principle Name (SPN) with the account that it is running on, such as a local system account or a domain user account.

The syntax for registering Kerberos SPN's is as follows:

```
SetSpn [-A SPN | -D SPN | -L SPN] serviceaccount
```

The `-A` adds the specified SPN account, `-D` deletes the specified SPN account, and `-L` lists all the SPNs registered to the specified account.

The following example sets the appropriate SPM to the local system account on the local box named `SQLBox2005` in the `Avalon` domain:

```
SetSpn -A http/SQLBox2005 Avalon\local_system_account
```

`INTEGRATED` authentication lets the endpoint support both NTLM (NT Lan Manager, the authentication method supported by Windows 95, 98, and NT 4.0) and `KERBEROS` authentication. The Kerberos protocol has better security, identifying both server and client at the authentication.

Endpoint Connect Permissions

This chapter also discussed setting permissions on endpoints. From a security perspective, a focus on `Connect` permissions is essential and must be constantly monitored and maintained. The best method of doing this is to grant the necessary permissions to a specific group or to specific users. For maintainability, managing a group is easier than managing individual users.

It should go without saying that granting access to the Public role is not recommended.

Endpoint State

Managing the endpoint state is critical to the security of your SQL Server. A newly created endpoint has a `STATE` of `stopped` unless it is specifically set to `started` in the `CREATE ENDPOINT` statement. If an endpoint is no longer needed, set its state to `stopped` or `disabled` to prevent security risks. It might also be wise to drop unused Web Methods.

Secure Endpoint Defaults

As explained earlier in this chapter, most of the options for creating an endpoint have defaults if a value is not specified. The majority of these defaults provide the most efficient security, so it is best to leave the defaults unless there is a reason for changing the default.

Two of the options should not be changed unless you have a very specific reason. The first option is the following:

```
BATCHES = DISABLED
```

The second option is as follows:

```
LOGIN_TYPE = WINDOWS
```

For endpoint users, only Windows Authentication allows for the `LOGIN_TYPE` options.

Deployment Scenarios

This chapter also briefly discussed the concept of using native XML Web Services and some reasons as to why they would be beneficial in your environment. This section builds on that and outlines some scenarios as to when and why your application environment would benefit from using native XML Web Services, as well as reasons why it would not make sense to deploy them.

Here are some *reasons for* deploying:

- **Your application uses stored procedures heavily.** This should almost be self-explanatory. SQL Server 2005 now makes it very easy to expose your business logic via stored procedures using HTTP endpoints regardless of the client. You also should determine how much of your business logic is currently in stored procedures.
- **You are looking for a better performance over the SQLXML solution.** The SQLXML provides a mid-tier solution that in previous versions of SQL Server required IIS setup and configuration. The SQL Server 2005 endpoint solution provides this same functionality on a single server, allowing for better performance.

- **Your application reads and writes XML data.** This is a given. Any application that consumes or returns XML data is a great candidate for a Web Service. Moving that functionality into a native XML Web Service provides even more robustness on all levels.
- **As an alternative to SQL Server Reporting Services (SSRS).** Native XML Web Services can provide the information and data necessary to produce a report for your application. SSRS adds resource overhead to SQL Server. Native XML Web Services can provide the same information without the additional overhead.
- **Service Oriented Architecture (SOA).** This allows you to combine and integrate your current Web Service architecture with a SQL Server Web Service architecture, enabling the two environments to work together.

The following are two *reasons against* deployment:

- **Your application currently reads and writes BLOB data.**
- **You require real-time transaction processing.** If your application is used for OLTP (Online Transaction Processing) then you ought to reconsider the use of Native XML Web Services.

Summary

SOAP is such a deep topic. Whole books have been written specifically on SOAP and Web Services. However, the intent of this chapter was to briefly introduce SOAP to give you a background on the technology so that the rest of the chapter made sense.

I hope you are starting to feel the excitement in the air over this topic. As explained previously, SOAP is not an end-all solution. You are not being asked to rip out your existing Web Services infrastructure. However, this is a great technology that will complement your existing solutions very well by providing access to data for a wide variety of clients.

The vast majority of this chapter focused on native XML Web Services in SQL Server 2005, introducing and digging into endpoints and Web Methods, as well as the important discussion of permissions for these objects.

As with most topics, the chapter closed with a couple of sections discussing some guidelines and limitations for native XML Web Services, along with some best practices to keep in mind when you are considering implementing this great technology.

In the next chapter, you learn how to access these native XML Web Services from the client.

18

SOAP at the Client

In Chapter 17, you learned about endpoints and native XML Web Services in SQL Server 2005, as well as how to create, modify, and manage them in your environment. You also learned a little bit about some of the reasons you might want to consider deploying endpoints alongside your existing Web Services infrastructure, and adding native XML Web Services as a complement to what you already have.

This chapter builds on the last chapter, focusing on what you can do with those newly created endpoints by providing a lot of examples, giving you an idea of how endpoints are used from the client side.

This chapter walks you through creating a Visual Studio 2005 application to consume the endpoint and then make changes to the endpoint to add functionality to the application. A few pages are dedicated to showing you how to secure an endpoint with SSL for secure communication of data between the client and SQL Server.

Two main topics are discussed in this chapter:

- How to consume and use an endpoint
- How to secure an endpoint

Consuming and Using an Endpoint

A review is necessary to look at the functionality that will be provided by the endpoint. Initially, the endpoint is going to expose an ordered list of all the product models as well as a count of the products associated with each product model. To supply the list of product models, you need to create the following stored procedure. If you have not yet created this stored procedure, open a query window in SQL Server Management Studio and run the following T-SQL:

```
USE AdventureWorks
GO
CREATE PROCEDURE GetProductModels
AS
  SELECT ProductModelID, Name
  FROM Production.ProductModel
  ORDER BY Name

GO
```

As you can see, the stored procedure queries the Production.Product table for the ProductModelID and Name columns, sorted alphabetically by the Name column. The endpoint also needs to expose a way to return the product count for a given ProductModelID. For this, use a user-defined function. Run the following T-SQL to create the necessary UDF:

```
USE AdventureWorks
GO
CREATE FUNCTION ProductByProductModelID(@ProductModelID int)
RETURNS int
AS
BEGIN
RETURN
(
  SELECT COUNT(*)
  FROM Production.product
  WHERE productmodelid = @ProductModelID
)
END
```

Looking at the code, you can see that it returns a count of the number of products for a given ProductModelID. To test this UDF, run the following T-SQL in a query window.

```
SELECT AdventureWorks.dbo.ProductByProductModelID(8)
```

Figure 18-1 shows that for the given ProductModelID of 8, there are 10 associated product records for that ProductModelID.

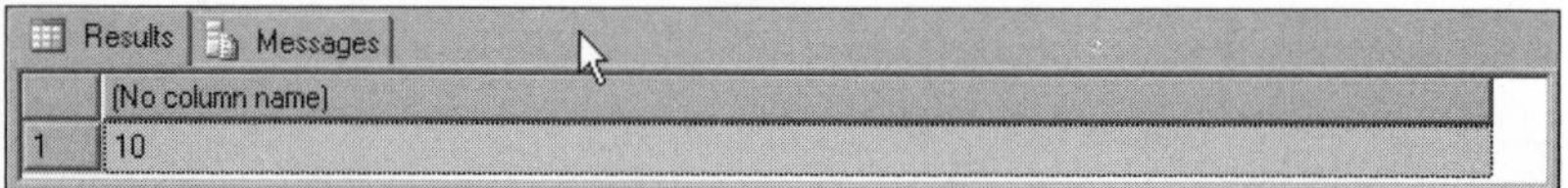

Figure 18-1

Both the stored procedure and the user-defined function are used in the initial creation of the endpoint.

The following SQL creates the endpoint needed to get the application started. In a query window, execute the following SQL statement:

```
USE AdventureWorks
GO
CREATE ENDPOINT Wrox_EndPoint
```

```
STATE = STARTED
AS HTTP
(
 SITE = 'localhost',
 PATH = '/Wrox',
 AUTHENTICATION = (INTEGRATED),
 PORTS = ( CLEAR )
)
FOR SOAP
(
 WebMethod 'GetProductCountByProductModelID'
 (
        NAME = 'adventureworks.dbo.ProductByProductModelID',
        SCHEMA = STANDARD
 ),
 WebMethod 'GetProductModels'
 (
        NAME = 'adventureworks.dbo.GetProductModels',
        SCHEMA = STANDARD
 ),
 WSDL = DEFAULT,
 BATCHES = ENABLED,
 DATABASE = 'AdventureWorks'
)
```

Notice that both the stored procedure and UDF are exposed by this endpoint as Web Methods. A Web Method in this context, as explained in the previous chapter, is similar to a Web Method you would normally create in Visual Basic or C# except for the fact that these Web Methods are stored procedures or User-Defined Functions (UDFs).

As explained in the previous chapter, the name of the Web Method does not necessarily have to match the name of the stored procedure or UDF. As you will see later in the chapter, what actually shows up in the `sys.endpoint_webmethods` system table is not the actual name of the SQL Server object (in this example, the function ProductsByProductModelID) but it is the Web Method name.

Granting Permissions

Now that you've created the endpoint, the next step is to give permissions to the appropriate users to access the endpoint. It does no good to create an endpoint if it can't be used or consumed. To grant permissions, expand the SQL Server Object Explorer Security node in the Management Studio. Underneath the Security node, expand the Logins node. Right-click the Logins node, and select New Login from the context menu.

In the Login - New dialog there are several options that allow you to create different types of SQL Server logins. For the purposes of this chapter, keep all of the defaults and create a Windows authentication login. When you select Windows Authentication, the New Login dialog does not create the Windows login. It merely points to a previously created Windows user account. In this example, the user account Scott had already been created as a local user on the machine in which SQL Server 2005 is running by using the Computer Management dialog, as shown in Figure 18-2.

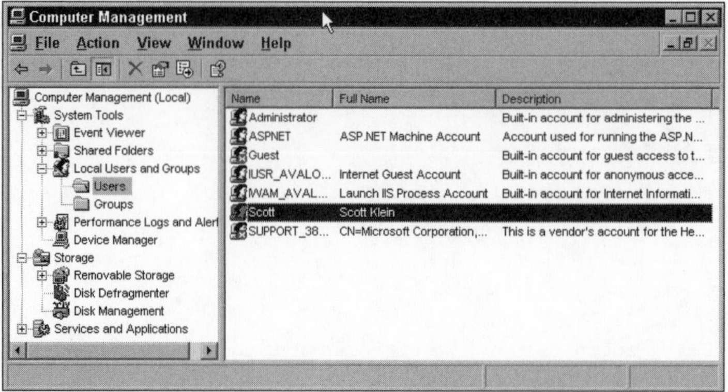

Figure 18-2

On the New Login - New form (shown in Figure 18-3), you can either type in the name of user or group, or you can click the Search button look for a specific user or group.

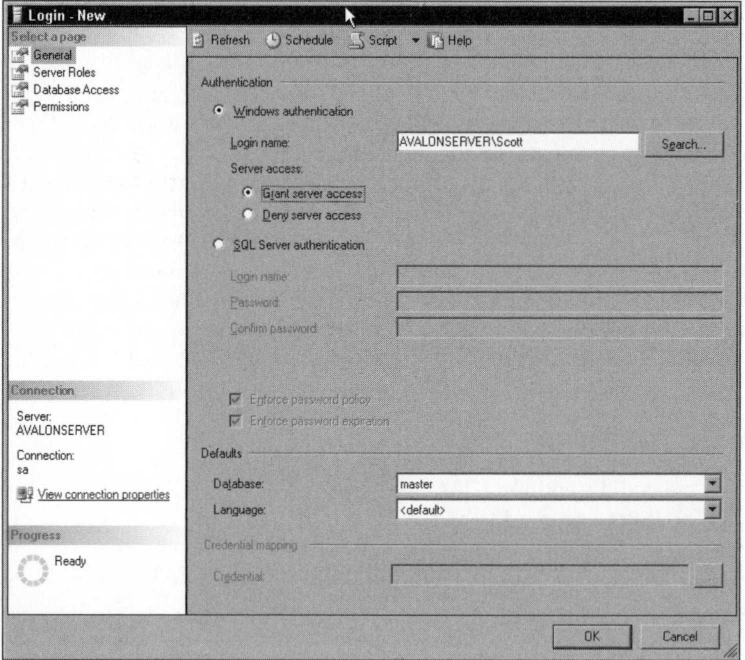

Figure 18-3

The format of the Login Name or username must follow one of these two options: either `Domain\username` or `Domain\GroupName`.

If the format is incorrect, SQL Server generates an error stating that the information entered is not a valid Windows NT name.

You can leave all the other information alone and accept the defaults. Once you have selected the user or group you wish to grant access to the endpoint, click OK. This essentially creates a mapping between SQL Server and Windows for user authentication. When the user tries to access the endpoint, SQL Server passes the user's credentials to Windows for authentication.

Figure 18-4 shows the user added to the Logins group in SQL Server.

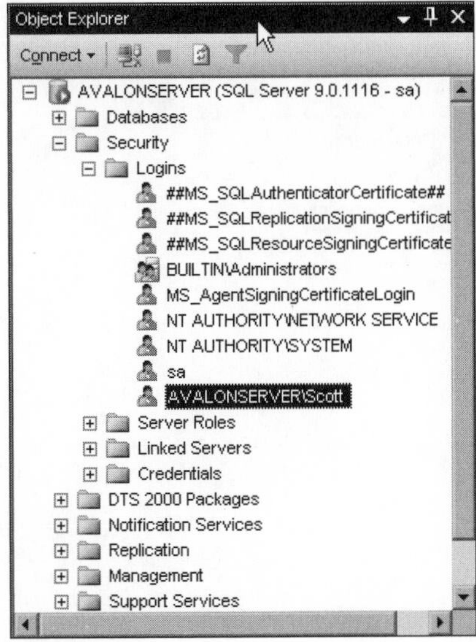

Figure 18-4

Can user Scott now access the endpoint? No, he cannot. There is still one more step to take.

The final step in this process is to tell SQL Server that user Scott has access to the endpoint Wrox_EndPoint. To do this, execute the following SQL Statement in a query window:

```
USE MASTER
GO
GRANT CONNECT ON ENDPOINT::Wrox_EndPoint TO [AVALONSERVER\Scott]
GO
```

As explained in Chapter 17, the `CONNECT` permission controls which logins have the ability to execute requests against an endpoint. Once this statement executes successfully, user Scott should have access to the Wrox_EndPoint created earlier and be able to execute any WebMethods associated with the Wrox_EndPoint endpoint.

Building the Client Application

It is now time to build the client application that will consume this Web Service and execute the Web Methods associated with the endpoint. Open Visual Studio 2005 and create a new Visual Basic (or C#) Windows project. The first step is to consume the SQL Server 2005 Web Service.

Consuming the SQL Server 2005 Web Service

Consuming a SQL Server 2005 Web Service is really no different than consuming a normal Web Service in an application. Once you've created the project, right-click the project name and select Add Web Reference from the context menu. This opens the Add Web Reference dialog shown in Figure 18-5.

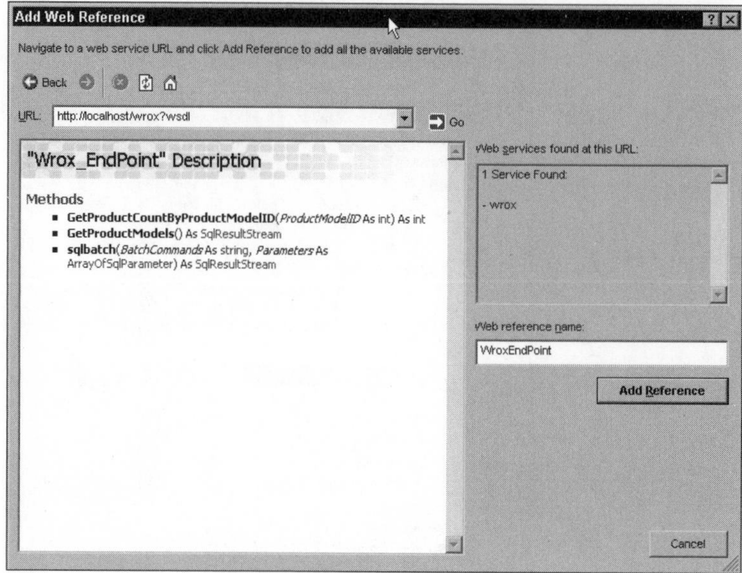

Figure 18-5

In the URL box, type **http://localhost/wrox?wsdl** and click the Go button. The URL needs to be manually typed in because the Web Service has not been set up to be published via any discovery methods such as UDDI. Also, look at the end of the URL. Unlike typical Web Services that are already aware of their interface, the WSDL for endpoints must be specified so that it can describe the endpoint interface to the client. In this example, the Default WSDL is used, which returns a full version of the WSDL file. You'll learn more about this later in the chapter.

The big thing to point out on the Add Web Reference dialog is the three methods listed. When the endpoint was created, two Web Methods were specified, so why are there three listed? If you remember when the endpoint was created, one of the arguments specified was `BATCHES = ENABLED`. By including this argument and setting it to `ENABLED`, SQL Server automatically adds a third method called `sqlbatch`. This method allows ad-hoc SQL queries to be sent to this endpoint for execution.

For the Web Reference Name, type **WroxEndPoint** and then click the Add Reference button. This adds the Web Service reference to the Visual Studio project as shown in Figure 18-6.

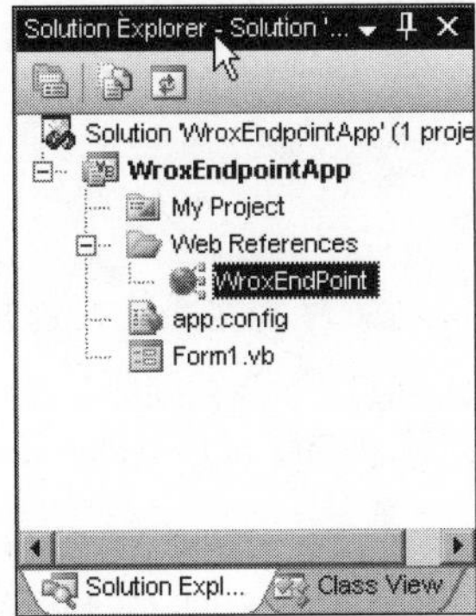

Figure 18-6

Now that the endpoint has been consumed by the application, all the exposed WebMethods are available. It will be beneficial to look at one more thing before beginning to write code.

In the Solution Explorer, click the Show All Files button — the second button from the left. This displays all the files in the solution, including all the files associated with the new Web Service you just added. There should be a plus (+) next to the WroxEndPoint Web Service. Click the plus to expand group, and you should see the wrox.wsdl file associated with this endpoint, as shown in Figure 18-7.

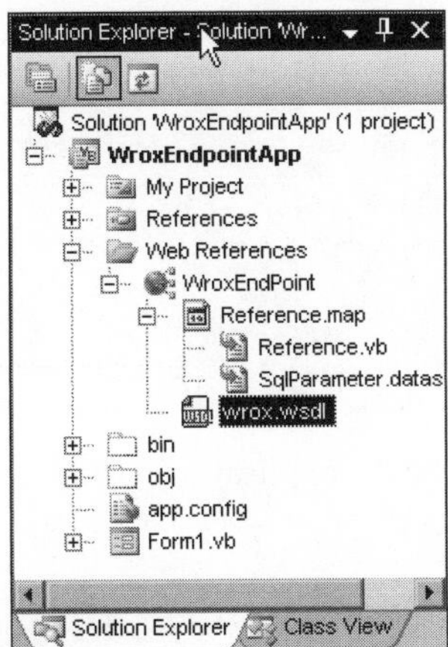

Figure 18-7

The next step is to design the form and add some code to it. The project was created with a default Form1 and that is what is used for these examples. Double-click Form1 to open it in Design Mode.

Once the form is open, place a button, two list boxes, and two text boxes on the form. Set the `Name` properties of the list boxes `lstProductModels` and `lstProducts`, and then set the `Name` properties of the text boxes `txtProductCount` and `txtProductNumber`. As a matter of UI, set the `Text` property of the button to `GetProducts`.

Next, right-click the form and select View Code from the context menu. Add the following three highlighted lines of code to the form:

```
Imports System.Data
Public Class Form1
Dim ws As New WroxEndPoint.Wrox_EndPoint
Dim ds As Dataset
```

The second highlighted line of code declares a new instance of the WroxEndPoint Web Service, which is used throughout the application. Also, a dataset is declared to which all data returned by the Web Service are sent.

Go back to Design View of the form and double-click the button to view the code behind the button. Add the following code to the button:

```
ws.Credentials = System.Net.CredentialCache.DefaultCredentials

Try

  Dim oa As Object

  oa = ws.GetProductModels

  If oa(0).ToString = "System.Data.DataSet" Then
    ds = DirectCast(oa(0), DataSet)

    Me.lstProducts.DataSource = ds.Tables(0)
    Me.lstProducts.DisplayMember = "Name"
    Me.lstProducts.ValueMember = "ProductModelID"

  End If

Catch ex As Exception
  MessageBox.Show(ex.Message.ToString)
End Try
```

Run the project by pressing F5. When the application has compiled and the form comes up, click the GetProducts button. Figure 18-8 shows the results as returned by the GetProductModels Web Method.

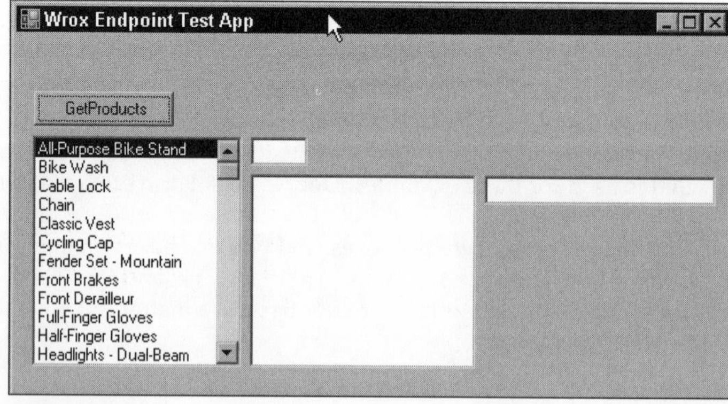

Figure 18-8

Clicking the Product Model list box does nothing right now but it will shortly.

The first line of code behind the button gets the system credentials for the current context in which the application is running. Typically, this is the username, password, and domain of the user running the application. Those are then passed to the Web Service reference and set using the `Credentials` property of the earlier declared Web Service:

```
ws.Credentials = System.Net.CredentialCache.DefaultCredentials
```

The next two lines of code call the GetProductModels Web Method on the endpoint and return the data:

```
Dim oa As Object

oa = ws.GetProductModels
```

In this example, an object array is declared and the results of the Web Service call are returned as a SQL dataset into the object array:

```
If oa(0).ToString = "System.Data.DataSet" Then
  ds = DirectCast(oa(0), DataSet)
```

By returning the results this way, the items in the object array can be examined. Here, the first item in the array is examined to see if it contains a dataset. If it does, the object has no idea what it is, so it needs to be converted to a dataset. Once that is done, the next few lines of code set the appropriate properties on the list box so the items in the result set can be displayed in the list box:

```
Me.lstProducts.DataSource = ds.Tables(0)
Me.lstProducts.DisplayMember = "Name"
Me.lstProducts.ValueMember = "ProductModelID"
```

It is time to add code to the click event of the Product Model list box. Close the form, stopping the application, and open the form in Design View. Double-click the `lstProductModels` list box and add the following code:

```
ws.Credentials = System.Net.CredentialCache.DefaultCredentials

Try

  Dim id As Integer = CInt(Me.lstProductModels.SelectedValue)

  Me.txtProductCount.Text = ws.GetProductCountByProductModelID(id).Value.ToString()

Catch ex As Exception
  MessageBox.Show(ex.Message.ToString)
End Try
```

Run the application again and click the GetProducts button. Select a product model from the list box by clicking its name. The Product Count text box should then display the count of associated products related to the selected product model as illustrated in Figure 18-9.

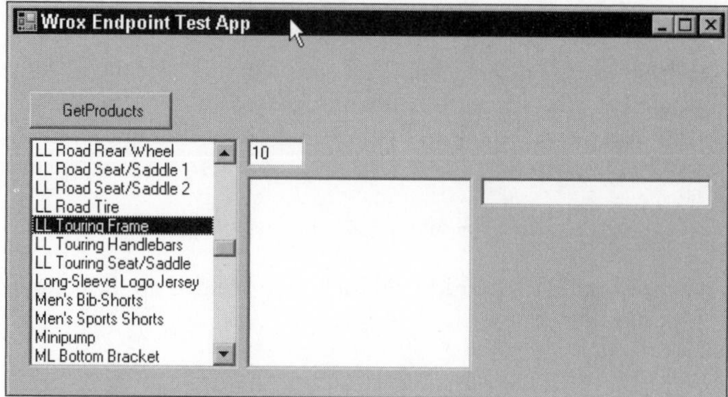

Figure 18-9

Looking at the code behind the list box shows the same `Credentials` statement, which is always needed when you execute a Web Method:

```
ws.Credentials = System.Net.CredentialCache.DefaultCredentials
```

Realistically, this same line of code could have been put in the `Form_Load` event so that it would only be run once.

The next two lines of code get the ProductModelID from the list box for the associated product model selected, and then pass that value to the GetProductCountByProductModelID Web Method:

```
Dim id As Integer = CInt(Me.lstProductModels.SelectedValue)

Me.txtProductCount.Text = ws.GetProductCountByProductModelID(id).Value.ToString()
```

That Web Method, if you remember, is a UDF that takes that ID value and queries the ProductionProduct table for all products that contain the passed-in ProductModelID. In this example, the function returned a count of 10.

Not good enough, you say? Okay, time to beef it up a bit. Open a query window and create the following stored procedure:

```
Use AdventureWorks
GO
CREATE PROCEDURE GetProductsByProductModelID
@ProductModelID int
AS
 SELECT ProductID, Name
 FROM Production.Product
 WHERE ProductModelID = @ProductModelID
 ORDER BY Name
GO
```

This stored procedure takes the same ProductModelID and query as the associated ProductID and Name. It also needs to be added to the endpoint, so in the same query window, execute the following SQL to add it to the endpoint:

```
Use AdventureWorks
GO
ALTER ENDPOINT Wrox_EndPoint
FOR SOAP
(
  ADD WEBMETHOD 'GetProductsByProductModelID'
 (
         NAME='AdventureWorks.dbo.GetProductsByProductModelID',
         SCHEMA = STANDARD
 )
)
```

In your Visual Studio project, right-click the WroxEndPoint Web Service and select Update Web Reference from the menu. This refreshes the Web Service reference in your project.

Next, add the following code (shown with the gray background) behind the ProductModel list box:

```
ws.Credentials = System.Net.CredentialCache.DefaultCredentials

Try

  Dim id As Integer = CInt(Me.lstProducts.SelectedValue)

  Me.txtProductCount.Text = ws.GetProductCountByProductModelID(id).Value.ToString()

  Dim oa As Object

  oa = ws.GetProductsByProductModelID

  If oa(0).ToString = "System.Data.DataSet" Then
    ds = DirectCast(oa(0), DataSet)

    Me.lstProducts.DataSource = ds.Tables(0)
    Me.lstProducts.DisplayMember = "Name"
    Me.lstProducts.ValueMember = "ProductModelID"

  End If

Catch ex As Exception
  MessageBox.Show(ex.Message.ToString)
End Try
```

This code should look very similar to the code that is behind the button. The only difference is that a different Web Method is being called, but the results are being returned the same way.

Now when you run the application and you click on an item in the list box, the associated ProductModelID is sent to the GetProductsByProductModelID WebMethod, returning the results and populating the lstProducts list box, as shown in Figure 18-10.

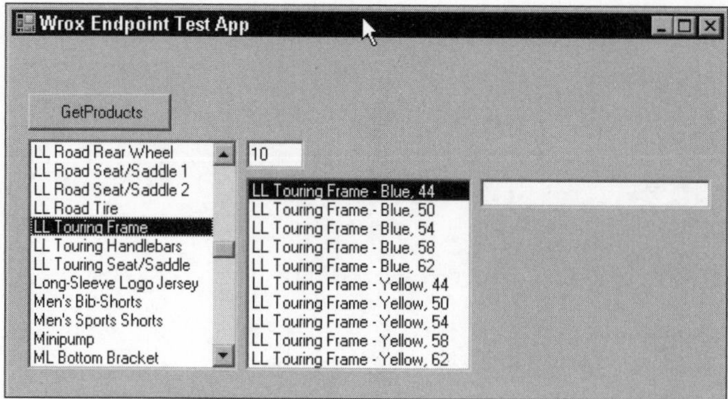

Figure 18-10

Still not good enough, you say? One more modification, then. In a query window, execute the following SQL Statement:

```
Use AdventureWorks
GO
CREATE FUNCTION ProductInfoByProductID
     ( @ProductID int )
RETURNS nvarchar(25)
AS
Begin
RETURN (
        SELECT ProductNumber
        FROM Production.Product
        WHERE ProductID = @ProductID
       )
End
```

This UDF is similar to the first UDF created near the beginning of the chapter, except that it returns a string instead of an integer.

Add the Web Method to the endpoint by running the following SQL:

```
Use AdventureWorks
GO
ALTER ENDPOINT Wrox_EndPoint
FOR SOAP
(
  ADD WEBMETHOD 'GetProductInfoByProductID'
 (
         NAME='AdventureWorks.dbo.ProductInfoByProductID',
         SCHEMA = STANDARD
 )
)
```

In your Visual Studio project, right-click the WroxEndPoint Web Service and select Update Web Reference from the menu. This refreshes the Web Service reference in your project.

If the application is still running, stop the application and double-click the lstProducts list box to view the code. Add the following code to the list box:

```
ws.Credentials = System.Net.CredentialCache.DefaultCredentials

Try

  Dim id As Integer = CInt(Me.lstProducts.SelectedValue)

  Me.txtProductNumber.Text = ws.GetProductInfoByProductID(id).Value.ToString()

Catch ex As Exception
  MessageBox.Show(ex.Message.ToString)
End Try
```

Run the application and select a product model. When the Product list box is populated, the associated ProductNumber is displayed in the ProductNumber text box as shown in Figure 18-11.

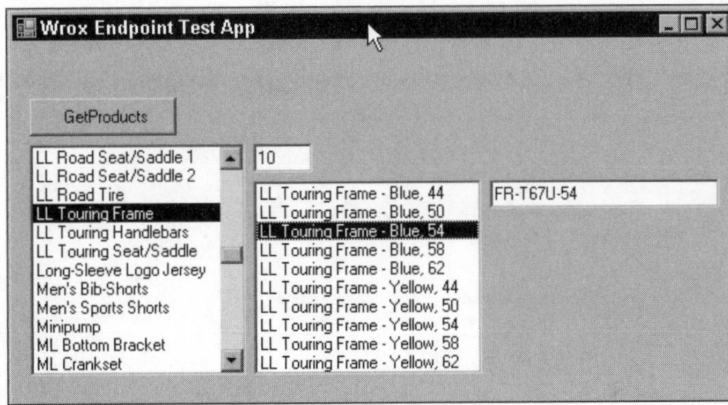

Figure 18-11

The code behind the Product list box is similar to the code behind the Product Model list box, which calls the GetProductInfoByProductID Web Method.

Comparing WSDL

At the beginning of the chapter, an endpoint was consumed using the default WSDL file. Figures 18-6 and 18-7 showed the result of specifying the default WSDL file when consuming a Web Service. The results are a bit different when specifying the Simple WSDL file. For example, create an endpoint using the following SQL:

```
CREATE ENDPOINT Test_EndPoint
STATE = STARTED
AS HTTP
(
 SITE = 'localhost',
 PATH = '/Test',
 AUTHENTICATION = (INTEGRATED),
 PORTS = ( CLEAR )
)
FOR SOAPz
```

```
(
 WebMethod 'GetProductCountByProductModelID'
 (
         NAME = 'adventureworks.dbo.ProductByProductModelID',
         SCHEMA = STANDARD
 ),
 WebMethod 'GetProductModels'
 (
         NAME = 'adventureworks.dbo.GetProductModels',
         SCHEMA = STANDARD
 ),
 WSDL = DEFAULT,
 BATCHES = ENABLED,
 DATABASE = 'AdventureWorks'
)
```

Add a reference to the Web Service to your Visual Studio application, but for this example, specify a Simple WSDL by specifying `http://localhost/Test?wsdlsimple` on the end of the URL as shown in Figure 18-12.

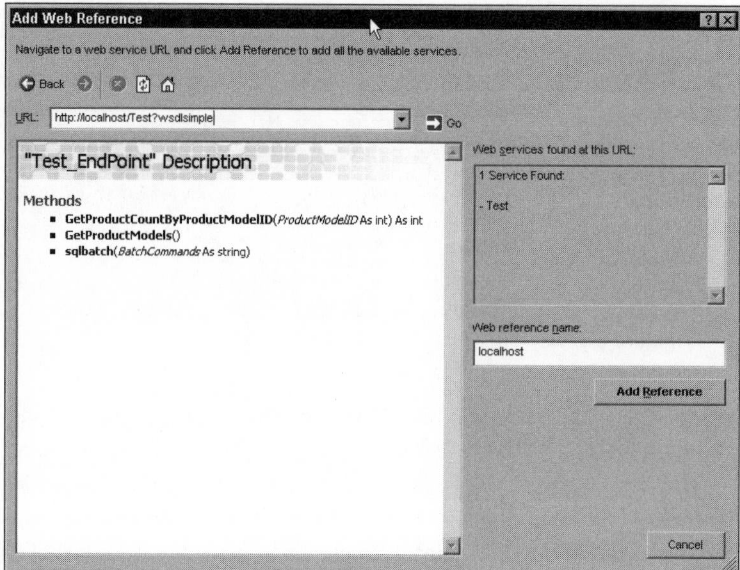

Figure 18-12

Now flip back a few pages to Figure 18-5 and look at the differences between the methods. The two that stand out are the GetProducts and sqlbatch Web Methods. The Default WSDL sets a response type to `SqlResultStream`, as shown in Figure 18-5, while a Simple WSDL does not, as shown in Figure 18-12.

This also applies to the sqlbatch WebMethod, but notice that the `Parameters As ArrayOfSqlParameter` that exists in Figure 18-5 no longer exists in the Simple WSDL in Figure 18-12.

Figure 18-13 shows the differences when viewed in Visual Studio. Notice that the Test reference localhost Web Service reference includes an extra reference map. The Reference.map and associated files map the endpoint URLs and contain the contract and binding information for the endpoint.

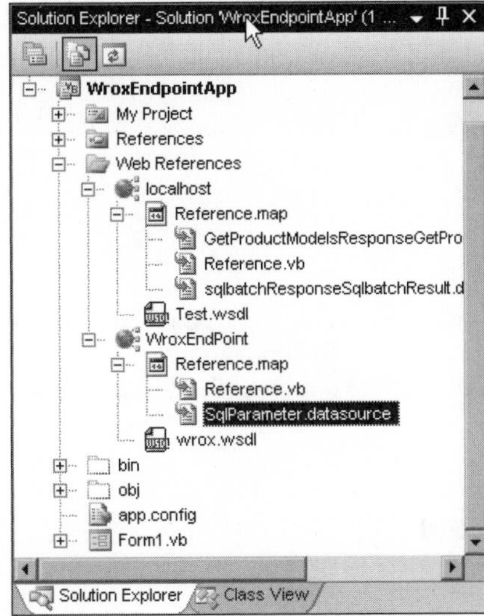

Figure 18-13

There is much more to discuss regarding WSDL files, but that is saved for the next chapter. For now, you should have a good, albeit brief, introduction to WSDL files and what they do. Also, you should have a good grasp of consuming and using endpoints. The next topic discusses securing your endpoints.

Securing an Endpoint

In SQL Server 2005, anonymous access is not allowed. Due to this amount of security, all connections are authenticated at the HTTP transport level. However, one of the supported authentication methods is BASIC authentication, which allows for the passing of clear text for credentials over the wire. Thus, when you create an endpoint using BASIC authentication, SSL is required.

For example, the following creates a valid endpoint:

```
CREATE ENDPOINT Wrox_EndPoint2
STATE = STARTED
AS HTTP
(
 SITE = 'localhost',
 PATH = '/Wrox',
 AUTHENTICATION = (BASIC),
 PORTS = ( SSL )
)
FOR SOAP
(
 WebMethod 'GetProductCountByProductModelID'
```

```
    (
            NAME = 'adventureworks.dbo.ProductByProductModelID',
            SCHEMA = STANDARD
    ),
    WebMethod 'GetProductModels'
    (
            NAME = 'adventureworks.dbo.GetProductModels',
            SCHEMA = STANDARD
    ),
    WSDL = DEFAULT,
    BATCHES = ENABLED,
    DATABASE = 'AdventureWorks'
)
```

However, this alone is not enough to secure the endpoint. SSL must be configured on the endpoint. This is accomplished using the `httpcfg` tool. This tool allows you to configure the HTTP API by wrapping the HTTP config APIs for SSL certificates (among other things). The `httpcfg` tool ships with Windows Server 2003.

The syntax for the `httpcfg` tool is as follows:

```
Httpcfg set ssl /I IP:Port /h Hash /g Guid
```

You can find the `hash` value by looking at the `Thumbprint` value of other SSL certificates used in your environment.

For the GUID, there are a number of tools that generate GUIDs. It is best that you use a single GUID for each instance of SQL Server.

For example, to enable SSL on an endpoint, you could execute the following command in a command window:

```
Httpcfg set sll /I 192.168.100.102:443 /h 2948458a2958767f810990 /g "{3cc61e0d-
8g7b-5e7g-984e-6bff8gc98701}"
```

What this does is point your endpoint to an existing SSL certificate within your organization that the endpoint can utilize for encryption.

There are a number of places to get certificates, including Microsoft Certificate Services, an installation option of Windows 2003, which installs a certificate authority (CA) to allow you to issue certificates for use with any number of public key security programs.

Summary

For any of you who have done any sort of Web Service development in Visual Studio, the technology in this chapter should be exciting. This chapter, as well as Chapter 17, was very fun to write because the technology is so interesting to explore.

Chapter 17 gave you the foundation for building and managing endpoints. The purpose of this chapter was to build on that foundation and show you how to use those endpoints, as well as how to secure endpoints should the need and requirements call for it. This chapter focused on two major topics:

- Consuming and using a Native SQL Server 2005 Web Service and associated Web Methods. Using Visual Studio 2005, you were able to consume a Web Service and use that Web Service to build an application that queries and returns data via a Web Method and populate a form. This functionality will provide a great benefit to non-Windows environments. Native XML Web Services also lends itself to better usability when working with the wide range of development environments and toolsets.
- Securing your Web Service. This chapter mentioned several key pieces of information that focused on securing your endpoints, including using SSL to exchange data, disabling the Guest account, and limiting access to endpoints to specific users and groups. These and the other security tools mentioned will help ensure a secure Web Service environment.

A few pages touched briefly on WSDL files and why they are used. If you don't understand them or still have questions about them, don't fret. The next chapter is dedicated completely to the topic of WSDL.

19

Web Service Description Language (WSDL)

Chapter 18 briefly discussed Web Service Description Language (WSDL) files as part of the SOAP topic. *WSDL files* are dynamically generated XML documents whose sole purpose is to define and describe the interface for RPC (Remote Procedure Call) method's SQL batch functionality exposed by HTTP endpoints. WSDL files are not handed out by default; the client must request them from the SQL Server. They are then used to generate RPC and SQL batch requests against SQL Server endpoints.

At the time of this writing, the W3C had just released the first complete draft of the *WSDL Primer for WSDL version 2.0* and the *First Public Working Draft of the SOAP 1.1 Binding*. Although SQL Server 2005 uses the WSDL 1.1 specification, it would be worthwhile reading up on the 2.0 specification.

This chapter takes a deeper look at WSDL support in SQL Server 2005, starting with the contents of a WSDL file and moving on to the different types of WSDL files, including creating your own custom WSDL file.

The following topics are covered in this chapter:

- An overview of a WSDL file
- The contents of a WSDL file
- Default WSDL file
- Simple WSDL file
- How to create custom WSDL files

WSDL File Overview

When you configure endpoints to support WSDL files, you can specify one of two configurations. If you remember back to Chapter 17's discussion of endpoints, one of the arguments that you can use is the `WSDL` argument, which specifies whether WSDL document generation is supported by the endpoint, as well as the two types that are supported (default and customized).

Both of those types are discussed in further detail later in this chapter, but this section discusses how they are supported by SQL Server 2005.

When you create and define an endpoint, the `WSDL` argument tells the server if a WSDL file needs to be generated and returned to the client so that the endpoint can describe its features. The WSDL files are generated and returned to the client when the connection is first made to an HTTP endpoint. Three values can be specified for this argument: `NONE`, `DEFAULT`, and a stored procedure. If you specify a value of `NONE`, the endpoint does not return a WSDL file.

If you specify a value of `DEFAULT`, the type of WSDL file returned depends on the URL string used to connect to the endpoint. The client application can request the WSDL file using one of two URL formats specified by the URL string: Default and Simple. Both of these are discussed in more detail later in the chapter.

WSDL File Contents

A WSDL file is simply an XML document that contains a root element that specifies the WSDL namespace and a set of defined Web Services within a collection of endpoints. The root element, `<definitions>`, defines the WSDL namespace as `http://schemas.xmlsoap.org/wsdl`.

A simple and typical WSDL file looks like the following:

```
<definitions>
  <types>
    ...
  </types>
  <message>
    ...
  </message>
  <portType>
    ...
  </PortType>
  <binding>
    ...
  </binding>
  <service>
    ...
  </service>
</definitions>
```

The elements within a WSDL file are summarized as follows:

- <types>: Contains data type definitions for exchanged messages.
- <message>: Defines the message data being sent.
- <portType>: A set of operations supported by the endpoint.
- <binding>: The protocol and data format for a defined port type.
- <service>: A collection of related endpoints.

The WSDL Namespace

The namespace of a WSDL file is very similar to a schema namespace in that it associates any names in the WSDL document to the target namespace. The ability to specify a namespace is critical for WSDL 2.0 because of the capability to import or inherit interfaces.

At the root of a WSDL file is the <definitions> element followed by a set of definitions inside. The definitions element contains a namespace, which, like a schema, is used to dictate the namespace of the elements being defined. A WSDL file with a specified namespace might look like the following:

```
<definitions name="Motocross"
  targetNamespace="http://dirtbikes.com/motocross.wsdl"
  xmlns:soap="http://schemas.xmlsoap.org/wsdl/soap"
  xmlns = "http://schemas.xmlsoap.org/wsdl">
</definitions>
```

The <types> Element

The <types> element contains the data type definitions that pertain to the messages exchanged between the client and the endpoint. For best results, it is recommended that you use XSD within the WSDL, as follows:

```
<definitions>
  <types>
    <xsd:schema>
  </types>
</definitions>
```

Using XSD ensures that any types defined in the message can be used even if the ending format is not XML. The following code fragment illustrates what a <types> element instruction would look like when requesting a WSDL file from the wrox_endpoint created in Chapter 17. This example has been simplified a bit for better readability, but it should illustrate how the element is used:

```
<types>
<xmlns:schema elementFormDefault="qualified"
  targetNamespace="http://">
  <xmlns:element name="GetProductInfo">
    <xmlns:complexType>
      <xmlns:sequence>
        <xmlns:element minOccurs="1" maxOccurs="1" name="ProductID"
```

```
            type="xmlns:int" />
        </xmlns:sequence>
      </xmlns:complexType>
    </xmlns:element>
    <xmlns:element name="GetProductInfoResponse">
      <xmlns:complexType>
        <xmlns:sequence>
          <xmlns:element minOccurs="1" maxOccurs="1" name="GetProductInfoResult"
  type="xmlns:int" />
        </xmlns:sequence>
      </xmlns:complexType>
    </xmlns:element>
  </xmlns:schema>
  </types>
```

The <message> Element

A message is a definition of the data being sent between two points, and is defined by the `<message>` element. A message can contain one or more parts, each part being associated to a type using a `message-typing` attribute. The `message-typing` attributes defined in WSDL are used in conjunction with XSD and are defined as the `element` and `type` attributes.

The general syntax for the `<message>` element is as follows:

```
<message name="messagename">
  <part name="partname" element="qname" type="qname" />
</message>
```

The `messagename` attribute provides a unique name between all the messages defined and enclosed in the WSDL document, while the `partname` attribute provides a unique name between all of the parts within the message. For example, the following code fragment shows the format of a WSDL message:

```
<message name="GetProductInfoSoapIn">
  <part name="parameters" element="xmlns0:GetProductInfo" />
</message>
<message name="GetProductInfoSoapOut">
  <part name="parameters" element="xmlns0:GetProductInfoResult" />
</message>
```

The `element` attribute refers to an XSD element using a qualified name, or QName. The `type` element refers to an XSD schema type, whether simple or complex, also using a QName. In the example code, the `element` attribute for the `SoapIn` message is referring to the XSD element name `GetProductInfo`, taken from the XSD schema shown in the previous section:

```
<xmlns:element name="GetProductInfo">
```

It is normal to allow and define other `message-typing` attributes as long as a different namespace is used from the original WSDL.

In the code examples, the `<message>` element includes the `<part>` element, which provides a way of describing the detail of a message. Each message has the capability to contain one or more `<part>` subelements if the message has more than one logical component. For example, the following contains a `GetProductInfo` part and a `GetCustomerInfo` part:

```
<types>
  <xmlns:schema elementFormDefault="qualified"
    targetNamespace="http://">
      <xmlns:element name="GetProductInfo">
        <xmlns:complexType>
          <xmlns:sequence>
            <xmlns:element minOccurs="1" maxOccurs="1" name="ProductID"
             type="xmlns:int" />
          </xmlns:sequence>
        </xmlns:complexType>
      </xmlns:element>
  <xmlns:element name="GetProductInfoResponse">
    <xmlns:complexType>
      <xmlns:sequence>
        <xmlns:element minOccurs="1" maxOccurs="1" name="GetProductInfoResult"
type="xmlns:int" />
      </xmlns:sequence>
    </xmlns:complexType>
  </xmlns:element>
</xmlns:schema>
  <xmlns:schema elementFormDefault="qualified"
    targetNamespace="http://">
      <xmlns:element name="GetCustomerInfo">
        <xmlns:complexType>
          <xmlns:sequence>
            <xmlns:element minOccurs="1" maxOccurs="1" name="CustomerID"
             type="xmlns:int" />
          </xmlns:sequence>
        </xmlns:complexType>
      </xmlns:element>
  <xmlns:element name="GetCustomerInfoResponse">
    <xmlns:complexType>
      <xmlns:sequence>
        <xmlns:element minOccurs="1" maxOccurs="1" name="GetCustomerInfoResult"
type="xmlns:int" />
      </xmlns:sequence>
    </xmlns:complexType>
  </xmlns:element>
</xmlns:schema>
</types>
```

```
<message name="customer">
  <part name="GetProductInfo" element="xmlns:GetProductInfo" />
  <part name="GetCustomerInfo" element=" xmlns:GetCustomerInfo" />
</message>
```

Alternatively, you can specify the parts like this:

```
<message name="product">
  <part name="GetProductInfo" element="xmlns:GetProductInfo" />
</message>
<message name="customer">
  <part name="GetCustomerInfo" element=" xmlns:GetCustomerInfo" />
</message>
```

Additionally, an input/output message can be created using the same logic, as follows:

```
<message name="productInput">
  <part name="GetProductInfo" element="xmlns:GetProductInfo" />
</message>
<message name="ProductOutput">
  <part name="GetCustomerInfo" element=" xmlns:GetCustomerInfo" />
</message>
```

portType

PortTypes are a named set of operations, or interfaces, and the messages involved for a given operation. The general syntax for the `<portType>` is as follows:

```
<definitions>
  <portType name="porttypename">
    <operation name="operationname"/>
  </portType>
</definitions>
```

For example, the following defines a `<portType>` named DataInterface that contains two operations, `Read` and `Write`:

```
<definitions>
  <portType name="DataInterface">
    <operation name="Read"/>
    <operation name="Write"/>
  </portType>
</definitions>
```

The `portType` name provides a unique name against all the other `portTypes` defined in the WSDL document. Equally, the `operation` name is supplied via the `name` attribute. These operations in WSDL refer to the four transmission operations that an endpoint can support. They are as follows:

- **One-way:** In a one-way operation, the endpoint receives the message. The syntax for a one-way operation is as follows:

```
<definitions>
  <portType name="porttypename">
    <operation name="operationname">
      <input name="inputname" message="messagename" />
    </operation>
  </portType>
</definitions>
```

In the following example, the `DataInterface` operation is used to define a one-way operation:

```
<definitions>
  <portType name="DataInterface">
    <operation name="Read">
      <input name="adm:GetData" />
    </operation>
  </portType>
</definitions>
```

In the one-way operation, the <input> element specifies the message format for this type of operation. The operationname value must be a qualified name.

- **Request-response:** In a Request-response operation, the endpoint receives a message, and then sends a corresponding message. The syntax for a Request-response operation is as follows:

```
<definitions>
  <portType name="porttypename">
    <operation name="operationname" parameterOrder="">
      <input name="inputname" message="messagename" />
      <Output name="outputname" message="messagename" />
      <fault name="faultname" message="messagename" />
    </operation>
  </portType>
</definitions>
```

In a Request-response operation, the <input> and <output> elements are required, but the <fault> element is not. In this operation, the <fault> element specifies the format for error messages returned as the result of the operation. The <input> and <output> elements specify the message format for the request and response. The messagename value must be a qualified name. The following example illustrates a Response-request operation using the GetProductInfo stored procedure:

```
<portType name="ProductInfoPortType">
  <operation name="GetProductInfo">
    <input message="adm:productInput"/>
    <output message="adm:ProductOutput"/>
  </operation>
</portType>
```

- **Solicit-response:** For the Solicit-response operation, the endpoint sends a message, and then receives a corresponding message. The syntax for a Solicit-response operation is as follows:

```
<definitions>
  <portType name="porttypename">
    <operation name="operationname" parameterOrder="">
      <Output name="outputname" message="messagename" />
      <Input name="inputname" message="messagename" />
      <fault name="faultname" message="messagename" />
    </operation>
  </portType>
</definitions>
```

In the following example, the endpoint sends a ProductOutput message and then receives a ProductInput message in response:

```
<portType name="ProductInfoPortType">
  <operation name="GetProductInfo">
    <output message="adm:ProductOutput"/>
    <input message="adm:productInput"/>
  </operation>
</portType>
```

Similar to the Request-response operation, the <input> and <output> elements for the Solicit-response operation are required, but the <fault> element is not. In this operation, the <fault> element specifies the format for error messages returned as the result of the operation. The <input> and <output> elements specify the message format for the request and response. The messagename value must be a qualified name.

- **Notification:** In a Notification operation, the endpoint sends a message. No message is received in response. The syntax for a Notification operation is as follows:

```
<definitions>
  <portType name="porttypename">
    <operation name="operationname">
      <Output name="outputname" message="messagename" />
    </operation>
  </portType>
</definitions>
```

In the following example, an Output message is sent from the endpoint via the SaveData message.

```
<definitions>
  <portType name="DataInterface">
    <operation name="Read">
      <Output name="adm:SaveData" />
    </operation>
  </portType>
</definitions>
```

While a Notification operation could be considered one-way since there is no response to the Output, this operation is considered a Notification operation because the endpoint is initiating the communication but not expecting a response.

Binding

Binding specifies the message format and protocol for the operations and messages for a specific portType. Each portType may have more than one binding element; thus the binding element is defined as follows:

```
<definitions>
    <binding name="uniquename" type="QName">
        <operation name="uniquename">
            <input name="uniquename" >
            </input>
            <output name="uniquename" >
            </output>
            <fault name="uniquename">
            </fault>
        </operation>
    </binding>
</definitions>
```

The name attribute on the binding element specifies a unique binding name against all other binding elementss in the WSDL document. The type attribute references the portType to which it is bound. QName refers to an XML qualified name.

Binding provides the ability to apply specific information regarding the method of transport (such as HTTP) and the type of protocol (such as SOAP) for the Web Service. A Web Service can support multiple transport methods and protocol types, and in cases such as these, you must provide a binding for each protocol type/transport method combination.

In the following code sample, HTTP is specified as the transport method and SOAP is specified as the protocol. The transport is specified by the value of the `transport` attribute, in this case `"http://schemas/xmlsoap.org/soap/http"`. The SOAP protocol is specified on the `<soap:binding>` element:

```
<binding name="ProductInfoSoap" type="adm:ProductInfoPortType">
  <soap:binding style="document" transport="http://schemas/xmlsoap.org/soap/http"/>
    <operation name="GetProductInfo">
      <input message="productInput ">
        <soap:body parts="body" use="literal"/>
        <soap:header message="" part="subscribeheader" use="literal"/>
      </input>
    </operation>
</binding>
```

Bindings can specify only a single protocol and cannot specify address information.

Services

A *service* is a group of related ports or endpoints. It is defined as follows:

```
<definitions>
  <service name="">
    <port.../>
  </service>
</definitions>
```

A port is what defines each individual endpoint specified by a single binding address. Ports cannot specify more than one address and cannot specify any binding information other than the specific address information. For example, the following defines a port on a single binding address:

```
<definitions>
  <service name="servicename">
    <port name="portname" binding="bindingname">
    </port>
  </service>
</definitions>
```

The `service name` attribute provides a unique service name against all other services defined in the WSDL document. The same goes for the `port name`:

```
<service name="GetProductInfoService">
  <port name="ProductInfoPort" binding="adm:ProductInfoSoap">
    <soap:address location="http://mysite.com/getproducts"/>
  </port>
</service>
```

Default WSDL File

The default WSDL file is returned when you specify the "wsdl" argument at the end of the HTTP argument string to the HTTP SOAP endpoint. Use the endpoint you created in Chapter 17 with the following T-SQL:

```
CREATE ENDPOINT wrox_endpoint
STATE = STARTED
AS HTTP(
   PATH = '/wrox',
   AUTHENTICATION = (DIGEST),
   PORTS = ( CLEAR ),
   SITE = 'vssql2005'
   )
FOR SOAP (
   WEBMETHOD 'GetProducts'
            (name='AdventureWorks.dbo.GetProducts',
             SCHEMA=STANDARD ),
   WSDL = DEFAULT,
   SCHEMA = STANDARD,
   DATABASE = 'AdventureWorks'
   )
GO
```

The URL `http://servername/wrox_endpoint/wrox?wsdl` is needed to access the Default WSDL.

Default WSDL files, which are generated by an endpoint, specify parameter types by either referencing the defined types or by referencing subtypes of the defined types, as discussed in the subsequent sections.

Mapping SQL Server to XSD Types

When Default WSDL files are returned, any parameter elements contain a type mapping, which maps the WSDL `sqltype` to the equivalent SQL Server type. The following table shows the related mappings.

SQL Server Type	XSD Type
BigInt	long
Binary	base64binary
Bit	boolean
Char	string
DateTime	datetime
Decimal	decimal
Float	double
GUID	string
Image	base64Binary
Int	int

SQL Server Type	XSD Type
Money	decimal
NChar	string
NText	string
Numeric	decimal
NVarchar	string
Real	float
SmallInt	short
SmallDateTime	datetime
SmallMoney	decimal
Sql_Variant	anyType
Text	string
TimeStamp	base64Binary
TinyInt	unsignedByte
UDT (CLR)	base64Binary
UDT (SQL)	Original base type
VarBinary	base64Binary
Varchar	string
XML	any
XML typed	any

Mapping SQL Server to CLR Types

The following table lists the WSDL mapping between a SQL type and its equivalent CLR type when a WSDL file is generated.

WSDL Type	CLR Type
sqltypes:char	System.Data.SqlTypes.SqlString
sqltypes:nchar	System.Data.SqlTypes.SqlString
sqltypes:varchar	System.Data.SqlTypes.SqlString
sqltypes:nvarchar	System.Data.SqlTypes.SqlString
sqltypes:text	System.Data.SqlTypes.SqlString
sqltypes:ntext	System.Data.SqlTypes.SqlString

Table continued on following page

WSDL Type	CLR Type
sqltypes:varbinary	System.Data.SqlTypes.SqlBinary
sqltypes:binary	System.Data.SqlTypes.SqlBinary
sqltypes:image	System.Data.SqlTypes.SqlBinary
sqltypes:timestamp	System.Byte
sqltypes:timestampnumeric	System.Int64
sqltypes:decimal	System.Data.SqlTypes.SqlDecimal
sqltypes:numeric	System.Data.SqlTypes.SqlDecimal
sqltypes:bigint	System.Data.SqlTypes.SqlInt64
sqltypes:int	System.Data.SqlTypes.SqlInt32
sqltypes:smallint	System.Data.SqlTypes.SqlInt16
sqltypes:tinyint	System.Data.SqlTypes.SqlByte
sqltypes:bit	System.Data.SqlTypes.SqlBoolean
sqltypes:float	System.Data.SqlTypes.SqlDouble
sqltypes:real	System.Data.SqlTypes.SqlSingle
sqltypes:datetime	System.Data.SqlTypes.SqlDateTime
sqltypes:smalldatetime	System.Data.SqlTypes.SqlDateTime
sqltypes:money	System.Data.SqlTypes.SqlMoney
sqltypes:smallmoney	System.Data.SqlTypes.SqlMoney
sqltypes:uniqueidentifier	System.Data.SqlTypes.SqlQuid
sqltypes:xml	System.Xml.XmlNode
sqltypes:Sql_Variant	System.Object
sqltypes:Udt	System.Xml.XmlElement

xml data type

`xml` data type parameters that are defined in the Default WSDL file are subsequently mapped to the equivalent `sqltypes:xml` WSDL type listed previously. The benefit of this mapping is that all well-formed XML can be specified without any more schema validation, resulting in better performance.

Simple WSDL File

The Simple WSDL file is a scaled-down version of the Default WSDL file. In the Simple WSDL file, all primitive XSD data types are automatically substituted for SQL types that are more richly described in the

Default WSDL file. In doing so, however, some of the flexibility is lost when dealing with SQL data types, yet it makes up this loss in simplicity when it comes to providing WSDL documents to the different types of clients.

The Simple WSDL file provides backward-compatibility for those clients that cannot understand the complexities of the Default WSDL file. An example of this would be those clients that have been built using the SOAP toolkit, which does not provide the capability to process Default WSDL files generated by SQL Server. The reason for this is due to the limitation to understand and interrogate some of the SQL native types.

An example of this can be seen in the following two WSDL files. The first is a Default WSDL file that shows a more complex type:

```
<xsd:simpleType name="money">
              <xsd:restriction base="xsd:decimal">
              <xsd:totalDigits value="19">
              </xsd:totalDigits>
              <xsd:fractionDigits value="4">
              </xsd:fractionDigits>
              <xsd:maxInclusive value="922337203685477.5807">
              </xsd:maxInclusive>
              <xsd:minInclusive value="-922337203685477.5808">
         </xsd:minInclusive>
      </xsd:restriction>
</xsd:simpleType>
```

This example illustrates a Simple WSDL file and a much simpler type:

```
<xsd:simpleType name="int">
    <xsd:restriction base="xsd:int">
    </xsd:restriction>
</xsd:simpleType>
```

Custom WSDL File

Creating a Custom WSDL file requires multiple steps, outlined here. First, you need to create the code for your Custom WSDL file. Next, you have to create and register an assembly containing the Custom WSDL file. Finally, you must create the necessary stored procedures and endpoints. Since you created an endpoint and corresponding stored procedures in Chapter 17, those are used for the examples in this section. For the purposes of this example, however, the T-SQL code drops and re-creates the necessary objects. Follow these steps:

1. Create a directory named Wrox on the root of your C: drive if you have not already done so. Underneath the Wrox directory, create a subdirectory called Chapter19.
2. Open your favorite text editor and type the following code:

```
Imports System
Imports System.Data
Imports System.Data.Sql
Imports System.Data.SqlTypes
Imports System.Data.SqlClient
```

```
Imports Microsoft.SqlServer.Server
Imports Microsoft.SqlServer

Partial Public Class WroxWSDL
    <Microsoft.SqlServer.Server.SqlProcedure()> _
    Public Shared Sub GenerateWSDL(ByVal iEndPointID As SqlInt32, ByVal bIsSSL As
SqlBoolean, ByVal strHost As SqlString, ByVal strQueryString As SqlString)
        Dim spPipe As SqlPipe = SqlContext.Pipe
        Dim strWSDL As String = RetrieveWSDL(iEndPointID, bIsSSL, strHost,
strQueryString, spPipe)
        If Nothing = strWSDL Then
            spPipe.Send("Error retrieving original WSDL.")
            Return
        End If
        strWSDL = UpdateWSDL(strWSDL, strQueryString.Value)
        If Nothing = strWSDL Then
            spPipe.Send("Error customizing WSDL.")
            Return
        End If
        ReturnWSDL(strWSDL, spPipe)
    End Sub

    Private Shared Function RetrieveWSDL(ByVal iEndPointID As SqlInt32, ByVal
bIsSSL As SqlBoolean, ByVal strHost As SqlString, ByVal strQueryString As
SqlString, ByVal spPipe As SqlPipe) As String
        Dim strReturnValue As String = Nothing
        Dim conn As SqlConnection = New SqlConnection("context connection=true")
        Dim myCommand As New SqlCommand("sys.sp_http_generate_wsdl_
defaultsimpleorcomplex", conn)
        If myCommand Is Nothing Then
            spPipe.Send("Error creating SqlCommand object.")
            GoTo ret
        End If
        myCommand.CommandText = "sys.sp_http_generate_wsdl_defaultsimpleorcomplex"
        myCommand.CommandType = CommandType.StoredProcedure
        If Not strQueryString.Value.StartsWith("wsdl", True, System.Globalization
.CultureInfo.InvariantCulture) Then
            spPipe.Send("Error: Not a WSDL request.")
            GoTo ret
        End If
        myCommand.Parameters.Add("@EndpointID", SqlDbType.Int)
        myCommand.Parameters(0).Value = iEndPointID
        myCommand.Parameters.Add("@IsSSL", SqlDbType.Bit)
        myCommand.Parameters(1).Value = bIsSSL
        myCommand.Parameters.Add("@Host", SqlDbType.NVarChar, strHost.Value.Length)
        myCommand.Parameters(2).Value = strHost
        If strQueryString.Value.ToLower(System.Globalization.CultureInfo
.InvariantCulture).IndexOf("extended") > 0 Then
            myCommand.Parameters.Add("@QueryString", SqlDbType.NVarChar, 11)
            myCommand.Parameters(3).Value = "wsdlcomplex"
        Else
            myCommand.Parameters.Add("@QueryString", SqlDbType.NVarChar, 4)
            myCommand.Parameters(3).Value = "wsdl"
        End If
```

```
        Dim oReader As SqlDataReader = myCommand.ExecuteReader
        If oReader Is Nothing Then
            spPipe.Send("Error occurred during execution of SqlCommand.")
            GoTo ret
        End If
        If oReader.HasRows Then
            If oReader.Read Then
                strReturnValue = oReader.GetSqlValue(0).ToString
            End If
        End If
ret:
        Return strReturnValue
    End Function

    Private Shared Function UpdateWSDL(ByVal strWsdlOrg As String, ByVal strQuery
As String) As String
        Dim strLCQuery As String = strQuery.ToLower
        If strLCQuery.IndexOf("wrox") > -1 Then
            Return UpdateWsdlForVS2005(strWsdlOrg)
        End If
        Return strWsdlOrg
    End Function

    Private Shared Sub ReturnWSDL(ByVal strWSDL As String, ByVal spPipe As SqlPipe)
        Dim iMaxLength As Integer = 4000
        Dim oMetaData(1) As SqlMetaData
        oMetaData(0) = New SqlMetaData("XML_F52E2B61-18A1-11d1-B105-00805F49916B",
SqlDbType.NVarChar, iMaxLength, 1033, SqlCompareOptions.None)
        If oMetaData(0) Is Nothing Then
            spPipe.Send("Error creating the required SqlMetaData object for
response.")
            GoTo ret
        End If
        If strWSDL.Length < iMaxLength Then
            iMaxLength = strWSDL.Length
        End If
        Dim aoResponse(1) As Object
        aoResponse(0) = New Object
        If aoResponse(0) Is Nothing Then
            spPipe.Send("Error creating the object to hold the SqlDataRecord
value.")
            GoTo ret
        End If
        aoResponse(0) = strWSDL.Substring(0, iMaxLength)
        Dim oRecord As SqlDataRecord = New SqlDataRecord(oMetaData)

        If oRecord Is Nothing Then
            spPipe.Send("Error creating SqlDataRecord.")
            GoTo ret
        End If
        spPipe.SendResultsStart(oRecord)
        Dim iccLeft As Integer = strWSDL.Length - iMaxLength
        Dim iLength As Integer = strWSDL.Length
        While iccLeft > 0
            If iccLeft > iMaxLength Then
```

```
                oRecord.SetString(0, strWSDL.Substring(iLength - iccLeft,
iMaxLength))
                spPipe.SendResultsRow(oRecord)
                iccLeft = iccLeft - iMaxLength
            Else
                oRecord.SetString(0, strWSDL.Substring(iLength - iccLeft, iccLeft))
                spPipe.SendResultsRow(oRecord)
                iccLeft = 0
            End If
        End While
        spPipe.SendResultsEnd()
ret:
        Return
    End Sub

    Private Shared Function UpdateWsdlForVS2005(ByVal strWsdlOrg As String) As
String
        Const strMaxOccurs As String = "maxOccurs=""unbounded"""
        Dim strReturn As String = strWsdlOrg
        If Nothing = strReturn Then
            GoTo ret
        End If
        Dim strTemp As String = "<xsd:any namespace=""http://www.w3.org/2001/
XMLSchema"" minOccurs=""0"" processContents=""lax"" />"
        Dim iIndex As Integer = strReturn.IndexOf("complexType name=""SqlRowSet""")
        If iIndex <= 0 Then
            strReturn = Nothing
            GoTo ret
        End If
        iIndex = strReturn.IndexOf(strTemp, iIndex)
        If iIndex <= 0 Then
            strReturn = Nothing
            GoTo ret
        End If
        strReturn = strReturn.Remove(iIndex, strTemp.Length)
        strTemp = "namespace=""urn:schemas-microsoft-com:xml-diffgram-v1"""
        iIndex = strReturn.IndexOf(strTemp, iIndex)
        If iIndex <= 0 Then
            strReturn = Nothing
            GoTo ret
        End If
        strReturn = strReturn.Remove(iIndex, strTemp.Length)
        strReturn = strReturn.Insert(iIndex, strMaxOccurs)
ret:
        Return strReturn
    End Function
End Class
```

3. Save this as WroxWSDL.vb in the Chapter19 directory.
4. Open a command prompt and navigate to your `C:\Wrox\Chapter19` directory. At the command prompt, type the following, making sure to replace the xxxxx value in the framework version with the version of the .NET Framework you are currently using, such as v2.0.50215:

```
C:\windows\Microsoft.Net\Framework\v2.0.xxxxx\vbc.exe /t:library /r:sqlaccess.dll
/r:system.dll /r:system.data.dll /r:system.xml.dll wroxwsdl.vb
```

If you receive an error stating that sqlaccess.dll cannot be found, copy the sqlaccess.dll from the SQL Server directory to the Chapter19 directory. The sqlaccess.dll file is located in `\Program Files\Microsoft SQL Server\MSSQL.1\MSSQL\Binn`.

5. Rerun the command at the command prompt. When this finishes executing, you should see wroxwsdl.dll in your Chapter21 directory.

6. Next, open a new query window in SQL Server Management Studio and execute the following T-SQL:

```
USE AdventureWorks
GO

DROP ASSEMBLY WroxCustomWSDL
GO

CREATE ASSEMBLY WroxCustomWSDL FROM 'C:\Wrox\Chapter19\WroxCustomWSDL.dll'
GO
```

This step registers the custom WSDL assembly created in the previous section with SQL Server so that it is aware that it exists and available for use.

7. Open a new query window and execute the following T-SQL to create the necessary stored procedures:

```
USE AdventureWorks
GO

DROP PROCEDURE WroxCustomWSDL
GO

CREATE PROCEDURE WroxCustomWSDL
(
  @endpointID as int,
  @isSSL as bit,
  @host as nvarchar(255),
  @querystring as nvarchar(255)
)
AS EXTERNAL NAME WroxCustomWSDL. WroxWSDL.GenerateWSDL
GO

GRANT EXEC on WroxCustomWSDL to [PUBLIC]
GO

DROP PROCEDURE GetProducts1
GO

CREATE PROCEDURE GetProducts1
  @ProductID int,
  @ProductName nvarchar(25) output
AS
```

```
    SELECT @ProductName = [Name] FROM Production.Product WHERE ProductID = @ProductID

GO

GRANT EXEC ON GetProducts1 TO [public]
GO
```

The first stored procedure maps directly to the CLR method and previously created assembly. Notice that the information for the external name in the procedure `WroxCustomWSDL` maps directly to the class name created first. This is how the mapping is applied.

The second stored procedure is the normal procedure, which queries and returns the product information from the Production.Product table.

8. Create the necessary endpoint by executing the following T-SQL in a query window:

```
DROP ENDPOINT wrox_endpoint2
GO

CREATE ENDPOINT wrox_endpoint2
STATE = STARTED
AS HTTP(
   PATH = '/wrox2',
   AUTHENTICATION = (DIGEST, INTEGRATED),
   PORTS = ( CLEAR ),
   SITE = 'localhost'
   )
FOR SOAP (
   WEBMETHOD 'GetProducts1'
            (name='AdventureWorks.dbo.GetProducts1'),
   WSDL = 'AdventureWorks.dbo.WroxCustomWSDL',
   SCHEMA = STANDARD,
   DATABASE = 'AdventureWorks'
   )
GO

Use Master
GO

GRANT CONNECT ON ENDPOINT::wrox_endpoint2 to [PUBLIC]
```

You have just created your own custom WSDL. Now, based on what you have learned so far, your homework assignment is to return the custom WSDL. How do you do this?

Hint: You don't need Visual Studio, just your Web browser. Plus, you'll need to use the word "wrox" in the URL somewhere (look at the code for the custom WSDL file).

What you should get back, displayed in the browser, is the custom WSDL file.

Summary

The entire purpose of this chapter was to give you a better understanding of WSDL and its inner workings so that you can get a better feel for how they interact with SQL Server endpoints. Granted, WSDL is a very deep and rich topic, and a whole lot more probably could have been covered, but that is not the intent of this chapter. Overall, you should now have some level of understanding of how endpoints utilize WSDL and what you can do with them.

To these ends, this chapter first gave a brief overview of what WSDL is and how it pertains to SQL Server 2005. From there, you learned what exactly is contained in a WSDL file that makes it so useful and robust. Starting with the namespace and moving on to each element that makes up a WSDL file, this section should have given you a better understanding of the makeup of a WSDL file so that if the occasion arises, you can generate your own.

From there, the different types of WSDL files were discussed, as well as the differences between them and why you would want to use one over the other. You learned about the Default and Simple WSDL file types, and if neither of those fit your fancy, you learned how to create your own.

The next chapter moves on to discuss SQLXML Managed Classes.

Part V: SQL Server 2005 and Visual Studio 2005

20

SQL Server 2005 SQLXML Managed Classes

Way back toward the beginning of the book, a number of chapters focused on SQLXML 4.0 that comes with SQL Server 2005 and the new support for the `xml` data type. Those chapters focused strictly on dealing with XML on the client side and using certain technologies to deal with XML data.

Recall from those chapters that SQLXML contains three separate data provider options that allow you to gain access to XML data from SQL Server 2005. The first option, the SQLXMLOEDB provider, lets you gain access to the SQLXML 4.0 functionality via ADO (ActiveX Data Objects). This option is good but it comes with its limitations, such as that it can only provide output via a stream.

The second option, the SQL Native Client, provides access to SQLXML functionality through a new data access technology that combines both the SQLOLEDB and SQLODBC drivers into single API. It provides additional functionality beyond what you would find in MDAC by exposing the new SQL Server 2005 XML features.

The third option is SQLXML Managed Classes, which provide SQLXML 4.0 functionality inside the .NET Framework.

This chapter focuses on the SQLXML 4.0 Managed Classes and the functionality they provide within .NET Framework. The following topics are covered in this chapter:

- ❑ Overview of the SQLXML Managed Classes object model
- ❑ Examples using the SQLXML Managed Classes

SQLXML Managed Classes Object Model

SQLXML Managed Classes are wrappers around the native SQLXML classes, exposing the SQLXML 4.0 functionality inside the .NET Framework. These Managed Classes make it easier for developers to move their current SQLXML native code to .NET.

The SQLXML Managed Classes object model exposes three objects that provide all of the SQLXML functionality needed to gain access to XML data from SQL Server from within your .NET application. The three objects are as follows:

- `SqlXmlCommand`
- `SqlXmlParameter`
- `SqlXmlAdapter`

SqlXmlCommand Object

The `SqlXmlCommand` object is the class that provides the avenue for executing T-SQL commands, stored procedures, and queries to the database via technologies such as XSD schemas and templates, and have the results returned back to the client as XML.

This class also provides the capability to send queries to the database and retrieve the results as a stream or even append the results to an existing stream. This class lets you parameterize queries via the associated `SqlXmlParameter` class by specifying values for each parameter.

The execution of ad hoc queries such as native T-SQL, schemas, and stored procedures is available, as well as Template and XPath queries. No matter the type of query, you have the ability to specify whether you want the results converted to XML either on the client or on the server via a property of this class.

The basic syntax of the `SqlXmlCommand` class is as follows:

```
Imports Microsoft.Data.SqlXml
Dim cmd As SqlXmlCommand = New SqlXmlCommand(ConnectionStrting)
```

The connection string specifies an OLEDB or ADO connection using the SQLOLEDB provider. The data provider should not be included in the provider string. For example, the following connection string connects to the AdventureWorks database on the local server using the SQLOLEDB provider:

```
Provider=SQLOLEDB; Server=(local); database=AdventureWorks; UID=userid;PWD=password
```

Methods and Properties

The `SqlXmlCommand` object contains a number of methods and properties that support the querying and XML formatting of data returned from SQL Server 2005.

Methods

The following sections contain a detailed explanation of the methods supported by the `SqlXmlCommand` class.

ClearParameters()

The `ClearParameters()` method, new to version 2.0 of the .NET Framework, clears any parameters previously created for a given command object. This method allows you to execute multiple queries on the same command object without the hassle of deleting the parameters. The syntax of this method is as follows:

```
cmd.ClearParameters()
```

CreateParameter()

The `CreateParameter()` method is used in conjunction with the `SqlXmlParameter` object. This method allows you to specify and set a Name/Value pair that you want to pass to a command.

The following code snippet illustrates the syntax for using the `CreateParameter()` method:

```
Dim cmd AS SqlXmlCommand = New SqlXmlCommand(ConnectionString)
cmd.CommandText = "SELECT Name FROM Production.Product WHERE ProductID = ?"
Dim Param As SqlXmlParameter
Param = cmd.CreateParameter()
Param.Value = "Scott"
```

A more detailed example is shown later in this chapter.

ExecuteNonQuery()

The `ExecuteNonQuery()` method executes a T-SQL command but does not return any results, such as an `INSERT` or `UPDATE` statement.

The following code snippet illustrates the syntax for using the `ExecuteNonQuery()` method:

```
Dim cmd AS SqlXmlCommand = New SqlXmlCommand(ConnectionString)
cmd.CommandText = "UPDATE Production.Product SET Name = 'Blade' WHERE
ProductID=316"
cmd.ExecuteNonQuery()
```

Since this is the chapter on SQLXML Managed Classes, a better example would be to use this method with an updategram or Diffgram to update data, which is what one of the examples later in the chapter demonstrates.

ExecuteStream()

The `ExecuteStream()` method comes in handy when you want query results returned to you as a stream. Since the `ExecuteStream()` method is part of the SQLXML Managed Classes, this allows you to return results to the client formatted as XML using the `FOR XML` clause.

For example, the following code snippet demonstrates executing a SQL query to a stream:

```
Dim MyStrm as Stream
Dim cmd AS SqlXmlCommand = New SqlXmlCommand(ConnectionString)
cmd.CommandText = "SELECT ProductID, Name FROM Production.Product WHERE ProductID =
1 FOR XML AUTO"
MyStrm = cmd.ExecuteStream()
```

ExecuteToStream()

The ExecuteToStream() method lets you return query results to an existing stream. Unlike the ExecuteStream() method, which returns the query results to a new stream, the ExecuteToStream() method lets you append query results to an existing stream.

The following code fragment returns the results of a query to an existing stream, appending the results:

```
Dim MyStrm as Stream
Dim cmd AS SqlXmlCommand = New SqlXmlCommand(ConnectionString)
cmd.CommandText = "SELECT ProductID, Name FROM Production.Product WHERE ProductID =
1 FOR XML AUTO"
cmd.ExecuteToStream(MyStrm)
```

Other Methods

There are a few other methods, such as GetType() and ToString(). For example, you could output the ToString() method to a message box or the immediate window as follows:

```
MessageBox.Show(cmd.ToString())
```

As a result, the following would be displayed in the message box:

```
"Microsoft.Data.SqlXml.SqlXmlCommand"
```

The GetType() method is useful if you want to look at the SqlXmlCommand system type information. For example, the following returns the SqlXmlCommand type information in a MessageBox:

```
MessageBox.Show(cmd.GetType())
```

A portion of the results are shown here:

```
System.RuntimeType: "Microsoft.Data.SqlXml.SqlXmlCommand"
Assembly: {System.Reflection.Assembly}
AssemblyQualifiedName: "Microsoft.Data.SqlXml.SqlXmlCommand, Microsoft.Data.SqlXml,
Version=9.0.242.0, Culture=neutral, PublicKeyToken=89845dcd8080cc91"
Attributes: 1048577
BaseType: "Microsoft.Data.SqlXml.SqlXmlCommand"
ContainsGenericParameters: False
DeclaringMethod: Exception of type: '{System.InvalidOperationException}' occurred.
DeclaringType: Nothing
DefaultBinder: {System.DefaultBinder}
Delimiter: "."c
```

There are also several properties supported by the SqlXmlCommand object, which are discussed next.

Properties

The SqlXmlCommand object supports the properties detailed in the following sections.

BasePath

The `BasePath` property is a directory path used in resolving the relative path when you specify an XSL file, a schema file, or an XML template. For example, when you specify an XSL file using the `XslPath` property, you can enter the value in one of two ways. The following method uses both the `XslPath` property and the `BasePath` property:

```
cmd.XslPath = "Motocross.xsl"
cmd.BasePath = "c:\temp\"
```

The second method is to specify both the directory and the XSL file in the `XslPath` property, as follows:

```
cmd.XslPath = "c:\temp\Motocross.xsl"
```

If the path specified in the `XslPath` property is relative, then the value specified in the `BasePath` property is used to correct the relative path.

ClientSideXml

The `ClientSideXml` property specifies whether or not the returned results are converted on the client instead of the server. When you set this property to `True`, the conversion happens on the client. If you set it to `False`, the XML formatting happens on the server.

For example, look at the following T-SQL statement:

```
SELECT FirstName, LastName, Title, EmailAddress, Phone
FROM Person.Contact
FOR XML AUTO
```

When you set the `ClientSideXml` property to `True`, the entire T-SQL statement is sent to the server, including the `FOR XML` clause, but the server ignores the `FOR XML` clause and sends the results of the query back as a result set for XML formatting on the client.

When you set the `ClientSideXml` property to `False`, the XML formatting is handled at the server.

The syntax is as follows:

```
cmd.ClientSideXml = True
```

CommandStream

The `CommandStream` property sets the stream for the `Command` object. It allows you to execute a command from an external source such as a file or an XML template.

The syntax for the `CommandStream` property is as follows:

```
cmd.CommandStream = InputStream
```

`InputStream` contains the query information, such as an XML template.

The following example executes a template file query to a CommandStream:

```
Dim MyStrm as MemoryStream = New MemoryStream
Dim cmd AS SqlXmlCommand = New SqlXmlCommand(ConnectionString)
cmd.CommandStream = FileStream("Motocross.xml", FileMode.Open)
cmd.BasePath = "c:\temp\"
```

When you use the CommandStream property, the only appropriate values for the CommandType property are Template, UpdateGram, and Diffgram.

CommandText

The CommandText property specifies the text of the command to be executed. The text of this property is of the CRUD (Create, Read, Update, Delete) type, allowing you to execute T-SQL queries. A simple example is as follows:

```
Dim cmd AS SqlXmlCommand = New SqlXmlCommand(ConnectionString)
cmd.CommandText = "SELECT ProductID, Name FROM Production.Product WHERE ProductID =
1 FOR XML AUTO"
```

CommandType

The CommandType property specifies the type of command to be executed. The available types are used to determine the type of command. They are:

- DiffGram: Specifies that a Diffgram will be executed.
- Sql: Executes a T-SQL command.
- Template: Executes an XML template command.
- TemplateFile: Executes a template file at a specified path.
- UpdateGram: Specifies that an updategram will be executed.
- XPath: Executes an XPath command.

NameSpace

The NameSpace property enables the execution of XPath queries that contain namespaces. In SQLXML 4.0, the wildcard character (*) is not supported, but a namespace prefix is still required in the XPath query. To overcome this issue, the Namespaces property is available to provide namespace binding, as follows:

```
Dim cmd AS SqlXmlCommand = New SqlXmlCommand(ConnectionString)
cmd.Namespaces = "xmlns:x='urn:schema:Products'"
```

OutputEncoding

When the results of a query are being returned to a stream, the OutputEncoding property specifies the encoding for that stream. The default and most common encoding is UTF-8, but ANSI and Unicode are also very common. The OutputEncoding property lets you specify a different encoding.

The syntax for setting this property is as follows:

```
cmd.OutputEncoding = "UTF-8"
```

RootTag

The `RootTag` property lets you specify a root element for any XML generated via the results of a query returning XML. For example, if the query returns an XML fragment, it does not contain a root element, making it an invalid XML document. The `RootTag` property lets you specify the name of the root element to ensure a valid XML document.

The following example uses the `RootTag` property to add a root element to the results of a query:

```
Dim cmd AS SqlXmlCommand = New SqlXmlCommand(ConnectionString)
cmd.CommandText = "SELECT ProductID, Name FROM Production.Product WHERE ProductID =
1 FOR XML AUTO"
cmd.RootTag = "Root"
```

SchemaPath

The `SchemaPath` property provides the name and location of the mapping schema for XPath queries. This path can be absolute or relative (if relative, this property is used in conjunction with the `BasePath` property). For example:

```
Dim cmd AS SqlXmlCommand = New SqlXmlCommand(ConnectionString)
cmd.CommandType = SqlXmlCommandType.XPath
cmd.SchemaPath = "Motocross.xml"
```

XslPath

The `XslPath` property contains name of the XSL file and corresponding directory. It is not necessary to specify a directory for the XSL file, but one can be included. (See the comments on the `BasePath` property for more information on specifying paths for these properties.)

The syntax for using the `XslPath` property is as follows:

```
Dim cmd AS SqlXmlCommand = New SqlXmlCommand(ConnectionString)
cmd.XslPath = "Motocross.Xsl"
```

SqlXmlParameter Object

The `SqlXmlParameter` object allows you to dynamically parameterize your query filter criteria and specify values for the query parameters at run time. You may know that you want to query the Person .Contact table based on specific criteria, but you won't know what those criteria are until run time.

For example, you may want to return the Title, EmailAddress, and Phone fields from the Person.Contact table, but you won't know for which person until run time, when a specific person is selected.

Properties

The following sections outline the properties that are supported by the `SqlXmlParameter` object.

Name

The `Name` property specifies the name of the parameter:

```
Dim cmd AS SqlXmlCommand = New SqlXmlCommand(ConnectionString)
cmd.CommandText = "SELECT Name FROM Production.Product WHERE ProductID = ? FOR XML
AUTO"
Dim Param As SqlXmlParameter
Param = cmd.CreateParameter()
Param.Name = "ProductID"
Param.Value = "320"
```

In most cases this property is not necessary. A few examples in the "Examples" section of this chapter demonstrate how to use this property.

Value

The `Value` property specifies the value of the parameter being passed to the `Command` object, as follows:

```
Dim cmd AS SqlXmlCommand = New SqlXmlCommand(ConnectionString)
cmd.CommandText = "SELECT Name FROM Production.Product WHERE ProductID = ? FOR XML
AUTO"
Dim Param As SqlXmlParameter
Param = cmd.CreateParameter()
Param.Value = "Scott"
```

SQLXMLAdapter Object

The `SqlXmlAdapter` object provides the functionality that allows the dataset object of the .NET Framework to work together with this and the other objects of the SQLXML Managed Classes.

Methods

The following sections explain the methods that are supported by the `SqlXmlAdapter` object.

Fill()

The `Fill()` method fills a .NET Framework dataset with the XML query results returned from SQL Server. The following example queries the Production.Product table for a specific ProductID and fills a dataset using the `Fill()` method:

```
Dim cmd AS SqlXmlCommand = New SqlXmlCommand(ConnectionString)
cmd.CommandText = "SELECT Name FROM Production.Product WHERE ProductID = 1 FOR XML
AUTO"
...
Dim ds As Dataset = New Dataset
Dim Adapt Ad SqlXmlDataAdapter
Adapt = new SqlXmlDataAdapter(cmd)
Adapt.Fill(ds)
```

Update()

The `Update()` method is used to update SQL Server data from data in the existing dataset. For example, the following code queries the Name column from the Production.Product table for a specific ProductID, uses the `Fill()` method to fill a dataset with the results, and then uses the `Update()` method to update the data in the dataset and update the database with the updated value:

```
Dim cmd AS SqlXmlCommand = New SqlXmlCommand(ConnectionString)
cmd.CommandText = "SELECT Name FROM Production.Product WHERE ProductID = 1 FOR XML
AUTO"
...
Dim ds As Dataset = New Dataset
Dim Adapt Ad SqlXmlDataAdapter
Adapt = new SqlXmlDataAdapter(cmd)
Adapt.Fill(ds)
Dim rw As DataRow
rw = ds.Tables(0).Rows(0)
rw("Name") = "Ball Bearing"
Adapt.Update(ds)
```

Examples

Now that you have an understanding of SQLXML Managed Classes and their methods and properties, it's time to build some examples and put this great technology to work. Open Visual Studio 2005 and create a new Visual Basic Windows application project. Name the project ManagedClasses.

Place a `Button` and a `TextBox` on the form. Set the properties of the controls to the following:

Control	Property	Value
`Form`	`Text`	`Managed Classes Example`
	`StartPosition`	`CenterScreen`
	`Size`	448, 288
`Button`	`Text`	`Get Results`
	`Size`	98, 28
	`Location`	12, 39
	`Name`	`"cmdGetResults"`
`TextBox`	`Multiline`	`True`
	`Size`	416, 113
	`Location`	12, 73
	`Name`	`"txtResults"`
	`ScrollBars`	`Vertical`

Now it's time to add code. Double-click the `Button` to display the click event code behind it and add the following code:

```
Dim MyStrm As Stream
Dim ConnectString As String

'Be sure to put in the correct Username and Password in the connect string!
ConnectString = _
"Provider=SQLOLEDB;Server=(local);database=AdventureWorks;UID=?;PWD=?"

Dim cmd As SqlXmlCommand = New SqlXmlCommand(ConnectString)

cmd.CommandText = "SELECT ProductID, Name FROM Production.Product " & _
"WHERE ProductID = 320 For XML Auto"

Try
  MyStrm = cmd.ExecuteStream
  MyStrm.Position = 0

  Dim StrRdr As StreamReader = New StreamReader(MyStrm)

  Me.TextBox1.Text = StrRdr.ReadToEnd()

Catch ex As Exception
  MessageBox.Show(ex.Message.ToString)
End Try
```

The first two lines declare the `Stream` object and set the connection string. The next line creates the `SqlXmlCommand` object, which is then used to set the `CommandText` property, which is the T-SQL statement to be executed. Once that is done, the `Command` is executed with the results returned in a Stream.

Run the project by pressing F5 or by selecting the Start Debugging option from the Debug menu. When the form opens, click the Get Results button to run the code. The results should be returned and displayed in the text box, as shown in Figure 20-1. In this example, the ProductID and Name columns are returned for ProductID 320.

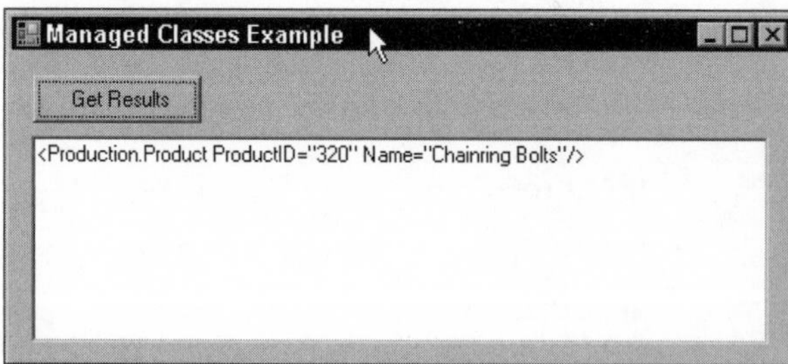

Figure 20-1

The previous example specified the ProductID in the T-SQL statement. The next example modifies the previous example a little bit by specifying the ProductID to query using a parameter and the `SqlXmlParameter` class.

Modify the code behind the button as follows:

```
Dim MyStrm As Stream
Dim ConnectString As String
Dim Param As SqlXmlParameter

'Be sure to put in the correct Username and Password in the connect string!
ConnectString = _
"Provider=SQLOLEDB;Server=(local);database=AdventureWorks;UID=?;PWD=?"

Dim cmd As SqlXmlCommand = New SqlXmlCommand(ConnectString)

cmd.CommandText = "SELECT Name FROM Production.Product " & _
" WHERE ProductID = ? For XML Auto"

Param = cmd.CreateParameter
Param.Value = 320

Try
  MyStrm = cmd.ExecuteStream
  MyStrm.Position = 0

  Dim StrRdr As StreamReader = New StreamReader(MyStrm)

  Me.TextBox1.Text = StrRdr.ReadToEnd()

Catch ex As Exception
  MessageBox.Show(ex.Message.ToString)
End Try
```

In this example, the `SqlXmlParameter` class is created and then used to create a parameter on the `Command` object in which to pass the desired ProductID.

Run the project again and click the Get Results button. The results from this query, specifically the Name column, are returned and displayed in the text box, as shown in Figure 20-2.

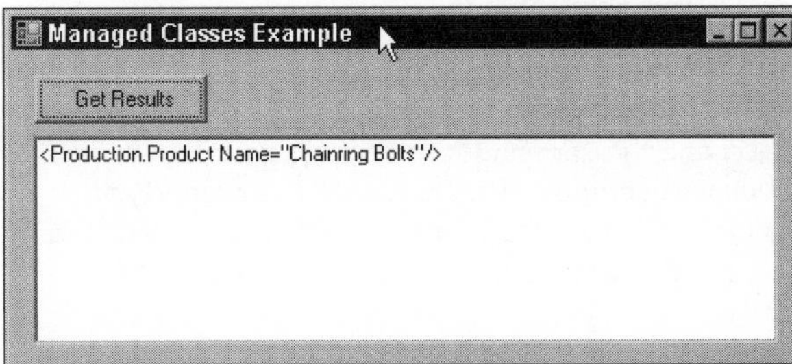

Figure 20-2

Both of the previous examples used inline T-SQL statements to query the data. The next example, however, takes it to the next step and queries the database using a template.

Open Notepad or your favorite text editor and type the following code, saving the file as Products.xml in the `C:\wrox\chapter20` directory:

```
<ROOT xmlns:sql="urn:schemas-microsoft-com:xml-sql">
  <sql:query>
    SELECT ProductID, Name
    FROM   Production.Product
    FOR XML AUTO
  </sql:query>
</ROOT>
```

Next, modify the `click` event code behind the Get Results button as follows:

```
Dim MyStrm As Stream
Dim ConnectString As String
Dim ms As MemoryStream = New MemoryStream
Dim sw As StreamWriter = New StreamWriter(ms)

'Be sure to put in the correct Username and Password in the connect string!
ConnectString = _
"Provider=SQLOLEDB;Server=(local);database=AdventureWorks;UID=?;PWD=?"

Dim cmd As SqlXmlCommand = New SqlXmlCommand(ConnectString)

cmd.CommandStream = New FileStream("c:\wrox\chapter21\Products.xml", FileMode.Open)
cmd.CommandType = SqlXmlCommandType.Template

Try
  MyStrm = cmd.ExecuteStream
  MyStrm.Position = 0

  Dim StrRdr As StreamReader = New StreamReader(MyStrm)

  Me.TextBox1.Text = StrRdr.ReadToEnd()

Catch ex As Exception
  MessageBox.Show(ex.Message.ToString)
End Try
```

In this example, a template (Products.xml) is provided, which contains the T-SQL that will be executed by the `SqlXmlCommand` object and the `CommandStream` property. The file mode is set to `Open`, which tells the operating system to open an existing file. The `CommandType` property is set to `SqlXmlCommandType.Template`, which tells the `Command` that a template is being executed, and then the template is executed with the results being returned to a stream.

Run the project again and click the Get Results button to run the code. Your results should look like Figure 20-3.

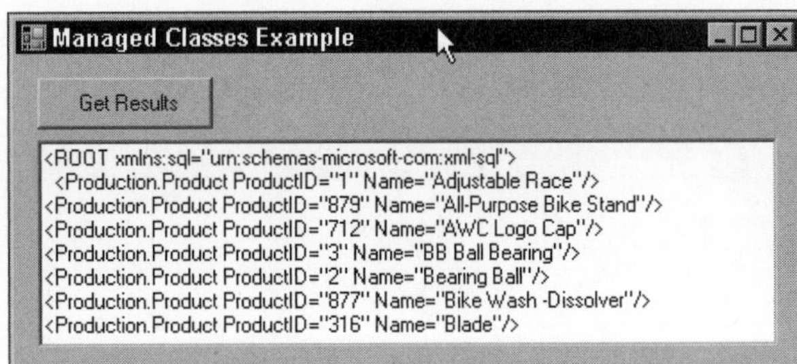

Figure 20-3

Building on the previous examples, this next example uses a parameter as well, but also uses the template technology found in the second example. To do that, modify the Products.xml file and add the following:

```
<ROOT xmlns:sql="urn:schemas-microsoft-com:xml-sql">
  <sql:header>
    <sql:param name= 'ProductID'>320</sql:param>
  </sql:header>
  <sql:query>
    SELECT ProductID, Name
    FROM   Production.Product
    WHERE  ProductID = @ProductID
    FOR XML AUTO
  </sql:query>
</ROOT>
```

Next, modify the `click` event code behind the Get Results button as follows:

```
Dim MyStrm As Stream
Dim ConnectString As String
Dim Param As SqlXmlParameter

'Be sure to put in the correct Username and Password in the connect string!
ConnectString = _
"Provider=SQLOLEDB;Server=(local);database=AdventureWorks;UID=?;PWD=?"

Dim cmd As SqlXmlCommand = New SqlXmlCommand(ConnectString)
cmd.CommandType = SqlXmlCommandType.TemplateFile
cmd.CommandText = "c:\Wrox\Chapter21\Products.xml"

Param = cmd.CreateParameter
Param.Name = "@ProductID"
Param.Value = 320

Try
  MyStrm = cmd.ExecuteStream
  MyStrm.Position = 0

  Dim StrRdr As StreamReader = New StreamReader(MyStrm)

  Me.TextBox1.Text = StrRdr.ReadToEnd()

Catch ex As Exception
  MessageBox.Show(ex.Message.ToString)
End Try
```

Run the project again and click the Get Results button to run the code. Your results should look like Figure 20-4.

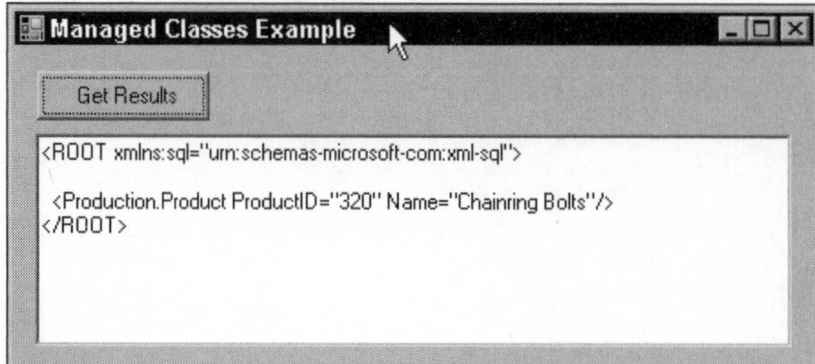

Figure 20-4

In this example, a parameter is passed to the template that is then used in the execution of the T-SQL statement. Parameters being passed to a template must begin with an at sign (@). In this example, the `Name` property of the `SqlXmlParameter` is set with the name `@productID` and then the `Value` property is set with the actual value that will be passed to the template.

The next example uses the stored procedure called `GetProductsByProductModelID` that was created in Chapter 19's discussion of endpoints. If the stored procedure exists, open a query window in SQL Server Management Studio and execute the following T-SQL, making sure the AdventureWorks database is selected:

```
Create Procedure GetProductsByProductModelID
@ProductModelID int
As

SELECT ProductID, Name
FROM Production.Product
WHRE ProductModelID = @ProductModelID
GO
```

Modify the `click` event code behind the Get Results button as follows:

```
Dim MyStrm As Stream
Dim ConnectString As String
Dim Param As SqlXmlParameter

'Be sure to put in the correct Username and Password in the connect string!
ConnectString = _
"Provider=SQLOLEDB;Server=(local);database=AdventureWorks;UID=?;PWD=?"

Dim cmd As SqlXmlCommand = New SqlXmlCommand(ConnectString)
cmd.ClientSideXml = True
cmd.CommandText = "EXEC GetProductsByProductModelID ? FOR XML NESTED"

Param = cmd.CreateParameter
Param.Value = 5

Try
```

```
        MyStrm = cmd.ExecuteStream
        MyStrm.Position = 0

        Dim StrRdr As StreamReader = New StreamReader(MyStrm)

        Me.TextBox1.Text = StrRdr.ReadToEnd()

    Catch ex As Exception
        MessageBox.Show(ex.Message.ToString)
    End Try
```

Run the project again and click the Get Results button to run the code. Your results should look like Figure 20-5.

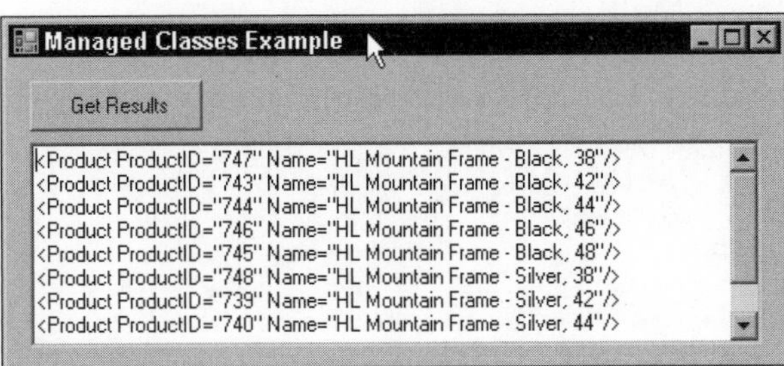

Figure 20-5

Here, the `CommandText` property is set to the name of the stored procedure, but in the place of the parameter value being passed to the stored procedure is a question mark (?). That is because the parameter is being passed using the `SqlXmlParameter` object. The placement of the parameter's value with the stored procedure is handled by the `SqlXmlCommand` object and is executed correctly.

Notice that the formatting of XML occurs on the server using the `FOR XML` clause at the end of the `CommandText` statement.

The next example uses the `SqlXmlAdapter` class to update data in a table. To begin with, query the Production.Product table, shown in Figure 20-6, and look at the first five rows, specifically row 5 where the ProductID is 316. The value of the Name column for ProductID 5 is Blade. This example uses the SqlXmlAdapter class to change that value.

Results | Messages

	ProductID	Name	ProductNumber	MakeFlag	FinishedGoodsFlag	C
1	1	Adjustable Race	AR-5381	0	0	N
2	2	Bearing Ball	BA-8327	0	0	N
3	3	BB Ball Bearing	BE-2349	1	0	N
4	4	Headset Ball Bearings	BE-2908	0	0	N
5	316	Blade	BL-2036	1	0	N

Figure 20-6

For this example, make sure you have a reference to the `System.Data` and `System.Xml` namespaces, and an `Imports` statement for the same in your Visual Studio application.

Open Notepad or your favorite text editor, type the following template schema, and save it as ProdSchema.xml in the `C:\wrox\chapter20` directory:

```
<xsd:schema xmlns:xsd="http://www.w3.org/2001/XMLSchema"
            xmlns:sql="urn:schemas-microsoft-com:mapping-schema">
  <xsd:element name="Prod" sql:relation="Production.Product" >
   <xsd:complexType>
     <xsd:sequence>
        <xsd:element name="ProdName"
                     sql:field="Name"
                     type="xsd:string" />
        <xsd:element name="ProdNum"
                     sql:field="ProductNumber"
                     type="xsd:string" />
     </xsd:sequence>
     <xsd:attribute name="ProductID" type="xsd:integer" />
     <xsd:attribute name="ProductModelID" type="xsd:integer" />
    </xsd:complexType>
  </xsd:element>
</xsd:schema>
```

Next, modify the `click` event code behind the Get Results button as follows:

```
Dim ConnectString As String
Dim rw as DataRow
Dim ad As SqlXmlAdapter

'Be sure to put in the correct Username and Password in the connect string!
ConnectString = _
"Provider=SQLOLEDB;Server=(local);database=AdventureWorks;UID=?;PWD=?"

Dim cmd As SqlXmlCommand = New SqlXmlCommand(ConnectString)
Dim myms as MemoryStream = New MemoryStream

Try
  cmd.RootTag = "Root"
  cmd.CommandText "Prod"
  cmd.CommandType = SqlXmlCommandType.XPath
  cmd.SchemaPath = "c:\wrox\chapter21\ProdSchema.xml"

  Dim ds as DataSet = New DataSet
  ad = New SqlXmlAdapater(cmd)
  ad.Fill(ds)
  rw = ds.Tables("Prod").Row(4)
  rw("ProdName") = "Blades"
```

```
    ad.Update(ds)

    'Let 'em know the process is done
    Me.TextBox1.Text = "Done"

  Catch ex As Exception
    MessageBox.Show(ex.Message.ToString)
  End Try
```

Run the project again and click the Get Results button to run the code. Notice in Figure 20-7 that for ProductID 316, the value in the Name column has been changed from Blade to Blades.

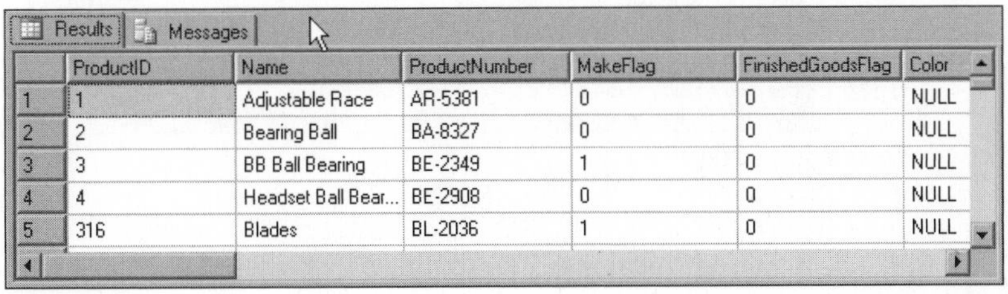

	ProductID	Name	ProductNumber	MakeFlag	FinishedGoodsFlag	Color
1	1	Adjustable Race	AR-5381	0	0	NULL
2	2	Bearing Ball	BA-8327	0	0	NULL
3	3	BB Ball Bearing	BE-2349	1	0	NULL
4	4	Headset Ball Bear...	BE-2908	0	0	NULL
5	316	Blades	BL-2036	1	0	NULL

Figure 20-7

In this example, an XPath query is executed against the schema, which returns an XML document containing the Product Name and ProductNumber columns. The returned XML data is then loaded into a dataset, and then the value of the Name column is changed. Finally, a `DiffGram` is internally generated and the changes are applied back to the database.

For this example, the same template schema is used but the results are returned via a `StreamReader`. Modify the click event code behind the Get Results button as follows:

```
Dim ConnectString As String
Dim MyStrm As Stream

'Be sure to put in the correct Username and Password in the connect string!
ConnectString = _
"Provider=SQLOLEDB;Server=(local);database=AdventureWorks;UID=?;PWD=?"

Dim cmd As SqlXmlCommand = New SqlXmlCommand(ConnectString)

Try
  cmd.RootTag = "Root"
  cmd.CommandText "Prod"
  cmd.CommandType = SqlXmlCommandType.XPath
  cmd.SchemaPath = "c:\wrox\chapter21\ProdSchema.xml"

  MyStrm = cmd.ExecuteStream

  Dim StrRdr As StreamReader = New StreamReader(MyStrm)

  Me.txtResults.Text = StrRdr.ReadToEnd

Catch ex As Exception
```

```
    MessageBox.Show(ex.Message.ToString)
  End Try
```

Run the project again and click the Get Results button to run the code. Your results should look like Figure 20-8.

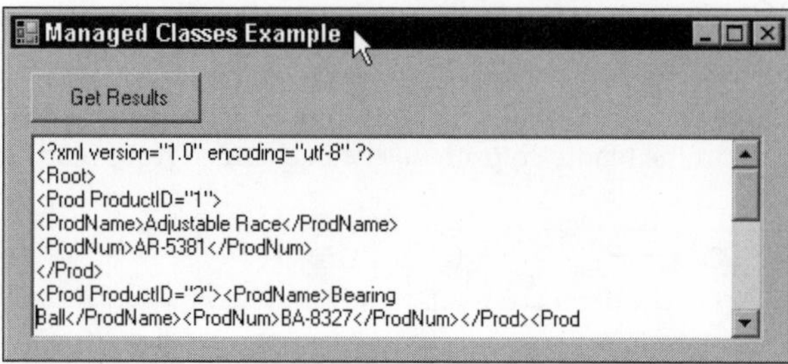

Figure 20-8

This example returns the results into a stream. The stream is then passed to a `StreamReader`, which reads the length of the stream and writes that to the text box.

Finally, one last example. This time, the steps are laid out, but the results are not shown. Your homework assignment is to figure out how to get the results and what the results will be.

The first step is to modify the Products.xml file to create an `UpdateGram`. (`UpdateGrams` were covered in Chapter 13 if you need to go back and refresh your memory.)

The next step is to modify the code behind the button to execute the template. The results aren't returned, but you can find out when the execution of code is finished by displaying a message in the text box.

Here is a hint:

```
<ROOT xmlns:sql="urn:schemas-microsoft-com:xml-sql" xmlaw:updg="urn:schemas-
microsoft-com:xml-updategram">
  WHAT GOES HERE?
</ROOT>
```

And another one:

```
Dim MyStrm As Stream
Dim ConnectString As String
Dim Param As SqlXmlParameter

'Be sure to put in the correct Username and Password in the connect string!
ConnectString = _
"Provider=SQLOLEDB;Server=(local);database=AdventureWorks;UID=?;PWD=?"

WHAT GOES HERE?

Try
```

```
    WHAT GOES HERE?

    Me.TextBox1.Text = "Done!"

  Catch ex As Exception
    MessageBox.Show(ex.Message.ToString)
  End Try
```

Summary

By the end of this chapter, you should have a pretty good handle on the different methods available to query XML data from SQL Server 2005. As discussed at the beginning of the chapter, there are three different avenues you can choose from. The first avenue mentioned was the `SQLXMLOEDB` provider, which provides SQLXML functionality via ADO. The second avenue mentioned was the new SQL Native Client, which gives access to SQLXML via a new DLL that wraps OLE DB and ODBC functionality into a single data access technology. The third avenue, discussed in this chapter, was SQLXML Managed Classes.

This chapter began by giving an overview of the SQLXML Managed Classes and the object model, then detailing the methods and properties of the `SqlXmlCommand`, `SqlXmlParameter`, and `SqlXmlAdapter` objects provided by the SQLXML Managed Classes.

The last half of the chapter provided a number of examples using the SQLXML Managed Classes, using a lot of the methods and properties discussed in the first half of the chapter.

It should be fairly apparent that all three options for accessing XML data are equally rich in functionality, but determining which one is right for you depends on your needs and your environment. The SQLXML Managed Classes allow you to migrate to the .NET Framework without having to do a ton of application rewrite, and without losing any functionality.

21

Working with Assemblies

With the integration of the Common Language Runtime (CLR) in SQL Server 2005, a means of providing access to the rich programming model of the .NET Framework functionality from within a SQL Server instance was necessary. To accomplish this, the concept of *assemblies* is introduced in SQL Server 2005.

Assemblies are .NET-compiled and -hosted DLL files used by SQL Server to deploy objects such as stored procedures, user-defined types, triggers, and user-defined functions that are typically written in T-SQL, but that can now be created and written using a number of managed code languages such as Visual Basic .NET or C#.

This new addition to SQL Server 2005 also provides the capability to access the very improved programming model of the .NET Framework from within database objects such as stored procedures, functions, and types. There have been many enhancements to version 2.0 of the .NET Framework and many of these new improvements are now made available via the integration of the CLR.

This chapter discusses the topic of assemblies as they pertain to SQL Server 2005, covering the following topics:

- ❑ Enabling CLR integration and using managed code in assemblies
- ❑ Securing your assemblies

Assemblies

Prior to SQL Server 2005, an assembly was known as, and really still is, a unit of code compiled into a .dll or .exe, also known as managed code. This terminology and functionality still exists with the .NET Framework. However, with SQL Server 2005, the term of assembly just got a little fuzzier.

In the realm of SQL Server, an *assembly* is an object that references a physical assembly .dll file. The managed code is a DLL file that is created using the .NET Framework CLR and accessible to other managed code, and more specifically, from within SQL Server. Each piece of managed code contains a couple of pieces of important information. The first is the metadata that describes the assembly, such as the methods and properties of the assembly, and the version number of the assembly. The second piece of information is the actual managed code, the methods and properties that make up the assembly.

The managed code within an assembly runs the functionality of SQL Server objects such as stored procedures, UDTs, CLR functions, and CLR triggers. More important, an assembly itself controls the permission level at which the managed code can access internal and external resources.

When an assembly is created in SQL Server via the `CREATE ASSEMBLY` statement, the .dll file is physically loaded into SQL Server so that it can be referenced and used by the SQL Server engine. Two tables exist in SQL Server 2005 that show the created assemblies. Those tables are called sys.assemblies and sys.assembly_files. At any time during the examples in this chapter, feel free to query those two tables to look at the information stored.

Enabling CLR Integration

Before you can start utilizing assemblies in SQL Server 2005, you need to tell SQL Server that it is okay to start talking the CLR/.NET jive. By default, CLR integration is turned off and needs to be enabled so that any of the .NET objects can be accessed from within SQL Server.

To enable CLR integration, run the following code in a query window in SQL Server Management Studio:

```
EXEC sp_configure 'show advanced options', 1
GO
RECONFIGURE
GO
sp_configure 'clr enabled', 1
GO
RECONFIGURE
GO
```

To enable CLR integration, you must have `ALTER SETTINGS` *server level permissions. These permissions are implicitly held by members of the sysadmin and serveradmin server roles.*

The other method of enabling CLR integration is to turn it on via the SQL Server Surface Area Configuration tool. To get to this tool, select the SQL Server Surface Area Configuration menu, shown in Figure 21-1, from the Microsoft SQL Server 2005 ⇨ Configuration Tools menu.

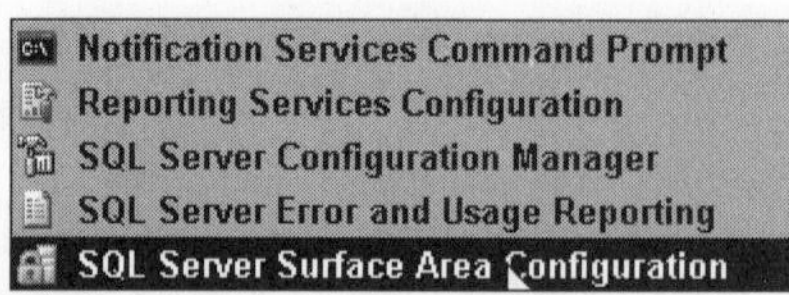

Figure 21-1

Selecting this menu opens the SQL Server 2005 Surface Area Configuration dialog, shown in Figure 21-2. To configure CLR integration, click the Surface Area Configuration for Features option at the bottom of the dialog. This opens the Surface Area Configuration for Features form, shown in Figure 21-3.

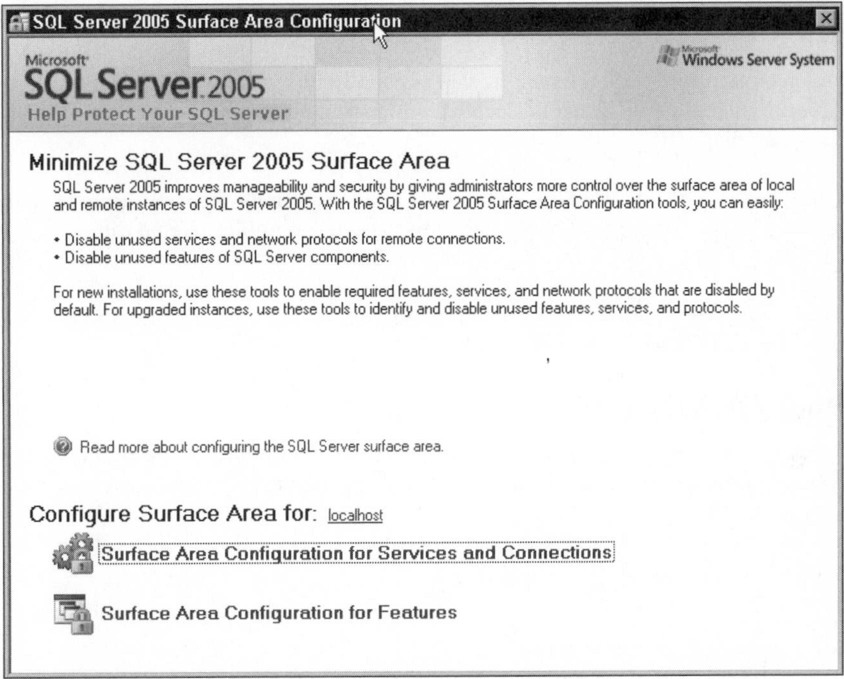

Figure 21-2

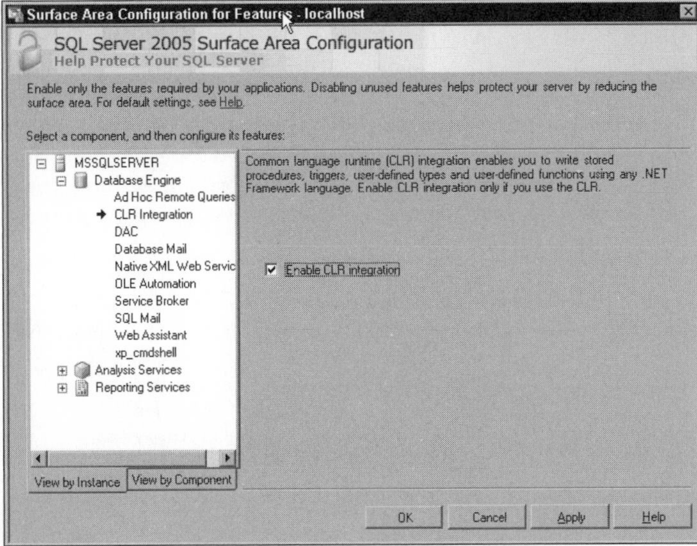

Figure 21-3

To configure CLR integration, select CLR Integration on the left under Database Engine, and then check the Enable CLR Integration box on the right. Click OK to enable the option and close the form. You are now ready to go.

Managed Code

The definition of managed code is usually given as code written in one of several high-level programming languages such as C# or Visual Basic .NET, which share class libraries and are compiled into an Intermediate Language (IL).

You have seen managed code used throughout the book, especially the last couple of chapters when the topics of the SqlXml Managed Classes were discussed. Assemblies are no different, except unlike Chapter 20 where you dealt with existing managed code, this chapter lets you create the managed code.

This section introduces you to assemblies and walks you through the creation and use of them through SQL Server 2005 and Visual Studio .NET 2005.

Stored Procedures

This first example is an easy one to help you get your feet wet in understanding how assemblies work with SQL Server 2005. To begin, create a directory called Chapter21 in the `C:\Wrox` directory.

Open your favorite text editor, enter the following code, and save it as HelloScott.vb:

```
Imports System
Imports System.Data
Imports Microsoft.SqlServer.Server
Imports System.Data.SqlTypes

Public Class HelloScottProc
  Public Shared Sub HelloScott()
    SqlContext.Pipe.Send("Hello Scott!")
  End Sub
End Class
```

The next step is where you create the managed code. To accomplish this you need to invoke the command line compiler, which compiles the file into the desired managed code. The compiler is located in the folder for the specific .NET version underneath the Windows directory. For example, these examples use version 2.0.50215 of the .NET Framework, so the compiler is located in `C:\Windows\Microsoft.Net\Framework\v2.0.50215`.

Open a command prompt and browse to the folder specific to the version of the .NET Framework you are running. In that directory, you should find a file called vbc.exe (for Visual Basic .NET) or csc.exe (for C#).

At the command prompt, type and execute the following:

```
vbc /target:library c:\wrox\chapter21\helloscott.vb
```

The results are shown in Figure 21-4.

```
C:\WINDOWS\system32\cmd.exe

C:\WINDOWS\Microsoft.NET\Framework\v2.0.50215>vbc /target:library c:\wrox\chapte
r22\helloScott.vb
Microsoft (R) Visual Basic Compiler version 8.0.50215.44
for Microsoft (R) .NET Framework version 2.0.50215.44
Copyright (C) Microsoft Corporation 1987-2003. All rights reserved.

C:\WINDOWS\Microsoft.NET\Framework\v2.0.50215>
```

Figure 21-4

A new file called HelloScott.dll is now in the `C:\wrox\Chapter21` directory where the HelloScott.vb file is located (see Figure 21-5). The HelloScott.dll file is the managed code.

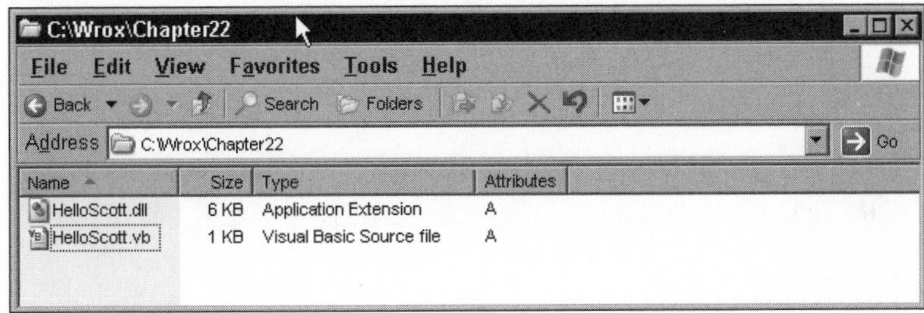

Figure 21-5

The next step is to create the assembly and reference in SQL Server. Open a query window in the SQL Server Management Studio, making sure the AdventureWorks database is selected, and execute the following T-SQL statement:

```
CREATE ASSEMBLY helloscott
FROM 'c:\wrox\chapter21\helloscott.dll'
WITH PERMISSION_SET = SAFE
```

The `CREATE ASSEMBLY` statement loads the compiled .dll into SQL Server that can now be referenced from within SQL Server. Multiple copies, or versions, of the assembly can be stored in SQL Server with the same file name as long as each .dll has a different file version number.

The code in this example creates an assembly called `helloscott` using the helloscott.dll and sets the permission to `SAFE`. `PERMISSION_SET` is discussed in detail later in this chapter.

With the assembly created, the next step is to create a simple stored procedure that will use the assembly. The following DDL statement creates the entry point for the assembly:

```
CREATE PROCEDURE HelloMe
AS
EXTERNAL NAME helloscott.HelloScottProc.HelloScott
```

To test this example, run the stored procedure by executing the following statement:

```
EXEC helloMe
```

Figure 21-6 shows all the code used in the example and the results from running the `EXEC` statement.

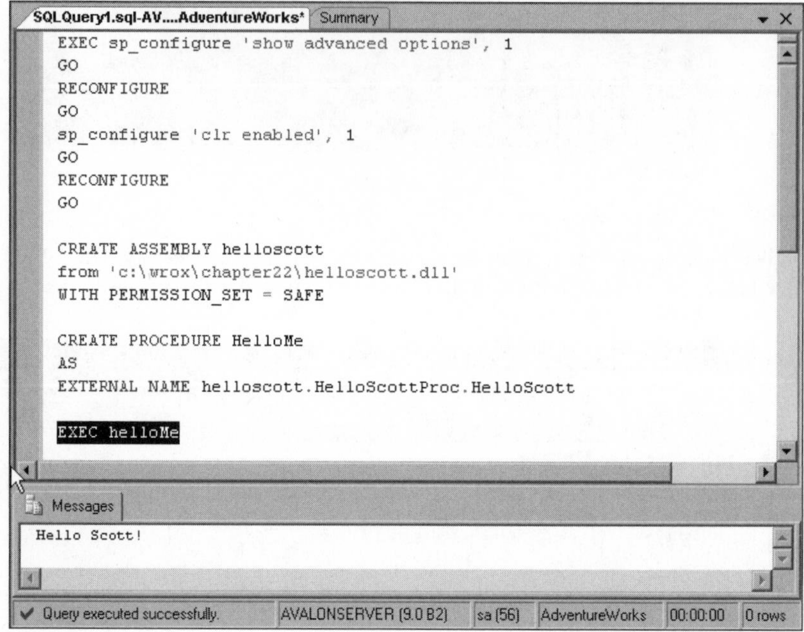
SQLQuery1.sql-AV....AdventureWorks*
Summary
EXEC sp_configure 'show advanced options', 1
GO
RECONFIGURE
GO
sp_configure 'clr enabled', 1
GO
RECONFIGURE
GO
CREATE ASSEMBLY helloscott
from 'c:\wrox\chapter22\helloscott.dll'
WITH PERMISSION_SET = SAFE
CREATE PROCEDURE HelloMe
AS
EXTERNAL NAME helloscott.HelloScottProc.HelloScott
EXEC helloMe
Messages
Hello Scott!
Query executed successfully.
AVALONSERVER (9.0 B2)
sa (56)
AdventureWorks
00:00:00
0 rows

Figure 21-6

While this example is quite simple, it does show the basic steps for creating and deploying assemblies. The next examples build on this code and demonstrate more complex functionality to access SQL Server data.

You must be thinking, "There must be an easier way to build and deploy these assemblies." Well, actually, there is. However, the reason these exercises have you building and deploying these assemblies manually is so that you understand what is happening behind the scenes when these assemblies are created. Don't worry, though, because at the end of Chapter 22, you'll see "the easy way."

In this next example, the assembly is used to access some data from a SQL Server instance. Open your text editor again and enter the following code, saving the file in the `C:\Wrox\Chapter21` directory as GetProducts.vb:

```
Imports System
Imports System.Data
Imports Microsoft.SqlServer.Server
Imports System.Data.SqlTypes
Imports System.Data.SqlClient

Public Class GetProductsProc
  Public Shared Sub GetProducts()
    Dim conn as SqlConnection = New SqlConnection("context connection = True")
    conn.Open()
    Dim cmd As SqlCommand = New SqlCommand("SELECT Name FROM Production.Product" &_
"WHERE ProductID = 1", conn)
```

```
        SqlContext.Pipe.ExecuteAndSend(cmd)
    End Sub
End Class
```

This code in this assembly creates a connection to the database and executes a T-SQL statement, returning the value of a column for a specified row.

In your command prompt, modify the command line as follows and run it:

```
vbc /target:library c:\wrox\chapter21\GetProducts.vb
```

You should now see a new DLL called GetProducts.dll in the Chapter22 directory. Again, this is the managed code piece of the assembly.

Now you need to create the assembly reference in SQL Server. In your query window, run the following T-SQL:

```
CREATE ASSEMBLY GetAWProducts
FROM 'c:\wrox\chapter21\GetProducts.dll'
WITH PERMISSION_SET = SAFE
```

One thing to notice about this `CREATE ASSEMBLY` statement is the `WITH PERMISSION_SET` clause at the end. This clause specifies the access permissions that are given to the assembly when it is used and accessed by SQL Server. The available values for this clause are `SAFE`, `EXTERNAL_ACCESS`, and `UNSAFE`. Each of these is explained in detail at the end of this chapter.

Now that the assembly reference is created, the next step is to create a SQL Server object that can use the assembly, again using a stored procedure. Run the following T-SQL in your query window to create the stored procedure:

```
CREATE PROCEDURE GetProducts
AS
EXTERNAL NAME GetAWProducts.GetProductsProc.GetProducts
```

Before you execute the stored procedure, take a look at the `EXTERNAL NAME` syntax of the `CREATE PROCEDURE` statement. This specifies the method of the .NET assembly. The format of the syntax is as follows:

```
Assembly_name.class_name.method_name
```

Using the previous example, the assembly name comes from the `CREATE ASSEMBLY` statement, which in this case is `GetAWProducts`. The second part is the class name, which comes from the code in the GetProducts.vb file in the statement `Public Class GetProductsProc`. The third part is the method name, which also comes from the GetProducts.vb, which in this example is `GetProducts` from the `Public Shared Sub GetProducts` declaration.

Putting these pieces of information together in the `EXTERNAL NAME` clause tells the stored procedure what to execute when the stored procedure is executed.

At this point you are ready to test the assembly and get data back. In your query window, execute the following T-SQL:

```
EXEC GetProducts
```

Figure 21-7 shows the results you should see.

Figure 21-7

A downside to using assemblies is that if you modify the managed code piece, the DLL, you need to drop the assembly reference in SQL Server. The problem is that you can't just delete the assembly because it is being referenced by the `GetProducts` stored procedure. So, to delete the assembly, you must first delete all objects that reference that assembly, which in this case, thankfully, is only the `GetProducts` stored procedure.

So, run the following code to first delete the stored procedure and then the reference to the assembly. You're doing this because some of the subsequent examples use the `GetProducts` assembly again with some modifications.

You are probably asking yourself, "Why isn't it possible to just modify and rebuild the assembly?" That would be nice, but if you remember some of the information from the discussion of assemblies at the start of this chapter, when you are creating an assembly and a reference to it, a lot of information about the assembly (the metadata) is stored with the assembly reference in SQL Server. It contains class metadata within the instance of SQL Server and therefore just recompiling the DLL does no good because SQL Server still has the metadata for the previous assembly.

First, drop the stored procedure and assembly, as follows:

```
DROP PROCEDURE GetProducts
GO
DROP ASSEMBLY GetAWProducts
GO
```

Now modify the assembly code as follows:

```
Imports System
Imports System.Data
Imports Microsoft.SqlServer.Server
Imports System.Data.SqlTypes
Imports System.Data.SqlClient

Public Class GetProductsProc
  Public Shared Sub GetProducts()
    Dim conn as SqlConnection = New SqlConnection("context connection = True")
```

```
        conn.Open()
        Dim cmd As SqlCommand = New SqlCommand("SELECT Name, ProductNumber FROM " & _
    "Production.Product ORDER BY ProductID", conn)
        SqlContext.Pipe.ExecuteAndSend(cmd)
      End Sub
    End Class
```

You have probably noticed in the previous examples that the results are being returned through a couple of objects called `SqlContext` and `SqlPipe`. Chapter 22 goes into much greater detail about these objects, but for now suffice it to say that any CLR objects running in a SQL Server instance return their results through a connect pipe. This pipe is a property of the `SqlContext` object. The `SqlPipe` object is very similar to the `Response` object in ASP.NET.

Realistically, this example is not much different from the first one except that instead of specifying a ProductID to return a specific record, the query is returning the Name and ProductNumber columns for all the rows. The rest of the code remains the same.

Don't forget to recompile the assembly, using the same syntax as in the previous examples.

The `CREATE ASSEMBLY` and `CREATE PROCEDURE` statements remain the same, so go ahead and execute those:

```
CREATE ASSEMBLY GetAWProducts
FROM 'c:\wrox\chapter21\GetProducts.dll'
WITH PERMISSION_SET = SAFE
GO
CREATE PROCEDURE GetProducts
AS
EXTERNAL NAME GetAWProducts.GetProductsProc.GetProducts
GO
```

Now, as before, execute the stored procedure:

```
EXEC GetProducts
```

Your results should show the Name and ProductNumber columns for all the records from the Production.Product table, as shown in Figure 21-8.

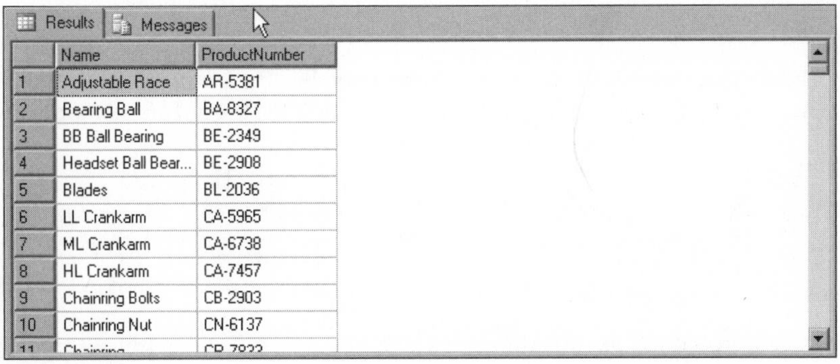

Results | Messages

	Name	ProductNumber
1	Adjustable Race	AR-5381
2	Bearing Ball	BA-8327
3	BB Ball Bearing	BE-2349
4	Headset Ball Bear...	BE-2908
5	Blades	BL-2036
6	LL Crankarm	CA-5965
7	ML Crankarm	CA-6738
8	HL Crankarm	CA-7457
9	Chainring Bolts	CB-2903
10	Chainring Nut	CN-6137

Figure 21-8

In this example, the Name and ProductNumber columns are returned for all the rows because the query does not specify a specific ProductID to return a single row. Thus, all the rows are returned.

However, there will be times where you will want to filter the query by specifying a filter criterion (such as specifying a ProductID as in the previous example), but you won't know that value until runtime. In cases like this, being able to specify a parameter to the assembly comes in handy.

This next example builds on the previous example, passing a parameter to the assembly. The same GetAWProducts assembly is used, so drop the stored procedure and assembly first:

```
DROP PROCEDURE GetProducts
GO
DROP ASSEMBLY GetAWProducts
GO
```

Modify the assembly as follows, adding a parameter and modifying the `SELECT` statement:

```
Imports System
Imports System.Data
Imports Microsoft.SqlServer.Server
Imports System.Data.SqlTypes
Imports System.Data.SqlClient

Public Class GetProductsProc
  Public Shared Sub GetProducts(ByVal ProductID As Integer)
    Dim conn as SqlConnection = New SqlConnection("context connection = True")
    conn.Open()
    Dim cmd As SqlCommand = New SqlCommand("SELECT Name, ProductNumber FROM " & _
"Production.Product WHERE ProductID = " & ProductID, conn)
    SqlContext.Pipe.ExecuteAndSend(cmd)
  End Sub
End Class
```

Recompile the assembly in the command window; the syntax hasn't changed for that yet. Additionally, create the assembly reference:

```
CREATE ASSEMBLY GetAWProducts
FROM 'c:\wrox\chapter21\GetProducts.dll'
WITH PERMISSION_SET = SAFE
GO
```

In this case, since a parameter is being passed to the assembly, the syntax for the `CREATE PROCEDURE` statement also needs to change. Modify the code for creating the procedure as follows:

```
CREATE PROCEDURE GetProducts
@ProductID int
AS
EXTERNAL NAME GetAWProducts.GetProductsProc.GetProducts
GO
```

Execute the stored procedure, but this time, pass a valid ProductID value (this example uses a ProductID of 1, but you could pass any valid ProductID to test the assembly):

```
EXEC GetProducts 1
```

The results of passing a ProductID of 1 are shown in Figure 21-9.

	Name	ProductNumber
1	Adjustable Race	AR-5381

Figure 21-9

The results returned from this procedure, the Name and ProductNumber columns, were returned for a single specific row, specified by the ProductID that was passed in via a parameter. The query was then executed using that parameter as filter criteria, with the results being returned via the `ExecuteAndSend` method.

Building on the last example, this next example also takes a parameter to query information from SQL Server and then write the results to a file.

Modify the assembly as follows:

```
Imports System
Imports System.Data
Imports Microsoft.SqlServer.Server
Imports System.Data.SqlTypes
Imports System.Data.SqlClient

Public Class GetProductsProc
  Public Shared Sub GetProducts(ByVal ProductModelID As Integer)
    Dim conn as SqlConnection = New SqlConnection("context connection = True")
    conn.Open()
    Dim cmd As SqlCommand = New SqlCommand("SELECT ProductID, Name, " & _
    " ProductNumber FROM Production.Product  WHERE ProductModelID = " & _
    ProductModelID, conn)

    Dim rdr As SqlDataReader = cmd.ExecuteReader

    Dim sw As StreamWriter = New StreamWriter("c:\wrox\chapter21\output.txt")
    If rdr.HasRows = True Then
      Do While rdr.Read
        sw.WriteLine(CType(rdr.Item(0), String) + "  " + rdr.Item(1) + "  " +
rdr.Item(2))
      Loop
    Else
      sw.WriteLine("No Rows")
    End If

    rdr.Close()
    conn.Close()
    sw.Close()

  End Sub
End Class
```

For this example, the `CREATE ASSEMBLY` and `CREATE PROCEDURE` code have not changed, so execute that code:

```
DROP PROCEDURE GetProducts
GO
DROP ASSEMBLY GetAWProducts
GO
CREATE ASSEMBLY GetAWProducts
FROM 'c:\wrox\chapter21\GetProducts.dll'
WITH PERMISSION_SET = SAFE
GO
CREATE PROCEDURE GetProducts
@ProductID int
AS
EXTERNAL NAME GetAWProducts.GetProductsProc.GetProducts
GO
```

Now execute the stored procedure to view the results. You should receive the message shown in Figure 21-10.

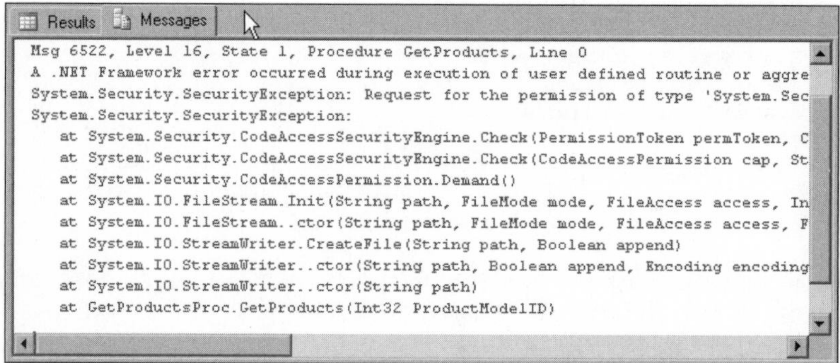

Figure 21-10

Do you know why it didn't work? The answer has to do with security. What `PERMISSION_SET` was used when creating the assembly?

As explained earlier, there are different `PERMISSION_SET` levels, and you will learn shortly what each of those means. In simple terms for now, `SAFE` mode is the stingiest with its access to external resources (such as file access), as demonstrated in this example. To gain access to external resources, the `PERMISSION_SET` needs to be changed to `EXTERNAL_ACCESS`.

This means that the permissions on the assembly need to change. In order to do that the assembly needs to be dropped and recreated (which means that the stored procedure needs to be dropped as well):

```
DROP PROCEDURE GetProducts
GO
DROP ASSEMBLY GetAWProducts
GO
```

Recreate the assembly with the following changes, using the `EXTERNAL_ACCESS` permission set, and then create the stored procedure:

```
CREATE ASSEMBLY helloscott
FROM 'c:\wrox\chapter21\GetProducts.dll'
WITH PERMISSION_SET = EXTERNAL_ACCESS
GO
CREATE PROCEDURE GetProducts
@ProductID int
AS
EXTERNAL NAME GetAWProducts.GetProductsProc.GetProducts
GO
```

Now execute the stored procedure again.

```
EXEC GetProducts 6
```

Once this has finished executing, you should be able to see a new file called output.txt in the `C:\Wrox\Chapter21` directory, as shown in Figure 21-11.

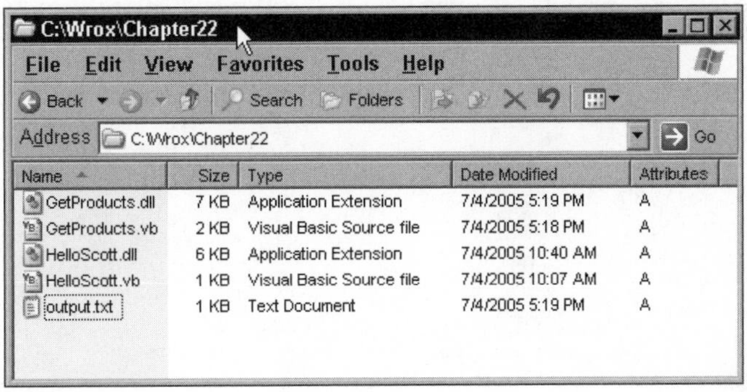

Figure 21-11

Open the output.txt file. As you can see, all the data returned from the execution of the assembly — the ProductID, Name, and ProductNumber for the given ProductModelID — was passed in to the assembly as a parameter. The text file should look like Figure 21-12.

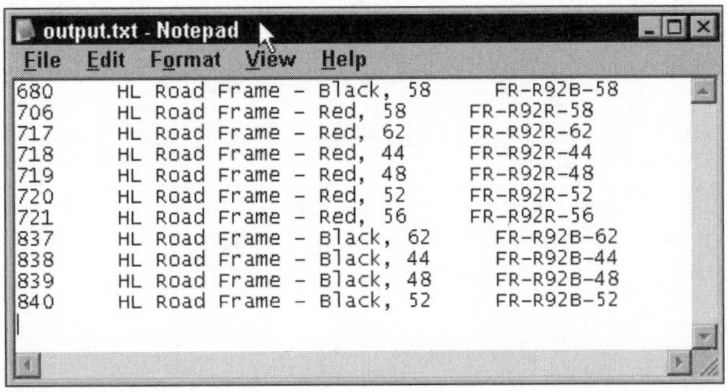

Figure 21-12

Something interesting to note here. This example returns the results to a text file and not the query window. You could do both, however, by leaving the line `SqlContext.Pipe.ExecuteAndSend(cmd)` in as follows:

```
Dim cmd As SqlCommand = New SqlCommand("SELECT ProductID, Name, " & _
" ProductNumber FROM Production.Product  WHERE ProductModelID = " & _
ProductModelID, conn)

SqlContext.Pipe.ExecuteAndSend(cmd)

Dim rdr As SqlDataReader = cmd.ExecuteReader
```

By including this line, you get the output.txt file and the results are sent to the query window as well.

User-Defined Functions

All of the examples thus far have used a stored procedure to execute the assembly, so it's time to shift directions a bit and employ user-defined functions to demonstrate how to use other SQL Server objects to execute an assembly.

These examples use a new assembly, so open your text editor and enter the following code, saving it as GetProductCount.vb in the `C:\Wrox\Chapter21` directory. This assembly returns a single integer value, the number of rows in the Production.Product table:

```
Imports System
Imports System.Data
Imports Microsoft.SqlServer.Server
Imports System.Data.SqlTypes
Imports System.Data.SqlClient

Public Class GetProductCountProc
    Public Shared Function GetProductCount() As Integer

        Dim conn As SqlConnection = New SqlConnection("context connection=true")
        conn.open()
        Dim cmd As SqlCommand = New SqlCommand("SELECT Count(*) AS ProductCount
FROM Production.Product", conn)
        Return CInt(cmd.ExecuteScalar())

    End Function
End Class
```

Change the command line compiler command so that it looks like this:

```
vbc /target:library c:\wrox\chapter21\GetProductCount.vb
```

Upon executing this command, a new DLL is created in the directory, so now you can create the assembly reference. Execute the following `CREATE ASSEMBLY` statement in a query window. The assembly is not going to access any external resources so the `PERMISSION_SET` can be set back to `SAFE`:

```
CREATE ASSEMBLY GetProductCount
from 'c:\wrox\chapter21\getproductcount.dll'
WITH PERMISSION_SET = SAFE
GO
```

Using a UDF (user-defined function) is not too different from using a stored procedure. The EXTERNAL NAME clause is the same and works the same. The only difference is that there are different kinds of functions: scalar-valued and table-valued.

Scalar-valued functions return a single value, such as an integer or string. A *table-valued* function returns a set of columns or a table.

This first example builds a scalar-valued function to return a single integer value, the count of rows in the Production.Product table.

Create the function by executing the following T-SQL in a query window:

```
CREATE FUNCTION GetProductCountUDF()
RETURNS INT
AS
EXTERNAL NAME GetProductCount.GetProductCountProc.GetProductCount
GO
```

Unlike stored procedures that use the EXEC command to run them, a function is executed by simply selecting from the function, as shown in the following code:

```
SELECT dbo.GetProductCountUDF()
```

Figure 21-13 shows the results of the execution of the function.

Figure 21-13

In this example, the assembly passes the results back to the function by using the ExecuteScalar method with the Return keyword as follows:

```
Return CInt(cmd.ExecuteScalar())
```

The ExecuteScalar method used in this example executes the query as defined in the SqlCommand, but returns only the first column of the first row of the result set. All other columns or rows are discarded. The Return statement returns the results of the query, in this case the value 504, via the function.

Building on the previous example, instead of returning the number of rows for the entire table, the next example passes a parameter into the assembly to return only the number of rows for a given ProductModelID.

As you might expect, the assembly and function need to be dropped first since you're using the same assembly:

```
DROP FUNCTION GetProductCountUDF
GO
DROP ASSEMBLY GetProductInfo
GO
```

Modify the assembly as follows, adding a parameter to the function and adding a `WHERE` clause to the `SELECT` statement:

```
Imports System
Imports System.Data
Imports Microsoft.SqlServer.Server
Imports System.Data.SqlTypes
Imports System.Data.SqlClient

Public Class GetProductCountProc
  Public Shared Function GetProductCount(ByVal ProductModelID As Integer) As _
  Integer

    Dim conn As SqlConnection = New SqlConnection("context connection=true")
    conn.open()
    Dim cmd As SqlCommand = New SqlCommand("SELECT Count(*) AS ProductCount " & _
    "FROM Production.Product WHERE ProductModelID = " & ProductModelID, conn)
    Return CInt(cmd.ExecuteScalar())

    End Function
End Class
```

Don't forget to compile the assembly. Once that is done you can recreate the assembly reference:

```
CREATE ASSEMBLY GetProductCount
from 'c:\wrox\chapter21\getproductcount.dll'
WITH PERMISSION_SET = SAFE
GO
```

The syntax for the `CREATE FUNCTION` statement needs to change to pass a parameter. The syntax is a bit different, as shown here:

```
CREATE FUNCTION GetProductCount (@ProductModelID int)
RETURNS INT
AS
EXTERNAL NAME GetProductCount.GetProductCountProc.GetProductCount
GO
```

This time, when you select from the function, be sure to pass a parameter value, as follows (this example uses the value of `6`, but you can use any valid number from the ProductModelID column):

```
SELECT dbo.GetProductCount (6)
```

This example returns a value of `11`, as shown in Figure 21-14.

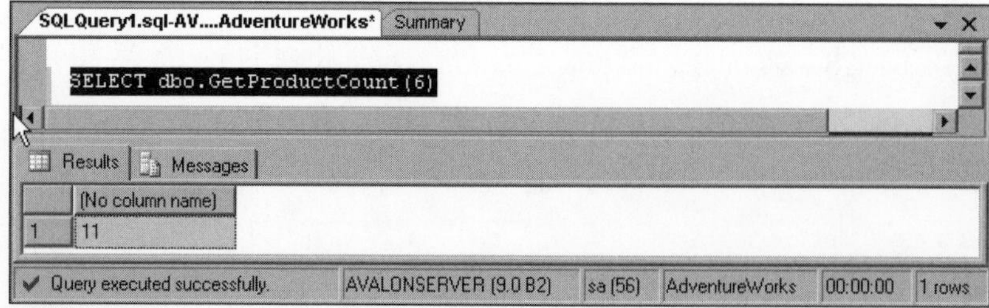

Figure 21-14

The results for this example are returned the exact same way as in the previous example, using the `ExecuteScalar` method, which allows the passing of a single return value to the calling function.

None of the examples have yet to return the data formatted as XML, so it is time to do that. This example uses the GetProducts assembly, so in order to use it you must first delete it:

```
DROP PROCEDURE GetProducts
GO
DROP ASSEMBLY GetAWProducts
GO
```

Next, modify the GetProducts.vb assembly as follows:

```
Imports System
Imports System.Data
Imports Microsoft.SqlServer.Server
Imports System.Data.SqlTypes
Imports System.Data.SqlClient

Public Class GetProductsProc
  Public Shared Sub GetProducts(ByVal ProductModelID As Integer)
    Dim conn as SqlConnection = New SqlConnection("context connection = True")
    conn.Open()
    Dim cmd As SqlCommand = New SqlCommand("SELECT ProductID, Name, " & _
      " ProductNumber FROM Production.Product  WHERE ProductModelID = " & _
    ProductModelID & " FOR XML AUTO, ELEMENTS", conn)

    SqlContext.Pipe.ExecuteAndSend(cmd)

    conn.Close()
```

As with the previous examples, create the assembly reference:

```
CREATE ASSEMBLY GetAWProducts
FROM 'c:\wrox\chapter21\GetProducts.dll'
WITH PERMISSION_SET = SAFE
GO
```

Use the `GetProducts` stored procedure for this example:

```
CREATE PROCEDURE GetProducts
@ProductID int
AS
EXTERNAL NAME GetAWProducts.GetProductsProc.GetProducts
GO
```

Execute the stored procedure to return the results and be sure to pass a value for the parameter that the assembly expects:

```
EXEC GetProducts 6
```

The XML is formatted on the server as specified by `FOR XML AUTO` in the `SELECT` statement, and the results returned are shown in Figure 21-15.

```
<Production.Product ProductID="680" Name="HL Road Frame - Black, 58" ProductNumber="FR-R92B-58'
<Production.Product ProductID="706" Name="HL Road Frame - Red, 58" ProductNumber="FR-R92R-58" /
<Production.Product ProductID="717" Name="HL Road Frame - Red, 62" ProductNumber="FR-R92R-62" /
<Production.Product ProductID="718" Name="HL Road Frame - Red, 44" ProductNumber="FR-R92R-44" /
<Production.Product ProductID="719" Name="HL Road Frame - Red, 48" ProductNumber="FR-R92R-48" /
<Production.Product ProductID="720" Name="HL Road Frame - Red, 52" ProductNumber="FR-R92R-52" /
<Production.Product ProductID="721" Name="HL Road Frame - Red, 56" ProductNumber="FR-R92R-56" /
<Production.Product ProductID="837" Name="HL Road Frame - Black, 62" ProductNumber="FR-R92B-62'
<Production.Product ProductID="838" Name="HL Road Frame - Black, 44" ProductNumber="FR-R92B-44'
<Production.Product ProductID="839" Name="HL Road Frame - Black, 48" ProductNumber="FR-R92B-48'
<Production.Product ProductID="840" Name="HL Road Frame - Black, 52" ProductNumber="FR-R92B-52'
```

Figure 21-15

In this example, the query included a `FOR XML` clause. When the procedure was executed, the query was sent to the server informing it to format the results as XML and return them to the client.

When you create the assembly, you need to establish a specific permission set on the assembly, which tells the assembly what level of permissions it has to operate within SQL Server. Those permission levels are discussed next.

Assembly Security

The CLR in the .NET Framework contains a security model for managed code named CAS (Code Access Security). This security model manages the security between the different types of CLR and non-CLR objects that are running within a SQL Server instance.

For assemblies, the following access permissions have been defined and implemented.

SAFE

The most restrictive permission, `SAFE` permissions allow access to internal and local data. No access to external resources such as files or directories, network resources, and the registry is permitted.

EXTERNAL_ACCESS

`EXTERNAL_ACCESS` permissions contain the same permissions as `SAFE`, but add the capability to access external resources such as files or directories, network resources, and the registry. Environment variables are also available with this level of permissions.

> `EXTERNAL_ACCESS` *assemblies are executed by the service account by default.*

UNSAFE

The least restrictive, and not recommended, `UNSAFE` permissions allow access to all resources internally as well as externally, and can call unmanaged code as well.

Summary

Assemblies provide tremendous value to the CLR integration with SQL Server 2005, and this chapter showed you various ways you can implement them in your environment and applications. These examples provided you with an understanding on how assemblies are implemented in SQL Server 2005. All of the examples were used for data access, but in reality, assemblies can play a much more important role. SQL Server is extremely good at data access. Why call out to an assembly only to have that assembly query back to SQL Server for data?

Where the CLR and assemblies show their strength are in things that SQL is not strong at, such as string manipulation and complex numerical computations. You saw how it is possible to pass in parameters to an assembly and return results. This is where assemblies should be used: to complement SQL Server.

Additionally, this chapter discussed the concept of managed code to give an overview of how assemblies work and what they contain. From there, you saw a number of examples using different SQL Server objects to gain access to the assemblies, such as user-defined functions and CLR procedures. Through this functionality you are able to take advantage of the CLR right within SQL Server to enhance SQL Server's already powerful functionality.

While the examples in this chapter demonstrated simple T-SQL statements, assemblies are extremely useful when your application requires high processor-intensive tasks, not simple T-SQL statements. Assemblies are very robust, but you must take care when developing and utilizing them to determine what permissions they need and what resources they might need access to.

Finally, you also saw an example that illustrated how to return XML formatted data. This is important because it might come in handy when you need to deal with XML formatted data.

The next chapter continues the discussion of managed code with a focus on .NET routines.

22

Creating .NET Routines

In Chapter 21, the discussion revolved around the topics of managed code and assemblies and how they work within an instance of SQL Server 2005. Really, this is just the tip of the iceberg in the whole managed code area that floats below the surface.

Chapter 21 defined the concept of managed code, and that same concept and terminology applies to this chapter. You learned that you could build database objects using the SQL Server integration with the .NET Framework CLR, basically called *managed code*. In these terms, managed code that runs within an instance of SQL Server is called a *CLR routine*.

This chapter focuses on a number of very common CLR routines that can add tremendous benefit to your application. The following topics are covered in this chapter:

- .NET routine overview
- User-defined procedures and triggers
- Scalar-value and table-value user-defined functions

Overview

A portion of Chapter 21 dealt with the concept of managed code. Chapter 21 defined managed code as code that is executed by the CLR rather than the operating system. Any managed code that runs within an instance of SQL Server is a CLR routine. CLR routines contain what is called a T-SQL declaration, which is equivalent to a normal T-SQL statement, and just like an assembly, CLR routines are mapped to publicly shared class method.

A routine is compiled into an assembly (which you learned about in the last chapter). In its simplest terms, assemblies contain classes, which contain methods. In other words, an assembly is made up of a class with each class containing one or more methods. The following example illustrates the basic construct of a CLR routine:

```
Public Class classname
  <Microsoft.SqlServer.Server.SqlFunction(DataAccess:=DataAccessKind.Read)>
  Public Shared Function FunctionName(arguments) As Integer

  End Function
End Class
```

Data Access

Data access in a routine is accomplished by using the SqlClient of ADO.NET, sometimes referred to as the Data Access Provider for SQL Server. Routines can access data from either the instance of SQL Server for which it is running, and they can also access data from other instances of SQL Server, depending on the user context.

New to SQL Server 2005 is a connection string keyword called `context connection`. You have seen this connection string used throughout a good number of examples in Chapter 21 and will see it more in this chapter. This connection string cannot be used with other connection strings. It takes the value `true` or `false`, and signifies that an in-process connection is or is not made to the database. The default is `false`.

Namespace Requirements

The following namespaces are required when building and compiling CLR routines. You also saw these in Chapter 21's discussion of assemblies, but they are listed here as a review:

- `Microsoft.SqlServer.Server`: This namespace is new to the .NET Framework 2.0.
- `System.Data`: Contains all of the classes the make up the ADO.NET architecture and is primarily responsible for the data access within managed applications.
- `System.Data.Sql`: This namespace is new to the .NET Framework 2.0.
- `System.Data.SqlTypes`: Provides the classes that support the native data types with SQL Server 2005.
- `System.Data.SqlClient`: The data provider for SQL Server. It allows applications to be able to access SQL Server 2005 databases, as well as SQL Server 7.0 and SQL Server 2000.

Before the examples begin, you need to understand the topic of data access as it pertains to CLR database objects. The following sections discuss the main in-process extensions of ADO.NET.

SqlContext Object

The `SqlContext` object is a new class in 2.0 of the .NET Framework and is part of the `Microsoft.SqlServer.Server` namespace. The `SqlContext` object provides the environment in which the assembly code is activated and running. The managed code is executed from the server thus running as part of the user connection, or within the user *context*. At this point the `SqlPipe` object is accessible.

SqlPipe Class

The SqlPipe class is a new addition to version 2.0 of the .NET Framework as part of the SqlContext object. In SQL Server, results from a query execution are sent back to the client via the caller's *pipe*. This is really no different for CLR database objects in that results are sent back to the client via the methods associated with the SqlPipe object.

The SqlPipe class has two methods associated with it: the Send method and the ExecuteAndSend method.

Send

The Send method sends data directly to the client. It can send a string type to the client, a single record back to the client using SqlDataRecord, or multiple records using the SqlDataReader.

For example, you use the Send method of the SqlPiple class to send query results from a SqlDataReader back to client:

```
Dim cmd As SqlCommand = New SqlCommand("SELECT Name, FROM Production.Product" & _
"ProductID = " & Convert.ToString(ProductID), conn)
Dim rdr As SqlDataReader = cmd.ExecuteReader
SqlContext.Pipe.Send(rdr)
```

ExecuteAndSend

The ExecuteAndSend method is used to execute a command from the SqlCommand object with the results being sent straight back to the caller.

In the following example, you return the results by using the ExecuteAndSend method of the SqlPipe class, which passes the SqlCommand object as a parameter. The SqlCommand object contains the query, which is sent to the server for execution by the ExecuteAndSend method:

```
Dim sqlComm As SqlCommand = conn.CreateCommand()
Dim sqlP As SqlPipe = SqlContext.Pipe
sqlComm.CommandText = "SELECT Name, FROM Production.Product"
sqlP.ExecuteAndSend(sqlComm)
```

SqlDataRecord Class

The SqlDataRecord object, as briefly described previously, allows a single row of data to be sent back to the caller.

The following code snippet shows the general syntax of the SqlDataRecord class:

```
Dim rec As SqlDataRecord
```

Examples later in this chapter illustrate how the SqlDataRecord class is used.

User-Defined Procedures

You saw quite a few examples using CLR stored procedures in the previous chapter, so only a couple of examples are shown here. In Chapter 21 the results were typically returned via the `SqlPipe` object, but in the following examples, the results are returned differently. Output parameters typically should be returned as an output parameter, using a by-reference variable, or using the `SqlDataRecord` object.

The `SqlDataRecord`, as explained previously, allows the return of a single row of data. While that may seem a bit limited, this method provides the capability to manipulate the data and the way the results are returned to the client prior to returning the data to the client.

For the examples in this chapter, create a directory called `Chapter22` as a subdirectory to the `C:\Wrox` directory as you have done with previous chapters.

ByRef Output Parameter

You can pass arguments into procedures in Visual Basic *by value* (ByVal) or *by reference* (ByRef). By reference means that that the value of the argument passed in to the procedure can be changed within the procedure and returned to the process that called the procedure. The process does not change for CLR routines.

For this example, the results are returned via an output parameter on the stored procedure call via a ByRef variable in the assembly method. Open a text editor, type in the following code, and save it as `C:\Wrox\Chapter22\GetProductInfoParam.vb`:

```
Imports System
Imports System.Data
Imports Microsoft.SqlServer.Server
Imports System.Data.SqlTypes
Imports System.Data.SqlClient

Public Class GetProductsProc
  Public Shared Sub GetProducts(ByVal ProductID As Integer, ByRef ProdName As
String)
    Dim conn as SqlConnection = New SqlConnection("context connection = True")
    conn.Open()
    Dim cmd As SqlCommand = New SqlCommand("SELECT Name, FROM " & _
"Production.Product WHERE ProductID = " & Convert.ToString(ProductID), conn)
    Dim rdr As SqlDataReader = cmd.ExecuteReader
    SqlContext.Pipe.Send(rdr)

    If rdr.HasRows = True Then
      rdr.Read()
      ProdName = rdr.Item(0)
    End If

    rdr.Close()
    conn.Close
  End Sub
End Class
```

This code should look very similar to the code from the last chapter. The difference this time is that there are two arguments being passed to the sub. One is `ByVal`, which is the value of the ProductID; and the other is `ByRef`, the variable that will be filled with the data being returned.

Next, compile the assembly. Open a command prompt, navigate to the appropriate .NET version directory, and enter the following:

```
Vbc /target:library c:\wrox\chapter22\GetProductInfoParam.vb
```

Once the assembly is built, open a query window in SQL Server Management Studio and execute the following (making sure that the AdventureWorks database is selected), which creates the reference in SQL Server to the physical assembly:

```
CREATE ASSEMBLY GetProductOutParam
FROM 'c:\wrox\chapter22\GetProductInfoParam.dll'
WITH PERMISSION_SET = SAFE
GO
```

The next step is to create the stored procedure. This should seem very familiar since this is a lot like the examples in the last chapter. The difference is that, as illustrated in the following code, the creation of the stored procedure now takes an output variable into which the return value is passed:

```
CREATE PROCEDURE GetProductInfoOutput
@ProductID int,
@ProductName nvarchar(50) OUTPUT
AS
EXTERNAL NAME GetProductOutParam.GetProductsProc.GetProducts
GO
```

To be able to view the returned value, you declare a variable, as shown in the following code, which is passed to the stored procedure and filled with the returned data from the assembly. The `PRINT` statement then prints the returned value to the query window:

```
DECLARE @ProductName nvarchar(50)
EXEC GetProductInfoOutput 942, @ProductName
PRINT @ProductName
GO
```

After executing the code, you should see results similar to those shown in Figure 22-1.

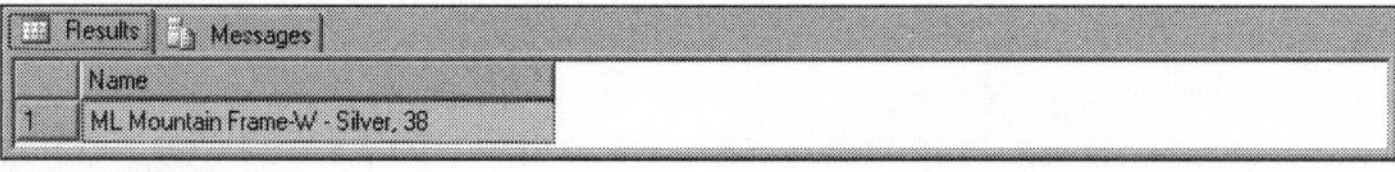

Figure 22-1

This example returned a single value via the `ByRef` parameter, but if needed to you could return results using multiple `ByRef` values. This works if you're returning a small handful of values. The more appropriate method, especially if you need to return a large number of columns, is the `SqlDataRecord` object, described in the next section.

Returning Results via SqlDataRecord

The `SqlDataRecord` object is very handy when your goal is to customize the way the results are returned to the client. This object, together with the `SqlMetaData` object, returns a tabular, single row of data in the order you specify. The `SqlMetaData` object is basically an array of the columns that are then added to the `SqlDataRecord` object. The following example uses the `SqlMetaData` object to build the array of columns with the associated data, which is then passed to the `SqlDataRecord` object for the building of the single row.

For this example, create a new document and type in the following code, saving it as GetProductInfoSDR.vb:

```
Imports System
Imports System.Data
Imports Microsoft.SqlServer.Server
Imports System.Data.SqlTypes
Imports System.Data.SqlClient
Imports System.IO

Public Class GetProductsProc
  Public Shared Sub GetProducts(ByVal ProductID As Integer)
    Dim conn As SqlConnection = New SqlConnection("context connection=true")
    conn.open()
    Dim cmd As SqlCommand = New SqlCommand("Select Name, ProductNumber, Color,
Class FROM Production.Product WHERE ProductID = " & ProductID, conn)
    Dim rdr As SqlDataReader = cmd.ExecuteReader
    SqlContext.Pipe.Send(rdr)

    If rdr.HasRows = True Then
      rdr.Read()
      Dim md As SqlMetaData = New SqlMetaData("Name", SqlDbType.NVarChar, 50)
      md = New SqlMetaData("ProductNumber", SqlDbType.NVarChar, 25)
      md = New SqlMetaData("Color", SqlDbType.NVarChar, 15)
      md = New SqlMetaData("Class", SqlDbType.NVarChar, 2)

      Dim rec As SqlDataRecord = New SqlDataRecord(md)

      rec.SetSqlString(0, rdr.Item(0))
      rec.SetSqlString(1, rdr.Item(1))
      rec.SetSqlString(2, rdr.Item(2))
      rec.SetSqlString(3, rdr.Item(3))

      'send it
      SqlContext.Pipe.Send(rec)

     End If

    rdr.Close()
    conn.Close()

  End Sub
End Class
```

Using the `SqlDataRecord` requires a few steps as shown in the code. First, like all the other examples, the data is returned via the `SqlDataReader`. However, what follows after that is somewhat tricky. First, you create the `SqlMetaData` object so that the desired number of columns can be created, passing the name of the desired column and corresponding data type.

Next, you create the `SqlDataRecord`, passing the array of columns in the `SqlMetaData` object. This tells the `SqlDataRecord` how many columns the single row needs to contain. The final step is to fill the columns with the desired data. In this example, all of the columns were of `String` type, so the `SetSqlString` property was used to set the values for each of the `NVarChar` columns.

Once the row is populated, it can be returned to the client via the `Pipe` object.

In order to test this example, compile the assembly prior to creating the assembly reference in SQL Server. The following code creates the assembly reference for the recently created assembly:

```
CREATE ASSEMBLY GetProductSDR
FROM 'c:\wrox\chapter22\GetProductInfoSDR.dll'
WITH PERMISSION_SET = SAFE
GO
```

Next create the procedure:

```
CREATE PROCEDURE GetProductInfoSDR
@ProductID int
AS
EXTERNAL NAME GetProductSDR.GetProductsProc.GetProducts
GO
```

Finally, call the stored procedure. You can pick any ProductID to try it out. This example uses ProductID 942:

```
EXEC GetProductInfoSDR 942
GO
```

Figure 22-2 shows the results returned from the stored procedure call.

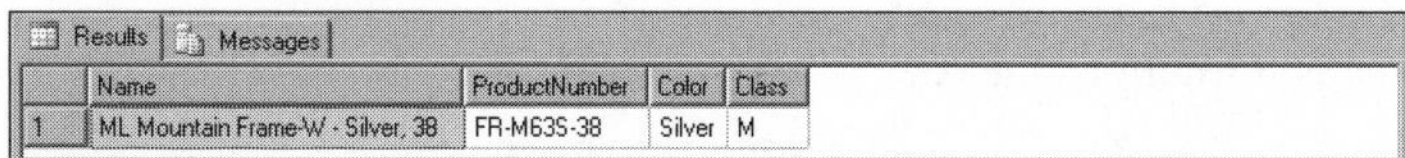

Figure 22-2

Once you have done this a few times, you begin to grasp the potential that this functionality provides, and really, this is just scratching the surface.

User-Defined Triggers

A *trigger* is a type of stored procedure that automatically fires when certain events happen, such as inserting, updating, or deleting data in a table. T-SQL triggers have the unique capability to determine the specific column from a table or view that fired the trigger. In addition, triggers have access to SQL

Server tables (specifically the INSERTED and DELETED tables) not accessible to other SQL Server objects such as normal stored procedures.

CLR triggers are in many ways similar to T-SQL triggers with a few differences. A CLR trigger can reference the data in the INSERTED and DELETED tables just like normal T-SQL triggers, but their method of determining which column fired the trigger is done as the result of an UPDATE operation. CLR triggers also have the capability to obtain information about database objects that were immediately affected by the result of a DDL statement.

The following illustrates the syntax for creating the trigger in SQL Server 2005:

```
CREATE TRIGGER trigger_name
ON table_name
FOR operation
AS
EXTERNAL NAME external_name
```

trigger_name is the name of the trigger. table_name is the name of table or view that the trigger is executed against. operation specifies the type of data modification statement that will fire the trigger. The available values for this are INSERT, UPDATE, and DELETE. external_name is the name of the assembly, and associated method, that will be bound to the trigger. The method cannot accept arguments and it cannot return a void.

How does the trigger know what type of action to perform? These are inherent capabilities provided by the SQlTriggerContext class, which is discussed next.

SqlTriggerContext Class

The SqlTriggerContext class, also new to version 2.0 of the .NET Framework, provides information about the corresponding trigger such as the type of trigger action that was fired (insert, update, or delete) and what modifications or changes were made to the corresponding table.

This class is not publicly available and can only be accessed from within the firing CLR trigger. It also can only be accessed from calling SqlContext.TriggerContext once inside the body of the CLR trigger.

In the previous trigger example, the type of trigger action was obtained from the SqlContext by calling the TriggerContext method, as follows:

```
Dim triggContext As SqlTriggerContext = SqlContext.TriggerContext
Select Case triggContext.TriggerAction
  Case TriggerAction.Insert
End Select
```

Once you have the SqlTriggerContext you can easily determine the action type that resulted in the firing of the trigger. The TriggerAction property of the SqlTriggerContext provides this information.

The following sections demonstrate how to insert, update, and delete data using the SqlTriggerContext class, beginning with INSERT.

INSERT

The example in this section demonstrates using a CLR trigger on an `INSERT` operation.

All of the trigger examples use three new tables that you will create shortly. The background behind these examples utilizes the motorcycle industry and the sport of motocross. The first table is the Manufacturer table, which holds all of the major motorcycle manufacturers that participate in the sport of motocross. The second table is the Riders table, which holds the names of the riders for the team or manufacturer for which they race. The third table is the WinBonus table. Each team pays the riders a base salary, as well as a bonus for each win. The WinBonus table holds the bonus amount for each win, per rider.

The following T-SQL creates the necessary tables and populates the Manufacturers table with the appropriate manufacturers:

```
CREATE TABLE [dbo].[Manufacturer](
  [ManufacturerID] [int] IDENTITY(1,1) NOT NULL,
  [ManufacturerName] [nvarchar](50) COLLATE SQL_Latin1_General_CP1_CI_AS NOT NULL,
  [ModifyDateTime] [datetime] NOT NULL CONSTRAINT [DF_Manufacturer_ModifyDateTime]
DEFAULT (getdate()),
 CONSTRAINT [PK_Manufacturer] PRIMARY KEY CLUSTERED
(
  [ManufacturerID] ASC
) ON [PRIMARY]
) ON [PRIMARY]

INSERT INTO Manufacturer (ManufacturerName) VALUES ('Yamaha')
GO
INSERT INTO Manufacturer (ManufacturerName) VALUES ('Honda')
GO
INSERT INTO Manufacturer (ManufacturerName) VALUES ('Suzuki')
GO
INSERT INTO Manufacturer (ManufacturerName) VALUES ('Kawasaki')
GO

CREATE TABLE [dbo].[Rider](
  [RiderID] [int] IDENTITY(1,1) NOT NULL,
  [ManufacturerID] INT NOT NULL,
  [RiderName] [nvarchar](50) COLLATE SQL_Latin1_General_CP1_CI_AS NOT NULL,
  [ModifyDateTime] [datetime] NOT NULL CONSTRAINT [DF_Rider_ModifyDateTime]
DEFAULT (getdate()),
 CONSTRAINT [PK_Rider] PRIMARY KEY CLUSTERED
(
  [RiderID] ASC
) ON [PRIMARY]
) ON [PRIMARY]

ALTER TABLE [dbo].[Rider]  WITH CHECK ADD  CONSTRAINT
[FK_Manufacturer_Rider_ManufacturerID] FOREIGN KEY([ManufacturerID])
REFERENCES [dbo].[Manufacturer] ([ManufacturerID])
GO

CREATE TABLE [dbo].[WinBonus](
  [WinBonusID] [int] IDENTITY(1,1) NOT NULL,
```

```
   [ManufacturerID] INT NOT NULL,
   [RiderID] INT NOT NULL,
   [Amount] INT NOT NULL,
   [ModifyDateTime] [datetime] NOT NULL CONSTRAINT [DF_WinBonus_ModifyDateTime]
DEFAULT (getdate()),
 CONSTRAINT [PK_WinBonus] PRIMARY KEY CLUSTERED
(
   [WinBonusID] ASC
) ON [PRIMARY]
) ON [PRIMARY]
```

Now that the infrastructure is in place, the first example inserts a record into the Riders table. When you insert a record, the requirements state that you must also insert a corresponding record into the WinBonus table for the given manufacturer and rider, along with the appropriate bonus amount.

The first step is to create the CLR trigger assembly. In a new document, enter the following code, saving it as UpdateRiderInfo.vb:

```
Imports System
Imports System.Data
Imports Microsoft.SqlServer.Server
Imports System.Data.SqlTypes
Imports System.Data.SqlClient
Imports System.IO

Public Class UpdateRiderTrig
  Public Shared Sub UpdateRider()

    Dim triggContext As SqlTriggerContext = SqlContext.TriggerContext
    Dim conn As SqlConnection = New SqlConnection("context connection = true")
    conn.Open()
    Dim ManufacturerID As Integer
    Dim RiderID As Integer
    Dim RiderName As String
    Dim sqlComm As SqlCommand = conn.CreateCommand()
    Dim sqlP As SqlPipe = SqlContext.Pipe
    Dim rdr As SqlDataReader

    Select Case triggContext.TriggerAction
      Case TriggerAction.Insert
        sqlComm.CommandText = "SELECT * from inserted"
        rdr = sqlComm.ExecuteReader()
        If rdr.HasRows = True Then
          rdr.Read()
          RiderID = rdr.Item(0)
          ManufacturerID = rdr.Item(1)
          RiderName = rdr.Item(2)
          rdr.close()
          Select Case ManufacturerID
            Case 1 'Yamaha
              sqlComm.CommandText = "INSERT INTO WinBonus (ManufacturerID, RiderID,
Amount) " & VALUES (" & ManufacturerID & ", " & RiderID & ", 5000)"
            Case 2 'Honda
              sqlComm.CommandText = "INSERT INTO WinBonus (ManufacturerID, RiderID,
Amount) " & "VALUES (" & ManufacturerID & ", " & RiderID & ", 4000)"
```

```
            Case 3 'Suzuki
              sqlComm.CommandText = "INSERT INTO WinBonus (ManufacturerID, RiderID,
Amount) " & "VALUES (" & ManufacturerID & ", " & RiderID & ", 2000)"
            Case 4 'Kawasaki
        sqlComm.CommandText = "INSERT INTO WinBonus (ManufacturerID, RiderID,
Amount) " & "VALUES (" & ManufacturerID & ", " & RiderID & ", 3000)"
          End Select
          sqlP.Send(sqlComm.CommandText)
          sqlP.ExecuteAndSend(sqlComm)
          sqlP.Send("You inserted: " & RiderName)
        End If

      Case TriggerAction.Update
        'We'll get to this next...

      Case TriggerAction.Delete
        'We'll get to this next...

    End Select

  End Sub

End Class
```

Take a minute and look at the code. The first line in the routine creates the `SqlTriggerContext` class. This is important because it tells the routine what type of operation was just performed. A connection is then made, followed by a `SELECT CASE` statement, which identifies the value of `SqlTriggerContext`. Once inside the appropriate action (in this case, an `INSERT`) the `INSERTED` table is then queried. The `INSERTED` table holds the information about the new record just inserted into the Riders table. Based on that information, the corresponding RiderName, RiderID, and ManufacturerID are obtained. The ManufacturerID is then used to determine, in a `SELECT CASE` statement, the appropriate WinBonus amount. Once that information is gathered, a new record is inserted into the WinBonus table.

You should also take note of two lines of code that return messages back to the client. This is for display purposes only. The first returns the T-SQL `INSERT` statement, and the second returns a generic message letting you know the operation was successful.

As usual, compile the assembly, and then create a SQL reference to it using the following code:

```
CREATE ASSEMBLY UpdateRiderInfoTrigg
FROM 'c:\wrox\chapter22\UpdateRiderInfo.dll'
WITH PERMISSION_SET = SAFE
GO
```

Just like a normal T-SQL trigger, three types of triggers can be created based on the assembly. In this example, an `INSERT` trigger is created on the Rider table using the following T-SQL code. The difference is that an extra clause is added at the end, which references the CLR trigger assembly:

```
CREATE TRIGGER I_RiderInfo
ON Rider
FOR INSERT
AS
EXTERNAL NAME UpdateRiderInfoTrigg.UpdateRiderTrig.UpdateRider
GO
```

The final step is to add a record to the Rider table. In a query window, execute the following INSERT statement on the Rider table:

```
INSERT INTO Rider (ManufacturerID, RiderName) VALUES (1, 'Chad Reed')
GO
```

When the statement executes successfully, you should see results in the result window that indicate one row was successfully inserted into the Rider table and one row was successfully inserted into the WinBonus table (see Figure 22-3). The extra comments, as explained earlier, are for display purposes.

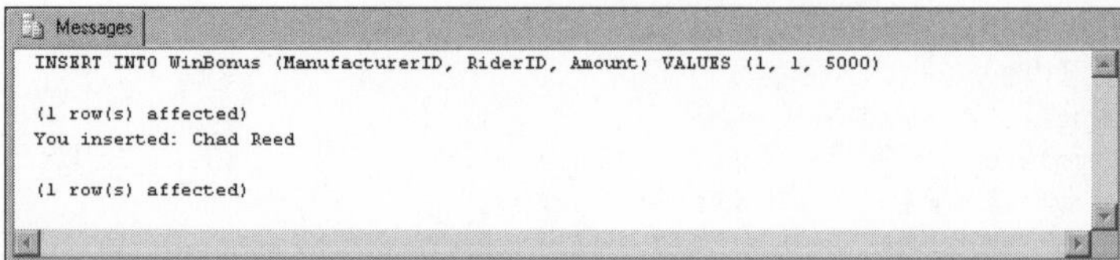

Figure 22-3

For verification, Figure 22-4 shows the results of querying the Rider and WinBonus tables.

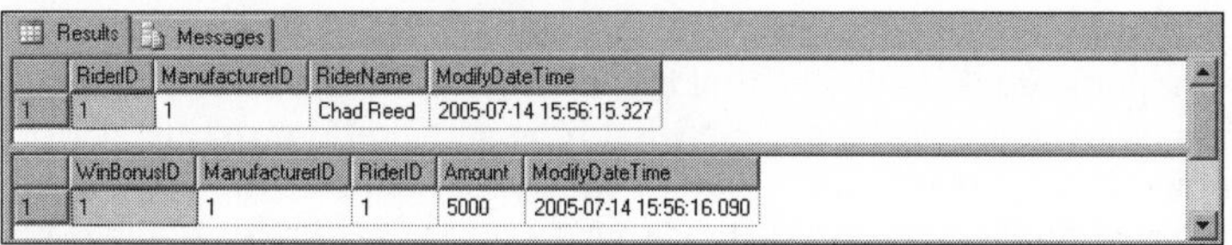

	RiderID	ManufacturerID	RiderName	ModifyDateTime
1	1	1	Chad Reed	2005-07-14 15:56:15.327

	WinBonusID	ManufacturerID	RiderID	Amount	ModifyDateTime
1	1	1	1	5000	2005-07-14 15:56:16.090

Figure 22-4

One of the things you might run into is the fact that a CLR trigger cannot stop an INSERT operation. For example, the code inside the INSERT portion of the preceding code cannot prevent the INSERT into the Rider table from taking place.

DELETE

The next example builds on the previous example, and takes into account a DELETE operation. When a rider is deleted, the corresponding WinBonus data also needs to be removed. This example illustrates how that is accomplished.

For the sake of extra data, add a second row:

```
INSERT INTO Rider (ManufacturerID, RiderName) VALUES (3, 'Ricky Carmichael')
GO
```

Since the same assembly is being used, the current trigger, assembly, and reference need to be deleted:

```
DROP TRIGGER I_RiderInfo
GO
DROP ASSEMBLY UpdateRiderInfoTrigg
GO
```

Modify the assembly code as follows, adding the DELETE portion of the routine:

```
        Case TriggerAction.Update
          'We'll get to this next...

        Case TriggerAction.Delete
          sqlComm.CommandText = "SELECT * from deleted"
          rdr = sqlComm.ExecuteReader()
          If rdr.HasRows = True Then
            rdr.Read()
            RiderID = rdr.Item(0)
            ManufacturerID = rdr.Item(1)
            RiderName = rdr.Item(2)
            rdr.close()
            sqlComm.CommandText = "DELETE FROM WinBonus WHERE RiderID = " & RiderID
            sqlP.Send(sqlComm.CommandText)
            sqlP.ExecuteAndSend(sqlComm)
            sqlP.Send("The following Rider has been deleted: " & RiderName)
          Else
            sqlP.Send("There is no rider by that name.")
          End If
      End Select

    End Sub

  End Class
```

Recompile the assembly, and run the following code to add back the reference and the INSERT trigger:

```
CREATE ASSEMBLY UpdateRiderInfoTrigg
FROM 'c:\wrox\chapter22\UpdateRiderInfo.dll'
WITH PERMISSION_SET = SAFE
GO

CREATE TRIGGER I_RiderInfo
ON Rider
FOR INSERT
AS
EXTERNAL NAME UpdateRiderInfoTrigg.UpdateRiderTrig.UpdateRider
GO
```

Next, you need to add the DELETE trigger. Just like the INSERT trigger, the syntax is the same except for the addition of the EXTERNAL NAME clause at the end, which references the external assembly:

```
CREATE TRIGGER D_RiderInfo
ON Rider
FOR DELETE
AS
EXTERNAL NAME UpdateRiderInfoTrigg.UpdateRiderTrig.UpdateRider
GO
```

If you query the Rider table, you should see two records. The WinBonus table should also have two records. Run the following T-SQL to delete the first row, which should delete Chad Reed:

```
DELETE Rider WHERE RiderID = 1
```

Figure 22-5 shows what the results look like when the execution is finished. The first results indicate that the row in the Rider table has been deleted, and the second results indicate that the WinBonus row has been deleted.

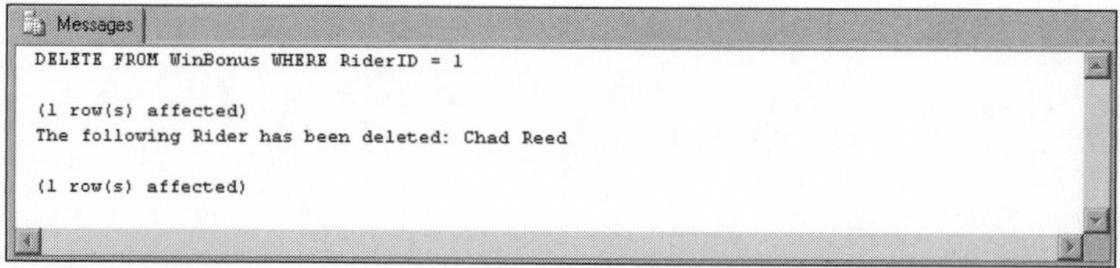

Figure 22-5

A quick query of both Rider and WinBonus tables again shows that the desired rider and corresponding WinBonus record have been deleted (see Figure 22-6).

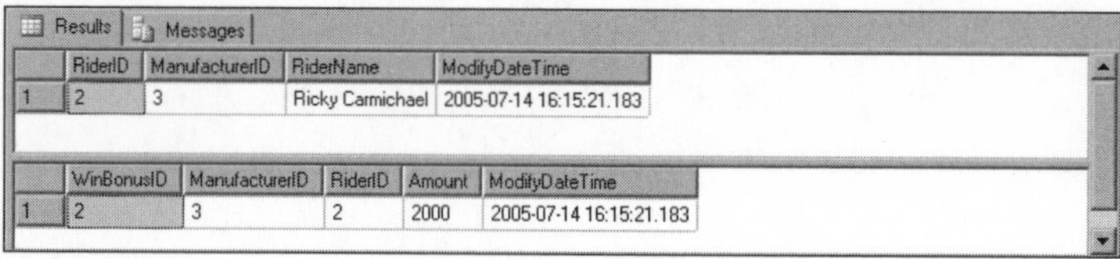

Figure 22-6

Realistically you would have some foreign keys that exist among all three tables to prevent someone deleting a Rider without first deleting the appropriate WinBonus rows.

UPDATE

The `UPATE` operation works the same way as `INSERT` and `DELETE`. In the next example, when a Rider record is updated the corresponding WinBonus record needs to be updated as well. For example, if a rider changes teams, the WinBonus for the new team most likely will not be the same as the previous team.

This example assumes that four riders exist in the Rider table. For simplicity's sake, start with a clean Rider table and insert four new records:

```
DELETE FROM RIDER
GO
INSERT INTO Rider (ManufacturerID, RiderName) VALUES (1, 'Chad Reed')
GO
INSERT INTO Rider (ManufacturerID, RiderName) VALUES (2, 'Kevin Windham')
GO
INSERT INTO Rider (ManufacturerID, RiderName) VALUES (3, 'Ricky Carmichael')
GO
INSERT INTO Rider (ManufacturerID, RiderName) VALUES (3, 'James Stewart')
GO
```

Now, for any of you that follow the sport of motocross, you know that James Stewart does not ride for Suzuki. However, for this example, he does. Don't worry, though; by the end of this example he will be on the correct team.

The first step is to modify the assembly routine to add the `UPDATE` logic. Add the following code:

```
            sqlP.Send("You inserted: " & RiderName)
          End If
      Case TriggerAction.Update
        sqlComm.CommandText = "SELECT * from inserted"
        rdr = sqlComm.ExecuteReader()
          If rdr.HasRows = True Then
            rdr.Read()
            RiderID = rdr.Item(0)
            ManufacturerID = rdr.Item(1)
            RiderName = rdr.Item(2)
            rdr.close()
            Select Case ManufacturerID
              Case 1 'Yamaha
                sqlComm.CommandText = "UPDATE WinBonus SET ManufacturerID = " &
ManufacturerID & ", Amount = 5000 WHERE RiderID = " & RiderID
              Case 2 'Honda
                sqlComm.CommandText = "UPDATE WinBonus SET ManufacturerID = " &
ManufacturerID & ", Amount = 4000 WHERE RiderID = " & RiderID
              Case 3 'Suzuki
                sqlComm.CommandText = "UPDATE WinBonus SET ManufacturerID = " &
ManufacturerID & ", Amount = 2000 WHERE RiderID = " & RiderID
              Case 4 'Kawasaki
                sqlComm.CommandText = "UPDATE WinBonus SET ManufacturerID = " &
ManufacturerID & ", Amount = 3000 WHERE RiderID = " & RiderID
            End Select
            sqlP.Send(sqlComm.CommandText)
            sqlP.ExecuteAndSend(sqlComm)
            sqlP.Send("Rider and Win Bonus Information has been updated for : " &
RiderName)
          End If
        Case TriggerAction.Delete
          sqlComm.CommandText = "SELECT * from deleted"
```

Upon examination, this code looks very similar to the `INSERT` code except that instead of inserting records into the WinBonus table, the code is updating the necessary record based on the ManufacturerID and RiderID.

Since the same assembly is being used, you need to delete the current trigger, assembly, and reference:

```
DROP TRIGGER I_RiderInfo
GO
DROP TRIGGER D_RiderInfo
GO
DROP ASSEMBLY UpdateRiderInfoTrigg
GO
```

Now put everything back. Again, be sure to recompile the assembly first:

```
CREATE ASSEMBLY UpdateRiderInfoTrigg
FROM 'c:\wrox\chapter22\UpdateRiderInfo.dll'
WITH PERMISSION_SET = SAFE
GO
CREATE TRIGGER I_RiderInfo
ON Rider
FOR INSERT
AS
EXTERNAL NAME UpdateRiderInfoTrigg.UpdateRiderTrig.UpdateRider
GO
CREATE TRIGGER D_RiderInfo
ON Rider
FOR DELETE
AS
EXTERNAL NAME UpdateRiderInfoTrigg.UpdateRiderTrig.UpdateRider
GO
```

Next, create the `UPDATE` trigger:

```
CREATE TRIGGER U_RiderInfo
ON Rider
FOR UPDATE
AS
EXTERNAL NAME UpdateRiderInfoTrigg.UpdateRiderTrig.UpdateRider
GO
```

Before you test the `UPDATE` trigger, query the Rider and WinBonus tables to verify that the data is indeed incorrect. James Stewart should have a ManufacturerID of 3 (Team Suzuki) and the goal is to change that to his correct team, Team Kawasaki (ManufacturerID 4) so that the correct WinBonus is paid.

Figure 22-7 shows the "before" image.

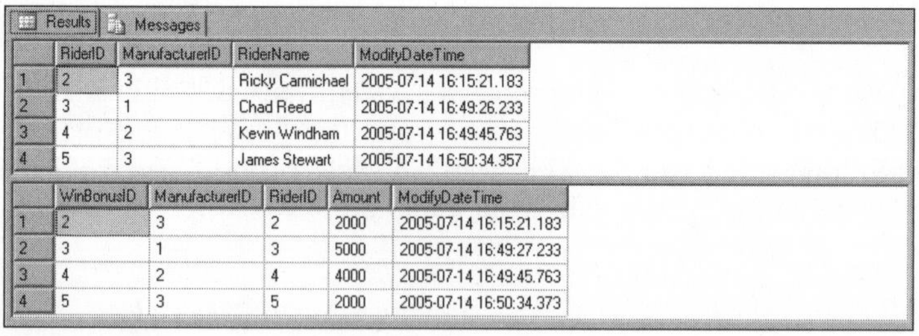

Results | Messages

	RiderID	ManufacturerID	RiderName	ModifyDateTime
1	2	3	Ricky Carmichael	2005-07-14 16:15:21.183
2	3	1	Chad Reed	2005-07-14 16:49:26.233
3	4	2	Kevin Windham	2005-07-14 16:49:45.763
4	5	3	James Stewart	2005-07-14 16:50:34.357

	WinBonusID	ManufacturerID	RiderID	Amount	ModifyDateTime
1	2	3	2	2000	2005-07-14 16:15:21.183
2	3	1	3	5000	2005-07-14 16:49:27.233
3	4	2	4	4000	2005-07-14 16:49:45.763
4	5	3	5	2000	2005-07-14 16:50:34.373

Figure 22-7

Before executing the following T-SQL, make sure that the RiderID for James Stewart is correct—in this example it is 5, but in your table it possibly could be 4:

```
UPDATE Rider SET ManufacturerID = 4 WHERE RiderID = 5
GO
```

Figure 22-8 shows the results of the `UPDATE` statement. As before, the first results illustrate that the update to the Rider table was successful, and the second results show that the `UPDATE` to the WinBonus table was successful.

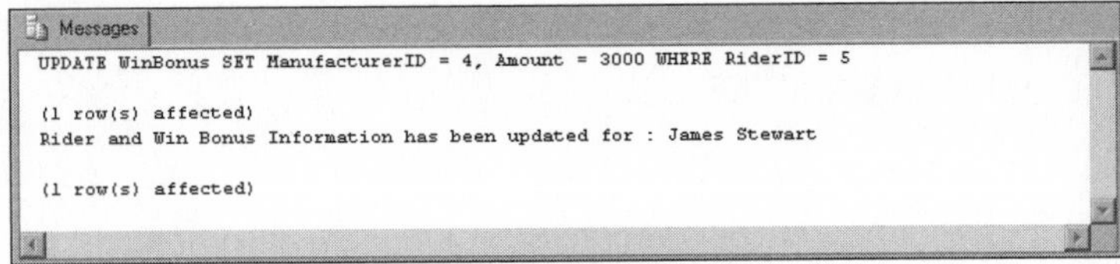

Figure 22-8

For verification, re-query the Rider and WinBonus tables. Figure 22-9 shows the correct data after the `UPDATE` statement execution.

Results | Messages

	RiderID	ManufacturerID	RiderName	ModifyDateTime
1	2	3	Ricky Carmichael	2005-07-14 16:15:21.183
2	3	1	Chad Reed	2005-07-14 16:49:26.233
3	4	2	Kevin Windham	2005-07-14 16:49:45.763
4	5	4	James Stewart	2005-07-14 16:50:34.357

	WinBonusID	ManufacturerID	RiderID	Amount	ModifyDateTime
1	2	3	2	2000	2005-07-14 16:15:21.183
2	3	1	3	5000	2005-07-14 16:49:27.233
3	4	2	4	4000	2005-07-14 16:49:45.763
4	5	4	5	3000	2005-07-14 16:50:34.373

Figure 22-9

In these examples, all the code for the `INSERT`, `UPDATE`, and `DELETE` operations were combined into a single assembly and routine. There is nothing preventing you from separating out the logic into different assemblies, or even separate routines in the same assembly. The purpose of these examples was to illustrate the possibilities and capabilities that the integration of .NET Framework CLR provides in SQL Server 2005 and CLR triggers.

That wasn't so hard was it? Actually, think about it. In reality you wouldn't use this to send a message back saying, "Hey, you just updated this record," but you would use it to perform tasks that the CLR is good at. For example, since you have access to the `INSERTED` and `UDPATED` records, you could use a CLR trigger to do data validation or data comparison work.

For ambitious readers, your homework assignment for this chapter is to modify the `INSERT` *portion of the CLR trigger to prevent multiple inserts of a Rider into the WinBonus table.*

Scalar-Valued UDFs

Scalar-valued UDF's were covered in Chapter 21, so you'll only see a brief discussion and example here. The purpose of scalar-valued functions is to return a single value such as an integer or Boolean (bit) value. It can even return a single string value.

This example queries the Rider table for the rider name and returns it using a scalar-valued UDF. First, enter the following code in a new text document and save it as `C:\Wrox\Chapter22\GetRiderBonusInfo.vb`:

```
Imports System
Imports System.Data
Imports Microsoft.SqlServer.Server
Imports System.Data.SqlTypes
Imports System.Data.SqlClient
Imports System.IO

Public Class GetRiderFunc
  <Microsoft.SqlServer.Server.SqlFunction(DataAccess:=DataAccessKind.Read)>
  Public Shared Function GetRider(ByVal ManufacturerID As Integer) As Integer

    Dim conn As SqlConnection = New SqlConnection("context connection=True")
    conn.open()

    Dim cmd As sqlcommand = New sqlcommand("SELECT SUM(Amount) FROM Winbonus where
ManufacturerID = " & Convert.ToString(ManufacturerID), conn)

    Return CInt(cmd.ExecuteScalar())

    Conn.close()

  End Function

End Class
```

This code should look no different from that of Chapter 21. Because they can return only a single value, UDFs are useful when needing to do computations such as a sum or count. This example sums the win bonuses for a particular manufacturer, so a UDF is perfect for this type of computation.

As with the previous examples, create and compile the assembly reference:

```
CREATE ASSEMBLY RiderBonus
FROM 'c:\wrox\chapter22\GetRiderBonusInfo.dll'
WITH PERMISSION_SET = SAFE
GO
```

The next step is to create the SQL Server function. This assembly takes a parameter and returns a value, so the function needs to reflect that when it is created, as shown in the following code:

```
CREATE FUNCTION GetRiderBonus(@ManufacturerID int)
RETURNS INT
AS EXTERNAL NAME RiderBonus.GetRiderFunc.GetRider
GO
```

Execute the function to return the results and be sure to pass a value for the parameter that the assembly expects. This example passes the value of ManufacturerID of 1:

```
SELECT dbo.GetRiderBonus(1)
```

Figure 22-10 shows the results of the function.

Figure 22-10

If you're interested in seeing an example of a table-valued user-defined function, head to `www.wrox.com` *and find this book's dedicated page.*

The Easy Way

As promised, this section will show you how to create the CLR triggers and UDFs used in this chapter and Chapter 21.

Start Visual Studio 2005 and create a new project. In the New Project dialog, expand either the Visual Basic or Visual C# project type. Under each language node is a Database option. Click the Database option for your preferred language. On the right side, under Templates, is displayed a list of database project templates. Select SQL Server Project, give the project a name (as shown in Figure 22-11), and click OK. After that, follow these steps:

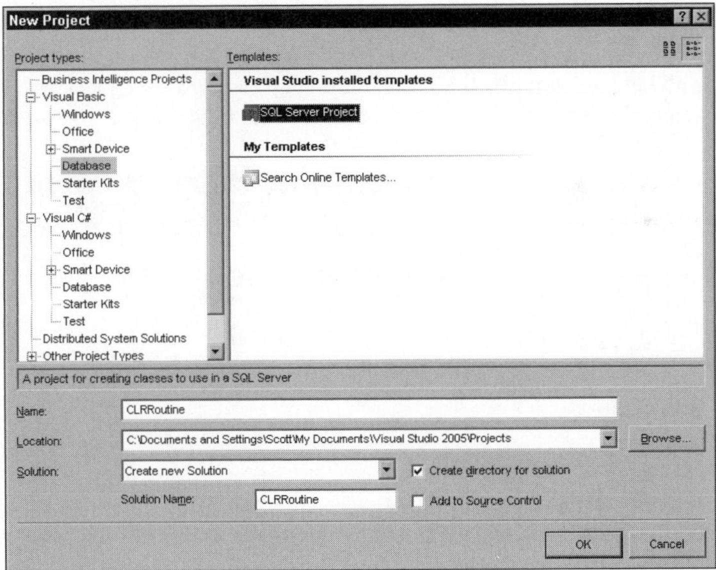

Figure 22-11

1. Visual Studio needs to know which database you will be working with, so it opens a Database Reference dialog for you to either pick an existing database reference or to create a new one. If you have already created one, select it from the list. Otherwise, click the Add New Reference button, which opens a dialog for you to enter the database connection information (see Figure 22-12).

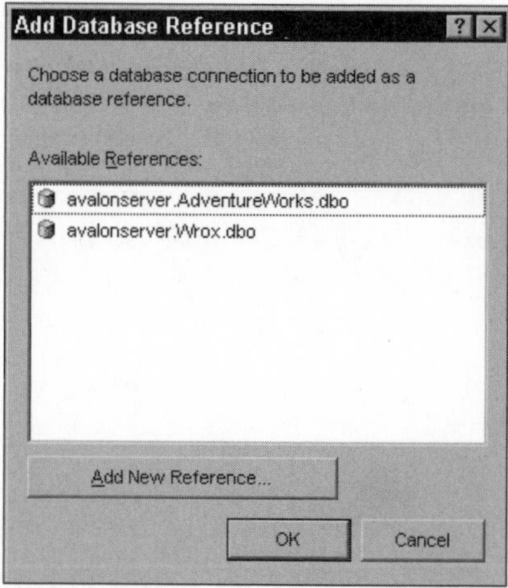

Figure 22-12

2. After you have selected your database reference, an empty database project is created. At this point you can select which type of CLR object you need to create. In the Solution Explorer for your project, right-click the project name and select Add from the context menu. Underneath the Add menu, select New Item. This opens the Add New Item dialog shown in Figure 22-13.

   In this dialog you have the option of selecting which type of CLR object you wish to create, and they are all here. As you can see in the figure, you can create a CLR Stored Procedure, CLR User-Defined Function, CLR Trigger, and other CLR templates.

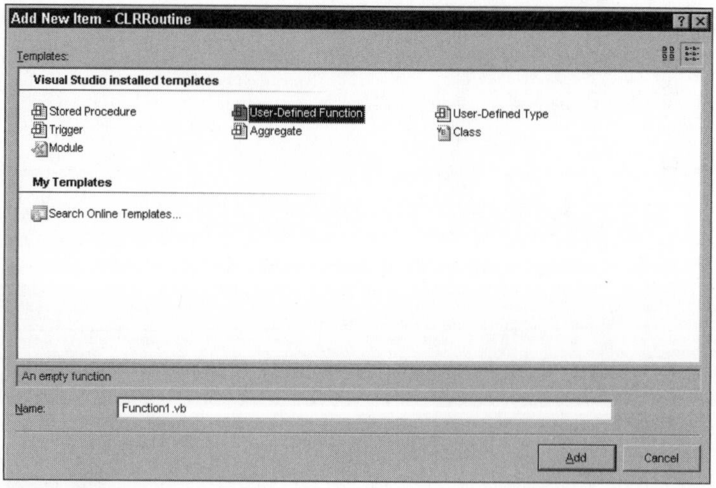

Figure 22-13

3. Select User-Defined Function and click OK. Visual Studio creates the User-Defined Function with all of the necessary code, as shown in Figure 22-14. All that is left is to put your specific code in where it says "Add your code here."

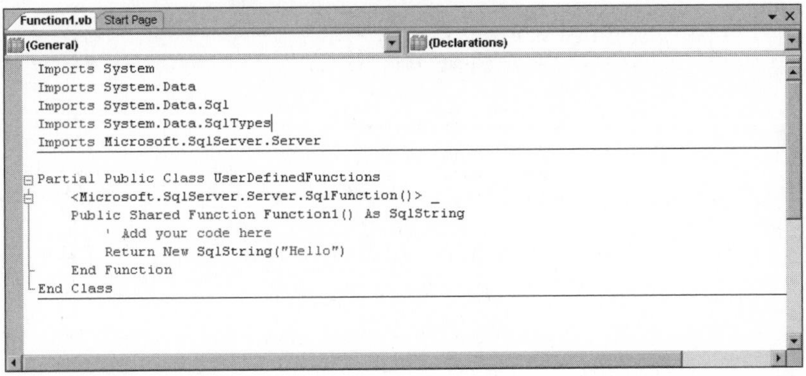
Function1.vb
Start Page
(General)
(Declarations)
Imports System
Imports System.Data
Imports System.Data.Sql
Imports System.Data.SqlTypes
Imports Microsoft.SqlServer.Server
Partial Public Class UserDefinedFunctions
<Microsoft.SqlServer.Server.SqlFunction()> _
Public Shared Function Function1() As SqlString
' Add your code here
Return New SqlString("Hello")
End Function
End Class

Figure 22-14

4. Figure 22-15 shows what a Visual Studio–generated CLR Trigger looks like. You need to un-remark the line directly above Public Shared Sub line and fill in the appropriate information. For example, in the figure, the `Target:` attribute points to Table1. Unless you have a table named Table1, this won't work, so you need to replace that with the appropriate table, as well as the appropriate event in the `Event` attribute and the `Name` attribute.

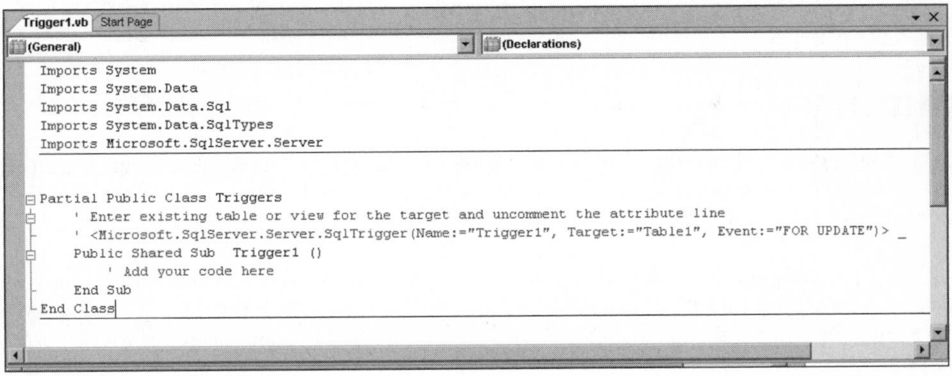
Trigger1.vb
Start Page
(General)
(Declarations)
Imports System
Imports System.Data
Imports System.Data.Sql
Imports System.Data.SqlTypes
Imports Microsoft.SqlServer.Server
Partial Public Class Triggers
' Enter existing table or view for the target and uncomment the attribute line
' <Microsoft.SqlServer.Server.SqlTrigger(Name:="Trigger1", Target:="Table1", Event:="FOR UPDATE")> _
Public Shared Sub Trigger1 ()
' Add your code here
End Sub
End Class

Figure 22-15

5. Remember all of that DOS prompt command code and T-SQL assembly code you had to do? Well, you don't need to do that here. Once you have saved and compiled the project successfully, the only thing you need to do is select Deploy from the Build menu in Visual Studio, as shown in Figure 22-16. This process creates the assembly DLL and creates the assembly in SQL Server. The only thing you need to do is to issue the `CREATE PROCEDURE` or `CREATE TRIGGER` statement depending on which type of CLR object you created.

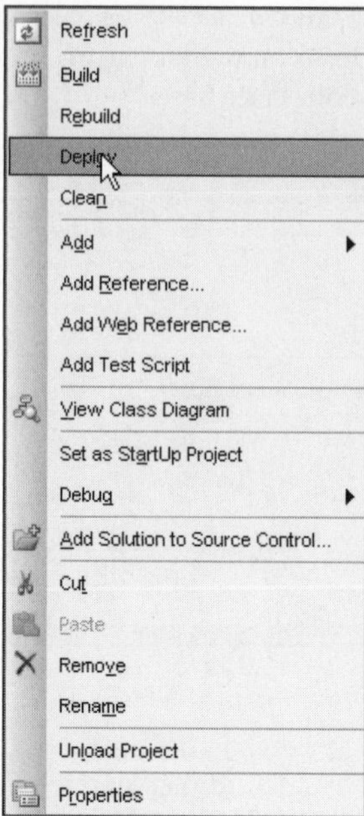

Figure 22-16

Pretty simple and efficient. After you have used the database templates you will have a hard time going back to the command prompt method.

Summary

This chapter focused on building different database objects using Common Language Runtime (CLR). These objects compile into managed code, which is then used from within an instance of SQL Server. CLR routines are managed code that runs from within an instance of Microsoft SQL Server.

There are a few different types of CLR routines such as user-defined procedures, user-defined triggers, and user-defined functions (both scalar-valued and table-valued). CLR routines provide a powerful and robust programming model that enables improved security and in some cases improved performance over its T-SQL equivalent.

This chapter focused on the different types of CLR routines and table-valued versus scalar-valued user-defined functions. This chapter also spent quite a bit of time discussing the different types of user-defined triggers such as `INSERT`, `UPDATE`, and `DELETE`, and showed you how to implement them.

From a security perspective, CLR routines are no different than the examples you created in Chapter 21. That is because when you create the assembly, just like you did in the last chapter, you have to specify the permission set, which specifies the level of security and permissions given to the assembly.

What about performance? Flip back to the summary section of Chapter 21 and re-read what is says about using CLR assemblies in SQL Server. The same concept applies here. You would not create a CLR trigger to do data reading and writing. But you could use it to add value to the existing T-SQL trigger functionality.

The next chapter discusses ADO.NET 2.0 and some of the new features that have been added that make working with data much more pleasant.

23

ADO.NET

If you were to count all the new features and enhancement made to ADO.NET 2.0, you would need all your fingers and toes, and even with that you would run out of digits. There are a lot. So many, in fact, that there are whole books dedicated to the topic.

A lot of the new ADO.NET 2.0 features require SQL Server 2005 to be able to take advantage of the new SQL Server 2005 features and enhancements. An example of this is support for the new SQL Server 2005 `xml` data type, which is provided by the new classes in the `System.Data.SqlTypes` namespace. Another example is the ability to have multiple result sets active on a single connection, known as MARS.

This chapter highlights and explains these and other new features and enhancements added to ADO.NET 2.0 and provides some examples of how they are used and what benefit they can provide to your application and environment. Specifically, this chapter covers the following topics:

- Dealing with the `xml` data type at the client
- Introduction to asynchronous operations
- Introduction to Multiple Active Result Sets (MARS)
- Using query notifications within your application

xml data type

The vast majority of this book has been dedicated to the new SQL Server 2005 `xml` data type and its related technologies. This new data type is not an afterthought or second-rate data type either; it is a first-rate data type that allows the storage, querying, and modification of XML documents and fragments. With its related methods, the `xml` data type integrates cleanly and efficiently into the realm of SQL Server.

This section discusses the new and enhanced functionality of ADO.NET 2.0 for the `xml` data type. For the examples in this chapter, you'll use a new Visual Studio 2005 project. Open Visual Studio 2005 and create a new Windows Application. You can give the project name any name that is meaningful to you.

Once the project is created, add a button and two text boxes onto Form1. Set the properties of each control as follows:

Control	Property	Value
Form1	FormBorderStyle	FixedSingle
	Size	513, 241
	StartPosition	CenterScreen
	Text	Chapter23
Button1	Location	12, 12
	Size	75, 34
	Text	XML DT
TextBox1	Name	txtResults
	Location	12, 52
	Multiline	True
	ScrollBars	Vertical
	Size	287, 77
TextBox2	Name	txtResults2
	Location	12, 135
	Multiline	True
	ScrollBars	Vertical
	Size	287, 77

Now add code behind the form. First, add the following `Imports` statements to the declarations section:

```
Imports System.Data
Imports System.Data.SqlClient
Imports System.Data.SqlTypes
Imports System.Data.Sql
Imports Microsoft.SqlServer.Server
```

Next, double-click the button on the form design to bring up the code for the button. Add the following code in the `Click` event of the button:

```
Dim ConnectString As String

ConnectString = "Persist Security Info=False;Server=(local);" & _
```

```
"database=AdventureWorks;Integrated Security=SSPI "

Dim conn As SqlConnection = New SqlConnection(ConnectString)
Dim cmd As SqlCommand = New SqlCommand

Try
  conn.Open()

  cmd.Connection = conn
  cmd.CommandType = CommandType.Text
  cmd.CommandText = "SELECT Name, Instructions FROM Production.ProductModel " & _
  "WHERE ProductModelID = 7"

  Dim rdr As SqlDataReader = cmd.ExecuteReader

  rdr.Read()
  Me.txtResults.Text = rdr.GetDataTypeName(1) & " - " & rdr(1)

  rdr.Close()
  conn.Close()

Catch ex As Exception
  MessageBox.Show(ex.Message.ToString)
End Try
```

Before you run the application, take a look at what the code is doing. Like most of the examples, a connection to the database is established and then a command is executed against the database, in this case, selecting the Name and Instructions columns from the Production.ProductModel table. The Name column is an `nvarchar` data type, but the Instructions column is the new `xml` data type.

This example returns a specific row in which there is an XML document in the Instructions column. When you use the `SqlDataReader` class, the XML is returned as a string even though the `GetDataTypeName` property of the `SqlDataReader` says that it is an `xml` data type.

Figure 23-1 shows the results of the execution of the code. The first part before the dash (-) is the column data type.

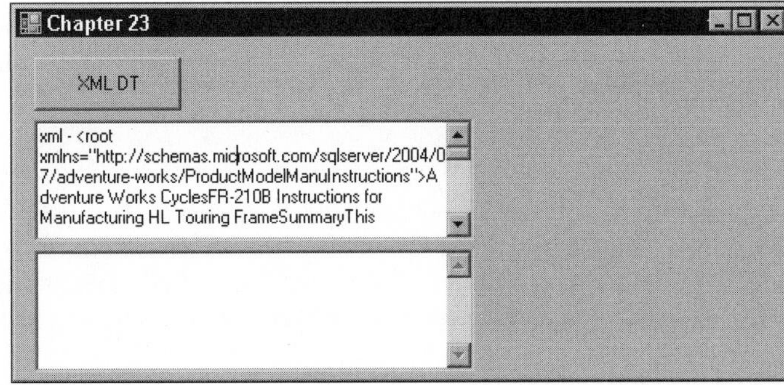

Figure 23-1

To return the value of a specified column as XML, you need to use the `GetSqlXml` method of the `SqlDataReader`. This method is new to version 2.0 of the .NET Framework and resides in the `System.Data.SqlClient` namespace (`System.data.dll`). The trick is that no conversions are performed, so the returned data must already be an XML value.

To return the data as XML, modify the code behind the button as follows:

```
Dim ConnectString As String

ConnectString = "Persist Security Info=False;Server=(local);" & _
"database=AdventureWorks;Integrated Security=SSPI "

Dim conn As SqlConnection = New SqlConnection(ConnectString)
Dim cmd As SqlCommand = New SqlCommand

Try
  conn.Open()

  cmd.Connection = conn
  cmd.CommandType = CommandType.Text
  cmd.CommandText = "SELECT Name, Instructions FROM Production.ProductModel " & _
  "WHERE ProductModelID = 7"

  Dim rdr As SqlDataReader = cmd.ExecuteReader

  rdr.Read()
  Me.txtResults.Text = rdr.GetDataTypeName(1) & " - " & rdr(1)

  Dim sqlx As SqlXml = rdr.GetSqlXml(1)
  Dim xr As XmlReader = sqlx.CreateReader
  xr.Read()
  Me.txtResults2.Text = xr.ReadOuterXml

  rdr.Close()
  conn.Close()

Catch ex As Exception
  MessageBox.Show(ex.Message.ToString)
End Try
```

In your declarations section of the form, add the following reference:

```
IMPORTS System.Xml
```

The example still returns the column as a string using the `SqlDataReader` and populates the first text box as it did before. It then uses the `GetSqlXml` method of the `SqlDataReader` to get the value as XML, which is then handed over to the `SqlXml` class for storage. The `SqlXml` class at this point contains the XML data retrieved from the server, and an `XmlReader` is created to read the XML data.

From there, the XML is read from the `SqlXml` class using the `ReadOuterXML` method of the `XmlReader` class. The results of that read are shown in Figure 23-2.

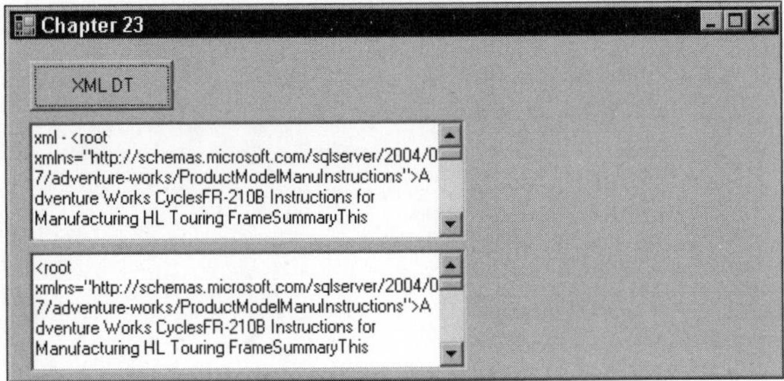

Figure 23-2

The other option is to use the `ExecuteXmlReader` method of the `SqlCommand` object. The caveat to using this method is that it can only be used to return a single row, single column XML result set. If your query returns multiple rows or columns, only the value of the first row is read, the rest is ignored, or basically thrown away. The upside, though, is that it is a quick way to return XML.

The following example illustrates the use of the `ExecuteXmlReader` method. Modify the code behind the button as follows:

```
Dim ConnectString As String

ConnectString = "Persist Security Info=False;Server=(local);" & _
"database=AdventureWorks;Integrated Security=SSPI "

Dim conn As SqlConnection = New SqlConnection(ConnectString)
Dim cmd As SqlCommand = New SqlCommand

Try
  conn.Open()

  cmd.Connection = conn
  cmd.CommandType = CommandType.Text
  cmd.CommandText = "SELECT Instructions FROM Production.ProductModel " & _
  "WHERE ProductModelID = 7"

  Dim xmlr As XmlReader = cmd.ExecuteXmlReader

  xmlr.Read()
  Me.txtResults.Text = xmlr.ReadOuterXml

  xmlr.Close()
  conn.Close()

Catch ex As Exception
  MessageBox.Show(ex.Message.ToString)
End Try
```

This code should be fairly straightforward. The `ExecuteXmlReader` method of the `SqlCommand` object is used to build and return an `XmlReader` object. The `ReadOuterXml` method is then used to read the contents of the XML, including the nodes and all of the children. Figure 23-3 shows the results of the query.

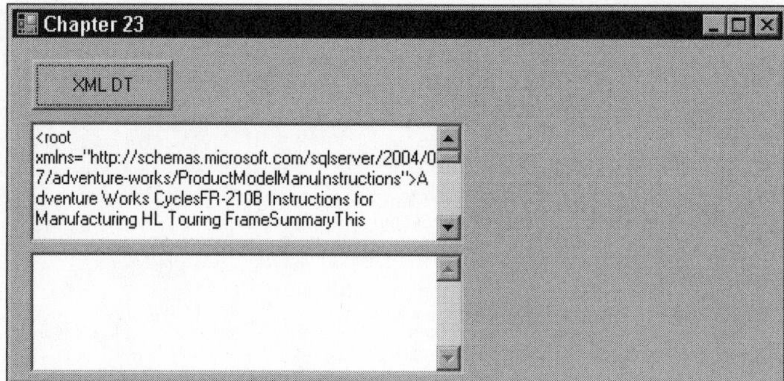

Figure 23-3

Version 2.0 of the .NET Framework has gone a long way to support the `xml` data type and it shows with all of the new classes that are included, such as the `SqlXml` class, which contains an instance of an `XmlReader` and contains XML data retrieved from SQL Server.

The next section introduces you to asynchronous operations.

Asynchronous Operations

Prior to ADO.NET 2.0, when a command was executed the application could not continue until the return of the command was complete. ADO.NET 2.0 solves that by allowing *asynchronous execution,* meaning that a command can be executed and yet the application can still continue processing other code. The key to this is the `Async=True` keywords in the connection string, which tell the connection to allow asynchronous command executions.

For this example, in the project you created earlier in the chapter, set the `Visible` properties of the two text boxes to `False` and then add a second button and two list boxes to the form with the following properties.

Control	Property	Value
`Button2`	`Location`	93, 12
	`Size`	75, 34
	`Text`	`Async Conns`
`ListBox2`	`Location`	12, 52
	`Size`	130, 160
`ListBox3`	`Location`	149, 52
	`Size`	130, 160

Next, add the following code behind `Button2`:

```
Dim ConnectString As String

ConnectString = "Persist Security Info=False;Server=(local); " & _
"database=AdventureWorks;Integrated Security=SSPI;async=true"

Dim conn1 As SqlConnection = New SqlConnection(ConnectString)
Dim conn2 As SqlConnection = New SqlConnection(ConnectString)

Try
  conn1.Open()

  Dim cmd1 As SqlCommand = New SqlCommand("SELECT Name, ProductNumber " & _
  "FROM Production.Product", conn1)
  cmd1.CommandType = CommandType.Text
  Dim Async1 As IAsyncResult = cmd1.BeginExecuteReader

  conn2.Open()

  Dim cmd2 As SqlCommand = New SqlCommand("SELECT ProductDescriptionID, " & _
  " Description FROM Production.ProductDescription", conn2)
  cmd2.CommandType = CommandType.Text
  Dim Async2 As IAsyncResult = cmd2.BeginExecuteReader()

  Dim rdr1 As SqlDataReader = cmd1.EndExecuteReader(Async1)
  Dim rdr2 As SqlDataReader = cmd2.EndExecuteReader(Async2)

  Do While rdr1.Read()
    Me.ListBox2.Items.Add(rdr1.Item(0) & "   " & rdr1.Item(1))
  Loop

  Do While rdr2.Read()
    Me.ListBox3.Items.Add(rdr2.Item(0) & "   " & rdr2.Item(1))
  Loop

  rdr1.Close()
  rdr2.Close()

Catch ex As Exception
  MessageBox.Show(ex.Message.ToString)
Finally
  conn1.Close()
  conn1.Dispose()
  conn2.Close()
  conn2.Dispose()
End Try
```

In this example, two connections are made to the database using the same connection. However, two separate commands are created, each querying different tables and returning different data. The `Begin` method returns an `IAsyncResult` reference, which tracks the state of the operation. This is also done for the second command. You must call the `EndExecuteReader` method to complete the execution of the operation. The results are then returned to the corresponding `SqlDataReader`.

Figure 23-4 shows the results of the query. The Production.Product query (the ListBox on the left) returns 504 rows and the Production.ProductDescription query (the ListBox on the right) returns 762 rows. When the query is run, both list boxes populate simultaneously.

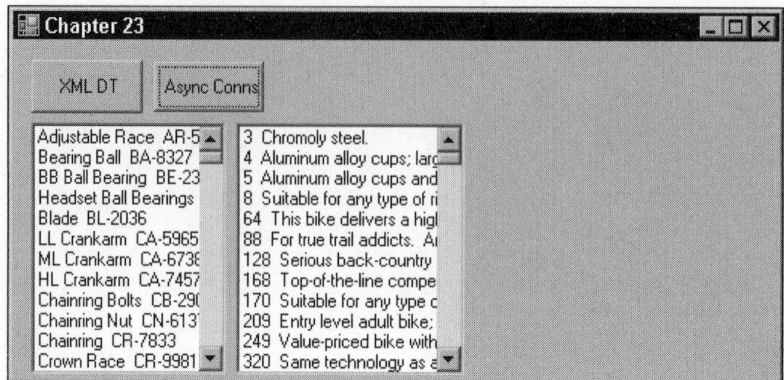

Figure 23-4

To further test this, replace the second command with the execution of a stored procedure instead of in-line T-SQL, as follows:

```
Dim cmd2 As SqlCommand = New SqlCommand("GetProductDescription", conn2)
Cmd2.CommandType = CommandType.StoredProcedure
```

Obviously, you need to create the stored procedure, but that is easy enough. Create a new stored procedure in the AdventureWorks database with the same T-SQL in the previous example.

There are corresponding methods that help with returning XML data: `BeginExecuteXmlReader` and `EndExecuteXmlReader`. The `BeginExecuteXMLReader` object initiates the asynchronous execution of a T-SQL or stored procedure, which returns the results as an `XmlReader` object. The `EndExecuteXmlReader` method finishes the execution and returns the requested XML.

The following code illustrates a simple example of how this is done:

```
Dim cmd1 As SqlCommand = New SqlCommand("SELECT Name, Instructions " & _
"FROM Production.ProductModel FOR XML AUTO, XMLData", conn1)
cmd1.CommandType = CommandType.Text
Dim Async1 As IAsyncResult = cmd1.BeginExecuteXmlReader

Dim xr As XmlReader = cmd1.EndExecuteXmlReader(Async1)
```

In this example, the `BeginExecuteXmlReader` method of the `SqlCommand` class initiates the asynchronous execution of the T-SQL statement. Those results are returned as an `XmlReader` object. The `EncExecuteXmlReader` method is then called to finish the asynchronous execution and return the results as XML.

Your homework assignment for this chapter is to modify the first example in this section to go against two separate databases.

Multiple Active Result Sets

Users of current and versions of ADO.NET and SQL Server are very familiar with this limitation and the "existing DataReader" message shown in Figure 23-5.

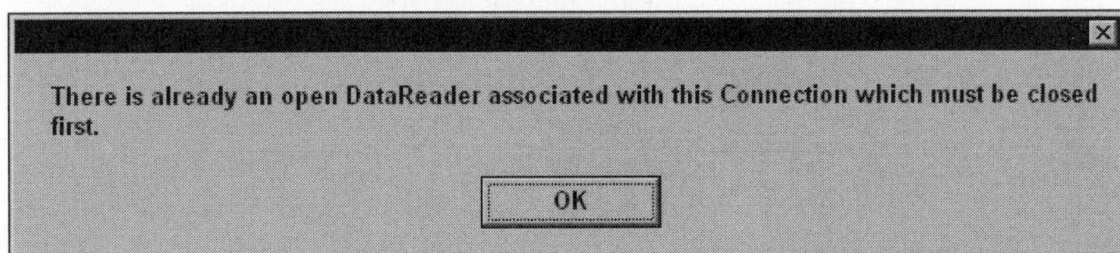
There is already an open DataReader associated with this Connection which must be closed first.
OK

Figure 23-5

The workaround for this problem was to create a whole new connection to the database. It wasn't the best solution, but it worked, and every programmer has either done it or knows someone who has.

New to SQL Server 2005 and ADO.NET 2.0 is the concept of Multiple Active Result Sets (MARS): the ability to have multiple result sets active on the same connection. MARS allow each connection to return results to individual corresponding `SqlDataReader` objects. Those `SqlDataReader` objects can work independently of the other `SqlDataReaders` or work together with the other `SqlDataReaders`. The magic word to active MARS in your application is to add `MultipleActiveResultSets=true` to your connection string. The following example illustrates how to implement MARS with SQL Server 2005 and Visual Studio 2005.

To begin, add one more button (Button4) to the form. Set its `Location` property to 305, 12. Set its `Size` property to 75, 34. Finally, set its `Text` property to `MARS`.

Next, add the following code behind Button4:

```
Dim ConnectString As String

ConnectString = "Data Source=(local);Initial Catalog=AdventureWorks;Integrated
Security=SSPI;MultipleActiveResultSets=true;"

Dim conn As SqlConnection = New SqlConnection(ConnectString)
Dim cmd As SqlCommand = New SqlCommand
Dim cmd2 As SqlCommand = New SqlCommand

Dim ProductModelID As Integer

Try
  conn.Open()

  cmd.Connection = conn
  cmd.CommandType = CommandType.Text
  cmd.CommandText = "SELECT ProductModelID, Name FROM Production.ProductModel" & _
  " ORDER BY ProductModelID"
  Dim rdr As SqlDataReader = cmd.ExecuteReader

  cmd2.Connection = conn
```

```
    cmd2.CommandType = CommandType.Text

    Do While rdr.Read
      ProductModelID = rdr.Item(0)
      Me.ListBox1.Items.Add(rdr.Item(1))
      cmd2.CommandText = "select Name, ProductNumber from production.product" & _
      " WHERE ProductModelID = " & ProductModelID
      Dim rdr2 As SqlDataReader = cmd2.ExecuteReader
      Do While rdr2.Read
        Me.ListBox1.Items.Add("     " & rdr2.Item(0))
      Loop
      rdr2.Close()
    Loop

    rdr.Close()
    conn.Close()

  Catch ex As Exception
    MessageBox.Show(ex.Message.ToString)
  End Try
```

As mentioned earlier the key is to add `MultipleActiveResultSets=true` to your connection string. As in many chapters, the example uses a normal connection string, but to activate MARS in the application the `MultipleActiveResultSets` keyword is used with a value of `True` passed to it.

A connection is then made to the database and two `SqlCommand` objects are created using the same connection to the database. The first `SqlCommand` queries the Production.ProductModel table and then loops through the results. For each record found in the Production.ProductModel table, the second `SqlCommand` queries the Production.Product table for the given ProductModelID. All of this from the same connection on two different `SqlCommands` and `SqlDataReaders`.

Figure 23-6 shows the results as they are written to the list box.

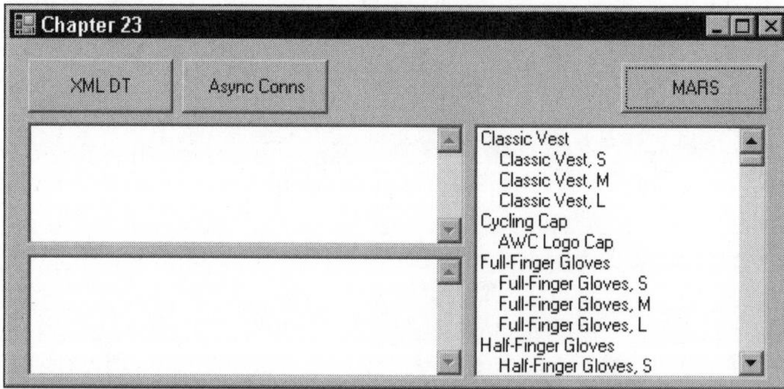

Figure 23-6

In the previous example, you used two T-SQL statements to demonstrate this functionality, but in fact you are not limited to just in-line T-SQL. The first command can use in-line T-SQL while the second command can use a stored procedure. The point is that regardless of the type of execution, multiple results can be returned via the same connection. It is even possible for each command to have more than one statement associated with it, returning multiple result sets per command.

Query Notifications

The concept of query notification, in its simplest terms, means that you can query a table and then be notified of any changes to that table. For example, you might have a table that is frequently updated and you would like other users of the application to see these changes without having to manually re-query to see if there are any changes to the underlying table. With query notifications, this is now possible.

Query notifications work in conjunction with the Service Broker to store and route the messages. Working with Service Broker, messages are stored and then sent to the caller informing them of any changes.

This example requires another button, called `Button5`. Yes, that's a lot of buttons but this way you won't have to modify your code from earlier examples and can use them for future reference. Set `Button5`'s `Location` property to 420, 12; set its `Size` property to 75, 34; and set its `Text` property to `Not. Service`.

The first step is to create a queue for the service to use. The purpose of the queue is to store messages sent by the Service Broker. The Service Broker places the messages in the queue for the appropriate service. Open a query window in SQL Server Management Studio and execute the following T-SQL (which also creates a queue for this example):

```
CREATE QUEUE ProductNotQue
GO
```

The next step is to create a Service Broker service. While this chapter does not go into the fine details of the Service Broker service, in simple terms the Service Broker service uses the name of the service to deliver messages to the appropriate queue in the database. The following example creates a service based on the queue you just created:

```
CREATE SERVICE ProductNotService
ON QUEUE ProductNotQue
([http://schemas.microsoft.com/SQL/Notifications/PostQueryNotification])
GO
```

The URL portion of the `CREATE SERVICE` statement specifies the contract. A contract specifies the message types used by an application to complete a specific task. It also defines an agreement between two services regarding the type of message used to complete a specific task. In the example, the contract used states that all messages of the `QueryNotification` be sent by the initiator of the conversation between the two services.

The next step is to create a `ROUTE`, which determines the routing of the message:

```
CREATE ROUTE ProductRoute
WITH SERVICE_NAME = 'ProductNotService',
ADDRESS = 'local'
GO
```

Now that the framework is in place, type the following code in the click event of Button5:

```
Dim ConnectString As String

ConnectString = "Persist Security Info=False;Server=(local);" & _
```

```
"Database=AdventureWorks;Integrated Security=SSPI;"

Dim conn As SqlConnection = New SqlConnection(ConnectString)

Try
  conn.Open()

  Dim cmd As SqlCommand = New SqlCommand("SELECT Name ProductNumber, Color," & _
  " Class, Style FROM Production.Product WHERE ProductModelID = 15", conn)
  Dim sqlnot As SqlNotificationRequest = New SqlNotificationRequest
  sqlnot.UserData = Guid.NewGuid.ToString

  sqlnot.Options =
"http://localhost/sql/MSSQLSERVER/AdventureWorks/ProductNotService"
  sqlnot.Timeout = 0

  cmd.Notification = sqlnot

  Dim rdr As SqlDataReader = cmd.ExecuteReader

  'Do something with the results
  Me.txtResults.Text = "SUCCESS!"

Catch ex As Exception
  MessageBox.Show(ex.Message.ToString)
Finally
  conn.Close()
End Try
```

As in all the other examples, this block of code starts by establishing a connection and using the `SqlCommand` object to execute some T-SQL. However, the difference here is that before the command is executed and returned to a `SqlDataReader`, a `SqlNotificationRequest` object is created with some properties set. The `Notification` method is then set on the command, which binds the `SqlNotificationRequest` object to the command.

All of this tells the command when it is executed that there could be changes made to the underlying data source and to be listening for those changes.

Just as a note, the other way to bind the `SqlNotificationRequest` object to the command is as follows:

```
Dim NotService As String = "ProductNotService"
cmd.Notification = New SqlNotificationRequest(Guild.NewGuid.ToString(),NotService,
0)
```

Once the query is made, the final step is to query the queue looking for messages that have been sent to the queue by the service. If it finds any changes, appropriate action can be taken to accommodate the changes. The following is a simple example that queries the queue looking for changes:

```
Dim cmd As SqlCommand = New SqlCommand("WAITFOR (RECEIVE message_body FROM
ProductNotQue)", conn)

cmd.CommandTimeout = 60000
```

```
Dim rdr As SqlDataReader = cmd.ExecuteReader

'Are there changes?  Take care of them here...
```

Now that you have a process listening for changes you are free to go off and do other tasks.

Summary

This short chapter may not seem adequate to discuss all the new ADO.NET 2.0 technologies, and in reality it isn't compared to what is out there on this subject. However, neither this chapter nor this book is focused on everything that is ADO.NET 2.0. This chapter introduced you to some of the new features and enhancements made to ADO.NET, how they interact with SQL Server 2005 to accomplish things people have been asking for, and to get excited about what is coming in the near future.

The chapter began by discussing some new features to ADO.NET 2.0 that support the `xml` data type, such as the `SqlXml` class.

Asynchronous operations offer a several options that allow developers to take full advantage of background threads. This functionality is provided via the `SqlCommand` class and this chapter provided some examples of how to utilize this functionality.

If you're tired of receiving the extremely irritating "existing DataReader for existing connection" error message, then reading the section on MARS was probably a welcome reprieve. Just the thought of being able to open multiple DataReaders on a single connection should be exciting. This chapter covered several ways to implement that technology.

Finally, query notifications can be an extremely beneficial addition to your application, but as you'll find out in the next chapter, there are several words of caution using this new technology. If you use them correctly, query notifications can add tremendous value to your application. If you do not use them correctly, your users will not be happy. Chapter 24 discusses some of the best practices when implementing much of the technology discussed in this chapter.

24

ADO.NET 2.0 Guidelines and Best Practices

Acting as a bookend to this part, this chapter discusses various ADO.NET guidelines and best practices you should follow when using some of the ADO.NET 2.0 functionality discussed in the Chapter 23.

The focus of this chapter deals specifically with some of the best practices for the following topics:

- `xml` data type
- Asynchronous operations
- MARS (Multiple Active Result Sets)
- Query Notification

xml data type

This section discusses a couple of items pertaining to dealing with the `xml` data type from the client using ADO.NET 2.0. Both of these topics were discussed in the Chapter 23, but the following sections highlight a couple of things that you should consider from a best practices perspective.

GetSqlXml

In the last chapter, you used the `GetSqlXml` method to return the value of an `xml` data type column as an XML value. The following code, for example, uses the `GetSqlXml` method to return the XML in the Instructions column from the Production.ProductModel table as an XML value:

```
Dim conn As New SqlConnection("Data Source=localhost;Initial _
Catalog=AdventureWorks;Integrated Security=SSPI")
Dim cmd As New SqlCommand()
```

```
cmd.Connection = conn
cmd.CommandType = CommandType.Text
cmd.CommandText = "SELECT Name, Instructions FROM Production.ProductModel" & _
"WHERE ProductModelID = 7"
Dim rdr As SqlDataReader = cmd.ExecuteReader

Dim dt As DataTable = rdr.GetSchemaTable

Do While rdr.Read()
  Dim sqlx As SqlXml = rdr.GetSqlXml(1)
  Dim xr As XmlReader = sqlx.CreateReader
  xr.Read()
Loop
```

This code uses the `GetSqlXml` method of the `SqlDataReader` to read the XML data out of the Instructions column, and then uses the `XmlReader` to read the content of the XML. There are a couple of things to consider when you use ADO.NET with XML, and the following section discusses each of those items.

Non-XML Values

The first thing you need to know is that when you call the `GetSqlXml` method, there is no conversion to XML when XML data is retrieved. The previous code example queries the Name and Instructions columns and uses the numeric ordinal of 1 to specify which column to return to the `GetSqlXml` method. The code executes successfully. However, if you were to change the column number to zero (0) as shown in the following code sample, the `GetSqlXml` method cannot correctly convert the value of column 0 to XML and returns the error shown in Figure 24-1:

```
Do While rdr.Read()
  Dim sqlx As SqlXml = rdr.GetSqlXml(0)
```

Figure 24-1

If you want to return the value as a string, the solution is to use the process described in the Chapter 23 and return the value directly from the `SqlDataReader` class.

Using IsDBNull

You may not always know if there is a value to be returned to the `GetSqlXml` method, and if you try to read the value without any sort of check first, you receive the error shown in Figure 24-2. The reason you receive the error is that, like the previous example, no conversions are performed and therefore the `GetSqlXml` method does not know how to deal with a null value. There must be a value and it must be an XML value.

Figure 24-2

If you are unsure if there is even a value to return, the solution is fairly simple. Use the `IsDBNull` method to check for a missing or non-existent value. Modify the example code as follows in order to solve this problem:

```
Do While rdr.Read()
  If IsDBNull(rdr.GetSqlXml(1)) = True Then
    MessageBox.Show("empty xml value")
  Else
    Dim sqlx As SqlXml = rdr.GetSqlXml(1)
    Dim xr As XmlReader = sqlx.CreateReader
    xr.Read()
  End If
Loop
```

This call returns `True` if the column value is null and `False` if it is not null.

ExecuteXmlReader

The purpose of the `ExecuteXmlReader` method is to tell the connection which type of command will be executed via the `CommandText` property, and then build an `XmlReader` object. The `CommandText` property can either be an in-line T-SQL statement or a stored procedure.

The `ExecuteXmlReader` method has been around for a while, but with ADO.NET 2.0 and SQL Server 2005, it gets even better. With SQL Server 2005, you now have the ability to retrieve an XML result set that contains a single row and single column.

So what happens if you your result set contains more than one row? The `ExecuteXmlReader` method associates the `XmlReader` to the first row, returns its value, and then dumps the rest of the results. A solution to this is to use MARS, which allows multiple commands using the same connection.

Pre-SQL Server 2005 versions do not have this capability, meaning that a connection that is actively performing actions for an existing `XmlReader` object cannot service any other `XmlReader` objects until the current `XmlReader` is closed. Again, MARS solves this problem, and is the subject of the next section.

MARS

Multiple Active Result Sets (MARS) allow you to run multiple commands simultaneously over the same database connection. This can have a positive performance impact on your application, but it can also have a negative performance impact if you are not careful.

Typically, default result sets are better performing over server-side cursors (whether it is a T-SQL cursor or an API cursor). Server-side cursors operate on complete sets of rows returned by the `SELECT` statement and provide a way for applications to work with one row or a set of rows at a time.

The syntax for creating server-side cursors is as follows:

```
DECLARE cursorname CURSOR
FOR SELECT * FROM Production.Product
OPEN cursorname
FETCH NEXT FROM cursorname
```

The difference between default result sets and server-side cursors is that default result sets send only the statement to be executed to the server one time. For server-side cursors, each time a `FETCH` statement is executed the statement is sent to the server and then parsed and compiled. Not good for performance.

In a normal scenario, default result sets can be used when the data you are returning is relatively small. The results can be then cached to memory and performance is improved.

The caveat here is that there are times when using MARS where a server-side cursor can be beneficial. Server-side cursors can be beneficial when your result set might take some time to execute or is returning a larger set of data and will take some time being read. You might also want to stick with a server-side cursor if you need cursor scrolling or locking. *Cursor scrolling* means that you can scroll back and forth between records, for example, move to the next record, or move to the previous record. *Locking* refers to the ability to lock a record when it is being accessed.

Another benefit of using server-side cursors is that there are no *orphaned* results on the connection between cursor operations. The upside to this is that you can then have multiple cursors running at the same time.

Asynchronous Operations

The following sections outline things to consider when coding asynchronous operations.

Blocking

Blocking occurs when one process blocks access to an object from another process. For example, a `SqlDataReader` could block the process of another `SqlDataReader` if they are trying to access the same table.

In asynchronous operations, there are some areas or situations that you should to be aware of that could cause blocking in certain scenarios. To begin with, there might be situations where the server just cannot keep up with the number of `reads()` sent by the client. The server can't send the results to the client fast enough, yet the client keeps issuing `reads()`. This situation could cause a read block to occur and prevent other processes from reading.

Second, a SQL statement that could take a bit of time to execute could cause some blocking problems, whether it is a read or write process.

Last, be careful how you use the `Close()` and `Dispose()` methods of the `SqlDataReader` class. If these methods are called during an execution process, it could leave pending rows out there that haven't been sent to the client yet. This could potentially cause a blocking problem for other processes coming in to access the same information.

Error Handling

There are two main places to be aware of where errors can occur during the execution of a command. Before asynchronous operations, most errors occurred at the execution of the command typically from an invalid connection or similar reason. The `begin()` method acts the same way and errors need to be handled similarly here.

However, with asynchronous operations, an error can be generated anywhere between the `begin()` and `end()` methods, and you won't know until the `end` method is called. When the error occurs, it is trapped and held on to but there is no way to return it to the calling client until the `end` method is called. For this reason, it is equally important to perform error handling on both methods, `begin()` and `end()`.

Canceling Commands

You should use the `cancel()` method of the `command` object to cancel any commands that have already been executed. This makes for an efficient cleanup and frees up processing. Simply disposing of the command without first canceling the command could have a negative effect on performance.

Query Notification

You have to admit that query notifications are cool. However, their coolness also allows them to be abused to the point of application degradation. There are right and wrong times to implement query notifications.

Query notifications are not meant as a catch-all for a high transaction, instant notification application. If you're thinking of using query notification with a high-level, on-demand application, think again. A network is a touchy thing. Too much network traffic is definitely not good and you know you want your application to perform at its best. However, slamming the network with a bunch of query notifications is asking for disaster and definitely won't make your users very happy. Each change initiates a query notification and request for query refresh.

This scenario multiplies exponentially if you have multiple users tracking the same data. Imagine the network traffic as each query notification triggers the users to re-query for the same data.

The ideal places for query notifications are lookup tables and areas where there are not a lot of continuous transactions. A high-transaction table would not be the place for a query notification. But a lookup table that gets updated infrequently would be perfect.

Summary

This technology is so new that there are many areas that have not been explored that can be added to the best practices. However, the pieces covered here are vital to the success of your application if you choose to implement these technologies.

While you many not immediately have any plans to implement the `xml` data type, this chapter covered a couple of things that should be considered when you do decide to start using the `xml` data type.

One of the best new features to ADO.NET 2.0 is the ability to run multiple commands simultaneously over the same database connection, know as MARS, and this chapter discussed some of the things to watch for when using MARS in your application.

Asynchronous operations were also discussed, pointing out some items to watch out for when utilizing these types of operations, such as blocking, error handling, and appropriately using the `cancel()` method.

Last, some thoughts on the query notifications were discussed. Query notifications can be a very useful addition to your applications, but as discussed in this chapter, they can also be a detriment if not correctly implemented.

The next, and final, chapter walks you through a case study implementing what you've learned in this book.

25

Case Study — Putting It All Together

With the release of SQL Server 2005, many companies will be asking the same question: "How can we implement this great new technology within our existing infrastructure?" This case study focuses on exactly that question, taking a look at those environments that are already using SQL Server 2000 and SqlXml in some fashion but would like to migrate to SQL Server 2005 and utilize the new technology found in it, specifically, the `xml` data type and the related technology.

The purpose of this case study is to give some examples of how a lot of the topics covered in this book can be implemented within an existing SQL Server 2000/XML environment. It utilizes much of the information from this book and all of the examples are done using the April 2005 TCP release of VB.NET 2005 and the June CTP release of SQL Server 2005.

This case study examines the current design and architecture of an application built and sold by the fictitious company 4FD, Fast Freddy's Five Finger Discount, a US-based company that has designed and developed its own procurement software package and is looking at further enhancements to the application supplied by SQL Server 2005 and Visual Studio 2005/ADO.NET 2.0.

This case study discusses the following topics:

- 4FD's existing applications and infrastructure
- Features of SQL Server 2005 that are utilized
- Integrating features of SQL Server 2005

Existing Application and Infrastructure

4FD has built a large scale purchasing application that they then sell to SMBs (Small to Medium Businesses). The application currently uses SQL Server 2000 as its database backend and Visual Basic.NET 2003 for the user interface.

4FD has also partnered with a second company, GPS (Guido's Pawn Shop), which provides document management services. This partnership has allowed for the integration of the two applications via a Web Service, which is described in more detail later.

Current Database Design

While this case study won't look at 4FD's entire database structure, it does look at the tables that are important to this case study. Those tables are shown in Figure 25-1.

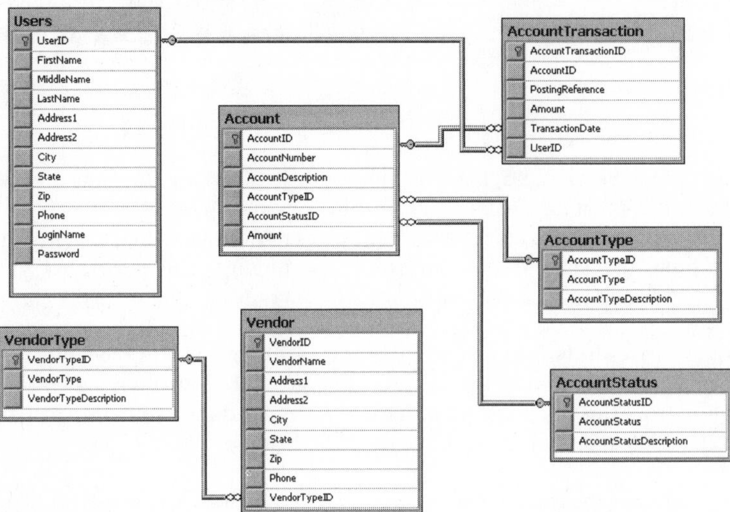

Figure 25-1

The three areas of focus for 4FD from a database aspect are the application user configuration information, reporting information, and account and vendor information.

Application User Configuration

In the current version of the application, certain user-specific application information is tracked and stored as XML documents. An example of the information tracked is form size and location, and grid column width so that when a user sizes a grid column on a particular form, the form remembers that information and when the form is opened again, the columns are sized and positioned as they were when the user last used the form.

The problem is that the XML document is stored on the user's local hard drive. This works, but the developers would like to remove any file system dependencies and move this information to the database. With the new `xml` data type and querying technologies, the users should see a performance increase when opening the forms.

Reporting Information

Similar to the application user configuration issue, certain details of the reporting aspect of the application need re-examination. Currently, the data for the reports are pulled from datasets, but the reporting requirements state that users must have the ability to save generated report data. This provides the users the ability to generate their own custom reports and if necessary, view the data outside of the base reports. When the user wants to print or print preview a specific report, they also have the ability to save the report data generated for that particular report. Currently, the data is saved as XML on the user's local hard drive.

Just like the application user configuration issue, the developers would like to remove any file system dependencies from the application as possible, and so the current thought process is to store this data as XML inside the database. This will provide a performance increase when pulling the saved data.

Account and Vendor Information

The current account and vendor information piece of the application really isn't a problem, but the team would like to implement some of the SqlXml 4.0 technology and SqlXml managed classes in a test environment on a small number of forms such as the Account and Vendor forms, and monitor the application over a period of time to see if there are performance ramifications. They currently use datasets to retrieve data and usher changes back to the database.

Current XML Use

Over the last couple of years, 4FD has been slowly integrating XML into their application, and has found that in certain scenarios it is quite useful. They currently use XML in the Web Service that provides the integration between the 4FD and GPS applications. This entails utilizing `XmlTextReader` and `XmlTextWriter` to read and generate XML documents, which are passed back and forth between the 4FD and GPS applications via the Web Service.

While this scenario works, it relies heavily on IIS, and with each customer purchase IIS must be configured and the Web Service installed. Because IIS is involved, security is a major factor. Equally, each environment is different with some having very tight IIS security and others having very loose IIS security, so dropping in a Web Service is not such a simple task since ICS has no control over the environment.

The other area where the application uses XML is to save the report data. As mentioned previously, when the users select the option to save the report data, the data is saved as an XML document to the user's local hard drive.

Partnership Information

The partnership between 4FD and GPS has been a success for both companies. This partnership allows for the modification of employee information in the 4FD application via the GPS Web interface even though the employee may not be a user of the 4FD application.

For example, Sally works for the ACME Company which has purchased both the 4FD and GPS applications. Sally has no need to use the 4FD application but on occasion has the need to submit purchase orders, or to change her benefit or demographic information.

A number of new online forms are in the process of being created, and in discussion with GPS, it was decided that this would be a great opportunity to implement a number of the new XML technologies that SQL Server 2005 provides, such as HTTP endpoints and the `xml` data type for data storage.

In the meetings between the two companies, it was decided that they would pick a number of the ESS (Employee Self Service) forms such as benefit change information, demographic change information, and employee deduction information forms to test the new SQL Server 2005 XML technologies.

Current Web Service Use

To facilitate the communication of data between the two applications, a .NET Web Service was created to handle the transportation of data. The data is formatted into XML documents by both applications as data is passed back and forth, and then the data is extracted using the `XmlTextReader` class by the receiving application.

The current design of the Web Service has all the Web methods contained into a single Web Service solely for the purpose of ease of installation and maintenance.

Shortcomings

There are several shortcomings with the current design that could benefit from a number of the new XML technologies in SQL Server 2005:

- New users need to be entered into both the 4FD and GPS applications manually, leaving room for input error. Customers would like to enter a new user into one of the applications and have it pushed to the other automatically, eliminating the need for double entry.
- Each time a new customer that requires ICS and GPS integration is acquired, the Web Service must be installed, making sure they have the latest incarnation of the Web Service. Even more critical is the issue of the different environments that the Web Service goes into, and the troubleshooting and support issues with the Web Service and IIS in each environment.
- Storing the report data on the user's local hard drive has severe security implications. It exposes the data to hacking, not to mention users who open the XML file and make changes not knowing XML.
- User application configuration has the same issue as the report data, but it's not as critical because the location of this file can be hidden fairly well. However, if the user were to know about the application configuration file and find it, they could cause some mischief.
- For many of 4FD's customers, the IIS server serves both internal and external users without the use of a firewall, which poses a huge security risk with sensitive data traveling over the wire.

Selecting SQL Server 2005 Features

After several meetings, management decided that the following features would be utilized in the revamp of the current 4FD application and database:

- The `xml` data type will be used in enhancing the current application in two major areas. The first area will be reporting. Current reporting functionality, while functional, could be improved both from a performance and security perspective. The second area is the application user configuration to improve application performance.

- HTTP endpoints will be utilized to add on to, and in some places replace, current Web Services for the integration between 4FD and GPS, eliminating the need for IIS. The first place this will be used is the automatic update of user information, eliminating double entry. When a new user is created in the GPS application, a call to a SQL Server 2005 Web Service (HTTP endpoint) will be made to update the 4FD application with the new user information. The second place HTTP endpoints will be used is in the new ESS forms created by GPS to pull information out of the 4FD application.
- SqlXml technology will be used in a few places: primarily on the Account and Vendor forms in the test environment to save the data back to the database. There are a couple of options 4FD could choose from, either updategrams or Diffgrams. 4FD decided to use Diffgrams initially and monitor the performance and functionality.
- SqlXml managed classes will be utilized to extend T-SQL functionality found in the current SQL Server 2000 database. As mentioned previously, 4FD currently uses datasets to retrieve this information, but they would like to modify these two areas to retrieve account and vendor information via SqlXml managed classes.
- .NET routines will be utilized to extend the functionality of SQL Server. Several stored procedures that perform some fairly intense calculations currently exist in the SQL Server 2000 version of the application. While T-SQL does a decent job, 4FD would like to try to move some of these calculations over to a .NET routine in an effort to boost performance, surmising that .NET might lend itself to performing these calculations better than the T-SQL counterparts.

Integrating Selected Features

This case study does not discuss the process of moving a SQL Server 2000 database to SQL Server 2005, so the rest of this case study assumes that the database has already been migrated and the additional features and changes are ready to be made.

Utilizing the xml data type

With the database moved over to SQL Server 2005 and the front-end application tested to make sure all the existing functionality is correct, the next step is to add the `xml` data type functionality to the database.

In the meetings to discuss what functionality of SQL Server 2005 would be useful in enhancing the current application, it was quite obvious that the `xml` data type would definitely be an asset to a few areas within the database. While many areas were discussed, two areas within the application were selected as an initial test to implement the `xml` data type, monitor the performance, and finish off the new functionality.

The first area is in reporting. In the current application, data for reports is generated and the user has the option of saving the data as XML format on the user's local file system. Users can then create their own custom reports based off that data, or re-run base reports off that data without the need to re-query the database. The downside to reading data off the file system is threefold. First is security. Storing sensitive data where it can be easily accessed is a no-no. The second is the possibility of XML document corruption, either the data or the validity of the XML document. Third is performance. Better application performance can be gained using the processing of SQL Server rather than reading off a file system.

The second area where 4FD decided to use the `xml` data type was in user configuration settings. The current application's requirements are that when a user changes a configuration item within the application, such as changing a column width of a grid on a form, that information needs to be saved so that when the user reopens that form, the grid column width is set to the width that the user set it to. Currently this information is being saved as XML to the local file system as well, and this has several problems: performance is the first problem, and the other problem, while less critical and highly unlikely, is having the user finding and modifying this file. The developers know that the second issue is akin to lightning striking the same place twice, but they would rather not take any chances. Moving this information to an `xml` data type column will eliminate these issues.

Setting Up the xml data type for Reporting

The first area of focus for the team is reporting. They have broken down the tasks to three main steps:

1. Creating the XML schema collection
2. Creating the necessary table
3. Modifying the application

Creating the XML Schema Collections

First, the team needs to create the schema collection that will be used for the selected reports. The developers have decided that they want the XML formatted specifically for each report, so they want the schemas created accordingly. Before creating the schemas, they decide what the XML for each report should look like.

The XML for the account transactions is to be formatted like the following:

```
<?xml version="1.0" encoding="UTF-8"?>
<AccountTrans AccountTransID="1">
  <Account>439-1277-66-29485-000</Account>
  <AccountDesc>Supplies</AccountDesc>
  <Amount>100.00</Amount>
  <TransDate>07-31-2005</TransDate>
  <User>14</User>
</AccountTrans>
```

Similarly, they want the XML for the Vendor information to be formatted as follows:

```
<?xml version="1.0" encoding="UTF-8"?>
<Vendor VendorID="1" VendorTypeID="1">
  <VendorName>Fast Freddy's Five Finger Discount</VendorName>
  <Address1></Address1>
  <City></City>
  <State></State>
  <Zip></Zip>
  <Phone></Phone>
</Vendor>
```

Given that information, they create the following schemas. First, the Account Transaction schema:

```
<xs:schema xmlns="" xmlns:xs="http://www.w3.org/2001/XMLSchema"
xmlns:msdata="urn:schemas-microsoft-com:xml-msdata" id="AcctTransDS">
 <xs:element name="AccountTrans">
  <xs:complexType>
   <xs:sequence>
    <xs:element name="Account" type="xs:string" minOccurs="0" msdata:Ordinal="0"/>
     <xs:element name="AccountDesc" type="xs:string" minOccurs="0"
msdata:Ordinal="1"/>
    <xs:element name="Amount" type="xs:string" minOccurs="0" msdata:Ordinal="2"/>
    <xs:element name="TransDate" type="xs:string" minOccurs="0"
msdata:Ordinal="3"/>
    <xs:element name="AcctType" type="xs:string" minOccurs="0" msdata:Ordinal="4/>
    <xs:element name="AcctStat" type="xs:string" minOccurs="0" msdata:Ordinal="5/>
    <xs:element name="User" type="xs:string" minOccurs="0" msdata:Ordinal="6/>
   </xs:sequence>
   <xs:attribute name="AccountTransID" type="xs:string"/>
  </xs:complexType>
 </xs:element>
 <xs:element name="AcctTransDS" msdata:IsDataSet="true"
msdata:UseCurrentLocale="true">
  <xs:complexType>
   <xs:choice minOccurs="0" maxOccurs="unbounded">
    <xs:element ref="AccountTrans"/>
   </xs:choice>
  </xs:complexType>
 </xs:element>
</xs:schema>
```

This schema validates any account transaction XML documents inserted into the ReportData column of the Reports table. When a user runs a report and selects the option to save the report data, an XML document in the form of the account transaction XML is generated and inserted into the Reports table. When the insert takes place, this schema validates the accuracy of the XML document.

Each element in the account transaction XML is validated against the corresponding element in the account transaction schema above. For example, the schema ensures that the XML contains a `<TransDate>` element, and that it is the third subelement of the `<AccountTrans>` element.

For the developers, this ensures the accuracy of the XML format by not letting any invalid XML documents for the Account Transaction report be saved.

Next, the vendor schema:

```
<xs:schema xmlns="" xmlns:xs="http://www.w3.org/2001/XMLSchema"
xmlns:msdata="urn:schemas-microsoft-com:xml-msdata" id="VendorDS">
 <xs:element name="Vendor">
  <xs:complexType>
   <xs:sequence>
    <xs:element name="VendorName" type="xs:string" minOccurs="0"
msdata:Ordinal="0"/>
    <xs:element name="Address1" type="xs:string" minOccurs="0" msdata:Ordinal="1"/>
    <xs:element name="City" type="xs:string" minOccurs="0" msdata:Ordinal="2"/>
    <xs:element name="State" type="xs:string" minOccurs="0" msdata:Ordinal="3"/>
    <xs:element name="Zip" type="xs:string" minOccurs="0" msdata:Ordinal="4"/>
    <xs:element name="Phone" type="xs:string" minOccurs="0" msdata:Ordinal="5"/>
```

```
    </xs:sequence>
    <xs:attribute name="VendorID" type="xs:string"/>
    <xs:attribute name="VendorTypeID" type="xs:string"/>
   </xs:complexType>
  </xs:element>
  <xs:element name="VendorDS" msdata:IsDataSet="true"
msdata:UseCurrentLocale="true">
   <xs:complexType>
    <xs:choice minOccurs="0" maxOccurs="unbounded">
     <xs:element ref="Vendor"/>
    </xs:choice>
   </xs:complexType>
  </xs:element>
</xs:schema>
```

Just like the account transaction schema, this vendor schema accomplishes the same goals, by not letting any vendor report XML documents be saved incorrectly. The same validation process that happens with the account transaction report happens with the vendor report.

Now that they have the schemas, the developers can create the XML schema collection. In SQL Server Management Studio, they run the following query to create the schema collection. From reading about schema collections, they know that they can use one statement with two schemas:

```
CREATE XML SCHEMA COLLECTION ReportSchemaCollection AS
'<xs:schema xmlns="" xmlns:xs="http://www.w3.org/2001/XMLSchema"
xmlns:msdata="urn:schemas-microsoft-com:xml-msdata" id="AcctTransDS">
 <xs:element name="AccountTrans">
  <xs:complexType>
   <xs:sequence>
    <xs:element name="Account" type="xs:string" minOccurs="0" msdata:Ordinal="0"/>
     <xs:element name="AccountDesc" type="xs:string" minOccurs="0"
msdata:Ordinal="1"/>
    <xs:element name="Amount" type="xs:string" minOccurs="0" msdata:Ordinal="2"/>
    <xs:element name="TransDate" type="xs:string" minOccurs="0"
msdata:Ordinal="3"/>
    <xs:element name="AcctType" type="xs:string" minOccurs="0" msdata:Ordinal="4"/>
    <xs:element name="AcctStat" type="xs:string" minOccurs="0" msdata:Ordinal="5"/>
    <xs:element name="Users" type="xs:string" minOccurs="0" msdata:Ordinal="6"/>
   </xs:sequence>
   <xs:attribute name="AccountTransID" type="xs:string"/>
  </xs:complexType>
 </xs:element>
 <xs:element name="AcctTransDS" msdata:IsDataSet="true"
msdata:UseCurrentLocale="true">
  <xs:complexType>
   <xs:choice minOccurs="0" maxOccurs="unbounded">
    <xs:element ref="AccountTrans"/>
   </xs:choice>
  </xs:complexType>
 </xs:element>
</xs:schema>
<xs:schema xmlns="" xmlns:xs="http://www.w3.org/2001/XMLSchema"
xmlns:msdata="urn:schemas-microsoft-com:xml-msdata" id="VendorDS">
 <xs:element name="Vendor">
```

```
    <xs:complexType>
     <xs:sequence>
      <xs:element name="VendorName" type="xs:string" minOccurs="0"
msdata:Ordinal="0"/>
      <xs:element name="Address1" type="xs:string" minOccurs="0" msdata:Ordinal="1"/>
      <xs:element name="City" type="xs:string" minOccurs="0" msdata:Ordinal="2"/>
      <xs:element name="State" type="xs:string" minOccurs="0" msdata:Ordinal="3"/>
      <xs:element name="Zip" type="xs:string" minOccurs="0" msdata:Ordinal="4"/>
      <xs:element name="Phone" type="xs:string" minOccurs="0" msdata:Ordinal="5"/>
     </xs:sequence>
     <xs:attribute name="VendorID" type="xs:string"/>
     <xs:attribute name="VendorTypeID" type="xs:string"/>
    </xs:complexType>
  </xs:element>
  <xs:element name="VendorDS" msdata:IsDataSet="true"
msdata:UseCurrentLocale="true">
    <xs:complexType>
     <xs:choice minOccurs="0" maxOccurs="unbounded">
      <xs:element ref="Vendor"/>
     </xs:choice>
    </xs:complexType>
  </xs:element>
</xs:schema>'
```

Now that the schema collection is created, the table can be created to hold the report information. As you recall from Chapter 7, the `CREATE XML SCHEMA COLLECTION` statement imports the schemas into the database for use with an `xml` data type columns or variables.

Creating the Table

The next step is to create the table that holds the report information and data. The goal of this table is to report information and data based on the specific report run (ReportNumber column) and the user who ran the report (UserID column). Since each user can run the same report but with different report filter criteria, the data is different and so the need to specify who ran the report is important.

The table will be called Reports, and besides the aforementioned ReportNumber and UserID columns, the table will also contain a report description column as well as the column that will hold the XML document containing the data. The developers create the table as follows:

```
CREATE TABLE [dbo].[Reports](
 [ReportID] [int] IDENTITY(1,1) NOT NULL,
 [UserID] [int] NOT NULL,
 [ReportNumber] [int] NOT NULL,
 [ReportDescription] [varchar](30) ,
 [ReportData] [xml](CONTENT [dbo].[ReportSchemaCollection]) NOT NULL,
 CONSTRAINT [PK_Reports] PRIMARY KEY CLUSTERED
(
 [ReportID] ASC
) ON [PRIMARY]
) ON [PRIMARY]
```

The developers run this query in SQL Server Management Studio to create the table and associate the XML schema collection to the ReportData column. Figure 25-2 shows what the table looks like in SQL Server Management Studio with the associated XML schema collection for the ReportData column.

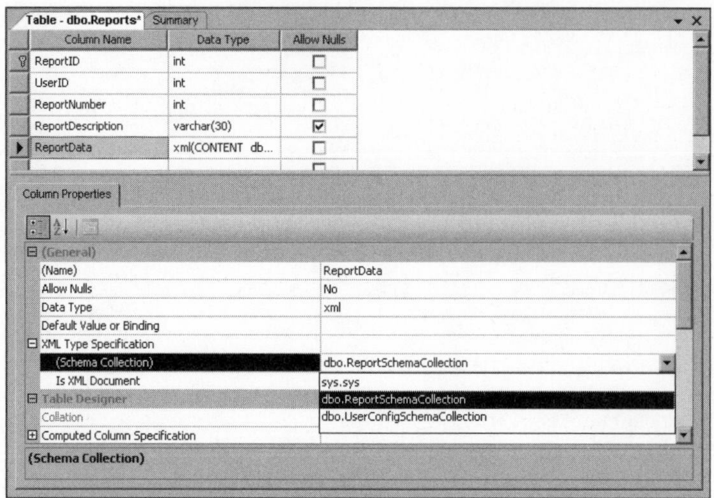

Figure 25-2

With the table created and some test data in the necessary tables (Account, AccountType, and AccountTransactions), the developers run a couple of tests to verify that the XML schema collection is working. The first test they run, shown here, should succeed:

```
INSERT INTO Reports (UserID, ReportNumber, ReportDescription, ReportData)VALUES (1,
1, 'this is a test',
  '<AccountTrans AccountTransID="1">
    <Account>111-1111-11-11111-000</Account>
    <AccountDesc>Donuts</AccountDesc>
    <Amount>100.00</Amount>
    <TransDate>07-31-2005</TransDate>
    <AcctType>3</AcctType>
    <AcctStat>2</AcctStat>
    <Users>1</Users>
</AccountTrans>')
```

The second test they run, shown here, should fail because the schema is looking for an element called <Account>, not <Accounts>:

```
INSERT INTO Reports (UserID, ReportNumber, ReportDescription, ReportData)
VALUES (1, 1, 'this is a test',
  '<AccountTrans AccountTransID="1">
    <Accounts>111-1111-11-11111-000</Accounts>
    <AccountDesc>Donuts</AccountDesc>
    <Amount>100.00</Amount>
    <TransDate>07-31-2005</TransDate>
    <AcctType>3</AcctType>
    <AcctStat>2</AcctStat>
    <Users>1</Users>
</AccountTrans>')
```

When the `INSERT` is executed, the schema validates the XML, finds that there is no element named `<Account>`, and rejects the `INSERT`.

With part two complete, the last step is to modify the application to write the data to the database instead of the local hard drive.

Modifying the Application

Modifying the application is the last step in this process, and after some discussion, 4FD decided to use a stored procedure to query the data and use the results to populate the Reports table.

The stored procedure they created (shown here) queries the AccountTransaction table for all transactions between a specific period of time and formats the results using the `FOR XML` clause:

```
CREATE PROCEDURE GetAccountTransactions
   @StartTranDate datetime,
   @EndTranDate datetime

AS
SELECT          Account.AccountNumber as Account,
                Account.AccountDescription As AccountDesc,
                AccountTransaction.Amount,
                AccountTransaction.TransactionDate As TransDate,
                AccountType.AccountType As AcctType,
                AccountStatus.AccountStatus As AcctStat,
                Users.LoginName As Users
FROM            AccountTransaction
INNER JOIN      Account ON AccountTransaction.AccountID = Account.AccountID
INNER JOIN      Users ON AccountTransaction.UserID = Users.UserID
INNER JOIN      AccountType ON Account.AccountTypeID = AccountType.AccountTypeID
INNER JOIN      AccountStatus ON Account.AccountStatusID =
AccountStatus.AccountStatusID
WHERE           AccountTransaction.TransactionDate BETWEEN @StartTranDate AND
@EndTranDate
FOR XML RAW, ROOT('AccountTrans'), ELEMENTS

GO
```

This stored procedure is simple in its filtering. It only filters by transaction date, but it could easily be modified to filter further by account type and account status, and even by user if needed. The intent here is to show how to return the desired data properly formatted in XML.

The developers test the stored procedure using some test data by executing the stored procedure through a query window in SQL Server Management Studio, as follows:

```
EXEC GetAccountTransactions '07/01/2005', '08/15/2005'
```

The results they get are as follows:

```
<AccountTrans>
  <row>
    <Account>1324</Account>
    <AccountDesc>Office Supplies</AccountDesc>
```

```
    <Amount>50.0000</Amount>
    <TransDate>2005-07-31T00:00:00</TransDate>
    <AcctType>1</AcctType>
    <AcctStat>1</AcctStat>
    <Users>scooter</Users>
  </row>
  <row>
    <Account>2345</Account>
    <AccountDesc>Book</AccountDesc>
    <Amount>29.9900</Amount>
    <TransDate>2005-08-01T00:00:00</TransDate>
    <AcctType>2</AcctType>
    <AcctStat>2</AcctStat>
    <Users>scooter</Users>
  </row>
</AccountTrans>
```

With the stored procedure working, the developers turn their attention to the application to modify the process of saving the data. Typically, the user can print or print preview the report, but they also have the option — regardless if they select to print or print preview the report — to save the data via a check box on the application report form.

The developers modify the code to verify if the check box has been checked. If it has, they take the results of the stored procedure and insert those results into the Report table, as follows:

```
INSERT INTO Reports ((UserID, ReportNumber, ReportDescription, ReportData)
VALUES (1, 1, 'Account Transaction Report',
'<AccountTrans>
  <row>
    <Account>1324</Account>
    <AccountDesc>Office Supplies</AccountDesc>
    <Amount>50.0000</Amount>
    <TransDate>2005-07-31T00:00:00</TransDate>
    <AcctType>1</AcctType>
    <AcctStat>1</AcctStat>
    <Users>scooter</Users>
  </row>
  <row>
    <Account>2345</Account>
    <AccountDesc>Book</AccountDesc>
    <Amount>29.9900</Amount>
    <TransDate>2005-08-01T00:00:00</TransDate>
    <AcctType>2</AcctType>
    <AcctStat>2</AcctStat>
    <Users>scooter</Users>
  </row>
</AccountTrans>')
```

This case study won't go into sending the results to the report. That is beyond the scope of this case study.

The developers could have also written the stored procedure to return the results via an `xml` data type variable output parameter as follows:

```
CREATE PROCEDURE GetAccountTransactions
   @StartTranDate datetime,
   @EndTranDate datetime,
   @x XML OUTPUT

AS
Set @x = (
SELECT          Account.AccountNumber as Account,
                Account.AccountDescription As AccountDesc,
                AccountTransaction.Amount,
                AccountTransaction.TransactionDate As TransDate,
                AccountType.AccountType As AcctType,
                AccountStatus.AccountStatus As AcctStat,
                Users.LoginName As Users
FROM            AccountTransaction
INNER JOIN      Account ON AccountTransaction.AccountID = Account.AccountID
INNER JOIN      Users ON AccountTransaction.UserID = Users.UserID
INNER JOIN      AccountType ON Account.AccountTypeID = AccountType.AccountTypeID
INNER JOIN      AccountStatus ON Account.AccountStatusID =
AccountStatus.AccountStatusID
WHERE           AccountTransaction.TransactionDate BETWEEN @StartTranDate AND
@EndTranDate
FOR XML RAW, ROOT('AccountTrans'), ELEMENTS)

GO
```

Both stored procedures accomplish the same thing, but the important thing here is that the data is now stored in a much more secure location.

With this task under their belt, the developers then move on to the task of addressing the application user configuration issue.

Setting Up the xml data type for User Information

The current Users table (shown in Figure 25-3) contains, among other data, information specific to users of the 4FD application, such as name and address information, as well as application logon information. This has worked well for the application, except for one area: The application tracks user-specific *application settings* information. For example, a lot of forms contain a number of sizable sections with one of those sections containing a data grid typically with two columns.

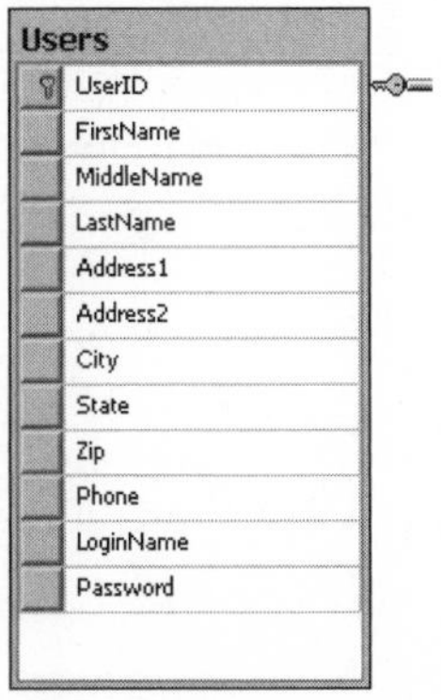

Figure 25-3

When a user sizes the data grid columns or changes the size of the form sections, that information is stored on the local hard drive in XML format. The XML format works, but storing it on the hard drive is not the best option. 4FD decided to store each user's settings along with their user information in the database. To accomplish this, a new `xml` data type column will be added to the Users table, which will store the application configuration information that can be easily read and saved by the application.

As before, this process is broken into three steps:

1. Creating the schema collection
2. Modifying the Users table to add the necessary column
3. Modifying the application to read from the Users table instead of the file system

Creating the XML Schema Collection

The first step again is to create the schema collection. For now, the team decided to make it pretty simple, so the XML document that they will use looks like the following:

```
<?xml version="1.0" encoding="UTF-8"?>
<FormConfigInfo FormID="1">
  <FormSection1Height>300</FormSection1Height>
  <FormSection2Height>400</FormSection2Height>
  <FormSection3Height>600</FormSection3Height>
  <FormWidth>800</FormWidth>
  <Column1Width>150</Column1Width>
  <Column2Width>250</Column2Width>
</FormConfigInfo>
```

The following code creates the XML schema collection used for this table:

```
CREATE XML SCHEMA COLLECTION UserConfigSchemaCollection AS
'<xs:schema xmlns="" xmlns:xs="http://www.w3.org/2001/XMLSchema"
xmlns:msdata="urn:schemas-microsoft-com:xml-msdata" id="FormConfig">
 <xs:element name="FormConfigInfo">
  <xs:complexType>
   <xs:sequence>
    <xs:element name="FormSection1Height" type="xs:string" minOccurs="0"
msdata:Ordinal="0"/>
     <xs:element name="FormSection2Height" type="xs:string" minOccurs="0"
msdata:Ordinal="1"/>
    <xs:element name="FormSection3Height" type="xs:string" minOccurs="0"
msdata:Ordinal="2"/>
    <xs:element name="FormWidth" type="xs:string" minOccurs="0"
msdata:Ordinal="3"/>
    <xs:element name="Column1Width" type="xs:string" minOccurs="0"
msdata:Ordinal="4/>
    <xs:element name="Column2Width" type="xs:string" minOccurs="0"
msdata:Ordinal="5/>
   </xs:sequence>
   <xs:attribute name="FormID" type="xs:string"/>
  </xs:complexType>
 </xs:element>
```

```
  <xs:element name="FormConfig" msdata:IsDataSet="true"
msdata:UseCurrentLocale="true">
    <xs:complexType>
      <xs:choice minOccurs="0" maxOccurs="unbounded">
        <xs:element ref="Users"/>
      </xs:choice>
    </xs:complexType>
  </xs:element>
</xs:schema>'
```

Now that the schema is defined, it is time to modify the Users table and add the appropriate column and schema.

Modifying the Users Table

The next step is to alter the table to add the `xml` data type column and associated schema defined in the previous section. The following query does just that:

```
ALTER TABLE Users
ADD UserAppConfig [xml](CONTENT [dbo].[UserConfigSchemaCollection])
GO
```

Once the column is added and the schema collection is associated to the new column, the table should look like Figure 25-4.

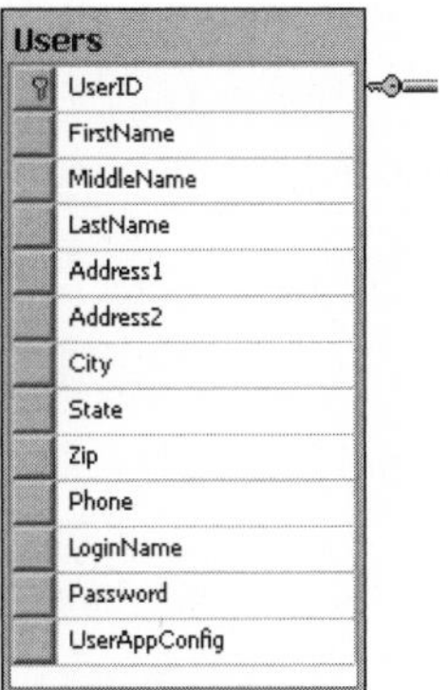

Figure 25-4

With the infrastructure in place, the application needs to be modified to now read and write to the new `xml` data type column.

Modifying the Application

The final step is to tell the application to retrieve information from the Users table instead of the file system. There are two areas of this piece. First, when the form loads, the developers want to retrieve the data for the specific form and set the properties accordingly. Second, when the form closes, the settings need to be written back to the database for the next time the user opens the form.

Form Load

After some discussion, the team decides the best method to achieve its goals is to use the `query()` method of the `xml` data type and return the XML document, which the developers can then parse through and pull out the information they need.

The developers created the following query to give them the XML document they need:

```
DECLARE @xmlvar xml
SET @xmlvar =
SELECT UserAppConfig.query ('
 For $var in FormConfigInfo
  where FormConfigInfo/@FormID="1"
   return($var)
') As Results
FROM Users
WHERE UserID = 1
```

The results are returned to the `@xmlvar` variable, which will be used shortly to extract the pertinent information to save back to the database.

When the results are returned, the developers have several options to parse through the XML document to pull out the information they need. After several discussions, the team decides that they will utilize the new features introduced in version 2.0 of the .NET Framework and use the `XmlReader` class to read in the results of the query and pull out the necessary information, as follows:

```
Dim ms As MemoryStream
Dim xtr As XmlTextReader
Dim FormSection1Height As String
Dim FormSection2Height As String
Dim FormSection3Height As String
Dim FormWidth As String
Dim Column1Width As String
Dim Column2Width As String
ms = New MemoryStream(@xmlvar)
xtr = New XmlTextReader(ms)
Do While xtr.Read
  If xtr.NodeType = XmlNodeType.Element Then
    Select Case xtr.Name
      Case "FormSection1Height"
        xtr.Read()
        FormSection1Height = Trim(xtr.Value)
      Case "FormSection2Height"
        xtr.Read()
        FormSection1Height = Trim(xtr.Value)
      Case "FormSection3Height"
        xtr.Read()
        FormSection3Height = Trim(Trim(xtr.Value))
      Case "FormWidth"
        xtr.Read()
        FormWidth = Trim(Trim(xtr.Value))
      Case "Column1Width"
        xtr.Read()
        Column1Width = Trim(Trim(xtr.Value))
      Case "Column2Width"
```

```
        xtr.Read()
        Column2Width = Trim(Trim(xtr.Value))
      End Select
    End If
  Loop
  xtr.Close()
```

The @xmlvar variable contains the information from the database for the specific user and form. A memory stream is created with the variable and that memory stream is then passed to the XmlTextReader for parsing. The XmlTextReader then parses the XML document stored inside the memory stream, looking for specific nodes. When it finds the nodes it is looking for, it saves the value of the node to a variable. That variable is used to set the specific form information when the form loads.

Once the information is extracted, the developers can use the data to set the appropriate properties on the form and datagrid. In their test environment, they do this on the Form_Load event for the forms they want to test.

Form Close

When the user closes the form, the developers utilize the modify() method of the xml data type to write the form information back to the database:

```
Update Users
Set UserAppConfig.modify ('
 replace value of (//FormConfigInfo/FormSection1Height)[1]
 with "100"
')
FROM Users
WHERE UserID = 2

Update Users
Set UserAppConfig.modify ('
 replace value of (//FormConfigInfo/FormSection2Height)[1]
 with "200"
')
FROM Users
WHERE UserID = 2

Update Users
Set UserAppConfig.modify ('
 replace value of (//FormConfigInfo/FormSection3Height)[1]
 with "300"
')
FROM Users
WHERE UserID = 2

Update Users
Set UserAppConfig.modify ('
 replace value of (//FormConfigInfo/FormWidth)[1]
 with "400"
')
FROM Users
```

```
WHERE UserID = 2

Update Users
Set UserAppConfig.modify ('
 replace value of (//FormConfigInfo/Column1Width)[1]
 with "500"
')
FROM Users
WHERE UserID = 2

Update Users
Set UserAppConfig.modify ('
 replace value of (//FormConfigInfo/Column2Width)[1]
 with "600"
')
FROM Users
WHERE UserID = 2
```

With these changes being written back to the database, the developers can now focus on their next task of integrating Native XML Web Services into their environment.

Building the HTTP Endpoints

The current integration between 4FD and GPS is done via a .NET Web Service. When a Web form is opened in the GPS application, it makes a call to the 4FD Web Service, which makes a connection to the current 4FD SQL Server 2000 database and retrieves the necessary data, formatted in XML using the `XMLTextWriter` property, and returns it to the GPS application.

One of the new forms that are in the process of being created is an Account Fund Transfer form. This form allows a dollar amount to be transferred from one account to another.

Again, there are three steps for this process:

1. Creating the stored procedure
2. Creating the HTTP endpoint
3. Modifying the application

Creating the Stored Procedure

The first step to this task is to create the following stored procedure that the endpoint will use to retrieve the data for the form:

```
CREATE PROCEDURE [dbo].[TransferAccountFunds]

@FromAccount varchar(30),
@ToAccount varchar(30),
@Amount money
AS
 BEGIN

  DECLARE  @FromValue money,
```

```
          @ToValue money

   SET @FromValue = (SELECT Budget FROM Account WHERE AccountNumber = @FromAccount)
   SET @ToValue = (SELECT Budget FROM Account WHERE AccountNumber = @ToAccount)

   IF @Amount <= @FromValue
     BEGIN
      BEGIN TRANSACTION AccountTransfer

     UPDATE Account SET Budget = @FromValue - @Amount WHERE AccountNumber =
@FromAccount
     UPDATE Account SET Budget = @ToValue + @Amount WHERE AccountNumber = @ToAccount

    COMMIT TRANSACTION AccountTransfer
   END
END

GO
```

After running a few tests and verifying that it works according to spec, the developers then turn their attention to creating the HTTP endpoint in SQL Server 2005.

Creating the Endpoint

The second part to this task is to create the HTTP endpoint, or native XML Web Service. The developers open a query window inside SQL Server Management Studio and type in the following T-SQL:

```
CREATE ENDPOINT 4FD_EndPoint
STATE = STARTED
AS HTTP
 (
  SITE = 'localhost',
  PATH = '/4FD',
  AUTHENTICATION = (INTEGRATED),
  PORTS = ( CLEAR )
 )
FOR SOAP
 (
  WebMethod 'TransferAccountFunds'
  (
  NAME = '4FD.dbo.TransferAccountFunds',
  SCHEMA = STANDARD
),
  WSDL = DEFAULT,
  BATCHES = ENABLED,
  DATABASE = '4FD'
)
```

They execute the preceding statement to create the endpoint. The query succeeds and the endpoint is created. The developers are not done, however, because even though the endpoint and Web Method are created, no one has permission to access it.

In this scenario, a small group will be using this application in a test environment at first, so the team creates a domain group called Test to which they add the small handful of users that will be testing the application.

With the group added and users added to the group, the development team then executes the following statement to grant everyone in the group permission to access and execute the Web Method:

```
USE MASTER
GO
GRANT CONNECT ON ENDPOINT::4FD_EndPoint TO [4FDSERVER\George]
GO
```

The third and final step is to consume the Web Service or endpoint. Since the consuming application will be a third-party application, there is nothing to do on the 4FD side except provide the necessary information GPS needs to consume the Web Method.

SqlXml Managed Classes

Several requirements have come in regarding some of the current vendor forms in the application, so 4FD needs to make some changes in this area of the application. The team decided this would be a good time to implement some of the new technology and roll it out in a small test environment and monitor it for a brief period of time and run some comparison tests.

The team has had its eye on SqlXml managed classes since the team members read about them a couple of years ago when they showed up in SqlXml 3.0. However, they just couldn't buy into them until they read about SQL Server 2005 and all the XML capabilities it provides.

Currently, when the form loads, the list of Vendors populates a list box or grid. When users click on a vendor in the list, they query the database for the specific vendor information for the selected vendor.

They are currently using ADO.NET and datasets to retrieve the information and save it back to the database if any changes are made.

What they would like to do is implement SqlXml managed classes in this scenario. When they select a vendor from the list, they want to retrieve the specific vendor information via SqlXml-managed classes, then if a changed is made to the vendor information on the form, they want to use an DiffGram to save the information back to the database.

Once the data is retrieved to populate the form, they decide to use the new and improved `XmlTextReader` and its new ADO.NET 2.0 improvements to that class.

Retrieving the Data

The team first modifies the Vendor form to use the `SqlXmlCommand` class to retrieve the data to populate the form. A portion of the code is shown here:

```
Imports System.Xml.SqlXml
Imports System.Xml
Imports System.IO
```

The developers first add these three lines to the declaration section of their application. They then modify the appropriate section of code in the application that needs to retrieve the data. A portion of the code is shown here:

```
Dim MyStrm As Stream
Dim ConnectString As String
Dim Param As SqlXmlParameter

'Be sure to put in the correct Username and Password in the connect string!
ConnectString = "Provider=SQLOLEDB;Server=(local);database=4FD;UID=?;PWD=?"

Dim cmd As SqlXmlCommand = New SqlXmlCommand(ConnectString)

cmd.CommandText = "SELECT VendorName, Address1, Address2, City, State, Zip, Phone
FROM Vendor WHERE VendorID = ? For XML Auto"

Param = cmd.CreateParameter
' Grab the VendorID from the form...
Param.Value = Me.txtVendorID.Text

Try
  MyStrm = cmd.ExecuteStream
  MyStrm.Position = 0

  Dim StrRdr As StreamReader = New StreamReader(MyStrm)

  Dim xtr As XmlTextReader = New XmlTextReader(StrRdr)

  xtr.Read()

  'Now populate the form with the info
  Me.txtVendorName.Text = xtr.Item(0)

  ...

Catch ex As Exception
  MessageBox.Show(ex.Message.ToString)
End Try
```

Now that the data is returned and the form populated, the developers turn their attention to saving the data back to the database if changes are made.

Building the Diffgram

The first step to saving the data is to build the mapping schema that the Diffgram will use to map to the appropriate table and columns in the database.

The team creates the following schema and saves it with the name VendorSchema.xml:

```
<xsd:schema xmlns:xsd="http://www.w3.org/2001/XMLSchema"
xmlns:sql="urn:schemas-microsoft-com:mapping-schema">
 <xsd:element name="Ven" sql:relation="Vendor" >
  <xsd:complexType>
   <xsd:sequence>
    <xsd:element name="Name"
        sql:field="VendorName"
        type="xsd:string" />
    <xsd:element name="Addr1"
```

```
            sql:field="Address1"
            type="xsd:string" />
        <xsd:element name="Addr2"
            sql:field="Address2"
            type="xsd:string" />
        <xsd:element name="City"
            sql:field="City"
            type="xsd:string" />
        <xsd:element name="State"
            sql:field="State"
            type="xsd:string" />
        <xsd:element name="Zip"
            sql:field="Zip"
            type="xsd:string" />
        <xsd:element name="Phone"
            sql:field="Phone"
            type="xsd:string" />
       </xsd:sequence>
       <xsd:attribute name="VendorID" type="xsd:integer" />
     </xsd:complexType>
   </xsd:element>
  </xsd:schema>
```

The next step is to modify the save routine to update the database based on the mapping schema and Diffgram. A portion of the code is shown here:

```
Dim ConnString As String =
"Provider=SQLOLEDB;Server=servername;database=4FD;Integrated Security=SSPI;"
Dim row As DataRow
Dim ad As SqlXmlAdapter
Dim ms As MemoryStream = New MemoryStream()
Dim cmd As SqlXmlCommand = New SqlXmlCommand(ConnString)

cmd.RootTag = "ROOT"
cmd.CommandText = "Ven"
cmd.CommandType = SqlXmlCommandType.XPath
cmd.SchemaPath = "C:\apppath\VendorSchema.xml"

Dim ds As DataSet = New DataSet()

Try
  ad = New SqlXmlAdapter(cmd)
  ad.Fill(ds)
  row = ds.Tables("Ven").Rows(0)
  row("Addr2") = "Suite 200"
  ad.Update(ds)

Catch ex As Exception
  MessageBox.Show(ex.Message)
End Try
```

This example uses the `SqlxmlCommand` class and a few of the associated properties to execute the Diffgram. The `CommandText` property maps the schema to the corresponding table in the database. The `CommandText` property contains the type of command, in this case an XPath command. Last, the `SchemaPath` property contains the location of the mapping schema created here.

The Diffgram, when executed, updates the Address2 field in the Users table.

Building the .NET Routines

The last remaining item of focus for the team is to move some of the processing logic from within T-SQL to .NET routines. The purpose of this task is to see if a gain in performance can be obtained by moving some of the processing into .NET. The developers know that this process is going to take some experimenting to find the right balance of T-SQL and .NET, so they thought they would start pretty simple and build from there.

They decide to start with moving some of the account transaction processing into .NET routines. Some of the logic calls for account transaction records to be summed up given a date range, and then based on those results, further processing takes place.

The first task at hand is to build the .NET routine and compile it into a DLL. The .NET code they write, shown here, takes two input parameters that contain the begin and end date in which to filter the account transaction records, and the last parameter returns the sum of the query:

```
Imports System
Imports System.Data
Imports Microsoft.SqlServer.Server
Imports System.Data.SqlTypes
Imports System.Data.SqlClient

Public Class SumAcctTransByDate
  Public Shared Sub SumTrans(ByVal BeginDate As Date, ByVal EndDate As Date, ByRef
Total As Decimal)
    Dim conn as SqlConnection = New SqlConnection("context connection = True")
    conn.Open()
    Dim cmd As SqlCommand = New SqlCommand("SELECT SUM(Amount) FROM " & _
"AccountTransaction WHERE TransactionDate BETWEEN = '" & BeginDate & "' AND '" &
EndDate & "'", conn)
    Dim rdr As SqlDataReader = cmd.ExecuteReader
    SqlContext.Pipe.Send(rdr)

    If rdr.HasRows = True Then
      Rdr.Read()
      Total = rdr.Item(0)
    End If

    rdr.Close()
    conn.Close
  End Sub
End Class
```

The developers then compile the routine into an assembly using the following syntax:

```
Vbc /target:library c:\wrox\chapter23\SumAccountTransactions.vb
```

The next step is to create the assembly reference. The following creates the reference in SQL Server to the physical assembly:

```
CREATE ASSEMBLY SumAccountTransDateRange
FROM 'c:\apppath\SumAccountTransactions.dll'
WITH PERMISSION_SET = SAFE
GO
```

The next step is to create the stored procedure. This stored procedure takes two input parameters, the beginning sum date and the ending sum date, and one output parameter, which is the total of the sum:

```
CREATE PROCEDURE SumTransactionsByDate
@BeginDate date,
@EndDate date,
@TotalAmount Money OUTPUT
AS
EXTERNAL NAME SumAccountTransDateRange.SumAcctTransByDate.SumTrans
GO
```

As good developers, the team then tests this stored procedure by running a couple of tests against some test data to verify that the stored procedure is indeed working the way they expect. One of the tests they run is as follows:

```
DECLARE @Total Mopney
EXEC SumTransactionsByDate '07/01/2005', '07/31/2005', @Total
PRINT @Total
GO
```

The next step is to integrate this stored procedure into the application. There are several ways the team can do this and it experiments with a couple of options. The first option they play with is to call this stored procedure from within the application. The other option is to call it from within another stored procedure so SQL Server can continue any processing it needs to do.

Both of these options have their advantages and disadvantages, so the developers experiment with both, and tests are still ongoing. They have determined that they need to experiment a bit more to find the right combination and mix of SQL and .NET/CLR.

Summary

This case study gave you some food for thought. The examples given don't provide the entire solution, but they do give a good foundation to how the `xml` data type can be implemented into an existing environment.

This case study focused on existing companies that already have a SQL Server/XML environment in place and want to utilize a number of the XML technologies found in SQL Server 2005.

You will find that it takes some investigation to decide how the xml data type can best benefit your current applications. The last thing you want to do is to force the technology into your environment. If it doesn't make sense, don't do it. If you are currently using XML in some fashion, then there is a good possibility that you can benefit from the `xml` data type and its related technologies.

For example, if you are storing XML as BLOBs, the `xml` data type may be right up your alley. But forcing XML into your application could have a negative impact in many areas, and that is not what you want.

XQuery in SQL Server 2005

It is no secret that XML is gaining popularity, a fact that becomes even more evident with the introduction of the `xml` data type in SQL Server 2005. As XML gains more popularity and becomes more of a mainstream technology in the workplace, there is an even bigger need to extract the data and information from XML.

Prior to SQL Server 2005, developers would resort to sticking XML documents into tables as BLOBs, using SqlXml, and at times tough query technology to extract and format the data that really did not provide a full XML data model support.

To solve this problem, Microsoft introduced not only the `xml` data type, but also support for XQuery, the language used for querying XML data.

This appendix discusses XQuery as it is used in SQL Server 2005, and covers the following topics:

- Introduction to and advantages of using XQuery
- XQuery expressions, including FLWOR, operators, and functions
- Creating XML using XQuery
- Relational variables and columns in XQuery

Advantages of XQuery

Before delving into the depths of XQuery, it is beneficial to answer a few questions as to the advantages of XQuery and why to use it over other technologies such as XSLT. XQuery provides a number of benefits:

- The amount of code it takes to write XQuery is much less than XSLT queries, making it easier and cheaper to maintain.
- XQuery is a strongly typed language, which improves query performance because implicit type casting doesn't need to take place, providing what is called type assurance.
- XQuery is a W3C recommendation and will thus see major support from most major database vendors.
- XQuery has the capability to be used as a weakly typed language for use with untyped XML data.

Now that SQL Server 2005 supports XQuery, what's better than being able to use XQuery at the server? This also provides a number of advantages over client-side XML processing. Some the advantages of using XQuery at the server include:

- **Reduced network traffic:** With the processing happening at the server, only the results are sent back to the client, resulting in less network traffic.
- **Better security:** Since only the data that is necessary is sent to the client, the risk of exposing unnecessary information and data is greatly lessened.
- **Improved performance:** Since the processing takes place at the server, the queries can take advantage of the query optimizations provided by the SQL Server engine. This process also allows for the query to take advantage of any indexes on the `xml` data type column.

Introduction to XQuery

To understand XQuery you must first understand a bit about XPath. The following sections introduce XPath and delve a bit into XPath expressions.

What Is XPath?

XPath (XML Path language) is a language that allows for locating specific parts of an XML document. It is able to accomplish this by using a path-based syntax, which identifies specified nodes within an XML document. The first version of XPath, 1.0, contained a set of functions to handle strings, Booleans, and numbers, as well as the ability to specify filter criteria.

XPath 2.0 builds on XPath 1.0 by adding more functionality such as a more detailed type system. XQuery 1.0 is built around XPath 2.0, adding functionality such as ordering, validation for filtering, construction, and reshaping capabilities.

XPath Expressions

XPath expressions are navigational directions in an XML document. They allow for the location of nodes and the navigation from one location to another within an XML document. This is accomplished via a sequence of steps, each step separated by a forward slash (/). Steps within an expression are evaluated from left to right, with each step setting the context (selected node) for the next step. Each step contains an axis, node test, and step qualifiers.

An *axis* specifies the direction of movement in relation to the context node. In SQL Server 2005, support axes are self, child, parent, descendant, attribute, and descendant-or-self.

A *node test* is the condition that all selected nodes by a step must satisfy, with the condition of the node based on a node name or node type.

A *step qualifier* is defined by either a *predicate*—an expression specified within square brackets that acts as a filter on a node—or a *dereference*, which maps the elements and attributes in a sequence to the nodes that they reference.

What Is XQuery?

XQuery is a fairly new language for querying XML data. It was designed from the ground up by the XML Query Working Group of the W3C with the sole purpose of querying data stored in XML format. It is essentially a superset of XPath 2.0 that gives it all the features of XPath 2.0 plus a long list of additional features. The list of features supported by SQL Server 2005 includes the following:

- Allows for the creation of new nodes
- Adds an order by clause to the `FLWOR` clause to provide the ability to sort

The great thing about XQuery is that it was built to work with all XML documents, whether they are untyped, typed, or a combination of both. In all cases, its job is to query data stored in XML format. It does this by using the XPath navigational functionality.

XQuery Expressions

Chapter 5 discussed XQuery expressions and their structure briefly, but they will be reviewed here in further detail to give you a better idea of how XQuery expressions work.

An XQuery expression has two parts, a prolog and a body. The first part is the XQuery Prolog, which is simply a namespace declaration, such as the following:

```
delcare namespace AW="http://schemas.microsoft.com/_
Sqlserver/2004/07/adventure-works/ProductModelManuInstructions");
```

The prolog can contain a namespace declaration, which is used to define the mapping between the prefix and namespace URI. The purpose of this is to let you use the prefix throughout the query instead of the entire namespace URI.

The body of the expression holds the query expression that defines the result of the query. For example:

```
/AW:root/AW:Employee[EmployeeID=32]
```

The body can be a `FLWOR` expression, an XPath expression, or any other XQuery expression. Putting the prolog and body together results in something like the following:

```
SELECT Instructions.query('
declare namespace AW="http://schemas.microsoft.com/sqlserver/2004/07/adventure-
works/ProductModelManuInstructions";
for $var in //AW:root/AW:Location[2]/AW:step
      return
           string($var)
') as Steps
FROM Production.ProductModel
WHERE ProductModelID=47
```

Using this query, the `FLWOR` statement is explained in the next section.

The FLWOR Statement

Similar to the T-SQL `SELECT` statement, XQuery `FLWOR` statements are the foundation for querying, filtering, and sorting results from an XML document. `FLWOR` stands for `FOR`, `LET`, `WHERE`, `ORDER BY`, and `RETURN`. As mentioned in Chapter 5, SQL Server 2005 supports all of these except `LET`.

The `LET` clause is used for binding a variable to the results of an expression. As this is not supported in SQL Server 2005, the workaround is to use an in-line expression.

FOR

The `FOR` clause lets users define and bind a variable to a sequence that is iterated through. While many developers new to XQuery and XPath assume that this is akin to a `For - Next` loop, that assumption is completely incorrect. A more correct comparison would be to the T-SQL `SELECT` statement, such as `SELECT fieldname FROM`. This is due to the input sequence being specified using XPath expressions, atomic values, or constructor functions.

The following example uses the `FOR` clause to return all the steps from the second location in the Instructions column. It does this by applying an XPath expression to the `FOR` clause, as follows:

```
SELECT Instructions.query('
declare namespace AW="http://schemas.microsoft.com/sqlserver/2004/07/adventure-
works/ProductModelManuInstructions";
for $var in //AW:root/AW:Location[2]/AW:step
      return
           string($var)
') as Steps
FROM Production.ProductModel
```

As shown in a previous example, this query could be filtered even further by appending a `WHERE` clause and specifying a specific ProductModelID.

WHERE

The `WHERE` clause, like a standard T-SQL `WHERE` clause, lets you filter the results of the query. Consider the following example:

```
SELECT Instructions.query('
declare namespace AW="http://schemas.microsoft.com/sqlserver/2004/07/adventure-
works/ProductModelManuInstructions";
```

```
for $var in //AW:root/AW:Location[2]/AW:step
      return
           string($var)
') as Steps
FROM Production.ProductModel
WHERE ProductModelID=47
```

This is nothing new. If you have been programming in T-SQL, you have been using the WHERE clause for quite a while.

order by

The order by clause for FLWOR expressions works similarly to the ORDER BY clause in T-SQL. Sorting is done by passing a sorting expression to the order by clause of the FLWOR expression. It allows you to sort the returned values from the query, as follows:

```
SELECT Instructions.query('
declare namespace AW="http://schemas.microsoft.com/sqlserver/2004/07/adventure-
works/ProductModelManuInstructions";
for $var in //AW:root/AW:Location[2]/AW:step
order by $var/AW:Location[2]
      return
           string($var)
') as Steps

FROM Production.ProductModel
```

In this case, the order by clause sorts the results returned by the FLWOR expression.

return

The return clause lets you define the results of the query. Think of it in a similar way as you think about the SELECT statement. What you put in the return clause determines the results you get back. In the return clause, you can specify any valid XQuery expression as well as build well-formed XML structures by specifying constructors for elements and attributes:

```
SELECT Instructions.query('
declare namespace AW="http://schemas.microsoft.com/sqlserver/2004/07/adventure-
works/ProductModelManuInstructions";
for $var in //AW:root/AW:Location[2]/AW:step
      return
           string($var)
') as Steps
FROM Production.ProductModel
WHERE ProductModelID=47
```

Later in this appendix, you'll delve deeper into how to build XML structures in the return clause.

XQuery Operators

SQL Server 2005 supports a number of XQuery operators, which fall into the following groups:

- Comparison operators
- Arithmetic operators
- Logical operators

The following sections discuss these operators in detail.

Comparison Operators

Comparison operators compare values, sequences, or a combination of both and are defined as follows:

- **Equal (=):** Compares the values of the left sequence to see if they match the values of the right sequence.
- **Not Equal (!=):** Compares the values of the left sequence to see if they do not match the values of the right sequence.
- **Less than (<):** Compares the values of the left sequence to see if they are less than the values of the right sequence.
- **Greater than (>):** Compares the values of the left sequence to see if they are greater than the values of the right sequence.
- **Less than or equal to (<=):** Compares the values of the left sequence to see if they are less than or equal to the values of the right sequence.
- **Greater than or equal to (>=):** Compares the values of the left sequence to see if they are greater than or equal to the values of the right sequence.

SQL Server 2005 has added support for all of these comparison operators. The following example uses the equal operator (=) to compare the value returned by the XPath statement with a literal string:

```
WITH XMLNAMESPACES ('http://schemas.microsoft.com/sqlserver/2004/07/adventure-
works/ProductModelDescription' AS PMD)
SELECT CatalogDescription.query('
    for $P in / PMD:ProductDescription/PMD:Manufacturer[PMD:Name =
"AdventureWorks"]
    return $P') as Result
FROM   Production.ProductModel
WHERE  ProductModelID=35
```

The results of this query are shown in Figure A-1.

```
<PD:Manufacturer xmlns:PD="http://schemas.microsoft.com/sqlserver/2004/07/adven
  <PD:Name>AdventureWorks</PD:Name>
  <PD:Copyright>2002</PD:Copyright>
  <PD:ProductURL>HTTP://www.Adventure-works.com</PD:ProductURL>
</PD:Manufacturer>
```

Figure A-1

In this example, the equal (=) operator is used to evaluate the value returned from the query expression with the value of `"AdventureWorks"`. If the comparison expression returns `True`, the query returns all the records where the match is found.

The next example uses a comparison operator for more than one record. First, query the ProductModel table as follows:

```
SELECT ProductModelID, CatalogDescription
FROM Production.ProductModel
```

Take a look primarily at ProductModelIDs 19, 23, and 25, shown in Figure A-2. If you look at the details of each catalogdescription for those three rows, you will notice that each has a different ProductPhotoID value.

Results | Messages

	productmodelid	catalogdescription
19	19	<?xml-stylesheet ...
20	20	NULL
21	21	NULL
22	22	NULL
23	23	<?xml-stylesheet ...
24	24	NULL
25	25	<?xml-stylesheet ...
26	26	NULL

Figure A-2

In SQL Server Management Studio, execute the following query, which queries only those records whose ProductPhotoID value is greater than 115. The XQuery query is not filtered by a `WHERE` clause so as to look at all the records. The XPath expression tells the query to look at all ProductPhotoID elements and return those records whose value for that element is greater than 115:

```
WITH XMLNAMESPACES ('http://schemas.microsoft.com/sqlserver/2004/07/adventure-
works/ProductModelDescription' AS PMD)
SELECT CatalogDescription.query('
    for $P in / PMD:ProductDescription/ PMD:Picture[PMD:ProductPhotoID > 115]
    return $P') as Result
FROM   Production.ProductModel
```

When you run the query, you will notice that only records 19 and 25 returned a result, as shown in Figure A-3. That is because the value of ProductPhotoID for ProductModelID 23 has a value less than 115.

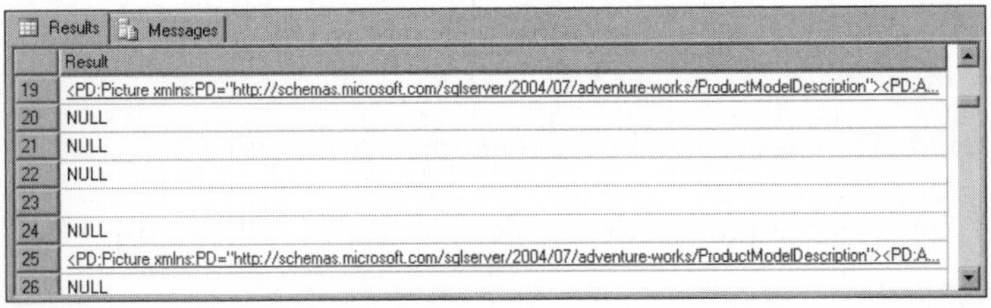

Results | Messages

	Result
19	<PD:Picture xmlns:PD="http://schemas.microsoft.com/sqlserver/2004/07/adventure-works/ProductModelDescription"><PD:A...
20	NULL
21	NULL
22	NULL
23	
24	NULL
25	<PD:Picture xmlns:PD="http://schemas.microsoft.com/sqlserver/2004/07/adventure-works/ProductModelDescription"><PD:A...
26	NULL

Figure A-3

Run the query again for values greater than 100 and look at the results. What you should get back is a value for row 28.

Value Comparison Operators

Value comparison operators are operators that compare atomic values. In SQL Server 2005, these operators are listed as follows:

- Equal (eq)
- Not equal (ne)
- Less than (lt)
- Greater than (gt)
- Less than or equal to (le)
- Greater than or equal to (ge)

The definitions of the value comparison operators are the same as those of the general comparison operators listed in the previous section. The difference between comparison operators and value comparison operators has to do with the handling of untyped atomic types. Consider this comparison:

```
for $P in / PMD:ProductDescription/ PMD:Picture[PMD:ProductPhotoID > 100]
```

In reality, it works the same as the following:

```
for $P in / PMD:ProductDescription/ PMD:Picture[PMD:ProductPhotoID gt 100]
```

The operators in these two examples are equivalent because of the way the XQuery/XPath language interprets the operators.

XQuery promotes the untyped type to the type of the other operand to ensure consistency.

Arithmetic Operators

Arithmetic, or numeric, operators are defined in SQL Server 2005 as follows:

- **Add (+):** Adds two or more numbers.
- **Subtract (-):** Subtracts two or more numbers.
- **Multiply (*):** Multiplies two or more numbers together.
- **Divide (div):** Divides two numbers.
- **Mod (mod):** Divides two numbers and returns the remainder.

For example, the following query uses the div operator to divide the returned value by 12.

```
SELECT demographics.query ('
 declare namespace ss="http://schemas.microsoft.com/sqlserver/2004/07/adventure-works/StoreSurvey";
 for $sa in /ss:StoreSurvey
 return
```

```
<StoreDetails
      AvgSalesPerMonth = "{$sa/ss:AnnualSales div 12}">
 </StoreDetails>
') as result
FROM sales.store
WHERE customerid = 1
```

Figure A-4 shows the results of the executed query. The value of AnnualSales is 30,000, but when the query is run, it divides that number by 12 and returns the results to the client.

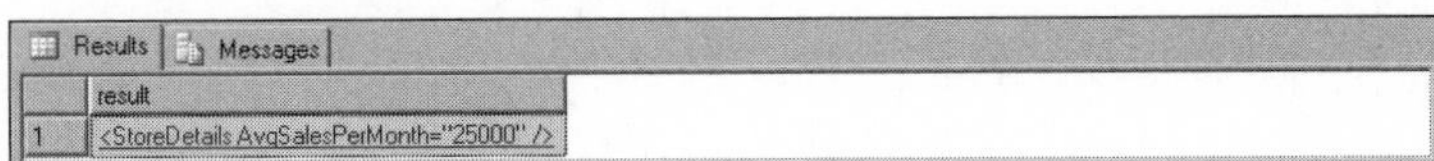

Figure A-4

All the other arithmetic operators listed previously behave in the same manner as `div`, and are fully supported by SQL Server 2005.

Logical Operators

Logical operators compare Boolean expressions, and the results of the query are returned as a Boolean. XQuery logical operators supported by SQL Server 2005 are the `and` and `or` operators.

The `and` operator compares two Boolean expressions. If both evaluate to `True`, then a `True` value is returned.

The `or` operator compares two Boolean expressions and if either expression evaluates to `True` then a `True` value is returned. If neither expression returns a `True` value, then a `False` value is returned.

And Or

This example uses the logical `and` operator to return a set of results based on two sets of criteria. First, query the Demographics column of the Sales.Individual table to get an idea of the data you will be working with. Run the following T-SQL in a query window:

```
SELECT Demographics FROM Sales.Individual
```

This query returns the Demographics column for all the rows in the table, as shown in Figure A-5. Clicking one of the rows displays the detail XML for that specific column and row.

Figure A-5

The next example filters the results, returning only those rows where the marital status is "M" and the occupation is "Professional," using the logical `and` operator. Type and execute the following XQuery in a query window:

```
SELECT demographics.query('
     declare namespace
IS="http://schemas.microsoft.com/sqlserver/2004/07/adventure-
works/IndividualSurvey";
     for $F in /IS:IndividualSurvey[IS:MaritalStatus="M"
     and IS:Occupation="Professional"]
     return
        $F
    ') as Result
FROM  sales.individual
```

The results show that there are at lease three records that meet the specified criteria (see Figure A-6). The empty rows signify that those records did not meet the specified criteria.

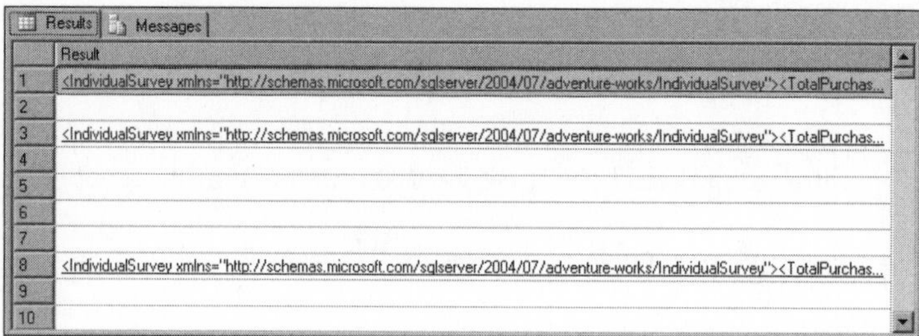

Figure A-6

Specifying `or` also works, but the results are different. Modify the query as shown follows:

```
for $F in /IS:IndividualSurvey[IS:MaritalStatus="M"
or IS:Occupation="Professional"]
```

Running this query returns a larger set of results since either the left expression or the right expression returns `True`.

If-Then-Else

The `if-then-else` construct of XQuery operates like that of other languages. It allows for the operations to be performed based on the condition of an expression. The following example uses the `if-then-else` construct to display the machine hours from the Instructions column if it exists for a location:

```
SELECT Instructions.query('declare namespace
PM="http://schemas.microsoft.com/sqlserver/2004/07/adventure-
works/ProductModelManuInstructions";
        for $WC in // PM:root/ PM:Location
        return
        if ( $WC[not(@MachineHours)] )
        then
          <WorkCenterLocation>
```

```
            { $WC/@LocationID }
          </WorkCenterLocation>
        else
          ()
') as Result
FROM Production.ProductModel
```

Figure A-7 shows the results of the query. If the query finds a `MachineHours` attribute, it displays the corresponding LocationID.

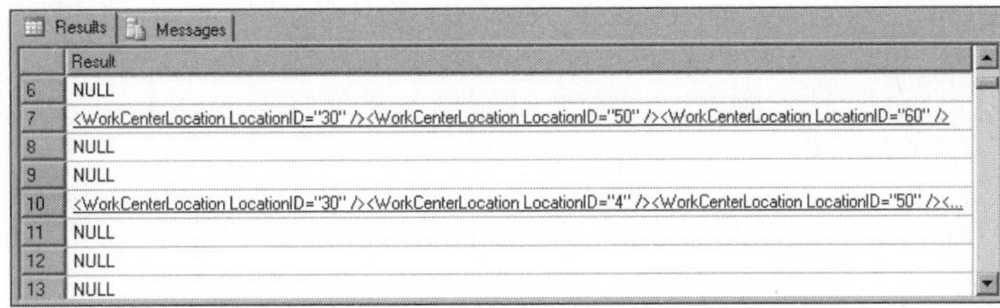

Figure A-7

A few more examples further on in this appendix demonstrate the `if-then-else` construct a bit more. Now, however, the discussion shifts toward the various XQuery functions supported by SQL Server 2005.

XQuery Functions

SQL Server 2005 supports a large number of built-in XQuery functions. These functions include a wide array of functionality, including aggregate functions, data accessor functions, numerical functions, context functions, and others. The following sections discuss the built-in XQuery functions.

data()

You can use the `data()` accessor to return values from nodes as typed values. For example, the following query uses the `data()` function to extract the catalog description information for any photos with a productphotoid less than 100. The `data()` function in this example returns the typed values:

```
SELECT CatalogDescription.query ('
    declare namespace pm="http://schemas.microsoft.com/sqlserver/2004/07/adventure-
works/ProductModelDescription";
        for $man in /pm:ProductDescription/pm:Picture
        where xs:integer (data($man/pm:ProductPhotoID) ) lt 100
        return
        element Picture
        {
         element Size {data($man/pm:Size) },
         element angle {data($man/pm:Angle) },
         element PhoneID {data($man/pm:ProductPhotoID) }
 }
') as Result
FROM production.productmodel
```

The results shown in Figure A-8 indicate that a couple of records match the specified criteria in the query.

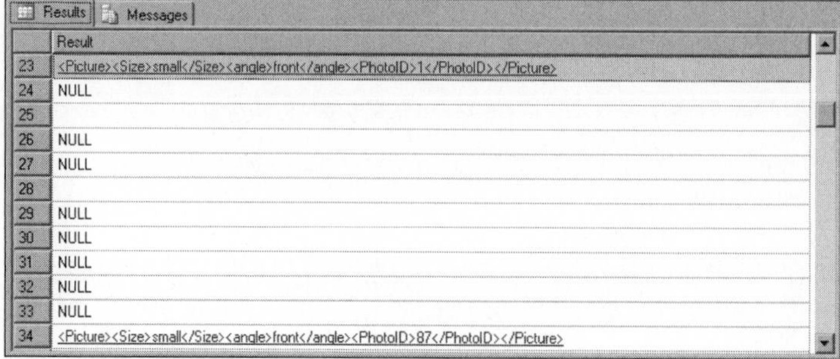

Figure A-8

string()

The `string()` function returns the string value of the item being returned. In the following example, three values are being returned, all of which are being returned as a string using the `string()` function, even the copyright value:

```
SELECT CatalogDescription.query ('
    declare namespace pm="http://schemas.microsoft.com/sqlserver/2004/07/adventure-
works/ProductModelDescription";
    for $man in /pm:ProductDescription/pm:Manufacturer
    return
    element Manufacturer
    {
        attribute Copyright {string($man/pm:Copyright) },
        element Manufacturer {string($man/pm:Name) },
        element ProductURL {string($man/pm:ProductURL) }
    }
') as Result
FROM production.productmodel
where productmodelid = 19
```

Figure A-9 shows the results of the query.

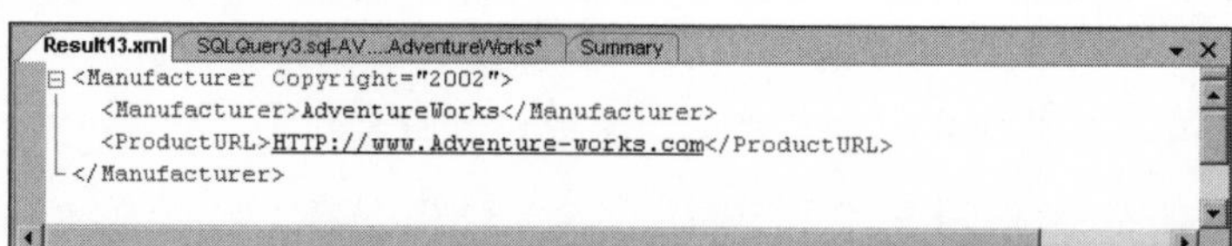

Figure A-9

Aggregate Functions

Aggregate functions act on a complete sequence of specified items and return the results of the aggregation. Those aggregate functions supported in SQL Server 2005 include `count()`, `min()`, `max()`, `avg()`, and `sum()`.

count()

The `count()` function returns the total number of items counted in a given sequence. For example, the following query counts the number of material elements for a given ProductModelID:

```
SELECT Instructions.query('
  declare namespace pm="http://schemas.microsoft.com/sqlserver/2004/07/adventure-
works/ProductModelManuInstructions";
  <Material>Total element count for material is { count(/pm:root/pm:Location)
}</Material>
') as Result
FROM Production.ProductModel
WHERE ProductModelID = 7
```

Figure A-10 show the results of the query. This query counted six material elements.

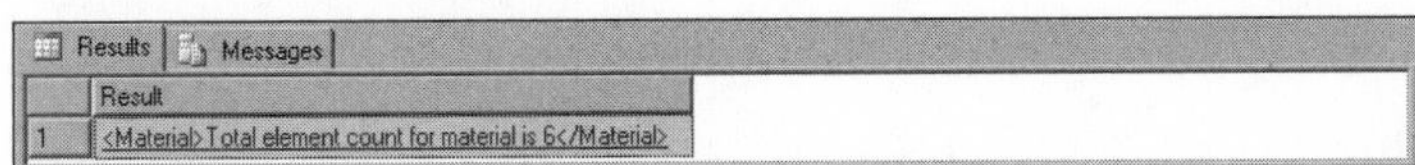

Figure A-10

min()

The `min()` function returns a single item from a sequence whose value is less than the other items in the sequence. The following example queries the Instructions column of the ProductModel table looking at all the `MachineHours` attributes of the Location element and returns the LocationID and MachineHours with the least (minimum) MachineHours value:

```
select Instructions.query('
  declare namespace pm="http://schemas.microsoft.com/sqlserver/2004/07/adventure-
works/ProductModelManuInstructions";
  for $Loc in /pm:root/pm:Location
  where $Loc/@MachineHours = min( /pm:root/pm:Location/@MachineHours )
return
  <Location LocationID="{ $Loc/@LocationID }"
            MachineHours= "{ $Loc/@MachineHours }" />
  ') as Result
FROM  Production.ProductModel
WHERE ProductModelID=10
```

Figure A-11 shows the results of the query.

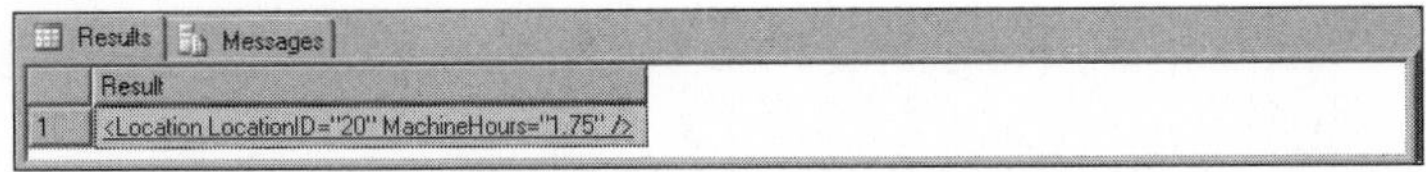

Figure A-11

max()

The `max()` function is the opposite of the `min()` function. It returns a single item from a sequence whose value is the most or greater than the others in the sequence. The following example returns the LocationID and MachineHours from the Location element with the greatest number of machine hours:

```
select Instructions.query('
  declare namespace pm="http://schemas.microsoft.com/sqlserver/2004/07/adventure-
works/ProductModelManuInstructions";
  for $Loc in /pm:root/pm:Location
  where $Loc/@MachineHours = max( /pm:root/pm:Location/@MachineHours )
return
  <Location LocationID="{ $Loc/@LocationID }"
              MachineHours= "{ $Loc/@MachineHours }" />
  ') as Result
FROM  Production.ProductModel
WHERE ProductModelID=10
```

Figure A-12 shows the results of the query.

Figure A-12

avg()

The `avg()` function returns the average of a given sequence. For example, the following query returns the average of the MachineHours for all the locations:

```
select Instructions.query('
  declare namespace pm="http://schemas.microsoft.com/sqlserver/2004/07/adventure-
works/ProductModelManuInstructions";
  <AverageMachineHours>
    { avg(//pm:Location/@MachineHours) }
  </AverageMachineHours>
  ') as Result
FROM  Production.ProductModel
WHERE ProductModelID=10
```

Figure A-13 shows the results of the query.

Figure A-13

sum()

The `sum()` function returns the sum of numbers for a given sequence. Keeping with the theme of machine hours, the following example sums the machine hours for all the locations for a given product model:

```
select Instructions.query('
  declare namespace pm="http://schemas.microsoft.com/sqlserver/2004/07/adventure-
works/ProductModelManuInstructions";
  <TotalMachineHours>
    { sum(//pm:Location/@MachineHours) }
  </TotalMachineHours>
  ') as Result
FROM  Production.ProductModel
WHERE ProductModelID=10
```

Figure A-14 shows the results of the query.

Figure A-14

Context Functions

Context functions are used to get relative properties for a given context item. The context functions supported by SQL Server 2005 are `last()` and `position()`.

last()

The `last()` function returns the position index of the last item in a sequence. For example, the following query returns the last instruction step for a given location. The location is specified by the value within the brackets (`[ ]`):

```
SELECT Instructions.query('
declare namespace pmi="http://schemas.microsoft.com/sqlserver/2004/07/adventure-
works/ProductModelManuInstructions";
   <LastStep>
     { (/pmi:root/pmi:Location)[1]/pmi:step[last()]/text() }
   </LastStep>
') as Result
FROM Production.ProductModel
WHERE ProductModelID=10
```

Figure A-15 shows the results of the query.

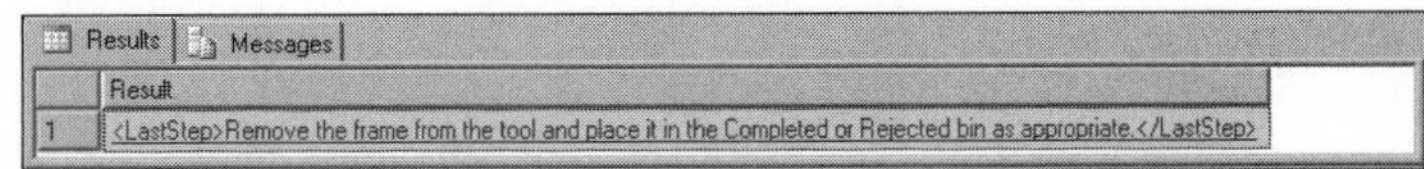

Figure A-15

You can even use the `last()` function to iterate backwards through the sequence. The following example uses the `last()` function to get the next-to-last step:

```
SELECT Instructions.query('
declare namespace pmi="http://schemas.microsoft.com/sqlserver/2004/07/adventure-
works/ProductModelManuInstructions";
   <SecondToLastStep>
     { (/pmi:root/pmi:Location)[1]/pmi:step[last()-1]/text() }
   </SecondToLastStep>
') as Result
FROM Production.ProductModel
WHERE ProductModelID=10
```

In this example, a value of one is subtracted from the `last()` function (`last() - 1`) to tell the last function to go to the next-to-last step.

As you have seen before, you can also change the location and go through the steps:

```
SELECT Instructions.query('
declare namespace pmi="http://schemas.microsoft.com/sqlserver/2004/07/adventure-
works/ProductModelManuInstructions";
   <SecondToLastStep>
     { (/pmi:root/pmi:Location)[2]/pmi:step[last()-1]/text() }
   </SecondToLastStep>
') as Result
FROM Production.ProductModel
WHERE ProductModelID=10
```

This example uses the same `last()` function, also subtracting one to go to the next-to-the step, but this time the second location was specified.

position()

The `position()` function specifies the position of an item within a sequence. The position is specified via an integer value. For example, the following query returns the first three steps for each location for a given product model:

```
SELECT Instructions.query('
     declare namespace
pd="http://schemas.microsoft.com/sqlserver/2004/07/adventure-
works/ProductModelManuInstructions";
     <Instructions>
          {
            for $f in /pd:root/pd:Location/*[position()<=3]
            return
            $f
          }
     </Instructions>
') as Result
FROM Production.ProductModel
WHERE ProductModelID = 10
```

Remember earlier where it was mentioned that the `if-then-else` constructor would be used again? Well, here it is. While iterating through the sequence, the query returns the first three steps for each location. The `if-then-else` constructor can be added to say that if there are more than three steps, then also return a value indicating that there are more. The following example shows how this is accomplished:

```
SELECT Instructions.query('
     declare namespace
pd="http://schemas.microsoft.com/sqlserver/2004/07/adventure-
works/ProductModelManuInstructions";
     <Instructions>
          {
            for $f in /pd:root/pd:Location/*[position()<=3]
            return
            $f
          }
          {
            if (count(/pd:root/pd:Location/*) > 3)
            then <DUDE-Theres-more/>
            else ()
          }
     </Instructions>
') as Result
FROM Production.ProductModel
WHERE ProductModelID = 10
```

Context functions are very useful to help you pinpoint a specific spot within the sequence. The `last()` function allows you to move to the last item in the sequence and from there, as you have seen, to navigate backwards through the sequence. The `position()` function allows you to move to a specific point within the sequence.

Using XQuery to Create XML

Through the power and flexibility of XQuery, you can build XML structures within a query. Thus is the nature of XQuery and its constructors. The constructors allow you to define the results of the query and can be used with elements, variables, comments, and text nodes.

A few of the examples in this appendix so far have built the XML manually, meaning the XML elements have been manually specified. For example, the following query returns the manufacturer information, building the XML with the results returned from the query:

```
SELECT CatalogDescription.query ('
  declare namespace pmi="http://schemas.microsoft.com/sqlserver/2004/07/adventure-
works/ProductModelDescription";
  for $man in /pmi:ProductDescription/pmi:Manufacturer
  return
  <ProductManufacturer Manufacturer = "{$man/pmi:Name}" >
    {$man/pmi:Copyright}
    {$man/pmi:ProductURL}
  </ProductManufacturer>
') as Result
FROM Production.ProductModel
WHERE ProductModelID = 19
```

The results from this query are shown in Figure A-16.

```
Result27.xml   SQLQuery3.sql-AV...AdventureWorks*   Summary
<ProductManufacturer Manufacturer="AdventureWorks">
   <pmi:Copyright xmlns:pmi="http://schemas.microsoft.com/sqlserver/2004/07/adv
   <pmi:ProductURL xmlns:pmi="http://schemas.microsoft.com/sqlserver/2004/07/ad
</ProductManufacturer>
```

Figure A-16

That's informative, but ugly. You can pretty this up by using some of the information you learned earlier in the appendix. Modify the query as follows:

```
SELECT CatalogDescription.query ('
  declare namespace pmi="http://schemas.microsoft.com/sqlserver/2004/07/adventure-
works/ProductModelDescription";
  for $man in /pmi:ProductDescription/pmi:Manufacturer
  return
    element Manufacturer
{
  element ManufacturerName {string($man/pmi:Name)},
  element Copyright {string($man/pmi:Copyright)},
  element ProductURL {string($man/pmi:ProductURL)}
}
') as Result
FROM Production.ProductModel
WHERE ProductModelID = 19
```

Now, rerun the query. You should see what appears in Figure A-17.

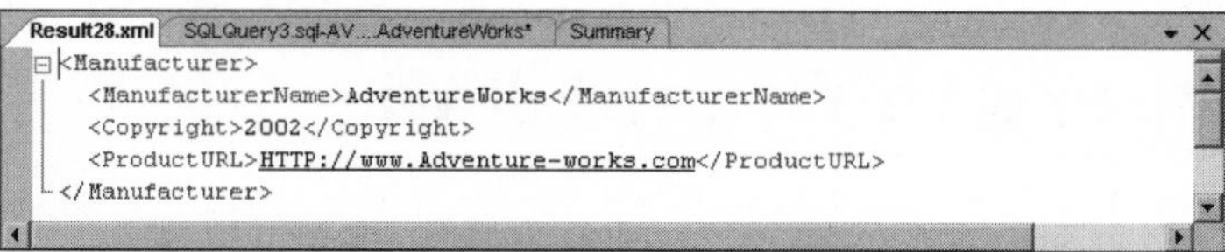

Figure A-17

That's better: same information, but much cleaner. Yet both Figure A-16 and Figure A-17 illustrate the ability of XQuery to return XML-formatted results.

In these examples, you have seen how to construct XML using XQuery. But the real question here is what does XQuery XML construction provide over XML shaping using `FOR XML`, and when would you use one over the other? The answer is, "It depends." First and foremost, XQuery cannot aggregate XML from multiple columns and multiple rows; `FOR XML` can. However, you can use both to format a single XML instance, and XQuery will probably be faster since `FOR XML` will need to hit the `xml` data type methods more than once for the XML instance. Likewise, XQuery is faster than its XML DML statement counterparts when constructing an XML instance.

Last, `FOR XML` has been enhanced and provides more functionality in SQL Server 2005 when it comes to building an instance of XML. The `TYPE` directive, new to SQL Server 2005, allows for better construction of XML results.

The real answer to the question lies with what you are attempting to do. You may need to experiment, but given some of this information, you may already have your answer.

Relational Variables and Columns

Nine times out of ten, you want to return additional information in your query that does not come from XML, but rather comes from standard relational columns. SQL Server 2005 fully supports this via the implementation of the `sql:column()` and `sql:variable()` functions.

sql:column()

The `sql:column()` function is used to return data from relational, non-XML columns. For example, the following query returns five relational columns from the Person.Contact table and constructs an XML instance with the results:

```
SELECT AdditionalContactInfo.query('
  declare namespace pc="http://schemas.microsoft.com/sqlserver/2004/07/adventure-
works/ContactInfo";
  element Person
  {
    element ContactID { sql:column("ContactID")},
    element FirstName { sql:column("FirstName")},
    element LastName { sql:column("LastName")},
    element Title { sql:column("Title")},
    element Email { sql:column("EmailAddress")}
  }
') AS Result
FROM Person.Contact
WHERE ContactID = 1
```

Figure A-18 shows the results of the query.

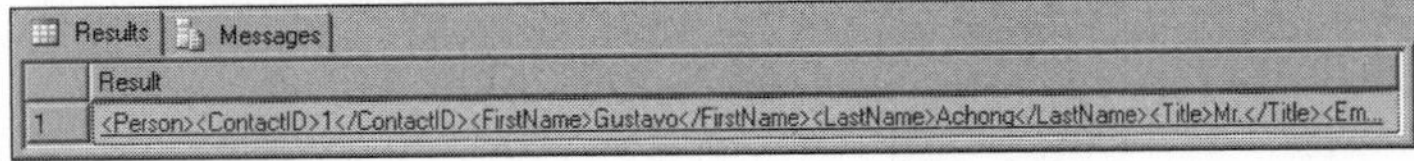

Figure A-18

In this example, the `sql:column` is used to return five relational columns. The five columns returned are enclosed in a `<Person>` element as specified by the query, as well as giving each column returned a name for the element from which the value for the column is returned.

sql:variable()

The `sql:variable()` function provides the ability to use a variable containing a value within an instance of an xml data type instance. The following code snippet example uses a variable to compare LocationID values:

```
/pi:root/pi:Location = sql:variable("@LocationID")
```

For example, you can create a stored procedure that takes an input parameter, and then use that parameter variable in the stored procedure within the XQuery query.

Before the stored procedure is created, the T-SQL to be used in the stored procedure needs to be tested outside of a stored procedure first. Using the previous example, open a query window and modify the previous example as follows:

```
DECLARE @EmailAddr varchar(15), @ContactID int
SET @EmailAddr = 'gustavo007@adventure-works.com'
SET @ContactID = 1
DECLARE @xml xml

SET @xml = (SELECT AdditionalContactInfo.query('
  declare namespace pc="http://schemas.microsoft.com/sqlserver/2004/07/adventure-
works/ContactInfo";
  element Person
  {
    element ContactID { sql:column("ContactID")},
    element FirstName { sql:column("FirstName")},
    element LastName { sql:column("LastName")},
    element Title { sql:column("Title")},
    element Email { sql:variable("@EmailAddr")}
  }
') AS Result
FROM Person.Contact
WHERE ContactID = @ContactID)

SELECT @xml
```

When you execute this query, you should get exactly the same results as you did in the previous example. First, a couple of variables are declared (`@EmailAddr` and `@ContactID`) and then some values are set to those variables, namely the e-mail address of Gustav and his ContactID number of 1. An `xml` data type variable is declared and then the `SELECT` statement used previously is set to that variable.

The thing to note is the highlighted line in the middle. Notice that, unlike the previous example, the `sql:variable` function is used here and the value of the `@EmailAddr` variable is used in the place of the actual value returned from the EmailAddress column.

Now you need to move this to a stored procedure. Create a new stored procedure in the AdventureWorks database and enter the following:

```
CREATE PROCEDURE SqlVariableSample
 @EmailAddr varchar(30),
 @ContactID int
AS
BEGIN

    -- Insert statements for procedure here
 SELECT AdditionalContactInfo.query('
  declare namespace pc="http://schemas.microsoft.com/sqlserver/2004/07/adventure-
works/ContactInfo";
```

```
  element Person
  {
    element ContactID { sql:column("ContactID")},
    element FirstName { sql:column("FirstName")},
    element LastName { sql:column("LastName")},
    element Title { sql:column("Title")},
    element Email { sql:variable("@EmailAddr")}
  }
') AS Result
FROM Person.Contact
WHERE ContactID = @ContactID

END
```

In a query window, execute the following T-SQL:

```
EXEC SqlVariableSample 'gustavo007@adventure-works.com', 1
```

What results did you get? You should see the same results as in the last two examples.

The `sql:column()` *and* `sql:variable()` *functions are not available via CLR UDF's and cannot be used with datetime and XML columns.*

Summary

This appendix, a primer of sorts, introduced you to the XQuery support in SQL Server 2005. Throughout this book, you encountered XQuery infrequently, so this appendix built on that information to give you a nice starting foundation for your XQuery journeys.

The more important things to take away from this appendix are the flexibility XQuery provides in querying the `xml` data type and some of the advantages XQuery has over related technologies such as XSLT. XQuery is much easier to learn and even at its initial 1.0 release has quite a bit of functionality.

The `FLWOR` statement alone gives XQuery much of its richness and provides much of the querying and filter capabilities. Not to take away from the other great functionality, but you have to admit that the `FLWOR` statement makes using XQuery very pleasant. Combine that with all the comparison operators and many functions available to XQuery and you have a full, powerful language that is a great complement to the `xml` data type.

Index

Symbols & Numerics

A

B

C

D

E

F

G

H

I

K

L

M

N

Q

R

S

T

U

V

W

X

Take your library wherever you go

Now you can access more than 70 complete Wrox books online, wherever you happen to be! Every diagram, description, screen capture, and code sample is available with your subscription to the **Wrox Reference Library**. For answers when and where you need them, go to wrox.books24x7.com and subscribe today!

Find books on

- ASP.NET
- C#/C++
- Database
- General
- Java
- Mac
- Microsoft Office
- .NET
- Open Source
- PHP/MySQL
- SQL Server
- Visual Basic
- Web
- XML

.wrox.com